TECHNICAL COMMUNICATION

A Reader-Centered Approach

Fourth Edition

Harcourt College Publishers

Where Learning Comes to Life

TECHNOLOGY

Technology is changing the learning experience, by increasing the power of your textbook and other learning materials; by allowing you to access more information, more quickly; and by bringing a wider array of choices in your course and content information sources.

Harcourt College Publishers has developed the most comprehensive Web sites, e-books, and electronic learning materials on the market to help you use technology to achieve your goals.

PARTNERS IN LEARNING

Harcourt partners with other companies to make technology work for you and to supply the learning resources you want and need. More importantly, Harcourt and its partners provide avenues to help you reduce your research time of numerous information sources.

Harcourt College Publishers and its partners offer increased opportunities to enhance your learning resources and address your learning style. With quick access to chapter-specific Web sites and e-books . . . from interactive study materials to quizzing, testing, and career advice . . . Harcourt and its partners bring learning to life.

Harcourt's partnership with Digital:Convergence™ brings :CRQ™ technology and the :CueCat™ reader to you and allows Harcourt to provide you with a complete and dynamic list of resources designed to help you achieve your learning goals. You can download the free :CRQ software from www.crq.com. Visit any of the 7,100 RadioShack stores nationwide to obtain a free :CueCat reader. Just swipe the cue with the :CueCat reader to view a list of Harcourt's partners and Harcourt's print and electronic learning solutions.

C 62 00 00 00 00 00 25 20

http://www.harcourtcollege.com/partners

TECHNICAL COMMUNICATION

A Reader-Centered Approach

Fourth Edition

PAUL V. ANDERSON
Miami University

HARCOURT BRACE COLLEGE PUBLISHERS

FORT WORTH   PHILADELPHIA   SAN DIEGO   NEW YORK   AUSTIN   ORLANDO   SAN ANTONIO
TORONTO   MONTREAL   LONDON   SYDNEY   TOKYO

PUBLISHER
Earl McPeek

ACQUISITIONS EDITOR
Julie McBurney

PRODUCT MANAGER
John Meyers

DEVELOPMENTAL EDITOR
Diane Drexler

ART DIRECTOR
Linda Beaupré

PRODUCTION MANAGER
Kathleen A. Ferguson

Address for Orders
Harcourt Brace College Publishers, 6277 Sea Harbor Drive, Orlando, FL 32887-6777
1-800-782-4479

Address for Editorial Correspondence
Harcourt Brace College Publishers, 301 Commerce Street, Suite 3700, Fort Worth, TX 76102

Web site Address
http://www.hbcollege.com

Harcourt Brace College Publishers will provide complimentary supplements or supplement packages to those adopters qualified under our adoption policy. Please contact your sales representative to learn how you qualify. If as an adopter or potential user you receive supplements you do not need, please return them to your sales representative or send them to: Attn: Returns Department, Troy Warehouse, 465 South Lincoln Drive, Troy, MO 63379.

Printed in the United States of America

1   2   3   4   5   6   7   039   9   8   7   6

Harcourt Brace College Publishers

FOR MY FAMILY

Margie, Christopher, Rachel

AND FOR MY TEACHERS

James W. Souther and Myron L. White

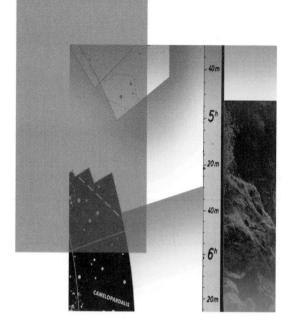

Preface

The world of technical communication has changed in dramatic and exciting ways since the appearance of this book's previous edition only four years ago. The explosive increase in use of the Internet is but one of several extraordinary events that have profoundly influenced the ways we communicate. Additionally, there have been substantial advances in the ways we think about and teach our subject. In creating this new edition of *Technical Communication: A Reader-Centered Approach,* I have introduced many innovations—including an extensive Web site for you and your students—that respond to these changes. At the same time, I've retained the book's distinctive strategies that, over the years, have proven successful for instructors and students alike.

New features include an extensive Web site for instructors and students.

READER-CENTERED APPROACH REMAINS

Most importantly, this remains a process-oriented textbook in which the central advice to students remains the same: think constantly about your readers—whether you are preparing messages that will be read on paper or viewed on a computer screen. As in earlier editions, every chapter, reference guide, and appendix conveys specific, useful advice built upon the hard-won insights that researchers have gained concerning the ways people read in the workplace.

The reader-centered approach unifies all of the book's advice.

By following the book's easy-to-remember guidelines, your students can become confident, flexible, resourceful writers who know how to size up a situation and then plan and draft a communication that will achieve an outcome that they and their readers both desire.

EXPANDED COVERAGE OF COMPUTER AND INTERNET COMMUNICATION

Many of the innovations to this edition reflect the significant increase in the use of computers as a tool for creating communications and as a medium for presenting them to readers. Here are some of the major new topics.

New chapter on electronic communication.

- **Creating e-mail, Web pages, and Web sites.** A new chapter (Chapter 15) on creating computer-based communications provides up-to-date advice for using e-mail, creating Web pages, and constructing informational Web sites of the kind prepared in the workplace. To illustrate, I've included many fully annotated screen shots. For students new to Web design, the chapter describes the most commonly used HTML tags.
- **Preparing electronic resumes.** At many companies, resumes from job applicants are scanned first by computers, not people. Chapter 2 includes a new section that tells students how to create effective computer-scannable resumes, ASCII resumes, and Web resumes.

Guidance for Web research.

- **Conducting research on the Internet.** A new section in the reference guide on research methods leads students through the process of conducting Internet research. To help students use the Web effectively, the section also explains how search engines work. In addition, it includes a new discussion that helps students perform the tricky task of evaluating information found on the Web.
- **Creating on-line instructions.** A new section in Chapter 20 supplements the coverage concerning paper-based instructions with advice for creating instructions that will be used on-screen.

Advice for taking fuller advantage of word-processing programs.

- **Using advanced word-processing features.** Standard word-processing programs now include several features—some very little used—that can aid writers at various stages of the writing process. Chapter 4 includes a new discussion of word-processing aids for outlining; Chapter 12 incorporates new advice on using "styles" when creating page designs, and Chapter 13 includes an updated discussion of features that check grammar, analyze writing style, and automatically compare two drafts of a communication to identify the differences between them.
- **Using electronic library resources.** Libraries are now as much on-line as on-the-shelf. A new section in the reference guide on research methods teaches students to use electronic card catalog systems and discusses other resources available in wired libraries.

ADDITIONAL COVERAGE OF OTHER TOPICS

I've also made numerous improvements in other areas, many based on suggestions generously provided by instructors and by students.

- **Writing collaboratively.** A new chapter consolidates the book's advice for working on collaborative writing teams. (Chapter 17)

- **Evaluating research results.** A new discussion helps students evaluate information they find through their research. (Chapter 6)
- **Citing sources.** A completely revised and updated appendix explains both the new MLA style and the current APA style. (Appendix B)
- **Designing pages and screens.** New guidelines for page design augment the already strong chapter on the visual design of technical communications. (Chapter 12)
- **Describing an object.** An expanded treatment of this important skill includes an extended example from the professional world. (Reference guide on organizational patterns)

Many sample documents.

In addition, a multitude of new, thoroughly annotated sample documents illustrate the practical application of the book's advice.

WEB SITE FOR INSTRUCTORS AND STUDENTS

Just as the Internet allows technical communication courses to move beyond classroom and library walls, so too has it allowed me to create a textbook that permits you and your students to move beyond its covers.

Located at http://english.harbrace.com/techw/anderson, the site offers the following for instructors:

- Complete instructor's manual.
- Sample syllabi created by faculty at a variety of colleges and universities.
- Additional exercises and cases.
- PowerPoint presentations that can be downloaded for use during class.
- Editable versions of various planning guides and checklists for distribution to students.
- An on-line forum where we instructors can exchange ideas, share teaching materials, answer one another's questions, and discuss issues of mutual interest.
- Links to other valuable sites.
- Bibliography of articles on technical communication and its teaching.

For students, the site offers:

Web site features for students.

- Career information and job-hunting tips.
- Links to Internet resources for projects.
- Additional sample documents.
- A forum for interacting with students at other schools.
- A chance to view outstanding work by other students and possibly display their own.

A printed instructor's manual is also available. Contact your Harcourt representative.

ADDITIONAL RESOURCES

Separately available are two popular supplements, written especially to accompany this book:

■ **Style and Usage Guide** by C. Gilbert Storms (Miami University, Ohio). If some or all of your students would benefit from extra study in this area, Dr. Storms' book provides a brief, inexpensive, and very effective supplement. Carefully coordinated with the textbook, it covers the points of grammar, punctuation, diction, and similar matters that most often puzzle technical-writing students. Where appropriate, it includes exercises.

■ **Technical Writing Guide for Nonnative Speakers of English,** by Robert M. Brown (Oklahoma State University), H. Young Kim (Cornell University), and Rebecca L. Damron (Oklahoma State University). This second, brief supplement enables you to provide rhetorically based instruction for your students who are second-language speakers of English. Fully coordinated with the textbook, it extends well beyond sentence-level issues to help international students understand such matters as typical reader preferences in the United States, as well as the organizational principles, rhetorical strategies, and conventions about visual aids that prevail here. It also includes special discussions of collaborative writing and plagiarism that are addressed to students from other cultures. If your class mixes native and non-native speakers, you can have both groups work with the same basic text, then use this supplement with those who were not born into our culture.

CONCLUSION

In sum, I feel particularly proud of this new edition of *Technical Communication: A Reader-Centered Approach.* I think you and your students will find it informative, useful, and fun.

My work on this edition has emphasized for me even more forcefully than before the extent to which every book is truly a collaborative effort. I've benefited from many forms of assistance, especially the advice of instructors and students who have graciously shared their ideas with me. I invite you to join the on-line forums at the book's Web site, and I assure you that I will read your contributions with interest. In addition, please feel welcome to contact me directly at any of the following addresses:

Please share your ideas with me.

English Department,
Miami University
Oxford, OH 45056

anderspv@muohio.edu

Web site for this book: http://english.harbrace.com/techw/anderson

ACKNOWLEDGMENTS

Writing a textbook is truly a collaborative effort to which numerous people make substantial contributions. I take great pleasure in this opportunity to thank the many persons who generously furnished advice and assistance while I was working on this fourth edition of *Technical Communication: A Reader-Centered Approach.*

At the top of my list are sixteen students at Iowa State University, who sent me thoughtful notes in which they identified the features of the third edition that they wanted me to retain and suggested innovations that they'd like to see me introduce in the fourth edition. Among the innovations emerging from their suggestions are the marginal annotations used throughout the chapters to highlight key points and provide easy access for readers who want to review particular points. These students are Dave Anstrom, Paula M. Culberton, Mojiboha T. Fasehune, Steve Groen, Eric Hillary, Scott W. Holtorf, I-Shin Hsu, John Eric Kurniawan, Ben Koch, Jake J. Kerber, Seung Lee, Bee-Hui Lim, Andrew Pospisal, Todd G. Shedeck, Jacob Wacker, and Yee Lam Wong.

I also gained much valuable advice from the following faculty who were willing to steal some time from the wonderful 1997 CCCC conference in Phoenix in order to participate in a sometimes irreverent focus group concerning this edition. They are Patricia Jenkins, University of Alaska-Anchorage; Johndan Johnson-Eilola, Purdue University; Dan Jones, University of Central Florida; Louise Rehling, San Francisco State University; Stuart Selber, Texas Tech University; and Diane Svoboda, Mesa Community College.

Equally helpful were the extensive, thoughtful written reviews of the third edition and of my preliminary plans for the fourth edition by the following individuals: Marcella Clark, Kansas State University; Anthony Flinn, Eastern Washington University; Roger Friedmann, Kansas State University; Judy Hakola, University of Maine; Sharon Irvin, Florida Institute of Technology; Judy Kaufman, Eastern Washington University; Nick Lilly, Tarleton State University; Walter Loscutoff, California State University-Fresco; Ronald Smith, University of Northern Alabama; Margaret Walters, University of Houston-Clear Lake; and Irene Ward, Kansas State University.

As I crystallized my plans for this edition and began drafting chapters, I benefited greatly from the insightful assistance and counsel of Mark Gallaher. I am also grateful to David Bruce, who has written and e-mailed many times over the years to share suggestions he has developed while teaching with the various editions of this book at Ohio University.

Much of my most valuable assistance has come from right here at Miami University. My technical communication colleagues—Jennie Dautermann, Bob Johnson, Jean Lutz, and Gil Storms—have been a fountain of inspiration and good counsel, both when they offered direct advice and when they shared their own teaching strategies and ideas. Many Miami staff members have also assisted me. Within the English department, these include Kathy Fox, Jackie Kearns, Trudi Nixon, and Leta Roberson. Among library staff, these include Belinda Barr, Lisa Santucci, and Bill Wortman. In our Computing and Information Services Department, they include Barbara Edwards and Gail Johnson.

In addition to drawing on the published research cited in the reference list, I garnered good ideas for this edition by examining the thoughtful work of several other researchers who have written textbooks in technical communication, including Deborah C. Andrews, Rebecca E. Burnett; Kenneth W. Houp, Thomas E. Pearsall, and Beth Tebeaux; Jimmy Killingsworth; and John M. Lannon; and Mike Markel. Deserving special mention for the help it gave me recasting the chapter on page design is Robin Williams' *The Non-Designer's Design Book* (Berkeley, CA: Peachpit Press, 1994).

While working on this edition, I have been blessed with the support of a wonderfully talented group at Harcourt. I am particularly grateful to Julie McBurney, who has very skillfully coordinated the many individuals and groups who worked on this project with me. I am also grateful to Linda Beaupré, who has brought the book's cover and interior designs to a new level. In addition, I want to thank Diane Drexler for the care she has devoted to the book, Matt Ball for his long hours and enthusiasm, and Kathy Ferguson for her flawless management of its production. I also want to thank Steven T. Jordan, John P. Meyers, and Karl Yambert for helping me formulate plans for this edition.

At York Production Services, I want to thank Nancy Whelan for her assistance in shepherding this edition from manuscript, through page proofs, and into the printing press.

Also I owe special thanks to Janel Bloch, whose skill and conscientious attention to detail and deadlines made it possible to complete this edition on schedule.

Finally, I thank my family for their unflagging encouragement, kindness, and good humor while I worked on this edition.

PAUL V. ANDERSON

Oxford, Ohio

Brief Contents

PART **I**   **Introduction**   1

   1   Communication, Your Career, and This Book   3

   2   Overview of the Reader-Centered Communication Process: Obtaining a Job   25

PART **II**   **Defining Objectives**   53

   3   Defining Your Objectives   55

PART **III**   **Planning**   79

   4   Planning to Meet Your Readers' Informational Needs   81

   5   Planning Your Persuasive Strategies   98

   6   Conducting Research   127

   Reference Guide: Five Research Methods   135

PART **IV**   **Drafting Prose Elements**   163

   7   Drafting Paragraphs, Sections, and Chapters   165

   Reference Guide: Six Patterns for Organizing   194

   8   Beginning a Communication   220

   9   Ending a Communication   238

   10   Creating an Effective Style   247

PART **V**   **Drafting Visual Elements**   271

   11   Drafting Visual Aids   273

   Reference Guide: Thirteen Types of Visual Aids   299

   12   Designing Pages and Documents   331

PART 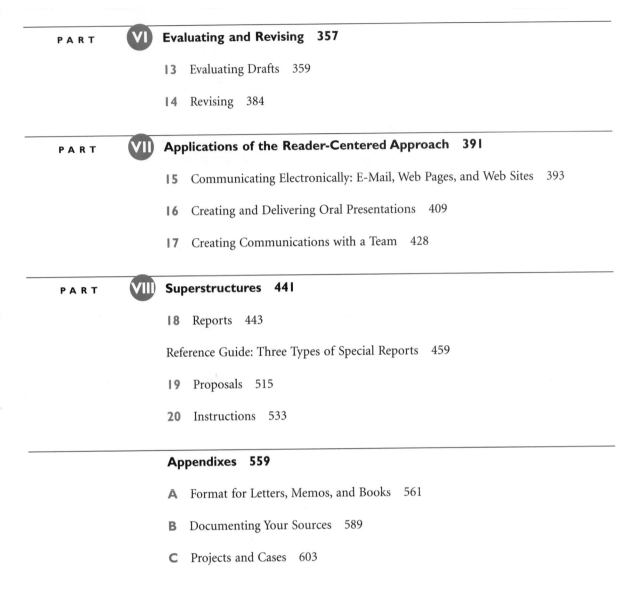 **VI** **Evaluating and Revising 357**

13 Evaluating Drafts 359

14 Revising 384

PART **VII** **Applications of the Reader-Centered Approach 391**

15 Communicating Electronically: E-Mail, Web Pages, and Web Sites 393

16 Creating and Delivering Oral Presentations 409

17 Creating Communications with a Team 428

PART **VIII** **Superstructures 441**

18 Reports 443

Reference Guide: Three Types of Special Reports 459

19 Proposals 515

20 Instructions 533

Appendixes 559

A Format for Letters, Memos, and Books 561

B Documenting Your Sources 589

C Projects and Cases 603

Contents

PART I   **Introduction**   1

CHAPTER 1   **Communication, Your Career, and This Book**   3

Your Communication Skills Will Be Critical to Your Success   4

Writing at Work Differs from Writing at School   5

At Work, Writing Is an Action   10

The Main Advice of This Book: Think Constantly about Your Readers   11

How People Read   11

Two Strategies for Keeping Your Readers in Mind   16

Some Reader-Centered Strategies You Can Begin Using Now   18

What Lies Ahead in This Book   22

Exercises   23

CASE: Selecting the Right Forklift Truck   23

FOCUS ON CAREERS: Technical Communication Careers   6

FOCUS ON ETHICS: Your Writing and Your Values   12

CHAPTER 2   **Overview of the Reader-Centered Communication Process: Obtaining a Job**   25

Writing Your Resume   26

Electronic Resumes: Special Considerations   39

Writing Your Job Application Letter   43

Writing for Employment in Other Countries   49

Conclusion   49

Exercises   50

CASE: Advising Patricia   50

FOCUS ON ETHICS: Ethics and the Job Search   34

PART II   **Defining Objectives**   53

CHAPTER 3   **Defining Your Objectives**   55

The Importance of Your Objectives   56

GUIDELINE 1:   Focus on What You Want to Happen While Your Readers Are Reading   57

GUIDELINE 2:   Identify the Tasks Your Readers Will Perform While Reading   58

GUIDELINE 3:   Tell How You Want to Change Your Readers' Attitudes   60

GUIDELINE 4:   Learn Your Readers' Important Characteristics   61

GUIDELINE 5:   Learn about the Context in Which Your Readers Will Read   64

GUIDELINE 6:   Learn Who *All* Your Readers Will Be   65

GUIDELINE 7:   Ask Others to Help You Understand Your Readers and Their Context   71

GUIDELINE 8:   Remain Open to New Insights and Information   71

Using Your Objectives to Guide Your Writing: An Example   71

Conclusion   72

Exercises   76

CASE: Announcing the Smoking Ban   76

FOCUS ON ETHICS: Identifying Stakeholders   70

PART **III**   **Planning   79**

CHAPTER 4   **Planning to Meet Your Readers' Informational Needs   81**

Benefits of Good Planning   82

Organization of This Book's Advice about Planning   82

GUIDELINE 1:   Answer Your Readers' Questions   83

GUIDELINE 2:   Include the Additional Information Your Readers Need   86

GUIDELINE 3:   Organize to Support Your Readers' Tasks   88

GUIDELINE 4:   Look for a Technical Writing Superstructure You Can Adapt   92

GUIDELINE 5:   Plan Your Visual Aids   93

GUIDELINE 6:   Outline, If This Would Be Helpful   94

GUIDELINE 7:   Take Regulations and Expectations into Account   94

How Much Time to Spend on Planning   96

Exercises   96

CASE: Filling the Distance-Learning Classroom   97

FOCUS ON ETHICS: Investigating Stakeholder Impacts   87

CHAPTER 5   **Planning Your Persuasive Strategies   98**

How Persuasion Works   99

GUIDELINE 1:   Emphasize Benefits for Your Readers   100

GUIDELINE 2:   Address Your Readers' Concerns and Counterarguments   103

GUIDELINE 3:   Show That Your Reasoning Is Sound   106

GUIDELINE 4:   Organize to Create a Favorable Response   109

GUIDELINE 5:   Create an Effective Relationship with Your Readers   112

GUIDELINE 6:   Adapt Your Persuasive Strategies to Your Readers' Cultural Background   119

Conclusion   120

Exercises   120

CASE: Debating a Company Drug-Testing Program   123

CASE: Increasing Organ Donations   124

FOCUS ON ETHICS: Ethics of Persuasion   119

CHAPTER 6 **Conducting Research   127**

Goals of Good Research   128

GUIDELINE 1: Define Your Research Objectives   128

GUIDELINE 2: Plan Before You Begin   129

GUIDELINE 3: Check Each Source for Leads to Other Sources   131

GUIDELINE 4: Carefully Evaluate What You Find   131

GUIDELINE 5: Begin Interpreting Your Research Results Even as You Obtain Them   131

GUIDELINE 6: Take Careful Notes   132

Conclusion   134

FOCUS ON ETHICS: Documenting Your Sources   133

REFERENCE GUIDE **Five Research Methods   135**

Exploiting Your Own Memory and Creativity   136

Searching the Internet   142

Using the Library   149

Interviewing   155

Conducting a Survey   158

PART **IV** **Drafting Prose Elements   163**

CHAPTER 7 **Drafting Paragraphs, Sections, and Chapters   165**

Applying This Chapter's Advice   166

GUIDELINE 1: Begin by Announcing Your Topic   167

GUIDELINE 2: Present Your Generalizations before Your Details   170

GUIDELINE 3: Move from Most Important to Least Important   173

GUIDELINE 4: Reveal Your Organization   174

GUIDELINE 5: Consult Conventional Strategies When Faced with Organizational Difficulties   189

GUIDELINE 6: Consider Your Readers' Cultural Background When Organizing   189

Conclusion   191

Exercises   191

FOCUS ON ETHICS: When Human Consequences Are Ignored   189

REFERENCE GUIDE **Six Patterns for Organizing   194**

Classification (Grouping Facts)   195

Description of an Object (Partitioning)   198

Description of a Process (Segmentation) 202

Comparison 208

Cause and Effect 210

Problem and Solution 212

Combinations of Patterns 215

Exercises 218

CHAPTER 8 **Beginning a Communication 220**

The Two Functions of a Beginning 221

GUIDELINE 1: Give Your Readers a Reason to Pay Attention 221

GUIDELINE 2: State Your Main Point 226

GUIDELINE 3: Tell Your Readers What to Expect 226

GUIDELINE 4: Encourage Openness to Your Message 227

GUIDELINE 5: Provide Necessary Background Information 231

GUIDELINE 6: Adjust the Length of Your Beginning to Your Readers' Needs 231

GUIDELINE 7: For Longer Communications, Begin with a Summary 232

GUIDELINE 8: Adapt Your Beginning to Your Readers' Cultural Background 236

Conclusion 237

Exercises 237

FOCUS ON ETHICS: How to Confront Unethical Practices—and Survive 229

CHAPTER 9 **Ending a Communication 238**

Introduction to the Guidelines 239

GUIDELINE 1: After You've Made Your Last Point, Stop 240

GUIDELINE 2: Repeat Your Main Point 240

GUIDELINE 3: Summarize Your Key Points 241

GUIDELINE 4: Refer to a Goal Stated Earlier in Your Communication 241

GUIDELINE 5: Focus on a Key Feeling 243

GUIDELINE 6: Tell Your Readers How to Get Assistance or More Information 243

GUIDELINE 7: Tell Your Readers What to Do Next 244

GUIDELINE 8: Identify Any Further Study That Is Needed 244

GUIDELINE 9: Follow Applicable Social Conventions 244

Conclusion 245

Exercises 245

FOCUS ON ETHICS: Avoiding Stereotypes 242

CHAPTER 10 **Creating an Effective Style 247**

Choosing Your Voice 248

GUIDELINE 1: Find Out What's Expected 249

GUIDELINE 2: Consider the Roles Your Voice Creates for Your Readers and You 250

GUIDELINE 3: Consider How Your Attitude toward Your Subject Will Affect
Your Readers 251

GUIDELINE 4: Say Things in Your Own Words   252

Constructing Sentences   252

GUIDELINE 1: Simplify Your Sentences   252

GUIDELINE 2: Put the Action in Your Verbs   254

GUIDELINE 3: Use the Active Voice Unless There Is Good Reason to Use
the Passive Voice   255

GUIDELINE 4: Emphasize What's Most Important   256

GUIDELINE 5: Smooth the Flow of Thought from Sentence to Sentence   257

GUIDELINE 6: Vary Your Sentence Length and Structure   260

Selecting Words   260

GUIDELINE 1: Use Concrete, Specific Words   260

GUIDELINE 2: Use Specialized Terms When—and Only When—Your Readers
Will Understand Them   262

GUIDELINE 3: Use Words Accurately   264

GUIDELINE 4: Choose Words With Appropriate Associations   264

GUIDELINE 5: Choose Plain Words over Fancy Ones   267

Conclusion   267

Exercises   268

FOCUS ON ETHICS: Avoiding Sexist Language   265

PART V Drafting Visual Elements   271

CHAPTER 11 Drafting Visual Aids   273

GUIDELINE 1: Look for Places Where Visual Aids Will Help You Achieve
Your Communication Objectives   274

GUIDELINE 2: Choose Visual Aids Appropriate to Your Objectives   279

GUIDELINE 3: Make Your Visual Aids Easy to Understand and Use   282

GUIDELINE 4: Use Color to Support Your Message   286

GUIDELINE 5: Adapt Existing Visual Aids to Your Purpose and Readers   294

GUIDELINE 6: Integrate Your Visual Aids with Your Text   295

GUIDELINE 7: When Addressing an International Audience, Check Your Visual Aids
with Persons from the Other Nations   296

Conclusion   298

REFERENCE GUIDE Thirteen Types of Visual Aids   299

Displaying Data   300

Showing How Something Looks or Is Constructed   312

Showing How to Do Something   321

Explaining a Process   321

Providing Management Information   325

FOCUS ON ETHICS: Avoiding Graphics That Mislead   313

Exercises   328

CHAPTER 12   **Designing Pages and Documents   331**

Importance of Good Design   332

Design Elements of a Communication   332

Four Basic Design Principles   333

GUIDELINE 1:   Begin by Considering Your Readers and Purpose   334

GUIDELINE 2:   Align Related Visual Elements with One Another   334

GUIDELINE 3:   Use Contrast to Establish Hierarchy and Focus   337

GUIDELINE 4:   Use Proximity to Group Related Elements   342

GUIDELINE 5:   Use Repetition to Unify Your Communication Visually   342

GUIDELINE 6:   Select Type That Is Easy to Read   344

Practical Procedures for Designing Pages   346

GUIDELINE 7:   Design Your Overall Package for Ease of Use and Attractiveness   348

Visual Design of On-Line Pages   350

Conclusion   350

Exercises   350

PART   **VI**   **Evaluating and Revising   357**

CHAPTER 13   **Evaluating Drafts   359**

Overview of Evaluation   360

Checking   361

GUIDELINE 1:   Check from Your Readers' Point of View—and Your Employer's   361

GUIDELINE 2:   Distance Yourself from Your Draft   362

GUIDELINE 3:   Read Your Draft More Than Once, Changing Your Focus Each Time   364

GUIDELINE 4:   Use Computer Aids to Find (But Not to Cure) Possible Problems   364

Reviewing   366

GUIDELINE 1:   Discuss the Objectives of the Communication and the Review   367

GUIDELINE 2:   Build a Positive Interpersonal Relationship with Your Reviewers or Writer   368

GUIDELINE 3:   Rank Suggested Revisions—And Distinguish Matters of Substance from Matters of Taste   369

GUIDELINE 4:   Explore Fully the Reasons for All Suggestions   370

User Testing   371

GUIDELINE 1:   Pick Test Readers Who Truly Represent Your Target Readers   373

GUIDELINE 2: Ask Your Test Readers to Use Your Draft in the Same Ways Your Target Readers Will Use It   373

GUIDELINE 3: Learn How Your Draft Affects Your Test Readers' Attitudes   378

GUIDELINE 4: Interview Your Test Readers After They've Used Your Draft   379

GUIDELINE 5: Test Early and Often, When Appropriate   380

Conclusion   380

Exercises   380

FOCUS ON ETHICS: Evaluating from an Ethical Perspective   363

CHAPTER 14 Revising   384

GUIDELINE 1: Adjust Your Effort to the Situation   385

GUIDELINE 2: Make the Most Significant Revisions First   387

GUIDELINE 3: Be Diplomatic   389

GUIDELINE 4: To Revise Well, Follow the Guidelines for Writing Well   390

GUIDELINE 5: Revise to Learn   390

Conclusion   390

PART VII Applications of the Reader-Centered Approach   391

CHAPTER 15 Communicating Electronically: E-Mail, Web Pages, and Web Sites

Using E-Mail   393

GUIDELINE 1: See What Other People Are Doing   396

GUIDELINE 2: Keep Your Messages Brief   396

GUIDELINE 3: Make Your Messages Easy to Read On Screen   396

GUIDELINE 4: Provide an Informative, Specific Subject Line   397

GUIDELINE 5: Take Time to Revise   397

GUIDELINE 6: Remember that E-Mail Isn't Private   397

Creating Informational Web Sites   398

Guidelines for Designing Web Pages   400

GUIDELINE 1: Make Your Pages Easy to Read   402

GUIDELINE 2: Keep Your Pages Short   403

GUIDELINE 3: Make Your Pages Attractive   403

GUIDELINE 4: Limit Loading Time   403

GUIDELINE 5: Keep Your Pages Up to Date   403

Guidelines for Creating Web Sites   403

GUIDELINE 1: Begin by Considering Your Site's Audience and Purpose   404

GUIDELINE 2: Meet Your Readers' Informational Needs   404

GUIDELINE 3: Organize Your Site Hierarchically   404

GUIDELINE 4:   Provide Useful Associative Links   405

GUIDELINE 5:   Label Your Links Clearly   405

GUIDELINE 6:   Provide Many Navigational Aids   406

GUIDELINE 7:   Use a Consistent Visual Design   406

GUIDELINE 8:   Enable Readers to Contact You   406

GUIDELINE 9:   Test Your Site   407

Exercises   408

FOCUS ON ETHICS: Ethics of Web Site Creation   407

CHAPTER 16   **Creating and Delivering Oral Presentations   409**

GUIDELINE 1:   Define Your Objectives   410

GUIDELINE 2:   Select the Form of Oral Delivery Best Suited to Your Purpose and Audience   410

GUIDELINE 3:   Focus on a Few Main Points   412

GUIDELINE 4:   Use a Simple Structure—and Help Your Listeners Follow It   412

GUIDELINE 5:   Use a Conversational Style   413

GUIDELINE 6:   Look at Your Audience   415

GUIDELINE 7:   Prepare for Interruptions and Questions—and Respond Courteously   416

GUIDELINE 8:   Fully Integrate Visual Aids into Your Presentation   417

GUIDELINE 9:   Rehearse   424

GUIDELINE 10:   Accept Your Nervousness—and Work with It   425

Making Team Presentations   425

Conclusion   427

Exercises   427

CHAPTER 17   **Creating Communications with a Team   428**

Special Challenges of Team Projects   429

GUIDELINE 1:   Begin by Creating a Consensus Concerning the Communication's Objectives   430

GUIDELINE 2:   Involve the Whole Team in Planning   431

GUIDELINE 3:   Make a Project Schedule   433

GUIDELINE 4:   Share Leadership Responsibilities   433

GUIDELINE 5:   Make Meetings Efficient   435

GUIDELINE 6:   Encourage Debate and Diversity of Ideas   435

GUIDELINE 7:   Be Sensitive to Possible Cultural and Gender Differences in Team Interactions   438

GUIDELINE 8:   Use Computer Support for Collaboration When It's Available   439

Conclusion   440

PART **VIII** **Superstructures** 441

CHAPTER 18 **Reports** 443
Your Readers Want to Use the Information You Provide 444
Readers' Six Basic Questions 444
General Superstructure for Reports 445
Sample Outlines and Reports 449
Conclusion 452

REFERENCE GUIDE **Three Types of Special Reports** 459
Empirical Research Reports 460
Feasibility Reports 487
Progress Reports 506

CHAPTER 19 **Proposals** 515
The Variety of Proposal-Writing Situations 516
Proposal Readers Are Investors 517
The Questions Readers Ask Most Often 518
Strategy of the Conventional Superstructure for Proposals 518
Superstructure for Proposals 520
Sample Proposal 527

CHAPTER 20 **Instructions** 533
Four Important Points 534
Superstructure for Instructions 535
Physical Construction of Instructions 547
Writing On-Line Instructions 549
Sample Instructions 549
Exercises 557

Appendixes 559

APPENDIX A **Formats for Letters, Memos, and Books** 561
Letter Format 562
Memo Format 567
Book Format 569

APPENDIX B **Documenting Your Sources 589**

Choosing a Format for Documentation 590

Deciding Where to Place In-Text Citations 590

Using the APA Documentation Style 591

Using the MLA Documentation Style 596

APPENDIX C **Projects and Cases 603**

Project 1:   Resume and Job Application Letter 604

Project 2:   Informational Web Site 605

Project 3:   Informational Page 606

Project 4:   Unsolicited Recommendation 607

Project 5:   Brochure 608

Project 6:   Instructions 608

Project 7:   User Test and Report 609

Project 8:   Project Proposal 610

Project 9:   Progress Report 611

Project 10:   Formal Report or Proposal 611

Project 11:   Oral Briefing I: Project Plans 612

Project 12:   Oral Briefing II: Project Results 613

Case 1:   Electromagnetic Fields 614

Case 2:   Company Day Care 616

Case 3:   Ethics Report 620

Case 4:   Corporate Credo 621

Case 5:   International Issue Report 621

Case 6:   Propose Your Own Business 622

Acknowledgments 625

References 629

Index 633

TECHNICAL COMMUNICATION

A Reader-Centered Approach

Fourth Edition

Introduction

CHAPTER 1
Communication, Your Career, and This Book

CHAPTER 2
Overview of the Reader-Centered Communication Process: Obtaining a Job

CHAPTER

Communication, Your Career, and This Book

CHAPTER OVERVIEW

Your Communication Skills Will Be Critical to Your Success

Writing at Work Differs from Writing at School

At Work, Writing Is an Action

The Main Advice of This Book: Think Constantly about Your Readers

How People Read

Two Strategies for Keeping Your Readers in Mind

Some Reader-Centered Strategies You Can Begin Using Now

What Lies Ahead in This Book

From the perspective of your professional career, communication is one of the most valuable subjects you will study in college.

Why? Imagine what your working days will be like. You'll spend much of your time using the special knowledge and skills you learned in college to answer questions asked by co-workers, develop recommendations requested by managers, and solve problems faced by customers. Furthermore, you will generate many good ideas on your own. Looking around, you will discover ways to make things work better or do them less expensively, to solve problems that have stumped others, or to bring about improvements that others haven't even begun to dream about.

Yet all your knowledge and ideas will be useless unless you communicate them to someone else. Consider the examples of Sarah Berlou and Larry Thayer.

A recent college graduate who majored in metallurgy, Sarah works on a research team that is developing an experimental automobile engine. For the past week, she has been analyzing a group of pistons that broke during a recent test. Her analysis has been skillful, but what she learns about why the pistons failed will be of no help to her team unless she communicates her results to the engineers who must re-design them.

Similarly, Larry, a newly hired dietitian, must communicate to accomplish his goal of improving operations in the kitchen of the hospital where he works. Larry has devised a way to reorganize kitchen operations that will save money and provide better service to patients. However, his ideas will lead to action only if he communicates his recommendations to people who have the power to implement them.

YOUR COMMUNICATION SKILLS WILL BE CRITICAL TO YOUR SUCCESS

Like Sarah and Larry, you will be able to make your work valuable to others only if you communicate it to them.

College graduates typically spend one day a week—or more—writing.

Consequently, you'll spend much of your time at work writing and speaking. Numerous studies indicate that if you are at all like the typical college graduate, you can expect to spend about 20 percent of your on-the-job time on writing (Barnum and Fischer; Beer and McMurrey; Northy; Pinelli, Glassman, Oliu, and Barclay; Roth). That's one full day out of every 5-day work week! And it doesn't include all the additional time you'll spend talking with other people—whether on the phone or in person, whether in groups and meetings or one-to-one.

Communication ability is critical to on-the-job success.

Moreover, your success in your career will depend largely on your ability to communicate effectively. For example, 94 percent of the graduates from seven departments that send students to technical writing classes reported that the ability to "write well" (not just write, but *write well*) is important to them in their jobs. More than half—58 percent—said it is of "great" or "critical" importance (Anderson). When communication researcher Lorie Roth asked college graduates in a variety of professions how important writing is to them, more than 75 percent responded "very important"—the highest level of importance they could check on their questionnaires.

Because communication is so critical in the workplace, your ability to write and speak effectively will be a major factor your employer considers when evaluating your performance (Beer and McMurrey).

Communication ability enables you to have an impact in your career.

In addition to helping you earn recognition and advancement, good communication skills can also bring you the satisfaction of having a personal impact in your career. Perhaps you will design a new product or service you believe your employer should offer. Maybe you will seek an increased budget to support an important project you are leading. To succeed in these endeavors, you will need to influence other people's decisions and actions through your writing and speaking.

You may also want to have an impact in another area. Many of the issues that arise on the job involve moral and ethical values. Companies sometimes consider modifying their operations in a way that will improve efficiency but displace workers. Government departments, such as environmental protection agencies, often develop regulations that will help some people but disadvantage others. And in any workplace, questions arise about whether certain decisions, policies, and practices are fair to various individuals or groups. Decisions involving ethical values are difficult to make because people have different ideas about what is the right thing to do. For your views to influence the outcome on such matters, you will need to express yourself clearly and persuasively.

This book will help you write and speak effectively at work.

This book will teach you how to succeed when you communicate at work. It concentrates on written communications to be read on paper or a computer screen, but the strategies and skills it describes apply also to oral communication. Also, Chapters 13 and 17 discuss oral communication strategies you can use when working with others, and Chapter 16 provides detailed advice for oral presentations.

WRITING AT WORK DIFFERS FROM WRITING AT SCHOOL

This book begins with the assumption that you already know a great many things about effective communication that will be indispensable in your career. However, it also assumes that you may need to learn new skills—and even some new ways of thinking about communication—in order to convey your ideas successfully on the job. That's because communication at work differs significantly from communication at school. The following sections discuss these differences with respect to writing, but similar differences also exist for oral communication.

PURPOSE

As a student, you write for *educational* purposes. Instructors ask you to compose term papers, prepare laboratory reports, and take written exams to help you learn the course material and give you a chance to demonstrate your mastery of a subject. They read primarily to assess your knowledge and assign a grade, and they are unlikely to alter their personal beliefs or actions as a result of what you say. In contrast, on the job, you will write for *practical* purposes, such as helping your employer improve a product or increase efficiency. Your readers will be co-workers, customers, or other individuals who need your information and ideas so that they can pursue their own practical goals.

At work, people write for practical purposes.

Technical Communication Careers

No discussion of workplace writing would be complete without a description of the profession of technical communication. "This is an ideal career for anyone who likes to write and enjoys science, technology, or some similar specialty," according to Jonathan Dinsmore, an award-winning writer of computer manuals for Structural Dynamics Research Corporation, a software development company. "I feel as though I'm contributing to important medical developments," adds Julie Neild, who works with research scientists as a medical writer at Eli Lilly, a major pharmaceutical company.

Rated in the top twenty of the best careers in America, technical communication includes a wide range of jobs (Gilbert). Jonathan and Julie both work with small groups of other professional communicators. In contrast, many large companies, such as AT&T and IBM, employ hundreds, even thousands of technical communication specialists. Other employers include the aircraft and automobile industries, environmental consulting firms, government agencies, hospitals, medical research centers, universities, and industrial research laboratories. In fact, in almost every field, technical communicators find interesting and challenging work. There are even companies whose sole business is to sell technical communication services to other organizations.

Although most technical communicators prepare print documents, an increasing number work with other media, preparing such things as on-line computer documentation, computer-based training programs, multimedia information systems, and videotape instructions.

In the United States, more than 100 colleges and universities offer degrees in technical communication, ranging from the associate degree to the Ph.D. Also, many people enter this profession from other fields, such as journalism, literature, and political science, as well as from various technical specialties, including engineering and the sciences.

For more information about careers in this field, talk with your technical writing instructor, librarian, or campus placement center. You can also contact the Society for Technical Communication (STC), an international organization, at Suite 904, 901 North Stuart Street, Arlington, VA 22203. The STC's Web site is at http://www.stc-va.org.

These differences in purpose have a profound impact on the kinds of communication you need to produce. Consider just one example. In college, where your aim is to show how much you know, one of your writing strategies is probably to say as much as you can about your subject. At work, where you will write to support or influence other people's actions, your strategy should be to include *only* the information your readers need—no matter how much more you know. Extra information will only clog your readers' path to what they need, thereby decreasing their efficiency and creating frustration.

At work, writers include only what their readers will find useful or persuasive.

AUDIENCE

When you write a paper in college, you most often write to a single person: your instructor. At work, however, you will often create a single communication that addresses a wide variety of people who differ from one another in many important ways, including their familiarity with your specialty, the way they will use your

Audiences for on-the-job writing are diverse in many ways.

information, and their professional and personal concerns. The audience for Larry's report recommending changes to the hospital kitchen is typically diverse.

Larry's readers differ widely in their responsibilities and concerns.

> Larry's first reader will be his supervisor, who will want to know how operations in her area would have to change if his recommendations were adopted.
>
> Some of his other readers will include the vice president for finance, who will want to verify Larry's cost estimates; the director of personnel, who will want to know whether she would need to rewrite any job descriptions; and members of the labor union, who will want assurances that the new work assignments will treat them fairly.

The audiences for on-the-job communications often reflect other kinds of diversity as well. Many organizations have clients, customers, and suppliers in other parts of the world. Thirty-three percent of U.S. corporate profits are generated by international trade (Lustig and Koester), and the economies of many other nations are similarly linked to distant parts of the globe. Moreover, many employers are themselves international, so that even when employees address their co-workers they are writing or speaking to persons in other countries. In addition, when communicating to co-workers working at their own locations, workers often address a multicultural audience—persons of diverse national and ethnic origin. Your ability to communicate successfully at work will probably depend partly on your ability to adapt to the multinational, multicultural nature of your audience.

TYPES OF COMMUNICATION

Also, on the job you will create a wide variety of communications that you probably don't prepare at school, including memos, business letters, instructions, project proposals, and progress reports. Each of these types of communication has its own conventions, which you need to learn in order to write successfully at work.

IMPORTANCE OF THE VISUAL DIMENSION

At work, writing often includes visual aids and page design.

When writing at school, you may be accustomed to writing assignments that involve only text, only words. On the job, however, you will often use visual aids such as drawings, charts, and tables to communicate facts and shape attitudes. Probably, you will also devote much effort to arranging text and visual aids on a page or computer screen in a way that makes the communication attractive, easy to understand, and easy to navigate for people who wish to locate and read only a particular part of the overall communication. Figure 1.1 shows a page from a computer manual that illustrates the importance of the visual dimension.

WRITING PROCESS

At work, you will probably use writing processes that differ substantially from those you are familiar with in college:

■ **FIGURE 1.1** **Some Visual Dimensions of Technical Communication** From Hewlett Packard, *HP Laserjet 5P and 5MP Printer User's Manual* (Boise, Idaho: Hewlett Packard, 1995) 4–19.

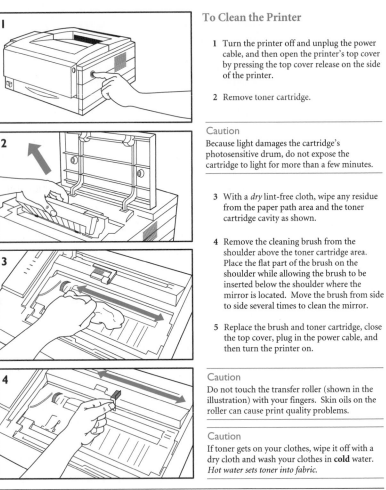

Visual features of this page help readers perform their task.

The large heading explains what readers will learn.

The drawings show exactly what the readers need to do; they even show a hand performing these tasks.

They include arrows to indicate the direction of movement.

Each numbered drawing corresponds to the step with the same number.

To help readers match each drawing with its step, the numbers in the drawings are very large, and the numbers for the steps are bold and in a column of their own.

Dark lines highlight the cautions; the word "caution" is printed in bold.

The rectangle at the side of the page helps readers flip to the specific information they need.

To Clean the Printer

1 Turn the printer off and unplug the power cable, and then open the printer's top cover by pressing the top cover release on the side of the printer.

2 Remove toner cartridge.

Caution
Because light damages the cartridge's photosensitive drum, do not expose the cartridge to light for more than a few minutes.

3 With a *dry* lint-free cloth, wipe any residue from the paper path area and the toner cartridge cavity as shown.

4 Remove the cleaning brush from the shoulder above the toner cartridge area. Place the flat part of the brush on the shoulder while allowing the brush to be inserted below the shoulder where the mirror is located. Move the brush from side to side several times to clean the mirror.

5 Replace the brush and toner cartridge, close the top cover, plug in the power cable, and then turn the printer on.

Caution
Do not touch the transfer roller (shown in the illustration) with your fingers. Skin oils on the roller can cause print quality problems.

Caution
If toner gets on your clothes, wipe it off with a dry cloth and wash your clothes in **cold** water. *Hot water sets toner into fabric.*

Troubleshooting and Maintenance 4-19

4 Troubleshooting and Maintenance

Collaborative writing is more common at work than in college.

■ **Collaboration.** Eighty-seven percent of the college graduates studied by researchers Lisa Ede and Andrea Lunsford reported that they work with co-writers at least some of the time. For long documents, the number of co-writers is sometimes astonishingly large. Martin Marietta Corporation's multivolume proposal to build a permanent space station contained text and drawings by more than 300 engineers (Mathes and Stevenson). Even when only one person prepares a communication, he or she consults others about it throughout the writing process. These other people may include the writer's boss and co-workers—and even members of the intended audience.

- **Reviews.** In one form of collaboration, writers submit their work for review by managers and others who have the power to demand certain changes. The number of reviewers may range from one to a dozen or more, and some drafts go through many cycles of review and revision before obtaining final approval. Carolyn Boiarsky, a communication expert, describes one document that went through more than 100 drafts!

- **Document families.** People at work often create families of related documents as they work on a project. For example, they may write a proposal seeking permission for the project, prepare interim reports to tell others about their progress, and compile a final report when the project is finished. Documents in these families often refer to one another and even borrow material from other "family" members.

- **Deadlines.** Whatever kind of communications you prepare at work, deadlines for completing them are likely to be much more significant—and changeable—than the deadlines for the papers you write at school. For example, if your company is preparing a proposal or sales document, it must reach the client on time. Otherwise, it may not be considered at all—no matter how good it is. Employers sometimes advise that "it's better to be 80 percent complete than 100 percent late." On the other hand, deadlines that initially seem firm are sometimes extended as new priorities arise with their own urgent deadlines.

At work, writing often must be reviewed and approved by others.

"It's better to be 80 percent complete than 100 percent late."

POLITICAL AND SOCIAL CONSIDERATIONS

Researcher Geoffrey A. Cross witnessed the production of a 504-word letter that took 8 people 51 days to write. One reason this letter took so long to write is that the various co-writers held different positions in the organization and had different views about what the letter should say. Such disagreements are common. Although individuals, departments, and divisions may share the same overall objectives, they may have very different ideas about how to achieve them. Moreover, some organizations are full of competitiveness and even intrigue, as individuals and groups vie for recognition, power, and money.

Even in the absence of conflict or competition, every communication situation has social dimensions. To begin, some sort of relationship exists between the writer and his or her readers: manager and subordinate, customer and supplier, co-worker and co-worker. In addition, every organization has a certain "style," which reflects the way the organization perceives itself and presents itself to outsiders. For example, an organization might be formal and conservative or informal and innovative. Individual departments within organizations may also have their own styles, which all members of the group are expected to reflect in the way they write. At work, you will need to take a wide range of political and social considerations into account when you write.

Different organizations have different customs about writing.

LEGAL AND ETHICAL CONCERNS

Everything you write at work is potentially a legal document.

Under the law, most documents written by employees are viewed as representing the position and commitments of the organization itself. Company documents can even be subpoenaed as evidence in disputes over contracts and in product liability lawsuits. These are among the reasons that certain documents are carefully reviewed before being sent to their intended readers.

Be alert to the ethical dimensions of your writing.

Even when the law does not come into play, many communications written at work have moral and ethical dimensions. The decisions and actions they advocate can affect many people for better or worse. Because of the importance of the ethical dimension of the writing you will do in your career, this book presents "Focus on Ethics" discussions throughout its chapters. The first is on page 12.

AT WORK, WRITING IS AN ACTION

Some people are hindered in their ability to write effectively on the job because they mistakenly think of writing as an afterthought, as merely recording or transporting information they developed while acting as specialists in their chosen fields.

Nothing could be further from the truth.

When you write at work, you act. You exert your power to achieve a specific result, to change things from the way they are now to the way you want them to be. Consider, again, the examples of Sarah and Larry.

In addition to acting as specialists, Sarah and Larry must perform *writing acts*.

Sarah wants to help her team develop a successful engine. Acting as a metallurgical specialist, she has tested the faulty pistons to determine why they failed. Her ultimate purpose is to help her employer design and produce pistons without flaws. To contribute to the success of the engine, she, too, must perform a *writing act*. She must compose sentences, construct tables of data, and perform other writing activities in order to present her results in a way the engineers will find useful.

Similarly, Larry believes that the hospital kitchen is run inefficiently. Acting as a dietetics specialist, he has devised a plan for improving its operation. For his plan to be put into effect, however, Larry must perform an *act of writing*. He must write a proposal that will persuade the hospital's decision-makers to implement his plan.

At work, writing is a social action.

The most important thing to remember about the "writing acts" you will perform at work is that they are *social* actions. Every communication you write will be an interchange between particular, individual people: you and your readers. Perhaps you will be a supervisor telling a co-worker what you want done, an adviser trying to persuade your boss to make a certain decision, an expert helping another person operate a certain piece of equipment. Your reader may be an experienced employee who is uncertain of the purpose of your request, a manager who has been educated to ask certain questions when making a decision, a machine operator who has a particular sense of personal dignity and a specific amount of knowledge about the equipment to be operated.

Even when you are writing to a group of people, your communication will establish an individual relationship between you and each person in the group. Each person will read with his or her own eyes, react with his or her own thoughts and feelings.

THE MAIN ADVICE OF THIS BOOK: THINK CONSTANTLY ABOUT YOUR READERS

The observation that writing is a social action leads to the main advice of this book: when writing, think constantly about your readers. Think about what they want from you—and why. Think about how you want to help or influence them and how they will react to what you have to say. Think about them as if they were standing right there in front of you while you talked together.

You may be surprised that this book emphasizes the personal dimension of writing more than such important characteristics as clarity and correctness. Although clarity and correctness are important, they cannot, by themselves, ensure that something you write at work will be successful.

For example, if Larry's proposal for modifying the hospital kitchen is to succeed, he will have to explain the problems created by the present operation in a way that his *readers* find compelling, he will have to address the kinds of objections his *readers* will raise to his recommendations, and he will have to deal sensitively with the possibility that his *readers* may feel threatened by having a new employee suggest improvements to a system they themselves set up. If his proposal fails to do these things, it will not succeed, no matter how "clear and correct" the writing is. A communication may be perfectly clear, perfectly correct, and yet be utterly unpersuasive, utterly ineffective.

Success is determined by the readers' response.

The same is true for all the writing you will do at work: what matters is how your readers respond. That's the reason for taking the reader-centered approach described in this book. This approach focuses your attention on the ways you want to help and influence your readers and teaches specific strategies that you can use to achieve those goals.

HOW PEOPLE READ

The detailed suggestions about on-the-job writing presented in this book are based, in part, on what researchers have learned about how people read. The following paragraphs describe three of their most important findings: readers construct meaning, readers' responses are shaped by the situation, and readers react moment by moment.

READERS CONSTRUCT MEANING

For readers, determining meaning requires mental work.

When researchers say that readers construct meaning, they are emphasizing the fact that the meaning of a written message doesn't leap into our minds solely from the words we see. Instead, we derive meaning from the message by actively interacting with it. In this interaction, we draw on and apply a great deal of knowledge that

Your Writing and Your Values

At work, you will sometimes write communications that could affect the happiness and even the health and well-being of other people. For example, you may write a proposal for a new product that can cause physical harm—at least if not handled properly. You may prepare a report that managers will use to make other people's jobs significantly more—or less—desirable, or even determine whether these people will continue to be employed.

Ethics and This Book

A major aim of this book is to help you deal with the ethical issues you may encounter when communicating at work. Of course, personal values differ at least somewhat from person to person. Consequently, this book won't tell you what your values ought to be. Instead, it will help

you see how you can act in accordance with your own values on the job.

Will Your Values Be Welcome at Work?

Some students wonder whether it will really be necessary for them to think about their values at work. Will you actually be asked to write unethically in your career? The answer depends largely on the company you work for and the managers to whom you report. Based on interviews with top executives, Charles E. Watson reports that 125 of the largest companies in the United States have a strong commitment to ethical behavior (Watson). Employees of these companies, one assumes, receive support and guidance when facing an ethical conflict. Similarly, in *Companies with a Conscience*, Mary Scott and

Howard Rothman describe many instances of values-minded management. And the Center for Business Ethics has a file with hundreds of ethics codes that corporations throughout the United States have adopted as their official policy (see page 102 for an example). Still, we all have read stories about companies that engage in bribery, price gouging, dumping of toxic wastes in public waterways, and other unethical practices. Further, even a company that has adopted an ethics code may have employees who act unethically. A nationwide survey indicates that 50 percent of U.S. employees have felt pressure on the job to act in ways they consider to be unethical (Golen, Powers, and Agnes).

(continued)

isn't on the page at all, but in our heads. Consider, for example, the amount of knowledge we must possess and apply to understand even such a simple sentence as "It's a dog." To begin, we must know enough about letters and language to decipher the three printed words *(it's, a,* and *dog)* and to understand their grammatical relationships. Children and people from some other cultures do not possess this knowledge and therefore cannot read the sentence. Moreover, to understand what a sentence means, we must also know the context in which it is made. For example, the word *dog* has several meanings, so we cannot know the meaning of the sentence "It's a dog" unless we know whether it answers the question, "What kind of animal is Jim's new pet?" or the question, "What do you think of the new computer made by ABC Corporation?"

Furthermore, we not only construct meaning from individual words and sentences, but we also build these smaller meanings into larger structures of knowledge. These structures are not merely our memories of the words we have read but rather our own creations. Here's a quick way to demonstrate this point to yourself.

(continued from previous page)

Bring Your Values to Work

Because they want to avoid conflicts over values in their careers, some employees have decided that their personal values have no place on the job. But that is a dangerous course. It can lead you into going along with actions at work that you would condemn at home. Furthermore, as companies decide what to do in certain situations, they sometimes discuss quite explicitly the ethical dimensions of the actions they might take. In these discussions, you can influence your employer's organization to act in accordance with your own ethical views—but only if you have brought your values with you to work.

Think of Yourself as a Citizen

The "Focus on Ethics" boxes throughout this book will help you integrate your values into your communication activities at work in ways that minimize unproductive conflict.

A helpful initial step is to think of yourself not only as an *employee* but also as a *citizen* of the organization for which you work. When we think of the qualities of a good employee, we often think of a narrow range of attributes, such as productivity, punctuality, cooperativeness, and willingness to comply with corporate policy. When we think of the qualities of a good citizen, we think of considerateness, willingness to help others, and concern for the group's welfare. Both sets of values are important on the job.

Thinking of yourself as a citizen doesn't mean that you must disregard traditional business values. You can still pursue such goals as making a profit, increasing efficiency, and competing successfully. By thinking of yourself as both an employee and a citizen, you consider both profits and people when you write.

Thinking of yourself as a citizen can help you fulfill your ethical obligations to people outside your employer's organization as well as those within it. We all have multiple citizenships. We are citizens of our family, community, state, and country. We are also citizens of various formal and informal groups and organizations. We don't shed one citizenship in order to assume another. When you are communicating as a member of your employer's organization, remember that your communication may affect outside people as well—and that you have an ethical obligation to take their well-being and point of view into account.

Where to Start

A first step in bringing your personal values to your on-the-job communication might be to list those values. Then, you might imagine some of the ways these values might influence the communicating you do in your career. It's never too early to start thinking about what your values mean in terms of your practical actions as a communicator in the workplace.

Imagine that someone has asked you to explain the meaning of the following statement made earlier in this chapter: "When you write at work, you act." First, write down a sentence that answers the request, then try to find a sentence in the book that exactly matches yours. Most likely, you won't be able to. The sentence you wrote is not one you remembered from the text. Rather, it expresses the book's meaning in your own words. It is, in fact, the meaning you constructed through your interaction with the text.

READERS' RESPONSES ARE SHAPED BY THE SITUATION

A second important fact about readers is that their responses to a communication are shaped by the total situation in which they read—including their purpose in reading the communication, their perception of the writer's purpose, their personal stake in the subject discussed, and their past relations with the writer.

To see how such factors can influence a reader's reaction, consider Kate's situation.

Kate's response to the
memo will be shaped by
her situation.

Kate's employer asked her to select the desktop computer to be purchased for fifty offices at corporate headquarters. After completing much of her research, Kate read a memo that said the ABC computer is "a dog."

Kate's response to this statement would depend on many things. Did the other opinions and data she had gathered support this assessment? Was the statement made by a computer specialist, a salesperson for one of ABC's competitors, or the president of Kate's company? Had she already announced publicly her own assessment of the computer, or was she still undecided about it? Depending on the answers to these questions, Kate's response might range anywhere from being pleased because her own judgments have been supported by a well-respected person to being embarrassed by having her publicly announced judgment called into question.

The range of situational factors that can affect a reader's response is obviously unlimited. The key point is that in order to predict how a reader might respond to something you are writing, you must understand the situation in which the person will read your communication.

READERS REACT MOMENT BY MOMENT

The third important fact about readers is that they react to communications moment by moment. When we read a humorous novel, we chuckle as we read a funny sentence. We don't wait until we finish the entire book. Similarly, people react to each part of a memo, report, or proposal as soon as they come to it. The following demonstration illustrates this point.

Imagine you are the manager of the personnel department in a factory. A few days ago you met with Donald Pryzblo, who manages the data processing department, to discuss a problem. Recently, the company's computer has been issuing some payroll checks for the wrong amount. Your department and Pryzblo's work together in preparing each week's payroll. First, your clerks collect a time sheet for each employee, check over the information, and transfer the information on those sheets to time tickets, which they forward to Pryzblo's department. His clerks enter the information into a computer program that calculates each employee's pay and prints the checks. The whole procedure is summarized in the following diagram:

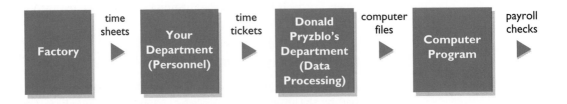

In your discussion with Pryzblo, you proposed a solution that he did not like. Because you two are at the same level in the company, neither of you can tell the other what to do. When you turn on your computer this morning, you find an e-mail message from Pryzblo.

Your task in this demonstration is to read the memo *very slowly*—so slowly that you can focus on the way you react, moment by moment, to each statement. First, turn to the e-mail message shown in Figure 1.2 on page 16. Cover it with a sheet of paper. Then slide the paper down the page, stopping after you expose the first sentence. Immediately after reading the sentence, write down your reactions (in your role as manager of the personnel department). Proceed in this way through the rest of the message. When you are finished, turn back here.

Finished? Now look back over your notes. Most people who participate in this demonstration find themselves responding strongly to almost every sentence. For example, they react to the quotation marks that surround the word *errors* in the first sentence. The word *insinuated* in the second sentence also draws an immediate response from most readers. (They laugh if they forget to play the role of personnel manager; they cringe if they remember to play the role.)

Readers respond on a moment-by-moment basis.

The fact that readers respond to a communication moment by moment is important to you as a writer because their reaction to any one sentence will influence their reaction to everything they read from that point forward. For example, most people who read Donald Pryzblo's memo while playing the role of personnel manager grow defensive the moment they see the quotation marks around the word *errors,* and they become even more so when they come to the word *insinuated.* After they read the third paragraph, their defensiveness hardens into a grim determination to resist any recommendation Pryzblo may make.

Readers' reactions in one moment shape their subsequent reactions.

A few readers are more even tempered. Instead of becoming defensive, they become skeptical. As they read the first two sentences, they realize that Pryzblo is behaving emotionally rather than intellectually, so they decide to evaluate his statements very carefully. When they read his accusation that the personnel department clerks are miscopying the time sheets, they want to know what evidence he has to support that claim. When the next sentence fails to provide any evidence, they feel disinclined to go along with any suggestions Pryzblo may make.

When writing, keep your readers foremost in mind.

Thus, even though different readers react to the first few sentences of this memo in different ways, their early reactions shape their responses to the sentences that follow. Consequently, even though Pryzblo's recommendation seems sensible enough in itself, no reader I've met feels inclined to accept it.

It is possible, of course, that Pryzblo had some other purpose in writing his memo. For example, he may have wanted to inflame the personnel manager into making a rash response that would get him or her into trouble with their boss. For that purpose, his memo might have worked very well. But even in that case, the basic points of this demonstration would remain unchanged: people react to what they read on a moment-by-moment basis, and their reactions at each moment shape their reactions to what follows.

The preceding discussion explains why it is so important for you to follow the main advice of this book—"Think constantly about your readers." Each reader will create his or her own response to your communications. To write effectively, you need to be able to predict these responses and design your messages accordingly. You will be best able to do this if you keep your readers—their needs and goals,

■ **FIGURE 1.2**

**E-mail Message for
Demonstration**

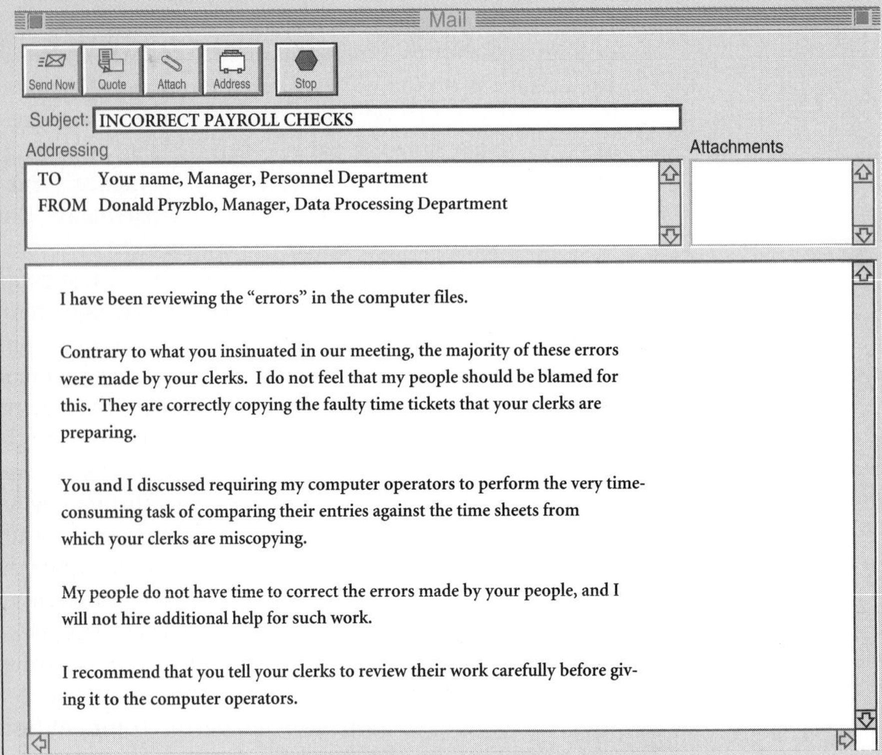

Mail

| Send Now | Quote | Attach | Address | | Stop |

Subject: INCORRECT PAYROLL CHECKS

Addressing   Attachments

TO   Your name, Manager, Personnel Department
FROM   Donald Pryzblo, Manager, Data Processing Department

I have been reviewing the "errors" in the computer files.

Contrary to what you insinuated in our meeting, the majority of these errors
were made by your clerks. I do not feel that my people should be blamed for
this. They are correctly copying the faulty time tickets that your clerks are
preparing.

You and I discussed requiring my computer operators to perform the very time-
consuming task of comparing their entries against the time sheets from
which your clerks are miscopying.

My people do not have time to correct the errors made by your people, and I
will not hire additional help for such work.

I recommend that you tell your clerks to review their work carefully before giving it to the computer operators.

feelings and situations, preferences and responsibilities—foremost in mind
throughout your work on each communication.

TWO STRATEGIES FOR KEEPING YOUR READERS IN MIND

Unfortunately, when writing you have so many things to do that it can be easy to
lose sight of your readers. To prevent this from happening, you can develop a reader-
centered writing process, and you can "talk" with your readers. These strategies are
explained in the following paragraphs and referred to throughout the rest of the
book.

USE A READER-CENTERED WRITING PROCESS

Your writing process is the set of activities you perform when you prepare a message. Although these activities are quite varied, they may be classified into five groups:

Activities of Writing

- Defining your objectives
- Planning your communication
- Drafting your communication
- Evaluating your draft
- Revising your draft based on the results of your evaluation

Define your objectives in a reader-centered way.

The strategy of a reader-centered writing process is to keep your reader primarily in mind during each of these activities. Thus, when defining your objectives, you focus on what you want to happen while your reader is reading. For example, instead of saying, "My purpose is to describe two companies from which we might buy supplies," you say, "My purpose is to present information about two suppliers to a manager who wants to quickly compare them on a point-by-point basis." Unlike the first statement, the second suggests what information you should include about the suppliers (the information related to your readers' selection criteria) and also how you should organize it (into a point-by-point comparison).

Refer to your reader-centered objectives throughout.

After you've defined your objectives in reader-centered terms, refer to your objectives continually so you can benefit from the practical insights they provide about how to write your message. Writers sometimes forget to do this. For example, when evaluating a draft, they concentrate on spelling and punctuation without asking whether their readers will respond to their message in the desired way. Avoid such mistakes. Throughout all your work on a communication, refer to your reader-centered objectives.

Use new insights that emerge.

In a reader-centered writing process, you must also remain open to new insights about your readers that you gain as you proceed. While planning, drafting, and evaluating a communication, writers often learn new things about their readers or the situational factors that will influence the readers' responses. When that happens, take advantage of what you've learned by altering your objectives, plans, and draft appropriately.

TALK WITH YOUR READERS

Aim for continuous reader involvement.

At work, it is often possible to speak directly with your readers about a communication that you are preparing. There is no better way to keep your readers in mind through the writing process than to discuss your communication with them as you create it. An ideal you should set for yourself is to achieve *continuous reader involvement,* in which you speak with your readers at every step in writing. Thus, when planning a report or set of instructions, you might ask them, "What do you want this communication to do for you? What kind of help do you want from it? How will you read it, and how will you use the information it presents?" When planning, you could discuss your ideas and perhaps show your readers an outline. When you've created a draft, you can ask for their reactions. If you are writing instructions, you might even ask members of your target audience to test out the draft to see if they can really perform the task by following what you've written.

Create an imaginary conversation if you can't actually talk with your readers.

In situations where you cannot talk directly with your readers, you may still benefit from conversing with them imaginatively. This strategy can be especially helpful when you are drafting. Think of your communication as a conversation in which you make a statement and your reader responds. Write each sentence, each paragraph, each chapter to create the interaction—the conversation—with your readers that will bring about the final result you desire.

Talk *with* your readers, not *to* them.

When following this strategy, it is crucial that you talk *with* your readers, not *to* them. When you talk *to* other people, you are like an actor reciting a speech: you stick to your script without regard to how your audience is reacting to your words. When you talk *with* others, you adjust your statements to fit their reactions. Does someone squeeze his brows in puzzlement? You explain the point more fully. Does someone twist her hands impatiently? You abbreviate your message. Are your listeners unpersuaded by one argument? Then you abandon it and try another.

Consider how much Donald Pryzblo could have benefited from "talking" with the personnel manager as he drafted his memo. After writing the first sentence, Pryzblo would have seen the manager wrinkle his or her forehead as the manager saw the quotation marks around the word *errors*. After writing the second sentence, Pryzblo would have seen the manager's jaw tighten and heard the manager exclaim, "What proof do you have that my clerks are making the mistakes?" Seeing these things, Pryzblo would have known that he could persuade the manager to accept his recommendation only if he changed his draft. Even better, Pryzblo could have considered the manager's reactions *before* drafting. Then he might have thought, "I want to begin this memo in a way that will make the personnel manager feel open-minded about my recommendation."

This strategy of imagining your readers in the act of reading works for any kind of communication, not just ones (like Pryzblo's) intended primarily to persuade. Figure 1.3 shows how another writer benefited from "talking" with her reader while writing a set of instructions. The strategy works so well because it enables you to anticipate your reader's moment-by-moment responses to your message and to write accordingly.

SOME READER-CENTERED STRATEGIES YOU CAN BEGIN USING NOW

Despite the many ways that readers' goals, concerns, feelings, and likely responses can vary from one situation to another, readers approach almost all on-the-job communications with several widely shared aims and preferences. The following paragraphs briefly introduce several reader-centered strategies that address these common aims and preferences so that you can begin using them immediately. All are discussed more fully later in this book:

- **Help your readers focus on key information quickly.** At work, readers are often looking for specific pieces of information. Sometimes what they most want is a particular fact. Sometimes it's the writer's conclusions or recommendations (not the thought processes that led up to these). Almost always it's something they

■ **FIGURE 1.3**

How One Writer "Talked" with Her Reader

Marty improved her draft by imagining her reader's reactions to what she wrote.

Marty's "Talk" with Her Reader

Marty, a young engineer, was writing instructions for calibrating an instrument for testing the strength of metal rods. One of her original instructions read like this:

15. Check the reading on Gauge E.

Marty then imagined how a typical user of her instructions would react after reading that instruction. She saw the reader look up and ask, "What should the reading be?" So Marty told the reader to look for the correct reading in the Table of Values.

Marty then imagined that when the reader looked at the Table of Values, the reader discovered that the value on Gauge E was incorrect. The reader then asked. "What do I do now?" So Marty revised again.

In the end, her instructions read as follows.

15. Check the reading on Gauge E to see if it corresponds with the appropriate value listed in the Table of Values (see Appendix IV, page 38).
   • if the value is <u>incorrect</u>, follow the procedures for correcting inbalances (page 28).
   • if the value is <u>correct</u>, proceed to Step 16.

intend to put to practical use as they perform some activity or make a decision. Instead of reading a communication from front to back in the way people do in college, readers at work often scan for the information they want and skip the rest of a communication entirely.

Help Your Readers Find Information Quickly

■ **State your main points up front, including your recommendations and conclusions.**

■ **In all other parts, state the information that is most important to your readers before presenting the less important information.**

■ **Use headings. Print them in bold to make them easy to spot.**

■ **Use topic sentences.**

■ **Use lists.**

■ **Eliminate irrelevant information that can hide what matters to your readers.**

These techniques are illustrated in Figure 1.4, which shows a memo written by Frank Thurmond, who was asked to find out whether his company could use a new,

■ FIGURE 1.4

Reader-Centered Strategies

Thurmond's first sentence explains the memo's relevance to the reader: it reports on tests the reader requested.

His next two sentences present the information his reader most needs: the new plastic won't work.

Headings and topic sentences tell the reader what each section contains, thereby helping him locate specific information quickly.

Headings are in boldface to make them stand out.

Thurmond uses a list to promote rapid reading.

In the list, Thurmond puts the most important problem first: the deformation of the bottles.

Thurmond explicitly states the significance of the facts he presents.

Throughout the memo, Thurmond uses lively, active verbs (highlighted in color).

PIAGETT HOUSEHOLD PRODUCTS
Intracompany Correspondence

October 12, 19—

To   Herman Wyatt
From   Frank Thurmond
Subject Test of Salett 321 Bottles for Use with StripIt

We have completed the tests you requested to find out whether we can package StripIt Oven Cleaner in bottles made of the new plastic, Salett 321. We conclude that we cannot, chiefly because StripIt attacks and begins to destroy the plastic at 100°F. We also found other significant problems.

Test Methods

To test Salett 321, we used two procedures that are standard in the container industry. First, we evaluated the storage performance of filled bottles by placing them in a chamber for 28 days at 73°F. We stored other sets of 24 bottles at 100°F and 125° for the same period. Second, we tested the response of filled bottles to environmental stress by exposing 24 of them for 7 days to varying humidities and varying tremperatures up to 140°F.

We also subjected glass bottles containing StripIt to the same test conditions.

Results and Discussion

In the 28 day storage tests, we discovered three major problems:

- StripIt attacked the bottles made from Salett 321 at 100°F and 125°F. At 125°F, the damage was particularly serious, causing localized but severe deformation. Most likely, StripIt's ketone solvents weakened the plastic. The deformed bottles leaned enough to fall off shelves in retail stores.

- The sidewalls sagged slightly at all temperatures, making the bottles unattractive.

- StripIt yellowed in plastic bottles stored at 125°F. No discoloration occured in glass bottles at this temperature. We speculate that StripIt interacted with the resin used in Salett 321, absorbing impurities from it.

In the environmental test, StripIt attacked the bottles at 140°F.

Conclusion

Salett 321 is not a suitable container for StripIt. Please call me if you want additional information about these tests.

---

inexpensive plastic to make the containers for a household oven cleaner it manufactures. Among other things, note how careful he was to include only the information his readers would find relevant. For example, he selected only the test results that would help his readers decide whether to use the new plastic. If he were writing to someone else—say, another researcher who wanted to understand the nature of the chemical reaction between the oven cleaner and the plastic—Thurmond would have included a different set of information.

■ **Tell your readers how your information is relevant to them.** When readers pick up a communication at work, they often ask, "Why should I read this? How does it relate to my needs or responsibilities?" If they decide to read on, they want to know the relevance of the facts being presented.

Explain Relevance to Your Readers

■ In the first sentence or paragraph, explicitly tell your readers how your communication relates to their goals and interests.

■ Wherever you state facts, also explain their significance from your readers' perspective.

To explain the relevance of his memo, Thurmond opened with a sentence that not only announces the topic (tests of the plastic), but also reminds his reader that the reader requested the tests. Thurmond also explains the significance of the various test results, for example, when he states that when the oven cleaner attacks the plastic, it deforms the bottles so that they might fall off the shelves in retail stores.

■ **Make your communication easy to read.** Help your readers get the information they want with as little effort as possible.

Make Your Writing Easy to Read

■ Trim away unnecessary words. For example, use "now" instead of "at this point in time," and use "because" instead of "due to the fact that."

■ Use the active voice, rather than the passive. Thus, instead of writing, "The tests *were* completed by our department," write, "Our department *completed* the tests."

■ Put the action in verbs rather than in other parts of speech. For example, write, "We *conclude*" rather than "We reached the *conclusion*."

How effective are these writing techniques? Researchers James Suchan and Robert Colucci created two versions of the same report. The "high-impact" version followed most of the techniques just described, and the "low-impact" version did not. The high-impact version reduced reading time by 22 percent, and tests showed that readers understood it better.

WHAT LIES AHEAD IN THIS BOOK

Throughout the rest of this book, you'll find detailed advice and information that will help you write effectively and ethically on the job. Figure 1.5 summarizes this book's overall organization.

Many of the chapters offer guidelines, which are brief summary statements designed to make the book's suggestions easy to remember and use. As you read the guidelines, remember that the guidelines are merely that: guidelines. They are not rules. Each one has exceptions, and some of them may even seem to conflict. To apply the guidelines successfully, you need to use good sense and creativity, guided always by thoughts of your readers and the specific ways you want to affect them.

This book's guidelines are not rules.

To help you learn how to apply the guidelines, the chapters describe many sample situations and show many example letters, memos, reports, and other communications. These reflect *typical* business concerns and practices. However, what's typical is not what's universal. The readers and circumstances you will encounter in your job will certainly differ to some extent from those described here. In fact, you may work for a boss or client whose regulations, values, or preferences are very *untypical*. To write successfully, then, you may need to *ignore* one or more of this book's guidelines.

■ **FIGURE 1.5** **Contents of this Book**	Part	Description
	I Overview	To provide you with a detailed example of the reader-centered writing process, Chapter 2 leads you through the writing of a resume and job application letter.
	II Reader-centered writing process	Chapters 3 through 14 present suggestions for performing each of the activities of the writing process, beginning with defining your objectives, and proceeding through planning, drafting, evaluating, and revising.
	III Special communication situations	Chapter 15 explains how to create business-oriented e-mail messages, Web pages, and Web sites.
		Chapter 16 tells how to prepare and deliver oral presentations.
		Chapter 17 provides advice for working on a team that is preparing a written or oral communication.
	IV Superstructures	Chapters 18 through 20 introduce you to the general frameworks—called *superstructures*—used for constructing six types of communication: reports (four types), proposals, and instructions.
	V Formats	Appendix A describes the conventional formats for business letters, memos, and similar communications.
		Appendix B explains two widely used formats for citing sources.

No matter what situation you find yourself in, however, the book's overall advice will guide you to success: size up your situation by focusing on your readers and the way you want to affect them, then use your objectives to shape your message in a way that will bring about the result you desire and also treat ethically all persons who might be affected by your message. If you learn how to apply this advice to the typical situations described here, you will have mastered the strategies needed to write successfully in any untypical situation you encounter.

In your efforts to prepare yourself to communicate successfully in your career, I wish you good luck.

EXERCISES

1. Interview someone who holds a job you might like to have. Ask about the kinds of communications the person writes, the readers he or she addresses, the writing process and technology the person uses, and the amount of time the person spends writing. Supplement these questions with any others that will help you understand how writing fits into this person's work. According to your instructor's directions, bring either notes or a one-page report to class.

2. Find a communication written by someone who has the kind of job you want, perhaps by asking a friend, family member, or your own employer. Explain the communication's purposes from the point of view of both the writer and the readers. Describe some of the writing strategies the writer has used to achieve these purposes.

3. a. Find a piece of writing that you believe to be ineffective. (You might look for an unclear set of instructions or an unpersuasive advertisement for some business or technical product.) Write a brief analysis of three or four "reading moments" in which you interact with the text in a way that works against the writer's desired results.

   b. Now analyze an effective piece of writing. This time, write about three or four "reading moments" in which you interact with the text in a way that helps the writer bring about the desired results.

CASE

SELECTING THE RIGHT FORKLIFT TRUCK

It has been two weeks since you received this assignment from your boss, Mickey Chelini, who is the Production Engineer at the manufacturing plant that employs you. "We've been having more trouble with one of our forklift trucks," he explained. You are not surprised. Some of those jalopies have been breaking down regularly for years.

"And Ballinger's finally decided to replace one of them," Mickey continued. Ballinger is Mickey's boss and the top executive at the plant. His title is Plant Manager.

"What finally happened to make him decide that?" you asked. "I thought he was going to keep trying to repair those wrecks forever."

"Actually, he wants to replace one of the newer ones that we bought just two years ago," Mickey replied. "That particular forklift was manufactured by a company that has since gone bankrupt. Ballinger's afraid we won't be able to get replacement parts. I think he's right."

"Hmm," you commented.

"Anyway," Mickey said, "Ballinger wants to be sure he spends the company's money more wisely this time. He's done a little investigation himself and has narrowed the choice to two machines. He's asked me to figure out which one is the best choice."

You could see what was coming. You've had a hundred assignments like this before from Mickey.

"I'd like you to pull together all the relevant information for me. Don't make any recommendation yourself; just give me all the information I need to make my recommendation. Have it to me in two weeks."

"Will do," you said, as you started to think about how you could squeeze this assignment into your already tight schedule.

YOUR ASSIGNMENT

It's now two weeks later. You've gathered the information given below in "Notes on Forklifts." First, plan your final report by performing the following activities:

- List the specific questions Mickey will want your report to answer. *Note:* Your boss does *not* want you to include a recommendation in your report.
- Underline the facts in your notes that you would include in your report; put an asterisk by those you would emphasize.
- Decide how you would organize the report.
- Explain which techniques from the list on pages 18 through 21 you would use when writing this report. What other things would you do to assist your readers?

Second, imagine that you have been promoted to Mickey's job (Production Engineer). Tell how you would write the report that you would send to Ballinger regarding the purchase of a new forklift. It must contain your recommendation.

NOTES ON FORKLIFTS

Present Forklift. The present forklift, which is red, moves raw material from the loading dock to the beginning of the production line and takes finished products from the Packaging Department back to the loading dock. When it moves raw materials, the forklift hoists pallets weighing 600 pounds onto a platform 8 feet high, so that the raw materials can be emptied into a hopper. When transporting finished products, the forklift picks up and delivers pallets weighing 200 pounds at ground level. The forklift moves between stations at 10 mph, although some improvements in the production line will increase that rate to 15 mph in the next two months. The present forklift is easy to operate. No injuries and very little damage have been associated with its use.

Electric Forklift. The electric forklift carries loads of up to 1,000 pounds at speeds up to 30 mph. Although the electric forklift can hoist materials only 6 feet high, a 2-foot ramp could be built beneath the hopper platform in three days (perhaps over a long weekend, when the plant is closed). During construction of the ramp, production would have to stop. The ramp would cost $1,600. The electric forklift costs $37,250, and a special battery charger costs $1,500 more. The forklift would use about $2,000 worth of electricity each year. Preventive maintenance costs would be about $700 per year, and repair costs would be about $800 per year. While operating, the electric forklift emits no harmful fumes. Parts are available from a warehouse 500 miles away. They are ordered by phone and delivered the next day. The electric forklift has a good operating record, with very little damage to goods and with no injuries at all. It comes in blue and red.

Gasoline Forklift. The gasoline forklift is green and carries loads of up to 1 ton as rapidly as 40 mph. It can hoist materials 12 feet high. Because this forklift is larger than the one presently being used, the company would have to widen a doorway in the cement wall separating the Packaging Department from the loading dock. This alteration would cost $800 and would stop production for two days. The gasoline forklift costs $49,000 but needs no auxiliary equipment. However, under regulations established by the Occupational Safety and Health Administration, the company would have to install a ventilation fan to carry the exhaust fumes away from the hopper area. The fan costs $870. The gasoline forklift would require about $1,800 of fuel per year. Preventive maintenance would run an additional $400 per year, and repairs would cost about $600 per year. Repair parts are available from the factory, which is 17 miles from our plant. Other owners of this forklift have incurred no damage or injuries during its operation.

2

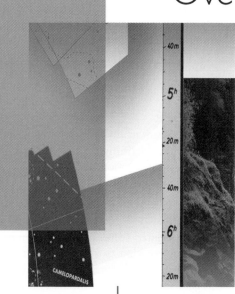

Overview of the Reader-Centered Communication Process: Obtaining a Job

CHAPTER OVERVIEW

Writing Your Resume

Electronic Resumes: Special Considerations

Writing Your Job Application Letter

Writing for Employment in Other Countries

T his chapter provides an overview of the reader-centered communication process. To illustrate this process, it shows how to create a resume and job application letter.

The resume and letter were chosen for this purpose for two reasons. The first is to provide you with detailed advice concerning two communications that will play important roles in your career. The second reason is this: these communications illustrate with special clarity how completely the success of your work-related writing depends on the response it elicits from your readers. When you finish reading this chapter, you should know not only how to take a reader-centered approach to communicating, but also why it is worthwhile to do so.

WRITING YOUR RESUME

The following advice for resume writing is organized around the five major activities of the reader-centered communication process: defining objectives, planning, drafting, evaluating your draft, and revising. A special section discusses the preparation of electronic resumes.

DEFINING YOUR RESUME'S OBJECTIVES

Qualities of a good statement of objectives

While preparing your resume or any other work-related communication, you must make a multitude of decisions about such things as what to say, how to organize your message, what style to use, and how to design your pages. A good statement of objectives contains enough specific information to serve as the basis for all of these decisions. It is *not* helpful to say simply that your resume's goal is to persuade an employer to give you a job or an interview for a job. To be truly useful, your objectives statement must identify the specific factors that will influence the employer's decision. For example, you must identify the exact qualifications the employer is seeking—because one of your resume's primary objectives is to persuade that you possess these qualifications. Your statement should also describe the way the employer will read your resume, because another of your resume's objectives is to highlight your qualifications for someone who reads in this particular way.

What Employers Look For
At a general level, the qualifications employers seek in job applicants fall into three categories:

Qualifications that employers seek

- **Technical expertise.** Employers want to hire people who, with a minimum of on-the-job training, can perform their jobs adeptly.
- **Supporting abilities.** Most jobs require a wide range of abilities beyond the purely technical ones. These often include communication, interpersonal, time management, and project management skills.
- **Favorable personal attributes.** Employers want to hire people they believe to be motivated, self-directed, and responsible. Because almost every job requires extensive, effective interaction with others, employers also want to hire people who will work well with co-workers, customers, and vendors, among others.

Try to learn exactly what the employer wants.

For any particular job, of course, employers will seek a specific set of technical know-how, collateral abilities, and personal attributes. Instead of asking, "Does this applicant have technical expertise?" an employer will ask, "Can this person analyze geological samples?" "Write computer programs in object-oriented C++?" "Manage a consumer electronics store?"

To identify the specific skills and personal qualities sought by the employers you'd like to work for, find out as much as possible about the daily work of people in the position you would like to hold. Gather this information by talking with instructors in your major, interviewing a person who now holds such a position, or reading materials about careers at your library or campus employment center. The more you understand about the job you want, the better prepared you will be to write a resume that demonstrates you have the qualities necessary to flourish in it.

How Employers Read Resumes

Employers often read resumes in a three-stage process.

Most employers use a three-stage process when selecting new employees. In the first stage, your resume may have different readers than in the latter two stages, and these readers may read in much different ways:

In stage one, the most promising applicants are quickly identified.

- **Initial screening.** Many employers receive hundreds, even thousands, of applications a week. Faced with this deluge of applications, these readers may scan quite rapidly through resumes, trying quickly to identify the best candidates. They can afford to mistakenly eliminate some good candidates from further consideration because there will still be more than enough to look at. Often these initial readers are employees in a personnel office, not specialists in the area where you are seeking a position.

  To succeed in this stage, your resume must make an immediate, positive impression on a reader who may be dulled by having read many other resumes in the previous hour or two. Moreover, your resume must be free from misspellings, grammatical errors, and any hint of sloppiness that would give this reader an excuse to shove your application into the rejection pile.

Stage-two readers seek an exact match with the employer's needs.

- **Detailed examination of the most promising applications.** Resumes that pass the initial screening are forwarded to stage-two readers: managers and others in the department with the opening. These persons, too, want to read rapidly because many other duties clamor for their attention. However, these readers have many fewer resumes to review, they know exactly what qualifications they desire, and they have a personal stake in the choice of the new employee because they will be working directly with this person. Consequently, they study resumes in detail, hoping to find a perfect match with their needs.

  To succeed with these readers, you must provide enough specific evidence to persuade them that you are extremely well suited for the position. Vagueness and generalities will not persuade that you have exactly the qualifications they seek.

- **In-depth interviewing.** Applicants whose resumes win favor with stage-two readers are invited for interviews so that the employer can assess their qualifications more completely. Resumes are often read with even greater care at this stage.

While writing your resume, focus on the readers in the first two stages: the personnel officer, who is trying to sort rapidly through an avalanche of applications, and the department manager, who is looking for someone whose qualifications exactly match the position to be filled. Your resume's primary goal is to make a rapid, distinctive, and favorable impression on these two readers so that you can proceed to stage three.

PLANNING

When planning a communication, you decide what to include and how to organize and present it. In a resume, of course, you include information about your education, activities, experiences, and talents that will persuade employers that you have the qualifications they desire. There are two general patterns for organizing this content:

Two basic types of resumes

- **Experiential resume.** In an experiential resume, you arrange information about yourself around your experiences: attending college, working, participating in campus or community activities. Then you describe each of these experiences in ways that demonstrate that you have the qualifications employers want. Figure 2.1 shows a resume organized around the writer's experiences.
- **Functional resume.** In a functional resume, you organize a key portion of your resume around your abilities and accomplishments. For instance, you might have headings entitled "Technical Abilities," "Management Experience," and "Communication Skills." Later in the resume you would list the college you attended and the jobs you've held. Figure 2.4 (page 37) shows a functional resume that is discussed later in this chapter.

Choosing the best resume pattern

For most college students, an experiential resume is the best choice. Functional resumes usually work best for individuals who have had enough professional experience to be able to list a substantial number of on-the-job responsibilities and accomplishments in several categories. Even if you write an experiential resume, however, concentrate on conveying the sense that you not only possess knowledge and skills but also that you can use them to accomplish an employer's goals.

Length depends on qualifications

How Long Should Your Resume Be?

People often ask, "How long should my resume be?" The answer is: as long as it takes to present your qualifications concisely but well. For many undergraduates, that's one page. However, undergraduates and others with extensive qualifications may need to use a second page. Employers realize this, as indicated by their response to a survey of more than 800 hiring officials by Harcourt, Krizan, and Merrier.

Employer Preferences	
Preferred Length	**Percentage of Hiring Officials**
■ No more than one page	23.6
■ No more than two pages	41.8
■ Depends on applicant's information	32.7
■ Other length	01.8

■ **FIGURE 2.1**

Experiential Resume

Jeannie Ryan

Present Address		**After May 28, —**
325 Foxfire Drive, Apt 214		85 Deitrich Court
Denver, Colorado 70962		Flint, Colorado 73055
(303) 532-1401	ryanja@acs.udenver.edu	(303) 344-7329

Jeannie tells where she can be reached before and after graduation.

She includes her e-mail address.

Jeannie states her specific objective and stresses her creativity and special abilities.

She names the employer's goal she will help the employer achieve.

Jeannie emphasizes her thorough preparation by listing many relevant courses.

She uses bullet lists throughout her resume to enable her readers to quickly scan her qualifications.

Jeannie describes a special course related to her career objective.

She tells what she learned that will be helpful to her in the job she desires.

Jeannie aligns dates against the right-hand margin to balance the two sides of her resume visually.

She highlights her management responsibilities.

Jeannie encloses her references with her resume.

Objective To conduct market research in a full-service marketing firm where I can use my creative and quantitative abilities to increase sales for clients.

Education **Bachelor of Science in Marketing**   May —
Minor in Computer Science
University of Denver

Related Courses
· Marketing Research
· Analytical Methods for Marketing
· Quantitative Analysis of Business Problems
· Programming in C++
· Stochastics
· Survey Sampling
· Strategic Marketing Management

Special Project In Advanced Marketing, we students worked in teams to analyze the potential Southwest market for Columbo Yogurt, a best-selling product on the East Coast. Then we produced a marketing strategy for Columbo in this region.

Work Experience **Ali Company,** Wilke, Colorado   Summer —
Sales Intern
· Built backroom inventories, stocked cases, and secured endcap displays for an ice cream manufacturer.
· Learned to see consumer marketing from the perspectives of both the manufacturer and the retailer.

Sears, Redvale, Colorado   Summer —
Retail Salesclerk
· Created displays, took inventory, and assisted customers.
· Learned how much advertising and marketing strategies affect consumer decisions.

Tels Marquart, Inc., Redvale, Colorado   Summer —
Receptionist
· Learned to work in a fast-paced office environment.

YWCA, Redvale, Colorado   Summer —
Aquatic Instructor
· Taught people of all ages.

Activities **Synchronized Swim Team**   All four years
Vice President (Senior Year)
· Planned and directed an hour-long public program for this 50-member club.

References See enclosed sheet.

DRAFTING

Drafting is the act of transforming your plan into a finished communication. This involves creating the text and also constructing an effective and appealing visual design.

Drafting the Text of an Experiential Resume

As you draft the text of your resume, your most valuable asset is the knowledge about your readers that you developed when defining your resume's objectives. Every word in your resume should help to persuade employers that you possess the technical qualifications, supporting abilities, and personal attributes required for the specific job you want. Figure 2.2 describes six general strategies for achieving this goal, and the paragraphs that follow detail ways to apply these strategies in a resume organized around your experiences.

Help employers contact you.

Include your e-mail address.

Identifying and Contact Information   Place your name prominently at the top of your page so employers can easily locate your resume in a stack of applications. Also provide your postal address, e-mail address, and phone number. If you will live away from school during the summer or other part of the year, give the relevant information so employers can also reach you at these times.

Most employers want you to state your objectives.

Professional Objective   In response to a survey, personnel officers from the 500 largest corporations in the United States reported that the most serious problem they find with resumes and letters of application is the applicants' failure to specify their job and career objectives (Wells, Spinks, and Hargrave). This surprises some students, who think, "After I present my qualifications, shouldn't an employer be able to match me to an appropriate opening?" Harried managers and personnel officers trying to work their way through a pile of applications don't have time to do that.

Tell what you will give, not what you want to get.

When writing your objective, avoid taking the writer-centered approach of telling what you want to *get from* your future employer. Instead, take the reader-centered approach of telling what you will *give to* the employer, focusing specifically on the results you will help to achieve. Here's a simple, two-step procedure for doing that:

Make it your objective to achieve results that the employer desires.

- **Identify the practical results you would help to produce if you worked in the department or unit to which you are applying.**   If you don't know what these results are, ask a professor, talk with someone in the kind of job you want, or contact your campus employment center for assistance.
- **State that your objective is to achieve those results.**

A senior in sports studies, Howard used this process while preparing a resume directed to fitness centers that specialize in serving competitive athletes. Howard's first draft read as follows:

Writer-centered objective | A position where I could extend my knowledge of nutrition and sports studies.

After considering this statement from his readers' perspective, Howard realized that it told merely what he wanted to gain from the job. It said nothing about how he would use his knowledge to benefit an employer. By focusing on what a fitness center would want him to accomplish with his knowledge, Howard created the following reader-centered, results-oriented objective:

Reader-centered revision | A position in which I develop individualized nutrition and exercise programs that enable competitive athletes to achieve peak performance.

■ FIGURE 2.2 **General Resume Strategies**	■ **Take an employer's perspective.**	Make all decisions concerning your resume by thinking about the qualities an employer will hope to find in a job applicant.
	■ **Show breadth as well as depth.**	Detail the full scope of your qualifications.
	■ **Think creatively about your qualifications.**	Think beyond course titles and job titles. Your challenge is to describe your knowledge and experience that relates to the job you want.
	■ **Put the most impressive information first.**	Make your first impression on your readers count. Busy readers may quit reading if the first things they encounter are ordinary and unimpressive.
	■ **Give specific details.**	Don't say that you are "proficient on the computer." Name the programs you've mastered. Don't say that you have "taken several courses" that focus on a certain subject. List the course titles or give the total number of credit hours.
	■ **Omit information that will not impress an employer.**	No matter how proud you are of some fact, leave it out if an employer won't care. Don't bury your good qualifications in items that are unimportant to your reader.

Jena, a computer science major, used the same strategy to improve her objective:

Vague, trite objective | A position as a computer systems analyst in the field of software development with an innovative and growing company.

Improved, results-oriented revision | To develop and maintain software systems that provide efficient, easy-to-use control of inventory, ordering, and billing for a mail-order business.

You can also create a results-oriented objective when applying for an internship, co-op, or summer job. Even though you will be assisting professionals and learning from them, you will still make valuable contributions to your employer.

Objective for internship | An internship in which I would help a team of aerospace engineers design high-quality components for commercial aircraft.

Education   When describing your education, name your college, degree, and graduation date. But don't stop there. Provide additional details that will help you persuade employers that you have the technical skills required by the job you want:

Special credentials that you may have

- Grade point average, if good.
- Academic honors.
- On-the-job educational experiences, such as a co-op assignment or internship.
- Advanced courses directly relevant to the job you want.
- Courses outside your major that broaden the range of abilities you would bring to an employer. For instance, if you are an engineering student with several business courses, state that fact.
- Special projects, such as a thesis or a design project in an advanced course.
- Additional college degrees, including associate degrees.
- Training programs provided by past employers.

Examples of education sections

The resumes of Jeannie Ryan (Figure 2.1) and Ramón Perez (Figure 2.3) show how two very different people elaborated on the ways their education qualifies them for the jobs they are seeking. Jeannie is a senior who has gone to college full-time (except summers) since graduating from high school. Like Ramón, she lists her school, major, and date of graduation. Because her grades are somewhat below average, she does not mention her grade point average.

Nevertheless, she lists courses she has taken in two areas—marketing management and analytical methods—that are critical to the job she wants. Furthermore, she describes in detail a course in which she worked on a major project that closely resembles the kind of assignment she might have at work.

Ramón completed most of his college work in the evening while holding a full-time job. Nevertheless, he earned excellent grades and therefore lists his grade point average. In addition, he lists his honors in a separate section to give them added prominence.

Work Experience   When preparing your work experience section, list the employers and their cities, and your job titles. Then begin thinking of facts about these jobs that you can highlight:

Highlight results you've achieved.

- **Accomplishments.** Describe any projects you worked on, problems you addressed, goals you pursued, and reports you helped write. Where possible, emphasize specific results—number of dollars saved, additional units produced, or extra customers served. Even if you worked only in unskilled jobs, you may have suggested a way to improve service at a restaurant or increase safety on a factory floor. Such accomplishments are well worth mentioning.

Tell what you learned.

- **Knowledge gained.** Be resourceful in telling what you have learned in your previous employment. Realizing that her duties of stacking ice cream packages neatly in supermarket freezers might not seem relevant to a job in marketing, Jeannie describes the insight she gained in that job: "Learned to see consumer marketing from the perspectives of both the manufacturer and the retailer" (Figure 2.1).
- **Skills, equipment, and computer programs used.** Mention all that are relevant to the job for which you are applying.
- **Responsibilities given.** There's no better way to demonstrate that you are a reliable person than to indicate that other employers have entrusted you with significant responsibility.

After you've assembled your notes concerning your jobs, follow this advice for presenting them in your resume:

- **Put your most impressive job first.** If your most recent job is your most impressive, list your jobs in reverse chronological order. To highlight an older job, create a special heading for it, such as "Related Experience." Then describe less relevant jobs under "Other Experience."

For more on putting actions in verbs, see Chapter 10.

- **Put your actions in verbs, not nouns.** Verbs portray you in action. Don't say you were responsible for the "*conversion* of manual accounting system to computer" but that you "*converted* manual accounting system to computer." Don't say you were responsible for the "*analysis* of test data" but that you "*analyzed* test data."

■ FIGURE 2.3

Resume of a Person Who Completed College While Working Full-Time

Ramón tells how he can be reached at work and home.

He identifies the job he desires and highlights his special abilities.

He tells what he will do to help the employer achieve its goals.

Ramón includes his excellent GPA.

He emphasizes his preparation in both computers and business.

Ramón highlights his achievement in completing his degree while working full-time.

He emphasizes his honors by giving them their own heading.

Ramón lists specific on-the-job accomplishments.

He establishes that he was recognized as a good employee.

Ramón tells substantial responsibilities he was assigned; he uses a technical term of the field ("proved the vault").

Ramón Perez

16 Henry Street
Brooklyn, New York 11231
Work: (212) 374-7631
Home: (718) 563-2291

Professional Objective

A position as a systems analyst where I can use my knowledge of computer science and business to develop customized systems for financial institutions

Education

New York University. *B.S. in Computer Science*
December —
GPA 3.4 overall; 3.7 in major

Computer classes include artificial intelligence and expert systems, computer security, data communication, deterministic systems, and stochastics

Business classes include accounting, banking, finance, and business law

Worked full-time while completing last half of course work

Honors

Dean's List three times
Golden Key National Honor Society

Related Work

Miller Health Spas, New York City, 1998–Present
Data Entry Clerk
• Helped convert to a new computerized accounting system
• Served on the team that wrote user documentation for the system
• Trained new employees
• Earned Employee of the Month Award twice

Meninger Bank, New York City, 1994–1998
Teller
• Performed all types of daily, night-deposit, and bank-by-mail transactions
• Proved the vault, ordered currency, and handled daily cash flow
• Learned how financial computer systems look from tellers' viewpoint

Activities

Juvenile Diabetes Foundation, 1997–Present
Volunteer
• Helped design a major fund-raising event two years in a row
• Successfully solicited two million dollars in contributions from sponsors

References

Professor Max Dobric	Professor R. Paul Berg	Wilson Meyerhoff
Computer Science Department	Finance Department	Senior Accountant
New York University	New York University	Miller Health Spas
New York, NY 12234	New York, NY 12234	3467 Broadway
(212) 998-1212	(212) 998-7635	New York, NY 12232
		(212) 671-9007

He describes something he learned that will help him in the job he wants.

Ramón emphasizes a specific achievement, naming the amount of money involved.

He includes his references in his resume.

Ethics and the Job Search

One of the most interesting—and perplexing—features of workplace writing is that the ethical standards differ from one situation to another. The resume and job application letter illustrate this point because the expectations that apply to them are significantly different from those that apply to other common types of on-the-job writing.

Ethical Expectations

For instance, when writing a resume you are permitted to present facts about yourself in a highly selective way that would be considered unethical in some other kinds of workplace writing. For example, imagine that you have suggested that your company reorganize its system for keeping track of inventory. Several managers have asked you to investigate this possibility further, then write a report about it. In this report, your readers will expect you to include unfavorable information about your system as well as favorable information. If you omit

the unfavorable information, your employer will judge that you have behaved unethically in order to win approval of your idea.

If you were to submit your resume to these same readers, however, they would not expect you to include unfavorable information about yourself. In fact, they would be surprised if you did.

Furthermore, these readers would expect you to present the favorable information about yourself in as impressive a language as possible, even though they might feel you were ethically bound to use cooler, more objective writing in your proposal about the inventory system.

Ethical Guidelines

How, then, can you distinguish an ethical presentation of your qualifications from an unethical one? Here are some guidelines:

1. Don't list degrees you haven't earned, offices you haven't served in, or jobs you haven't held.

2. Don't list awards or other recognition you haven't actually received.
3. Don't take sole credit for things you have done as a team member.
4. Don't give yourself a job title you haven't had.
5. Don't phrase your statements in a way that is intended to mislead your readers.
6. Don't list references who haven't agreed to serve as references for you.

If you are unsure whether you are writing ethically in some part of your resume, ask your instructor or someone else who is familiar with workplace expectations about this type of communication. More generally, you might also ask for advice from more experienced people whenever you are unsure about the ethical expectations that apply to any communication you write at work.

- **Use strong verbs.** When choosing your verbs, choose specific, lively verbs, not vague, lifeless ones. Avoid saying simply that you "worked with merchandise displays." Say that you "designed" or "created" those displays. Don't say that you "interacted with clients" but that you "responded to client concerns."
- **Use parallel constructions.** If you make a series of parallel statements, be sure to use the correct parallel construction. Nonparallel constructions slow reading and indicate a lack of writing skill. Here's an example from a list of major job responsibilities.

Changing *correspondence* to *corresponded* makes it parallel with *helped* and *prepared*.

Not Parallel	**Parallel**
■ Help_ed_ train new employees.	■ Help_ed_ train new employees.
■ Correspondence with customers.	■ Correspond_ed_ with customers.
■ Prepar_ed_ loan forms.	■ Prepar_ed_ loan forms.

Similarly, use parallel constructions within sentences or sentence fragments. For example, revise the following:

<table>
<tr><td>Not parallel</td><td>My responsibilities included demonstrating the equipment, order preparation, and following up after delivery.</td></tr>
</table>

to read:

<table>
<tr><td>Parallel</td><td>My responsibilities included demonstrating the equipment, preparing orders, and following up after delivery.</td></tr>
</table>

Activities   At the very least, participation in group activities indicates that you are a pleasant person who gets along with others. Beyond that, it may show that you have acquired certain abilities that are important in the job you want. Notice, for instance, how Jeannie Ryan describes her participation in one of her extracurricular activities (Figure 2.1):

Emphasis on management responsibilities	**Synchronized Swim Team** *Vice President (Senior Year)* ■ Planned and directed an hour-long public program for this 50-member club.

This statement suggests that Jeannie has been entrusted with considerable responsibility by people who know her well and that she has had experience in an essentially managerial position.

Special Abilities   Include unusual abilities of any sort, such as being selected for a high school choir that toured Europe or playing varsity sports at your college. You can give these abilities special emphasis by presenting them in a section of their own, labeled with a title such as "Computer Skills" or "Foreign Languages."

Interests   A brief mention of your special interests will give evidence that you are a person who can talk about something other than studies and jobs. If the information you include under the "Activities" heading provides information about your interests, a separate section is unnecessary.

Personal Data   Federal law prohibits employers from discriminating on the basis of sex, religion, color, age, or national origin. It also prohibits employers from inquiring about matters unrelated to the job a person has applied for. For instance, employers cannot ask if you are married or plan to be married. Many students welcome these restrictions on employers because they consider such questions to be personal or irrelevant. On the other hand, federal law does not prohibit you from giving employers information of this sort if you wish. And many students do. If you include such information, you should probably place it at the end of your resume, just before your references. It is almost certainly less impressive than the things you say in the other sections.

References   Your first step in deciding how to present your references is deciding whether to list them in your resume or whether to add a line to your resume that says, "References available on request." There are three reasons for including them with your resume:

- The majority of employers want references with the resume, according to a recent survey (Patterson).
- Including your references makes it easier for employers to contact these persons. Employers don't have to take the extra steps of requesting the names from you and then awaiting your reply.
- The appearance of the references helps to make your resume persuasive because it shows that people are willing to speak on your behalf.

Select references who can give a well-rounded portrait of your qualifications and who will seem credible to employers:

- **Select people who can speak about the range of your *professional* qualifications.** Choose college instructors, employers, and advisers of campus organizations. Select a mix of people who can speak about different qualifications you possess. Avoid listing your parents and their friends, who (an employer might feel) are going to say nice things about you no matter what.
- **Choose at least three references.** That number is so common that you may appear deficient with fewer. Additional references are fine.
- **Check with each person before listing him or her as a reference.** Ask, "Do you think you know me well enough to give me a strong recommendation?" This allows a person who wouldn't be helpful to decline gracefully. Give your resume to your references so they can review your qualifications when an employer calls.
- **Make your references look important and easy to contact.** Don't list your references like this:

Poor presentation of references

John Douglas	Walter Williamson
Laws Hall	6050 Busch Boulevard
Miami University	Fort Worth, Texas 76104
Oxford, Ohio 45056	

For all an employer will know, Laws Hall is a dormitory, John Douglas is the applicant's roommate, and Walter Williamson is a neighbor on Busch Boulevard. Give titles, full business addresses, and phone numbers (including area codes). Add an e-mail address if appropriate.

Better presentation

Dr. John Douglas, Chairperson	Mr. Walter Williamson, Director
Management Department	Corporate Services Division
Laws Hall	Orion Oil Company
Miami University	6050 Busch Boulevard
Oxford, Ohio 45056	Fort Worth, Texas 76104
(513) 529–5265	(817) 376–2554

Drafting the Text for a Functional Resume

A functional resume has the same aims as an experiential one. The chief difference is that in a functional resume, you consolidate the presentation of your accomplishments and experience in a special section located near the beginning, rather than weave this information into your sections on education, work experience, and activities. Figure 2.4 shows an example.

■ **FIGURE 2.4**

Functional Resume

George creates a distinctive design for his resume by putting his address and phone number at the bottom.

George names the job he seeks.

He names the employer's goal that he will help the employer achieve.

In this functional resume, George highlights his special qualifications in a separate section.

He describes a major accomplishment.

George uses the present tense in his "Management" and "Budgetary" entries because these are continuing duties; he uses the past tense in his entry about "Innovation" because it describes a completed project.

He provides information about the budget's size.

Because he presented information about substantial on-the-job responsibilities and achievements above, he does not elaborate on his jobs here.

Because he has substantial professional experience, George deemphasizes his college experiences by giving only basic facts.

GEORGE SHRIVER

Objective

Senior management position where I can lead a technical communication department that assists a computer manufacturer in achieving high quality and productivity.

Skills and Accomplishments

Management	Supervise a team of six specialists who create print and on-line user documentation and also develop and deliver training programs for in-house use.
Innovation	Proposed and oversaw the development of an interactive videodisc training program for process engineers in a small factory that manufactures computer components.
Technical Expertise	Familiar with latest developments in both hardware and software. Programming knowledge of Visual C++, Java, and various proprietary computer languages.
Budgetary Responsibility	Manage an annual budget of nearly one-half million dollars.

Employment History

Training Director, Saffron Computer Technology, Inc., Anaheim, CA, 1997-Present
Training Specialist, Calpon Software Systems, Deer Park, NJ, 1994-1997

Education

B.A. in Technical and Scientific Communication, Miami University (OH), 1994
Numerous professional development courses

Professional Societies

Society for Technical Communication (Chapter President, 1998)
American Society for Training and Development

Special Qualifications

Fluent in German   Trained in conflict resolution   Certified to teach CPR

References available upon request

1734 Everet Avenue   Pasadena, CA 91101   (314) 417-7787
GShriver@nettlink.com

He names a leadership position in his professional society.

George shows commitment to continued professional development.

George lists additional qualifications that may interest an employer.

He includes his e-mail address.

Headings for functional resumes

This special section needs a title that emphasizes its contents, such as "Skills" or "Skills and Achievements." Within the section, use headings that identify the major areas of ability and experience that you would bring to an employer. Typical headings include "Technical," "Communication," "Management," and "Financial." However, the specific headings that will work best for you will depend on the nature of your abilities and on the job you are seeking. Notice that the headings on George Shriver's resume (Figure 2.4) are quite specific to skills required of the manager of a technical communication department.

Because you are aggregating your skills and accomplishments in the special "Skills" section, the other sections of your functional resume should be brief in order to avoid redundancy.

Designing Your Resume's Appearance

On the job, good visual design can be crucial to a communication's success. Nowhere is that more true than with a resume, whose design must do the following:

- Emphasize your most impressive qualifications
- Support rapid reading
- Look attractive

The resumes shown in this chapter achieve these objectives through a variety of methods.

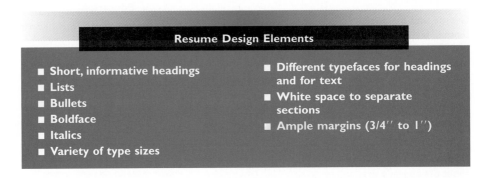

Resume Design Elements

- Short, informative headings
- Lists
- Bullets
- Boldface
- Italics
- Variety of type sizes
- Different typefaces for headings and for text
- White space to separate sections
- Ample margins (3/4″ to 1″)

To check the visual balance of your resume, fold your resume vertically. Both sides should have a substantial amount of type. Neither should be primarily blank.

EVALUATING

Review from an employer's perspective.

When you evaluate a draft of any communication, you look it over for potential problems and for possible improvements. With your resume, start by checking for misspellings and grammatical errors. Then use your knowledge about your readers to predict how they will respond to each feature of your resume. Will they understand the things you say? Find them impressive? Respond favorably to your resume's appearance?

Ask someone else to review your resume.

Unfortunately, as writers we all have difficulty seeing our own work in just the way our readers will. We often see what we intended—which is not always the same as what we accomplished. Show your draft to other people. Be sure to tell these reviewers about your target readers so they, too, can try to read from your target readers' perspective. Good people to ask for this help include your classmates, your writing instructor, instructors in your major department, and advisers from your campus career services center.

REVISING

Revising would be easy if it involved only making corrections in matters where there is a clear right and wrong. However, the review of your resume may turn up problems for which there's no immediately obvious answer. You may even get contradictory advice from different reviewers. Here, too, let your judgment and creativity be guided by knowledge of your readers. After all, their responses are what really matter.

ELECTRONIC RESUMES: SPECIAL CONSIDERATIONS

Increasingly, job applicants and employers are using electronic resumes rather than paper ones. The following sections provide advice about three types: scannable resumes, resumes submitted via the Internet, and Web page resumes.

SCANNABLE RESUMES

Many employers ask computers, not people, to be the first readers of your resume. They feed your resume to a scanner, which enters it into a computer's database. To find applicants who might be invited for a job interview, the employers ask the computer to search its database for resumes that have words—called *keywords*— that the employers believe would appear in the resumes of good candidates for the opening they want to fill. The computer displays a list of the resumes with the most matches, called *hits*.

If you suspect that your resume might be scanned, call the employer to ask or else enclose both a regular resume and a scannable one. To create an effective scannable resume, follow the advice below.

Making Your List of Keywords

Even when preparing a scannable resume, take a reader-centered approach to writing. In this case, begin by identifying the keywords an employer might use for the job you want.

Keywords to Use

- **Attributes you have that you feel any employer would desire from a college-educated employee:** leadership, responsibility, writing ability, interpersonal skills, etc.
- **Degrees, certifications, and licenses:** B.A., B.S., R.N. (registered nurse), P.E. (professional engineer license), C.P.A. (certified public accountant).
- **Words in an advertisement you've found for the position.**
- **Specialized equipment and techniques you've used in school or at work:** X-ray machine, PK/PD analysis, ladderlogic.
- **Computer programs and operating systems:** Microsoft Word, Excel, Autocad II, C++, UNIX.
- **Course titles and the major topics you studied within the courses.**
- **Job titles and the tasks you performed.**
- **Buzzwords in your field:** *client server, LAN, low-impact aerobics, TQM* (total quality management).
- **Professional and honor societies.** Join these groups, especially those related to your major, because they are often entered as keywords.
- **Foreign languages you know and countries you've lived in.** These can be especially important to employers with facilities, suppliers, or customers in other countries.

To increase the chances that the computer will pick out your keywords, do the following:

Ways to increase the number of hits your resume receives

- **Put your keywords in nouns, not verbs.** Do this, even if the writing in your scannable resume becomes wordy as a result. Some computer programs have difficulty with verbs.
- **Be redundant.** For instance, write "Used Lotus 1-2-3 spreadsheet program" rather than "Used spreadsheet program" or "Used Lotus 1-2-3." You don't know which term an employer will use, and if both terms are used, you will have two hits.
- **Create a "Keywords" section.** In it, list keywords you can't easily work into any of your resume's other sections. Place this section after your name or after your objective.
- **Proofread carefully.** Computer programs don't match misspellings.

Persuading Your Scannable Resume's Human Readers

After the initial evaluation by a computer, your resume will be read by humans. Therefore you must also write it in a way that will be understandable and persuasive to people:

- **Work your keywords into sentence-like statements that are easy to read.**
- **Use the advice for paper resumes, except where it contradicts the specific needs of a scannable resume.**   Note that you will have to work creatively to strike a balance between the wordiness and redundancy that get lots of hits from a computer and the brevity that adds punch for human readers.

Preparing for Flawless Scanning

Every error a scanner makes when reading your resume reduces the chances that your resume will be plucked from the employer's computer database.

Make each letter and word stand out distinctly.

- Use only 12-point or 14-point type in a standard typeface (e.g., Times or Helvetica).
- Be sure that adjacent letters don't touch. Two letters that touch will appear to be one (very puzzling) letter to a scanner.
- Avoid italics and underlining. Bold and all-caps are okay.

Use a simple visual design.

- Eliminate decorative elements, such as lines, dots, or borders. Bullets are fine.
- Use only a single column of text. Some scanners cannot understand or reproduce a multicolumn format.
- Use ragged right margins. Justified margins create large spaces between words that can perplex scanners.
- Use blank lines and headings in bold to separate sections and increase readability.
- Don't worry about how many pages you use. Computers don't care.
- Put your name at the top of every page, on a line of its own.

Submit a sharp, clean copy.

- Use laser printing or high-quality photocopying. Broken letters, fuzzy letters, and stray marks can confuse scanners.
- Use white or light paper to provide a high contrast with the printed words. Avoid shading and textured paper.
- Mail your resume flat. Folds can fool scanners.

Figure 2.5 shows Ramón Perez's resume in a scannable form. Notice how different it looks from the resume he designed to be read first by a person (Figure 2.3).

RESUMES SUBMITTED VIA THE INTERNET

Some employers ask applicants to submit their resumes via the Internet. When doing this, follow the advice for scannable resumes, not paper ones. Almost certainly your resume will be read directly into a computer database in either of the following circumstances:

- **If the employer requests your resume in ASCII.** In most desktop publishing programs, you can respond to this request by saving the file that contains your resume as a "Text" or "Text Only" file. This removes all formatting, so follow the advice concerning the layout of scannable resumes.

■ FIGURE 2.5

Scannable Resume

Ramón includes a list of keywords that don't appear elsewhere in his resume.

To assure that a scanner could read his resume, Ramón uses a single-column format rather than the two-column format he created for his print resume.

He also eliminates the italics that appeared in his print resume (see page 33).

Throughout this resume, Ramón uses 12-point Times, a typeface scanners can read without difficulty.

To make his resume easy for humans (as well as scanners) to read, Ramón relies on:

- capital letters
- bold
- bullets
- blank lines

To be read by a scanner, Ramón's resume requires two pages, but that is fine because scanners don't care how many pages they read.

RAMÓN PEREZ
16 Henry Street
Brooklyn, New York 11231
Work: (212) 374-7631
Home: (718) 563-2291

KEYWORDS
Responsible, financial management, banking experience, accounting, auditing, high motivation, communication ability

PROFESSIONAL OBJECTIVE
A position as a systems analyst where I can use my knowledge of computer science and business to develop customized systems for financial institutions

EDUCATION
New York University
B.S. in Computer Science
December 19—
GPA 3.4 overall; 3.7 in major

Computer classes include artificial intelligence and expert systems, computer security, data communication, deterministic systems, and stochastics

Business classes include accounting, banking, finance, and business law

Worked full-time while completing last half of course work

HONORS
Dean's List three times
Golden Key National Honor Society

RELATED WORK
Miller Health Spas, New York City, 1998–Present
Data Entry Clerk
- Helped convert to a new computerized accounting system
- Served on the team that wrote user documentation for the system
- Trained new employees
- Earned Employee of the Month Award twice

Meninger Bank, New York City, 1994–1998
Teller
- Performed all types of daily, night-deposit, and bank-by-mail transactions
- Proved the vault, ordered currency, and handled daily cash flow
- Learned how financial computer systems look from tellers' viewpoint

ACTIVITIES
Juvenile Diabetes Foundation, 1997–Present
Volunteer
- Helped design a major fund-raising event two years in a row
- Successfully solicited two million dollars in contributions from sponsors

(Ramón uses a second page for his references)

■ **If the employer wants your resume submitted as an e-mail message.** Include your resume in the message itself, not as an enclosure. Many employers use resume processing systems that will not read enclosures.

At their Web sites, some employers provide application forms that you can fill out on-line. When doing so, use the same strategies you would for a scannable resume.

WEB PAGE RESUMES

Although most employers do not read Web page resumes, a few do. If you create a resume accessible via the World Wide Web, consider the following advice:

Chapter 15 provides additional advice about creating effective Web pages.

- **Keep your design simple, uncluttered.** Although you can do many fancy things with a Web page, don't let your readers be distracted from your qualifications by fancy embellishments.
- **Include a hyperlink to your e-mail address.** Employers cannot readily download your Web page into their recruitment databases, and printing a paper copy of it would require many pages. By including a hyperlink to your e-mail address, you make it easy for them to ask for another form of your resume.
- **Protect yourself.** If you are going to post your resume with an on-line resume service, choose one that provides security. Some of these services have no security, so that other people can alter your resume.

WRITING YOUR JOB APPLICATION LETTER

Importance of a job application letter

Your job application letter is a critically important part of the package you submit to employers. In response to a survey of 150 executives from the nation's 1,000 largest employers, 60 percent indicated that a job application letter is just as or more important than the resume (Patterson).

Reflecting the approach of many employers, corporate recruiter Richard Berman reports that if a letter doesn't grab him, he merely gives the enclosed resume a quick scan to see if it might turn his opinion around. In contrast, when he discovers a particularly effective letter, he goes immediately to colleagues to announce that he's "found a good one" (Patterson 37).

DEFINING YOUR LETTER'S OBJECTIVES

Your letter should be tailored to the single employer you are addressing.

Your job application letter has somewhat different work to do than does your resume. Of course, both have the same general objective: to get you the interview—and job—you want. But your resume concentrates on persuading that you would be good at the *type* of job you want. In contrast, your letter's primary objective is to persuade that you would make a positive contribution to the *particular employer* to whom you are applying.

Published remarks by employers as well as surveys of them suggest that successful application letters provide positive and persuasive answers to the following employer questions:

Employer's questions when reading a job application letter

- **Why do you want to work for me instead of someone else?** In response to a survey by Wells, Spinks, and Hargrave, 81 percent of the personnel directors at the 500 largest corporations in the United States either "agreed" or "strongly agreed" that applicants should explain why they chose to apply to this specific company.
- **How will you contribute to my organization's success?** In the Wells, Spinks, and Hargrave survey, 88 percent of the personnel directors "agreed" or "strongly

agreed" that job application letters should tell how the job seeker's qualifications match the organization's needs. Corporate recruiter Kirk Newsome recommends that job seekers do the research necessary to clearly connect their knowledge and experiences with what's happening in the company (Patterson).

■ **Will you work well with my other employees and the persons with whom we do business?** From your tone and writing style, employers will draw inferences about your ability to interact effectively and pleasantly with others.

PLANNING

The first step in planning your job application letter is to conduct the research necessary to answer the reader's first question, "Why do you want to work for me instead of someone else?" When conducting this research, it's helpful to categorize each fact you discover as either writer-centered or reader-centered. Writer-centered facts involve such things as the benefits the organization gives employees or the appealing features of its co-op program. You won't gain anything by mentioning such things in your letter because whenever you talk about them, you are saying, in essence, "I want to work for you because of what you will give me." When employers are hiring, they are not looking for people to give things to.

Look for information about things the organization is proud of.

In contrast, reader-centered facts concern things the organization is proud of—a specific innovation it has created, a novel process it uses, a goal it has achieved. These are facts you can build on to create a reader-centered letter.

In addition to looking for things you can praise, research the goals and activities of people who hold the job you want. The more you know about the specific job you want, the more persuasively you will be able to answer the reader's second question, "How will you contribute to my organization's success?"

For detailed advice on how to conduct research, see Chapter 6 and Reference Guide: Five Research Methods.

Figure 2.6 lists several ways you can obtain specific, reader-centered information about an employer. Look especially for things to praise that are related to the particular job you want. If you want to be an electrical engineer, it won't help much for you to praise the accounting system.

DRAFTING

When drafting your letter, think of it as having three parts: introduction, qualifications section, and closing.

Introduction
The major thing to accomplish in your introduction is to indicate the job you want and why. Here's a weak, but very common, way to do that.

Weak introduction | I wish to apply for a position as _____. I am a senior at _____ majoring in _____.

You can begin your letter much more effectively by using the reader-centered facts you discovered:

■ Praise the accomplishment, project, or activity you learned about. Praise is almost always welcomed by a reader, provided that it seems sincere.
■ State that your reason for applying for the job is your desire to contribute to these or similar efforts.

■ FIGURE 2.6

Ways to Learn about an Employer

■ **Draw on your own knowledge.**	Especially if you've already worked for the company as an intern or interim employee, you may already know what you need to know. Remember, however, that you need information related to the specific area of activity in which you'd like to work.
■ **Ask an employee, professor, or other knowledgeable person.**	People often have information that isn't available in print or on-line.
■ **Contact the company.**	It might send you publications about itself. It's possible that the information in the publications may be too general to be helpful, but maybe you'll find exactly what you need.
■ **Search the Web.**	Some sites provide information about thousands of companies. An example is Hoover's On-line: http://hoovweb.com. You can also use a search engine such as AltaVista or Yahoo to look for the employer's Web site. Chapter 6 provides advice about using search engines.
■ **Consult your campus's placement office or career services center.**	It may have information about the employer that interests you.
■ **Visit the library.**	Business newspapers and magazines, as well as trade and professional journals, are excellent sources of information. A reference librarian can be of great help in locating these materials.

Here's an introduction in which the writer uses this strategy.

Shawana gives specific praise related to the job she wants.

She introduces herself and expresses her desire to contribute.

She identifies the job she wants.

> While reading the August issue of *Automotive Week*, I learned that you needed to shut down your assembly line for only 45 minutes when switching from making last year's car model to this year's model. This 500 percent reduction in shutdown time over last year is a remarkable accomplishment. As a senior in manufacturing engineering at Western University, I would welcome a chance to contribute to further improvements in the production processes at your plant. Please consider me for the opening in the Production Design Group that you advertised through the University's Career Services Center.

Note that Shawana isn't praising the features of the car or the huge profit the company made. That would be superficial praise anyone could give without having any real understanding of the organization. Instead, Shawana focuses on a specific accomplishment, discovered through her research, that is directly related to her own specialty.

Qualifications Section

In your letter's qualifications section, discuss your knowledge and experience in ways that make clear how they would enable you to contribute to the employer's organization. Some job applicants divide this section into two parts: one on their education and the other on their work experience or personal qualities. Other applicants devote a paragraph to their knowledge and skills in one area and a second paragraph to their knowledge and skills in another area. Many other methods of organizing are also possible.

Whichever method of organizing you use, be sure to relate the specific facts you convey about yourself to the demands of the position you want. Don't merely list courses you've taken. Tell also how the knowledge you gained will help you to do a good job. Don't merely list previous job titles and areas of responsibility. Indicate how the skills you gained will enable you to succeed in the job you are seeking.

What the student learned

In my advanced physical chemistry course, I learned to conduct fluoroscopic and gas chromatographic analyses similar to those used in your laboratory to detect contaminants in the materials provided by your vendors.

How this will enable the student to contribute

In one course, we designed a computer simulation of the transportation between three manufacturing facilities, two warehouses, and seventeen retail outlets. Through this class, I gained substantial experience in designing the kinds of systems used by your company.

Conclusion

In the conclusion of your letter, look ahead to the next step. If you are planning to follow up your letter with a phone call, indicate that. In some situations, such a call can be helpful in focusing an employer's attention on your resume. If you are planning to wait to be contacted by the employer, indicate where you can be reached and when.

Using a Conventional Format

Finally, when drafting a letter of application, be sure to use a conventional format. Standard formats are described in Appendix A and are used in the sample letters in this chapter.

EVALUATING

Don't skip this step when preparing your job application letter. This letter is an especially challenging communication to write. Look it over very carefully yourself, and ask others to help you determine whether your letter is coming across in the way you intend. The following paragraphs discuss some of the most important things to look for.

Review the Personality You Project

Employers will examine everything you say for clues to your personality. When you say what appeals to you about the organization and explain why you are well suited for the job, you are revealing important things about yourself. Notice, for instance, how the first sentence of the second paragraph of Jeannie Ryan's letter (Figure 2.7) shows her to be a goal-oriented person who plans her work purposefully. Also, notice how the first paragraph of Ramón's letter (Figure 2.8) shows him to be an enthusiastic person with a firm sense of direction. When reviewing your own draft, pay special attention to the personality you project.

Review Your Tone

Some people have difficulty indicating an appropriate level of self-confidence. You want the tone of your letter to suggest to employers that you are self-assured but not brash or overconfident. Thus you want to avoid statements like this:

Overconfident tone

I am sure you will agree that my excellent education qualifies me for a position in your Design Department.

■ **FIGURE 2.7**

Letter of Application to Accompany the Resume Shown in Figure 2.1

Jeannie addresses a specific person.

She shows specific knowledge of the company and offers praise related to it.

Jeannie states that she wishes to pursue a goal that the employer pursues.

Jeannie lists specific courses that prepare her for the specific job she wants.

She describes one way her job experience will benefit the employer.

Jeannie tells how abilities she developed in a college activity will benefit the employer.

She highlights a specific accomplishment.

She requests an interview.

325 Foxfire Drive, Apt. 214
Denver, Colorado 70962
February 8, —

Ms. Nancy Zwotny, Manager
Employment and Employee Relations
Burdick Marketing
650 Broadway
Denver, CO 70981

Dear Ms. Zwotny:

I was very impressed last October when I read in *Retail News* that in one year your firm added seven large national accounts to its client list. And I was especially interested to learn that this success is built upon the power and rapid response of computerized tools for marketing analysis that your personnel have developed. As a senior marketing major at the University of Denver who has a solid background in computerized decision-making, I would very much like to work for Burdick as a research assistant dedicated to developing effective marketing strategies for clients.

To prepare myself for employment in marketing research, I have taken several classes in data analysis, including two classes in quantitative methods, four in computer science, and one in survey sampling. Also, my many management courses include several in strategic marketing management.

To learn the practical application of concepts I've studied in school, I have worked in selling to consumers and to retailers. Both jobs taught me how unreliable our common-sense predictions about consumer behavior can be and how important it is to research the market before introducing a new product. In addition, my position as vice president of the university's synchronized swim team has helped me develop my leadership and communication skills that will assist me in working effectively with other Burdick employees and with Burdick's clients. One of my responsibilities has been to help this diverse group of fifty people work together to prepare programs they can present proudly to the public.

I'm sure you realize that a letter and resume (which I've enclosed) can convey only a limited sense of a person's motivation and qualifications. I would welcome the opportunity to meet with you in person to explain my credentials more fully. Next week, I will call your secretary to see if you are able to grant me an interview. I hope that I may look forward to speaking with you.

Sincerely yours,

Jeannie Ryan

Jeannie Ryan

Enclosure

The phrase "I am sure" is certain to offend some readers. And the sentence as a whole pushes the readers out of consideration by asserting that the writer has already performed for them their job of evaluating the writer's qualifications. The tone of the following sentence is more likely to create a favorable response:

Tells how this will enable the student to contribute | I hope you will find that my education qualifies me for a position in your Design Department.

■ **FIGURE 2.8**

Letter of Application to Accompany the Resume Shown in Figure 2.3

Ramón addresses a specific person.

He demonstrates a specific knowledge of the company and conveys his enthusiasm for it.

Ramón states that he wishes to achieve results that the employer desires to achieve.

Ramón conveys his determination to prepare for the job for which he is applying.

Ramón explains how his job experience would benefit the employer.

He also tells how two classes he took would benefit the employer.

He provides specific evidence of personal characteristics he thinks the employer will view favorably.

Ramón asks for an interview.

---

16 Henry Street
Brooklyn, New York 11231
September 24,—

Estelle Ritter
Financial Systems Division
Medallion Software, Inc.
1655 Avenue of the Americas
New York, New York 11301

Dear Ms. Ritter:

About a year ago, I met David Yang, a systems analyst in your department, who told me about Medallion's highly successful efforts to create integrated computer systems for banks and other financial institutions. I was particularly intrigued when he explained that many of the programs you design for international corporations must conform to government banking regulations—which differ from country to country. What a challenge! As a systems analysis major with a considerable interest in meeting the needs of clients in the financial services industry, I would like to be considered for a position in your division.

Since talking with David, I have sought out courses that would prepare me for exactly the kind of work your division performs. This semester, for example, I am taking a course in computer security and another in international finance. In addition, I have gained considerable insight into the structure and uses of two sophisticated financial systems while working as a data entry clerk for the Miller Health Spas chain and as a teller for the Meninger Bank. I have also completed several classes in written and oral communication, which would help me present Medallion effectively to clients. You will find additional details about my qualifications in the enclosed resume.

I feel that I am a well-disciplined, highly motivated person with a strong desire to excel. I have taken the last half of my college courses while working full-time to support my wife and young son. After I become settled into a permanent job, I plan to begin graduate study in computer science so that I continue to develop my skills in systems analysis and design.

Would it be possible for me to meet with you to discuss what I have to contribute to Medallion? If so, please call me at (212) 374-7631 during the day.

Sincerely,

Ramón Perez

Ramón Perez

Enclosure

Achieving just the right tone in the conclusion of a letter is also rather tricky. You should avoid ending your letter like this:

Ineffective, demanding tone

I would like to meet with you at your earliest convenience. Please let me know when this is possible.

To sound less demanding, the writer might revise the second sentence to read, "Please let me know *whether* this is possible" and add "I *look forward* to hearing from you."

Finally, remember that you must assure that each sentence states your meaning clearly and precisely. And you must eradicate *all* spelling and grammatical errors.

REVISING

When revising your drafts, you may encounter the same difficulties you encounter when revising your resume. The people who help you evaluate your letter may identify problems but not tell you how to solve them, or they may give you conflicting advice. To revise well, you have to use your own creativity and good judgment. And you need to think constantly about how your readers will react, moment by moment, to what you have written.

WRITING FOR EMPLOYMENT IN OTHER COUNTRIES

In many other countries, resumes and job application letters look very different from those used in the United States. In Asian cultures, for instance, letters focus more on personal qualities than on skills and accomplishments. In France, many employers want job application letters written by hand so they can subject the letters to handwriting analysis. French employers believe that this analysis enables them to learn about the applicant's personal traits, which they weigh heavily when making employment decisions.

Because customs differ from country to country, if you apply for a job in another country you will need to produce a resume and job application letter that differ significantly from the ones described in this chapter. However, you will still be able to succeed if you follow the reader-centered writing process described here—one in which you use your understanding of your readers' needs, expectations, preferences, and other important characteristics to guide your writing.

CONCLUSION

This chapter has had three major purposes:

- To show how a reader-centered approach can help you make important decisions when writing a resume and a letter of application.
- To illustrate the writing process and show how its various activities are related to one another. In particular, this chapter has emphasized the importance of defining your objectives, which involves understanding your readers and deciding how you want to affect them. That early work will provide you with sound guidance throughout the later stages of the writing process.
- To show how completely the design of a communication depends on your particular purpose and readers.

The reader-centered strategy described here is fundamentally the same as the strategy for creating any other kind of communication related to your job. This strategy is explained in more detail in the rest of this book.

E X E R C I S E S

1. Find a sample resume at your college's career services center or in a book about resume writing. Evaluate it from the point of view of its intended reader. How could it be improved?

2. Complete the assignment in Appendix C on writing a resume and a letter of application.

C A S E

ADVISING PATRICIA

This morning you stopped outside the library to talk with Patricia Norman, a senior who is majoring in marketing. She told you with a mixture of excitement and anxiety that she has finally decided to join the many other seniors who are busily looking for a job. She's even drafted a resume and begun writing letters to employers listed in a publication she picked up at the Career Services Center.

"Look," she exclaimed. "One of the department store chains I'm writing to is mentioned in this article that Professor Schraff asked us to read." She held out an article from *Retail Management*. "They've begun opening free-standing specialty shops in their stores. The managers order their own merchandise and run their own advertising campaigns. It's been a huge success. This sounds like such a great place to work. A big chain that welcomes innovators." Then her excitement turned to anxiety. "I'm worried they won't like my resume and application letter, though. I've gone over both again and again, and my roommate has, too. But I'm still worried."

As you tried to reassure her, she pulled out her drafts and put them into your hand. "Take a look at them and tell me what you really think. I need all the help I can get." You had to leave for an appointment, but you agreed to look over her drafts and meet her again this evening.

Now it's afternoon, and you've started to read Patricia's resume and letter. As you do, you think back over some of the things you know about her. She's an active and energetic person, talkative, and fun to be with. Throughout her years in college, she has spent lots of time with a group called Angel Flight, a volunteer organization that sponsors service activities on campus and off. In fact, this past year you've seen less of her because she has spent so much time serving as the organization's president. "As President, I'm responsible for *everything*," she once told you. "Everything from running meetings, to getting volunteers, to seeing that the volunteers have done what they said they would." While a junior she held some other office, you recall—also a time-consuming one. But she's like that. In the Marketing Club, she edited the newsletter and handled lots of odd jobs, like putting up posters announcing speakers and meetings. She was also treasurer of the Fencing Club, another of her interests. Once when you marveled at how many things she was able to do, she responded, "It's not so much, if you're organized."

Despite all the time she spends on such activities, Patricia earns good grades, a 3.6 average, she told you once. Although she's had to take lots of business courses, she's also squeezed in a few electives in one of her favorite subjects: art history. One Saturday last year, she even got you to travel 200 miles with her to see an art exhibit—a "major" exhibit, she had assured you.

But the trip you most enjoyed with her was to a shopping center, where she spent more time commenting on how the merchandise was displayed than looking for things to buy. She talked a lot about the way they did things at a Dallas department store where she's worked the past three summers. She must have some interesting opportunities there, you note; after all, one of the people she lists as a reference is the store manager. Her other references are professors who've taught classes that you and Patricia have taken together. They were fun. Everything's fun with Patricia.

YOUR ASSIGNMENT

Decide what you will say to Patricia about her letter (Figure 2.9) and resume (Figure 2.10). What strengths will you praise? What changes will you suggest? What questions will you ask to determine whether she might include additional information? Assume that her resume will be read first by a person, not by a scanner.

■ FIGURE 2.9

Letter of Application for Use with Case

Box 88
Wells Hall
University of Washington
Seattle, Washington 98195
February 12, 19—

Kevin Mathews, Director
Corporate Recruiting
A. L. Lambert Department Stores, Inc.
Fifth and Noble Streets
San Diego, California 92103

Dear Mr. Mathews:

I saw A. L. Lambert's advertisement in the *College Placement Annual.* I was very impressed with your company. I hope that you will consider me for an opening in your Executive Develepment Program.

In June, I will graduate from the University of Washington's retailing program, where I have focused my study on marketing management.   I have learned a great deal about consumer behavior, advertising, and inovative sales techniques. Furthermore, I have gained a through overview of the retailing industry, and I have studied successful and unsuccessful retailing campaigns through the case-study method.

In addition to my educational qualifications, I have experience both in retail sales and in managing volunteer organizations. While working in a Dallas department store for the past four summers, I had many opprtunities to apply the knowledge and skills that I have learned in college. Likewise, in my extracurricular activities, I have gained experience working and communicating with people. For instance, I have been the president of Angel Flight, a volunteer service organization at the University of of Washington. Like a manager, I supervised many of the organization's activities. Similarly, while holding offices in two campus organizations, I have developed my senses of organization and responsibility.

I would like to talk with you in person about my qualifications. Please tell me how that can be arranged.

Sincerely yours,

Patricia Norman
Patricia Norman

■ **FIGURE 2.10**

Resume for Use with Case

PATRICIA NORMAN
Box 80, Wells Hall
University of Washington
Seattle, Washington 98195
(206) 529-5097

PERSONAL
Born: March 17, 19—
Health: Excellent
Willing to relocate

PROFESSIONAL OBJECTIVE
To work for an innovative and growing retailer.

EDUCATION
University of Washington, Seattle, Washington, B.S. in Retailing,
May 19—.

Earned 23 credit hours in marketing management, obtaining a working knowledge of the factors motivating today's consumer. Also learned how a product is marketed and distributed to the consumer. Took eight credit hours of study focused specifically on principles and problems of retail management

WORK EXPERIENCE
Danzig's Department Store, Dallas, Texas,
Summers 19— through 19—.

Worked as a sales clerk. Helped customers choose their purchases and listened politely to their complaints. Cash register operation. Stocked shelves and racks. Provided assistence to several department managers.

ACTIVITIES
Fencing Club, served as treasurer
Angel Flight, President.
Marketing Club, member

REFERENCES
Derek Yoder, *Store Manager*   Gregory Yule
Danzig's Department Store   Pinehurst Hall
11134 Longhorn Drive   University of Washington 98195
Dallas, Texas 75220   (206) 579-9481

Lydia Zelasko
Putman hall
University of Washington
Seattle, Washington 98195

Defining Objectives

CHAPTER 3
Defining Your Objectives

Defining Your Objectives

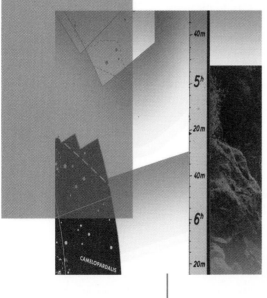

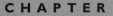

GUIDELINES

1	Focus on what you want to happen while your readers are reading
2	Identify the tasks your readers will perform while reading
3	Tell how you want to change your readers' attitudes
4	Learn your readers' important characteristics
5	Learn about the context in which your readers will read
6	Learn who *all* your readers will be
7	Ask others to help you understand your readers and their context
8	Remain open to new insights and information

CHAPTER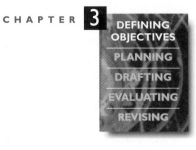

You are now beginning a new portion of this book. In it you will find twelve chapters that present detailed, practical advice about each of the five major activities you will perform when writing on the job:

- Defining your objectives
- Planning your communication
- Drafting your prose and visual aids
- Evaluating your draft
- Revising

In this chapter, you'll learn a reader-centered approach to the first of these activities: defining your objectives.

THE IMPORTANCE OF YOUR OBJECTIVES

All five writing activities are important, but defining objectives deserves your special attention. To see why, consider Todd's situation.

Todd needs a basis for deciding how to write his report.

A recent college graduate, Todd has been assigned to investigate ways of applying a more chip-resistant paint to his employer's products, which include washing machines, refrigerators, and other large appliances. This morning, Todd's boss dropped by his office. After reassuring Todd that such requests are routine in this company, Todd's boss told him that two vice presidents have asked Todd to write a report on his progress.

"How should I write this report?" Todd asks himself. "What should I tell the vice presidents, and how should I say it?"

To answer these questions, Todd must determine what he wants to accomplish in his report: he must define his objectives. Doing so will require some effort, but the result will guide him throughout the rest of his work on the report. When he plans and drafts, his objectives will help him decide how long the report should be, what to say in it, what to present in prose or in tables and illustrations—how, in fact, to handle every aspect of his message. Similarly, when Todd evaluates his draft, his objectives will help him determine what needs to be improved. And when he revises, his objectives will help him focus on the goal toward which all his revisions are directed.

This chapter provides eight guidelines that will enable Todd—and you—to gather information that will enable you to make sound decisions about the content and design of your communications.

Focus on What You Want to Happen While Your Readers Are Reading

When describing the purpose of a communication they are preparing, people often state its topic: "I'm going to write about orbiting, inhabited space stations." Or they name the type of document they are going to prepare: "I'm going to write a proposal" or "I'm going to write instructions." Perhaps the most important thing to remember as you define your communication's objectives is that you should focus not on your topic or document type but on *people.*

Your writing goal is to bring about change.

Here's why. As explained in Chapter 1, when you write on the job, you will be taking an action intended to bring about a change. You will be endeavoring to transform some aspect of the current situation—the way things are now—into a more desirable state.

The desire for this change may originate from your boss, other persons in your employer's organization, even you yourself. No matter where it originates, however, you will be able to achieve this change only with the aid of other people: your readers. After all, if you could make the change by yourself, you'd have no need to write.

Change requires the aid of other people.

Suppose you wish to obtain funding for a project. Your project will be funded only if your proposal persuades your boss to allocate the money you desire. Maybe you wish to help one of your employer's clients choose between two computers. The client will be able to select wisely only if your report enables readers to understand these alternatives fully and compare them meaningfully.

The outcome depends on what happens when your readers are reading.

Consequently, the true purpose of your writing is to enable or persuade your readers to act in a way that leads to the change you desire. And there's only one time when your communication has the power to directly affect your readers' actions: when they are actually reading it. If things go well during these moments, your communication will succeed.

However, if things don't go well during your readers' reading moments, your communication won't be successful.

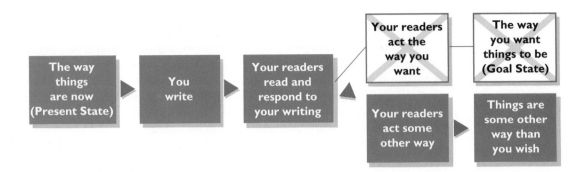

Because the success or failure of your writing depends on your readers' responses during this critical time, focus your objectives on what you want to happen while your readers are in the act of reading your message.

Create a mental portrait of your readers in the act of reading.

An excellent way to establish this focus is to follow a suggestion offered in Chapter 1: create a mental portrait of your readers in the act of reading. Use this portrait to consolidate the important insights you develop while defining your objectives. It will help you to predict your readers' specific responses to each particular writing strategy you develop as you plan, draft, and revise your communication.

The next five guidelines describe techniques you can use to construct such a mental portrait of your readers.

GUIDELINE **2** **Identify the Tasks Your Readers Will Perform While Reading**

Begin constructing your mental portrait of your readers by identifying the purposes they will have in mind when they pick up and begin to read your communication. Almost certainly, they will be attempting to gain information they can use in some practical way. A manager might read a report to gather information needed to make a decision. An engineer might consult a computer reference manual to solve a specific programming problem. To write successfully, you must design your communications so they help your readers locate and use the information they need.

At work, people read for practical purposes.

The following three-step procedure will help you do this.

Identifying Your Readers' Tasks

1. Identify the information your readers want your communication to provide.
2. Determine how your readers will look for this information.
3. Determine how they will use the information.

Identifying the Information Your Readers Want

Imagine the questions your readers will ask.

To identify the information your readers will seek, think of them primarily as persons who ask questions they want your communication to answer. Their questions, of course, are determined in large part by their purpose in reading, as Todd's situation illustrates.

Todd has identified two reasons the vice presidents might have for requesting that he write a report on his investigation of new methods for applying chip-resistant paint. First, they might want to decide which approach they want him to concentrate on in his future work. In this case, their questions are likely to be "Which alternative appears to produce the best results?" "Which ones appear to be least costly?" and "How will our production line need to be altered if we employ each of the most promising alternatives?"

To write effectively, Todd must determine which set of questions his readers want his report to answer.

Alternatively, the vice presidents may have asked Todd to write because they are worried that he won't complete his work in time for them to use his results on a new line of products they will begin manufacturing next year. In this instance, their questions will probably be "What work do you still have to do?" "How long will it take you?" and "If you can't be done by May 30 without extra help, how much help will you need?"

If Todd writes a report that answers one set of questions, but the vice presidents are asking the other set, he will not write successfully.

Determining How Your Readers Will Look for Answers

Once you've identified your readers' questions, imagine the ways they will look for and use the answers. Here are three search strategies readers often use on the job:

Three ways readers search for information

- **Thorough, sequential reading.** Todd's readers are likely to read his progress report this way because the report will probably be short, and they will want to understand every detail in order to make their decision.
- **Reading for key points only.** If Todd were later to write a lengthy report detailing all that he found out through his investigation, the vice presidents might scan for the key points, then pass the report along to technical specialists for more detailed analysis and follow-through.
- **Reference reading.** After the new painting process has been instituted, an engineer might read in this way, looking only for specific pieces of information in order to troubleshoot a problem that cropped up with a piece of equipment.

Different search methods require different writing strategies.

Knowing how your readers will look for information can help you make many important writing decisions. If your readers will read sequentially, you can build ideas from paragraph to paragraph and section to section, but if they will engage in reference reading you cannot rely on some sections to provide background information for others, and you will need to provide headings and other guides to help your readers rapidly locate the information they seek. People read some communications, such as computer manuals, in different ways at different times. These communications need to be designed to support more than one kind of reading.

Determining How Your Readers Will Use the Answers

Knowing how your readers will use the information they find in your communications can help you decide how best to organize and present information to your readers. Here are three common ways people use written information on the job—together with example writing strategies appropriate to each:

Readers want to use the information you provide.

- **To compare alternatives.** If the vice presidents were reading Todd's report to determine which process to adopt, he should organize in a way that would enable them to easily compare the alternatives on a point-by-point basis (cost, implementation time, etc.).
- **To determine how the information will affect them and their organization.** The engineer in charge of the production line in Todd's company might want to know how the new process would affect his responsibilities. Todd could organize a report to this individual around the types of changes that might be involved, such as those in equipment and personnel.
- **To perform a procedure.** A technician might need directions for performing some part of the new process. Todd could most effectively assist this person by preparing step-by-step instructions in a numbered list.

Enabling element of purpose

When you use the techniques just described to identify your readers' questions, methods of looking for the answers, and ways of using the answers, you are defining your communication's *enabling element* of purpose. That is, you are determining what you want your communication to *enable* your readers to do while reading. Advice throughout the rest of this book will help you craft communications that achieve the enabling element of their purpose.

G U I D E L I N E 3 Tell How You Want to Change Your Readers' Attitudes

Persuasive element of purpose

When creating your mental portrait of your readers, you should also tell how you want your communication to alter your readers' attitudes. In doing so, you define the *persuasive element* of your communication's purpose.

Every communication written at work has an important persuasive aim. Sometimes this persuasive aim is subordinated to an informational aim, but it is always present. Consider what happens when you read directions from your instructor for a homework assignment. The assignment might seem strictly informational because your primary purpose in reading is to understand what your instructor wants. As you read, however, you also respond emotionally. Perhaps you feel eager because the assignment sounds interesting, or maybe you feel indifferent because you don't see the point of the work. Because your emotions are part of your response as a reader, your instructor cannot achieve his or her desired outcome solely by making the directions understandable. To achieve his or her goal of having you complete the assignment correctly and thoughtfully, your instructor must also write in a way that encourages you to approach the assignment in a positive frame of mind.

As you define the persuasive element of purpose, remember that your readers' attitudes may focus on any of the following objects:

Things your readers may have attitudes about

- **Your subject matter.** Many of the topics you write about will be ones your readers have thought about already and so have already formed attitudes about.
- **You.** As one recent college graduate observed, "As soon as I started my job, I realized that every time I communicate, people judge me based upon how well they think I write or speak." Even when you are merely answering factual questions or reporting raw data, you will want your communication to inspire a favorable opinion of you as a person.
- **Your department or organization.** When writing to people outside your immediate working group, your communications will represent not only you but also your co-workers. Impressions your readers have of your department or company will shape their response to your message, and you will certainly want to influence their attitude toward these organizations.
- **The communication itself.** Readers can come to a communication with very high—or very low—motivation to read it. For example, many people are uninterested in reading instructions. When writing instructions, therefore, you will want to employ writing strategies that create the missing motivation.

You may wish to *change*, *reinforce*, or *shape* attitudes.

When incorporating their attitudes into your mental portrait of your readers, determine how your communication must *change* these attitudes in order to bring about the outcome you desire. That is, think about what these attitudes are now and also what you want them to be after your readers have finished reading. Often, you will need to *reverse* negative attitudes and also *reinforce* positive ones. You may also need to *shape* your readers' attitudes concerning topics they don't have opinions about at present.

The distinction among these three kinds of attitude change will be important to you because different kinds of change are best addressed by different persuasive strategies. For example, to reinforce an attitude, you can build on the existing attitude and expect little resistance. Consequently, you can usually present only positive points without trying to rebut arguments against your position. In contrast, if you want to reverse an attitude, you can expect your readers to be resistant. Consequently, you must not only cite positive points, but also address the counterarguments your readers will raise.

Figure 3.1 illustrates some ways you might want to alter your readers' attitudes in several typical communications.

GUIDELINE **4** **Learn Your Readers' Important Characteristics**

Different readers respond differently to the same writing strategies. Consequently, when constructing your mental portrait of your readers, you should incorporate the characteristics of your particular readers that will influence the way they will respond to your communication. The following paragraphs discuss six reader characteristics that are especially important to include.

Professional Role

By learning your readers' professional roles, you can often infer the kinds of information they will seek from your communication and the ways they will use it. For

■ **FIGURE 3.1** **Ways in Which Communications Prepared at Work Can Alter Readers' Attitudes**

The Way Things Are Now	You Act (You Write)	The Way You Want Things to Be
Your reader is a manager who wants to decide whether or not to purchase a certain piece of equipment.	You write a memo evaluating the equipment in terms of the benefits it will bring the company.	The manager decides to buy the equipment and feels confident that he or she has made a good decision based on information you provided.
Your reader is the director of a plant that is using an outdated process. The director feels that the process is fine.	You write a report on problems with the current process and the ways they can be overcome by various new processes.	After reading your report, the plant director feels that the process being used now may be faulty and that one of the new ones is worth investigating further.
Your readers are bank clerks who will be using a new computer system. They are afraid it will be significantly more complicated than the present system.	You write a procedures manual that shows how easy it is to use the new system.	The bank clerks feel relaxed and self-confident after learning how to use the new system from your manual.

People in different roles ask different questions.

instance, when reading a report on the industrial emissions from a factory, an environmental engineer working for the factory might ask, "How are these emissions produced, and what ideas does this report offer for reducing them?" whereas the corporate attorney might ask, "Do these emissions exceed standards set by the Environmental Protection Agency and, if so, how can we limit our legal liability for these violations?"

The most obvious clues to your readers' roles are their job titles—for example, systems analyst, laboratory technician, bank cashier, or director of public relations. However, be sure not to settle for a merely general sense of your readers' responsibilities with respect to your communication. Determine as precisely as possible why each person will be reading your communication and exactly what information he or she will be looking for.

Familiarity with Your Topic

Readers unfamiliar with your topic need background information.

Your readers' familiarity with your topic—company inventory levels, employee morale on the second shift, software problems, or whatever—will determine how much background information you need to provide to make your communication understandable and useful to them. When writing about a topic they know well, you need to include no background at all. However, if you are treating a topic they don't know much about, you may have to explain the general situation before you can proceed to the heart of your message. Also, if your readers are unfamiliar with your topic, you may need to explain how it relates to them so they can judge whether to bother reading about it.

Knowledge of Your Specialty

To use the information you provide, readers need to understand the terms and concepts you employ. Consider, for example, an instruction manual for a computer-controlled machine that directs the reader to "zero the tool along the Z-axis." Readers unfamiliar with this type of equipment might ask, "What is zeroing? What is the Z-axis?" If the instructions do not answer these questions, the readers will have to ask someone else for help, which defeats the purpose of the instructions. On the other hand, the instructions writer would not want to provide these definitions if all of his or her readers are already familiar with these terms. Coming upon such explanations, these readers would ask, "Why is this writer making me read about things I already know?"

Relationship with You

When conversing, you adjust your speech to your relationship with the other person. You talk with a friend more informally than with a college instructor you don't know well—and both your friend and your instructor might be startled if you didn't make such adjustments. Similarly, when writing at work, you should write in a way that reflects the relationships you have with your readers.

Personal Preferences

A variety of personal characteristics can also influence readers' responses to your writing. For example, you may be writing to an individual who detests the use of certain words or insists on particular ways of phrasing certain statements. Or you might be writing to someone who is keenly interested in information you would not have to supply to most people. Some readers favor brief messages, and some insist on more detail. Some prefer reading prose, and some like tables, graphs, and other visual aids. Some like a formal writing style, and others prefer informality. It only makes sense for you to accommodate such personal preferences where feasible.

Accommodate your readers' preferences when you can.

To a certain extent, people's preferences are shaped by the customary practices employed where they work. This is important to keep in mind as you begin to work for a new company, whether you have just graduated from college or have moved from another employer. When people say, "That's not the way we write here," they may be expressing preferences shared by many other people in the company.

Cultural Background

Different cultures have radically different customs about writing.

People's cultural backgrounds can also influence their response to your writing. For example, in the dominant business culture in the United States, people prefer blunt, brisk communication, but in Japan, Korea, Thailand, and China, communication is much more indirect and polite (Lustig and Koester 123). In the United States, business decisions are typically made on the basis of the impersonal needs or objectives of the organization, but in Arab cultures, where personal relations are extremely important in all aspects of life, businesspeople typically decide whether they would like to work with the person who represents an organization that wants to do business with them (Ruch 240).

When you are addressing readers in other countries, it will be critical for you to learn as much as you can about their culture. One excellent source is the *International Handbook of Corporate Communication,* which describes on-the-job communication in more than 100 nations (Ruch). Where possible, it can be very helpful to ask someone from the culture to read over your draft to help you avoid sending an ineffective, difficult-to-understand, or even inadvertently offensive communication.

Remember, too, that the workplace in many countries is becoming increasingly multicultural. In the United States, for instance, it's common to find in a single building employees raised in families and communities with Northern European, African-American, Latino, and Asian heritage. Consequently, even the responses of people working in your own building may be influenced by communication traditions in their families or communities that are substantially different from those to which you are accustomed.

Special Considerations

This is a catchall category. It is a reminder that each reader is unique. You should always be on the lookout for reader characteristics you would not normally need to consider. For example, you may be addressing individuals with an especially high or low reading level, weak eyesight, or color blindness—and it will be essential for you to take these characteristics into consideration when writing.

Sometimes you need to consider where your readers will read.

It is also wise to consider the setting in which your readers will be reading, in case this suggests ways you can adapt your communication to make it more useful for them. For example, if you are writing a manual for a computer program, you might want to design it in a small format to help conserve desk space for your readers. If writing a repair manual for hydraulic pumps, you might print your manual on paper coated to resist the moisture, oil, and dirt that is unavoidable in that reading environment.

Ordinarily you will not need to consider special factors of this sort. However, each time you prepare a communication, you should ask yourself, "Are there any special factors I should take into account when addressing these readers?"

GUIDELINE **5** **Learn about the Context in Which Your Readers Will Read**

Each message is part of an ongoing story.

At work, people interpret what they read as a chapter in an ongoing story. Consequently, they interpret and respond to each message in light of prior events as well as their understanding of the people and groups involved. Fill out your mental portrait of your readers by imagining how the following circumstances might influence their response to your communication:

- **Recent events related to your topic.** Maybe you are going to announce the reorganization of a department that has just adjusted to another major organizational change. You'll need to make a special effort to present the newest change in a positive light. Or maybe you are requesting money to attend an important professional meeting. If your department has just been reprimanded for excessive travel expenses, you will have to make an especially strong case.

- **Interpersonal, interdepartmental, and intraorganizational relationships.** If you are requesting cooperation from another department that has long been a competitor of yours for company resources, you will need to call upon special diplomacy. Political conflicts between individuals and groups can also create delicate writing situations in which certain ways of expressing your message can appear to support one faction and to insult or weaken another—even if you have no intention of getting involved at all.

GUIDELINE **6** **Learn Who *All* Your Readers Will Be**

So far, this chapter has assumed that you will know from the start just who your readers will be. That may not always be the case. Communications you prepare on the job may find their way to many people in many parts of your organization. Numerous memos and reports prepared at work are routed to one or two dozen people—and sometimes many more. Even a brief communication you write to one person may be copied or shown to others. To write effectively, you must know who *all* your readers will be so you can keep them all in mind when you write. The following discussion will help you identify readers you might otherwise overlook.

Phantom Readers

The most important readers of a communication may be hidden from you. That's because at work, written communications addressed to one person are often *used* by others. Those real but unnamed readers are called *phantom readers.*

Examples of times you might have phantom readers

Phantom readers are likely to be present behind the scenes when you write communications that require some sort of decision. One clue to their presence is that the person you are addressing is not high enough in the organizational hierarchy to make the decision your communication requires. Perhaps the decision will affect more parts of the organization than are managed by the person addressed, or perhaps it involves more money than the person addressed is likely to control.

Much of what you write to your own boss may actually be used by phantom readers. For instance, your boss may be a manager who accomplishes work by assigning it to assistants. Thus, your boss may check over your work and then pass it along to his or her superiors.

People who have worked at a job for a while usually learn which communications are likely to be passed up the organizational hierarchy, but a new employee may be chagrined to discover that a hastily written memo has been read by executives at very high levels. To avoid such embarrassment, you need to identify phantom readers so that you can write in a way that meets their needs, as well as the needs of the less influential person you are addressing.

Future Readers

Your future readers may include lawyers and judges.

Your communications may be put to use weeks, months, or even years after you imagined their useful life was over. Lawyers say that the memos, reports, and other documents that employees write today are evidence for court cases tomorrow. Most company documents can be subpoenaed for lawsuits concerning product liability, patent violation, breach of contract, and other issues. If you are writing a communication that could have such use, remember that lawyers and judges may be your future readers.

Your future readers also may be employees of your company who might retrieve your old communications for information or ideas. By thinking of their needs, you may be able to save them considerable labor, as the following example illustrates.

> Employed by a pharmaceutical company, a group of chemists analyzed plants from around the world, looking for compounds with medicinal value. Such analyses can be extremely complex. For instance, the chemists once searched through some plant samples for a compound whose presence was hidden by other compounds. They finally isolated the compound through an ingenious procedure and dutifully placed a record of the results in the company's files.
>
> Three years later, they encountered a similar problem with another plant. Remembering their earlier success, they went to the files to see what they had done in the past.
>
> To their dismay, they discovered that they had recorded only the results of their analysis, not the procedures they had used. Consequently, they had to spend two weeks re-creating by a hit-and-miss method the procedure they could have imitated in a day if only they had considered themselves as future readers.

When writing "for the record," remember that there would be no reason to make such a record unless there will be future readers whose needs you should understand and support.

Complex Audiences

Writers sometimes overlook important members of their audience because they assume that all their readers have identical needs and concerns. Actually, audiences often consist of diverse groups of people with widely varying backgrounds and responsibilities.

Complex audiences are very common at work.

That's partly because decisions and actions at work often have an impact on many people and departments throughout the organization. For instance, a proposal to change a company's computer system will affect persons throughout the organization, and people in different areas will have different concerns—some with recordkeeping, some with data communication, some with security, and so on. People in each area will read and comment on your proposal.

Even when only a few people are affected by a decision, many employers expect widespread consultation and advice on it. Each person consulted will have his or her own professional role and area of expertise, and each will play that role and apply that expertise when studying your communication.

When you address a group of people who will be reading from many perspectives, you are addressing a *complex audience*. To do that effectively, you need to write in a way that will meet each person's needs without reducing the effectiveness of your communication for the others. Sometimes you may have to make a tradeoff by focusing on the needs and concerns of the most influential members of your audience. In any case, the first step in writing effectively to a complex audience is to identify each of its members or groups.

Identifying Readers: An Example

The following example describes how one writer identified a complex audience and then creatively addressed the needs of his various readers.

Thomas McKay's employer, Midlands Research Corporation, has a contract to test emissions from thirteen hundred smokestacks in the Midwest. His company lost a substantial amount of money because of flaws in an air sampler it purchased from Aerotest Corporation. As Vice President of the Environmental Division, McKay was responsible for writing to Aerotest to request compensation.

To identify the specific people who would be his readers, he sketched out the diagram shown in Figure 3.2. As it indicates, McKay discovered that although his letter was addressed to a single person, Robert Fulton, Aerotest's Vice President of the Sales Division, it would have a wide readership in Aerotest. He also determined that his letter would have several readers at Midlands and the Environmental Protection Agency (EPA), which is the government agency that had paid for the work that Midlands could not complete on time because of the equipment's failure.

McKay identified several groups of phantom readers at Aerotest.

McKay predicted that Fulton would pass his letter along to several other Aerotest readers, including persons in the departments that engineered and manufactured the faulty equipment because their work was being criticized. He also guessed that Fulton would give the letter to Aerotest's repair shop, asking it to examine the costs Midlands said it had incurred in repairing the equipment. And McKay foresaw Fulton might give copies of the letter to some of Aerotest's sales force, especially the sales engineer who sold the product to Midlands. Finally, McKay felt certain that Aerotest's lawyers would read the letter carefully because Fulton might feel that Aerotest's failure to fulfill Midlands' request might lead to legal action.

McKay thought also about the readers in his own company to whom he would send a copy of his letter.

Within his own company, McKay himself would pass his letter to several people whose names did not appear in it. These persons included Midlands' lawyers, the field teams that had encountered the problem and would want to know what was done about it, and Midlands' Purchasing Department, which needed to be alerted that Aerotest could be a company to avoid.

McKay realized that he would also have phantom readers at the EPA.

McKay decided to send a copy of the letter to the EPA as a way of supporting his earlier explanations for Midlands' inability to complete its work on time. In addition to the EPA administrator in charge of the contract, he predicted that EPA readers would include the contracting officer and the enforcement officers who had been unable to get in a timely manner the emissions data they needed.

To see how McKay designed a communication to meet the needs of this diverse group of readers, see Figure 3.3. Overall, he employed a common technical communication strategy of devoting different, readily distinguishable parts of his communication to different elements of his readership. In the letter itself, he lays out the essential request and the reasons for it, something of interest to most of these readers. In addition, he has attached supplementary information of special interest to some (but not all) readers. For instance, for the lawyers and the EPA contracting officer, he has enclosed two detailed accounts of the problems encountered. These serve to answer the question, "What evidence does McKay have that the problems encountered by Midlands were caused by poor work on Aerotest's part?"

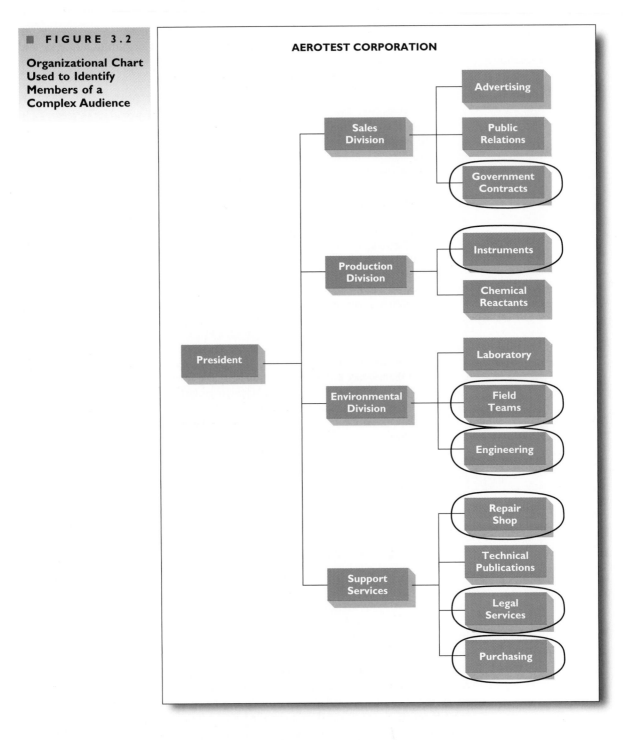

Organizational Chart Used to Identify Members of a Complex Audience

■ FIGURE 3.3

Letter to a Complex Audience (Enclosures not Shown)

McKay explains the problem, a subject of interest to all his phantom readers.

McKay includes several enclosures, each designed to meet the needs of a specific subgroup of his phantom readers.

MIDLANDS RESEARCH INCORPORATED
2796 Buchanan Boulevard   Cincinnati, Ohio 45202

Mr. Robert Fulton   October 17, 19—
Vice President for Sales
Aerotest Corporation
485 Connie Avenue
Sea View, California 94024

Dear Mr. Fulton:

In August, Midlands Research Incorporated purchased a Model Bass 0070 sampling system from Aerotest. Our Environmental Monitoring Group has been using—or trying to use—that sampler to fulfill the conditions of a contract that MRI has with the Environmental Protection Agency to test for toxic substances in the effluent gases from thirteen industrial smokestacks in the Cincinnati area. However, the manager of our Environmental Monitoring Group reports that her employees have had considerable trouble with the sampler.

These difficulties have prevented MRI from fulfilling some of its contractual obligations on time. Thus, besides frustrating our Environmental Monitoring Group, particularly the field technicians, these problems have also troubled Mr. Bernard Gordon, who is our EPA contracting officer, and the EPA enforcement officials who have been awaiting data from us.

I am enclosing two detailed accounts of the problems we have had with the sampler. As you can see, these problems arise from serious design and construction flaws in the sampler itself. Because of the strict schedule contained in our contract with the EPA, we have not had time to return our sampler to you for repair. Therefore, we have had to correct the flaws ourselves, using our Equipment Support Shop, at a cost of approximately $1,500. Because we are incurring the additional expense only because of problems with the engineering and construction of your sampler, we hope that you will be willing to reimburse us, at least in part, by supplying without charge the replacement parts listed on the enclosed page. We will be able to use those parts in future work.

Thank you for your consideration in this matter.

Sincerely,

Thomas McKay
Vice President
Environmental Division

Enclosures: 2 Accounts of Problems
             1 Statement of Repair Expenses
             1 List of Replacement Parts

Similarly, because he predicted that Aerotest's repair shop would ask, "Did the repairs made by Midlands really cost $1,500?" McKay prepared a detailed statement of repair expenses. Had he left out any of the information in his letter and enclosures, he would have significantly decreased his chances of obtaining the reimbursement he desired and of maintaining the good graces of the EPA.

Of course, McKay could not have developed these writing strategies if he had been unaware of the complexity of the audience for his letter. When defining your objectives, you should be equally careful to identify all of your readers.

Identifying Stakeholders

There are many strategies for assuring that on-the-job writing is ethical. Some writers use an "alarm bell" strategy. They trust that if an ethical problem arises in their writing, an alarm bell will go off in their heads. Unless they hear that bell, however, they don't think about ethics. Other writers use a "checkpoint" strategy. At some predetermined point in the writing process, they review their work from an ethical perspective.

This book teaches a process strategy for ethical writing. In it, you integrate an ethical perspective into every stage of your work on a communication. It's important to follow a process strategy because at every step of writing you make decisions that shape the way your communication will affect other people. Accordingly, at every step you should consider your decisions from the viewpoint of your personal ethical beliefs about the ways you should treat others.

Stakeholders

In a process approach to ethical writing, no step is more important than the first: defining objectives. When you are defining your communication's objectives, you are (in part) identifying the people you will keep in mind throughout the rest of your writing effort. When you follow the reader-centered approach to writing that is explained in this book, you begin by identifying your readers.

To write ethically, you must also identify another group of people: the individuals who will gain or lose because of your message. Collectively, these people are called *stakeholders* because they have a stake in what you are writing. Only by learning who these stakeholders are can you assure that you are treating them in accordance with your own ethical values.

How to Identify Stakeholders

Because communications written at work often have far-reaching effects, it's easy to overlook some stakeholders. If that happens, a writer risks causing accidental harm that could have been avoided if only the writer had thought through all the implications of his or her communications.

To identify the stakeholders in your communications, begin by listing the people who will be *directly* affected by what you say and how you say it. In addition to your readers, these individuals may include many other people. For instance, when Craig was preparing a report for his managers concerning the development of a new fertilizer, he realized that his stakeholders included not only the managers but also the farmers who would purchase the fertilizer and the factory workers who would handle the chemicals used to manufacture it.

Next, list people who will be affected *indirectly*. For example, because fertilizers run off the land into lakes and rivers, Craig realized that the stakeholders of his report included people who use these lakes and rivers for drinking water or recreation. Indeed, as is the case with many other communications, the list of indirect stakeholders could be extended to include other species (in this case, the aquatic life in the rivers and lakes) and the environment itself.

Finally, think of the people who may be *remotely* affected. These people may include individuals not yet born. For example, if Craig's fertilizer does not break down into harmless elements, the residue in the soil and water may affect future generations.

Continuous Stakeholder Involvement

As just explained, the reason for identifying stakeholders at the very beginning of your work on a communication is to enable you to take them into account throughout the rest of the writing process. The "Focus on Ethics" boxes in later chapters will explain how to do that. By following their advice, you will be able to achieve a "continuous stakeholder involvement" in your writing that parallels the "continuous reader involvement" described in Chapter 1.

GUIDELINE **7**   **Ask Others to Help You Understand Your Readers and Their Context**

Like most activities of writing, defining objectives is one where you can benefit greatly from the assistance of other people. Obvious sources of assistance are your boss and co-workers, who may have valuable insights into the needs, attitudes, preferences, and situations of your readers.

Ask your target readers what they want and how they will use it.

When possible, also speak directly to your target readers. Better than anyone else, they know what they want from your communication and how they will use it. Contacting them about your communication's objectives is one of the many ways you can follow the strategy, described in Chapter 1, of continuously involving your readers in your writing process.

GUIDELINE **8**   **Remain Open to New Insights and Information**

This final guideline serves to remind you of a simple but important point: although defining your objectives is the first activity that you should perform when writing on the job, it's also one you should treat as an ongoing effort. As you plan, draft, evaluate, and revise, you will continue to refine your sense of what you want to accomplish and deepen your understanding of your readers. Make good use of what you learn. Let your new insights guide your future work, even when this means modifying a plan or draft you've already made.

Use what you learn as you work on your communication.

USING YOUR OBJECTIVES TO GUIDE YOUR WRITING: AN EXAMPLE

The following paragraphs tell how one author skillfully analyzed her audience and then used that information to write a successful communication.

Stephanie works for the Kansas City office of a nonprofit organization that provides Braille translations for textbooks and other reading material requested by blind people. The translations are created entirely by volunteers, and Stephanie believes she knows how to improve the way translation assignments are made. At present, assignments go to each of the volunteers in turn, regardless of the volunteer's speed or reliability. Stephanie has decided to write a memo to her boss, Mrs. Land, suggesting that when a translation is needed very quickly, it be assigned to a volunteer who has worked rapidly and dependably in such situations in the past. To define the objectives of her memo, Stephanie has filled out a worksheet based on the guidelines given in this chapter.* That worksheet, with her notes, is shown in Figure 3.4 (page 73).

While defining the persuasive element of her

The information Stephanie recorded on the worksheet has provided her with many important insights about how to write her memo. Most importantly, when filling

---

* **Note to the Instructor:** A reproducible copy of this worksheet is contained in the *Instructor's Manual.* Also, you may download an editable copy of this worksheet from the Web site for this book.

proposal's purpose, Stephanie developed an understanding of her readers that enabled her to choose effective writing strategies.

out the section on her reader's attitudes, Stephanie realized how much she would have to consider Mrs. Land's possible defensiveness. Mrs. Land set up the present system and believes it works very well. Furthermore, she is the type of person who resists suggestions for change. After considering these characteristics, Stephanie concluded that she could not assume that Mrs. Land would even agree that a problem existed, and that she would have to present the problem without seeming to criticize Mrs. Land.

Stephanie realized that she needed to be especially careful to identify and answer all of Mrs. Land's questions about the change's impact on the organization.

The worksheet also helped Stephanie focus on the fact that Mrs. Land feels Stephanie doesn't understand all the considerations that go into running the agency. Therefore, Stephanie determined that she would have to show in her memo that she has carefully considered all the organizational ramifications of the change she wants to propose.

By thinking about the context in which Mrs. Land would read, Stephanie avoided an ineffective strategy.

When filling out the section related to the general situation in which she would be writing, Stephanie noted that two months earlier Mrs. Land had successfully resisted pressure from several members of the agency's board of directors to force her to retire so that a younger person might take over. Stephanie realized that any reference to these board members or their wishes for streamlined operations might arouse a very hostile response from Mrs. Land.

By considering the stakeholders in her situation, Stephanie found a way to avoid hurting them.

Finally, when trying to fill out the section concerning stakeholders, Stephanie discovered that she needed to talk with some of the translators to find out what they thought of her proposal. Through these interviews, she learned that those who might be judged less reliable and less speedy would be deeply offended. To avoid hurting their feelings, Stephanie modified her proposed plan in the following way: the agency would ask all the translators to tell how many pages they could commit to translating in a week. Urgent translations would go to those who made the largest commitments. Translators who failed to meet their original commitment would be invited to specify a lower commitment that would better suit their personal schedules.

With these considerations in mind, Stephanie wrote a detailed, diplomatic, four-page memo. After several months of deliberation, Mrs. Land accepted Stephanie's proposal.

For your convenience, Figure 3.5 (pages 75 and 76) lists the questions that appear in the worksheet used by Stephanie. Answering them will help you define your communication's objectives in a reader-centered way.

CONCLUSION

The activity of defining objectives is more than an academic exercise. As Stephanie's example shows, it can provide you with valuable insights about the best way to write your communication. Throughout the rest of this book, you will learn specific ways you can use your analysis of your purpose, readers, stakeholders, and situation to help you make good decisions throughout all your work on any communication you prepare at work.

■ **FIGURE 3.4   Stephanie's Completed Worksheet for Defining Objectives for Her Unsolicited Recommendation**

DEFINING OBJECTIVES

Overall Purpose

What are you writing?
A proposal for a new method of assigning Braille translations, in which the most urgent requests go to the quickest and most reliable volunteers.

What prompts you to write?
I believe the new method will improve our service.

What outcome do you desire?
I would like the new method to be put into effect, at least on a trial basis.

Reader Profile

Who is your primary reader?
Mrs. Land.

What is your reader's relationship to you?
She is my boss, and she likes to maintain a formal superior-subordinate relationship.

What are your reader's job title and responsibilities?
She is Director of the Braille Division, responsible for recruiting and maintaining a large group of volunteer Braille translators, advertising translation services to blind people, and responding to requests for translations by assigning volunteers the work of making them.

Who else might read your communication?
Rich Seybold and Mina Williams, Mrs. Land's chief assistants.

How familiar is your reader with your subject?
Mrs. Land knows the present system of assigning Braille translations as well as anyone because she set it up and has run it for the past twelve years. She does not know that I am thinking of proposing an alternative but does know that systems similar to mine are used by some other offices of the Society for the Blind.

How familiar is your reader with your specialty?
Very familiar.

Does your reader have any communication preferences you should take into account?
She likes all communications to look "business-like." She does not like informality.

Should you take into account any other things about your reader when writing?
Mrs. Land gives the impression of being very sure of herself but feels threatened by suggestions for change.

Situational Analysis

What events and circumstances influence the way you should write?
Mrs. Land was recently asked by three board members to retire. She successfully resisted.

■ **FIGURE 3.4** *(continued)*

Reader's Informational Needs

What are the key questions your reader will ask while reading?
What makes you think anything is wrong with the present system?
How, exactly, would your new system work?
What would I have to do differently?
How would the operations of this office be changed?
How would we determine which translations deserve highest priority?
How would we decide which translators are placed in our top group?
Would it cost anything?

How will your reader search for the answers? (The reader may use more than one strategy.)

___X___ Sequential reading from beginning to end
___X___ Selective reading, as when using a reference book (what key terms will your reader
       look for?)
_____ Other (explain)
       Mrs. Land will probably skip around through the memo at first, but will later read it from
       front to back.

How will your reader use the information you provide?

___X___ Compare point by point (what will be the points of comparison?)
___X___ Attempt to determine how the information you provide will affect him or her
___X___ Attempt to determine how the information you provide will affect his or her organization
___X___ Follow instructions step by step
_____ Other (explain)
       She will compare her system with mine in terms of cost, speed of producing translations,
       and effect on volunteer morale. Although she won't exactly look for instructions
       in my proposal, she will want to know in detail how the process would work.

Reader's Attitudes

What is your reader's attitude toward your subject? Why? What do you want it to be?   Mrs. Land
thinks the present system runs as well as one possibly could. I want her to see that a better system
is possible.

What is your reader's attitude toward you? Why? What do you want it to be?   Although I have
worked for her for three years, Mrs. Land still thinks of me as a newcomer who knows little and
has impractical ideas. I want her to think that I am a helpful, knowledgeable, sensible person.

Stakeholders

Who, besides your readers, are the stakeholders in your communication?   The Society's clients.
The translators—including those who would be given priority assignments and those who
wouldn't.

How will they be affected by it?   I don't know. I'd better investigate this.

■ **FIGURE 3.5**

Worksheet for Defining Objectives

Defining Objectives

Overall Purpose

What are you writing?

What prompts you to write?

What outcome do you desire?

Reader Profile

Who is your primary reader?

What is your reader's relationship to you?

What are your reader's job title and responsibilities?

Who else might read your communication?

How familiar is your reader with your subject?

How familiar is your reader with your specialty?

Does your reader have any communication preferences you should take into account?

Should you take into account any other things about your reader when writing?

Situational Analysis

What events and circumstances influence the way you should write?

Reader's Informational Needs

What are the key questions your reader will ask while reading?

How will your reader search for the answers? (The reader may use more than one strategy.)

_____ Sequential reading from beginning to end

_____ Selective reading, as when using a reference book (what key terms will your reader look for?

_____ Other (explain)

How will your reader use the information you provide?

_____ Compare point by point (what will be the points of comparison?)

_____ Attempt to determine how the information you provide will affect him or her

_____ Attempt to determine how the information you provide will affect his or her organization

_____ Follow instructions step by step

_____ Other (explain)

Reader's Attitudes

What is your reader's attitude toward your subject? Why? What do you want it to be?

What is your reader's attitude toward you? Why? What do you want it to be?

Stakeholders

Who, besides your readers, are stakeholders in your communication?

How will they be affected by it?

EXERCISES

1. Find an example of a communication you might write in your career. Following the guidelines in this chapter, define its objective. Be sure to identify each of the following:

- The readers and their characteristics
- The stakeholders and the ways they might be affected by the communication
- The final result the writer desires
- The enabling elements of the communication's purpose

- The persuasive elements of its purpose

Then explain how the communication's features have been tailored to fit its objectives. If you can think of ways the communication might be improved, make recommendations.

2. Define the objectives of an assignment you are preparing for your technical communication class.

CASE

ANNOUNCING THE SMOKING BAN

As you sit in your office on the top floor of the four-story building owned by your employer, you look up from the draft of a memo that company president C. K. Mitchell dropped onto your desk a few minutes ago. He asked you for your opinion of it.

The memo announces a new no-smoking policy for the company, which employs about 250 people who work in your building or the one next door. Formulating the policy has been difficult. Recently, the state legislature passed a law requiring all employers to establish a policy on smoking. The law doesn't say what the policy should be, only that every employer must have one.

C. K. appointed a team of top managers to discuss the matter and make a recommendation. One possibility would be to permit smoking everywhere. That is the current policy, but a very vocal group of nonsmokers clearly expects something else. This group numbers nearly half the workforce, including many influential members of the company.

Another possibility would be to allow smoking only in private offices. At first, that seemed like a great idea and was almost announced as the new policy. At the last minute, however, Maryellen Rosenberg, Director of Personnel, pointed out that many of the employees don't have private offices. In fact, only salaried employees do. The secretaries, mail clerks, janitors, and others without private offices would surely complain that the policy discriminated against them.

After considering and rejecting several other plans, C. K. finally decided that the only thing to do would be to ban smoking altogether. "What could be more appropriate," he asked at a managers' meeting yesterday, "for a company that tries to make people healthier?" Your company designs and markets exercise equipment for homes and fitness centers. After prompting from you and several others, C. K. decided to hire a consulting firm that offers a course to help employees stop smoking. The course will be offered to employees free of charge.

"C. K.'s memo on this had better be good," you thought as he gave you the draft. Although the employees know that C. K. has been meeting with you and others to work out a policy, the details have been kept secret. The publicity surrounding the new law has sparked some heated controversies. Some employees have talked of quitting if they can't smoke at work, and others have talked of quitting if smoking isn't prohibited.

The controversies are harming morale, which is already low because C. K. recently reduced the company's contribution to the profit-sharing plan despite a steady rise in revenues. The money saved is being used to buy the building next door, a move that will save the company money in the long run. However, C. K.'s action is widely viewed as yet another example of his heavy-handed, insensitive style.

YOUR ASSIGNMENT

First, to fashion a reasonable set of objectives for C. K.'s memo, fill out the Worksheet for Defining Objectives (Figure 3.5). Remember that the memo must somehow satisfy all the employees. Second, evaluate the draft of C.K.'s memo (Figure 3.6) in light of the objectives you have established, and then revise the draft to make it more effective. Be prepared to explain your revisions to C. K.

■ **FIGURE 3.6**

Memo for Use with Case

MEMORANDUM

TO: All Employees

FROM: C. K. Mitchell

RE: Smoke-Free Environment

I hereby notify you that beginning September 1 of this year, Fitness Exercise Equipment, Inc. will institute a smoke-free environment. To wit, smoking will <u>not</u> be allowed anywhere inside the main building or the satellite building next door.

The delay between this announcement and the beginning date for this new policy will allow any employees who smoke the chance to enroll in courses which, I hope, will help them break or curtail their habit. In accordance with our concern for the wellness of all our employees, we will enhance our working environment by prohibiting all smoking.

All employees are thanked for their cooperation, understanding, and dedication to better health.

PART III

Planning

CHAPTER 4
Planning to Meet Your Readers'
Informational Needs

CHAPTER 5
Planning Your Persuasive Strategies

CHAPTER 6
Conducting Research

REFERENCE GUIDE
Five Research Methods

Planning to Meet Your Readers' Informational Needs

GUIDELINES

1 | Answer your readers' questions

2 | Include the additional information your readers need

3 | Organize to support your readers' tasks

4 | Look for a technical writing superstructure you can adapt

5 | Plan your visual aids

6 | Outline, if this would be helpful

7 | Take regulations and expectations into account

CHAPTER 4

DEFINING OBJECTIVES

PLANNING

DRAFTING

EVALUATING

REVISING

In the preceding chapter, you learned how to define objectives for the communications you write at work. This chapter is the first of three that will help you translate your objectives into a successful plan of action.

BENEFITS OF GOOD PLANNING

Planning is an inevitable part of writing. Whenever you start to write to a friend, instructor, or co-worker, you begin with at least *some* idea of what you will say and how you will say it. However, there is a great difference between good planning and poor planning. Good planning can benefit you in two ways:

- **Good planning saves time.** Consider some of the difficulties Charlotte encountered when she drafted a report without first planning it carefully. She spent more than an hour writing and then polishing three long paragraphs she later decided she didn't need. She also spent half an hour revising two pages before she discovered that they would be much more effective if reorganized and moved to another place. Had she spent fifteen minutes planning before she began to write, Charlotte could have saved herself much time and effort.
- **Good planning helps you increase the effectiveness of your writing.** When Charlotte showed her report to her boss, he pointed out several places where she had failed to present and support her major points clearly and forcefully. How did that happen? Charlotte had focused on each sentence and paragraph without giving much thought to her overall strategy. With better planning, she would have paid attention to larger questions, such as how she could make her points fit together and how she could most persuasively present her conclusions.

In a way, Charlotte was lucky. Her boss gave her time to rework her report before she sent it to its intended readers. Consequently, she suffered only a loss of time and effort, and some loss of pride. However, at work people often have no time to rewrite their communications. They must get them right the first time. If they don't, the communications are sent anyway. The costs of poor planning in such situations can be much greater than those Charlotte experienced.

ORGANIZATION OF THIS BOOK'S ADVICE ABOUT PLANNING

To help you plan effectively, this book presents two complementary sets of planning guidelines that correspond to the enabling and persuasive elements of purpose explained in Chapter 3. The seven guidelines in this chapter will help you design plans for achieving the enabling element of purpose, which is to enable your readers to locate, understand, and use the information and ideas that they need from you. The six guidelines in Chapter 5 will help you create plans for achieving the persuasive element of purpose, which is to influence your readers' attitudes and actions in the ways you desire.

GUIDELINE **1**   ## Answer Your Readers' Questions

If possible, ask your readers what they want.

The first step in achieving the enabling element of purpose is to identify the information your readers need from you. The surest way to do this is to ask your readers directly. However, that's not always possible on the job. When it's not, you can gain enormously helpful guidance about what to include in your communications by following Chapter 3's advice to think of your readers as persons who ask questions. The answers to these questions are the content you need to provide.

On the job, readers' questions usually arise from three reader characteristics discussed in Chapter 3: professional roles, unfamiliarity with the subject of your communication, and limited knowledge of your specialty.

Questions Arising from Your Readers' Professional Roles

As explained in Chapter 3, the most important thing to think about when identifying your readers' questions is their professional roles. For this reason, it's always important for you to understand as fully as you can what your readers' responsibilities are with respect to the issues you discuss in your communication.

Readers' three major roles: decision-maker, adviser, implementer

However, it's also helpful to focus on the general use your readers will make of your communication. Regardless of the particularities of their job responsibilities, people at work usually read in order to make a decision, advise others about a decision, or implement a decision. The following paragraphs describe the kinds of questions they typically ask when playing the roles of decision-maker, adviser, and implementer.

Decision-makers   The decision-makers' role is to say how the organization will act when confronted with a particular choice. They determine what the company should do in the future—next week, next month, next year. Consequently, decision-makers usually ask questions shaped by their need to choose between alternative courses of action:

Decision-makers want conclusions, not details.

- **What are your conclusions?** Decision-makers are much more interested in your conclusions than the raw data you gathered or the particulars of your procedures. Conclusions can serve as the basis for decisions; details cannot.
- **What do you recommend?** Decision-makers usually ask you about a topic because you have special knowledge of it. This knowledge makes your recommendation especially valuable to decision-making readers.

Decision-makers look to the future.

- **What will happen?** Decision-makers want to know what will occur if they follow your recommendations—and what will happen if they don't. How much money will be saved? How much will production increase? How will customers react?

Decision-makers prize brevity.

Decision-makers are often in managerial or executive positions, where they are pulled by responsibilities in many areas. Consequently, they usually prefer brief answers to their questions. As the director of one government research office declared, "If it can't be held together with a paper clip, it is too long for me to read." Many organizations require that reports to management be no more than a page or two long, even if the reports represent several months of work.

However, even as you strive for brevity, be sure to be specific. Include the details necessary to guide decisions. For example, if you are predicting sales and income for the next three years, don't say merely that both will rise. Decision-makers will want to know how large the increases will be and which products will generate them.

Many decision-makers prefer nontechnical answers, especially if they are unfamiliar with the technical terms and concepts used in a specialized field. Even decision-makers who once specialized in the field may have lost touch with new developments. They will depend on you to use terms they understand and to provide the background they need in order to grasp technical content.

Advisers   Advisers provide information and advice for decision-makers to consider when deciding what the organization should do. Unlike decision-makers, advisers *are* interested in details. They need to analyze and evaluate the evidence supporting your general conclusions, recommendations, and projections.

Consequently, advisers ask questions that touch on the thoroughness, reliability, and impact of your work:

Advisers want the details, not just generalizations.

- Did you use a reasonable method to obtain your results?
- Do your data really support your conclusions?
- Have you overlooked anything important?
- If your recommendation is followed, what will be the effect on other departments?
- What kinds of problems are likely to arise?

Though advisers want detailed answers to these questions, they are not likely to want every last particular of the procedures you used or every last piece of data you collected. They need just enough detail to assess the quality and consequences of your ideas and information.

How to address decision-makers and advisers in one document

Often you will have to write a single report that must meet the needs of both decision-makers and advisers. Usually such a report consists of two parts: (1) a very brief summary—called an *executive summary* or *abstract*—at the beginning of the report, designed for decision-makers and (2) the body of the report, designed for advisers. Typically, the executive summary is only a page or a few pages long, whereas the body may exceed a hundred pages.

Researcher James W. Souther asked a large group of managers how often they read each of the parts of a long report. As Figure 4.1 indicates, they reported that they read the summary 100 percent of the time, but the body only 15 percent of the time. When decision-makers want more information than the summary provides, they usually go to the introduction (which provides background information) and to the recommendations (where the writers explain their suggestions fully). The rest of the report is read by advisers.

Implementers   Decisions, once made, must be carried out by someone. Implementers are these individuals.

The most important questions asked by implementers are these:

Implementers want to know what to do—and why.

- **What do you want me to do?** Whether you are writing step-by-step instructions, requests for information, or policies that others must follow, you must provide implementers with clear, exact, easy-to-follow directions. Be sure to say *explicitly* what you want. All too often, people fail to get what they want because their readers cannot tell exactly what they are being asked to do.

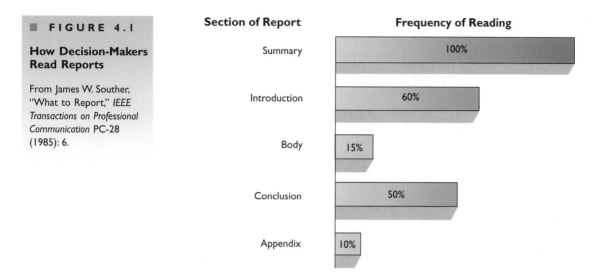

■ **FIGURE 4.1**

How Decision-Makers Read Reports

From James W. Souther, "What to Report," *IEEE Transactions on Professional Communication* PC-28 (1985): 6.

Section of Report   **Frequency of Reading**

Summary — 100%

Introduction — 60%

Body — 15%

Conclusion — 50%

Appendix — 10%

■ **What is the purpose of the actions you are asking me to perform?** Readers of policy statements and general directives often must know the intent of a policy if they are to produce satisfactory results. Imagine, for instance, the situation of the managers of a factory who have been directed to cut by 15 percent the amount of energy used in production. They will want to know whether they are to make a long-term energy saving or to compensate for a short-term shortage. If the latter, they might take some temporary actions, such as altering work hours and curtailing certain operations. However, if the reduction is to be long-term, they might take such measures as purchasing new equipment and modifying the factory building.

If you want it done one way, tell your readers.

■ **How much freedom do I have in deciding how to do this?** People often devise shortcuts or alternative ways of doing things. When any one of several ways is acceptable, you may not need to specify one over another. But when you have a preference, you should state it explicitly.

Name the deadline.

■ **When must I complete this task?** To be able to adjust their schedules to include a new task along with their other responsibilities, readers need to know when the new task must be completed.

Questions Arising from Your Readers' Unfamiliarity with Your Subject

Sometimes readers need background.

Some of the questions your readers ask may arise from their lack of familiarity with your subject. Imagine, for example, that you are going to recommend to executives at corporate headquarters some ways of improving management in a branch office. If they already know how that office operates and why management there needs to be improved, you can proceed directly to your recommendations. But if they know little or nothing about that particular office, they will probably ask a good many questions about the situation.

When furnishing such background information, remember to provide only what your readers need in order to understand your message and its significance to them. Don't provide unnecessary details or information unrelated to their needs.

Questions Arising from Your Readers' Limited Knowledge of Your Specialty

Sometimes you must educate your readers.

On occasion, you may need to use a term that some of your readers won't understand. To answer the readers' question, "What does that mean?" you might provide a definition:

> A *headgate* is a gate for controlling the amount of water flowing into an irrigation ditch.
> A *rectifier* is an electrical device for converting alternating current to direct current.

Or you might use an analogy:

> Wood sorrel is a plant that resembles clover.
> On the proposed extruders, we will use a feed system much like that found on a Banbury mixer.

You will find more advice on defining and explaining unfamiliar terms in Chapter 10.

On occasion, you may need to give a much longer explanation of some mechanism, process, or concept. Chapter 7 provides advice you can use when you need to explain at length.

Of course, the preceding descriptions of three readers' roles are greatly simplified. Any individual reader's questions will be shaped by his or her specific responsibilities within the organization. Moreover, these roles often overlap and intertwine. Often, a person asked to advise about a particular decision will also be asked to carry it out. Nevertheless, the roles of decision-maker, adviser, and implementer can help you understand the ways your readers will want to use your communications—and hence what you should include in them.

GUIDELINE **2** **Include the Additional Information Your Readers Need**

Ask yourself, "What else should my readers know?"

Although your efforts to decide what to say to your readers should certainly include an attempt to identify your readers' likely questions, remember that sometimes readers don't know all the questions they should ask. For example, imagine Toni's situation.

Research often turns up facts that are important to readers even though the readers would not know to ask for them.

Toni has been asked to investigate three computer programs her employer might purchase for use in designing products. While gathering information about the programs, she learned that the company that makes one of them is in financial trouble. If it goes out of business, Toni's employer will not be able to obtain the assistance and improved versions of the program it would normally expect to receive. Even though Toni's readers are not likely to ask, "Are any of the programs made by companies that appear to be on the verge of bankruptcy?" Toni should include that information in her report.

Investigating Stakeholder Impacts

As Chapter 3 explained, the first step in writing ethically is to identify your communication's stakeholders—the people who will be affected by what you say and how you say it. Next, learn how your communication will impact these people and how they feel about these potential effects.

Asking Stakeholders Directly

The best way to learn how your communication will affect its stakeholders is to talk to these individuals directly. In many organizations, such discussions are a regular step in the decision-making process that accompanies the writing of reports and proposals. When an action is considered, representatives of the various groups or divisions that might be affected meet together to discuss the action's potential impacts on each of them.

Similarly, government agencies often solicit the views of stakeholders. For example, the federal agencies that write environmental impact statements are required to share drafts of these documents with the public so that concerned citizens can express their reactions. The final draft must respond to the public's comments.

Even in situations that are tra-ditionally viewed as one-way communications, many managers seek stakeholder inputs. For instance, when conducting annual employee evaluations, some managers draft their evaluation, then discuss it with the employee before preparing the final version.

Action You Can Take

If you are writing a communication for which there is no established process for soliciting stakeholders' views, you can initiate such a process on your own. To hear from stakeholders in your own organization, you can probably just visit or call. To contact stakeholders outside your organization, you may need to use more creativity and also consult with your co-workers.

If you already know the stakeholders well, you may be able to find out their views very quickly. At other times, an almost impossibly large amount of time would be needed to thoroughly investigate stakeholders' views. When that happens, the decision about how much time to spend can itself become an ethical decision. The crucial thing is to make as serious an attempt as circumstances will allow. There's all the difference in the world between saying that you can spend only a limited amount of time investigating stakeholders' views and saying that you just don't have any time to find out what the stakeholders are thinking.

Speaking for Others

To save time, you might try to imagine what the stakeholders would say if you spoke to them directly. Clearly this course of action is superior to ignoring stakeholders altogether. But you can never know exactly what others are thinking. The greater the difference between you and the stakeholders—in job title, education, and background—the less likely you are to guess correctly. So, it's always best to let stakeholders speak for themselves.

Conclusion

On many issues, different people are likely to have different opinions about what is the most ethical course of action. Asking stakeholders for their input does not guarantee that they all will be happy with what you ultimately write. But it does guarantee that you have heard their opinions. Without this step, you can scarcely attempt to take their needs and concerns into account.

In considering information you might include even though your readers probably won't ask for it, be careful to avoid the temptation to include information that interests you but will be of no use to your readers.

GUIDELINE 3 **Organize to Support Your Readers' Tasks**

Organize in a way that helps readers find and use your information.

To fully meet your readers' informational needs, you must not only include the information your readers need but also organize this material in a helpful way. An excellent way to develop a reader-centered organization is to think once again about the enabling element of your communication's purpose. In particular, think about the ways your readers will search for and use the information you will provide, and then organize in a way that will help them perform these tasks.

Note that this guideline's advice is very different from the typical advice about organization. When asked what method of organization a writer should use, most people reply, "A logical organization, of course." Unfortunately, a logical organization is not necessarily helpful to the reader.

Organize in the way your readers will find most helpful when they try to use your information to fulfill their own goals.

Imagine, for example, that you work in the registrar's office of a small college. The college's computer has broken down; some files have been lost. You have been asked to work manually to fulfill a request from the college president for a list of the home addresses, majors, and class standings (first-year, sophomore, junior, senior) of all students enrolled in a technical writing course. The instructors in this course have circulated sign-up sheets to their students. Now, with the completed sheets in front of you, you must combine all the information into a single list for the president.

How will you organize the list? By major? By class standing? By hometown? By some other principle of organization? Although any of these choices would be *logical*, they would not be equally *useful*. The most useful organization would be the one most compatible with the *use* the president will make of the list. If the president plans to send out a series of letters, one to all the seniors, another to all the juniors, and so on, you would organize the list according to class standings. If the president wants to determine which departments send the most students to technical writing classes, you would arrange the list according to the students' majors. Each of these patterns is not only logical in itself but also succeeds in supporting the president's reading task.

Of course, readers' tasks vary greatly from situation to situation. Nevertheless, some tasks are common enough to make it possible to identify a few widely applicable strategies for organizing messages. The following paragraphs describe these strategies.

Organize Hierarchically

Readers build mental hierarchies.

When we read, we encounter small bits of information one at a time: first what we find in this sentence, then what we find in the next sentence, and so on. One of our major tasks is to build these small bits of information into larger structures of meaning that we can store and work with in our own minds. Researchers have found that one of the major cognitive strategies we use to do these things is to create mental hierarchies of meaning. Represented on paper, these mental hierarchies look like outlines (Figure 4.2) or tree diagrams (Figure 4.3) (page 90), with the overall topic divided into subtopics, and some or all of the subtopics broken down into still smaller units.

■ **FIGURE 4.2**

Outline Showing the Hierarchical Organization of a Report

Parking Recommendations to
Greenwood Area Council

Topic	I. Introduction
Topic	II. Problems
Subtopic	A. Insufficient parking
	1. Shoppers complain about inconvenience
Smaller parts	2. Shop owners complain about lost sales
	3. Police report many parking violations
Subtopic	B. Traffic congestion
	1. People circle through the area waiting for a parking space to open up
Smaller parts	2. Additional on-street parking impedes the free flow of traffic
	3. Though illegal, some double-parking occurs, clogging streets
Topic	III. Possible solutions
Subtopic	A. Build a parking garage in the center of the shopping area
	1. Advantages
Smaller parts	2. Disadvantages
	3. Cost
Subtopic	B. Build a parking lot on the edge of the shopping area and run shuttle buses to major stores
	1. Advantages
Smaller parts	2. Disadvantages
	3. Cost
Topic	IV. Recommendations

For readers, building these hierarchies can be hard work, as we've all experienced when we've had to reread a passage because we can't figure out how its sentences fit together.

Help readers by organizing hierarchically.

The easiest and surest way to help your readers build mental hierarchies from your communications is simply to present the information already organized this way. This doesn't mean that you need to start every writing project by making an outline (see Guideline 6). Often, you may be able to achieve a hierarchical organization without outlining. But you should always organize hierarchically.

Group Together the Items Your Readers Will *Use* Together

Organize to support your readers' way of using your communication.

Creating a hierarchy involves grouping facts. You assemble individual facts into small groups and then gather these groups into larger ones. When grouping your facts, be sure to group together the information your readers will *use* together.

To do this, think about the mental tasks your readers will want to perform in order to use the information you provide. Consider the way Daniel was able to find an effective organization for a report based on his understanding of the ways his readers would use the information he provided.

■ **FIGURE 4.3**   **Tree Diagram Showing the Hierarchical Organization of a Report**

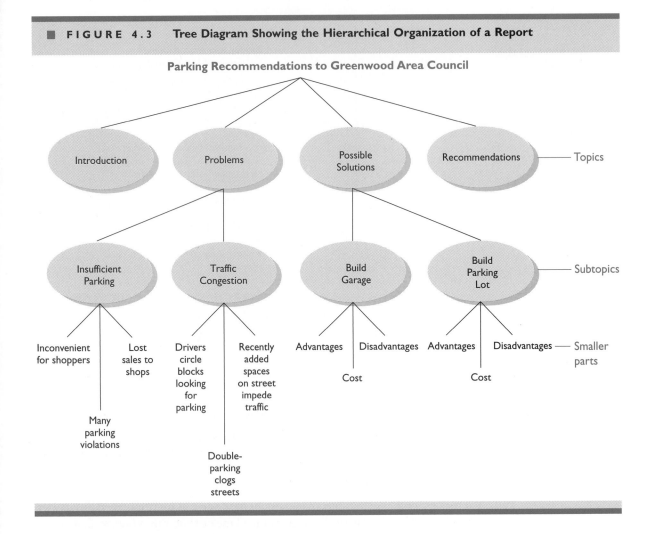

Daniel works for a federal task force that has assigned him to write the final report on its efforts to determine the effects of sulfur dioxide (SO_2) emissions from automobiles and factories. The report will summarize the findings of hundreds of research projects conducted over many years.

Daniel might organize his report in several ways. If the purpose of the report is to review the history of research on SO_2 emissions, his readers will want to understand the relationships over time of the various studies he summarizes. To help them do that, he could organize his report chronologically, with such chapter titles as "Research from 1970 to 1990" and "Research from 1990 to the Present."

> However, suppose the purpose of Daniel's report is to help legislators evaluate the effects of SO_2 emissions so they can enact appropriate regulations. Then, his readers will want a summary of each kind of impact, regardless of when the studies exploring the impact were published. To help his readers with this task, Daniel organized his report in the following way:
>
> I. Effects on Human Health
>   A. Effects on skin
>
>   B. Effects on internal organs
>   1. Heart
>   2. Lungs
>   3. Etc.
>
> II. Effects on the Environment
>   A. Effects on human-made objects
>   1. Buildings
>   2. Cars
>
>   B. Effects on nature
>   1. Lakes, rivers, and oceans
>   2. Forests
>   3. Wildlife
>   4. Etc.

Daniel devised his outline based on his understanding of the ways his readers would use the information in his report.

Of course, you can't plan a useful organization simply by imitating the one Daniel created, but you can do it by following his procedure: think about how your readers will use the information and ideas you provide, and group your material accordingly.

Give the Bottom Line First
Readers at work want to find the main point of a communication as swiftly as possible. To express this desire, they often urge writers to "put the bottom line first."

What Is the Bottom Line?   The *bottom line,* of course, is the last line of a financial statement. Literally, the writers are being told, "Before you swamp me with details on expenditures and sources of income, tell me whether we made a profit or took a loss."

Readers want the main point quickly.

That advice can be applied figuratively to many kinds of communication prepared at work. Before people at work read the details of a report, proposal, or other decision-making communication, they want to know what its main point is.

To say that you should put the bottom line first doesn't necessarily mean that you must state your main point in the very first sentence. It's still appropriate to provide relevant background information at the outset. But don't keep your readers in suspense. As soon as possible, state the main point: Is the project on schedule, or must we take special action to meet the deadline? Will the proposed design for our product work, or must it be modified?

Is It Illogical to Put the Bottom Line First?   Putting the most important information first seems illogical to some writers. They reason that the most important information is generally some conclusion they reached fairly late in their thinking about their subject matter. Before reaching it, they had to gather and analyze facts, and they therefore reason that they should give their readers those facts to consider before telling them what conclusions they reached.

Focus on use, not logic, when organizing.

Such a view is writer-centered. It assumes that because the writer gained information in a certain way, that is the way the information should be presented. Although such an organization has logic, it is also *logical* to state a conclusion or recommendation and then to follow with explanations and supporting details. And when the reader is *first* interested in the conclusion or recommendation, then it is certainly more reader-centered to accommodate the reader.

Should You *Always* Put the Bottom Line First?   "Do I always need to give the bottom line first?" you may be asking. Not necessarily. The importance of doing so depends on your readers and the situation. Some readers are more patient than others when the main point is delayed, especially when the communication is brief. Furthermore, in some special situations, giving the bottom line first can undermine the success of your communication. You will find a discussion of such situations in the fourth guideline of Chapter 5. As a general rule, however, you can increase your readers' satisfaction with your writing by giving the bottom line first.

In some circumstances, you should delay the main point.

GUIDELINE 4   Look for a Technical Writing Superstructure You Can Adapt

Superstructures are conventional patterns for writing.

At work, you will often write in a situation that closely resembles circumstances encountered by other people many times before. Like other people, you may need to report on a business trip, tell someone how to operate a piece of equipment, or request funds for a project you would like to conduct. For many of these recurring situations, writers employ conventional patterns for constructing their communications. These patterns go by several names, such as *genres* and *formats*. Here, they are called *superstructures* (van Dijk).

At work, you will encounter many superstructures: the business proposal, budget report, computer manual, feasibility report, project proposal, and environmental impact statement, to name a few. Carolyn R. Miller, Graham Smart, and other researchers suggest that each superstructure exists because writers and readers agree that it provides an effective pattern for meeting some particular communication need that occurs repeatedly. Figure 4.4 shows how the superstructure for proposals accommodates readers (by answering their questions) and also writers (by providing them with a framework for presenting their persuasive claims).

Superstructures assist both readers and writers.

Because superstructures serve the needs of both readers and writers, they are ideal for writing reader-centered communications. They can be especially helpful at the planning stage because they suggest the kinds of information your readers probably want and the manner in which the information should be organized and presented. However, superstructures are not surefire recipes for success. Each represents a general framework for constructing messages in a *typical* situation. But no two situations are exactly alike. Moreover, for many situations no superstructure

■ FIGURE 4.4

Superstructure for Proposals

Topic	Readers' Question	Writer's Persuasive Point
Introduction	What is this communication about?	Briefly, I propose to do the following.
Problem	Why is the proposed project needed?	The proposed project addresses a problem, need, or goal that is important to you.
Objectives	What features will a solution to this problem need in order to be successful?	A successful solution can be achieved if it has these features.
Product or Outcome	How do you propose to do those things?	Here's what I plan to produce and how it has the features necessary for success.
Method	Are you going to be able to deliver what you describe here?	Yes, because I have a good plan of action (method); the necessary facilities, equipment, and other resources; a workable schedule; appropriate qualifications; and a sound management plan.
Costs	What will it cost?	The cost is reasonable.

exists. To use superstructures effectively, look for an appropriate one; if you find one, adapt it to your particular purpose and readers.

Chapters 18 through 20 describe the general superstructures for reports, proposals, and instructions. At work, you may encounter more specialized superstructures developed within your profession or industry—or even within your own organization.

GUIDELINE **5**   **Plan Your Visual Aids**

Visual aids are very common in on-the-job writing.

On-the-job communications often use visual aids to supplement the text. Tables, graphs, drawings, and photographs convey certain kinds of information more succinctly and forcefully than words. So when you are planning a communication, look for places where you can use visual aids to show how something looks (in drawings or photographs), explain how something is organized (flow charts), make detailed information readily accessible (tables), or clarify the relationship among groups of data (graphs).

Chapter 11 provides detailed advice about where to use visual aids and how to construct them effectively. However, don't wait until you read that chapter to begin incorporating visual aids into your communication plans.

GUIDELINE 6 ## Outline, If This Would Be Helpful

When they talk about planning a communication, many people mention outlining—and ask, "Is outlining worth the work it requires?" No single answer to this question is valid for all writers and all situations. The following general observations about outlining practices at work may help you determine when (and if) outlining might be worthwhile for you.

Outlining is rare for some types of communication.

On the job, outlining is rarely used for short or routine messages. However, many writers outline longer, more complex communications, especially if they expect to have difficulties in organizing. They use outlining as a way of experimenting with alternative ways of structuring their message before they begin to invest time in drafting. Similarly, if they encounter problems when drafting, some writers will try to outline the troublesome passage.

Outlining is common for reviews and team writing.

Also, writers sometimes wish to—or are required to—share their organizational plans with a superior or co-worker. Outlining provides them with a convenient way of explaining their plans to such individuals.

Finally, outlining can help writing teams negotiate the structure of a communication they must create together (see Chapter 17).

When creating an outline, remember that the kind of tidy structure shown in Figure 4.2 represents the product of the outlining process. Many writers begin organizing by making lists or diagrams, drawing arrows and pictures, and using many other techniques to think through possible ways of putting their information together for their readers.

Using Computers to Outline

Your word processor can help you outline.

Most word-processing programs include special tools for outlining. With these tools, you can, for instance, make an outline and then convert it immediately into the headings for your document. These tools will also allow you to convert from the normal view of your document to an outline view, so you can review the organizational structure that is evolving as you write. When you move material in the outline, the program automatically moves the corresponding parts of your full text, which can sometimes make for an extremely efficient way to revise a draft. Figure 4.5 shows some of the features of one widely used word-processing program's outlining tool.

GUIDELINE 7 ## Take Regulations and Expectations into Account

Many organizations have strong expectations—and even regulations—that constrain what writers can say and how they can say it. These constraints can affect *any* aspect of a communication—even tone, use of abbreviations, layout of tables, size of margins, and length (usually specifying a *maximum* length, not a minimum).

■ **FIGURE 4.5**

Outlining Function of a Word-Processing Program

The outlining function of Microsoft Word enables you to:

■ Create your outline.

■ Add text under your headings.

■ Shift instantly to a finished communication.

You can easily switch between viewing the outline and the full text.

You can reorganize your communication simply by moving a heading; the subheadings and text automatically move also.

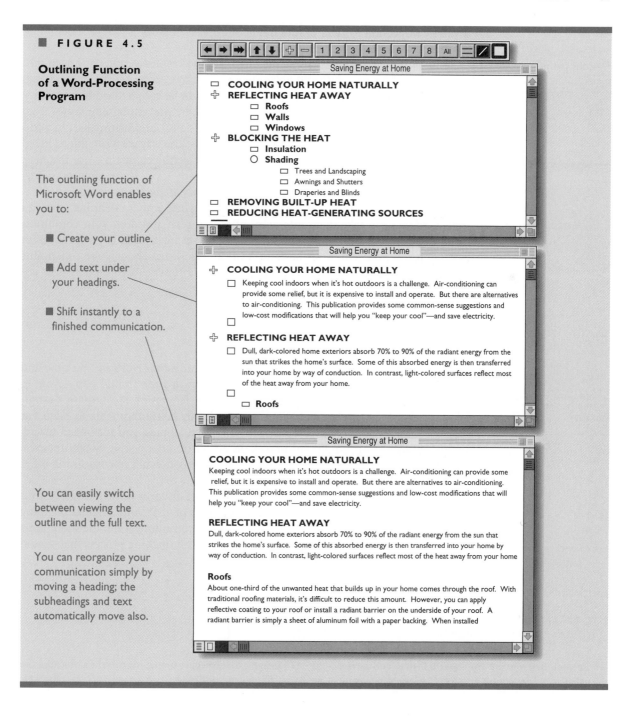

It will be important for you to find out about these constraints and take them into account as you plan your communications.

Reasons for organizational expectations about writing

Some of these constraints come directly from the employer, reflecting such motives as the company's desire to cultivate a particular corporate image, to protect its legal interests (because any written document can be subpoenaed in a lawsuit), and to preserve its competitive edge (for example, by preventing employees from accidentally tipping off competitors about technological breakthroughs). In addition, most organizations develop writing customs—"the way we write things here."

Writing constraints also can originate from outside the company—for instance, from government regulations that specify how patent applications, environmental impact reports, and many other types of documents are to be prepared.

Be sure to find out what these constraints are when you are defining your objectives so you can take them into account as you plan and draft your communication. Many companies publish *style guides* that set forth their regulations about writing. Ask if your employer has one. You can also learn about these constraints by asking co-workers and reading communications similar to yours that your co-workers have written in the past.

HOW MUCH TIME TO SPEND ON PLANNING

Time needed for planning can vary.

This chapter has presented many planning suggestions that will save you time and enhance the effectiveness of your writing. How much time should you devote to following these suggestions? If you are writing a brief communication on a familiar topic that is easy to explain, you may need only a few moments to plan. For longer communications on complex and unfamiliar topics, you may need several hours—or days—including time to seek the advice of other people. Sometimes you can plan by making a few mental notes or by jotting down a few words. At other times, you may have to work out a detailed outline.

As you work on successive drafts, you are likely to discover ways to improve your plans. That doesn't mean that you planned poorly or that your original planning was a waste of time. The more you think about a communication, the more ideas you will have on ways to strengthen it. Planning is an ongoing process that should continue until you have completed your final draft.

EXERCISES

1. Imagine that you are employed full-time and have decided to take a course at a local college. First, name a course you might like to take. Next, by following Guidelines 1 and 2, list the information you would include in a memo in which you ask your employer to pay your tuition and permit you to leave work early two days a week to attend class.

2. Imagine that you have been hired to write a brochure that will present your college department in a favorable light to entering first-year students and students who are thinking of changing their majors. Following the guidelines in this chapter, generate a list of things you would want to say. How would you group and order your material?

CASE

FILLING THE DISTANCE-LEARNING CLASSROOM

You knock on the office door softly, unsure why the Chair of the English Department has asked to meet with you.

"Welcome," Professor Rivera says, immediately putting you at ease. "I'm glad you could come. Professor Baldwin suggested you might be able to help me with a sort of marketing project."

What a relief. At least you haven't done anything wrong.

"Have you heard about our new distance-learning classroom?" Professor Rivera asks. You tell her you know that a large room in the English building is being redesigned as a computerized classroom.

"Well, in addition to computers, the room will have video cameras, projection equipment, special software, and a very large screen. By means of this equipment, it can be paired with a similar classroom elsewhere in the world so that students in both locations can become part of the same class.

"In fact, we're getting ready to conduct a few experimental sections of First-Year English in which students here will be paired with students in a similar course at a university in Brazil. A team of faculty from both schools has planned a common syllabus and paired sections here and in Brazil to meet at the same hours. When the Brazilian instructor or students speak, the students and instructor here will be able to see and hear them. And vice versa. Also, students in the two locations will exchange drafts via the Internet, and they will even be able to project a draft of a student's paper in both locations so that all the students can talk jointly about it."

"But isn't Portuguese the native language of Brazil?" you ask.

"Yes," Professor Rivera replies. "All of the Brazilian students will be studying English as a second language, although they will also have studied several years of it before attending their university. Of course, English is a second language for many students here at our own university as well."

"What an interesting project," you observe.

"Yes," Professor Rivera responds. "The faculty members involved think it will have several benefits for students. It's increasingly important for college graduates to be able to work in an international economic and intellectual environment. This course will help prepare them for such work. In addition, many businesses are now using exactly the kind of technology we have placed in the distance-learning classroom to hold meetings that involve employees or clients located at various points around the globe. Students in the experimental classes will gain experience with such technology that could give them a tremendous boost in the job market."

"Sounds great," you say. "But what does it have to do with me? I've already completed that course."

"What we'd like you to do is to write a pamphlet we can send this summer to incoming students to entice some of them to sign up for the experimental distance-learning sections of First-Year English."

"Sounds easy," you say.

"Well, there are some complications," Professor Rivera explains. "This is an experiment of sorts. Many tests will be run to determine the effects of the distance-learning environment. The experiment is important because some faculty members are skeptical about the program, worried that it might focus on technology in ways that will detract from the quality of the writing instruction.

"Because this is an experiment, the faculty members who designed the program want the students in the distance-learning sections to represent a cross-section of students in First-Year English. It can't be populated with just students who have a high interest in technology or international studies. Therefore, they have asked the Admissions Office to generate a list of 240 randomly selected incoming students to whom the pamphlet will be sent. The aim of the pamphlet is to persuade at least half of the recipients to enroll in six special sections."

"In that case, writing the pamphlet will be a challenge," you agree.

"Will you accept the challenge?" Professor Rivera asks.

"Sure. Why not?"

YOUR ASSIGNMENT

Following the guidelines in Chapter 3, define the objectives for your pamphlet. Then, by following the guidelines in this chapter, list the things you would say in the pamphlet to the incoming students. Identify the things you would need to investigate further before writing.

Planning Your Persuasive Strategies

GUIDELINES

1	Emphasize benefits for your readers
2	Address your readers' concerns and counterarguments
3	Show that your reasoning is sound
4	Organize to create a favorable response
5	Create an effective relationship with your readers
6	Adapt your persuasive strategies to your readers' cultural background

CHAPTER **5** DEFINING OBJECTIVES
PLANNING
DRAFTING
EVALUATING
REVISING

As explained in Chapter 3, persuasion is a crucial component in almost all on-the-job writing. In some communications, such as requests to management and proposals to clients, persuasion is of paramount importance. In other communications, such as instructions and technical reports, the persuasive aim is less obvious but still present. At the very least, writers want to create a favorable impression of themselves, their departments, and their companies.

Whether in the foreground or the background, your persuasive aims are important enough for you to develop specific plans for achieving them. This chapter begins with a practical discussion of how persuasion works and then presents six guidelines for influencing your readers' thoughts, feelings, and actions.

HOW PERSUASION WORKS

According to researchers, the best way to influence how people think, feel, or act is to concentrate on shaping their *attitudes* (Petty and Cacioppo, "Elaboration"). At work, you will be concerned with your readers' attitudes toward a wide variety of subjects, such as products, policies, actions, and other people. As Chapter 3 explained, you may use your persuasive powers to influence your readers' attitudes in any of the following ways:

Ways to change readers' attitudes.

- **Reverse** an attitude you want your readers to abandon.
- **Reinforce** an attitude you want them to hold even more firmly.
- **Shape** their attitude on a subject about which they currently have no opinion.

Attitude is determined by the sum of thoughts about a topic.

What determines a person's attitude toward something? Researchers have found that it isn't a single thought or argument, but the *sum* of the various thoughts the person associates with the person or thing under consideration (Petty and Cacioppo, *Attitudes*). This is a critical point to remember as you plan your persuasive strategies. Consider the following example.

Edward's overall attitude is determined by his many thoughts related to the puchase.

The sum of his positive and negative thoughts will determine whether his overall attitude is positive or negative.

Edward is thinking about purchasing a particular photocopy machine for his department. As he deliberates, a variety of thoughts cross his mind: the amount of money in his department's budget, the machine's special features (such as automatic sorting), its appearance and repair record, his experience with another product made by the same company, and his impression of the marketing representative who sells the machine. Each of these thoughts will make Edward's attitude more positive or more negative. He may think his budget has enough money (positive) or too little (negative); he may like the salesperson (positive) or detest the salesperson (negative); and so forth.

Some of these thoughts will probably influence Edward's attitude more than others. For instance, Edward may like the machine's special features and color, but those two factors may be outweighed by reports that the machine's repair record is very poor. If the sum of Edward's thoughts associated with the machine is positive, he will have a favorable attitude toward it and may buy it. If the sum is negative, he will have an unfavorable attitude and probably will not buy it.

Whether in the background or the foreground, your persuasive aims are important enough to deserve special attention when you are planning your communication.

Emphasize Benefits for Your Readers

The most obvious way to prompt your readers to experience favorable thoughts is to tell them how they will benefit from taking the position, performing the action, or purchasing the product you are recommending. That's what companies do in advertisements that emphasize the whitener in their toothpaste that will brighten your teeth, or describe the computer-controlled braking system in their cars that will protect you from skidding.

Focus on professional benefits.

The strategy behind such ads is to stress *personal* benefits that readers will enjoy in their private lives. In many working situations, you are more likely to achieve your persuasive aims if you focus instead on benefits related to your readers' *professional* responsibilities. You can do this in two ways: by stressing organizational goals and by stressing your readers' growth needs.

Stress Organizational Goals

At work you will often write to co-workers in your company and to employees in other organizations. These people have been hired to advance their employer's interests. Consequently, you can often persuade them to look favorably at an action or decision if you can convince them it will help them achieve their employer's objectives.

All organizations have goals.

Most business organizations have the same general goals: to operate efficiently, increase income, reduce costs, keep employee morale high, and so on. However, each company also has its own unique goals. A company might be seeking to control 50 percent of its market, to have the best safety record in its industry, or to expand into ten states in the next five years. Moreover, each department within a company has specific objectives. Thus, the research department aims to develop new and improved products, the marketing department seeks to identify new markets, and the accounting department strives to manage financial resources prudently.

Help your readers achieve these goals.

When planning a communication, think about the organizational goals—both general and specific—your readers are pursuing. Then tell them how your proposed action or decision will help them achieve those goals.

Figure 5.1 shows a marketing brochure that uses organizational objectives to persuade its intended readers (purchasing managers for supermarkets and supermarket chains) to carry a certain product. Notice the boldfaced statements that proclaim how the product will build sales volume, stimulate impulse buying, and deliver profits.

Some organizational goals reflect broad values.

Most companies have goals that involve social, ethical, and aesthetic values not directly related to profit and productivity. Some companies spell out these values in corporate credos; Figure 5.2 (page 102) is an example. Even in companies that do not have an official credo, broad human and social values may provide an effective foundation for persuasion, especially when you are advocating a course of action that seems contrary to narrow business interests. For example, by pointing to the benefits to be enjoyed by a nearby community, you might be able to persuade your employer to strengthen its water pollution controls beyond what is required by law.

■ FIGURE 5.1

Brochure That Stresses Organizational Objectives

In order to persuade supermarkets to sell a nonalcoholic beverage, this brochure promises to help the markets achieve the following organizational objectives:

■ Build sales volume.

■ Stimulate impulse buying.

■ Deliver increased profits.

It even provides a place for stores to calculate their potential profits.

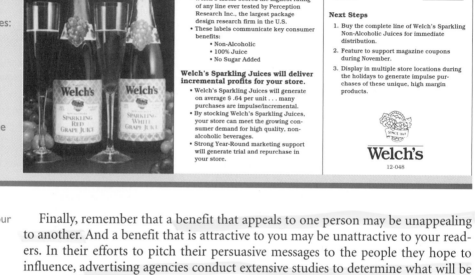

Pitch your appeals to your particular readers.

Finally, remember that a benefit that appeals to one person may be unappealing to another. And a benefit that is attractive to you may be unattractive to your readers. In their efforts to pitch their persuasive messages to the people they hope to influence, advertising agencies conduct extensive studies to determine what will be most appealing to their target markets. Follow their lead. Learn as much as you can about the organizational benefits that your target readers value most highly.

Stress Growth Needs

Studies of employee motivation by Abraham Maslow and by Frederick Herzberg suggest another type of benefit you can use in your persuasive strategies. Both researchers confirmed that, as everyone knew, employees are motivated by such considerations as pay and safe working conditions. However, the studies also found that after most people feel they have an adequate income and safe working conditions, they become less easily motivated by these factors. Consequently, such factors are called *deficiency needs:* they motivate principally when they are absent.

People seek more than pay from their jobs.

Once their deficiency needs are met—and even before—most people are motivated by so-called *growth needs,* including the desire for recognition, good relationships at work, a sense of achievement, personal development, and the enjoyment of work itself.

Many other studies have confirmed these findings. For instance, a study of supervisors showed that recognition, achievement, and personal relationships are much more powerful motivators than money (Munter). Another found that computer professionals are less motivated by salary or status symbols than by the

Responsibilities to users of the company's products

Responsibilities to employees

Responsibilities to communities

Responsibilities to stockholders

Our Credo

We believe our first responsibility is to the doctors, nurses and patients, to mothers and all others who use our products and services. In meeting their needs everything we do must be of high quality. We must constantly strive to reduce our costs in order to maintain reasonable prices. Customers' orders must be serviced promptly and accurately. Our suppliers and distributors must have an opportunity to make a fair profit.

We are responsible to our employees, the men and women who work with us throughout the world. Everyone must be considered as an individual. We must respect their dignity and recognize their merit. They must have a sense of security in their jobs. Compensation must be fair and adequate, and working conditions clean, orderly and safe. Employees must feel free to make suggestions and complaints. There must be equal opportunity for employment, development and advancement for those qualified. We must provide competent management, and their actions must be just and ethical.

We are responsible to the communities in which we live and work and to the world community as well. We must be good citizens—support good works and charities and bear our fair share of taxes. We must encourage civic improvements and better health and education. We must maintain in good order the property we are privileged to use, protecting the environment and natural resources.

Our final responsibility is to our stockholders. Business must make a sound profit. Research must be carried on, innovative programs developed and mistakes paid for. New equipment must be purchased, new facilities provided and new products launched. Reserves must be created to provide for adverse times. When we operate according to these principles, the stockholders should realize a fair return.

Johnson & Johnson

opportunity to gain new skills and knowledge in their field (Warren, Roth, and Devenna).

These studies demonstrate that one powerful persuasive strategy is to show how the decisions or actions you are advocating will help your readers satisfy their growth needs. When you request information or cooperation from a co-worker, mention how much you value his or her assistance. When you evaluate a subordinate's performance, discuss accomplishments as well as shortcomings. When you ask someone to take on additional duties, emphasize the challenge and opportunities for achievement that lie ahead.

Figure 5.3 shows a recruiting brochure distributed by Procter & Gamble to attract new employees. Notice the many ways it appeals to college graduates by emphasizing the opportunities they would have with the company to assume responsibility, take on challenges, and grow professionally.

Appeal to your readers' desire for growth.

■ **FIGURE 5.3**

First Page from a Recruiting Brochure That Stresses Growth Needs

This page from a recruiting brochure appeals to the growth needs of potential employees.

Opportunities for professional development:
- Mentoring by managers.
- Ongoing education.

Opportunities for achievement:
- Promise of substantial responsibility.
- Promise of recognition by others.
- Policy of promoting from within.

Pleasure of the work:
- Chance to use your talents.
- Option of learning new technologies.

The quotation from the new employee, Liz, highlights personal achievement and satisfaction.

P&G
CAREER OPPORTUNITIES

PRODUCT SUPPLY–ENGINEERING

OPPORTUNITIES FOR CAREER DEVELOPMENT

Your success at Proctor & Gamble depends on your abilities and aspirations. Our global scope, wide range of products, and diverse fields of endeavor offer you a world of choices in job assignments and career paths. P&G's commitment to career development is reflected in three long-standing policies:

PROMOTION FROM WITHIN
This policy is a cornerstone of our business. All managers start in entry-level positions and rise on the basis of their performance at P&G. You can expect to take on increased responsibilities as you demonstrate your abilities to do so. This policy, coupled with P&G's record of expanding the business, continually creates opportunities for advancement and broadening.

EARLY AND MEANINGFUL RESPONSIBILITY
From the very beginning, you will have a significant share of your department's responsibilities. You will be able to demonstrate and expand your talents as you learn by doing. You will see the difference you're making and know that others recognize your efforts.

TRAINING AND DEVELOPMENT
Due to our promotion from within policy, it is crucial that we develop the full potential of every person. Managers take this responsibility very seriously, and the result is a full range of support you need to enhance your professional development.

"My first assignment was helping roll out a new product initiative. I assessed project feasibility by analyzing the cost to develop and install the equipment that the new process required. Even though it was my first project, I was solely responsible for my function's deliverables. Being able to contribute to a multi-million dollar product initiative after only a few months with P&G was a rewarding experience that built my confidence about what I can accomplish."

Liz Fikes

Continuing education programs, on-going coaching from your manager and other technical experts, as well as performance feedback will help build your skills. Your first assignments give you the chance to immediately contribute to the business, while developing your professional skills. You have clear project responsibilities of your own, and are involved in other projects that stretch your engineering abilities. You take part in an extensive new engineering training program covering topics ranging from project management techniques to advanced engineering technologies, to effective interpersonal skills. You will learn to incorporate Total Quality Management principles into your daily work. Also, your colleagues and technology leader will provide

valuable mentoring to accelerate your development.

After completing your initial assignments, you can further develop your technical mastery in the field you've chosen or learn a different technology. You might move to one of P&G's many manufacturing sites to perform on-site engineering support work. Whatever your path, you will encounter new technical challenges.

GUIDELINE ② **Address Your Readers' Concerns and Counterarguments**

When people read, they not only pay attention to the writer's statements but also generate their own thoughts. For example, as Edward reads a brochure about a copy machine he may purchase, he responds to a description of some special feature by thinking, "Hey, that sounds useful" (positive) or "I don't see what good that will do me" (negative). Some of a reader's thoughts even arise independently of any specific statement the writer makes. For instance, while reading the brochure, Edward may remember a comment about the machine made by a manager whose department already owns one.

Whether readers' self-generated thoughts are favorable or unfavorable, research shows that they can have a greater influence on the readers' attitude toward the writer's subject than any point made in the communication itself (Petty and Cacioppo, "Elaboration"). Consequently, when you are trying to persuade, avoid saying anything that might prompt negative thoughts. And try to counteract any negative thoughts that seem likely to arise in your readers' minds despite your best efforts.

One way to avoid arousing negative thoughts is to answer all the important questions your readers are likely to ask while reading your communication. Most of these questions will simply reflect the readers' efforts to understand your position or proposal thoroughly. "What are the costs of doing as you suggest?" "What do other people who have looked into this matter think?" "Do we have employees with the education, experience, or talent to do what you recommend?" If you answer such questions satisfactorily, they create no problem whatever. But if you ignore them, they may prompt negative thoughts. Readers may think you have overlooked some important consideration or have decided to ignore evidence that might weaken your position. The remedy, quite simply, is to anticipate these questions and answer them satisfactorily.

In addition to asking questions, readers may generate arguments against your position. For example, if you say there is a serious risk of injury to workers in a building used by your company, your readers may think to themselves that the building has been used for three years without an accident. If you say a new procedure will increase productivity by at least 10 percent, your readers may think to themselves that some of the data on which you are basing your estimate are inaccurate. Readers are especially likely to generate counterarguments when you attempt to *reverse* their attitudes. Research shows that people resist efforts to persuade them that their attitudes are incorrect (Petty and Cacioppo, "Elaboration").

To deal effectively with counterarguments, you must offer some reason for relying on your position rather than on the opposing position. For example, imagine that you are proposing the purchase of a certain piece of equipment and that you predict your readers will object because it is more expensive than a competitor's product they believe to be its equal. You might explain that the competitor's product, though less expensive to purchase, is more expensive to operate and maintain. Or you might point out that the equipment you are recommending has certain capabilities that make it well worth the additional cost.

To anticipate the questions and counterarguments you must address, follow Chapter 3's advice for identifying readers' questions, but focus specifically on questions that *skeptical* readers might ask. Another way of anticipating readers' counterarguments is to learn their reasons for holding their present attitudes. Why do they do things the way they do? What arguments do they feel most strongly support their present position? At times, you may have to show the weaknesses of your readers' reasons in order to demonstrate the superiority of your own. But do so diplomatically. The last thing you want to do is arouse the defensiveness of the persons you are trying to persuade.

Marginal notes:

Readers' self-generated thoughts are very influential.

Avoid inspiring negative thoughts.

Address objections your readers might raise.

Imagine that you are addressing highly skeptical readers.

■ **FIGURE 5.4**

Letter That Addresses Counterarguments

WGWG
12741 Vienna Boulevard
Philadelphia, PA 19116

August 17, 19—

Mr. Roger L. Nordstrom
Llat Marketing, Inc.
1200 Langstroth Avenue
Philadelphia, Pennsylvania 19131

Dear Mr. Nordstrom:

What a lucky coincidence that we should have met at Shelby's last week. As I told you then, I believe you can improve the advertising service you provide many of your clients by switching to our station some of the radio advertising that you presently place for your clients with WSER and WFAC. Since we met, I have put together some figures.

The primary advantage of advertising with us is that you will extend the size of your audience considerably. As an example, consider the reach of the campaign you are now running for Fuller's Furniture Emporium. You currently buy 45 spots over four weeks on the other two stations. According to Arbitron market analysis, you thereby reach 63% of your target market—women in the 25–54 demographic group—an average of 16 times per week. However, there is a lot of overlap in the audiences of those two stations: many listeners switch back and forth between them.

Writer states a counterargument that might occur to the reader.

Writer specifies a benefit to the reader that will outweigh the objection.

In contrast, we serve a very distinct audience. By using only 30 spots on those two stations and giving 15 to us, you would increase your reach to 73% of the 25–54 group. It's true, of course, that this change would reduce from 16 to 13 the number of times the average listener hears your message. However, this is an increase of 8% in the portion of your target audience that you would reach.

But there's more. At the same time that you increased your audience, you would also decrease your costs. For example, if you switched the Fuller's Furniture Emporium spots in the way described, your costs would drop from $6,079 to $4,850. Our audience is smaller than the audiences on those stations, but our rates are only about half of theirs.

In your efforts to address your readers' concerns and counterarguments, be careful not to mention objections your readers are unlikely to raise on their own. There's always the chance that they will find the objection more persuasive than your rebuttal.

Figure 5.4 shows a letter in which the Marketing Director of a radio station attempts to persuade an advertising agency to switch some of its ads to her station. Notice how she anticipates and addresses possible counterarguments.

FIGURE 5.4
(continued)

Roger L. Nordstrom   – 2 –   August 17, 19—

As you consider these figures and others that might be given to you by other radio stations, be careful to evaluate them carefully. As we are all aware, anyone can manipulate statistics to their advantage. We recently discovered that one of our competitors was circulating data regarding the portion of the audiences of Philadelphia stations that are "unemployed." In that analysis, our station had a significantly higher portion of "unemployed" listeners than did either WSER or WFAC.

However, after some investigation, we discovered that in those statistics, "unemployed" meant "unemployed outside the home." That meant that people "unemployed" are not necessarily breadwinners who are unable to provide an income for their families. They could be housewives with considerable power over family decisions about spending. In fact, surveys indicate that housewives are often the <u>primary</u> decision-makers about such things as household furnishings—a point that is quite important with respect to your account with Fuller's Furniture Emporium.

I suggest that we get together soon so that we can sketch out the details of some radio advertising schedules that would include WGWG. I'll call you next week.

Cordially,

Ruth Anne Peterson
Ruth Anne Peterson
Marketing Director

Writer states a counterargument the reader is likely to hear from competitors.

Writer exposes faulty reasoning underlying the counterargument.

GUIDELINE **3**   **Show That Your Reasoning Is Sound**

A third strategy for writing persuasively is to show that your reasoning is sound. In most working situations, one of the most favorable thoughts your readers could possibly have is, "Yeah, that makes sense"—and one of the most unfavorable is, "Hey, there's a flaw in your reasoning."

Sound reasoning is especially important when you are trying to influence your readers' decisions and actions. In addition to identifying potential benefits that will appeal to your readers, you also must persuade them that the decision or action you advocate will actually bring about these benefits—that the proposed new equipment really will reduce costs enough to pay for itself in just eighteen months, or that the product modification you are recommending really will boost sales 10 percent in the first year.

Sound reasoning is also essential when you are describing conclusions you have reached after studying a group of facts, such as the results of a laboratory experiment or consumer survey. In such cases, you must persuade your readers that your conclusions are firmly based on the facts.

Notice that in each of the situations just mentioned (as well as in any other you might encounter on the job), you must not only *use* sound reasoning, but also *convince your readers* that your reasoning is sound. The ability to do so is one of the most valuable writing skills you can develop. The following discussion, based largely on the work of Stephen Toulmin, will help you master this skill (Toulmin, Rieke, and Janik).

How Reasoning Works

To accept your reasoning as sound, your readers must feel that they understand the following elements:

- **Your claim.** The position you want your readers to accept.
- **Your evidence.** The facts, observations, or other information you offer in support of your claim.
- **Your line of reasoning.** The connection linking your claim and your evidence; the reasons why your readers should agree that your evidence proves your claim.

The following diagram illustrates the relationship among these three elements:

Evidence ——————————————→ Claim
The following facts, observations, and other evidence support the claim.   Such and such should be done.

Line of Reasoning
The evidence should be accepted as adequate support for the claim for the following reasons.

Imagine that you work for a company that manufactures cloth. You have found out that one of your employer's competitors recently increased its profits by installing computers to run some of its textile mills. If you were to recommend that your employer buy similar computers, your argument could be diagrammed as follows:

```
Evidence ══════════════════════▶ Claim
Our competitor has increased          By using computers we will
profits by using computers.           increase our profits.
                          ▲
                          │
                          │
                    Line of Reasoning
                    Experience has shown that
                    actions that increase the profits
                    of one company in an industry
                    will usually increase the profits
                    of other companies in the
                    same industry.
```

To accept your claim, readers must be willing to place their faith in *both* your evidence and your line of reasoning. The next two sections offer advice about how to persuade them to do so.

Present Sufficient and Reliable Evidence

First you must convince your readers that your evidence is both sufficient and reliable.

How to provide sufficient evidence

To provide *sufficient* evidence, you must furnish all the details your readers are likely to want. For instance, in the example of the textile mills, your readers would probably regard your evidence as skimpy if you produced only a vague report that the other company had somehow used computers and saved some money. They would want to know how the company had used computers, how much money had been saved, whether the savings had justified the cost of the equipment, and so forth.

How to provide reliable evidence

To provide *reliable* evidence, you must produce the type of evidence your readers are likely to accept. The type of evidence varies greatly from field to field. For instance, in science and engineering, certain experimental procedures are widely accepted as reliable, whereas common wisdom and unsystematic observation usually are not. In contrast, in many business situations, personal observations and anecdotes provided by knowledgeable people often are accepted as reliable evidence.

Explicitly Justify Your Line of Reasoning Where Necessary

To argue persuasively, you must not only present sufficient and reliable evidence, but also convince your readers that you are using a valid line of reasoning to link your evidence to your claim. Writers often omit any justification of their line of reasoning in the belief that the justification will be obvious to their readers. In fact, that is sometimes the case. In the construction industry, for example, people generally agree that if an engineer uses the appropriate formulas to analyze the size and shape of a bridge, the formulas will accurately predict whether or not the bridge will be strong enough to support the loads it must carry. The engineer doesn't need to justify the formulas themselves.

Avoid false assumptions.

In many cases, however, readers search aggressively for a weak line of reasoning. In particular, they are wary of arguments based on false assumptions. For example, they may agree that if another textile mill like yours saved money by computerizing, then your mill would probably enjoy the same result; however, your readers may question the assumption that the other mill truly is like yours. Maybe it makes a different kind of product or employs a different manufacturing process. If you think your readers will suspect that you are making a false assumption, offer whatever evidence or explanation you can to dispel their doubt.

Avoid overgeneralizing.

Readers also look for places where writers have overgeneralized by drawing broad conclusions from too few specific instances. If you think your readers will raise such an objection to your argument, mention additional cases. Or, narrow your conclusion to better match the evidence you have gathered. For example, instead of asserting that your claim applies to all textile companies in all situations, argue that it applies to particular companies or particular situations.

GUIDELINE **4** **Organize to Create a Favorable Response**

Organization can affect persuasiveness.

The way you organize a communication may have almost as much effect on its power to persuade as what you say. That point was demonstrated by researchers Sternthal, Dholakia, and Leavitt, who presented two groups of people with different versions of a talk urging that a federal consumer protection agency be established. One version *began* by saying that the speaker was a highly credible source (a lawyer who graduated from Harvard and had extensive experience with consumer issues); the other version *ended* with that information.

Among people initially opposed to the speaker's recommendation, those who learned about his credentials at the beginning responded more favorably to his arguments than did those who learned about his credentials at the end. Why? This outcome can be explained in terms of two principles you learned in Chapter 1. First, people react to persuasive messages moment by moment. Second (and here's the key point), their reactions in one moment will affect their reactions in subsequent moments. In this experiment, those who learned of the speaker's credentials before hearing his arguments were relatively open to what he had to say. But those who learned of the speaker's credentials only at the end worked more vigorously at creating counterarguments as they heard each of his points. After those counterarguments had been recorded in memory, they could not be erased simply by adding information about the speaker's credibility.

Thus, it's not only the array of information that is critical in persuasion, but also the way readers process the information. The following sections suggest two strategies for organizing to elicit a favorable response: choose carefully between direct and indirect organizational patterns, and create a tight fit among the parts of your communication.

Choose Carefully between Direct and Indirect Organizational Patterns

The direct pattern goes directly to the main point.

As you learned in Chapter 4, the most common organizational pattern at work begins by telling the bottom line—the writer's main point. Communications organized this way are said to use a *direct* pattern of organization because they go directly to the main point and only afterward present the evidence and other information related to it. For example, in a memo recommending the purchase of

■ **FIGURE 5.5**

Comparison of Direct and Indirect Patterns for Organizing Leah's Memo

The direct pattern presents the recommendation first.

The indirect pattern delays the recommendation; it's for use where the reader may react unfavorably.

Direct Pattern	Indirect Pattern
I. Leah presents her recommended strategy.	I. Leah discusses the goals of the present system from the *readers' point of view.*
II. Leah explains why her way of warehousing is superior to the present way.	II. Leah discusses the ways in which the present system does and does not achieve the readers' goals.
III. Leah explains in detail how to implement her system.	III. Leah presents her recommended strategy for achieving those goals more effectively, focusing on the ways her recommendation can overcome the shortcomings of the present system.
	IV. Leah explains in detail how to implement her system.

a new computer program, you might begin with the recommendation and then explain why you think the new program is desirable.

The indirect pattern delays the main point.

The alternative is to postpone presenting your main point until you have presented your evidence or other related information. This is called the *indirect* pattern of organization. For example, in a memo recommending the purchase of a new computer program, you might first explain the problems created by the current program, withholding until later your recommendation that a new one be purchased. Figure 5.5 compares direct and indirect organizational patterns.

To choose between the direct and indirect organizational patterns, focus your attention on your readers' all-important initial response to your message. The direct pattern will start your readers off on the right foot when you have good news to convey: "You're hired," "I've figured out a solution to your problem," or something similar. By starting with the good news, you put your readers in a favorable frame of mind as they read the rest of your message.

Use the direct pattern when expecting a favorable response.

The direct pattern also works well when you are offering an analysis or recommending a course of action that you expect your readers to view favorably—or at least objectively—from the start. Leah is about to write such a memo, in which she will recommend a new system for managing the warehouses for her employer, a company that manufactures hundreds of parts used to drill oil and gas wells. Leah has chosen to use the direct pattern shown in the left-hand column of Figure 5.5. This is an appropriate choice because her readers (upper management) have expressed dissatisfaction with the present warehousing system. Consequently, she can expect a favorable reaction to her initial announcement that she has designed a better system.

Use the indirect pattern when your readers might react unfavorably.

The direct pattern is less effective when you are conveying information your readers might view as bad, alarming, or threatening. Imagine, for example, that Leah's readers are the people who set up the present system and that they believe it is working well. If Leah begins her memo by recommending a new system, she might put her readers immediately on the defensive because they might feel she is criticizing their competence. Then she would have little hope of receiving an open and objective reading of her supporting information. By using an indirect pattern, however, Leah can *prepare* her readers for her recommendation by first getting them to agree that it might be possible to improve on the present system. The right-hand column of Figure 5.5 shows an indirect pattern she might use.

You may wonder why you shouldn't simply use the indirect pattern all the time. It presents the same information as the direct organization (plus some more), and it avoids the risk of inciting a negative reaction at the outset. The trouble is that this pattern frustrates the readers' desire to learn the main point first.

In sum, the choice between direct and indirect patterns of organization can greatly affect the persuasiveness of your communications. To choose, you need to follow the basic strategy suggested throughout this book: think about your readers' moment-by-moment reactions to your message.

Create a Tight Fit among the Parts of Your Communication

When organizing a communication, you can also strengthen its persuasiveness by ensuring that the parts fit together tightly. This advice applies particularly to longer communications, where the overall argument often consists of two or more subordinate arguments. The way to do this is to review side by side the claims made in the various parts of a communication.

Every part must match up with all the other parts.

For example, imagine that you are writing a proposal. In an early section, you describe a problem your proposed project will solve. Here, your persuasive points are that a problem exists and that the readers should view it as serious. In a later section you describe the project you propose. Check to see whether this description tells how the project will address each aspect of the problem that you described. If it doesn't, either the discussion of the problem or the discussion of the project needs to be revised so the two match up. Similarly, your budget should include only expenses that are clearly related to the project they describe, and your schedule should show when you will carry out each activity necessary to complete the project successfully.

Of course, the need for a tight fit applies not only to proposals but also to any communication whose various parts work together to affect your readers' attitudes. Whenever you write, think about ways to make the parts work harmoniously together in mutual support of your overall position.

GUIDELINE **5**   **Create an Effective Relationship with Your Readers**

One of the most important factors influencing the success of a persuasive communication is how your readers feel about you. You will remember from Chapter 1 that you should think of the communications you prepare at work as interpersonal interactions. If your readers feel well-disposed toward you, they are likely to consider your points openly and without bias. If they feel irritated, angry, or otherwise unfriendly toward you, they may immediately raise counterarguments to every point you present, making it extremely unlikely that you will elicit a favorable reaction, even if all your points are clear, valid, and substantiated. Good points rarely win the day in the face of bad feelings.

The following sections describe two ways you can present yourself to obtain a fair—or even a favorable—hearing from your readers at work: present yourself as a credible person, and present yourself as nonthreatening.

Present Yourself as a Credible Person

The more credible you are, the more persuasive you are.

Your credibility is your readers' beliefs about whether or not you are a good source for information and ideas. If people believe you are credible, they will be relatively open to what you say. They may even accept your judgments and recommendations without inquiring very deeply into your reasons for making them. If people do not find you credible, they may refuse to give you a fair hearing no matter how soundly you state your case.

To see how much your readers' perception of you can affect the way they respond to your message, consider the results of the following experiment. Researchers H. C. Kelman and C. I. Hovland tape-recorded a speech advocating lenient treatment of juvenile delinquents. Before playing their tape for one group, they identified the speaker as an ex-delinquent out on bail. They told another group that the speaker was a judge. Only 27 percent of those who heard the "delinquent's" talk responded favorably to it, while 73 percent of those who heard the "judge's" talk responded favorably.

Several factors that influence credibility

Researchers have conducted many studies on the factors that affect an audience's impression of a person's credibility. In summarizing this research, Robert Bostrom has identified five key factors. Figure 5.6 explains these factors and describes strategies you can use to build your credibility. Figure 5.7 (page 114) shows a letter that puts many of these strategies into action. In it, an advertising company attempts to persuade a bank to let it make a sales presentation.

Present Yourself as Nonthreatening

Readers may see you as threatening even when you wish to help.

Psychologist Carl Rogers has identified another important strategy in fostering open, unbiased communication: reduce the sense of threat that people often feel when others are presenting ideas to them. According to Rogers, people are likely to feel threatened even when you make *helpful* suggestions. As a result, your readers may see you as an adversary even though you don't intend at all to be one.

(Text continued on page 116)

■ FIGURE 5.6

Strategies for Building Credibility

Factor	Explanation/Action
Expertise	Expertise is the relevant knowledge, education, and experience that readers perceive you to possess. Writing Strategies • Mention your credentials. • Demonstrate a command of the facts. • Avoid oversimplifying. • Mention or quote experts in the field so their expertise supports your position.
Trustworthiness	Trustworthiness depends largely on your readers' perception of your motives. If you seem to be acting out of self-interest, your credibility is low; if you seem to be acting objectively or for goals shared by the audience, your credibility is high. Writing Strategies • Stress values and objectives that are important to your readers. • Avoid drawing attention to personal advantages to you. • Demonstrate a knowledge of the concerns and perspectives of others.
Group membership	You will have more credibility if you are a member of the readers' own group or of a group admired by your readers. Writing Strategies • If you are associated with a group admired by your readers, allude to that relationship. • If you are addressing members of your own organization, affirm that relationship by showing that you share the group's objectives, methods, and values. • Use terms that are commonly employed in your organization.
Dynamic appeal	An aggressive, forceful, frank person has much higher credibility than a passive, forceless, guarded person. Writing Strategies • State your message simply and directly. • Show enthusiasm for your ideas and subject.
Power	Readers assign high credibility to writers who control what the readers want. Thus, simply by virtue of his or her position, a boss acquires some credibility with subordinates. Writing Strategies • If you are in a position of authority, identify your position if your readers don't know it. • If you are not in a position of authority, associate yourself with a powerful person by quoting the person or by saying that you consulted with him or her or were assigned the job by that individual.

Tal, Inc

3645 WEST LAKE ROAD • ERIE, PENNSYLVANIA 16505 • 814/838-4505

30 May, 19—

Mr. Jeff Frances
Vice President, Marketing
First Federal Savings and Loan
724 Boardman-Poland Road
Youngstown, OH 44512

Dear Mr. Frances:

Our firm is very interested in presenting its financial advertising and marketing credentials to you for consideration.

While you may never have heard about Tal, Inc., chances are you're familiar with our work. Here in Youngstown, Tal, Inc. has been responsible for recent marketing communications programs of the Western Reserve Care System that includes Northside and Southside Medical Centers, Tod Children's Hospital, and Beeghly Medical Park.

But more important to you as Vice President of Marketing at First Federal Savings and Loan is Tal, Inc.'s experience as a full-service financial advertising agency. That experience includes work for such clients as Pennbank; The First National Bank of Pennsylvania; Permanent Savings Bank, Buffalo, NY; North Star Bank, Buffalo, NY; and Citizens Fidelity Bank, Louisville, KY.

Our growth mission is to expand our financial client base to the Youngstown market. Toward that end, our firm is interested in presenting our award-winning financial portfolio and case histories for your review. The portfolio features a broad range of financial capabilities. In addition to TV, radio, newspaper, and outdoor advertising, you'll find samples of P.O.S., Collateral Brochures and Pamphlets, Annual Reports, Direct Mail, and Sales Support Materials. We're confident you'll like what you see and hear. But we're also confident you'll recognize the possibilities a Tal, Inc./First Federal Savings and Loan relationship would afford.

ADVERTISING

BUFFALO • ERIE • LANCASTER

Writer emphasizes experience in reader's city.

Writer demonstrates experience with reader's type of company.

Writer cites evidence of his company's standing.

Writer expresses enthusiasm and confidence.

FIGURE 5.7
(continued)

Writer closes on
goal-oriented
energetic note.

Mr. Jeff Frances   30 May 19—   – 2 –

Our goal is to apply our capability to the marketing challenges in the Youngstown
market during the coming year. Please let me know how I might proceed in
presenting our qualifications to you. I can be contacted during regular business
hours at 814/838-4505.

Thank you for your consideration of Tal, Inc.

Sincerely,

Peter M. Sitter
Financial Services
Account Supervisor

Nonthreatening Strategies

Praise Your Readers
- When writing to an individual, mention one of his or her recent accomplishments.
- When writing to another organization, mention something it prides itself on.
- When praising, be sure to mention specifics. General praise sounds insincere.

Present Yourself as Your Readers' Partner
- Identify some personal or organizational goal of your readers that you will help them attain.
- If you are already your readers' partner, mention that fact and emphasize the goals you share.

Show That You Understand Your Readers
- Even if you disagree with your readers, state their case fairly.
- Focus on areas of agreement.

Maintain a Positive and Helpful Stance
- Present your suggestions as ways of helping your readers do an even better job.
- Avoid criticizing or blaming.

Here are four methods, based on the work of Rogers, that you can use to present yourself as nonthreatening to your readers. To see how to apply this advice, consider the following situation.

Although she is presenting complaints from student employees, Marjorie wisely frames her memo in a nonthreatening way.

Marjorie Lakwurtz is a regional manager for a company that employs nearly 1,000 students in many cities during the summer months to paint houses and other large structures. Each student is required at the beginning of the summer to make a $100 deposit, which is returned at the end of the summer. Students complain that the equipment they work with isn't worth anywhere near $100 so the deposit is unjustified. Furthermore, they believe that the company is simply requiring the deposit so it can invest the money during the summer. The company keeps all the interest on the deposits, not giving any to the students when it returns their deposits at the end of the summer.

Marjorie agrees that the students have a good case, so she wants to suggest a change. She could do that in a negative way by telling the company that it should be ashamed of its greedy plot to profit by investing other people's money. Or she could take a positive approach, presenting her suggested change as a way the company can better achieve its own goals. In the memo shown in Figure 5.8, she takes the latter course. Notice how skillfully she presents herself as her readers' partner.

■ FIGURE 5.8

Memo in Which the Writer Establishes a Partnership with the Reader

---

PREMIUM PAINTING COMPANY

February 12, 19—

TO: Martin Sneed

FROM: Marjorie Lakwurtz

RE: Improving Worker Morale

Marjorie opens by praising the reader.

> Now that I have completed my first year with the company, I have been thinking over my experiences here. I have enjoyed the challenges that this unique company offers, and I've been very favorably impressed with our ability to find nearly 1000 temporary workers who are willing to work so energetically and diligently for us.

In fact, it's occurred to me that the good attitude of the students who work for us is one of the indispensable ingredients in our success. If they slack off or become careless, our profits could drop precipitously. If they become careless, splattering and spilling paint for instance, we would lose much of our profits in cleaning up the mess.

Marjorie presents herself as the reader's partner in the mutual goal of raising worker morale.

> Because student morale is so crucial to us, I would like to suggest a way of raising it even further—and of ensuring that it won't droop. From many different students in several cities, I have heard complaints about the $100 security deposit we require them to pay before they begin work. They feel that the equipment they work with is worth much less than that, so that the amount of this security deposit is very steep. Furthermore, there is a widespread belief that the company is actually cheating them by taking their money, investing it for the summer, and keeping the profits for itself.

Marjorie uses "we" to reinforce the sense of partnership.

> Because the complaints are so widespread and because they can directly affect the students' sense of obligation to the company, I think we should try to do something about the security deposit. First we could reduce the deposit. If you think that would be unwise, we could give the students the interest earned on their money when we return the deposits to them at the end of the summer.

A Caution against Arousing Negative Thoughts

Sympathetic statements can arouse negative thoughts.

One caution is in order here. When you are trying to show how much you sympathize with your readers or understand their position, be careful not to arouse negative thoughts accidentally. For example, imagine that you are writing a memo notifying employees in your company that their office will be moving to a new city. You will

FIGURE 5.8
(continued)

Martin Sneed
February 12, 19—
Page 2

Marjorie shows that she understands the reader's perspective.

I realize that it would be difficult to calculate the precise amount of interest earned by each student. They begin work at different times in May and June, and they end at different times in August and September. However, we could establish a flat amount to be paid each student, perhaps basing it on the average interest earned by the deposits over a three-month period.

Marjorie counters a possible objection by making a positive suggestion.

Marjorie states and addresses another counterargument.

I'm sure that it has been somewhat beneficial for the company to have the extra income produced by the deposits. But the amount earned is still rather modest. The additional productivity we might enjoy from our students by removing this irritant to them is likely to increase our profits by much more than the interest paid.

Marjorie closes on a positive note, reemphasizing her desire to work as her reader's partner.

If you would like to talk to me about this idea or about the feelings expressed by the students, I would be happy to meet with you.

want the employees to feel favorably inclined toward the move. For that reason, you would want to avoid saying things like, "I know you are anxious about the move," which would bring their anxiety to the forefront, or "I know you have heard rumors about the move for weeks," which might make them resentful for those weeks they have had to rely on rumors rather than hard facts from management.

This caution doesn't mean you should ignore your readers' counterproductive feelings. You should, for example, do what you can to reduce their anxiety by telling

Ethics of Persuasion

Nowhere are the ethical dimensions of on-the-job writing more evident than when you are trying to persuade other people to take a certain action or adopt a certain attitude. Here are four guidelines for ethical persuasion that you might want to keep in mind: don't mislead, don't manipulate, open yourself to your readers' viewpoint, and argue from human values.

Don't Mislead

When you are writing persuasively, respect your readers' right to evaluate your arguments in an informed and independent way. If you mislead your readers by misstating facts, using intentionally ambiguous expressions, or arguing from false premises, you deprive your readers of their rights.

Don't Manipulate

The philosopher Immanuel Kant originated the enduring ethical principle that we should never use other people merely to get what we want. Whenever we try to influence our readers, the action we advocate should advance their goals as well as our own.

Under Kant's principle, for instance, it would be unethical to persuade readers to do something that would benefit us but harm them. High-pressure sales techniques are unethical because their purpose is to persuade consumers to purchase something they may not need or even want. Persuasion is ethical only if it will lead our readers to get something they truly desire.

Open Yourself to Your Readers' Viewpoint

To keep your readers' goals and interests in mind, you must be open to their viewpoint. Instead of regarding their counterarguments as objections you must overcome, try to understand what lies behind their concerns. Consider ways of modifying your original ideas to take your readers' perspective into account.

In this way, rather than treat your readers as adversaries, accept them as your partners in a search for a course of action acceptable to you all (Lauer). Management experts call this the search for a "win-win" situation—a situation in which all parties benefit (Covey).

Argue from Human Values

Although many organizations realize that they need to consider human values when making a decision, others do not. In fact, some organizations would consider it inappropriate to argue that money should be invested in improvement because the change would make work easier for employees who perform routine tasks or are easily replaceable. In other organizations, human values are sometimes overlooked when people begin to focus too sharply on business objectives.

Whenever human values are relevant, don't hesitate to mention them when you are writing to persuade. Even if your remarks are overlooked, you will have succeeded in introducing a consideration of such values into your working environment. Your action may even encourage others to follow your lead.

them favorable and reassuring things about the move. But avoid triggering or reinforcing negative thoughts.

GUIDELINE **6**   **Adapt Your Persuasive Strategies to Your Readers' Cultural Background**

What's persuasive in one culture may not be in another.

The persuasive strategies you've just read about may need to be adjusted in light of the cultural background of your readers. For example, what readers consider to be benefits vary from nation to nation. In Denmark, Germany, Holland, and the United States, companies sell fluoride toothpaste by emphasizing its decay prevention benefits. However, to sell the same products in England, France, and Italy, the companies must emphasize the way the toothpaste enhances the consumer's appearance (Roth). To appeal to car buyers, Volvo focuses on safety and durability in the United States, status and leisure in France, and performance in Germany (Ricks).

Also, people from different cultures have different views about what constitutes a good reason for taking a particular action. Whereas many Western cultures base their arguments on facts, international communication expert R. W. Brislin reports that in Arab cultures people support their positions through emotions so that "facts seem to take second place to feelings" (153).

Similarly, what readers consider to be an appropriate role for a writer differs from culture to culture. For example, in the United States, writers often "tell it like it is." But in many Asian cultures, a writer would not do anything to cause the reader or anyone else to lose face (Lustig and Koester).

These cultural differences mean that you must study the cultural norms of your readers whenever you hope to persuade someone from another country.

CONCLUSION

This chapter has focused on writing persuasively. As you can see, nearly every aspect of your communication affects your ability to influence your readers' attitudes and actions. Although the guidelines in this chapter will help you write persuasively, the most important persuasive strategy of all is to keep in mind your readers' needs, concerns, values, and preferences whenever you write.

EXERCISES

1. a. Using your common sense about how people react, rewrite the e-mail message by Donald Pryzblo (Figure 1.2, page 15) so that it will be more likely to persuade the personnel manager to follow his recommendation. Assume that Pryzblo knows that the manager's clerks are miscopying because he has examined the time sheets, time tickets, and computer files associated with 37 incorrect payroll checks; in 35 cases, the clerks made the errors. Take into account how you expect the personnel manager to react to finding an e-mail message from Pryzblo in his or her in-box. Make sure that the first sentence of your revision addresses a person in that frame of mind and that your sentences lead effectively from there. Leave the last sentence unchanged.

   b. In the margin of your revision or on a separate sheet

of paper, state what you expect the personnel manager's reaction will be after reading each sentence.

2. Find two persuasive messages, including one that contains at least 25 words of prose. The messages may be advertisements, marketing letters, memos from school or work, or business communications. Examine the persuasive strategies used in each. What are they? Do they work well? What other strategies might have been used? Present your responses in a memo addressed to your instructor and attach copies of the messages. For a brief assignment, write 200 to 500 words. For a long assignment, write 800 to 1,200 words.

3. Analyze the letter shown in Figure 5.9 and identify its strengths and weaknesses. Relate your points to the guide-

■ FIGURE 5.9

Letter for Exercise

616 S. College #84
Oxford, Ohio 45056

Georgiana Stroh
Executive Vice President
Thompson Textiles Incorporated
1010 Note Ave.
Cincinnati, Ohio 45014

Dear Mrs. Stroh:

As my junior year draws to a close, I am more and more eager to return to our company, where I can apply my new knowledge and skills. Since our recent talk about the increasingly stiff competition in the textile industry, I have thought quite a bit about what I can do to help Thompson continue to prosper. I have been going over some notes I have made on the subject, and I am struck by how many of the ideas stemmed directly from the courses I have taken here at Miami University.

Almost all of the notes featured suggestions or thoughts I simply didn't have the knowledge to consider before I went to college! Before I enrolled, I, like many people, presumed that operating a business required only a certain measure of commonsense ability—that almost anyone could learn to guide a business down the right path with a little experience. However, I have come to realize that this belief is far from the truth. It is true that many decisions are common sense, but decisions often only appear to be simple because the entire scope of the problem or the full ramifications of a particular alternative are not well understood. A path is always chosen, but often is it the BEST path for the company as a whole?

In retrospect, I appreciate the year I spent supervising the Eaton Avenue Plant because the experience has been an impetus to actually learn from my classes instead of just receiving grades. But I look back in embarassment upon some of the decisions I made and the methods I used then. I now see that my previous work in our factories and my military experience did not prepare me as well for that position as I thought they did. My mistakes were not so often a poor selection among known alternatives, but were more often sins of omission. For example, you may remember that we were constantly running low on packing cartons and that we sometimes ran completely out, causing the entire line to shut down. Now I know that instead of haphazardly placing orders for a different amount every time, we should have used a forecasting model to determine and establish a reorder point and a reorder quanitity. But I was simply unaware of many of the sophisticated techniques available to me as a manager.

I respectfully submit that many of our supervisory personnel are in a similar situation. This is not to downplay the many contributions they have made to the company. Thompson can directly attribute its prominent position in the industry to the devotion and hard work of these people. But very few of them have more than a high school education or have read even a single text on management skills. We have always counted on our supervisors to pick up their

lines in this chapter. The following paragraphs describe the situation in which the writer, Scott Houck, is writing.

Before going to college, Scott worked for a few years at Thompson Textiles. In his letter, he addresses Thompson's Executive Vice President, Georgiana Stroh. He is writing because in college he learned many things that made him think Thompson would benefit if its managers were better educated in modern management techniques. Thompson Textiles could enjoy these benefits, Scott believes, if it would offer management courses to its employees and if it would fill job openings at the managerial level with college graduates. However, if Thompson were

FIGURE 5.9
(continued)

management skills on the job without any additional training. Although I recognize that I owe my own opportunities to this approach, this comes too close to the commonsense theory I mentioned earlier.

The success of Thompson depends on the abilities of our managers relative to the abilities of our competition. In the past, EVERY company used this commonsense approach, and Thompson prospered because of the natural talent of people like you. But in the last decade, many new managerial techniques have been developed that are too complex for the average employee to just "figure out" on his or her own. For example, people had been doing business for several thousand years before developing the Linear Programming Model for transportation and resource allocation problem-solving. It is not reasonable to expect a high school graduate to recognize that his or her particular distribution problem could be solved by a mathematical model and then to develop the LP from scratch. But as our world grows more complex, competition will stiffen as others take advantage of these innovations. I fear that what has worked in the past will not necessarily work in the future: We may find out what our managers DON'T know CAN hurt us. Our managers must be made aware of advances in computer technology, management theory, and operations innovations, and they must be able to use them to transform our business as changing market conditions demand.

I would like to suggest that you consider the value of investing in an in-house training program dealing with relevant topics to augment the practical experience our employees are gaining. In addition, when management or other fast-track administrative positions must be filled, it may be worth the investment to hire college graduates whose coursework has prepared them to use state-of-the-art techniques to help us remain competitive. Of course, these programs will initially show up on the bottom line as increased expenses, but it is reasonable to expect that, int the not-so-long run, profits will be boosted by newfound efficiencies. Most important, we must recognize the danger of adopting a wait-and-see attitude. Our competitors are now making this same decision; hesitation on our part may leave us playing catch-up.

In conclusion, I believe I will be a valuable asset to the company, in large part because of the education I am now receiving. I hope you agree that a higher education level in our employees is a cause worthy of our most sincere efforts. I will contact your office next week to find out if you are interested in meeting to discuss questions you may have or to review possible implementation strategies.

Sincerely,

Scott Houck

to follow Scott's recommendations, it would have to change its practices considerably. Thompson has never offered courses for its employees and has long sought to keep payroll expenses low by employing people without a college education, even in management positions. (In a rare exception to this practice, the company has guaranteed Scott a position after he graduates.)

To attempt to change the company's policies, Scott decided to write a letter to one of the most influential people on its staff, Mrs. Stroh. Unfortunately for Scott, throughout the three decades that Stroh has served as an executive officer at Thompson, she has consistently opposed company-sponsored education and the hiring of college graduates. Consequently, she has an especially strong motive for rejecting Scott's advice: she is likely to feel that, if she agreed that Thompson's educational and hiring policies should be changed, she would be admitting that she had been wrong all along.

C A S E

DEBATING A COMPANY DRUG-TESTING PROGRAM

"Have you read your e-mail yet this afternoon?" Hal asks excitedly on the telephone. The two of you started working at Life Systems, Inc. in the same month and have become good friends even though you work in different departments. By now you've both risen to management positions.

"Not yet. What's up?"

"Wait 'til you hear this," Hal replies. "Tonti's sent us all a message announcing that she's thinking about starting a company drug-testing program." The person Hal calls "Tonti" is Maria Tonti, the company president, who has increased the company's profitability dramatically over the past five years by spurring employees to higher productivity while still giving them a feeling they are being treated fairly.

"A what?"

"Drug testing. Mandatory urine samples taken at unannounced times. She says that if she decides to go ahead with the program, any one of our employees could be tested, from the newest stockroom clerk to Tonti herself."

"You're kidding!" you exclaim as you swivel around and look out your window and across the shady lawn between your building and the highway.

"Nope. And she wants our opinion about whether she should start the program or not. In the e-mail she says she's asking all of her 'key managers' to submit their views in writing. She wants each of us to pick one side or the other and argue for it, so that she and her Executive Committee will know all the angles when they discuss the possibilities next week."

Hal pauses, waiting for your reaction. After a moment, you say, "Given the kinds of products we make, I suppose it was inevitable that Tonti would consider drug testing sooner or later." Life Systems, Inc. manufactures highly specialized, very expensive medical machines, including some that keep patients alive during heart and lung transplant operations. The company has done extremely well in the past few years because of its advanced technology and—more important—its unsurpassed reputation for reliable machines.

You add, "Does she say what started her thinking about drug testing? Has there been some problem?"

"I guess not. In fact, she says she hasn't had a single report or any indication that any employee has used drugs. I wonder what kinds of response she'll get."

You speculate, "I bet she gets the full range of opinions—all the way from total support for the idea to complete rejection of it."

Just then someone knocks at your door. Looking over your shoulder, you see it's Scotty with some papers you asked him to get.

"I've got to go, Hal. Talk to you later."

"Before you hang up," Hal says, "tell me what you're going to say in your reply to Tonti."

"I don't know. I guess I'll have to think it over."

YOUR ASSIGNMENT

Write a reply to Maria Tonti's e-mail message. Begin by deciding whether you want to argue for or against the drug-testing program. Then think of all the arguments you can to support your position. Next, think of the strongest counter arguments that might be raised against your position. In your memo, argue persuasively on behalf of your position, following the guidelines in Chapters 4 and 5. Remember to deal with the arguments on the other side.

CASE

INCREASING ORGAN DONATIONS

Case created by Gail S. Bartlett

You've been working for the past six months at Organ Replacement Gives a New Start (ORGANS), a regional clearinghouse for information about organ donation. At any given moment, 30,000 people in the United States are on a waiting list for organ transplants. Seven of them will die today, and every 20 minutes another will join the waiting list. It is believed that from 12,000 to 15,000 potential organ donors die each year in the United States, but only 4,500 of them actually donate. One donor may provide as many as six organs for transplant.

To discover ways of increasing the number of potential organ donors in the area, Eleanor Gaworski, executive director of ORGANS, asked staff member Aaron Nicholson to study and report on a recent Gallup survey of attitudes toward organ donation. However, Aaron suddenly left ORGANS to take another job. Eleanor has asked you to prepare the report using the information he has collected. The information includes the following tables and notes.

YOUR ASSIGNMENT

According to your instructor's directions, do one of the following:

A. For one of the tables, or for a group of the tables, identified by your instructor, state the important conclusion or conclusions that you draw, explain the evidence that supports your conclusion, and make a recommendation.

B. Using all the tables or a group identified by your instructor, write a full report to Eleanor. Include an introduction; a brief explanation of the survey method used; the key conclusions you draw, together with the specific results that support them; and your recommendation.

C. Make a bar chart, pie chart, or other visual aid that highlights the results presented in one of the tables.

Notes Aaron Left

Largest survey ever conducted on attitudes about organ donation

National survey—6,127 people interviewed

Procedures used make results representative of the U.S. adult population

Telephone survey

In tables, not all percentages total 100% because of rounding

Organs taken only from people who are brain-dead

Brain-dead means there is no hope of recovery

Younger people have more organs to donate; as people get older, fewer of their organs are suitable for donation

People do *not* need to sign an organ donor card or to indicate on their driver's license their desire to donate organs

Next of kin's permission is *always* needed even if a person has indicated a desire to donate organs

1. Do you support or oppose the donation of organs for transplants?

	Support	Oppose	Don't Know
Total	85%	6%	9%
Age 18–24	81%	10%	9%
25–34	85	7	8
35–44	91	4	5
45–54	86	4	9
55+	81	7	11

2. How likely are you to want to have your organs donated after your death?

	Very Likely	Some-what Likely	Not Very/ Not at All Likely	Don't Know
Total	37%	32%	25%	6%
Age 18–24	33%	41%	22%	5%
25–34	38	40	17	5
35–44	50	28	17	5
45–54	41	36	18	5
55+	27	26	38	9

3. Is there a particular reason you are not likely to want to have your organs donated upon your death? What might that reason be? (Asked of persons who reported they are not likely to want to have their organs donated)

Response	% of Times Mentioned
Medical reasons	13%
Believe I'm too old	10
Don't want body cut up/want to be buried as a whole person	9
Don't feel right about it	6
Against religion	5
Other	10
No reason/don't know/haven't given much thought	47

4. Have you made a personal decision about whether or not you would want your or your family members' organs donated in the event of your or their deaths?

Percent Who Have Made Decision About:

	Own Organs	Family Members' Organs
Total	42%	25%
Age 18–24	40%	23%
25–34	43	26
35–44	49	32
45–54	46	33
55+	36	17

Attitude toward Organ Donation

Support	45%	27%
Oppose	39	25

5. Have you told some member of your family about your wish to donate your organs after your death? (Asked of respondents who reported themselves likely to wish to become organ donors)

	Yes
Total	52%
Age 18 – 24	39%
25 – 34	52
35 – 44	58
45 – 54	51
55+	52

6. How willing are you to discuss your wishes about organ donation with your family? Would you say very willing, somewhat willing, not very willing, or not at all willing? (asked of those who have not discussed wishes with family)

Response	Likely to Donate	Not Likely to Donate
Very willing	36%	23%
Somewhat willing	53	35
Not very willing	7	13
Not at all willing	3	23
Don't know	2	4

7. If you had *not discussed* organ donation with a family member, how likely would you be to donate his or her organs upon death?

	Very/Some-what Likely	Not Very/Not at All Likely	Don't Know
Total	47%	45%	7%
Age 18 – 24	44%	52%	4%
25 – 34	51	44	5
35 – 44	54	42	4
45 – 54	51	43	6
55+	38	49	13

Attitude toward organ donation

Support	52%	41%	7%
Oppose	11	84	5

8. If a family member *had requested* that his or her organs be donated upon death, how likely would you be to donate the organs upon death?

	Very/Some-what Likely	Not Very/Not at All Likely	Don't Know
Total	93%	5%	2%
Age 18 – 24	94%	5%	1%
25 – 34	94	5	2
35 – 44	97	2	1
45 – 54	96	3	1
55+	87	8	3

Attitude toward organ donation

Support	95%	3%	1%
Oppose	69	24	6

9. Most of the people who need an organ transplant receive a transplant.

	Strongly Agree/Agree	Disagree/Strongly Disagree	Don't Know
Total	20%	68%	12%
Age 18 – 24	32%	54%	14%
25 – 34	19	72	9
35 – 44	14	74	12
45 – 54	12	75	13
55+	24	63	13

Attitude toward organ donation

Support	19%	70%	11%
Oppose	32	55	14

10. It is possible for a brain-dead person to recover from his or her injuries.

	Strongly Agree/ Agree	Disagree/ Strongly Disagree	Don't Know
Total	21%	63%	16%
Age 18 – 24	28%	52%	19%
25 – 34	25	60	15
35 – 44	20	65	15
45 – 54	16	71	13
55+	18	64	17
Attitude toward organ donation			
Support	20%	65%	15%
Oppose	33	51	15

11. I am going to read you a couple of statements. For each one, please tell me if that particular statement must be true or not true before an individual can donate his or her organs.

Statement	True	False	Don't Know
The person must carry a signed donor card giving permission.	79%	15%	5%
The person's next of kin must give his or her permission.	58%	34%	8%

12. In the past year, have you read, seen, or heard any information about organ donation?

	Yes
Total	58%
Age 18 – 24	36%
25 – 34	47
35 – 44	61
45 – 54	65
55+	68
Attitude toward organ donation	
Support	61%
Oppose	38

Survey results are from the Gallup Organization, Inc., *The American Public's Attitudes toward Organ Donation and Transplantation,* conducted for The Partnership for Organ Donations, Boston, MA, February 1993. Used with permission.

CHAPTER 6

Conducting Research

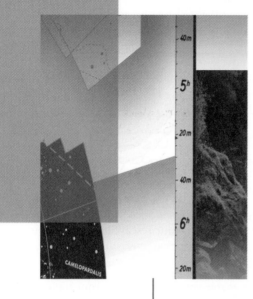

G U I D E L I N E S

1	Define your research objectives
2	Plan before you begin
3	Check each source for leads to other sources
4	Carefully evaluate what you find
5	Begin interpreting your research results even as you obtain them
6	Take careful notes

127

DEFINING
OBJECTIVES
PLANNING
DRAFTING
EVALUATING
REVISING

For many writers, research is an especially pleasurable part of writing. They enjoy learning new things. They delight in using their expertise and ingenuity to uncover novel facts. And they find a sense of achievement in determining how to make their discoveries useful and persuasive to their readers.

Of course, research can also be highly frustrating—if it produces poor results or takes too much time.

This chapter presents six guidelines that will help you become a highly productive researcher, one who achieves excellent results in as little time as possible. Its advice will apply to the majority of writing-related research that you do on the job. In addition, the Reference Guide following this chapter provides detailed suggestions for using five methods of gathering information and ideas often employed at work.

Exploiting your memory
Searching Internet
Using the Library
Interviewing
Conducting a Survey

GOALS OF GOOD RESEARCH

Take a reader-centered approach to research.

The first thing to remember about research is that it needs to be just as reader-centered as any other writing activity. Your research is successful only if it produces results that your readers will value. In particular, your research should provide you with information and ideas that have the following characteristics—from your readers' perspective (see Figure 6.1):

Characteristics of good research

- **Right scope.** The research results enable you to write about your topic with sufficient breadth to meet your readers' needs.
- **Right depth.** The research provides sufficient detail to allow your readers to understand your topic to the level necessary for them to perform their tasks and appreciate the validity of your persuasive points.
- **Right treatment.** The research results approach your topic in the same way that your readers will approach it. For example, if your readers are persons who will install a large computer system, your research produces results that will assist them with installation rather than help them administer or use the system.

In research, efficiency is required.

At work, time is always at a premium. Consequently, research must produce information of the right scope, depth, and treatment with a minimum expenditure of time. Delays caused by inefficient research not only postpone the time when your readers can use the fruits of your efforts but also rob your other projects of attention they need.

GUIDELINE 1   **Define Your Research Objectives**

You can streamline your research by defining in advance what you want to find. After all, you are not trying to dig up everything that is known about your subject. You are seeking only information and evidence that will help you achieve your communication's objectives.

■ **FIGURE 6.1**

Characteristics of Good Research

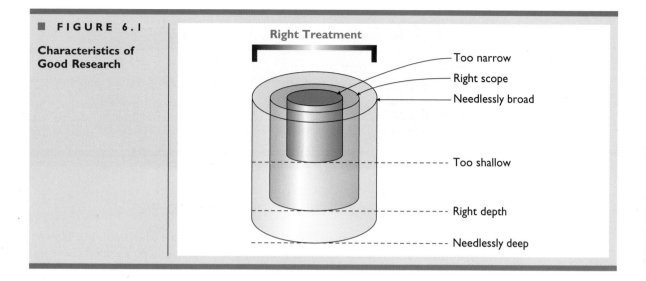

Begin by reviewing your communication's objectives. Your research objectives should be squarely built on them. Who are your readers? What questions will they ask? The questions you can't answer immediately are the ones your research needs to investigate.

Base your research objectives on your readers' needs.

Consider also the kinds of answers your readers will want to their questions. Will they want general information or specific details? Will they want you to treat your topic from the standpoint of the engineer or the accountant, the consumer or the producer? The kinds of answers your readers desire will determine the types of sources you consult during your research.

Be ready to modify your objectives as you proceed.

Although you should define your research objectives at the outset, you should also be ready to revise them as you proceed. Research is all about learning. One of the things you may learn along the way is that you need to investigate something you hadn't originally thought important—or even thought about at all.

GUIDELINE ② **Plan Before You Begin**

Many people conduct research haphazardly. They dash off to the library or log onto the Internet in the hopes of quickly finding just the right book or Web site. If the first source fails, they scoot off to another one. Such an approach can waste time and cause you to overlook very helpful sources, including (perhaps) the one that includes exactly the information you need.

You will research much more efficiently and effectively if you begin by making a plan.

Making a Research Plan

- Identify all sources that might be helpful. Include people and organizations as well as publications.
- Identify the most promising sources. It only makes sense to focus your efforts on them.
- Determine the most productive order in which to consult your sources.
- Make a schedule so you can apportion your time wisely. Include the time needed for interpreting results.

As you make your research plan, consider the following advice:

- **Consult general sources first.** Imitate movie directors who begin their films with a panoramic overview of a scene before zooming in on a central character or action. By starting with a general view of your subject, you increase the ease with which you can locate, comprehend, and interpret the more detailed facts you will later encounter. Useful general sources are encyclopedias (including the specialized ones that exist for many subjects), articles in popular magazines, and review articles published in specialized journals for the purpose of summarizing research on a particular subject.
- **Conduct preliminary research when appropriate.** In some situations, it will be helpful for you to conduct some research in preparation for other research.

    Imagine, for instance, that your key source is an executive or expert you can contact only once. You wouldn't want to misuse your time with this person by asking for information you could easily obtain elsewhere. Instead, you should gather that readily available information in advance. This will enable you to focus your conversation with your key source on facts this person alone can supply.

While making your plan, you might find it helpful to use a planning guide like this one:

Readers' Question	Possible Sources	Assessment of Each Source	When to Consult
Are our competitors developing this technology more rapidly than we are?	Competitor reports to stockholders	Biased	Next week
	Trade journals	Probably reliable	Immediately
When will our design be ready?	Kami Mason, Project Coordinator	Objective, informed	Close to completion of report

GUIDELINE **3**   **Check Each Source for Leads to Other Sources**

One good source can lead you to others.

Conducting research is like solving a crime. You don't know exactly what the outcome will be—or where to find the clues. Consequently, it makes sense to check every source for leads to other sources. Scrutinize the footnotes and bibliographies of every book, article, and report you consult. When you locate a book in the library stacks, browse through books that are nearby. And when you interview people, ask them to suggest additional places to look and persons to speak with. Be sure to schedule time to follow up on promising leads.

GUIDELINE **4**   **Carefully Evaluate What You Find**

You have no use for information that your readers won't find useful or persuasive or that you yourself don't believe to be credible. Consequently, you should evaluate continuously the facts and ideas you discover. If you find that a book about your topic treats it at the wrong level or from the wrong perspective, put it back on the shelf. If you discover that your readers will perceive a particular person to be biased, move on to someone with more credibility.

To evaluate what you find, ask the same questions that a skeptical reader would ask.

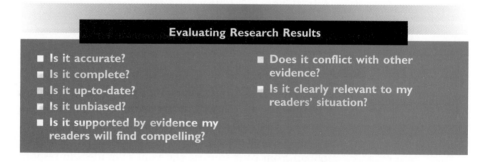

Evaluating Research Results

- Is it accurate?
- Is it complete?
- Is it up-to-date?
- Is it unbiased?
- Is it supported by evidence my readers will find compelling?

- Does it conflict with other evidence?
- Is it clearly relevant to my readers' situation?

When evaluating sources, be as cautious about your own biases as you are about any biases your sources may possess. Don't dismiss a source simply because it contradicts your views or presents data that fail to support your conclusions. Your readers depend on your thoroughness and integrity.

GUIDELINE **5**   **Begin Interpreting Your Research Results Even as You Obtain Them**

Research involves more than just amassing information. To make your results truly useful and persuasive to your readers, you must also interpret them in light of your readers' desires, needs, and situation. For example, imagine that you have been asked to study two computer programs that might replace an existing one used by your employer. One program, you discover, performs a certain function 9 percent more rapidly than the other. This fact alone would not be sufficient for a decision-making reader. You need to interpret the fact by telling the reader whether the greater speed would improve operations significantly enough to justify the added cost of the quicker program. And answering this secondary—but crucial—question may require additional research.

Here are some questions that will help you interpret your research results:

Interpreting Research Results

- **What do I conclude from them—and what else might I need to learn to test these conclusions?**
- **Are other interpretations possible—and do I need to explore them?**
- **What are the implications for my readers—and what else must I learn to explore these implications thoroughly?**
- **What are the implications for stakeholders who are not my** readers—and what else can I learn that will enable me to suggest ways to avoid undesirable consequences for them?
- **What does this mean my readers should do—and what do I need to investigate to assure that they have the information necessary to persuade them to take this action and to enable them to carry it out?**

GUIDELINE 6   Take Careful Notes

A simple but critical technique for researching productively is to take careful notes at every step of the way. When making notes on the facts and opinions you discover, be sure to distinguish quotations from paraphrases so you can properly identify quoted statements in your communication. Also, clearly differentiate ideas you obtain from your sources and your own ideas in response to what you find there.

Careful notes can prevent wasteful backtracking.

In addition, make careful bibliographic notes about your sources. Include all the details you will need when documenting your sources (see the "Focus on Ethics" box on page 133). For books and articles, this includes the following:

Books	Articles
• Author's or editor's full name	• Author's full name
• Exact title	• Exact title
• City of publication	• Journal name
• Publisher	• Volume (and issue unless pages are numbered consecutively throughout the volume)
• Year of publication	
• Edition	• Year of publication
• Page numbers	• Page numbers

Documenting Your Sources

FOCUS ON ETHICS

On the job, as in college, you have an ethical obligation to credit the sources of your ideas and information by listing those sources in a reference list, footnotes, or bibliography. However, the standards for deciding exactly what sources need to be listed at work differ considerably from the standards that apply at school.

The discussion of the five questions that follow will help you determine whether you need to document a particular source when writing at work.

Is This Information Common Knowledge?

Both in college and at work, you must indicate the source of ideas and information (1) that you have derived from someone else and (2) that are not common knowledge.

However, what's considered "common knowledge" at work is different from what's considered common knowledge at school. At school, it's knowledge every person possesses without doing any special reading. Thus, you must document any material you find in print.

At work, however, common knowledge is knowledge that is possessed by or readily available to people in your field. Thus, you do not need to acknowledge material you obtained through your college courses, your textbooks, the standard reference works in your field, or similar sources.

Does My Employer Own It?

As explained in Chapter 1, employers consider that they own the writing done at work by their employees. Consequently, it is usually considered perfectly ethical to incorporate information from one proposal or report into another without acknowledging the source.

Am I Taking Credit for Someone Else's Work?

On the other hand, you must be careful to avoid taking credit for ideas that aren't your own. In one case, an engineer was fired for unethical conduct because he pretended that he had devised a solution to a technical problem when he had actually copied the solution from a published article.

Am I Writing for a Research Journal?

In articles to be published in scientific or scholarly journals, ethical standards for documentation are far more stringent than for on-the-job reports and proposals. In such articles, thorough documentation is required even for ideas based on a single sentence in another source. Thus, you must document any information materials you find in print or on-line.

Also, in research labs where employees customarily publish their results in scientific or scholarly journals, even information drawn from internal communications may need to be thoroughly documented.

Whom Can I Ask for Advice?

Because expectations about documentation can vary from company to company and from situation to situation, the surest way to identify your ethical obligations is to determine what your readers and employer expect. Consult your boss and co-workers, and examine communications similar to the one you are preparing.

You will find information about how to write bibliographic citations in Appendix B.

For interviews, record the person's full name (verify the spelling!), title, and employer, if different from your own. Special considerations apply when your sources are on the Internet; they are described in Appendix B.

It is equally important for you to record the information you will need if you later find that you need to consult this source again. For instance, when working in a library, jot down the call number of each book; when interviewing someone, get the person's phone number or e-mail address; and when using a site on the World Wide Web, copy the universal resource locator (URL).

As you proceed, be sure to keep a list of sources that you checked but found useless. Otherwise, you may find a later reference to the same sources but be unable to remember that you have already looked at them.

CONCLUSION

This chapter's six guidelines apply to all your research efforts regardless of the research method you employ. Following this chapter is a Reference Guide that provides additional advice concerning five specific research techniques that are frequently used in the workplace.

Reference Guide: Five
Research Methods

CONTENTS

Exploiting Your Own Memory and Creativity

Searching the Internet

Using the Library

Interviewing

Conducting a Survey

T his Reference Guide tells how to use five research methods commonly employed on the job. Each method is discussed separately to create a reference source that allows you quickly to access the advice about the particular method you select.

Research Methods	
■ Exploiting your own memory and creativity	Page 136
■ Searching the Internet	Page 142
■ Using the library	Page 149
■ Interviewing	Page 155
■ Conducting a survey	Page 158

EXPLOITING YOUR OWN MEMORY AND CREATIVITY

Almost always, your best research aids will include your own memory and creativity. The following sections discuss four methods of exploiting the power of these mental resources. Each method can be useful at the beginning of your research and at many points along the way:

- Brainstorming
- Freewriting
- Drawing a picture of your topic
- Creating and studying a table or graph of your data

BRAINSTORMING

When you brainstorm, you generate thoughts about your subject as rapidly as you can through the spontaneous association of ideas, writing down whatever thoughts occur to you.

Brainstorming lets your thoughts run free.

The power of brainstorming arises from the way it unleashes your natural creativity. By freeing you from the confines imposed by outlines or other highly structured ways of organizing your ideas, brainstorming lets you follow your own creative lines of thought.

Brainstorming is especially helpful in enabling you to focus in on the core ideas you want to communicate to your readers, whether in an overall message or in one part of a longer message. It also works well in group writing projects: when the members brainstorm aloud, the ideas offered by one person often spark ideas for the others.

Brainstorming Procedure

1. **Review your knowledge of your readers and communication situation.**
2. **Ask yourself, "What do I know about my subject that might help me achieve my communication purpose?"**
3. **As ideas come, write them down as fast as you can, using single words or short phrases. As soon as you list one idea, move on to the next thought that comes to you.**
4. **When your stream of ideas runs dry, read back through your list to see if your previous entries suggest any new ideas.**
5. **When you no longer have any new ideas, gather related items in your list into groups to see if this activity inspires new thoughts.**

When brainstorming, avoid evaluating your ideas.

The key to brainstorming is to record ideas quickly without evaluating any of the thoughts that come to mind. Record *everything*. If you shift your task from generating ideas to evaluating them, you will disrupt the free flow of associations on which brainstorming thrives.

Here's the first part of a brainstorming session by Nicole. She wanted to write her boss about ways to improve the quality control procedures at her company, which makes machines that keep patients alive during organ transplant operations. Sitting at her computer, Nicole began by simply tapping out her initial thoughts on her subject.

While brainstorming, Nicole sometimes moved from one idea to a related one. At other times, she jumped to a completely unrelated thought.

Ideas for Quality Control Recommendations

Problem: Present system is unreliable
Everyone is "supposed" to be responsible for quality
No one has specific responsibilities
Workers feel rushed, sometimes ignore quality checks
People's lives are at stake
Near-fatal failure last year in Tucson
Need procedures to test critical components when they arrive from supplier
People follow their own shortcuts, using personal assembly techniques
Don't realize harm they could do
Product's overall record of performance is excellent

After running out of ideas, Nicole grouped related items under common headings. Note how organizing her notes around her three main topics spurred her to develop additional thoughts.

REFERENCE GUIDE: Five Research Methods

Ideas for Quality Control Recommendations

Importance of Quality Control
 Lives depend on it (near-fatal failure in Tucson)

New ideas suggested by outlining
 Avoid product liability lawsuits
 Keep sales up

Present System
 Overall record is excellent, but could easily fail
 Everyone is supposed to be responsible for quality, but no one is
 Workers follow their own shortcuts and personal assembly techniques
 Workers feel rushed, sometimes ignore quality control checks

New idea
 Only consistent test is at end of building the machine (some parts may cause the machine to fail due to flaws that are not detectable in whole-machine test)

Strategies for a Better System
 Test critical parts as they are delivered from the supplier

New idea
 Insist that standard assembly procedures be followed

New idea
 Assign specific responsibilities—and rewards

FREEWRITING

Freewriting is very much like brainstorming. Here, too, you tap your natural creativity free from the confines of structured thought. You rapidly record your ideas as they pop into your mind. Only this time, you write prose rather than a list. The goal is to keep your ideas flowing.

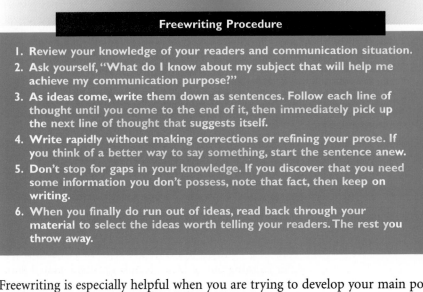

Freewriting Procedure

1. Review your knowledge of your readers and communication situation.
2. Ask yourself, "What do I know about my subject that will help me achieve my communication purpose?"
3. As ideas come, write them down as sentences. Follow each line of thought until you come to the end of it, then immediately pick up the next line of thought that suggests itself.
4. Write rapidly without making corrections or refining your prose. If you think of a better way to say something, start the sentence anew.
5. Don't stop for gaps in your knowledge. If you discover that you need some information you don't possess, note that fact, then keep on writing.
6. When you finally do run out of ideas, read back through your material to select the ideas worth telling your readers. The rest you throw away.

Freewriting can help you develop your main ideas.

Freewriting is especially helpful when you are trying to develop your main points. Use it when writing brief communications or parts of a long communication when you still need to interpret your data or formulate your recommendations.

Below is a sample freewriting done by Miguel, an employee of a company that makes precision instruments. He had spent two weeks investigating technologies to be placed aboard airplanes for detecting microbursts and wind shear, two dangerous atmospheric conditions that have caused several crashes. Miguel wrote this freewriting draft when deciding what to say in the opening paragraph of his report.

In Miguel's freewriting, ideas are jumbled together, but they are now recorded so he can sort through and organize them.

> Wind shear and microbursts have been blamed for several recent airline crashes (find out which ones—Dallas?). People are studying several technologies for detecting these conditions. Then pilots can fly around them. The technologies might be used on the ground or in planes. On-board devices would be much more helpful to pilots. Several technologies are being studied. The equipment would need to be approved by the Federal Aviation Administration. It is eager for such devices to be developed. There would be a high demand for on-board devices from airlines. Many companies are working on them. The key point is we could make a lot of profit if we develop the right instrument first. We need to pick the most promising technology and develop it.

Freewriting produces ideas, not a draft.

The following passage shows the paragraph Miguel wrote after freewriting. Note that it further develops some ideas from his freewriting, and it omits others. It is a fresh start—but one built on the ideas Miguel generated while freewriting.

Through freewriting, Miguel realized that profitability was a key point, and so placed it first in his subsequent draft.

His ideas are now organized and clearly developed.

> We have a substantial opportunity to develop and successfully market instruments that can be placed aboard airplanes to detect dangerous wind conditions called wind shear and microbursts. The conditions have been blamed for several recent air crashes, including one of a Lockheed L-1011 that killed 133 people. Because of the increasing awareness of the danger of these wind conditions, the Federal Aviation Administration is encouraging research into a variety of technologies for detecting them. Most concern systems placed at airports or in large airplanes. We could establish a highly profitable niche by developing a system for use in small, private aircraft. In this report, I will review four major technologies, assessing the suitability of each for development by our company.

DRAWING A PICTURE OF YOUR TOPIC

Try thinking visually.

Another effective strategy for exploiting your memory and creativity is to explore your topic visually. Here are four kinds of diagrams that writers at work have found to be useful.

Flow Chart

When you are writing about a process or procedure, try drawing a flow chart of it. Leave lots of space around each box in the flow chart so you can write notes next to it. Here's a flow chart that Nicole used to generate ideas for a report recommending improved quality control procedures in the manufacture and delivery of the medical equipment sold by her employer.

Above the flow chart, Nicole wrote the ideas that occurred to her as she studied the chart.

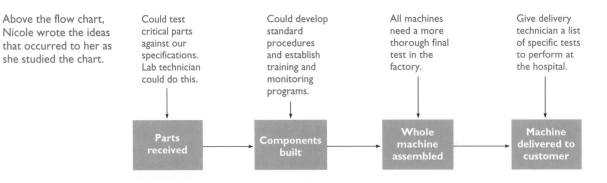

Could test critical parts against our specifications. Lab technician could do this.

Could develop standard procedures and establish training and monitoring programs.

All machines need a more thorough final test in the factory.

Give delivery technician a list of specific tests to perform at the hospital.

Matrix

A matrix is a table used to generate and organize ideas.

When you are comparing two or more alternatives in terms of a common set of criteria, drawing a matrix can aid you in systematically identifying the key features of each item being compared. Make a table in which you list the alternatives down the left-hand side, and write the topics or issues to be covered across the top. Then, fill in each cell in the resulting table by brainstorming. Blank boxes indicate information you need to obtain. Miguel created the following matrix on his computer, but he could also have done so with pencil and paper.

System	How It Works	Limitations	Potential Competition
Doppler Radar	Detects rapidly rotating air masses, like those found in wind shear	Technology still being researched	General Dynamics Hughes
Infrared Detector	Detects slight increases in temperature that often accompany wind shear	Temperature doesn't always rise	None—Federal Aviation Administration suspended testing
Laser Sensor	Sudden wind shifts affect reflectivity of air that lasers can detect	Provides only a 20-second warning for jets traveling at typical speed	Walton Electronic Perhaps Sperry

Cluster Sketch

Your ideas radiate from the center of the page.

Creating a cluster sketch is a simple, powerful technique for exploring a topic visually. Write your overall topic in a circle at the center of a piece of paper, then add circles around the perimeter that identify the major issues or subtopics, joining them with lines to the main topic. Continue adding satellite notes, expanding outward as far as you find productive. Figure RM.1 shows a cluster sketch created by Carol, an engineer who is leading a team assigned to help a small city locate places where it can drill new wells for its municipal water supply.

■ **FIGURE RM.1**

Cluster Sketch

Cluster sketches allow you to "draw" a map of your topics.

■ **FIGURE RM.2**

Idea Tree

Idea trees help you develop the hierarchical structure of your communications.

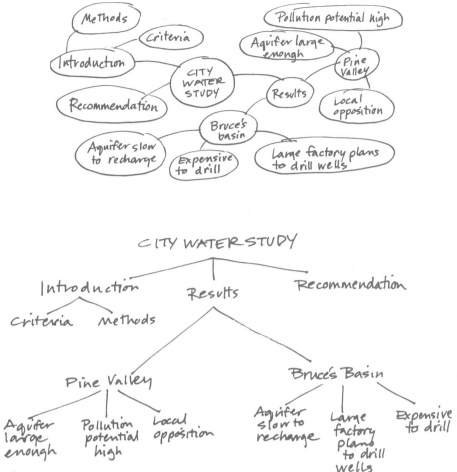

A variation of the cluster sketch is the idea tree, shown in Figure RM.2. At the top of a sheet of paper, write your main topic. Then list the main subtopics or issues horizontally below, joining them to the main topic with lines. Continue this branching as long as it is fruitful.

Table or Graph

Often, at work, you will need to write communications about data, such as the results of a test you have run, costs you have calculated, or production figures you have gathered. In such cases, many people find it helpful to begin their writing process by making the tables or graphs that they will include in their communication. Then they can begin to interpret the data arrayed before them, making notes about the data's meaning and significance to their readers.

SEARCHING THE INTERNET

The explosive growth of the Internet has created a rich and continuously evolving aid to researchers. From your computer at home, school, or work, the Internet lets you read technical reports from companies such as IBM, download software, view pictures taken by NASA spacecraft in remote areas of the solar system, or join on-line discussions on an astonishing array of topics. Figure RM.3 lists just a few of the resources the Internet makes available to you.

As wonderfully helpful as the Internet can be, it also poses two substantial challenges to you as a researcher:

Two challenges of Internet research

- **You may have difficulty finding helpful sites.** There are millions of sites on the Internet, with millions more added annually. Navigating through these sites to locate the ones that present useful information on your topic can be difficult.
- **You must carefully evaluate the sites you locate.** Anyone can post information on the Internet, regardless of his or her purpose, bias, or level of expertise. Because no one prevents unreliable information from appearing, you must carefully evaluate the credibility of each site you encounter.

SEARCH TOOLS

To assist people in conducting Internet research, two types of tools have been developed: search engines and Internet directories.

Search Engines

Search engines have three elements: spider, database, and robot.

Search engines have three basic elements (Gralla). The first is a computer program, called a *spider*, that crawls across the World Wide Web, extracting the words, Internet address, and possibly other information from each site it visits. The spider delivers this information to the second element, a *database*, which indexes and stores the information.

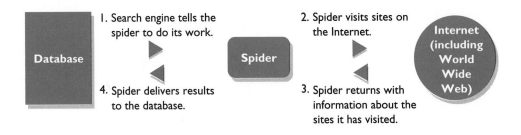

Database

1. Search engine tells the spider to do its work.

4. Spider delivers results to the database.

Spider

2. Spider visits sites on the Internet.

3. Spider returns with information about the sites it has visited.

Internet (including World Wide Web)

To conduct a search, you use keywords.

A search engine's third element is a *robot.* You interact with the robot by giving it one or more words that are associated with your research topic. These are called *keywords.* The robot looks through the database (not the Internet itself) for sites that contain the keywords you submitted. At the completion of its search, the robot tells you the number of matches it has found and provides a link to each site, possibly with some additional information about it. See the diagram at the top of page 144.

■ **FIGURE RM.3**

Some Major Internet Resources for Research

Internet Resource	Examples
Corporate reports and information	IBM posts technical documents, Microsoft offers detailed information on its products, and the World Wildlife Fund reports on its environmental projects. Thousands of other profit and nonprofit organizations do the same. Examples IBM Research Papers on Networking http://www.networking.ibm.com Microsoft product information and downloading http://www.microsoft.com World Wildlife Fund for Nature http://www.panda.org
Technical and scientific journals	Many technical and scientific journals are available on-line, though often only to people or through libraries that pay an on-line subscription fee. Examples *Journal of Cell Biology* http://www.jcb.org *IEEE Transactions on Software Engineering* http://www.computer.org/tse
Government agencies	Many government agencies have Web sites at which they provide reports, regulations, forms, and similar resources. Examples NASA http://www.nasa.gov National Institutes of Health http://www.nih.gov National Park Service http://www.nps.gov
Interest group discussions	Internet sites called *newsgroups* enable people to ask questions, offer advice, and share insights on-line. Newsgroups exist on thousands of topics, many organized around professional or research interests. Browser to try Dejanews http://www.dejanews.com
Texts of scientific, historical, and literary documents	From Shakespeare to Jane Austen, from Darwin to Newton, full texts of works of many important authors are available for on-screen reading and downloading. Browsers to try Archie http://archie.rutgers.edu Veronica gopher://gopher.unr.edu
Locator services	Services such as Four11 help you to find e-mail addresses. Browser to try Four11 http://www.four11.com

REFERENCE GUIDE: Five Research Methods

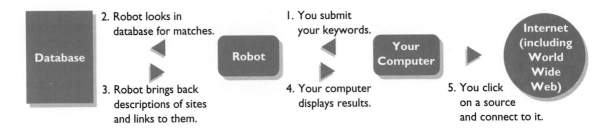

Figure RM.4 shows the home page for the search engine AltaVista. Figure RM.5 shows the results produced by an AltaVista search for the keywords "basking shark" (the second largest of all sharks), and Figure RM.6 shows a Web site accessed through a link from one of the AltaVista results.

Internet Directories

Internet directory databases are created by humans.

Internet directories depend on humans rather than spiders to build their databases. If the creators of Web sites wish to have their sites included in a directory's database, they submit the sites to the directory's research staff. The staff may also search the Web for additional sites that are likely to interest users. For the sites they select, the staff write brief descriptions, which then get entered into the database.

With Internet directories, you browse through menus.

The staff place the descriptions within a highly structured framework, which enables you to locate sites on a particular topic by browsing through a series of hierarchically organized menus. For instance, using the popular directory Yahoo to find information on basking sharks, you would first choose the category "Science," then "Biology," then "Zoology," then "Animals, Insects, Pets," then "Marine Life," then "Fish," then "Basking Shark." Figure RM.7 (page 146) shows the initial menu for Yahoo.

Some directories, including Yahoo, provide the option of conducting a keyword search. These searches look only at the directories' own databases, which contain the brief descriptions of the selected sites, as explained above.

CHOOSING A SEARCH TOOL

Search engines and directories each have distinct advantages.

Search engines and Internet directories provide distinctly different kinds of support for your research. Directories will enable you to avoid many of the useless sites you will bump into with a search engine, but a search engine will provide access to many sites that are missed by directories. A search for "basking sharks" with the search engine AltaVista produced 403 sites, including some written by elementary school children, while the Internet directory Yahoo produced just 2 sites, missing some maintained by research and wildlife organizations.

Search engines and Internet directories come in both generic and custom versions. Generic tools create their databases from general searches on the Internet, and they include pages on a wide array of topics.

■ **FIGURE RM.4**

Home Page for a Search Engine (AltaVista)

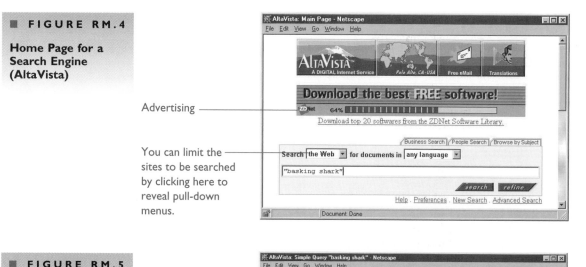

Advertising —

You can limit the sites to be searched by clicking here to reveal pull-down menus.

■ **FIGURE RM.5**

Results of an AltaVista Search for the Keywords "Basking Shark"

Total number of matches (403)

Blue type indicates links you can click on.

Title of the Web page

First words on the page

Address

■ **FIGURE RM.6**

Web Site Accessed through the AltaVista Search for the Keywords "Basking Shark" (This site contains photos of the sharks on one of its pages.)

Title of the Web page —

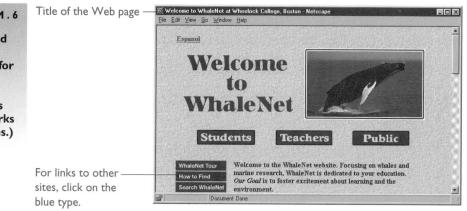

For links to other sites, click on the blue type.

■ **FIGURE RM.7**

**Home Page for an
Internet Directory
(Yahoo)**

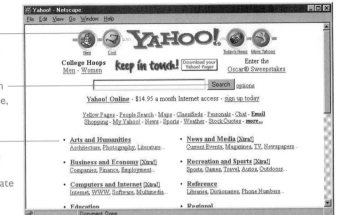

For links to sites
selected by Yahoo,
click on these icons.

For a keyword search
of the Yahoo database,
click here.

To begin a search
through Yahoo's
hierarchical menus,
click on the appropriate
topic.

Some Generic Search Tools

Search Engines

AltaVista	http://www.altavista.digital.com
Excite	http://www.excite.com
HOTBOT	http://www.hotbot.com
Infoseek	http://www.guide.infoseek.com

Internet Directory

| Yahoo | http://www.yahoo.com |

Use custom search tools
when possible.

Search tools differ in many
ways.

Custom search tools build specialized databases about specific topics. They can speed your research on many technical topics, as well as on topics of general interest, such as health, U.S. cities, and renaissance literature. Reference librarians are an excellent source of information about custom search tools.

Even among generic search tools, there are substantial differences that impact the kind of results they produce. As mentioned above, a search for "basking shark" with AltaVista produced 403 sites. The same search with HOTBOT produced 122. In addition to the number of sites identified, these differences can affect such things as the types of site found, the types of information included with the search results, the order in which the sites are listed, and the freshness of the sites (how recently the spider or research staff have updated the database). Because of such differences, it's often worthwhile to use more than one search tool.

CONDUCTING KEYWORD SEARCHES

Whether you are using a keyword search with a search engine or an Internet directory, the following strategies will help you work efficiently and productively:

Robots conduct searches by matching words.

1. **Brainstorm a list of keywords.** Identify words that would be associated with your topic, words that you think others might use, and synonyms for all those words. For more ideas on keyword searches, see page 151.

2. **Read the "Tips."** Most robots enable you to streamline your search. For example, many enable you to instruct them to show you only sites that contain *any* of several words you submit or only sites that contain *all* of several words you submit. To see the advantage of such features, consider the number of sites returned by AltaVista for three searches concerning laser eye surgery.

You can request different kinds of searches.

Match on any word ("laser" *or* "eye" *or* "surgery")	3,886 sites
Match on all words ("laser" *and* "eye" *and* "surgery")	66 sites
Match on the complete phrase (the words next to each other in the exact order)	5 sites

You can customize your search in other ways.

Some search tools allow you to sharpen your search by doing such things as asking only for sites that are in a particular language or that have been added to the database in a specified period (month, year). You can also customize the way that information about sites is displayed. To locate information about these features, look on the main menu for "Tips," "Help," "Advanced Search," or similar terms.

3. **Submit your search.** Within several seconds, the search tool should return its results, showing both the number of matches and displaying information about them.

EVALUATING YOUR SEARCH RESULTS

Whether you are using a search engine or an Internet directory, you need to evaluate the results you receive.

Use the list of results to target the most promising sites.

Your first evaluation should occur when the search tool produces its list of sites. You can save considerable time by using the information provided in this list to determine which sites are worth visiting. If it appears that none are, you are probably better off refining your search rather than peering into each site in the hope of finding something useful.

Although different search tools display different sets of information, the following result from AltaVista illustrates the kind of information you can use for this evaluation.

Number of the site in the list of matches

Title of the site

First words of the text on the site's page

1. Basking Shark – Scientific Information – Reproduction
Reproduction. Sharks are generally long lived (12–17 years), grow slowly, and produce small numbers of young (2–50) each year. By comparison, most bony fish
http://www.isle-of-man.com/interests/shark/repro.htm - size 5k - Apr-96 - English — Language used in the site

Address for the site

Domain

Size

Date the site was entered in the database

REFERENCE GUIDE: Five Research Methods

Check addresses before you visit sites.

In addition to reading the description of the site, look at its address:

- **Check the domain.** On the Internet, different types of organizations are assigned to different domains, which are included in the addresses of the sites created by those organizations.

Sample Internet Domains	
.com	commercial (sites for businesses)
.org	not-for-profit organizations
.edu	educational (sites for colleges and universities)
.gov	government (sites for local, state, and federal governments)

- Depending on what you are looking for, a commercial source may be good or it may be bad. For information about features of products, for instance, a company's Web site is usually a good source. For information about problems with the products, lawsuits against the company, or other unfavorable information, it's probably a bad source.
- **Look for the tilde: ~.** A tilde often indicates that the site is a personal site. For instance, an official Web site created for my university is:

| http://www.muohio.edu/aboutmiami

- In contrast, all files created as part of personal sites by faculty, staff, and students include a tilde:

| http://www.muohio.edu/~filename

- After you visit a promising site, carefully evaluate what you find there.

Evaluating Web Sites
■ Is the person or organization that created it identified?
■ Does the site allow you to contact the creator?
■ Does this person or organization have the necessary expertise?
■ Is the site likely to reflect personal or organizational bias?
■ Can you tell when it was last modified—and is it up-to-date?

TWO MORE TIPS FOR INTERNET RESEARCH

Here are two more tips for the research you conduct on the Internet:

- **Bookmark valuable sites.** It's easy to lose your way when linking from site to site on the Internet. Fortunately, Netscape and other browsers provide a bookmark feature that lets you add any page you are visiting to a personalized menu. By later selecting the title of the site from the menu, you can return immediately to the site. Some browsers also have a "Go" feature that lists the sites you have visited during your current session.

■ **Record bibliographic information as you proceed.** Even if you have created a bookmark for a site from which you have gathered information, the site may have changed or even disappeared the next time you look for it. Consequently, it's crucial for you to obtain the bibliographic information you will need from it at the same time you are gathering your information. In addition to the other information described in Appendix B, be sure to record the date of your visit.

USING THE LIBRARY

For many communications, the library will be your best source of information and ideas.

Libraries are as much on-line as on-the-shelf.

The first step in using the library effectively is to discard the old image of a library as a place that primarily houses books and periodicals. Although libraries still feature these publications, most are now as much on-line as on-the-shelf. In fact, many libraries are so computerized that you don't even need to enter the buildings to use their resources. You can access many of their resources through a computer in your classroom, home, or office.

Library resources fall into two broad categories:

Major library resources

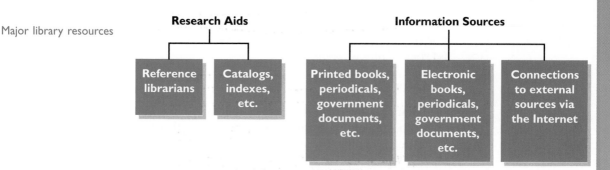

Generally, your excursions in library research will begin with one of the research aids, which can guide you to the most productive information sources. The following sections will help you use the research aids productively and also introduce some of the information sources with which you may not be familiar.

REFERENCE LIBRARIANS

When researching, you will rarely find any resource more helpful than reference librarians. They can tell you about specialized resources that you may not be aware of, and they can explain how to use the time-saving features of these resources.

FIGURE RM.8

Menu for Typical On-Line Library Catalog

If you aren't looking for a specific author or title, use the *subject* or the *word(s)* search.

Tell the reference librarian your communication's objectives.

Reference librarians will be able to give you the best help if you indicate very specifically what you want. In addition to telling your topic, describe what the purpose of your communication is, who your readers are, and how your readers will use your communication.

LIBRARY CATALOG

The library catalog lists the complete holdings of a library, including books, periodicals, pamphlets, recordings, videotapes, and other materials. In most libraries, the catalog is computerized so that you can search for items of interest to you in any of several ways. See Figure RM.8.

If you are looking for a particular book whose title you know or for work written or edited by a person whose name you know, library catalogs are very simple to use. However, when you begin by looking for information about a particular topic, your success may depend on your ingenuity and knowledge of how to use the computerized catalog that most libraries have.

To search for a specific topic, you have two choices:

Two kinds of library searches

■ **Subject search.** To aid researchers, librarians include subject headings in the record for each library item. When you indicate that you want to do a subject search, the computer will prompt you to enter the words that identify the subject you are looking for. The computer will search through all items that have been tagged with the exact words you entered.

- **Word search.** When you indicate that you wish to conduct a word search, you will also be prompted to enter the words that identify your subject. This time, however, the computer will search the title, author, and subject lines of all its records. Some systems will also search every word in the entry, including (for example) a book's table of contents if the system's entries include this information.

GUIDELINES FOR USING THE LIBRARY CATALOG

The following strategies will help you conduct efficient, productive subject and word searches of computerized library catalogs. The same general strategies also work with card catalogs.

Using a library catalog is like playing a word game.

1. **Develop a list of keywords and synonyms.** Subject searches and word searches are like word games. They will locate items on your topic only if the word you enter exactly matches the word used by the librarians (in a subject search) or author (in a word search). If you enter "gene splicing," and the librarians or author used "genetic engineering," you'll miss some potentially important items.

   Accordingly, your first step should be identifying the words that librarians and authors probably used to describe your topic. These words are called *keywords*.

Creating a Keyword List for Library Research

- Start with the words you would intuitively use to identify your subject.
- Then think of words you've heard other people use.
- Think of synonyms for the words you've listed.
- Ask a reference librarian, who can consult various sources that list standard subject terms.
- Scan through an article on the general area of your topic in an encyclopedia or other source of general information.
- Look for additional keywords in the list of subject headings of the items your search produces.

---

2. **Submit your keywords.** Figure RM.9 shows a computer screen used to submit a request for items that contain the words "World Wide Web." Even if your first keywords turn up a number of promising sources, try others. They may produce sources even more valuable than any in the first group.

3. **Evaluate your results.** When you submit words in a search, the computer will produce a list that briefly describes the items it has found. Figure RM.10 shows the results of the search for "World Wide Web." The first things to do when you receive your results are to check the titles to see if they are likely to be useful and to check the dates to see if the items listed are current enough for your purposes.

   For entries that look promising, examine the full record by clicking the mouse button or entering the item number. See Figure RM.11. The entry will provide

■ **FIGURE RM.9**

Request for a Word Search for "World Wide Web"

The search request is entered here.

Tips for narrowing a search

Click here for additional tips.

■ **FIGURE RM.10**

Results of a Word Search for "World Wide Web"

The system reminds you of your keywords.

It tells you how many matches it found (398).

Matches are listed with titles and (sometimes) authors.

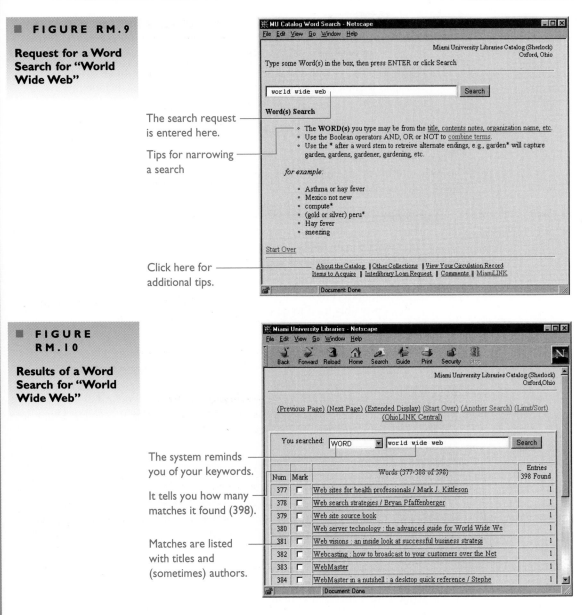

details about the book and whether it is available in the library or has been checked out.

4. **Refine your search as you proceed.** The first keywords you submit may produce the results you want. If you receive none (or too few), try other keywords or consult a reference librarian.

If you receive too many (some searches can produce thousands), you may narrow the search by specifying additional keywords. A search for "chess" produces 1,000 hits; by entering "computer chess" you might whittle that number to 80.

■ **FIGURE RM.11**

Catalog Entry for One Book Listed in a Search for "World Wide Web"

Bibliographic information about the book

The book is available (check shelves).

Note that the words "World Wide Web" appear in the book's contents, not its title (this was a *word* search, not a *title* search).

```
Miami University Libraries · Netscape
File Edit View Go Window Help

Author   Cotton, Eileen Giuffré, 1947-
Title    The online classroom : teaching with the Internet / by Eileen Giuffré Cotton
Imprint  Bloomington, Ind. : ERIC Clearinghouse on Reading, English, and Communication :
         EDINFO Press, 1997
Edition  2nd ed

LOCATION              CALL NO.              STATUS
King Reserve          LB1044.87 .C68 1997   CHECK SHELVES

Descript  vi, 234 p. : ill. ; 24 cm
Note     Includes bibliographical references and index
         Introduction to the Internet -- The World Wide Web -- Wealth of Web sites -- Searching
         on the Web -- Developing and designing a Web page -- Advanced Web -- The other
         Internet tools -- E-pals and keypals -- A whale of a time -- The news -- Look who's
         talking! -- Virtually together in D.C. -- The games people play -- The ABCs of the
         Internet -- Get a job! -- Book an hour -- Just for the little kids
Subject  Teaching -- Computer network resources
         Internet (Computer network) in education
         Education -- Computer network resources
Call #   LB1044.87 .C68 1997

Document: Done
```

You can also limit the boundaries of your search, for instance, by specifying that you want items published only before or after a certain date.

5. **Use other resources.** Don't limit yourself only to resources you locate through the library catalog. Your best source of information may be a journal article or other item not listed there. A reference librarian can help you identify other aids to use.

6. **When you go to the library shelves, browse.** Sometimes books that will assist you are located right next to books you found through the library catalog. Don't miss the opportunity to discover them.

INDEXES

Indexes are research aids that focus on specific topics or specific types of publications. Most catalog the contents of periodicals, but some include television programs, films, and similar items. Many indexes are available on-line or on CD-ROM. At some libraries they can be accessed through the same computer screens that provide access to the catalog.

To use indexes well, you need to select ones that cover the kinds of material you want:

■ **General periodical indexes.** They index the contents of publications directed to a general audience. The familiar *Reader's Guide to Periodical Literature* is an example.

■ **Specialized periodical indexes.** Almost every field has at least one. Examples are *Applied Science and Technology Index, Biological and Agricultural Index, Business Periodicals Index,* and *Engineering Index.*

■ **Newspaper indexes.**

Some indexes include abstracts.

Some indexes not only list articles, but also provide an abstract (or summary) of each one. Figure RM.12 shows an index entry that includes an abstract. By scan-

■ **FIGURE RM.12**

Abstract from an Abstracting Index

Bibliographic information, including full information on the article's location

Abstract summarizing the article

Subject headings are given as links to facilitate the location of related articles.

ning through an abstract, you can usually tell whether reading the entire article would be worthwhile.

Find out what indexing terms are used.

Whether you are using a printed or a computerized index, you can often speed your search by looking at the index's thesaurus. Different indexes use different sets of terms. Most publish this list in a thesaurus that can be accessed through a menu selection in the on-line version or found in the front or back of the printed version.

Use "Help" to customize a search.

Computerized indexes work the same way as the library catalog so that you can search by the same variables: author, title, words. Searches can also be limited in similar fashion, although different indexes do this in different ways, so you should look at the "Help" feature for instructions.

REFERENCE WORKS

When you hear the term *reference works*, you probably think immediately (and quite correctly) of encyclopedias, dictionaries, and similar storehouses of knowledge, thousands of pages long. What you may not realize is that many of these resources, such as the *Encyclopedia Americana*, are now available on-line or on CD-ROM, so that finding information in them can be very quick and easy.

In addition to such familiar reference works as the *Encyclopedia Britannica*, thousands of specialized reference works exist, some of which surely relate to your specialty. For example, there are the *Encyclopedia of the Biological Sciences*, *McGraw-Hill Encyclopedia of Science and Technology* (20 volumes), *Elsevier's Medical Dictionary*, *Harper's Dictionary of Music*, and the *Petroleum Dictionary*.

GOVERNMENT DOCUMENTS

Every year, the U.S. Government Printing Office distributes millions of copies of its publications, ranging from pamphlets and brochures to periodicals, reports, and books

(DiMario). Some are addressed to the general public, while others are addressed to specialists in various fields. Sample titles include: *Acid Rain, Chinese Herbal Medicine, Poisonous Snakes of the World,* and *A Report on the U.S. Semiconductor Industry.*

Government publications that may be especially useful to you are reports on research projects undertaken by government agencies or supported by government grants and contracts. Annually, the National Technical Information Service acquires more than 150,000 new reports on topics ranging from nuclear physics to the sociology of Peruvian squatter settlements (DiMario). Chances are great that some relate to your subject.

The following indexes are especially helpful.

Indexes to U.S. Government Publications

- **Monthly Catalog of U.S. Government Publications**
  Publications handled by the Government Printing Office
  http://www.access.gpo.gov/su_docs/dpos/adpos400.html

- **Government Reports Announcements and Index (GRAI)**
  Technical and research reports handled by the National Technical Information Service
  http://www.ntis.gov/search.htm

- **Lists of Publications by Specific Agencies**
  EPA http://www.epa.gov/ncepihom/
  NASA http://techreports.larc.nasa.gov/cgi-bin/NTRS
  National Institutes of Health http://www.nih.gov

- **A reference librarian can help you find many others.**

COMPUTERIZED FULL-TEXT SOURCES

You can download full texts.

Many libraries also offer computer access to the full text of various sources. These include standard reference works, such as the *Encyclopedia Britannica*, and specialized publications such as scientific journals. These utilities allow you to search for topics in the same sorts of ways described in the discussion of the library catalog. When you locate an article of interest, you can read the text on your computer screen, download it to your computer's memory, or print a copy of it.

INTERVIEWING

At work, your best source of information will often be another person. In fact, people will sometimes be your only source of information because you'll be researching situations unique to your organization or its clients and customers. Or you may be asking an expert for information that this person possesses that is not yet available in print or from an on-line source.

The following advice focuses on face-to-face interviews, but it applies also to telephone interviews, which are quite common in the workplace.

PREPARING FOR AN INTERVIEW

Preparing for an interview involves three major activities:

Take a reader-centered approach to selecting your interviewee.

- **Choose the right person to interview.** Approach this selection from your readers' perspective. Pick someone you feel confident can answer the questions your readers are likely to ask in a way that your readers will find useful and credible. If you are seeking someone to interview who is outside your own organization, the directories of professional societies may help you identify an appropriate person.
- **Make arrangements.** If you expect the interview to take more than a few minutes, contact the person in advance to make an appointment. Let the person know the purpose of the interview. This will enable him or her to start thinking about how to assist you before you arrive. Be sure to say how long you think the interview will take. This will enable your interviewee to carve out time for you from all of his or her other responsibilities. Also, if you would like to record the interview, ask permission in advance.

Decide in advance what you hope to learn from the interview.

- **Plan the agenda.** As the interviewer, you will be the person who must identify the topics that need to be discussed. Often, it's best simply to generate a list of topics to inquire about. But if there are specific facts you need to obtain, identify them as well. To protect against forgetting during the interview, bring a written list of your topics and specific questions.

CONDUCTING THE INTERVIEW

Do only 10 percent to 20 percent of the talking.

Unless you are seeking a simple list of facts, your goal in an interview should be to engage the other person in a conversation, not a question-and-answer session. In this conversation, your goal should be to have the other person do 80 percent to 90 percent of the talking—and to have him or her focus on the information you need. To achieve these goals, you will need to ask your questions well and maintain a productive interpersonal relationship with your interviewee. Figure RM.13 suggests practical steps that you can take.

It's especially important that you assume leadership for guiding the interview. You are the person who knows what information you need to obtain on your readers' behalf. Consequently, you may need to courteously redirect the conversation to your topics.

CONCLUDING THE INTERVIEW

End on time.

During the interview, keep your eye on the clock so that you don't take more of your interviewee's time than you requested. As the time limit approaches, do the following:

- **Check your list.** Make sure that all your key questions have been answered.
- **Invite a final thought.** One of the most productive questions that you can ask

■ **FIGURE RM.13**

Creating a Productive Conversation during an Interview

Goal	Guidelines
Establish rapport.	■ Arrive on time.
	■ Thank the person for agreeing to meet with you.
Explain your goal.	■ Tell what you are writing and who your readers will be.
	■ Explain the use your readers will make of your communication.
	■ Describe the outcome you desire.
Ask questions that encourage discussion.	■ Use open questions that ask the interviewee to explain, describe, and discuss. They can elicit valuable information that you might not have thought to ask for. Avoid closed questions that request a yes/no or either/or response.
	Closed question Does the present policy create any problems?
	Open question What are your views of the present policy?
	■ Use neutral, unbiased questions.
	Biased question Don't you think we could improve operations by making this change?
	Neutral question If we made this change, what effect would it have on operations?
	■ Begin with general questions, supplemented by more specific follow-up questions that seek additional details important to you.
	General question Please tell me the history of this policy.
	Follow-up question What role did the labor union play in formulating the policy?

(continued on next page)

near the end of an interview is, "Can you think of anything else I should know?"

■ **Open the door for follow-up.** Ask something like this: "If I find that I need to know a little more about something we've discussed, would it be okay if I called you?"

■ **Thank your interviewee.** If appropriate, send a brief thank-you note by letter, memo, or e-mail.

FIGURE RM 13 *(continued)*	**Show that you are attentive and appreciative.**	• Maintain eye contact and lean forward.
		• Respond with an occasional "uh-huh" or "I see."
		• Comment favorably on the interviewee's statements.
		Examples "That's helpful." "I hadn't thought of that." "This will be useful to my readers."
	Give your interviewee room to help you.	• If the interviewee pauses, be patient. Don't jump in with another question. Assume that he or she is thinking of some additional point. Look at him or her in order to convey that you are waiting to hear whatever he or she will add.
		• If the interviewee begins to offer information out of the order you anticipated, adjust your expectations.
	Keep the conversation on track.	• Preview the topics at the onset.
		• If the interviewee strays seriously from the topic, find a moment to interrupt politely in order to ask another question. You might preface the question by saying something like this: "My readers will be very interested to know..."
	Be sure you understand and remember.	• If anything is unclear, ask for further explanation.
		• On complicated points, paraphrase what your interviewee has said and then ask, "Have I understood correctly?"
		• Take notes. Jot down key points. Don't try to write down everything because that would be distracting and slow the conversation.
		• Double-check the spelling of names, people's titles, and specific figures.

CONDUCTING A SURVEY

Surveys support practical decision-making.

While an interview enables you to gather information from one person, a survey enables you to gather information from *groups* of people.

On the job, surveys are almost always used as the basis for practical decision-making. Manufacturers survey consumers when deciding how to market a new product, and employers survey employees when deciding how to modify personnel policies or benefit packages. Some surveys, such as those used to predict the outcomes of state and national elections, require the use of specialized techniques that are beyond the scope of this book. However, in many situations, you will be able to conduct surveys that provide a solid basis for on-the-job decision-making if you follow the suggestions given in the following sections.

WRITING THE QUESTIONS

The first step in writing survey questions is to decide exactly what you want to learn. Begin by focusing on the decisions that your information will help your readers make. This will help you determine what sorts of information your survey must yield. Consider the following example.

> Roger works for a small restaurant chain that has asked him to study the feasibility of opening a doughnut shop next to a college campus. He already has investigated possible sites and looked into licensing, insurance, wholesale suppliers, and related matters. Now he must find out if there would be enough business to make the shop profitable. As he thinks about the decisions that will be based on his report, he realizes that his employer will be interested not only in predicting the amount of sales but also in learning what kinds of doughnuts, pastries, coffee, and other products to offer; what prices to charge; and even what the opening and closing hours should be. Consequently, Roger must design questions on each of these areas.

Formulate survey questions based on the factors your readers will consider when making their decision.

The following suggestions will help you create an effective questionnaire that provides useful information and elicits the cooperation of the people you ask to fill it out.

- **Mix closed and open questions.** *Closed questions* allow only a limited number of possible responses. They provide answers that are easy to tabulate. *Open questions* allow the respondent freedom in devising the answer. They provide respondents an opportunity to react to your subject matter in their own terms. See Figure RM.14.
- You may want to follow each of your closed questions with an open one that simply asks respondents to comment. A good way to conclude a survey is to invite additional comments.
- **Ask reliable questions.** A *reliable* question is one that every respondent will understand and interpret in the same way. For instance, if Roger asked, "Do you like high quality pastries?" different readers might interpret the term "high quality" in different ways. Roger might instead ask how much the respondents would be willing to pay for pastries or what kinds of snacks they like to eat with their coffee.
- **Ask valid questions.** A *valid* question is one that produces the information you are seeking. For example, to determine how much business the doughnut shop might attract, Roger could ask either of these two questions:

Invalid　| How much do you like doughnuts?

Valid　| How many times a month would you visit a doughnut shop located within three blocks of campus?

- The first question is invalid because the fact that students like doughnuts does not necessarily mean that they would patronize a doughnut shop. The second question is valid because it can help Roger estimate how many customers the shop would have.

REFERENCE GUIDE: Five Research Methods

■ FIGURE RM.14

Closed and Open Questions for Surveys

Closed Questions

Forced Choice
- Respondents must select one of two choices (yes/no, either/or).

  Example
  Would you buy doughnuts at a shop near campus, yes or no?

Multiple Choice
- Respondents select from several predefined alternatives.

  How many times a month would you visit the shop?
  _____ I to 2   _____ 3 to 4   _____ 5 or more

Ranking
- Respondents indicate an order of preference.

  Example
  Please rank the following types of doughnuts, using a I for your favorite, and so on...

Rating
- Respondents pick a number on a scale.

  Example
  Please circle the number on the following scale that best describes the importance of the following features of a doughnut shop:

  Music   Unimportant   I   2   3   4   5   Important
  Tables   Unimportant   I   2   3   4   5   Important

Open Questions

Fill in the Blank
- Respondents complete a statement.

  Example
  When deciding where to eat a late-night snack, I usually base my choice on _____ .

Essay
- Respondents can frame responses in any way they choose.

  Example
  Please suggest ways we could make a doughnut shop that would be appealing to you.

- **Avoid biased questions.** Don't phrase your questions in ways that seem to guide your respondents to give a particular response.

  Biased | Wouldn't it be good to have a coffee shop near campus?
  Unbiased | How much would you like to have a coffee shop near campus?

- **Place your most interesting questions first.** Save questions about the respondent's age or similar characteristics until the end.
- **Limit the number of questions.** If your questionnaire is lengthy, people may not complete it. Decide what you really need to know and ask only about that.

Be sure that your questionnaire works before you distribute it.

- **Test your questionnaire.** Even small changes in wording may have a substantial effect on the way people respond. Questions that seem perfectly clear to you may appear puzzling or ambiguous to others. Before completing your survey, try out your questions with a few people from your target group.

CONTACTING RESPONDENTS

There are three methods for presenting your survey to your respondents:

Don't bias your respondents' answers.

- **Face-to-face.** In this method, you read your questions aloud to each respondent and record his or her answers on a form. It's an effective method of contacting respondents because people are more willing to cooperate when someone asks for their help in person than they are when asked to fill out a printed questionnaire. The only risk is that your intonation, facial expressions, or body language may signal that you are hoping for a certain answer. Research shows that respondents tend to give answers that will please the questioner.
- **Telephone.** Telephone surveys are convenient for the writer. However, it can sometimes be difficult to use a phone book to identify people who represent the group of people being studied.

Response rates can be very low.

- **Mail or handout.** Mailing or handing your survey forms to people you hope will respond is less time consuming than conducting a survey face-to-face or by telephone. Generally, however, only a small portion of the people who receive survey forms in these ways actually fill them out and return them. Even professional survey specialists typically receive responses from only about 20 percent of the people they contact.

SELECTING YOUR RESPONDENTS

At work, writers sometimes present their survey questions to every person who belongs to the group whose attitudes or practices they want to learn about. For example, an employee assigned to learn what others in her company feel about a proposed change in health care benefits or a switch to flextime scheduling might send a survey questionnaire to every employee.

Your sample should reflect the composition of the overall group.

However, surveys are often designed to permit the writers to generalize about a large group of people (called a *population*) by surveying only a small portion of individuals in the group (called a *sample*). To ensure that the sample is truly representative of the population, you must select the sample carefully. Here are four types of samples you can use:

- **Simple random sample.** Here, every member of the population has an equal chance of being chosen for the sample. If the population is small, you could put the name of every person into a hat, then draw out the names to be included in your sample. If the population is large—all the students at a major university, for example—the creation of a simple random sample can be difficult.
- **Systematic random sample.** To create a systematic random sample, you start with a list that includes every person in the population—perhaps by using a phone book or student directory. Then you devise some pattern or rule for

REFERENCE GUIDE: Five Research Methods

choosing the people who will make up your sample. For instance, you might choose the fourteenth name on each page of the list.

Convenience samples can give unreliable results.

- **Convenience sample.** To set up a convenience sample, you select people who are handy and who resemble in some way the population you want to survey. For example, if your population is the student body, you might knock on every fifth door in your dormitory, or stop every fifth student who walks into the library. The weakness of such samples is obvious: from the point of view of the attitudes or behaviors you want to learn about, the students who live with their parents or in apartments may be significantly different from those who live in dorms, just as those who don't go to the library may differ in substantial ways from those who do.

- **Stratified sample.** Creating a stratified sample is one way to partially overcome the shortcomings of a convenience sample. For instance, if you know that 15 percent of the students in your population live at home, 25 percent live in apartments, and 60 percent live in dormitories, you would find enough representatives of each group so that they constituted 15 percent, 25 percent, and 60 percent of your sample. Even if you can't choose the people in each group randomly, you would have made some progress toward creating a sample that accurately represents your population.

Use enough respondents to persuade your readers.

When creating your sample, you must determine how many people to include. On the one hand, you want a manageable number, but on the other hand, you also want enough people to form the basis for valid generalizations. Statisticians use formulas to decide on the appropriate sample size, but in many on-the-job situations, writers rely on their common sense. One good way to decide is to ask what number of people your readers would consider to be sufficient.

PART IV

Drafting Prose Elements

CHAPTER 7
Drafting Paragraphs, Sections, and Chapters

REFERENCE GUIDE
Six Patterns for Organizing

CHAPTER 8
Beginning a Communication

CHAPTER 9
Ending a Communication

CHAPTER 10
Creating an Effective Style

Drafting Paragraphs, Sections, and Chapters

GUIDELINES

1 | Begin by announcing your topic

2 | Present your generalizations before your details

3 | Move from most important to least important

4 | Reveal your organization

5 | Consult conventional strategies when faced with organizational difficulties

6 | Consider your readers' cultural background when organizing

CHAPTER

DEFINING OBJECTIVES
PLANNING
DRAFTING
EVALUATING
REVISING

This chapter marks a major transition in your study of on-the-job writing. In the preceding four chapters, you learned how to define your objectives and create plans for achieving them. In this chapter, you will learn how to transform your plans into action as you draft your communication.

Sometimes you will draft your communication very rapidly. You will simply sit down, write your draft, and send it off without making any changes at all. That will usually happen, however, only when you are writing very short communications on

Writers spend varying amounts of time drafting— sometimes hours per page.

routine matters. Longer, less routine, more critical messages require greater effort. For example, in response to a survey, 122 professional and managerial personnel said that when they prepare reports they spend an average of three hours on each page (Kelton).

This chapter and the next five will help you draft clear, persuasive messages— and do so as efficiently as possible. Four chapters (plus a reference guide) focus on your prose, and two focus on visual elements of your communication: your visual aids and your page design.

APPLYING THIS CHAPTER'S ADVICE

This chapter will help you draft paragraphs. Its advice will also help you construct the groups of paragraphs that make up the sections of larger communications, and its advice applies even to whole communications in their entirety. For convenience's sake, this chapter uses the word *segments* to designate these variously sized units.

Why can this chapter's advice apply with equal validity to segments that range in size from a few sentences to an entire communication that may be tens or hundreds of pages long? There are two reasons:

- **All segments, regardless of size, have the same basic structure.** You may have heard a paragraph defined as a group of sentences about the same subject. With only slight variation, that definition applies equally well to larger segments: a subsection is a group of paragraphs on the same subject, a section is a group of subsections on the same subject, and so on.
- **All segments make the same basic demand on readers.** To understand a segment, whether it is a short paragraph or an entire communication, readers must determine what its topic is and how its various parts (sentences, paragraphs, etc.) fit together. This includes knowing which of the points discussed is most important, which of the problems identified is most serious, and which of the recommended actions is most urgent.

Longer segments usually have a hierarchical structure.

Longer communications usually contain several sizes of segments, with smaller ones embedded in larger ones—paragraphs embedded in sections, sections embedded in chapters, and chapters embedded in the overall communication. This embedding occurs when writers follow Chapter 4's suggestion that they aid their readers by organizing their communications hierarchically.

You will find the suggestions in this chapter to be especially helpful when you wish to transform a hierarchically organized outline into smooth, easy-to-read prose. Creating this transformation is no easy task because the outline and the prose will differ in many important ways. Consider the following example.

This chapter's guidelines are especially helpful for long, hierarchically organized communications.

Jonathan works for an engineering consulting firm whose clients include amusement parks, museums, and similar businesses. For his first major writing assignment, he was asked to create a proposal that would persuade a financially troubled zoo to undertake a series of construction projects that would increase the zoo's revenue by attracting more visitors. Figures 7.1 and 7.2 show the complex relationship between his outline and his prose. For example, some elements that are distinct in the outline are joined in the prose under the same heading—and even in the same paragraph.

Yet the prose flows smoothly and is easy to follow. Jonathan was able to achieve this result throughout his proposal by applying this chapter's advice to all the proposal's segments—from the report in its entirety to the individual chapters, sections, subsections, and paragraphs.

This chapter's six guidelines will assist you with the following writing activities:

- Organizing the contents of your segments—Guidelines 1 through 3.
- Making this organization evident to your readers—Guideline 4.
- Using a helpful source of organizational patterns—Guideline 5.
- Organizing for readers from a culture different from your own—Guideline 6.

GUIDELINE **1** **Begin by Announcing Your Topic**

You have undoubtedly heard that you should begin your paragraphs with topic sentences. This guideline extends that advice to all your segments, large and small. Begin every segment with a topic statement that tells your readers what the segment is about.

How Topic Statements Help Readers

Why are topic statements so important? In order to understand a segment, readers must establish in their own minds a meaningful pattern to the various pieces of information conveyed within it. Unless the writer helps, this task of meaningful construction can be very difficult. Consider, for example, the following sentences from a technical report written by an engineer at a coal-fired electric plant.

Paragraphs without topic statements can be difficult to understand.

Companies that make cement and wallboard cannot use wet gypsum cakes. The cakes must be transformed into dry pellets, using a process called agglomeration. We could enter the agglomeration business ourselves or hire another company to agglomerate the gypsum for us. Also, the chloride content of the cakes is too high for use in wallboard. Our engineers can probably devise inexpensive cake-washing equipment that will reduce the chlorides to an acceptable level.

■ FIGURE 7.1 Chapters, Sections, and Subsections as Planned in an Outline

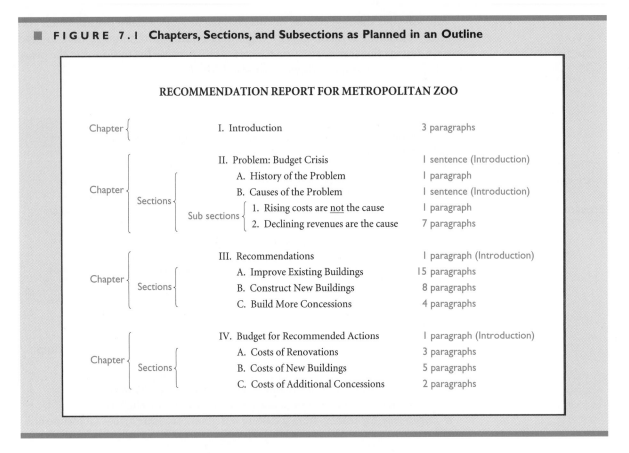

You could probably figure out what this paragraph is about if you studied it long enough. But your job as a reader would be much easier if the writer had added a statement telling you what it is about. Read the following topic statement and then read the paragraph again:

Topic statement | Before we can sell the gypsum produced by our stack scrubbers, we will have to process the wet gypsum cakes they produce.

Why Topic Statements Help Most at the Beginning of a Segment

Topic statements are helpful no matter where they appear in a segment, but they are especially helpful at the beginning. To understand why, consider two thinking strategies people use when reading:

- **Bottom-up processing.** In bottom-up processing, readers proceed in much the same way as people who are working a jigsaw puzzle without having seen a picture that tells them what the finished puzzle will look like. As they read, they try to guess how the small bits of information they gather from individual sentences fit together to form a general meaning for the paragraph, section, or chapter.
- **Top-down processing.** In top-down processing, readers proceed like people who have seen a picture of the finished jigsaw puzzle before they begin. Because

■ **FIGURE 7.2**

The Sections and Subsections of a Report (Compare with Figure 7.1)

Corresponds to section II.A. in outline

Corresponds to section II.B. in outline

Corresponds to section II.B.1. in outline

Corresponds to section II.B.2. in outline

Chapter 2
PROBLEM: BUDGET CRISIS

The Metropolitan Zoo faces a severe budget crisis. The crisis first surfaced last August, when the zoo discovered that operating expenses for the year were going to exceed income by $247,000. Emergency measures, including a reduction in working hours for some employees, lowered the actual loss by December 31 to $121,000. However, the zoo faces similar difficulties again this year—and in future years—unless effective measures are taken.

Causes of the Problem

What is causing this budget crisis, which first appeared in a year when the zoo thought it would enjoy a large profit? The crisis is <u>not</u> caused by rising costs. In fact, the zoo actually reduced operating costs by 3% last year. (This figure does not include the additional reduction brought about by the emergency measures taken in August.) The greatest savings in operating costs were related to energy expenses. The new power plant began operation, reducing fuel consumption by 15%. Also, design changes in the three largest animal houses conserved enough heat to reduce their heating expenses by 9%, which is 2% more than the zoo itself first estimated. Finally, a new method of ordering and paying for supplies has lowered expenses by enough to offset inflation.

The budget crisis is caused instead by declining revenues. During the past year income from admission fees, concession sales, and donations has dropped. Because of the decline in paid admissions, overall income from this source was $57,344 less last year than the year before.
[This discussion of falling revenue continues for two pages.]

they know the communication's overall structure in advance, they know immediately where to place the information they obtain from individual sentences.

Top-down processing is more efficient than bottom-up processing.

Although readers engage continuously in both processes, the more top-down processing they can perform while reading, the more easily they can understand and remember the message. To demonstrate that, researchers asked two groups of people to listen to the following passage being read aloud (Branford and Johnson).

Passage used in an
experiment that
demonstrated the
importance of top-down
processing

The procedure is actually quite simple. First you arrange things into different groups. Of course, one pile may be sufficient depending on how much there is to do. If you have to go somewhere else due to lack of facilities, that is the next step; otherwise you are pretty well set. It is important not to overdo things. That is, it is better to do too few things at once than too many. In the short run this may not seem important but complications can easily arise. A mistake can be expensive as well. At first the whole procedure will seem complicated. Soon, however, it will become just another facet of life. . . . After the procedure is completed, one arranges the materials into different groups again. Then they can be put into their appropriate places. Eventually they will be used once more and the whole cycle will then have to be repeated. However, that is part of life.

Initial topic statements
promote top-down
processing.

The researchers told one group the topic of this passage in advance; they told the other group afterwards. Then they asked both groups to write down everything they remembered from what they had heard. People who had been told the topic (washing clothes) before hearing the passage remembered much more than those who were told afterwards.

Topic statements placed at the beginning of segments also help readers who are skimming through your communication for particular facts or who want to spot your main points without reading the whole text.

As a general rule, use topic statements at the beginning of all segments, small and large. When you do this, you will create a hierarchy of topic statements. Figure 7.3 shows how Jonathan, in a passage from his report to the zoo, provided topic statements that interlock to form a hierarchy that corresponds to what he planned in Section II of his outline (Figure 7.1).

How to Indicate Your Topic

There are many ways to indicate the topic of a segment:

- **Use a sentence.** An example is the first sentence of the paragraph you are now reading.
- **Use a single word.** For example, the first word ("First") of the second sentence in the passage about washing clothes tells the reader, "You are now going to read a segment that explains the steps in the 'simple procedure' just mentioned."
- **Use a question.** For example, the question ("Why are topic statements so important?") that begins the second paragraph in the discussion of this guideline told you that you were about to read a segment explaining the importance of topic statements.

Whether you use a sentence, a word, a question, or some other device, remember to help your readers understand each segment by telling them at the outset what the segment is about.

GUIDELINE ② **Present Your Generalizations before Your Details**

When announcing the topic at the beginning of a segment, it is usually helpful to also state the general point you want to make about your topic. For instance, instead of saying only, "The topic of this section is the relative costs of shipping our

■ **FIGURE 7.3**

Topic Statements Used in Three Levels of the Report Outlined in Figure 7.1

Topic announced for chapter (whole discussion of the budget crisis)

Topic announced for first section (history of the crisis)

Topic announced for second section (causes of the crisis)

Topic announced for first subsection (one possible cause: rising costs)

Topic announced for second subsection (second possible cause: falling revenues)

Chapter 2
PROBLEM: BUDGET CRISIS

The Metropolitan Zoo faces a severe budget crisis. The crisis first surfaced last August, when the zoo discovered that operating expenses for the year were going to exceed income by $247,000. Emergency measures, including a reduction in working hours for some employees, lowered the actual loss by December 31 to $121,000. However, the zoo faces similar difficulties again this year—and in future years—unless effective measures are taken.

Causes of the Problem

What is causing this budget crisis, which first appeared in a year when the zoo thought it would enjoy a large profit? The crisis is <u>not</u> caused by rising costs. In fact, the zoo actually reduced operating costs by 3% last year. (This figure does not include the additional reduction brought about by the emergency measures taken in August.) The greatest savings in operating costs were related to energy expenses. The new power plant began operation, reducing fuel consumption by 15%. Also, design changes in the three largest animal houses conserved enough heat to reduce their heating expenses by 9%, which is 2% more than the zoo itself first estimated. Finally, a new method of ordering and paying for supplies has lowered expenses by enough to offset inflation.

The budget crisis is caused instead by declining revenues. During the past year income from admission fees, concession sales, and donations has dropped. Because of the decline in paid admissions, overall income from this source was $57,344 less last year than the year before.
[This discussion of falling revenues continues for two pages.]

company's products by truck and by train," you might say, "We can save 15 percent on transportation costs by shipping certain products by train rather than by truck."

How Initial Generalizations Strengthen Your Writing

Presenting your generalizations before your details strengthens your writing in three ways:

- **Initial generalizations make writing more understandable.** When you present your generalizations first, you save your readers the work of figuring out what your main point is. Imagine, for instance, that you are a manager who finds the following sentences in a report:

> Using the sampling technique described above, we passed a gas sample containing 500 micrograms of VCM through the tube in a test chamber set at 25°C. Afterwards, we divided the charcoal in the sampling tube into two equal parts. The front half of the tube contained approximately 2/3 of the charcoal while the back half contained the rest. Analysis of the back half of the tube revealed no VCM; the front half contained the entire 500 micrograms.

As you read these details, you probably find yourself asking, "So what?" Because you are concentrating on trying to discern the answer, you will probably remember fewer details from the passage than if the writer had begun the segment with the following statement:

> We have conducted a test that demonstrates the ability of our sampling tube to absorb the necessary amount of VCM under the conditions specified.

- **Initial generalizations make your writing more useful.** Placement of the generalization at the head of the paragraph would also help you perform your managerial task of determining whether the conclusion is valid, based on the evidence. You may ultimately reject the writer's inference, but at least the writer has lightened your task by announcing it up front so that you know in advance what conclusion each piece of the writer's evidence is supposed to support.
- **Initial generalizations make writing more persuasive.** Left to themselves, readers are capable of deriving all sorts of generalizations from a passage. Consider the following sentences:

> Richard moved the gas chromatograph to the adjacent lab.
> He also moved the electronic balance.
> And he moved the experimental laser.

Left to themselves, different readers will draw different conclusions from the same facts.

One reader might note that everything Richard moved is a piece of laboratory equipment and might generalize that "Richard moved some laboratory equipment from one place to another." Another reader might observe that everything Richard moved was heavy and might generalize that "Richard is strong." A member of a labor union in Richard's organization might generalize that "Richard was doing work that should have been done by a union member, not by a manager" and might file a grievance. Different generalizations lead to different outcomes.

Present your generalization before your readers begin to formulate contradictory ones.

A key point is that readers naturally formulate generalizations even if none are provided. Of course, when you are writing persuasively you will want your readers to draw one particular conclusion — and not other possible ones. You can increase your chances of succeeding by stating your desired generalization explicitly and by placing that generalization ahead of your supporting details so that your readers encounter it before forming a different generalization on their own.

When Not to Present Your Generalizations First

Although it is usually best to present your generalizations at the beginning of a segment, it is sometimes better to withhold them until later. As you found in Chapter 5, you would probably not want to launch a segment with a generalization that is likely to provoke a negative reaction from your readers. In such a case, it would be better to wait until you have laid the relevant groundwork. Review Chapter 5's discussion of the indirect organizational pattern for advice about what to do under such circumstances.

How Guideline 2 Relates to Guideline 1

Taken together, Guidelines 1 and 2 advise you to begin your segments by announcing your topic and also to state your main point about your topic in that place. Often, you will be able to make your writing more concise and forceful by doing both in a single sentence. Consider, for instance, the opening of a two-page discussion of experimental results.

Separate sentences state the topic and the writer's generalization.

> We conducted tests to determine whether the plastic resins can be used to replace metal in the manufacture of the CV-200 housing. The tests showed that there are three shortcomings in plastic resins that make them unsuitable as a replacement for the metal.

In this first draft, the first sentence announces the topic of the segment (the tests), and the second states the writer's generalization about the topic (the resins are not a good substitute for metal). When revising, the writer saved words by combining both topic and generalization in a single sentence:

Topic and generalization are combined in one sentence.

> Our tests showed three shortcomings in plastic resins that make them unsuitable as a replacement for metal in the manufacture of the CV-200 housing.

GUIDELINE 3 ### Move from Most Important to Least Important

Guidelines 1 and 2 discussed the way you begin your segments. This guideline focuses instead on the way you order the material that follows your opening sentence or sentences. It applies particularly to passages in which you present parallel pieces of information, such as a list of five recommendations or an explanation of three causes of a problem. Whether you present each item in a single sentence or in several paragraphs, put the most important item first and then proceed in descending order of importance.

Initial placement gives emphasis and helps readers who scan.

Putting the most important information first emphasizes that information and helps readers (such as decision makers) who are scanning your communication find the key points. Moreover, it increases the likelihood that this most important information will be read. At work, people frequently suffer interruptions when they are reading and may never get back to what they were doing. Moreover, if you start off with unimportant points, your readers may quit paying attention before they reach the important ones.

Determine what's most important by considering your readers' viewpoint.

To decide what information is most important, consider your readers' viewpoint. What information will they be most interested in or find most persuasive? For example, in the segment on the three shortcomings of plastic resins, readers will certainly be more interested in the major shortcoming than in the minor ones. Similarly, if they have to be persuaded to accept the writer's generalization that plastic resins aren't a good substitute for metal, they are sure to find the major shortcoming more compelling than the others.

Sometimes the most important information shouldn't be first.

In some situations, however, you may need to withhold your most important information in order to present your overall message clearly and economically. For instance, if you are listing the causes of something and their historical relationship is significant, the second cause may be the most important; however, because it is an outgrowth of an earlier, less significant development, you must present the lesser cause first. In general, though, presenting the most important information first will be most persuasive and helpful to your readers.

GUIDELINE 4   **Reveal Your Organization**

In addition to organizing your segments, you need to "reveal" that organization by drawing a "map" of it for your readers.

"But," you may ask, "if I've organized my communication carefully, why will my readers need a map of it? Won't a good, sensible organization be obvious to them?" Not necessarily. Communications contain two distinct kinds of information:

A communication's two kinds of information

- Information about the subject matter
- Information about how the writer has organized the discussion of this subject matter

Figure 7.4 illustrates the relationship between these two kinds of information.

When you read something that you yourself wrote, you see clearly both kinds of information, even if you included only subject-matter information and no organizational information. That's because you created the organization yourself.

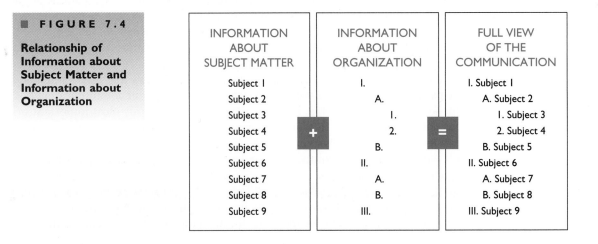

■ FIGURE 7.4

Relationship of Information about Subject Matter and Information about Organization

■ **FIGURE 7.5** **Comparision of the Writer's View and the Reader's View of a Communication if the Writer Neglects to Include Organizational Information**

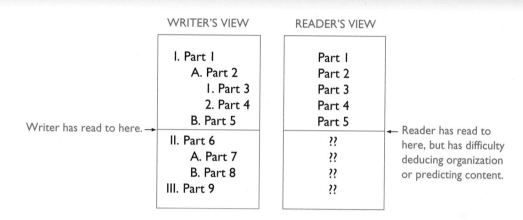

Forecasting Statements

Your readers, however, must construct a mental map of your organization as they read. As Figure 7.5 indicates, their map can look very different from yours if you don't supplement information about your subject matter with information about your organization. To puzzle out the organization of such a document, readers must perform a lot of difficult work. To see how much work is required, try to convert the table of contents shown in Figure 7.6 (page 176) into an outline. (The topics are listed in the correct order; your job is simply to reveal the hierarchical relationships among them.)

Readers need your help in constructing a mental map of your communication.

In contrast, when a writer provides a good map of his or her message, readers can discern the organization without knowing anything at all about the content. Look, for example, at Figure 7.7 (page 177), which shows a page written in Japanese. Even if you cannot read the language, the writers have provided enough organizational information for you to grasp the structure of the presentation.

The following sections discuss four techniques you can use simultaneously to reveal the organization of a communication.

Forecasting Statements

Forecasting statements tell readers what's coming up.

Although your topic statement tells your readers what the segment is about, it tells them nothing about how you have *organized* the segment. Consider the following sentence, which opens a section of a brochure published by a large chain of garden nurseries:

| Our first topic is the trees found in the American Southwest.

This sentence is a straightforward statement of what the section is about, but it gives no hint of the way in which the section has been organized. It might, for example, discuss evergreen trees first and then deciduous trees. Or it might first discuss healthy trees and then diseased ones. Or it might be organized in any of various other ways. Readers would have no way of knowing.

■ **FIGURE 7.6**

Table of Contents from an Instruction Manual Whose Writer has Failed to Provide Organizational Information

<table>
<tr><td colspan="3" align="center">**Pegasus Automatic Balance**</td></tr>
</table>

1.	Introduction	1
2.	Right-Hand Application Knob	2
3.	Left-Hand Application Knob	2
4.	Micrometer Knob	3
5.	Zero-Point Adjustment Knob	4
6.	Right-Hand and Left-Hand Weight Dials	5
7.	Projection Weight Dial	5
8.	General Features of the Weighing Components	6
9.	Special Features of the Weighing Pan	6
10.	Special Features of the Weighing Stirrup	7
11.	Adjusting the Sensitivity	8
12.	Adjusting the Zero Point	9
13.	Determining Weight	9
14.	Weighing to a Preselected Weight	10

To tell your readers in advance about the organization of a passage, begin with a *forecasting statement.* You might use a full sentence to supplement your topic statement:

Forecasting statement | Our first topic is the trees found in the American Southwest. <u>Some of the trees are native, some imported.</u>

Or you might announce the topic and forecast the organization in a single sentence:

Forecasting statement | Our first topic is the trees—<u>both native and imported</u>—found in the American Southwest.

Forecasting statements may vary greatly in the amount of detail they provide. The sample sentences above provide both the number and the names of the categories to be discussed. A more general preview is the one below, which tells its readers to expect a list of actions but not what these actions are or how many will be discussed:

Forecasting statement | To solve this problem, the department must take the following actions.

When deciding how much detail to include in a forecasting statement, consider the following points:

- **Provide enough detail so that your readers will know something specific about the arrangement of the section that follows.** Usually, the more complex the relationship among the parts, the greater the amount of detail that is needed.
- **Do not provide more detail than your readers can easily remember.** The purpose of a forecasting statement is to help your readers to understand what is to come, not to test their memory. If you are introducing the three steps of a solu-

■ **FIGURE 7.7**

Page Printed in Japanese

From *Dell Computer, Dell Ultra Scan 1000HS; Model D1025TM Color Monitor User's Guide* (Austin, Tx: Dell Computer, 1998) 61.

The gray block gives primary emphasis to the page's title.

Large, bold type shows where major sections begin.

Indentation signals subordination.

A table provides another way of using visual design to signal the organization of information.

画面の調整

調整のしかた

1 色温度調整画面を操作する

色温度調整画面では色温度を変えることができます。画面の色を印刷したものと同じ色になるように変えたいときなどに使います。色温度は9300K（青みがかった白）から5000K（暖色の赤）まで調整できます。
この調整はすべての入力信号に対して有効です。

1　MENUボタンを押す。MENU画面が表示されます。
2　ブライトネスまたはコントラストボタンを押して 色温度調整を選び、MENU ボタンを押す。
3　ブライトネスボタン☼↓/↑を押して9300K、5000K、あるいは🔳のオプションのどれかを選択します。
　● お買い上げ時は、2種類の色温度が設定されています。出荷時の設定は9300K、5000Kです。
　● 🔳のオプションでは、全色温度を使ってディスプレイの設定が可能です。コントラストボタンを押してご希望の色温度に調整してください。
4　MENUボタンを一度押すとMENU画面 に戻ります。二度押すと、通常の画面に戻ります。

ご注意
GEM（Graphic Enhancement Mode）を使用時の色温度調整は9300Kから11000Kの間での調整となります。GEMについて詳しくは、64ページの「Graphic Enhancement Mode（GEM）」の項を参照してください。

2 位置調整画面を操作する

位置調整画面では画像の位置を調整できます。この調整は現在受信している入力信号に対してのみ有効です。

1　MENUボタンを押す。MENU画面表示されます。
2　ブライトネスおよびコントラストボタンを押して、「位置調整」を選び、MENUボタンを押す。
3　垂直方向は、ブライトネスボタン☼↓/↑で調整する。
4　水平方向は、コントラストボタン◐←/→で調整する。
5　MENUボタンを一度押すとMENU画面 に戻ります。二度押すと、通常の画面に戻ります。

3 画調整画面を操作する

画調整画面では、コンバージェンスの調整とモアレ調整ができます。コンバージェンスが良い場合は画面上の赤、緑、青の電子ビームが正しく整列しています。コンバージェンスが正しく整列していない場合は、赤または青の影が見えること（特にテキストで）があります。これは画像の明瞭度、またはフォーカスに影響を与えます。モアレは画面上に現れる波模様や点状模様です。モアレを少なくするために、モアレのキャンセル調整を行います。
この調整はすべての入力信号に対して有効です。

1　MENUボタンを押す。MENU画面が表示されます。
2　ブライトネスまたはコントラストボタンを押して、「画調整」を選び、MENUボタンを押す。
3　ブライトネスボタン☼↓/↑を押して希望の調整項目を選びます。
4　コントラストボタン◐←/→を押して調整する。
5　MENUボタンを一度押すとMENU画面に戻ります。二度押すと、通常の画面に戻ります。

項目	機能
⊞ Hコンバージェンス	水平方向のコンバージェンスを調整します。
⊟ V コンバージェンス	垂直方向のコンバージェンスを調整します。
▥ モアレキャンセル	画面上の点状あるいは波形の線を少なくします。
▥ * モアレ調整	モアレキャンセルの効果を調整します。

* ▥ （モアレ調整）は、モアレキャンセルが「オン」の状態のときに現れます。

J

61

tion, you might want to name them before explaining them. However, if the solution contains eight steps, you will be better off stating the number of steps without naming them.

■ **Do not forecast more than one level at a time.** Don't try to list all the contents of a communication at its outset. That will only confuse your readers. Tick off only the major divisions of a particular section. If those divisions are themselves divided, provide each of them with its own forecasting statement.

Like topic statements, forecasting statements give readers a sense of the meaning and organization of what follows and help them to read and remember your message.

Transitions

As readers proceed from one part of a communication to another—from sentence to sentence, paragraph to paragraph, and section to section—they must figure out how these parts relate to one another. Chapter 10 ("Creating an Effective Style") tells how to lead readers smoothly from one sentence to the next. The discussion that follows explains how to construct transitional statements that help readers move between larger units of prose—from one paragraph or group of paragraphs to the next.

Transitional statements indicate two things. First, they tell what the upcoming segment is about. In this way, they often serve as topic sentences. Second, they indicate the relationship of what is coming and what has just ended.

How to Write a Transition   You can write transitions in a variety of ways. For example, you can be quite literal: "We are now making a transition from one topic to the next." You might take two sentences to do that:

Transition statement | In our guidelines for handling Exban, we have now completed our suggestions for guarding against accidental spills during transportation. We turn now to our guidelines for storing the product.

In more subtle transitions, you might use only a word or a phrase to allude to the discussion just completed:

Transition statements | After we developed our hypothesis, we were ready to design our experiment.
Having described the proposed accounting procedure, we will now discuss its advantages over the present one.

In the examples above, the introductory phrase reminds readers of what was described in the preceding section. The rest of the sentence tells what will be discussed in the next section.

Or you might include the reference to the section just completed in the main clause rather than in an introductory phrase:

Transition statements | We then designed an experiment to test our hypothesis.
The proposed accounting procedure has several advantages over the present one.

These sample transitions all would appear at the opening of the passage. However, transitions occasionally come at the end of a passage. Here is the last sentence of a section in a report about the sales performance of Big Q soft drinks over the past year:

Transition statement at the end of a segment | Against this background information concerning the factors affecting the soft-drink market overall, the performance of the Big Q line can be interpreted more precisely.

The following section then begins with a topic statement:

Topic statement for next segment | During the past twelve months, Big Q soft drinks performed extremely well in the parts of the market that were generally weak, but they performed below average in those that were strong.

Other Means of Making Transitions   Sometimes you can signal transitions without using any words at all. For example, in a report that presents three brief recommendations, you might arrange the recommendations in a numbered list. The numbers themselves would provide the transition from one recommendation to the next. Similarly, in a memo covering a number of separate topics, the transition from one to the next might be provided by a simple heading for each topic (see the discussion of headings below).

You can also make transitions through visual design.

Headings

A third technique for revealing organization is to use headings. Headings are signposts that tell readers what the successive parts of a communication are about. At work, writers use headings not only in long documents, such as reports and manuals, but also in short ones, such as letters and memos. To see how effectively the insertion of headings can reveal organization, look at Figures 7.8 (page 180) and 7.9 (page 181), which show two versions of the same memo, one without headings and one with headings.

Headings are used extensively in on-the-job writing.

How to Phrase Headings   Usually, headings are simply inserted into the text, with no change in the accompanying prose. To be helpful, they must tell clearly and specifically what kind of information is included in the passages they label. Vague headings provide no aid at all. Here are three strategies for writing headings that your readers will find helpful:

- **Ask the question that the segment will answer for your readers.** Headings that ask questions such as, "What happens if I miss a payment on my loan?" or "Can I pay off my loan early?" are especially useful in communications designed to help readers decide what to do.
- **State the main idea of the segment.** This strategy was used by the person who wrote the brochure on bicycling safety shown in Figure 7.10 (page 182). Headings such as "Ride with the Traffic" and "Use Streets with Parked Cars" are particularly effective in focusing readers' attention on the key point of a passage.
- **Use a key word or phrase.** This type of heading is especially effective when you are writing a communication in which a full question or statement would be unnecessarily wordy. Imagine, for instance, that you are writing a feasibility report on purchasing a multimedia production system for the sales department you manage. For the section that discusses prices, you might use this heading: "How Much Will This Equipment Cost?" The simple heading "Cost" would serve the same purpose.

Should you restrict yourself to only one type of heading in a particular communication, so that the headings are all questions, all statements, or all key words? Not necessarily. Each heading has its own function—to announce the topic of the following section clearly and usefully. In many communications, different sections require different types of headings.

Often, however, your best choice is to use parallel headings for parallel segments, such as when you are describing a series of steps in a process (opening the computer program, entering the data, and so on). The parallel phrasing cues readers that the sections being labeled are logically parallel.

Parallelism in headings is often desirable.

Text continued on page 183

■ **FIGURE 7.8**

Memo without Headings (Compare with Figure 7.9)

The lack of visual cues hides the organization of this memo's contents.

Garibaldi Corporation
INTEROFFICE MEMORANDUM

June 15, 19—

TO   Vice Presidents and Department Managers
FROM   Davis M. Pritchard, President
RE   PURCHASES OF COMPUTER AND FAX EQUIPMENT

Three months ago, I appointed a task force to develop corporate-wide policies for the purchase of computers and fax equipment. Based on the advice of the task force, I am establishing the following policies.

The task force was to balance two possibly conflicting objectives: (1) to ensure that each department purchase the equipment that best serves its special needs and (2) to ensure compatibility among the equipment purchased so the company can create an efficient electronic network for all our computer and fax equipment.

I am designating one "preferred" vendor of computers and two "secondary" vendors.

The preferred vendor, YYY, is the vendor from which all purchases should be made unless there is a compelling reason for selecting other equipment. To encourage purchases from the preferred vendor, a special corporate fund will cover 30% of the purchase price so that individual departments need fund only 70%.

Two other vendors, AAA and MMM, offer computers already widely used in Garibaldi; both computers are compatible with our plans to establish a computer network. Therefore, the special corporate fund will support 10% of the purchase price of these machines.

We will select one preferred vendor and no secondary vendor for fax equipment. The task force will choose between two candidates: FFF and TTT. I will notify you when the choice is made early next month.

■ **FIGURE 7.9**

Memo with Headings (Compare with Figure 7.8)

Garibaldi Corporation
INTEROFFICE MEMORANDUM

June 15, 19—

TO   Vice Presidents and Department Managers
FROM   Davis M. Pritchard, President
RE   PURCHASES OF COMPUTER AND FAX EQUIPMENT

Three months ago, I appointed a task force to develop corporate-wide policies for the purchase of computers and fax equipment. Based on the advice of the task force, I am establishing the following policies.

Objectives of Policies

The task force was to balance two possibly conflicting objectives: (1) to ensure that each department purchase the equipment that best serves its special needs and (2) to ensure compatibility among the equipment purchased so the company can create an efficient electronic network for all our computer and fax equipment.

Computer Purchases

I am designating one "preferred" vendor of computers and two "secondary" vendors.

Preferred Vendor: The preferred vendor, YYY, is the vendor from which all purchases should be made unless there is a compelling reason for selecting other equipment. To encourage purchases from the preferred vendor, a special corporate fund will cover 30% of the purchase price so that individual departments need fund only 70%.

Secondary Vendor: Two other vendors, AAA and MMM, offer computers already widely used in Garibaldi; both computers are compatible with our plans to establish a computer network. Therefore, the special corporate fund will support 10% of the purchase price of these machines.

Fax Purchases

We will select one preferred vendor and no secondary vendor for fax equipment. The task force will choose between two candidates: FFF and TTT. I will notify you when the choice is made early next month.

Headings help reveal the memo's organization.

Indenting indicates that these are the two parts of the policy.

Headings are bold to make them stand out.

■ **FIGURE 7.10 Brochure with Two Levels of Headings** Courtesy of State of Ohio Department of Public Safety.

WELCOME TO THE WORLD OF CYCLING

Welcome to the world of bicycling! As a bike rider you're one of a fast-growing group of vigorous outdoors-loving people.

Bicycling in America has been growing at an amazing rate. Many young executives ride bikes to work as an alternative to adding to the smog of smoky cities, and to fighting traffic jams. Young parents are finding a way to do their shopping, complete with child carrier and shopping baskets, without having to fight for a parking space at the shopping center. College and high school students find bikes an economical alternative to cars or buses.

Unfortunately, the rise of ownership and riding of bicycles has seen a corresponding rise in traffic accidents involving bicyclists.

According to the National Safety Council, 1,000 U.S. bicyclists were killed and 60,000 injured in bicycle-motor vehicle accidents during a recent year. Over the same period, Ohio recorded 36 cyclist fatalities and 2,757 injuries.

This brochure is presented in an attempt to show how more people can happily enjoy the sport of biking without suffering needless tragedy.

GUIDES FOR SAFE RIDING

In traffic situations, the bicyclist must remain as alert as the driver of a car or other motor vehicle. For adult cyclists, this means applying defensive driving techniques to cycling as well as auto driving.

Ride with the Traffic

Riding in the same direction as the traffic on your side of the road minimizes the speed at which oncoming cars approach you. It unnerves drivers to see a cyclist heading toward them, yet this seems to be the most common mistake of young riders. One should always ride in the right hand lane, as close to the curb as possible. If you have to walk your bike, however, you become a pedestrian, and you should walk facing traffic, the same as any other pedestrian.

Use Hand Signals

Signals should be given with your left hand, well before you get to the place where you want to stop or turn. Keep your hand out until you start to make your move, or until you need to put on the hand brakes, if you have them. A straight-out arm indicates a left turn, a right turn is signaled by holding your arm up bent at the elbow, with your thumb pointing to the right. (Don't use your right hand to signal right, because drivers can't see it as well.) A stop is signaled by holding your left hand straight down and out from your side.

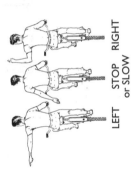

LEFT   STOP   RIGHT
            or SLOW

Ride One on a Bike

You may "look sweet upon the seat of a bicycle built for two" but unless you have a tandem, only one will do. Carrying passengers on handlebars or luggage carrier makes the bike unwieldy, hard to handle in traffic, and easy to spill. The same rule should apply to large packages. Put packages on the luggage carrier and don't tie up your hands with bulky objects.

A child can be carried safely in a child seat attached to the bicycle. Expert riders recommend rear child carriers because front seats make it difficult to steer and offer less protection for the child.

Ride Single File

Always ride single file in congested areas. Double-file riding is safe only on deserted country roads or special bike paths where cars aren't allowed.

Use Streets with Parked Cars

Expert cyclists say city cycling is safest on streets with parked cars. A lane about three feet wide is left between the parked cars and the moving traffic, so you should be able to maneuver easily between the parked cars and the traffic.

Watch out for car doors opening, however. Always use extra caution when you see people sitting in a parked car; they might just open the door and jump out without warning, throwing you into moving traffic.

Exercise Care at Intersections

The safest way to cross an intersection is to walk your bike across with the pedestrians. Left turns can be made from the center lane, as a car does, or by walking across one street and then the other. The latter procedure is safer for busy intersections and less experienced riders.

Figure 7.11 shows the table of contents from a booklet titled *Getting the Bugs Out.* Notice that all three types of headings are used. Notice also where parallel headings are used—and where they are not.

How to Design Headings Visually So That They Stand Out　Headings are usually bold and placed on their own line either at the left-hand margin or centered. When you want to create more than one level of heading in order to reveal your communication's organizational hierarchy, do the following:

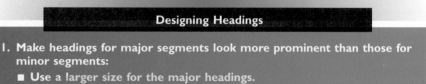

A heading's visual design can indicate its place in the communication's hierarchy.

> **Designing Headings**
>
> 1. **Make headings for major segments look more prominent than those for minor segments:**
>   - **Use a larger size for the major headings.**
>   - **Center the major headings and tuck the others against the left-hand margin.**
>   - **Use all capital letters for the major headings and only initial capital letters for the others.**
>   - **Give the major headings a line of their own and follow the others with text on the same line.**
> 2. **Make headings for segments at the same level in the hierarchy look the same:**
>   - **Give them the same visual treatment in every detail.**

Usually, you can use two or more of these techniques together so that they reinforce one another. By doing so, you can readily create two or three easily distinguishable levels of headings to reveal the organizational hierarchy of your communication. Figure 7.12 (page 185) shows an example.

Chapter titles are a form of heading.

If you feel that additional levels are needed, try making the most important sections into separate chapters, with the chapter titles serving as the highest level of heading. Figure 7.12 illustrates this also. Alternatively, you can reinforce the headings with letters and numbers in outline fashion, as shown in Figure 7.13 (page 186). In most circumstances, however, the numbers and letters of an outline diminish the effectiveness of headings by distracting the readers' eyes from the headings' key words.

How Many Headings Should You Use?　The exact number of headings appropriate for a given communication depends on the readers' needs. In communications that will be read straight through, you can usually meet your readers' needs by using a heading every few paragraphs. Major shifts in topic occur frequently in on-the-job writing, and headings help to alert readers to those shifts. In addition, frequent headings help hurried readers find specific pieces of information and review parts of a discussion that they have already read.

It's unusual for writers to use a heading for every paragraph.

On the other hand, writers rarely use headings for every paragraph. If they did, their headings would emphasize not the connectedness of the prose but its disjointedness; every paragraph would begin a major new topic.

Text continued on page 187

■ FIGURE 7.11

Table of Contents That Contains All Three Kinds of Headings (Question, Statement, Key Word or Phrase)

Copyright © National Audubon Society. Used with permission.

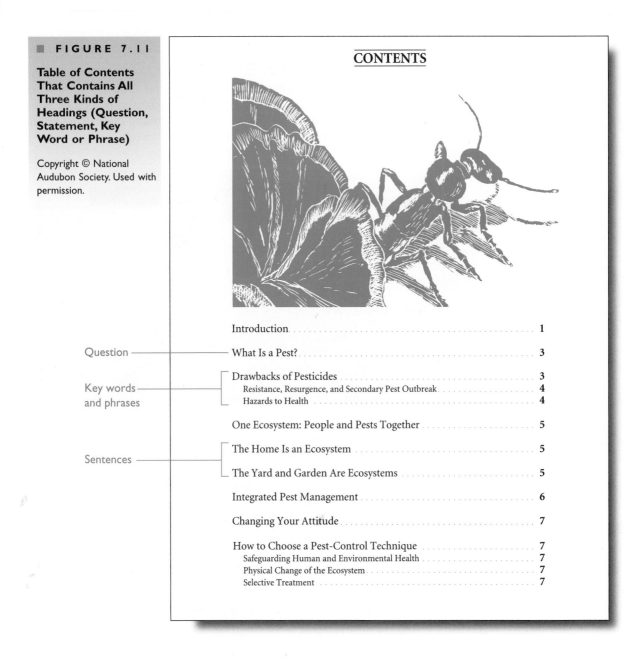

CONTENTS

Question ————

Key words and phrases ———

Sentences ———

Introduction 1

What Is a Pest? 3

Drawbacks of Pesticides 3
   Resistance, Resurgence, and Secondary Pest Outbreak 4
   Hazards to Health 4

One Ecosystem: People and Pests Together 5

The Home Is an Ecosystem 5

The Yard and Garden Are Ecosystems 5

Integrated Pest Management 6

Changing Your Attitude 7

How to Choose a Pest-Control Technique 7
   Safeguarding Human and Environmental Health 7
   Physical Change of the Ecosystem 7
   Selective Treatment 7

■ FIGURE 7.12

Headings That Indicate Organizational Hierarchy

Section heading ————

A-level heading ————

A-level heading ————

B-level heading ————

B-level heading ————

Section 1

INTRODUCTION

Southwestern Senior Services, Inc., is requesting support to develop an innovative behavior-management approach for nursing home residents who wander. The approach will be tested at Locust Knoll Village, a comprehensive philanthropic retirement community in the Chicago area.

"Wandering" Defined

Wandering is one of several deviant behaviors associated with the aging process. The term refers to disoriented and aimless movement toward undefinable objectives and unattainable goals. Snyder et al. (1998) describe the wanderer as moving about and traversing locations 32.5% of waking hours, as opposed to 4.2% for nonwanderers. Wanderers differ significantly from nonwanderers on a number of psychological variables and, overall, have more psychological problems, as assessed by the Human Development Inventory (Pyrek and Snyder, 1997).

Causes

The limited research on wandering has focused on organic and psychosocial factors.

Organic Factors. Early research typically attributed wandering behaviors to damage to the brain as a result of disease, rather than to cognitive impairment. More recently geropsychologists and gerontologists are beginning to believe that organic pathologies do not explain functional disorders or disruptive behavior (Monsour and Robb, 1992). The main reason for this shift in thinking is the research by Busse (1997) and Verwoerdt (1976), who found no consistent relationship between impairment and organic changes in the brain vessels.

Psychosocial Factors. Monsour and Robb (1992) and Snyder et al. (1998) suggest that the following three psychosocial factors are associated with wandering:

1. Lifelong patterns of coping with stress. Wanderers, as opposed to nonwanderers, typically respond to dramatic changes in routine or environment through motoric responses. Releases from tension developed early in life may have been brisk walks or long strolls.

2. Previous work roles. High rates of physical activity required by jobs held early in life may permanently influence behaviors, so that, for example, a mail carrier who delivered on foot may experience a compulsion to walk long after retirement.

3. Search for security. Some wanderers call out to dead parents or spouses, indicating that they are searching for security.

■ **FIGURE 7.13**

Table of Contents from a Research Report That Uses a Decimal Outlining System

From Ohio River Valley Sanitation Commission, *Assessment of Nonpoint Source Pollution of the Ohio River* (Cincinnati, Ohio: ORSANCO), 1990

TABLE OF CONTENTS

Section		Page
1.0	**INTRODUCTION**	
1.1	Objective	1
1.2	Definition of Nonpoint Source Pollution	1
1.3	Overview of the Problem	1
1.4	Assessment Method	2
2.0	**BASIN DESCRIPTION**	
2.1	Background	4
2.2	Current Land Use	4
3.0	**CHARACTERIZATION OF NONPOINT SOURCE POLLUTION**	
3.1	Background	9
3.2	Major Land Use Patterns Associated With Nonpoint Pollution	9
3.2.1	Agriculture	9
3.2.2	Silviculture	10
3.2.3	Mining	11
3.2.4	Construction	11
3.2.5	Urban Runoff	11
4.0	**STATE-BY-STATE NONPOINT SOURCE ASSESSMENTS**	
4.1	Background	14
4.2	Pennsylvania	15
4.3	West Virginia	21
4.4	Ohio	28
4.5	Kentucky	31
4.6	Indiana	35
4.7	Illinois	36
5.0	**DATA ANALYSIS**	
5.1	Introduction	38
5.2	Methodology	38
5.3	Results of the Analysis	42
5.3.1	Correlation Analysis	42
5.3.2	Limitations to the Correlation Analysis	50
5.3.3	Stepwise Regression	56
6.0	**CONCLUSION**	
6.1	Summary	64
6.2	Recommendations	65
	BIBLIOGRAPHY	67

v

An exception involves communications in which you are cataloging information, such as in warranties, contracts, troubleshooting guides, technical reference manuals, and fact sheets. In these documents, writers even use headings to label sentence fragments or brief bits of data. The effect, often, is to turn such a communication into something very much like a table of facts.

Are Headings Redundant with Topic Statements?   Because headings and topic statements both announce the subject of the section that follows, you may be wondering whether it is redundant to include a topic statement when a heading is used. It is not. The two usually reinforce each other, with the topic statement repeating one or more key words from the heading. For example, the heading "Method" might be followed immediately by a topic statement that says, "To test the three hypotheses described in the preceding section, we used a *method* that has proven reliable in similar situations."

Here, too, however, there are exceptions, including communications that catalog information.

In the end, of course, your key consideration in handling the relationship between headings and topic statements should be the needs of the readers you are addressing.

Visual Design

You can also enhance your readers' awareness of your communication's organization through the visual arrangement of your text on the page:

- **Adjust the location of your blocks of type.**   Here are three adjustments you can make:
  - Indent paragraphs lower in the organizational hierarchy. See Figure 7.14.
  - Leave extra space between the end of one major section and the beginning of the next.
  - In long communications, begin each new chapter or major section on its own page, regardless of where the preceding chapter or section ended.
- **Use lists.**   By placing items in a numbered or bullet list, you signal readers that items hold a parallel place in your organizational hierarchy.

Numbered List	Bullet List
The three steps we should take are:	Three features of the product are:
1. _____	■ _____
2. _____	■ _____
3. _____	■ _____

When constructing a list, give the entries a parallel grammatical construction: all the items should be nouns, or all should be full sentences, or all should be questions, and so on. Mixing grammatical constructions distracts readers and sometimes indicates a shift in point of view that breaks the tight relationship that should exist among the items in the list.

■ **FIGURE 7.14**

Indentation of Text Used to Indicate Organizational Hierarchy

From Robert Cowart and Kenneth Gregg, *Windows NT Server 4.0 Administrator's Bible* (Foster City, CA: IDG Books, 1996) 274.

Subordinate material is indented.

To emphasize this caution, the writer uses an icon and moves the text margin farther left.

A second level of indentation signals a second level of subordination.

---

274 Part II ◆ Getting Your NT Server Network Up and Running

Managing Disk Partitions

Use extreme caution when navigating through this next portion of Setup. You can easily create, destroy, and reformat entire disk partitions with a couple of keystrokes. Keep in mind that you're running a cousin of the powerful and potentially destructive DOS FDISK utility.

12. Setup lists hard disks, partitions, and unpartitioned areas on your computer. It then asks you where to install NT 4.0. Use the UP and DOWN ARROW keys to scroll through the list and highlight a partition. Go to step 12a.

   You'll need to find a destination partition with at least 115MB of free space on which to install Windows NT Server.

   In the list, all non-SCSI drives are displayed as "IDE/ESDI Disk." A SCSI drive is displayed as "Disk # at id # on bus # on" followed by the name of the SCSI adapter driver. The ID number is the SCSI ID assigned to the drive.

   Areas of your disks that contain no partition are displayed as "Unpartitioned space." Partitions that have been created but not yet formatted are displayed as "New (Unformatted)" or as "Unformatted or Damaged." Don't worry about the latter. This is just NT's generic way of saying that it doesn't recognize a partition as formatted.

   If you're installing Windows NT Server on a computer that contains a previous version of Windows NT and you were using disk stripes, mirrors, or volume sets, these partitions are shown as "Windows NT Fault Tolerance" partitions. Don't delete any of these partitions. See the section entitled "Migrating Fault Tolerance from Windows NT 3.x" in Chapter 19 for details on using existing fault-tolerance partitions.

   If you don't see all of your partitions listed, you may just need to use the UP and DOWN ARROW keys to scroll and display them. Only hard disks are included in this list.

   Don't panic if the drive letter assignments seem out of whack. They probably don't match the drive letters that you see under DOS or even under another version of NT. Once you've got NT up and running, you'll be able to change drive letter assignments very easily.

   12a. If you're ready to select a partition on which NT 4.0 will be installed, highlight that partition, press ENTER, and go to step 13. If you're not, go to step 12b to delete an existing partition or step 12c to create a new partition.

      You can select an unformatted partition or an existing formatted FAT or NTFS partition. Unpartitioned space isn't a valid destination for NT installation. You need to partition it first, in step 12c.

      If the partition that you select isn't large enough, Setup will complain and send you back to step 12.

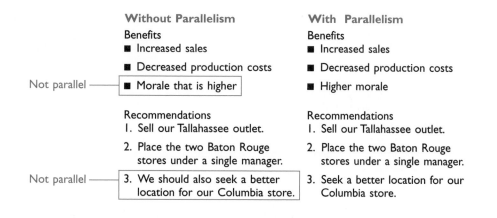

GUIDELINE 5   Consult Conventional Strategies When Faced with Organizational Difficulties

Every writer occasionally gets stumped when trying to organize a particular paragraph, section, or chapter. Often the organizational problem is one that many others have faced, such as how to describe a certain process or how to explain the causes of a particular event. For many commonly encountered organizational problems, there are conventional strategies for arranging material in ways that will be understandable and useful to readers. By consulting these strategies, you will often find a quick and effective solution to your own problem.

The Reference Guide following this chapter tells how to use six of these strategies that are especially useful on the job. As you study the strategies, remember to use them only as guides. To make them work in your particular context, you will need to adapt them to your purpose and the needs of your readers.

GUIDELINE 6   Consider Your Readers' Cultural Background When Organizing

The advice you have read so far in this chapter is based on the customs of readers in the United States and other Western countries where readers expect and value what might be called a "linear" organization. In this organizational pattern, writers express their main ideas explicitly and develop each one separately, carefully leading readers from one to another. As international communication experts Myron W. Lustig and Jolene Koester explain, this pattern can be visualized as "a series of steps or progressions that move in a straight line toward a particular goal or idea" (218).

In other cultures, writers and readers are accustomed to different patterns. For example, the Japanese use a nonlinear pattern that Satoshi Ishii calls a "gyre." The writer approaches a topic by indirection and implication because in Japanese culture it's rude and inappropriate to tell the reader the specific point being conveyed. Communication specialist Kazuo Nishiyama gives an example: when a Japanese manager says, "I'd like you to reflect on your proposal for a while," the manager can mean, "You are dead wrong, and you'd better come up with a better idea very soon. But I don't say this to you directly because you should be able to understand what I'm saying without my being so rude."

Different cultures use different organizational patterns.

When Human Consequences Are Ignored

FOCUS ON ETHICS

Employees sometimes become so engrossed in the technical aspects of their job that they lose track of the human consequences of their work. When this happens, they write communications in which their stakeholders are overlooked. Depending on the situation, the consequences can be quite harmful or relatively mild—but they can always lead to the unethical treatment of other people.

Mining Accidents

An example is provided by Beverly A. Sauer, who has studied the reports written by the federal employees who investigate mining accidents in which miners are killed. In their reports, as Sauer points out, the investigators typically focus on technical information about the accidents, without paying sufficient attention to the human tragedies caused by the accidents. In one report, for example, the investigators describe the path of an underground explosion as it traveled through an intricate web of mine shafts and flamed out of various mine entrances. At one entrance, investigators write, "Debris blown by the explosion's forces damaged a jeep automobile parked near the drift openings." The investigators don't mention in this passage that in addition to damaging the jeep, the explosion killed sixteen miners who were in the mine shafts.

In addition to overlooking the victims of the disasters, the investigators' reports often fail to identify the human beings who created the conditions that caused the accidents. One report says, "The accident and resultant fatality occurred when the victim proceeded into an area of known loose roof before the roof was supported or taken down." This suggests that the miner was crushed to death by a falling mine roof because he was careless. Sauer's research showed, however, that in the same mines ten fatalities had occurred in five years— and seven resulted from falling roofs. Managers of the mines were not following safety regulations, and mine-safety inspectors were not enforcing the law.

Stakeholders

Of course, there's nothing the inspectors' reports can do on behalf of the deceased miners or their families. However, the stakeholders in the inspectors' reports include other miners who continue to work in what is the most dangerous profession in the United States. As Sauer points out, the investigators' readers include the federal officials responsible for overseeing the nation's mining industry. If the inspectors wrote in ways that made these readers more aware of the human consequences of mining accidents—and of the human failings that often bring them about—the federal officials might be more willing to pass stricter laws and insist that existing regulations be strictly enforced.

As Sauer explains, in Europe, where government regulation of mining is much stronger, death and injury of miners are much rarer than in the United States. The high accident rate that makes mining so dangerous in the United States, she argues, results in part from the way mining investigators write their reports.

Responsibilities to People

Of course, most people aren't in professions where lives are at stake. In any profession, however, it's possible to become so focused on your technical subject matter that you forget the human consequences of your writing.

To avoid accidentally treating others unethically, first, always begin your writing by identifying your communication's stakeholders (page 75). Certainly, the stakeholders of the mining disaster reports include miners whose lives are endangered if government officials don't enact and enforce life-saving safety measures.

Second, determine how the stakeholders will be affected by your communication (page 95).

Third, draft your communication in a way that reflects proper care for these individuals. Be sure that all your decisions about what to say, what *not* to say, and how to present your message are consistent with your personal beliefs about how you should treat other people.

Similarly, in Hindi (one of the major languages of India), paragraphs do not stick to one unified idea or thought, as they do in the United States and many other Western nations. Jamuna Kachru explains that in the preferred Hindi style, the writer may digress and introduce material related to many different ideas.

Use appropriate organizational patterns when addressing persons from other cultures.

Because of these cultural differences, serious misunderstandings can arise when your readers are employed by other companies in another country, work for your own company in another country, or even work in your own building but were raised observing the customs of another culture. Such misunderstandings cannot be avoided simply by translating the words of your communication: the whole message must be structured to suit the customs of your readers' culture.

CONCLUSION

This chapter has suggested that in many situations you can make your writing more easily understandable and more persuasive if you begin your segments with topic statements; present generalizations before details; organize from most important to least important; and use headings, forecasting statements, and similar devices to reveal the organization of your communication to your readers.

Remember that the guidelines given in this chapter are suggestions, not rules. The only "rule" for writing segments is to be sure your readers know what you are talking about and how your various points relate to one another. Sometimes you will be able to do this without thinking consciously about your techniques. Often, however, you will be able to increase the clarity and persuasiveness of your segments by drawing on the advice presented here.

EXERCISES

1. Circle the various parts and subparts of the passage in Figure 7.15 to show how the smaller segments are contained within larger ones.

2. Identify the topic statements in Figure 7.15 by putting an asterisk before the first word of each sentence that indicates the topic of a segment.

3. Circle all the forecasting statements in Figure 7.12 (page 185). For those segments that lack explicit forecasting statements, explain how readers might figure out the way in which they are organized.

4. Figure 7.16 shows a memorandum whose contents have been scrambled. Each statement has been assigned a number.
   a. Write the numbers of the statements in the order in which the statements would appear if the memorandum were written in accordance with the guidelines

   in this chapter. Place an asterisk before each statement that would begin a segment. (When ordering the statements, ignore their particular phrasing. Order them according to the information they provide the reader.)
   b. Using the list you just made, rewrite the memorandum by rephrasing the sentences so that the finished memorandum conforms with all the guidelines in this chapter.

5. Figure 7.6 shows a table of contents from an instruction manual for an electronic balance, a device used to weigh samples in a laboratory. The writer has done a good job of listing the contents but has done a poor job of indicating coordination and subordination. Use the techniques described in Guideline 4 (page 174) to create a table of contents that reveals the organization more effectively. Note that after the "Introduction," the contents fall into two major parts, each with subparts. You will need to add some headings to these groupings.

■ **FIGURE 7.15**

**Passage Containing
Several Levels of
Segments**

Importing Insects

By importing insects from other parts of the world, nations can sometimes increase the productivity of their agricultural sector, but they also risk hurting themselves. By importing insects, Australia controlled the infestation of its continent by the prickly pear, a cactus native to North and South America. The problem began when this plant, which has an edible fruit, was brought to Australia by early explorers. Because the explorers did not also bring its natural enemies, the prickly pear grew uncontrolled, eventually rendering large areas useless as grazing land, thereby harming the nation's farm economy. The problem was solved when scientists in Argentina found a small moth, Cactoblastis cactorum, whose larvae feed upon the prickly pear. The moth was imported to Australia, where its larvae, by eating the cactus, reopened thousands of acres of land.

In contrast, the importation of another insect, the Africanized bee, could threaten the well-being of the United States. It once appeared that the importation of this insect might bring tremendous benefits to North and South America. The Africanized bee produces about twice as much honey as do the bees native to the Americas.

However, the U.S. Department of Agriculture now speculates that the introduction of the Africanized honey bee into the U.S. would create serious problems. The problems arise from the peculiar way the Africanized honey bee swarms. When the honey bees native to the United States swarm, about half the bees leave the hive with the queen, moving a small distance. The rest remain, choosing a new queen. In contrast, when the Africanized honey bee swarms, the entire colony moves, sometimes up to fifty miles. If Africanized bees intermix with the domestic bee population, they might introduce these swarming traits. Beekeepers could be abandoned by their bees, and large areas of cropland could be left without the services of this pollinating insect. Unfortunately, the Africanized honey bee is moving slowly northward to the United States from Sao Paulo, Brazil, where several years ago a researcher accidentally released 27 swarms of the bee from an experiment.

Thus, while the importation of insects can sometimes benefit a nation, imported insects can also alter the nation's ecological system, thereby harming its agricultural business.

■ FIGURE 7.16

Memo for Exercise 4

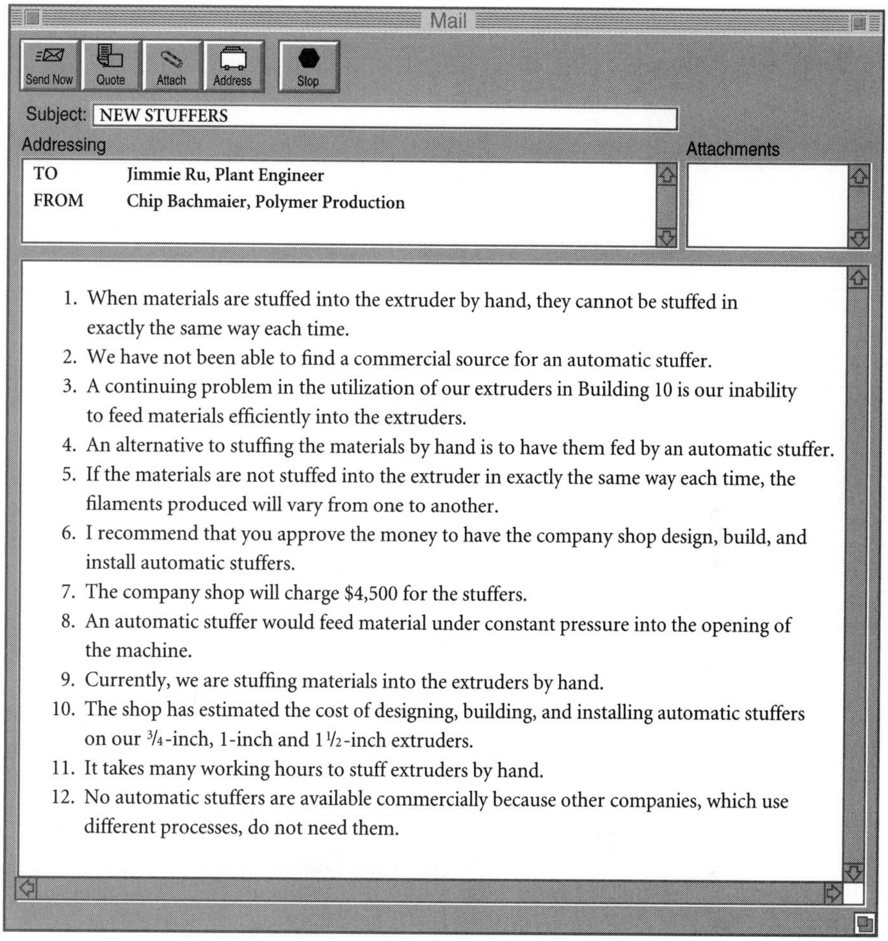

Mail

Send Now   Quote   Attach   Address   Stop

Subject: NEW STUFFERS

Addressing   Attachments

TO   Jimmie Ru, Plant Engineer
FROM   Chip Bachmaier, Polymer Production

1. When materials are stuffed into the extruder by hand, they cannot be stuffed in exactly the same way each time.

2. We have not been able to find a commercial source for an automatic stuffer.

3. A continuing problem in the utilization of our extruders in Building 10 is our inability to feed materials efficiently into the extruders.

4. An alternative to stuffing the materials by hand is to have them fed by an automatic stuffer.

5. If the materials are not stuffed into the extruder in exactly the same way each time, the filaments produced will vary from one to another.

6. I recommend that you approve the money to have the company shop design, build, and install automatic stuffers.

7. The company shop will charge $4,500 for the stuffers.

8. An automatic stuffer would feed material under constant pressure into the opening of the machine.

9. Currently, we are stuffing materials into the extruders by hand.

10. The shop has estimated the cost of designing, building, and installing automatic stuffers on our $3/4$-inch, 1-inch and $1\frac{1}{2}$-inch extruders.

11. It takes many working hours to stuff extruders by hand.

12. No automatic stuffers are available commercially because other companies, which use different processes, do not need them.

Reference Guide:
Six Patterns
for Organizing

CAMELOPARDALIS

CONTENTS

Classification (Grouping Facts)

Description of an Object (Partitioning)

Description of a Process (Segmentation)

Comparison

Cause and Effect

Problem and Solution

Combinations of Patterns

This Reference Guide describes six patterns for organizing information and arguments. These patterns work with segments of any size, whether a group of related sentences, a paragraph, a chapter, or even an entire communication.

Each pattern is discussed separately so that you can quickly access advice about the particular one you wish to use. A final section discusses the ways that several patterns are woven together in longer communications.

Patterns for Organizing

- **Classification**   Page 195
- **Description of an Object**   Page 198
- **Description of a Process**   Page 202
- **Comparison**   Page 208
- **Cause and Effect**   Page 210
- **Problem and Solution**   Page 212
- **Combinations of Patterns**   Page 215

CLASSIFICATION (GROUPING FACTS)

When writing on the job, you will sometimes have to deal with what seems to be a miscellaneous set of facts. Your challenge will be to arrange them in a way that will be meaningful and useful to your readers.

One way to address this challenge is to use a strategy called *classification*, in which you arrange your material into parallel groups of related items. Your goal would be to create the groups so that they meet the following criteria:

Criteria for classification

- **Every item has a place.** In one group or another, every item fits.
- **Each item has only one place.** If there were two logical places for an item, either the communication would be redundant because the item would be mentioned twice or readers would have to guess which of the two locations really presented the item.
- **The groupings are useful to your readers.** Items that readers will use together are grouped together.

There are two types of classification patterns: formal and informal.

FORMAL CLASSIFICATION

In formal classification, you group items according to a *principle of classification*— that is, according to some observable characteristic that every item in the group possesses. Consider Esther's situation.

Esther must select a principle of classification for a brochure.

Esther has been asked to write a brochure for consumers that describes the adhesives manufactured by her employer, a chemical company. As her principle of classification, she might choose any number of characteristics, including price, color, date first manufactured, and the type of material each was designed to bond (wood, metal, ceramic). Because each adhesive has one price, one color, one date of first manufacture, and one bonding application, any of these characteristics would produce an organization with a place for each adhesive. Also, because each adhesive has *only one* price, one color, one date, and one bonding application, each of these characteristics is a principle of classification that would produce an organization with only one place for each adhesive.

Esther makes her final choice by considering her readers' needs.

To decide which of these possible principles of classification would be most helpful to her readers, she thought about what they wanted to learn from the brochure. Realizing that they would want to know which adhesive was best for a particular job, she organized around the type of material each was designed to bond.

Create a hierarchy for a large set of facts.

When you are organizing a large set of facts, you can use classification to divide your groups into subgroups. For instance, within the section on adhesives for wood, metal, and ceramic, Esther might have grouped the adhesives according to any of the other principles she identified. Where appropriate, you can subdivide again and again to create a multilevel organizational hierarchy.

GUIDELINES FOR FORMAL CLASSIFICATION

1. **Choose a principle of classification that is suited to your readers and your purpose.** Every subject matter can be classified according to a variety of principles. The one you are accustomed to using may not be the one that's best suited to your communication. Follow Esther's example in considering your readers' needs.

2. **Use only one principle of classification at a time.** In order to create a hierarchical organization that has only one place for each item, you must use only one principle of classification at a time. For example, you might classify the cars owned by a large corporation as follows:

Valid classification

Cars built in the United States
Cars built in other countries

In this classification, you use only one principle of classification—the country in which the car was manufactured. Because each car was built in only one country, each would fit into only one group. Suppose you classified the cars this way:

Faulty classification

Cars built in the United States
Cars built in other countries
Cars that are expensive

This classification is faulty because two principles are being used simultaneously—country of manufacture and cost. An expensive car built in the United States would fit into two categories.

Of course, you can use different principles at different levels in a hierarchy:

Corrected classification

> Cars built in the United States
> > Expensive ones
> > Inexpensive ones
>
> Cars built in other countries
> > Expensive ones
> > Inexpensive ones

In this case, an expensive car built in the United States would have only one place at each level of the hierarchy.

INFORMAL CLASSIFICATION

In some situations, it is impossible or undesirable to classify according to objective characteristics. Consider, for example, the organization of a report Calvin needed to write.

Calvin must organize items where there is no objective principle of classification.

> Calvin's employer asked him to analyze advertisements appearing in several trade journals in the heavy-equipment industry. Calvin might have classified the ads according to such objective characteristics as size of ad or number of words of copy. However, because he knew that his employer wanted to begin advertising in those journals and wanted some advice about ad design, Calvin decided to classify the ads according to the type of advertising appeal used. Obviously, "type of advertising appeal" is not an objective characteristic. It requires subjective interpretation and judgment. When writers classify facts without using objective characteristics as their principle of classification, they are said to be using *informal classification*.

GUIDELINES FOR INFORMAL CLASSIFICATION

1. **Group your items in a way that is suited to your readers and your purpose.** Calvin organized his analysis around "type of advertising appeal" because he knew his employer was looking for advice about the design of ads.
2. **Use parallel groups at each level.** For instance, if you were classifying advertisements, you wouldn't use a list of categories like this:

Categories not parallel with the others

> Focus on price
> Focus on established reputation
> Focus on advantages over a competitor's product
> Focus on one of the product's key features
> Focus on several of the product's key features

The last two categories are at a lower hierarchical level than the other three. To make the categories parallel, you could combine them in the following way:

Categories correctly subordinated to a lower level

> Focus on price
> Focus on established reputation
> Focus on advantages over a competitor's product
> Focus on the product's key features
> > Focus on one key feature
> > Focus on several key features

3. **Avoid overlap among groups.** Even when you cannot use strict logic in classifying items, strive to provide one and only one place for each item. To do this, you must avoid overlap among categories. For example, in the following list, the last item overlaps the others because photographs can be used in any of the other types of advertisements listed.

Focus on price
Focus on established reputation
Focus on advantages over a competitor's product
Focus on the product's key features
Use photographs

SAMPLE CLASSIFICATION SEGMENTS

Figure PO.1 shows a passage organized according to *formal classification*. It describes various methods of detecting coronary heart disease. The writer chose to organize around the extent to which the methods require physicians to introduce something into the patient's body. The writer selected this principle of classification because he wants to focus on a new method whose advantage is that nothing needs to be placed in the patient's body.

Figure PO.2 (page 200) shows the outline of a research report organized according to *informal classification*. The writers describe the ways investigators should go about identifying water plants that might be cultivated, harvested, and dried to serve as fuel for power generators. Because the actual selection of plants would require the expertise of specialists from many fields, the writers have organized their communication in a way that helps people from each field find the information they need: there is a section on chemistry for chemists, one on economics for economists, and so on.

DESCRIPTION OF AN OBJECT (PARTITIONING)

At work you will often need to describe a physical object for your readers. If you write about an experiment, for example, you may need to describe your equipment. If you write instructions, you may need to describe the machines your readers will be using. If you propose a new purchase, you may need to describe the object you want to buy.

To organize such descriptions, you can use a strategy called *partitioning*. In partitioning, you divide your subject into its major components and (if appropriate) divide those into their subcomponents.

HOW PARTITIONING WORKS

Partitioning is a form of classification.

When partitioning, you follow the same basic procedure you use in classification. You think of the object as a collection of parts and use some principle to identify groups of related parts. Most often, that principle is either function or location. Consider, for instance, how each of those two principles might be used to organize a discussion of the parts of a car.

■ FIGURE PO.1

Passage Organized According to Formal Classification

Metin Akay, "Wavelet Applications in Medicine," *IEEE Spectrum* 34.5 1997: 50–1.

The principle of classification is the extent to which the methods involve placing something in the person's body ("invading" it).

The first group of methods involves no invasiveness.

The second group does involve invasiveness.

The second group is subdivided according to the amount of invasiveness.

Detecting Coronary Artery Disease

Coronary artery disease (CAD) is the leading cause of death in industrialized countries. In fact, one-third of all deaths in the U.S. are attributable to it. For this reason, the early detection of CAD has long been regarded as among the most vital areas of medical research, and several moderately invasive diagnostic methods have been developed.

Non-invasive methods gather diagnostic information without introducing anything into a patient's body. These methods include traditional physical examinations and history taking, electrocardiography, and echocardiography (ultrasonic imaging).

In contrast, invasive methods involve introducing a substance or object into the person's body. A moderately invasive method is the thallium test, in which a compound of radioactive thallium-201 is injected into the patient and then distributes itself throughout the myocardium (heart muscle) in proportion to the myocardial blood flow. The low-flow regions are detectable as cold spots on the image obtained from a radioisotope camera set over the chest. Although quite sensitive and accurate, the thallium test is also costly and time-comsuming.

As far as invasive techniques are concerned, the most reliable way to diagnose CAD is by means of cardiac catheterization, in which a catheter is inserted into a large artery (usually in the upper arm or thigh) and advanced to the heart. Once the catheter is positioned in the heart, a radio-opaque dye is released through it, making it possible to observe the condition of the coronary arteries with X-rays. Although it produces excellent images and definitive diagnoses, cardiac catheterization is expensive, painful, and time-consuming—and it carries an element of risk. For these reasons, an equally accurate, non-invasive method for early detection of coronary artery disease is greatly to be preferred.

[The article continues with a description of a new technology that may provide a highly accurate, non-invasive early detection method.]

Partitioning by location

If you organize your discussion by location, you might talk about the interior, the exterior, and the underside. The interior would be those areas under the hood, in the passenger compartment, and in the trunk. The exterior would be the front, back, sides, and top. The underside would include the parts under the body, such as the wheels and transmission.

Partitioning by function

However, if you were to organize your discussion by function, you might focus on parts that provide power and parts that guide the car. The parts that provide

■ **FIGURE PO.2**

Outline of a Report Organized According to Informal Classification

From S. Kresovich et al., *The Utilization of Emergent Aquatic Plants for Biomass Energy Systems* (Golden, CO: Solar Energy Research Institute, 1982).

IDENTIFYING EMERGENT AQUATIC PLANTS THAT MIGHT BE USED AS FUEL
FOR BIOMASS ENERGY SYSTEM

Introduction

Botanical Considerations
    Growth Habitat
    Morphology
    Genetics

Physiological Considerations
    Carbon Utilization
    Water Utilization
    Nutrient Absorption
    Environmental Factors Influencing Growth

Chemical Considerations
    Carbohydrate Composition
    Crude Protein Content
    Crude Lipid Content
    Inorganic Content

Agronomic Considerations
    Current Emergent Aquatic Systems
        Eleocharis dulcis
        Ipomoea aquatica
        Zizania palustris
        Oryza sativa
    Mechanized Harvesting, Collection, Densification, and
        Transportation of Biomass
    Crop Improvement
    Propagule Availability

Ecological Considerations
    Water Quality
    Habitat Disruption and Development
    Coastal Wetlands

Economic Considerations
    Prior Research Efforts
        Phragmites communis
        Arundo donax
        Other Research
    Production Costs for Candidate Species
        Planting and Crop Management
        Harvesting
        Drying and Densification
        Total Costs
    End Products and Potential Competition

Selection of Candidate Species

power are in several places (the gas pedal and gear shift are in the passenger compartment, the engine is under the hood, and the transmission, axle, and wheels are on the underside). Nevertheless, you could discuss them together because they are related by function.

Often, these two commonly used principles of classification—location and function—coincide. For instance, if you were to partition the parts of a stereo system, you could identify the following major components: the compact disc player (whose function is to create electrical signals from the impressions made on the surface of a disc), the amplifier (whose function is to increase the amplitude of those signals), and the speakers (whose function is to convert those signals into sound waves).

Of course, other principles of classification are possible. You could organize your description of the parts of a car according to the materials they are made from—a classification that could be useful to someone looking for ways to decrease the cost of materials in a car. You could also partition the parts of a car according to the countries in which they were manufactured—a classification that could be useful to an economist studying the effects of import tariffs or quotas on U.S. manufacturers.

GUIDELINES FOR PARTITIONING AN OBJECT

1. **Choose a basis for partitioning suited to your readers and purpose.** For instance, if you are trying to describe a car for new owners who want to learn about what they have purchased, you might organize according to location, so your readers will learn about the comforts and conveniences available to them when sitting in the passenger compartment, when using the trunk, and so on. In contrast, if you are describing a car for mechanics who will have to diagnose and correct problems, you would organize your description according to function. Thus, when the mechanics must correct a steering problem, they will learn about all the parts that make up the steering system.

2. **Use only one basis for partitioning at a time.** To assure that you have one place and only one place for each part you describe, use only one basis for partitioning at a time, just as you use only one basis for classifying at a time.

   In some communications, you may need to describe the same object from more than one point of view. For instance, in the introduction to an advertising brochure for a new car, you might describe the parts of the car from the point of view of their comfort and visual appeal to the owner. In this instance, you could organize by location. Later in the same brochure, you might describe the car from the point of view of performance, in which case you could organize by function. Each part of the car would appear in both sections of the brochure but would have only one place in each section.

3. **Arrange the parts of your description in a way your readers will find useful.** For instance, if you are partitioning by location, you might move systematically from left to right, front to back, or outside to inside. If you are describing things by function, you might treat the parts in the order in which they function in an activity of interest to your readers. For instance, if you are describing the parts that power a car, you might discuss them in the order in which the power flows through them: from engine to transmission, to drive shaft, to axle, and so on. At times, you can arrange material from most important to least important. For instance, if you are writing a repair manual, you might first describe the parts that cause the most problems.

The following outline shows how a computer could be partitioned into its major components and subcomponents.

Introduction
  Keyboard
    Regular Keys
    Function Keys
  Mouse
    Buttons
    Trackball
  Electronics Unit
    System Card
      Diskette Drive
      CD-ROM Drive
    Expansion Slots
  Monitor
    Screen
    Controls

EXTENDED DESCRIPTIONS OF AN OBJECT

In some situations, you may need to describe an object in an extended fashion. For instance, in some instruction manuals, it's necessary to provide detailed information about the construction and function of the various parts of the equipment being used. Similarly, product descriptions sometimes involve detailed discussions that are organized by partitioning. In addition to information about the parts of the object, such descriptions may include a title, introduction, drawing or other visual aid, and a conclusion.

Figure PO.3 presents an example of an extended description of an object.

DESCRIPTION OF A PROCESS (SEGMENTATION)

A description of a process explains the relationship of events over time. You may have either of two purposes in describing a process:

- **To enable your readers to *perform* the process.** For example, you may be writing instructions that will enable your readers to analyze the chemicals present in a sample of liver tissue, make a photovoltaic cell, apply for a loan, or run a computer program.
- **To enable your readers to *understand* the process.** For example, you might want your readers to understand the following:
  - **How something is done.** For instance, how coal is transformed into synthetic diamonds.
  - **How something works.** For instance, how the lungs provide oxygen to the bloodstream.
  - **How something happened.** For instance, how the United States developed the space programs that eventually landed astronauts on the moon.

■ **FIGURE PO.3**

Extended Description of an Object (Mechanism)

Based on Götz Wange, "Airbus for Tomorrow," *Daimler-Benz Technology '96* (Stuttgart, Germany: Daimler-Benz, 1996) 28–32.

Overall topic is introduced.

Forecasting statement indicates the organization of the rest of the description.

First major component is described: construction and operation.

Second major component is described: construction and operation.

Third major component is described: construction, operation, benefits.

ADAPTIVE AIRCRAFT WINGS

Until now, commercial airplanes have relied on rigid wings designed for a compromise between the requirements of take-off, landing, and cruising. In an effort to increase fuel efficiency, scientists at Daimler-Benz and the German Aerospace Research Center are experimenting with an "adaptive wing" that is capable of changing its geometry automatically during flight so that the best possible performance is always achieved. This new concept involves four major components: a sensor network, processor, intelligent flap, and adjustable contour region.

Sensor Network

The sensor network consists of dozens of sensors located at widely differing points under the wing skin. Throughout a flight, they continuously collect information about such things as airflow, laminar flow length, possible turbulence, and pressure distribution.

Processor

Information from the sensor network is fed to a special computer processor, which is linked to—but separate from—the flight management computer through which the pilot flies the plane. The special processor calculates the ideal geometry for the wing, taking into account the plane's desired speed, altitude, and actual weight as provided by the pilot and the flight management computer. Once the processor has determined the ideal wing shape, it transmits the necessary instructions to the two remaining components of the system: the intelligent flap and the moveable contours.

Intelligent Flap

Located at the rear of a wing, flaps are currently extended only during the take off and landing. The adaptive wing involves two important flap modifications. First, it puts the flaps into use throughout the flight, extending them in the manner calculated by the processor. Second, the flaps on the adaptive wing have a deformable trailing edge. This edge is constructed with small electrical actuators integrated into an elastic, shape-memory material. According to the amount of current that is applied, these materials change shape so that the trailing edge of the flap can be "tuned" to meet the demands of specific flight conditions.

A major benefit of the intelligent flap is that it could provide maximum lift with minimum drag for all flight situations, thereby saving fuel. Another benefit is an increased margin for safety during extreme in-flight maneuvers. For example, should a sudden loss of cabin pressure necessitate a rapid descent to an altitude where there is enough oxygen for breathing, the intelligent flap can reduce stressful loads on the wings. The intelligent flap can also alleviate the severity of the problems encountered when a plane flies into the vortex of turbulent air caused by another jet's engines.

In either case, you want to explain the overall structure of the process to your readers. To do that, you segment the process. You begin with the list of steps or events involved in the process, then you separate those steps or events into related groups. If the process is long enough, you may divide those groups of steps into subgroups, thereby creating an organizational hierarchy. In outlining instructions for building a cabinet, for instance, you would set forth the sequence of steps or events:

REFERENCE GUIDE: Six Patterns for Organizing

■ **FIGURE PO.3**
(continued)

Fourth major component is described: construction, operation, benefits.

Conclusion ties the entire segment together by highlighting benefits.

Figure helps to explain the components and their relationship.

Adjustable Contour Region

Midway back on its upper surface, the adaptive wing has an adjustable contour region that can be adjusted to lie smooth or bulge, thereby changing the wing's shape. Based on information provided by the sensor network, the processor would instruct actuators to thicken the upper surface of the wing at specific areas where doing so would increase the wing's aerodynamic efficiency. Scientists have identified two means of accomplishing this change in wing shape. First, tensioning elements placed under the wing's skin could act on a precalculated area of the wing like a bicep, causing the skin to bulge as they contract. Second, small electrical actuators integrated into an elastic wing surface could provide the same effect.

The advantage of adjustable contour region is that it would weaken the effect of the "compression wave" that forms at the leading edge of a jet's wing. Even when an aircraft flies below the speed of sound, the convex profile of the upper wing surface forces air flowing over it to travel at supersonic speeds, creating this compression wave, which exerts draft on the wing.

Conclusion

Although the adaptive wing is still under development, Project Leader Dr. Joseph Mertens estimates it will reduce wing resistence by fifteen percent. The benefits could snowball from there, he adds. For example, less drag means less fuel consumption, which in turn means less weight of fuel to be transported, which itself results in lower fuel consumption.

Adaptive Wing

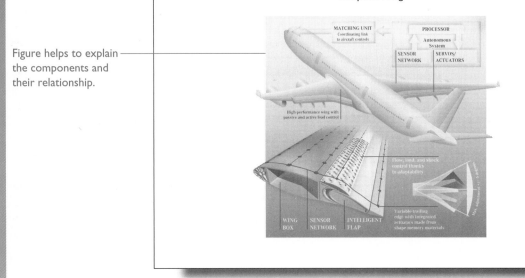

Example of segmenting a process

Obtaining Your Materials
Building the Cabinet
    Cutting the wood
    Routing the wood
    Assembling the parts
       Making the frame
       Mounting the doors
Finishing the Cabinet
    Sanding
    Applying the stain
    Applying the sealant

Use a principle of classification to group the steps.

As with partitioning, you need a principle of classification to guide you in segmenting a process. Commonly used principles include the time when the steps are performed (first day, second day; spring, summer, fall), the purpose of the steps (to prepare the equipment, to examine the results), and the tools used to perform the steps (for example, the function keys on a word processor, the numeric pad, and so on).

GUIDELINES FOR SEGMENTING

1. **Choose a principle for segmenting suited to your readers and your purpose.** If you are writing instructions, group them in ways that support an efficient or comfortable rhythm of work. If you are trying to help your readers understand a process, build your organization around concerns that are of interest or use to your readers. For example, imagine that you are writing a history of the process by which the United States placed a man on the moon. If your readers are legislators or government historians, you might segment your account according to the passage of various laws and appropriation bills, or according to the terms of the various administrators who headed the National Aeronautics and Space Administration (NASA). If your readers are scientists and engineers, you might focus on efforts to overcome various technical problems.

2. **Make your smallest groupings manageable.** One of the most important things for you to do when segmenting a process is to make your smallest groupings manageable. If they include too many steps or too few, your readers will not see the process as a structured hierarchy of activities or events but as a long, unstructured list of steps—first one, then the next, and so on. If you are writing instructions, the lack of structure will make it harder for your readers to learn the task. If you are describing a process, the lack of structure will make the process more difficult for them to comprehend.

3. **Make clear the relationships among the steps.** Finally, keep in mind that your segments should help your readers understand and remember the entire process. That means that readers will need to understand the relationships among the events and steps that make up the process.

   There are many ways of making those relationships clear. Where they are obvious, you can simply provide informative headings. At other times, you will need to explain them in an overview at the beginning of the segment, weave additional explanations into your discussions of the steps themselves, and explain the relationships again in a summary at the end.

■ **FIGURE PO.4**

Instructions Organized by Segmenting a Process

From *Apple Computer Power Macintosh User's Manual for 7300 Series* (Cupertino, CA: Apple Computer, 1997) 1, 3, 4, 7, 11, 14.

The instruction booklet organizes the process of setting up a computer by segmenting the process into several subtasks.

The overall process is described in 14 pages; some of the subtasks are explained on more than one page.

Each heading begins with a word describing the reader's action, thereby maintaining a focus on the process that the reader is to perform.

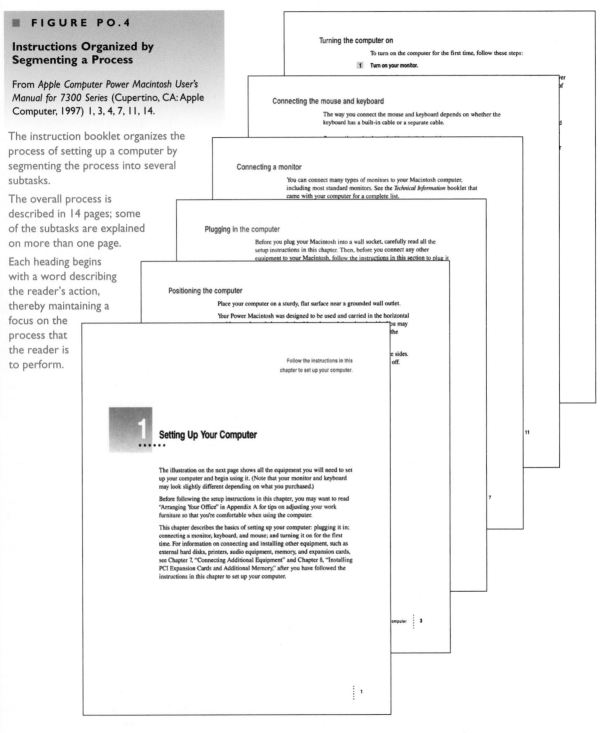

Turning the computer on

To turn on the computer for the first time, follow these steps:

1 Turn on your monitor.

Connecting the mouse and keyboard

The way you connect the mouse and keyboard depends on whether the keyboard has a built-in cable or a separate cable.

Connecting a monitor

You can connect many types of monitors to your Macintosh computer, including most standard monitors. See the *Technical Information* booklet that came with your computer for a complete list.

Plugging in the computer

Before you plug your Macintosh into a wall socket, carefully read all the setup instructions in this chapter. Then, before you connect any other equipment to your Macintosh, follow the instructions in this section to plug it

Positioning the computer

Place your computer on a sturdy, flat surface near a grounded wall outlet.

Your Power Macintosh was designed to be used and carried in the horizontal

Follow the instructions in this chapter to set up your computer.

1 Setting Up Your Computer

The illustration on the next page shows all the equipment you will need to set up your computer and begin using it. (Note that your monitor and keyboard may look slightly different depending on what you purchased.)

Before following the setup instructions in this chapter, you may want to read "Arranging Your Office" in Appendix A for tips on adjusting your work furniture so that you're comfortable when using the computer.

This chapter describes the basics of setting up your computer: plugging it in; connecting a monitor, keyboard, and mouse; and turning it on for the first time. For information on connecting and installing other equipment, such as external hard disks, printers, audio equipment, memory, and expansion cards, see Chapter 7, "Connecting Additional Equipment" and Chapter 8, "Installing PCI Expansion Cards and Additional Memory," after you have followed the instructions in this chapter to set up your computer.

■ **FIGURE PO.5**

Explanation Organized by Segmenting a Process

From William Cochran "Extrasolar Planets," *Physics World,* 10.7 1997: 31-5.

The topic is introduced. —

First stage is described. —

Alternative outcomes are identified. —

Second stage is described. —

Headings help to distinguish the stages. —

Third stage is described in two parts, with separate paragraphs devoted to planetesimals and to planets. —

A concluding sentence summarizes the overall process. —

How Planets Are Formed

Theoretical astrophysicists have developed an elaborate model describing the formation of stars like our Sun. In this theory, planet formation is a natural and almost necessary result of the process of star formation.

A Proto-Star is Born

These astrophysicists believe that the process of star formation begins when a dense region of gas and dust in an interstellar cloud becomes gravitationally unstable. The cloud begins a slow, quasistatic contraction as both its internal turbulent and magnetic support are gradually lost through cooling and the outward diffusion of the magnetic field. The core of this cloud condenses to form a proto-star.

If there is sufficient angular momentum, the collapsing cloud may fragment into two or more smaller pieces, thus leading to the formation of a binary or multiple star.

A Rotating Disc Forms

The remaining gas and dust from the cloud continue to fall inwards. Because this material must conserve the initial angular momentum of the cloud, it forms into a rotating disc around the proto-star in accordance with Kepler's laws, with the inner portion of the disc rotating more rapidly than the outer region.

Planets Are Created

The process of planet formation occurs within this rotating disc. Dust grains collide and stick together, forming larger particles. This collisional growth continues over millions of years and eventually results in the creation of rocky bodies a few kilometers in diameter, known as "planetesimals." At this point the gravitational attraction of the planetesimals begins to dominate their random velocities, increasing their growth rate to the point where planetary cores about a thousand kilometers across can form rapidly.

As the proto-planetary disc continues to evolve, the planetary cores in the inner portion of the disc collide, merge and grow to become terrestrial planets such as Earth and Mars. In the outer disc, the cores grow to larger masses. Once the planetary core reaches about 10 Earth masses, its gravity is sufficient to capture gaseous hydrogen and helium from the disc, forming a gas-giant planet such as Jupiter or Saturn. This rapid-growth phase removes most of the material near the orbit of the growing planet, forming a gap in the disc and effectively shutting off the growth process.

Thus, scientists think that planets are built from their cores outward by accretion processes in the disc of gas and dust that surrounds a star during its creation.

SAMPLE PROCESS DESCRIPTIONS

Figure PO.4 (on the facing page) shows a sample set of instructions that uses segmenting to identify the major parts of the process. Figure PO.5 shows a group of paragraphs that describe one theory about the process by which planets are formed. Notice how the writer uses headings to help signal the major phases of the process.

COMPARISON

At work, you will often be writing comparisons between two or more things. Such occasions fall into two categories:

Purposes of comparisons

- **You want to help your readers make a decision**. The workplace is a world of choices. People are constantly choosing among courses of action, competing products, alternative strategies. To help them choose, you will often write comparisons.
- **You want to help your readers understand something by means of an analogy.** One of the most effective ways to help your readers understand something new is to explain the ways in which it resembles—or differs from—something they are familiar with.

HOW COMPARISONS WORK

In some ways, a comparison is like a classification. You begin with a large set of facts about the things you are comparing and then group the facts around points that enable your readers to see how the things are like or unlike one another.

When writing a comparison, you can choose from two basic patterns: alternating pattern and divided pattern. Both include the criteria (or points of comparison) and information about each alternative in terms of each criterion. Consider, for example, Lorraine's situation.

Lorraine must organize her data so that her readers can make their decision easily.

Lorraine works for a steel mill that has decided to build a new blast furnace. She has been asked to study the two types of furnaces the mill is considering and then present her results in a report that will help the mill's upper management decide which furnace to construct. Having amassed hundreds of pages of information, Lorraine must now decide how to organize the body of her report.

For organizing her comparison, Lorraine has the two basic choices: the divided pattern and the alternating pattern.

Divided Pattern	Alternating Pattern
Furnace A	**Cost**
Cost	Furnace A
Efficiency	Furnace B
Construction time	**Efficiency**
Air pollution	Furnace A
Et cetera	Furnace B
Furnace B	**Construction time**
Cost	Furnace A
Efficiency	Furnace B
Construction time	**Air pollution**
Air pollution	Furnace A
Et cetera	Furnace B
	Et cetera
	Furnace A
	Furnace B

The alternating pattern is best for point-by-point comparisons.

As you can see, the alternating pattern is organized around the criteria, making it ideal for readers who want to make point-by-point comparisons. After thinking about how her readers would use her long report on the blast furnaces, Lorraine selected this pattern. This pattern would allow her readers to find the information about the costs of both blast furnaces or the efficiency of both without the flipping back and forth that the divided pattern would require.

The divided pattern works best when readers want to size up all facts about an alternative at once.

The divided pattern is well suited to situations where readers want to see all the information about each alternative at one time. Typically, this occurs when both the general nature and the details of each alternative can be described in a short space, say one page or so. The divided pattern was used, for instance, by an employee of a restaurant who was asked to investigate the feasibility of buying a new sound system for the restaurant. He described each of the systems in a single page.

When using either the alternating or divided pattern you can assist your readers by incorporating two kinds of preliminary information:

- **Description of the criteria.** This lets your readers know from the start what the relevant points of comparison are.
- **Overview of the alternatives.** This provides your readers with a general sense of what each alternative entails before they focus on the details you provide.

In both patterns, the statement of criteria would precede the presentation of details.

Taking these additional elements into account, the general structure of the two patterns is as follows:

Ways of Organizing Comparisons	
Divided Pattern	**Alternating Pattern**
Statement of Criteria	**Statement of Criteria**
Overview of Alternatives (optional)	**Description of Alternatives**
Evaluation of Alternatives	**Alternative A**
Criterion 1	**Criterion 1**
Alternative A	**Criterion 2**
Alternative B	**Alternative B**
Criterion 2	**Criterion 1**
Alternative A	**Criterion 2**
Alternative B	**Conclusion**
Conclusion	

GUIDELINES FOR WRITING COMPARISONS

1. **Choose points of comparison suited to your readers and your purpose.** When you are preparing comparisons for decision-makers, be sure to include not only the criteria they consider important but also any additional criteria that you—with your expert knowledge—regard as significant.

When you are writing comparisons to create analogies, be sure to compare and contrast only those features that will help your readers understand the points you are trying to make. Avoid comparing extraneous details.

2. **If you are making complex comparisons, arrange the parts of your comparisons hierarchically.** For example, group information on all aspects of cost (purchase price, operating cost, maintenance cost, and so on) in one place, information on all aspects of performance in another place, and so on.

3. **Arrange the parts in an order your readers will find helpful.** When your comparison is intended to help readers make a decision, lead off with the criteria that reveal the most significant differences between the things you are comparing. When your comparison is designed to aid understanding, discuss points of similarity first. In this way, you begin with what your readers will find familiar and then lead them to the less familiar.

SAMPLE COMPARISONS

Figure PO.6 shows a segment that compares two methods of studying the ways that mothers might affect their children if they take drugs during pregnancy.

CAUSE AND EFFECT

You may use the cause-and-effect strategy in two different ways:

Purposes of cause-and-effect explanations

- **To help your readers understand the cause or consequences of some action or event.** For example, you may need to explain the causes of solar flares, earthquakes, or the birth of identical twins.
- **To persuade.** For example, you might need to persuade your readers that the damage to a large turbine generator (effect) resulted from metal fatigue in a key part (cause) rather than from a failure to provide proper lubrication. Or you might try to persuade your readers that cutting the selling price of a product (cause) will increase sales and produce a greater profit (effect).

GUIDELINES FOR DESCRIBING CAUSES AND EFFECTS

1. **Begin by identifying the cause or effect that you are going to describe.** Your readers will want to know from the beginning of your segment exactly what you are trying to explain so that they will know what they should be trying to understand as they read it. Sometimes a single sentence will be enough. At other times you may need several sentences.

2. **Carefully explain the links in the chain of cause and effect that you are describing.** Remember that you are not simply listing the steps in a process. You want your readers to understand how each step leads to the next step or is caused by the preceding step.

3. **If you are dealing with several causes or effects, group them into categories.** Categories help readers to understand a complex chain of events.

■ **FIGURE PO.6**

Passage Organized by Comparison

From Ernest L. Abel, "Effects of Prenatal Exposure to Cannabinoids," *Current Research on the Consequences of Maternal Drug Abuse*, Theodore M. Pinkert, Ed. (Washington, DC: U.S. Department of Health and Human Services, 1985).

The need for epidemiological studies is explained.

Comparison of two types of epidemiological studies is announced.

First type is discussed: strength, then weaknesses.

Second type is discussed: strength matched to weakness of first type.

CLINICAL AND EPIDEMIOLOGICAL STUDIES OF THE EFFECTS OF PRENATAN EXPOSURE TO DRUGS

Since experimental administration of drugs to pregnant women is unethical, studies of the effects on their children of their using drugs are limited to clinical observation and epidemiological investigations. Although clinical reports can be of considerable importance in alerting physicians and health care providers to possible agents causing abnormal development, they are difficult to evaluate. For example, two early clinical reports of malformations in children born to marijuana users (Hecht et al. 1968; Carakushansky et al., 1969) were inconclusive since the mothers of these children used other drugs as well.

When clinical reports are followed by epidemiological studies involving larger numbers of patients, a better appreciation of incidence and causation is possible. Such epidemiological studies can be divided into two types, retrospective and prospective, each of which has its own strengths and shortcomings.

In most retrospective studies, information from large numbers of cases is obtained from hospital records. However, such records are often inadequate or incomplete, thoroughness of reporting varies widely, and criteria for assessment of anomalies may also vary. In contrast to retrospective studies, prospective studies carefully establish criteria and protocols for maternal histories and examination of infants in prenatal health clinics. However, women who are usually most seriously at risk for giving birth to infants with drug-related anomalies may not attend prenatal health care facilities and, therefore, do not participate in prospective studies, resulting in underestimation of whatever problem is being investigated. Because prospective studies are so rigid in their design, they also are less flexible in allowing for changes to be incorporated as new information is obtained. Also prospective studies cannot anticipate knowledge. For example in the U. S. Collaborative Perinatal Project (Heinonen et al. 1977) which prospectively evaluated 55,000 consecutive births, no information was obtained with respect to maternal marijuana consumption because, at the time of the original protocol, marijuana was not a suspected teratogen.

GUIDELINES FOR PERSUADING READERS TO ACCEPT YOUR VIEW OF CAUSE AND EFFECT

1. **State your claim at the beginning of your passage.** Your claim will be that some particular effect was created by some particular cause, or that some particular cause will lead to some particular effect.

2. **Present your evidence and lines of reasoning.** Where possible, focus on undisputed evidence because your readers' willingness to agree with you depends largely on their willingness to accept your evidence. Use lines of reasoning that your readers will accept as logically sound and appropriate to the situation.

Avoid the *post hoc ergo propter hoc* fallacy.

3. **Anticipate and respond to objections.** In cause-and-effect segments, as in any persuasive segment, your readers may object to your evidence or to your line of reasoning. Be particularly careful to avoid the *post hoc ergo propter hoc* fallacy. In this form of faulty reasoning, a writer argues that *because* an event occurred after another event, it was *caused* by that event. Consider this example. In an attempt to persuade his employer, a furniture company, to use computerized machinery for some of its manufacturing operations, Samuel argued that a competitor's profits had risen substantially after it made that move. Samuel's boss pointed out that the increase in sales might have been caused by other changes made over the same period, such as new designs or a reconfiguration of its sales districts. To persuade his boss that the computerization had *caused* the increase in sales, Samuel would have to do more than just state that it had preceded the increase.

You may want to review Guideline 3 in Chapter 5 for ways to assure your readers that your reasoning is sound.

SAMPLE CAUSE-AND-EFFECT SEGMENT

Figure PO.7 shows a segment in which the writer explains one theory about the cause of the extinction of dinosaurs.

PROBLEM AND SOLUTION

When you are talking about a problem and its solution, you may have either of two purposes:

- **To describe.** When talking about past events, you may want to describe the measures you, your co-workers, or your organization took to solve some problem that has now been eliminated.
- **To persuade.** When looking to the future, you may want to persuade your readers that the actions you are recommending will solve a problem they want to overcome.

■ **FIGURE PO.7**

Passage Organized around Cause and Effect

From Boyce Rensberger, "Death of Dinosaurs: A True Story?" *Science Digest* 94(5) 1986: 28–32.

Effect to be explained is announced.

Possible cause is announced.

Link between effect and cause is explained: asteroid created dust cloud that killed dinosaurs.

Evidence of link is presented: rare molecules in sediment indicate an asteroid may have hit Earth when dinosaurs died.

Additional evidence of link

WHAT CAUSED THE DEATH OF THE DINOSAURS?

One theory is that a comet, asteroid or other huge extraterrestrial body slammed into the Earth 65 million years ago and ended the 160-million year reign of the dinosaurs. According to this theory, the extraterrestrial body raised a huge dust cloud. Within days the black cloud spread over the Earth, darkening the sun. The air turned cold, and many dinosaurs died. Snow fell. Freezing darkness gripped the Earth for weeks. Plants, cut off from the sunlight that feeds them, couldn't survive. Without plants, the rest of the herbivorous dinosaurs followed, and the carnivores soon afterward. Along with a number of other species, the dinosaurs were gone forever.

Although many leading paleontologists and evolutionary biologists now accept the asteroid-impact theory, and despite popular accounts implying that the question is settled, it is not. A scattering of critics continue to challenge the whole notion.

Still, the theory is compelling. Every few months a new piece of evidence is added to the list, and most, to the critics' consternation, support the idea of an extraterrestrial impact.

Just recently, for example, scientists at the Scripps Institute of Oceanography, in La Jolla, California, found evidence of organic molecules in the layer of sediments laid down at the time the dinosaurs died; the molecules are exceedingly rare on Earth but relatively common in some meteorites and so, presumably, in some asteroids.

To put the discovery in perspective, and to appreciate the arguments on both sides of the impact debate, one must first understand the nature of the original finding.

In 1980, Luis Alvarez, a Nobel laureate in physics, his son Walter, a geologist, both at the University of California, Berkeley, and two associates published the theory that a massive impact took place at the end of the Cretaceous Period. The team had found a rare substance in the thin layer of sedimentary clay deposited just on top of the highest, and therefore the most recent, stratum of rock contemporary with those bearing dinosaur fossils. It was the element iridium, which is almost nonexistent in the Earth's crust but 10,000 times more abundant in extraterrestrial rocks such as meteorites and asteroids. Deposits above and below the clay which is the boundary layer separating the Cretaceous layer from the succeeding Tertiary, have very little iridium.

REFERENCE GUIDE: Six Patterns for Organizing

■ **FIGURE PO.7**
(continued)

Additional evidence continued —

Because the same iridium anomaly appeared in two other parts of the world, in clay of exactly the same age, the Alvarez team proposed that the element had come from an asteroid that hit the Earth with enough force to vaporize, scattering iridium atoms in the atmosphere worldwide. When the iridium settled to the ground, it was incorporated in sediment laid down at the time.

Link is restated. —

More startling was the team's proposal that the impact blasted so much dust into the atmosphere that it blocked the sunlight and prevented photosynthesis (others suggested that a global freeze would also have resulted). They calculated that the object would have had to be about six miles in diameter.

Additional evidence of link —

Since 1980, iridium anomalies have been found in more than 80 places around the world, including deep-sea cores, all in layers of sediment that formed at the same time.

Challenge to link is explained: molecules perhaps from volcano, not asteroid.

One of the most serious challenges to the extraterrestrial theory came up very quickly. Critics said that the iridium could have come from volcanic eruptions, which are known to bring up iridium from deep within the Earth and feed it into the atmosphere. Traces of iridium have been detected in gases escaping from Hawaii's Kilauea volcano, for example.

Challenge is refuted by new evidence: other molecules couldn't have come from volcano.

The new finding from Scripps appears to rule out that explanation, though, as a source for iridium in the Cretaceous–Tertiary (K–T) boundary layer. Chemists Jeffrey Bada and Nancy Lee have found that the same layer also contains a form of amino acid that is virtually nonexistent on Earth—certainly entirely absent from volcanoes—but abundant, along with many other organic compounds, in a type of meteor called a carbonaceous chondrite.

GUIDELINES FOR DESCRIBING PROBLEMS AND THEIR SOLUTIONS

1. **Begin by identifying the problem that was solved.** Make the problem seem significant to your readers and emphasize the aspects of the problem that were affected most directly by the solution.
2. **Explain the links between the problem and the solution.** You want your readers to understand *how* the problem was overcome by the solution.
3. **If the solution consisted of several actions, group them into categories.** The resulting hierarchy will help your readers to understand the complex solution.

GUIDELINES FOR PERSUADING READERS TO ACCEPT YOUR SOLUTION TO A PROBLEM

1. **Describe the problem in a way that makes it seem significant to your readers.** Remember that your aim is to persuade them to take the action you recommend. They will not be very interested in taking action to solve a problem they regard as insignificant.

2. **Present your evidence and indicate your line of reasoning.** Use evidence that your readers will find sufficient and reliable and a line of reasoning they will accept as logically sound and appropriate to the situation.

3. **Anticipate and respond to objections.** As with any segment designed to persuade, your readers may object to your evidence or your line of reasoning. Devote special attention to determining what those objections are so you can respond to them (see pages 103).

When writing problem-and-solution passages designed to persuade, you may want to refer to Guideline 3 in Chapter 5, which discusses ways to convince your readers that your reasoning is sound.

SAMPLE PROBLEM-AND-SOLUTION SEGMENT

Figure PO.8 shows a memo organized around a problem and a possible solution.

COMBINATIONS OF PATTERNS

Long communications usually mix several of the patterns described in this Reference Guide.

So far, this Reference Guide has treated the six organizational patterns in isolation from one another. In practice, they are often mixed with one another and with passages using other patterns.

This will happen, for instance, in a report that Gene is writing to tell decision-makers in his organization about a new technique for applying coatings to the insides of television screens. Like many technical reports, his will employ a problem-and-solution pattern for its overall structure. First, he will describe the problem that makes the old technique undesirable for his employer, then he will describe the technique he has developed as a solution to that problem. Within this overall pattern, Gene will use many others, including the ones for describing an object (the equipment used in his technique), explaining a process (the way his technique works), and making a comparison (the performance of his new technique versus the performance of the current one). Similarly, when you write at work, you will often weave together various patterns, each one suited to a special aim of one particular part of your message.

Figure PO.9 (page 216) shows the outline for a report that mixes several of the organizational patterns.

(Exercises for this chapter begin on page 218.)

REFERENCE GUIDE: Six Patterns for Organizing

■ **FIGURE PO.8**

Memo Organized around a Problem and Its Solution

MANUFACTURING PROCESSES INSTITUTE
Interoffice Memorandum   June 21, 19—

To   Cliff Leibowitz

From   Candace Olin

RE   Suggestion to Investigate Kohle Reduktion Process for Steelmaking

As we have often discussed, it may be worthwhile to set up a project investigating steelmaking processes that could help the American industry compete more effectively with the more modern foreign mills. I suggest we begin with an investigation of the Kohle Reduktion method, which I learned about in the April 1999 issue of High Technology.

Problem is identified. —

A major problem for American steelmakers is the process they use to make the molten iron ("hot metal") that is processed into steel. Relying on a technique developed on a commercial scale over 100 years ago by Sir Henry Bessemer, they make the hot metal by mixing iron ore, limestone, and coke in blast furnaces. To make the coke, they pyrolyze coal in huge ovens in plants that cost over $100 million and create enormous amounts of air pollution.

Problem is explained. —

Solution is announced. —

In the Kohle Reduktion method, developed by Korf Engineering in West Germany, the hot metal is made without coke. Coal, limestone, and oxygen are mixed in a gasification unit at 2500°. The gas rises in a shaft furnace above the gasification unit, chemically reducing the iron ore to "sponge iron." The sponge iron then drops into the gasification unit, where it is melted and the contaminants are removed by reaction of the limestone. Finally, the hot metal drains out of the bottom of the gasifier.

Solution is explained. —

Link between problem and solution is explained. —

The Kohle method, if developed satisfactorily, will have several advantages. It will eliminate the air pollution problem of coke plants, it can be built (according to Korf estimates) for 25% less than conventional furnaces, and it may cut the cost of producing hot metal by 15%.

This technology appears to offer a dramatic solution to the problems with our nation's steel industry: I recommend that we investigate it further. If the method proves feasible and if we develop an expertise in it, we will surely attract many clients for our consulting services.

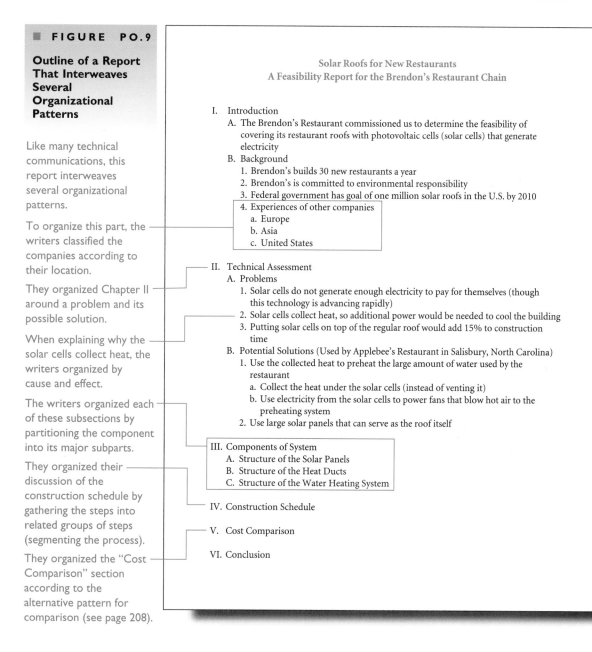

■ FIGURE PO.9

Outline of a Report That Interweaves Several Organizational Patterns

Like many technical communications, this report interweaves several organizational patterns.

To organize this part, the writers classified the companies according to their location.

They organized Chapter II around a problem and its possible solution.

When explaining why the solar cells collect heat, the writers organized by cause and effect.

The writers organized each of these subsections by partitioning the component into its major subparts.

They organized their discussion of the construction schedule by gathering the steps into related groups of steps (segmenting the process).

They organized the "Cost Comparison" section according to the alternative pattern for comparison (see page 208).

Solar Roofs for New Restaurants
A Feasibility Report for the Brendon's Restaurant Chain

I. Introduction
   A. The Brendon's Restaurant commissioned us to determine the feasibility of covering its restaurant roofs with photovoltaic cells (solar cells) that generate electricity
   B. Background
      1. Brendon's builds 30 new restaurants a year
      2. Brendon's is committed to environmental responsibility
      3. Federal government has goal of one million solar roofs in the U.S. by 2010
      4. Experiences of other companies
         a. Europe
         b. Asia
         c. United States

II. Technical Assessment
   A. Problems
      1. Solar cells do not generate enough electricity to pay for themselves (though this technology is advancing rapidly)
      2. Solar cells collect heat, so additional power would be needed to cool the building
      3. Putting solar cells on top of the regular roof would add 15% to construction time
   B. Potential Solutions (Used by Applebee's Restaurant in Salisbury, North Carolina)
      1. Use the collected heat to preheat the large amount of water used by the restaurant
         a. Collect the heat under the solar cells (instead of venting it)
         b. Use electricity from the solar cells to power fans that blow hot air to the preheating system
      2. Use large solar panels that can serve as the roof itself

III. Components of System
   A. Structure of the Solar Panels
   B. Structure of the Heat Ducts
   C. Structure of the Water Heating System

IV. Construction Schedule

V. Cost Comparison

VI. Conclusion

EXERCISES

1. To choose the appropriate principle of classification for organizing a group of items, you need to consider your readers and your purpose. Here are three topics for classification, each with two possible readers. First, identify a purpose that each reader might have for consulting a communication on that topic. Then identify a principle of classification that would be appropriate for each reader and purpose.

   Types of instruments or equipment used in your field
   Student majoring in your field
   Director of purchasing in your future employer's organization
   Intramural sports
   Director of intramural sports at your college
   Student
   Flowers
   Florist
   Owner of a greenhouse that sells garden plants

2. Use a principle of classification to create a hierarchy having at least two levels. Some topics are suggested below. After you have selected a topic, identify a reader and a purpose for your classification. Depending on your instructor's request, show your hierarchy in an outline or use it to write a brief discussion of your topic. In either case, state your principle of classification. Have you created a hierarchy that, at each level, has one and only one place for every item?

   Boats   Computers
   Cameras   Physicians
   The skills you will need on the job
   Tools, instruments, or equipment you will use on the job
   Some groups of items used in your field (for example, rocks if you are a geologist, or power sources if you are an electrical engineer)

3. Partition an object in a way that will be helpful to someone who wants to use it. Some objects are suggested below. Whichever one you choose, describe one specific instance of it. For example, describe a particular brand and model of food processor, rather than a generic food processor. Be sure that your hierarchy has at least two levels, and state the basis of partitioning you use at each level. Depending upon your instructor's request, show your hierarchy in an outline or use it to write a brief discussion of your topic.

   Aqualung   Microwave oven
   Graphing calculator   Bicycle
   Some instrument or piece of equipment used in your field that has at least a dozen parts

4. Segment a procedure to create a hierarchy you could use in a set of instructions. Give it at least two levels. Some topics are listed below. Show the resulting hierarchy in an outline. Be sure to identify your readers and purpose. If your instructor requests, use the outline to write a set of instructions.

   Changing an automobile tire
   Making homemade yogurt
   Starting an aquarium
   Rigging a sailboat
   Developing a roll of film
   Some procedure used in your field that involves at least a dozen steps
   Some other procedure of interest to you that includes at least a dozen steps

5. Segment a procedure to create a hierarchy you could use in a general description of a process. Give it at least two levels. Some suggested topics are listed below. Show the resulting hierarchy in an outline. Be sure to identify your readers and purpose. If your instructor requests, use the outline to write a general description of the process addressed to someone unfamiliar with it.

   How the human body takes oxygen from the air and delivers it to the parts of the body where it is used
   How television signals from a program originating in New York or Los Angeles reach television sets in other parts of the country
   How aluminum is made
   Some process used in your field that involves at least a dozen steps
   Some other process of interest to you that includes at least a dozen steps

6. One of your friends is thinking about making a major purchase. Some possible items are listed below. Create an outline with at least two levels that compares two or more good alternatives. If your instructor requests, use that outline to write your friend a letter.

Stereo   Personal computer
Binoculars   Bicycle
CD player

Some other type of product for which you can make a meaningful comparison on at least three important points

7. Think of some way in which things might be done better in a club, a business, or some other organization. Imagine that you are going to write a letter to the person who can bring about the change you are recommending. Create an outline with at least two levels in which you compare the way you think things should be done and the way they are being done now.

8. A friend has asked you to explain the causes of a particular event. Some events are suggested below. Write your friend a brief letter explaining the causes.

Static on radios and televisions
Immunization from a disease
Freezer burn in foods
Yellowing of paper

9. Think of a problem you feel should be corrected. The problem might be noise in your college library, shoplifting from a particular store, or the shortage of parking space on campus. Briefly describe the problem and list the actions you would take to solve it. Next, explain how each action will contribute to solving the problem. If your instructor requests, use your outline to write a brief memo explaining the problem and your proposed solution to a person who could take the actions you suggest.

CHAPTER 8

Beginning a Communication

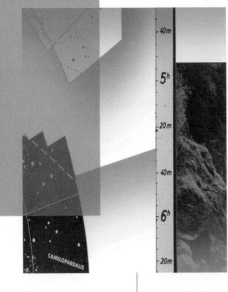

CAMELOPARDALIS

GUIDELINES

1 | Give your readers a reason to pay attention

2 | State your main point

3 | Tell your readers what to expect

4 | Encourage openness to your message

5 | Provide necessary background information

6 | Adjust the length of your beginning to your readers' needs

7 | For longer communications, begin with a summary

8 | Adapt your beginning to your readers' cultural background

220

CHAPTER

Imagine that you are attending the first day of a new course. You don't know any of the other students. Afterwards, the person sitting next to you starts a conversation. How will you respond?

Your response will probably depend upon the other person's opening words. The subject this person talks about, the person's tone of voice, even the way the person phrases his or her comments may all determine whether you linger to chat or rush off to your next destination. If you stay, you will probably shape your own comments in light of the first things the other person says.

The opening words of the communications you write at work will be much like the opening words of a conversation. They will influence greatly the way your readers react to your overall message. They may even determine whether your readers decide to keep on reading.

This chapter presents eight guidelines for creating beginnings that will elicit the response you want from your readers.

THE TWO FUNCTIONS OF A BEGINNING

Before reading these guidelines, however, you may find it helpful to think about the two distinct functions performed by the beginning of a communication:

- **A beginning introduces your message.** You use it to persuade your readers to pay close attention and to respond favorably to what you have to say. The guidelines in this chapter will help you achieve those objectives.
- **A beginning introduces a group of paragraphs.** In this case, the group consists of *all* the paragraphs in your communication. For this reason, several of the strategies Chapter 7 suggests you employ at the beginning of paragraphs, sections, and chapters apply equally to the beginning of your whole communication:
  - Announce the topic.
  - Begin with your main point.
  - Provide a forecasting statement.

These important pieces of advice from Chapter 7 are incorporated into Guidelines 1 through 3 of this chapter so that you can see how to apply them when writing the beginning of a communication.

GUIDELINE 1 | **Give Your Readers a Reason to Pay Attention**

People sometimes feel they are too busy to read.

The most important function of a beginning is to attract your readers' attention.

This may be a very difficult task. At work, people often complain that they receive too many memos, too many reports, too many e-mail messages. As they sift through the envelopes delivered to their desks or scan through the lists of e-mail messages recently received by their computers, the first question they ask about each item is, "Why should I read this?" If they don't find a persuasive answer quickly, they may file the communication unread or else throw it away.

In the face of these difficult circumstances, you must strive to gain not merely *some* attention from your audience, but their *close* attention. Doing so will be especially important when your communication's overall purpose is primarily persuasive. Research has shown that the more deeply people think about a message while reading or listening to it, the longer they are likely to adopt the attitudes it advocates, the more likely they are to resist attempts to reverse those attitudes, and the more likely they are to act upon those attitudes (Petty and Cacioppo).

People are more likely to be persuaded by messages they think deeply about.

To attract readers' close attention, you must usually do two things at the very beginning of your communication:

- Announce your topic.
- Tell your readers how they will benefit from the information you are providing.

Be sure to do *both* things. Don't assume that your readers will automatically see the value of your information after you have stated your topic. The benefit that appears obvious to you may not be obvious to them. Compare the following sets of statements:

State reader benefits explicitly.

Statements of Topic Only (Avoid Them)	Statements of Topic and Benefit (Use Them)
This memo tells about the new technology for making computer memory chips.	This memo answers each of the five questions you asked me last week about the new technology for making computer memory chips.
This report discusses step-up pumps.	Step-up pumps can save us money and increase our productivity.
This manual concerns the Cadmore Industrial Robot 2000.	This manual tells how to prepare the Cadmore Industrial Robot 2000 for difficult welding tasks.

Two strategies are particularly effective in persuading people that they will benefit from reading your communication: referring to your readers' request and offering to help your readers solve a problem.

Refer to Your Readers' Request

At work, you will often write in response to a request. A simple reference to the request will establish the benefit of your communication:

References to the readers' request

Here are the test results you asked for.

As you requested, I am enclosing a list of the steps we have taken in the past year to tighten security in the Data Processing Department.

Thank you for your inquiry about the capabilities of our Model 1770 color laser printer.

Offer to Help Your Readers Solve a Problem

A second strategy for persuading readers to devote serious attention to your communication is to explain that your communication will help them solve a problem they are dealing with. This strategy can be especially effective at work because most

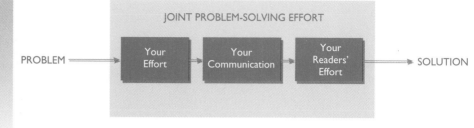

FIGURE 8.1

The Writer and the Readers Are Problem-Solving Partners

Based on J. C. Mathes and Dwight W. Stevenson, *Designing Technical Reports*, 2nd ed. (Indianapolis: Bobbs-Merrill, 1991).

employees see themselves as problem-solvers. Sometimes the problem will be technical, such as detecting flaws in airplane wings or preserving the freshness of the company's meat products without using harmful chemicals. Other problems may be organizational, such as improving morale or increasing the efficiency of the quality-assurance department. Still others may be ethical problems, such as ensuring that temporary employees are treated fairly. Whatever the problem, your readers will welcome communications that help them find a solution.

Readers welcome problem-solving ideas.

Communication experts J. C. Mathes and Dwight W. Stevenson have suggested an especially powerful approach to writing beginnings that builds on readers' concerns with problem-solving. First, think of a list of problems that are important to the people you are going to address in your communication. Then, identify from that list a problem that you will help your readers solve by presenting them with the information and ideas to be included in your communication. When you've done that, you have begun to think of yourself and your readers as partners in a joint problem-solving effort in which your communication plays a critical role. Figure 8.1 illustrates this relationship.

Once you have determined how to describe a problem-solving partnership between you and your readers, you are ready to draft the beginning of your communication. In it, you would typically explain the following three things:

Tell your readers these three things.

- **What the problem is.** Be careful to identify a problem your readers deem important.
- **What you have done toward solving the problem.** Review the steps you have taken as a specialist in your own field, such as developing a new feature for one of your employer's products, investigating products offered by competitors, or writing a new policy for handling purchase orders. Limit yourself to the activities that will be significant to your readers, rather than listing everything you may have done.
- **How your communication will help them.** Let your readers know what your communication will do for them as they perform their part of your joint problem-solving effort. For example, you might say that it will help them compare competing products or help them to understand a new policy for handling purchase orders or give them ideas for a new marketing plan.

Figure 8.2 shows the relationships among the three elements of a beginning.

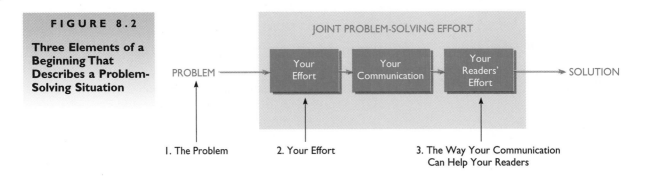

FIGURE 8.2

Three Elements of a Beginning That Describes a Problem-Solving Situation

For example, consider the way that Carla, a computer systems analyst, wrote the beginning of a report.

Carla thought of her trip as a problem-solving effort.

> Carla's report concerns her trip to Houston, where she studied the billing system at a hotel that her employer recently purchased. As she prepared to draft the report's beginning, she identified the problem that her communication would help her readers solve: the Houston hotel is making little money, perhaps because its billing system is faulty.
>
> She then thought of what she did in Houston and afterwards to help her readers solve this problem: she evaluated the billing system and formulated possible improvements.
>
> Finally, she determined what her report would offer her readers to help them perform their own problem-solving activities: it would help them choose the best course of action by providing data and recommendations on which they could base their decision.

Here is how Carla wrote the beginning of her report:

Carla names the problem her report will help solve.

> Over the past two years, our Houston hotel has shown a profit of only 4 percent, even though it is almost always 78 percent filled. A preliminary examination of the hotel's operations suggests that its billing system may be inadequate: it may be too slow in billing customers, and it may be inefficient and needlessly ineffective in collecting overdue payments.

Carla describes her work toward solving the problem.

> Therefore, I have thoroughly examined the hotel's billing cycle and its collection procedures, and I have considered ways to improve them.

Carla tells how her report will help her readers do their part toward solving the problem.

> In this report, I present the results of my analysis, together with my recommendations. To aid in the evaluation of my recommendations, I have included a discussion of the costs and benefits of each.

Must You Always Provide All This Information? Beginnings that use this strategy may be shorter or longer than Carla's. The crucial point is to make sure your readers understand all three elements of the problem-solving situation. One of the elements may be obvious to them. For example, if they asked for the information you are providing, simply refer to their request. Moreover, some of your readers may already be aware of what you have done to solve the problem. If Carla's only reader had been her boss, she could have written a very brief beginning, such as the following:

> In this report, I evaluate the billing system in our Houston hotel and recommend ways of improving it.

She included more explanation because she knew her report would also be read by people who were hearing about her trip for the first time.

Similarly, before using an abbreviated beginning, be sure that all your readers will understand immediately your communication's relevance to them even if you don't state it explicitly. Here are some situations in which a full description of the problem-solving situation is desirable:

- **Your communication will be read or heard by people outside your immediate working group.** The larger your audience, the less likely it is that all of them will be familiar with the context of your message.
- **Your communication will have a binding and a cover.** Bound documents are usually intended for large groups of readers. Such documents may also be filed to make them available for future reference. Unless you define the problem-solving situation, many readers will have no idea of what it was.
- **Your communication will be used to make a decision involving a significant amount of money.** Such decisions are often made by high-level managers who usually need to be told of the organizational context of the reports they read. For example, although Carla's boss asked her for the report, the people who will make a decision based on her recommendations have responsibility for the operation of the entire chain of hotels—247 in all. Carla cannot assume that they know about the Houston hotel's situation.

Defining the Problem in Unsolicited Communications   According to a survey, the majority of college graduates write on their own initiative (unsolicited) at least as often as they write on assignment (Anderson). When writing unsolicited requests or recommendations, you may sometimes encounter a special problem as you write the beginning: persuading your readers that a problem even exists.

Consider the way Roberto accomplished this goal:

Roberto works for a company that markets computer programs used to control manufacturing processes. One program contained bugs that Roberto wanted to fix because he sympathized with the customers who called for help when one of the bugs caused them difficulty and because he knew the company was losing sales due to the bugs. However, Roberto also knew that his boss did not believe the bugs really posed a problem—or, at least, one serious enough to require action.

Her top priority was developing new products rapidly.

Consequently, Roberto wrote his boss a memo that opened by discussing problems that the company had been having in releasing new products on time. He then showed how much of the systems analysts' time was spent helping customers with problems caused by the bugs. By tying his request to a problem that his reader found significant (not to the problems that actually prompted him to write), Roberto succeeded in being assigned to fix the two most serious bugs.

Roberto had to persuade his boss that a problem existed that was important to her.

In sum, to describe the benefit your readers will gain from reading your communication, adopt your readers' view of both the situation you are addressing and the communication itself. There is no task for which a reader-centered approach is more critical than explaining the significance of your message to your audience.

GUIDELINE **2**   **State Your Main Point**

At the beginning of a communication, it is often helpful to state your main point. In earlier chapters, you learned three major reasons for doing so:

> **Reasons for Stating Your Main Point at the Beginning**
>
> - You help your readers find what they most want or need.
> - You increase the likelihood that your readers will actually read your main point, instead of putting your communication aside before they get to it.
> - You provide your readers with a context for viewing the details that follow.

Choose Your Main Point Thoughtfully

Choose the main point of your communication in the same way you choose the main point of each segment. If you are responding to a request, your main point will be the answer to the question your reader asked. If you are writing on your own initiative, your main point might be what you want your readers to think or do after reading your communication.

Here are some sample statements:

From the beginning of a memo written in a manufacturing company: We should immediately suspend all purchases from Cleves Manufacturing until it can guarantee us that the parts it supplies will meet our specifications.

From the beginning of a memo written to a department head in a food services company: I request $1,200 in travel funds to send one of our account executives to the client's Atlanta headquarters.

From a research report: The test results show that the walls of the submersible room will not be strong enough to withstand the high pressures of a deep dive.

GUIDELINE **3**   **Tell Your Readers What to Expect**

In addition to stating your main point, the beginning of a communication should tell readers what to expect in the segments that follow. This guideline echoes the advice given in Chapter 7: "Use forecasting statements." When positioned at the beginning, forecasting statements should focus on the organization and scope of the overall communication.

Tell about Your Communication's Organization

The major reason for telling your readers about the *organization* of your communication is to provide them with a framework for understanding the connections among the various pieces of information you convey.

You can tell your readers about the organization of your communication in various ways:

Forecasting statement	In this report, we state the objectives of the project, compare the three major technical alternatives, and present our recommendation. The final sections include a budget and a proposed project schedule.
Forecasting list	This booklet covers the following topics: ■ Principles of Sound Reproduction ■ Types of Speakers ■ Choosing the Speakers That Are Right for You ■ Installing the Speakers

Tell about Your Communication's Scope

Readers want to know from the beginning what a communication does and does not contain. Even if they are persuaded that you are addressing a subject relevant to them, they may still wonder whether you will discuss the specific aspects of the subject they want to know about.

Often, you will tell your readers about the scope of your communication when you tell them about its organization: when you list the topics it addresses, you indicate its scope.

However, there will be times when you will need to include additional information. That happens when you want your readers to understand that you are not addressing your subject comprehensively or that you are addressing it from a particular point of view. For instance, you may be writing a troubleshooting manual to help factory workers solve a certain set of problems that often arise with the manufacturing robots they monitor. Other problems—ones your manual doesn't address—might require the assistance of a computer programmer or an electrical engineer. In that case, you should tell your readers explicitly about the scope of your manual:

Statement of scope	This manual treats problems you can correct by using tools and equipment normally available to you. It does not cover problems that require work by computer programmers or electrical engineers.

Use your judgment in deciding how much to say in your beginning about the organization and scope of your communication. For brief communications, readers don't need any information at all about such matters. But for longer ones, they will benefit from knowing at the start what lies ahead.

G U I D E L I N E 4 Encourage Openness to Your Message

Other chapters in this book have mentioned that readers can respond in different ways as they read a communication. For example, when they read a set of recommendations you are making, they can try to understand your arguments, or they can search for flaws. When they read a set of instructions you have prepared, they can follow your directions in every detail, or they can attempt the procedure on their own, consulting your instructions only if they get stumped.

Because the way you begin a communication has a strong effect on your readers' response, begin in a way that encourages them to be open and receptive to the points you will be making.

Situations Vary

Ordinarily, you will have no trouble eliciting a receptive response because you will be communicating with fellow employees, customers, and others who want the information you are providing. In certain circumstances, however, your readers may have a more negative attitude toward your message. For example, your report may reveal shortcomings in a plan devised by your readers themselves. Or you may be making a recommendation that, if followed, will have undesirable consequences for some of your readers. Or you may be writing to a customer who is dissatisfied with the products or services provided by your company. In such situations, you will need to take special care in drafting the beginning of your communication if you are to win a fair hearing for your message.

Special strategies are needed when readers might resist your message.

How to Predict Your Readers' Initial Attitude

Your readers' initial attitude toward your message will be negative if the answer to any of the following questions is "yes." In this case, try to pinpoint the attitudes that are likely to shape your readers' reactions to your communication. Then devise your beginning accordingly.

Predicting Whether Your Readers Will Resist Your Message

- Does your message contain bad news for your readers?
- Does your message contain ideas or recommendations that will be unwelcome to your readers?
- Do your readers have any feelings of distrust, resentment, or competitiveness toward you, your department, or your company?
- Are your readers likely to be skeptical of your knowledge of your subject or of the situation?
- Are your readers likely to be suspicious of your motives?

Some Strategies for Encouraging Openness

The strategy that is most likely to prevent or counteract an initial negative reaction differs from situation to situation. However, here are three strategies that often work:

- **Present yourself as a partner, not as a critic or a competitor.** Suggest that you are working with your readers to help solve a problem they want to solve or to achieve a goal they want to achieve. (See Guideline 1.)
- **Delay the presentation of your main point.** An initial negative reaction may prompt your readers to aggressively devise counterarguments to each point that

How to Confront Unethical Practices—and Survive

Suppose you learn that your employer is engaged in an action you consider to be unethical. Or suppose you are asked to write something that violates your sense of what is ethical. What should you do?

Don't Wait

New employees are sometimes advised to wait until they have achieved security and status before trying to bring about change. But that means you could spend years before addressing a practice you regard as unethical. Ignoring an unethical act is itself unethical.

The following paragraphs discuss some ways you can act ethically without jeopardizing your future with your employer's organization.

Take the Long View, But Begin Now

Instead of trying to change the situation immediately, make it your long-term goal to bring about change—but begin now. Here are some actions you can take.

1. Call attention, perhaps subtly, to the ethical issues involved. You might just ask a question. For example, if your employer is thinking of making a change that will adversely alter working conditions in a plant, you might ask, "How would this affect workers on the night shift?" You can even introduce a consideration of value: "Would that be fair to them?"

2. Mention the ethical issues that you think are involved. Let people know the values you bring to your understanding of the situation.

3. State your position, but be patient. Remember that change often comes slowly. Taking the initiative to improve a situation is an ethical act in itself.

Avoid Polarizing

You are much more likely to prevail if you invite people with other views to engage in a reasoned discussion than if you accuse and condemn them. It's not usually possible to persuade people by attacking them. They merely become defensive. Instead, ask them to share their sense of the values that apply to the situation. Appeal to their sense of fairness and of what is right and wrong.

Remain Open to Other Views

One reason to avoid polarizing is that it impairs your ability to understand others' views of the situation. People regularly differ on ethical matters, and your own view is not necessarily shared by others. Strive for solutions that will satisfy both yourself and others.

Blow the Whistle

You may someday witness a practice that is so outrageous that you will be willing to risk future promotions and even your job in order to stop it. If you come to that decision, seek the aid of influential people inside your company. If the practice you object to violates the law or a government regulation, alert the appropriate agency. This is called *whistle-blowing*.

Federal law and some state laws are intended to protect whistle-blowers, and some laws even reward whistle-blowers by giving them a portion of any financial settlement that is made. Still, many whistle-blowers do lose their jobs or continue to work under hostile conditions. If you are thinking of whistle-blowing, consider the possibility of first taking a nonconfrontational approach to the problem.

See also Chapter 5's discussion of the indirect pattern of organization (page 109).

follows. Therefore, if you believe that your readers may react negatively to your main point, consider making an exception to Guideline 2, which tells you to state your main point in your beginning. If you delay the presentation of your main point, your readers may consider at least some of your other points objectively before discovering your main point and reacting against it.

See also Chapter 5's suggestions for building credibility (page 112).

■ **Establish your credibility.** As Chapter 5 suggests, people are more likely to respond favorably to a message if they have confidence in the person who is delivering it. Consequently, you can promote openness to your message if you begin by convincing your readers that you are expert in your subject and knowledgeable about the situation. Does this mean that you should announce your credentials in the beginning of every communication? No. When you are writing to co-workers, they will already have formed an opinion about your credibility. Also, when you are taking a position with which your readers already agree, your credentials aren't likely to matter much. Needlessly presenting your credentials merely burdens your readers with unnecessary information. In some situations, however, some mention of your credentials will make your readers more receptive to your message.

Tell Yourself a Story

Although the strategies suggested above will often encourage openness, don't employ them mechanically. Always keep in mind the particular attitudes, experiences, and expectations of your readers as you devise the beginning of a communication.

Telling a story helps you focus on your particular readers.

You might do this by telling yourself a story about your readers. The central figure in your story should be your reader if you are writing to one person, or a typical member of your audience if you are writing to a group. Begin your story a few minutes before this person picks up your communication and continue it to the moment he or she reads your first words. Although you would not actually include the story in your communication, creating it can help you decide how to begin.

Here is a sample story, written by Jolene, a manager in an insurance company. Jolene wrote this story to help herself understand the readers of an instruction manual she is preparing. The manual will teach new insurance agents how to use the company's computer system.

Jolene predicts her readers' attitudes by imagining a story about one of them.

It's Monday afternoon. After half a day of orientation meetings and tours, Bob, the new trainee, sits down at the computer terminal for the first time to try to learn this system. He was a French major who has never used a data-entry program. Now, in two hours, he is supposed to work his way through this manual and then enter some sample policy information. He feels rushed, confused, and quite nervous. He knows that the information is critical, and he does not want to make an error.

Despite his insecurity, Bob will not ask questions of the experienced agent in the next office because (being new to the company) he doesn't want to make a bad impression by asking dumb questions.

Bob picks up the instruction manual for the SPRR program that I am writing: he hopes it will tell him quickly what he needs to know. He wants it to help him learn the system in the time allotted without his making any mistakes and without his having to ask embarrassing questions.

This story helped Jolene to focus on several important facts: the reader will be anxious, hurried, and uncertain. Those insights helped her write an effective opening for her manual:

Jolene adopts a helpful tone.

Jolene reassures her readers.

This manual tells you how to enter policy information into our SPRR system. It covers the steps for opening a file for a new policy, entering the relevant information, revising the file, and printing a paper copy for your permanent records.

Be sure to follow the instructions carefully, so that you can avoid making time-consuming errors. At the same time, you should know that the SPRR system is designed to flag possible errors so you can double-check them.

By identifying her readers' probable feelings, Jolene was able to reduce their anxiety and encourage them to be more open to her instructions.

GUIDELINE 5 **Provide Necessary Background Information**

As you draft the beginning of a communication, ask yourself whether your readers will need any background information to understand what you are going to tell them.

Here are some examples of situations that might require such information at the beginning:

Signs that your readers need background information

- **Your readers need to grasp certain general principles in order to understand your specific points.** For instance, your discussion of the feasibility of locating a new plant in a particular city may depend on a particular analytical technique that you will need to explain to your readers.
- **Your readers are unfamiliar with technical terms you will be using.** For example, as a specialist in international trade, you may need to explain certain technical terms to the board of directors before you present your strategies for opening up foreign markets.
- **Your readers are unfamiliar with the situation you are discussing.** For example, imagine that you are reporting to the executive directors of a large corporation about labor problems at one of the plants it recently acquired in a takeover. To understand and weigh the choices that face them, the directors will need an introduction to the plant and its labor history.

Not all background information belongs at the beginning of your communication. Information that pertains only to certain segments should appear at the beginning of those segments. In the beginning of your communication, include only background information that will help your readers understand your overall message.

GUIDELINE 6 **Adjust the Length of Your Beginning to Your Readers' Needs**

There is no rule-of-thumb that tells how long the beginning should be. A good, reader-centered beginning may require only a phrase or may take several pages. You need to give your readers only the information they don't already know. Just be sure they know the following:

> **What Your Readers Need to Know**
>
> - The reason they should read the communication (Guideline 1)
> - The main point of the communication (Guideline 2)
> - The organization and scope of the communication (Guideline 3)
> - The background information they need in order to understand and use the communication (Guideline 5)

If you have given your readers all this information—and have encouraged them to receive your message openly (Guideline 4)—then you have written a good beginning, regardless of how long or short it is.

Here is an opening prepared by a writer who followed all the guidelines given in this chapter:

Brief beginning

In response to your memo dated November 17, I have called Goodyear, Goodrich, and Firestone for information about the ways they forecast their needs for synthetic rubber. The following paragraphs summarize each of those phone calls.

The following opening, from a two-paragraph memo, is even briefer:

Briefer beginning

We are instituting a new policy for calculating the amount that employees are paid for over-time work.

At first glance, this single sentence may seem to violate all the guidelines. It does not. It identifies the topic of the memo (overtime pay), and the people to whom the memo is addressed will immediately understand its relevance to them. It also declares the main point of the memo (a new policy is being instituted). Moreover, because the memo itself is only two paragraphs long, its scope is readily apparent. The brevity of the memo also suggests its organization, namely, a brief explanation of the new policy and nothing else. The writer has correctly judged that his readers need no background information.

Examples of longer beginnings are shown in Figures 8.3 and 8.4.

Figure 8.3 shows a relatively long beginning from a report written by a consulting firm hired to recommend ways to improve the food service at a hospital. Like the brief beginnings given above, it is carefully adapted to its readers and to the situation.

Figure 8.4 (page 234) shows the long beginning of a 500-page service manual for the Detroit Diesel Series 53 engine manufactured by General Motors.

GUIDELINE **7** **For Longer Communications, Begin with a Summary**

At work, it's quite common for communications more than two pages long to start off with a brief summary of the entire message. These summaries serve two purposes:

Purposes of initial summaries

- They help busy managers learn the main points without reading the entire document.
- They help all readers build a mental framework for organizing and understanding the detailed information they will encounter as they read on.

In short communications, such as memos and letters, opening summaries are often only a few sentences incorporated in the opening paragraph or paragraphs. In longer communications, they may be a page or longer and may be printed on separate sheets that precede the body of the document.

Features of a Good Summary

No single pattern is appropriate for all summaries. However, readers usually want summaries to tell them something from each of a communication's main sections, so your summary's organization should ordinarily parallel the organization of the communication itself.

Informative summaries state the main points.

What you report from each section depends on what your readers will find most useful. One type of summary, the *informative summary,* states the main point or points from each section and emphasizes results, conclusions, and recommendations. Informative summaries are ideally suited to the needs of readers who are seek-

Text continued on page 235

FIGURE 8.3

Beginning of a Recommendation Report

Problem ————————————

Subparts of the overall problem ————————————

What the writers have done to help solve the problem ————————————

How this report will help the readers ————

How the report is organized ————————

Scope ————————

Main points ————————————

INTRODUCTION

Wilton Hospital has added 200 patient beds through construction of the new West Wing. Since the wing opened, the food-service department has had difficulty meeting this extra demand. The director of the hospital has also reported the following additional problems:

1. Difficulties operating at full capacity. The equipment, some of it thirty years old, breaks down frequently. Absenteeism has risen dramatically.

2. Costs of operation that are well above average for the hospital industry nationally and in this region.

3. Frequent complaints about the quality of the food from both the patients and the hospital staff who eat in the cafeteria.

To study these problems, we have monitored the operation of the food-service department and interviewed patients, food-service employees, and staff who eat in the cafeteria. In addition, we have compared all aspects of the department's facilities and operations with those at other hospitals of roughly the same size.

In this report, we discuss our findings concerning the food-service department's kitchen facilities. We briefly describe the history and nature of these facilities, suggest two alternative ways of improving them, and provide a budget for each. In the final section of this report, we propose a renovation schedule and discuss ways of providing food service while the renovation work is being done. (Our recommendations about staffing and procedures will be presented in another report in thirty days.)

The first alternative costs about $730,000 and would take four months to accomplish. The second costs about $1,100,000 and would take five months. Both will meet the minimum needs of the hospital; the latter can also provide cooking for the proposed program of delivering hot meals to housebound persons in the city.

FIGURE 8.4

Beginning of a Service Manual

From Detroit Diesel Corporation, *Detroit Diesel Engines Series 53 Service Manual* (Detroit, MI, 1990) 4.

What this manual is ————
about

Scope ————

Organization ————

Background information ————
to help readers use the
manual

Background information ————
that is implicit throughout
the rest of the manual

Additional background ————
information, including
cautions

General Information   DETROIT DIESEL 53

• SCOPE AND USE OF THE MANUAL

This manual covers the basic Series 53 Diesel Engines built by the Detroit Diesel Corporation. Complete instructions on operation, adjustment (tune-up), preventive maintenance and lubrication, and repair (including complete overhaul) are covered. The manual was written primarily for persons servicing and overhauling the engine and, in addition, contains all of the instructions essential to the operators and users. Basic maintenance and overhaul procedures are common to all Series 53 engines and, therefore, apply to all Inline and Vee models.

The manual is divided into numbered sections. The first section covers the engine (less major assemblies). The following sections cover a complete system such as the fuel system, lubrication system or air system. Each section is divided into subsections which contain complete maintenance and operating instructions for a specific subassembly on the engine. For example, Section 1, which covers the basic engine, contains subsection 1.1 pertaining to the cylinder block, subsection 1.2 covering the cylinder head, etc. The subjects and sections are listed in the Table of Contents on the preceding page. Pages are numbered consecutively, starting with a new Page 1 at the beginning of each subsection. The illustrations are also numbered consecutively, beginning with a new Fig. 1 at the start of each subsection.

Information regarding a general subject, such as the lubrication system, can best be located by using the Table of Contents. Opposite each subject in the Table of Contents is a section number which registers with a tab printed on the first page of each section throughout the manual. Information on a specific subassembly or accessory can then be found by consulting the list of contents on the first page of the section. For example, the cylinder liner is part of the basic engine. Therefore, it will be found in Section 1. Looking down the list of contents on the first page of Section 1, the cylinder liner is found to be in subsection 1.6.3. An Alphabetical Index at the back of the manual has been provided as an additional aid for locating information.

SERVICE PARTS AVAILABILITY

Genuine Detroit Diesel service parts are available from authorized Detroit Diesel distributors and service dealers throughout the world. A complete list of all distributors and dealers is available in the Worldwide Distributor and Dealer Directory, 6SE280. This publication can be ordered from any authorized distributor.

CLEARANCES AND TORQUE SPECIFICATIONS

Clearances of new parts and wear limits on used parts are listed in tabular form at the end of each section throughout the manual. It should be specifically noted that the "New Parts" clearances apply only when all new parts are used at the point where the various specifications apply. This also applies to references within the text of the manual. The column entitled "Limits" lists the amount of wear or increase in clearance which can be tolerated in used engine parts and still assure satisfactory performance. It should be emphasized that the figures given as "Limits" must be qualified by the judgment of personnel responsible for installing new parts. These wear limits are, in general, listed only for the parts more frequently replaced in engine overhaul work. For additional information, refer to the paragraph entitled *Inspection* under *General Procedures* in this section.

Bolt, nut and stud torque specifications are also listed in tabular form at the end of each section.

PARTS REPLACEMENT

Before installing a new or used part, check it thoroughly to make sure it is the proper part for the job. The quality of the replacement part must be equivalent to the quality of the original Detroit Diesel component being replaced and must meet DDC specifications for new or reusable parts.

Parts must also be clean and not physically damaged or defective. For example, bolts and bolt hole threads must not be damaged or distorted. Gasketing must have all holes completly punched with no residual gasket material left clinging to the top or bottom. Flatness and fit specifications in the service manual must be strictly adhered to.

CAUTION: Failure to inspect parts thoroughly before installation, failure to install the proper parts, or failure to install parts properly can result in component or engine malfunction and/or damage and may also result in personal injury.

Page 4   May, 1990   © Copyright 1990 Detroit Diesel Corporation

FIGURE 8.5

Summary of a Report Directed Primarily to Decision-Makers

Main point of report

Background concerning the problem addressed

Source of problem

Possible solutions

Recommendation and reason for it

EXECUTIVE SUMMARY

The Accounting Department recommends that Columbus International Airport purchase a new operating system for its InfoMaxx Minicomputer. The airport purchased the InfoMaxx Minicomputer in 1996 to replace an obsolete and failing Hutchins computer system. However, the new InfoMaxx computer has never successfully performed one of its key tasks: generating weekly accounting reports based on the expense and revenue data fed to it. When airport personnel attempt to run the computer program that should generate the reports, the computer issues a message stating that it does not have enough internal memory for the job.

Our department's analysis of this problem revealed that the InfoMaxx would have enough internal memory if the software used that space efficiently. Problems with the software are as follows:

1. The operating system, BT/Q-91, uses the computer's internal memory wastefully.
2. The SuperReport program, which is used to generate the accounting reports, is much too cumbersome to create reports this complex with the memory space available on the InfoMaxx computer.

Consequently, we evaluated three possible solutions:

1. Buying a new operating system (BT/Q-101) at a cost of $3500. It would double the amount of usable space and also speed calculations.
2. Writing a more compact program in BASIC, at a cost of $5000 in labor.
3. Revising SuperReport to prepare the overall report in small chunks, at a cost of $4000. SuperReport now successfully runs small reports.

We recommend the first alternative, buying a new operating system, because it will solve the problem for the least cost. The minor advantages of writing a new program in BASIC or of revising SuperReport are not sufficient to justify their cost.

---

ing advice about a decision or course of action. These summaries are sometimes called *executive summaries* because they are favored by decision-makers (executives) who rely on their advisers to read and evaluate the rest of the communication. Figure 8.5 shows an executive summary.

Descriptive summaries indicate the topics discussed.

Another type, the *descriptive summary*, identifies the topics covered in a communication without telling the main points made about each topic. Consequently, a descriptive summary resembles a prose table of contents. The summaries included

■ **FIGURE 8.6**

Descriptive Summary

From U.S. Environmental Protection Agency, *Handbook of Suggested Practices for the Design and Installation of Groundwater Monitoring Wells* (Washington, D.C.: Government Printing Office, 1991) iii.

> This handbook is intended to assist personnel involved with the design, construction, and installation of wells drilled for the purpose of monitoring groundwater for pollutants. It presents state-of-the-art technology that may be applied in diverse hydrogeologic situations and focuses on solutions to practical problems in well construction rather than on idealized practice. The information in the handbook is presented in both matrix and text form. The matrices use a numerical rating scheme to guide the reader toward appropriate drilling technologies for particular monitoring situations. The text provides an overview of the criteria that influence design and construction of groundwater monitoring in various hydrogeologic settings.

in printed or on-line bibliographic resources are often descriptive summaries. Because users of these resources are primarily interested in locating articles on the topic of their research, descriptive summaries, which focus on topics, are well suited to their needs. Figure 8.6 shows a descriptive summary.

Summaries exhibit purposeful redundancy.

By convention, nothing appears in the summaries that isn't also in the body of the communication. This purposeful redundancy enables the summary to present a complete and understandable message to the reader who reads nothing else in the communication. It also means that the summary can't serve as the introduction, even though the introduction that follows it will seem somewhat repetitious.

Summaries that appear in printed and on-line bibliographic resources are usually called *abstracts*. In many scientific and engineering fields, the term *abstract* is also used for the summary that appears at the front of long reports and proposals. Regardless of the name, they follow the conventions just described.

How Long Should Your Summary Be?   In many situations, someone (such as your boss) will specify the length of your summary. If you have no such guidance, you might follow this rule-of-thumb: make your summary roughly 5 to 10 percent of the length of the entire communication.

GUIDELINE **8**   **Adapt Your Beginning to Your Readers' Cultural Background**

Readers' expectations and preferences about the beginning of a communication are shaped by their cultures. The suggestions you have just read are suitable for readers in the United States and some other Western countries. However, customs vary widely. For example, communication researcher Iris I. Varner reports that the French open their business correspondence in a more formal way than do people in the United States. The Spanish are offended if a business letter does not begin in an extremely flowery manner (Ruch). In Japan, business letters typically begin with a reference to the season, followed by congratulations on the reader's prosperity. Japanese communication experts Saburo Haneda and Hirosuke Shima provide this example, written in April:

Beginning of a Japanese
business letter | The season for cherry blossoms is here with us and everybody is beginning to feel refreshed. We sincerely congratulate you on becoming more prosperous in your business.

Next, the letter moves indirectly to the main topic:

> By the way, our humble company has recently developed a new product, and we are submitting a sample for your kind inspection.

Clearly, you must have a good understanding of the communication customs of your readers' culture in order to create an effective opening.

CONCLUSION

The beginning is probably the most important segment of a communication. That's because it can influence the ideas and attitudes your readers derive from the rest of your communication, and it can even determine whether or not they will read further.

This chapter has suggested that in writing a beginning you start by trying to identify your readers' attitudes toward your message and by determining what you can say to help them understand and use what follows. This reader-centered approach will enable you to create beginnings that prompt your readers to pay careful attention, encourage them to treat your information and ideas with an open mind, and help them read efficiently.

EXERCISES

1. Select a communication written to people in your field of expertise. This might be a letter, a memo, a manual, or a report. (Do not choose a textbook.) Analyze the beginning of this communication in terms of the guidelines discussed in this chapter.

2. The instructions for many consumer products contain no beginning section at all. For instance, the instructions for some lawnmowers, cake mixes, and detergents simply provide a heading that says "Instructions" and then start right in. Find such a set of instructions and—in terms of the guidelines given in this chapter—evaluate the writer's decision to omit a beginning.

3. The following paragraphs are from the beginning of a report in which the manager of a purchasing department asks for better quality from the department in the company that is providing abrasives. Is this an effective beginning for what is essentially a complaint? Why or why not? Analyze this beginning in terms of the guidelines given in this chapter.

I am sure you have heard that the new forging process is working well. Our customers have expressed pleasure with our castings. Thanks again for all your help in making this new process possible.

We are having one problem, however, with which I have to ask once more for your assistance. During the seven weeks since we began using the new process, the production line has been idle 28 percent of the time. Also, many castings have had to be remade. Some of the evidence suggests that these problems are caused by the steel abrasive supplies we get from your department. If we can figure out how to improve the abrasive, we may be able to run the line at 100 percent of capacity.

I would be most grateful for help from you and your people in improving the abrasive. To help you devise ways of improving the abrasive, I have compiled this report, which describes the difficulties we have encountered and some of our thinking about possible remedies.

Ending a Communication

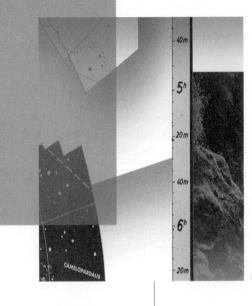

GUIDELINES

1	After you've made your last point, stop
2	Repeat your main point
3	Summarize your key points
4	Refer to a goal stated earlier in your communication
5	Focus on a key feeling
6	Tell your readers how to get assistance or more information
7	Tell your readers what to do next
8	Identify any further study that is needed
9	Follow applicable social conventions

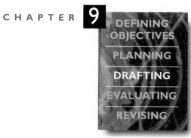

DEFINING
OBJECTIVES
PLANNING
DRAFTING
EVALUATING
REVISING

Imagine you are talking with a friend. Suddenly, without any warning, she turns around and leaves. Or, imagine that at the time set for the end of your class, your instructor simply stops talking and walks out of the room, without making any concluding remarks. Situations like these would probably leave you a little unsettled, a little uncertain. Why didn't your friend say good-bye? Why didn't your instructor bring the class to a close? What do they want you to think? To do?

As these examples suggest, the end of a conversation is very special. We expect other people to end their conversations with us in certain ways, and they expect the same of us. Similar expectations apply to much of the writing you will do on the job. To maintain an effective relationship with your readers, you need to satisfy these expectations.

People expect certain kinds of endings.

The endings of on-the-job communications are important for several other reasons as well:

Other reasons why endings are important

- **An ending is a place of emphasis.** Readers are more likely to remember a point made at the end of a communication than one made in the middle.
- **An ending creates your readers' final impression of your communication.** That impression may be crucial in shaping their attitudes toward you and your subject matter.
- **An ending provides a transition.** So long as your readers are reading your message, they are absorbed in what you have to say. The ending leads them out of the communication and into the larger stream of activities. They ask, "What should I do next?" How you answer that question can help determine what actions they will take.

For all these reasons, the endings of your communications deserve your special care and attention.

INTRODUCTION TO THE GUIDELINES

This chapter's guidelines describe a variety of ways to end the communications you prepare at work. Despite the important role that endings play, sometimes your best strategy will be to say what you have to say and then stop, *without* providing a separate ending (Guideline 1). Other times, you can use one or more of the strategies described in Guidelines 2 through 9.

How can you know which strategies to choose?

How to choose among possible strategies for endings

1. **Think about your readers in the act of reading. Decide what you want them to think, feel, and do as they finish your communication.** Then decide which strategy or strategies for endings are most likely to bring about that result.
2. **Second, look at what other people in your organization and your field have done in similar situations.** This will help you determine which kinds of ending your readers might be expecting.

GUIDELINE **1**   **After You've Made Your Last Point, Stop**

As mentioned above, sometimes you should end your communications without doing anything special at all. That happens when you use a pattern of organization that brings you to a natural stopping place. Here are some examples:

Communications that you may want to end after the last point

- **Proposals.** You will usually end a proposal with a detailed description of what you will do and how you will do it. Because that's where your readers expect proposals to end, they will enjoy a sense of completion if you simply stop after presenting your last recommendation. Furthermore, by ending after your recommendations, you will have given them the emphasis they require.
- **Formal reports.** When you prepare a formal report (a report with a cover, title page, and binding), the convention is to end either with your conclusions or your recommendations—both appropriate subjects for emphasis.
- **Instructions.** You will usually end instructions by describing the last step.

These are just some examples of communications that you may decide to end directly after making your last point. However, if your analysis of your purpose, readers, and situation convinces you that you should add something after your last point, use the other guidelines in this chapter to select strategies that will best help you meet your objectives.

GUIDELINE **2**   **Repeat Your Main Point**

Because the end of a communication is a point of emphasis, you can use it to focus your readers' attention on the points you want to be foremost in their minds as they finish reading.

Consider, for instance, the final paragraph of an article on "Preventing Wound Infections" written for family physicians (Mancusi-Ugaro and Rapport). The point made in this final paragraph was stated in the abstract at the beginning of the article and again in the fourth paragraph, where it was supported by a table. It was also referred to several other times in the article. Nevertheless, the writers considered it to be so important that in the final paragraph they stated it again:

Ending that repeats the communication's main point

Perhaps the most important concept to be gleaned from a review of the principles of wound management is that good surgical technique strives to maintain the balance between the host and the bacteria in favor of the host. The importance of understanding that infection is an absolute quantitative number of bacteria within the tissues cannot be overemphasized. Limiting, rather than eliminating, bacteria allows for normal wound healing.

You can use the same strategy in communications intended to help your readers make a decision or to persuade them to take a certain action. Here, for instance, is the final paragraph of a memo urging new safety measures:

Another example

I cannot stress too much the need for immediate action. The exposed wires present a significant hazard to any employee who opens the control box to make routine adjustments.

GUIDELINE **3**   ## Summarize Your Key Points

The strategy suggested by this guideline is closely related to the preceding one. The difference is that, in repeating your main point, you emphasize only the information you consider to be of paramount importance. In summarizing, you are concerned that your audience has understood the general thrust of your communication.

Here, for example, is the ending of a 115-page book entitled *Understanding Radioactive Waste,* which is intended to help the general public understand the impact of the nuclear power industry's plans to open new plants (Murray):

> It may be useful to the reader for us to now select some highlights, key ideas, and important conclusions for this discussion of nuclear wastes. The following list is not complete— the reader is encouraged to add items.

Key points are summarized.

> 1. Radioactivity is both natural and manmade. The decay process gives radiations such as alpha particles, beta particles, and gamma rays. Natural background radiation comes mainly from cosmic rays and minerals in the ground.
> 2. Radiation can be harmful to the body and to genes, but the low-level radiation effect cannot be proved. Many methods of protection are available.
> 3. The fission process gives useful energy in the form of electricity from nuclear plants, but it also produces wastes in the form of highly radioactive fission products. . . .

This list continues for thirteen more items, but this sample should give you an idea of how this author ended with a summary of key points.

Notice that a summary at the end of a communication differs significantly from a summary at the beginning. Because a summary at the beginning is meant for readers who have not yet read the communication, it must include some information that will be of little concern at the end. For example, the beginning summary of a report on a quality-control study will describe the background of the study. In contrast, an ending summary usually focuses more sharply on conclusions and recommendations.

GUIDELINE **4**   ## Refer to a Goal Stated Earlier in Your Communication

Many communications begin by stating a goal and then describing or proposing ways to achieve it. If you end a communication by referring to that goal, you remind your readers of the goal and sharpen the focus of your communication. In the following examples, notice how the ending refers to the beginning.

This first example comes from a seventeen-page proposal prepared by operations analysts in a company that builds customized, computer-controlled equipment used in print shops and printing plants:

Beginning states a goal.

> To maintain our competitive edge, we must develop a way of supplying replacement parts more rapidly to our service technicians without increasing our shipping costs or tying up more money in inventory.

Ending refers to the goal.

> The proposed reform of our distribution network will help us meet the needs of our service technicians for rapidly delivered spare parts. Furthermore, it does so without raising either our shipping expenses or our investment in inventory.

Avoiding Stereotypes

A man and a boy are riding together in a car. As they approach a railroad crossing, the boy shouts, "Father, watch out!" But it is too late. The car is hit by a train. The man dies, and the boy is rushed to a hospital. When the boy is wheeled into the operating room, the surgeon looks down at the child and says, "I can't operate on him. He's my son."

When asked to explain why the boy would call the deceased driver "Father" and the living surgeon would say "He's my son," people offer many guesses. Perhaps the driver is a priest or the boy's stepfather or someone who kidnapped the boy as a baby. Few guess that the surgeon must be the boy's mother. Why? Our culture's stereotypes about the roles men and women play are so strong that when people think of a surgeon, many automatically imagine a man.

Stereotypes and Ethics

What do stereotypes have to do with ethics? Stereotypes have serious consequences for both individuals and groups. People who are viewed in terms of stereotypes lose their ability to be treated as individual human beings. Further, if they belong to a group

that is unfavorably stereotyped, they may find it nearly impossible to get others to take their talents, ideas, and feelings seriously.

Of course, the groups that are disadvantaged by stereotyping extend well beyond women. For example, people are also stereotyped on the basis of their race, religion, age, sexual orientation, weight, physical handicap, and ethnicity. In some workplaces, manual laborers, union members, clerical workers, and others are the victims of stereotyping by people in white-collar positions.

Of course, one way to treat people ethically is to treat them as individuals, rather than as members of a stereotyped group. Another way is to avoid writing and speaking in ways that perpetuate stereotypes in the minds of your readers.

Actions You Can Take

Here are three ways you can avoid perpetuating harmful stereotypes:

- **Avoid describing people in terms of stereotypes.** In your reports, sales presentations, policy statements, and other communications, avoid giving examples that rely upon or reinforce stereotypes. For

example, don't make all the decision-makers men and all the clerical workers women.

- **Mention a person's gender, race, or other characteristic only when it is relevant.** To determine whether it's relevant to describe someone as a member of a minority group, ask yourself if you would make a parallel statement about a member of the majority group. If you wouldn't say, "This improvement was suggested by Jane, a person without any physical disability," don't say, "This improvement was suggested by Margaret, a handicapped person." If you wouldn't say, "The Phoenix office is managed by Brent, a hard-working white person," don't say, "The Phoenix office is managed by Terry, a hard-working Mexican-American."

- **Avoid humor that relies on stereotypes.** Humor that relies on stereotypes reinforces the stereotypes. Refrain from such humor not only when members of the stereotyped group are present, but at all times.

The second example is from *Biotechnology,* a journal concerned with the synthesis of new organisms that are commercially useful (Filho et al.). Note that the highly technical language is appropriate because the writers are addressing people knowledgeable in this field.

Beginning states a goal.	Given the necessity of producing alcohol as an alternative fuel to gasoline, especially in countries like Brazil, where petroleum is scarce, it is important to have a yeast strain able to produce ethanol directly from starchy materials.
Ending refers to the goal.	We are convinced that the stable pESA transformants can be of technological value in assisting ethanol fermentation directly from starchy materials, and we have described the first step towards this end. Continuing this work, genetic crosses with different *Saccharomyces distaticus* strains are presently being carried out to introduce maltase and glucomylase genes into the stable transformants that secrete functional α-amylase.

GUIDELINE 5   Focus on a Key Feeling

Sometimes you may want to focus your readers' attention on a feeling rather than on a fact. For instance, if you are writing instructions for a product manufactured by your employer, you may want your ending to encourage your readers' goodwill toward the product. Consider this ending of an owner's manual for a clothes dryer. Though the last sentence provides no additional information, it seeks to shape the readers' attitude toward the company.

Ending designed to build goodwill	The GE Answer Center™ consumer information service is open 24 hours a day, seven days a week. Our staff of experts stands ready to assist you anytime.

The following passage is the ending of a booklet published by the National Cancer Institute for people who have apparently been successfully treated for cancer but do not know how long the disease will remain in remission. It, too, seeks to shape the readers' feelings.

Ending designed to shape complex attitudes	Cancer is not something anyone forgets. Anxieties remain as active treatment ceases and the waiting stage begins. A cold or cramp may be cause for panic. As 6-month or annual check-ups approach, you swing between hope and anxiety. As you wait for the mystical 5-year or 10-year point, you might feel more anxious rather than more secure.
	These are feelings that we all share. No one expects you to forget you have had cancer or that it might recur. Each must seek individual ways of coping with the underlying insecurity of not knowing the true state of his or her health. The best prescription seems to lie in a combination of one part challenging responsibilities that require a full range of skills, a dose of activities that seek to fill the needs of others, and a generous dash of frivolity and laughter.
	You still might have moments when you feel as if you live perched on the edge of a cliff. They will sneak up unbidden. But they will be fewer and farther between if you have filled your mind with other thoughts than cancer.
	Cancer might rob you of that blissful ignorance that once led you to believe that tomorrow stretched on forever. In exchange, you are granted the vision to see each today as precious, a gift to be used wisely and richly. No one can take that away.

GUIDELINE 6   Tell Your Readers How to Get Assistance or More Information

At work, a common strategy for ending a communication is to tell your readers how to get assistance or more information. These two examples are from a letter and a memo:

Endings that offer help | If you have questions about this matter, call me at 523–5221.

If you want any additional information about the proposed project, let me know. I'll answer your questions as best I can.

By ending in this way, you not only provide your readers with useful information, but also you encourage them to see you as a helpful, concerned individual.

GUIDELINE **7** **Tell Your Readers What to Do Next**

Another strategy for effective endings is to tell your readers what you think should be done next. If more than one course of action is available, tell your readers how to follow up on each of them:

Ending that tells readers exactly what to do | To buy this equipment at the reduced price, we must mail the purchase orders by Friday the 11th. If you have any qualms about this purchase, let's discuss them. If not, please forward the attached materials, together with your approval, to the Controller's Office as soon as possible.

GUIDELINE **8** **Identify Any Further Study That Is Needed**

Much of the work that is done on the job is completed in stages. For example, one study might answer preliminary questions and, if the answers look promising, an additional study might then be undertaken. Consequently, one common way of ending is to tell readers what needs to be found out next:

Ending that identifies next question needing study | This experiment indicates that we can use compound deposition to create microcircuits in the laboratory. We are now ready to explore the feasibility of using this technique to produce microcircuits in commercial quantities.

Such endings are often combined with summaries, as in the following example:

Another example | In summary, over the past several months our Monroe plant has ordered several hundred electric motors from a supplier whose products are inferior to those we require in the heating and air conditioning systems we build. Not only must this practice stop immediately, but also we should investigate the situation to determine why this flagrant violation of our quality-control policies has occurred.

GUIDELINE **9** **Follow Applicable Social Conventions**

All the strategies mentioned so far focus on the subject matter of your communications. It is also important for you to observe the social conventions that apply in a given situation.

Some of those conventions involve customary ways of closing particular kinds of communication. For example, letters usually end with an expression of thanks, a statement that it has been enjoyable working with the reader, or an offer to be of further help if needed. In contrast, formal reports and proposals rarely end with such gestures.

Other conventions about endings are peculiar to the organization in which they are found. For example, in some organizations writers rarely end their memos with the kind of social gesture commonly provided at the end of a letter. In other organizations, memos often end with such a gesture, and people who ignore that convention risk seeming abrupt and cold.

Social conventions also apply to personal relationships between you and your readers. Have they done you a favor? Thank them. Are you going to see them soon? Let them know that you look forward to the meeting.

CONCLUSION

The endings of communications you prepare at work will help you achieve four aims:

1. Provide your readers with a sense of completion.
2. Emphasize key material.
3. Shape your readers' attitudes toward you and your subject matter.
4. Direct your readers' attention to future action.

This chapter has described nine ending strategies. By considering your readers, your objectives, and the social conventions that apply in your situation, you will be able to choose the strategy or combination of strategies most likely to succeed in the particular communication you are writing.

EXERCISES

1. The following paragraphs constitute the ending of a report to the U.S. Department of Energy concerning the economic and technical feasibility of generating electric power with a special type of windmill (Foreman). The windmills are called *diffuser augmented wind turbines* (DAWT). In this ending, the writer has used several of the strategies described in this chapter. Identify each of them.

Section 6.0
Concluding Remarks

We have provided a preliminary cost assessment for the DAWT approach to wind energy conversion in unit systems to 150 kw power rating. The results demonstrate economic viability of the DAWT with no further design and manufacturing know-how than already exists. Further economic benefits of this form of solar energy are likely through:

- Future refinements in product design and production techniques
- Economies of larger quantity production lots
- Special tax incentives

Continued cost escalation on nonrenewable energy sources and public concern for safeguarding the biosphere environment will surely make wind energy conversion by DAWT-like systems even more attractive to our society. Promotional actions by national policy makers and planners as well as industrialists and entrepreneurs can aid the emergence of the DAWT from its research phase to a practical and commercial product.

2. Describe the strategies for ending used in the following figures in this text:

FIGURE	PAGE	FIGURE	PAGE
1.4	20	10.3	269
2.7	47	18.3	453
2.8	48	SR.1	469
5.4	105	SR.5	499
5.8	117	SR.8	514
7.9	181	19.1	528
7.10	182		

3. Find examples of endings that use four of the nine strategies described in this chapter by looking in magazines, textbooks, instruction manuals, and other publications. If you find an ending that uses more than one of these strategies, count it as more than one example. For each example, explain why the writer chose the ending strategy that he or she used. Did the writer make a good choice? Explain why or why not.

Creating an Effective Style

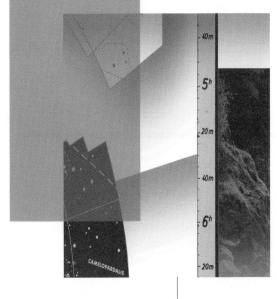

CAMELOPARDALIS

GUIDELINES

Guidelines for Choosing Your Voice

1   Find out what's expected

2   Consider the roles your voice creates for your readers and you

3   Consider how your attitude toward your subject will affect your readers

4   Say things in your own words

Guidelines for Constructing Sentences

1   Simplify your sentences

2   Put the action in your verbs

3   Use the active voice unless there is good reason to use the passive voice

4   Emphasize what's most important

5   Smooth the flow of thought from sentence to sentence

6   Vary your sentence length and structure

Guidelines for Selecting Words

1	Use concrete, specific words
2	Use specialized terms when—and only when—your readers will understand them
3	Use words accurately
4	Choose words with appropriate associations
5	Choose plain words over fancy ones

CHAPTER **10**

DEFINING
OBJECTIVES

PLANNING

DRAFTING

EVALUATING

REVISING

When we talk about "writing style," we can mean many things. For example, when we speak of Shakespeare's style or Jane Austen's style, we are referring to the features that make that person's writing unique. In contrast, when we speak of legal style or scientific style, we are referring to writing characteristics shared by groups of people, such as lawyers or scientists. We also use the word *style* to talk about a communication's readability and impact, saying that a communication is written in a clear or muddy style, an inspiring or boring style. We even use the word *style* to express judgments that are really about the writer, not the writing, as when we say that a style is friendly or stuffy, relaxed or stiff, helpful or condescending.

When writing at work, you will need to juggle all these dimensions of style at once, striving simultaneously to express your individuality, observe the stylistic conventions of your profession and your employer's organization, make reading easy for your readers, and create the impact you desire. The job isn't easy. These goals sometimes conflict. Furthermore, one style won't suit all occasions. At work, you need to be able to use different styles in different situations.

This chapter's guidelines will help you create an effective style for each communication you write on the job. They focus on voice, sentence construction, and word choice.

CHOOSING YOUR VOICE

Whenever you write, your readers "hear" your voice—and, based on what they hear, they draw conclusions about you and your attitudes. The conclusions they draw can greatly influence the success or failure of your communication.

GUIDELINE **1**   **Find Out What's Expected**

To a large extent, an effective voice is one that matches your readers' sense of what's appropriate. When reporters for the *Wall Street Journal* asked corporate executives to identify the major weaknesses in the writing of inexperienced employees, one of the items at the top of the list was "style or tone inappropriate for the intended audience" ("Weak Writers").

Here are three questions to ask yourself when determining how to match your voice to your readers' expectations:

Questions for determining what your readers expect

- **How formal do my readers think my writing should be?** An informal style sounds like conversation. You use contractions *(can't, won't)*, short words, and colloquial words and phrasing. A formal style sounds more like a lecture or speech, with longer sentences, formal phrasing, and no contractions.
- **How subjective or objective do my readers believe my writing should be?** In a subjective style, you would introduce yourself into your writing by saying such things as "I believe . . ." and "I observed . . ." In an objective style, you would mask your presence by stating your beliefs as facts ("It is true that . . .") and by reporting about your own actions in the third person ("The researcher observed . . .") or the passive voice ("It was observed that . . .").
- **How much "distance" do my readers expect me to establish between them and me?** In a personal style, you appear very close to your readers because you do such things as use personal pronouns *(I, we)* and address your readers directly. In an impersonal style, you distance yourself from your readers—for instance, by avoiding personal pronouns and by talking about yourself and your readers in the third person ("The buyer agrees to pay the seller the full amount by October 1").

Here are some factors that may influence your readers' expectations about style:

Factors Influencing Expectations about Style

- Your professional relationship with your readers (customers? supervisors? subordinates?)
- Your purpose (requesting something? apologizing? advising? ordering?)
- Your subject (routine matter? urgent problem?)
- Type of communication (e-mail? letter? formal report?)
- Your personality
- Your readers' personalities
- Customs in your employer's organization
- Customs in your profession

To learn what style your readers expect, follow the advice in Chapter 3: ask people who know (including even your readers) and look for communications similar to the one you are writing.

Expectations Are Different in Other Cultures

You should take special care to learn about your readers' expectations when you address people in a different country or culture. From country to country, the style of workplace writing varies considerably. For example, the Japanese write in a more personal style than do people from the United States, whose direct, blunt style the Japanese find abrupt (Ruch). Like business people in the United States, the Dutch also use a straightforward style that causes the French to regard writers from both countries as rude (Mathes and Stevenson). When writing to people in other countries, learn and try to use the styles that are customary there.

What If an Ineffective Style Is Expected?

Note that sometimes the expected style may be less effective than another style you could use. For example, in some organizations the customary and expected style is a widely (and justly) condemned style called *bureaucratese.* Bureaucratese is characterized by wordiness that buries significant ideas and information, weak verbs that disguise action, and abstract vocabulary that detaches meaning from the practical world of people, activities, and objects. Often, such writing features an inflated vocabulary and a general pomposity. Here's an example:

Bureaucratese | According to good quality-control practices in manufacturing any product, it is important that every component part that is constituent of the product be examined and checked individually after being received from its supplier or other source but before the final, finished product is assembled. (45 words)

The writer simply means this:

Plain English | Good quality-control requires that every component be checked individually before the final product is assembled. (16 words)

Another example:

Bureaucratese | Over the most recent monthly period, there has been a large increase in the number of complaints that customers have made about service that has been slow. (27 words)

Plain English | Last month, many more customers complained about slow service. (10 words)

The rest of this chapter's guidelines for constructing sentences and choosing words will help you avoid bureaucratese.

But what should you do if your manager or company advocates the use of bureaucratese, thinking it sounds impressive? Try to explain why a straightforward style is more effective, perhaps even showing people this book. If you fail to persuade, however, be prudent. Use the style that is required. Even within the confines of a generally bureaucratic style, you can probably bring about some improvements. For instance, if your employer expects a wordy, abstract style, you may still be able to use a less inflated vocabulary.

GUIDELINE **2** **Consider the Roles Your Voice Creates for Your Readers and You**

Through the voice you choose, you indicate the particular role you see yourself playing with respect to your readers. For example, when writing to workers in the department you manage, you might assume the voice of a stern authority or that of an open-minded leader. When instructing a new employee, you might assume the voice of a demanding instructor or a helpful guide.

The voice you choose indicates not only the role you assign yourself but also the one you assign to your readers. If you assume the voice of an equal writing to respected peers, your readers will probably accept their implied role as your equals. But if you assume the voice of a superior, unerring authority, they may resent their implied role as error-prone inferiors. Although they may not speak the words, they may think, "You have no right to talk to me like that." If your readers respond to your voice in that way, they are unlikely to receive your message in the way you desire.

Your voice can come across in as short a space as a single sentence. Compare the following statements:

Supportive voice	Let's meet tomorrow to see if we can figure out why people in your department had difficulty meeting last month's production targets.
Domineering voice	I have scheduled an hour for us to meet tomorrow to discuss the failure of your department to meet production targets last month.

The first sentence portrays the writer as a supportive person who wants to work as an equal with the reader, who is in turn portrayed as someone who would like to solve a problem that stumps both individuals. The second sentence portrays the writer as a powerful person who considers the reader to be someone who can be bossed around and blamed, a role the reader probably does not find agreeable.

GUIDELINE **3**   **Consider How Your Attitude toward Your Subject Will Affect Your Readers**

In addition to communicating attitudes about yourself and your readers, your voice communicates an attitude toward your subject. Feelings are contagious. If you write enthusiastically, your readers may catch your enthusiasm. If you seem indifferent, they may adopt the same attitude.

Writers are especially prone to problems with voice when writing on the spur of the moment. E-mail presents a special temptation to be careless about voice because it encourages spontaneity. As Laura B. Smith says, "Staring at e-mail can make users feel dangerously bold; they sometimes blast off with emotions that they probably would not use in a face-to-face meeting. It's sort of like being in the driver's seat of a car with the windows rolled up." Whenever you sense that your emotions are running high, give yourself time to revise and reflect before sending a message. Also, check carefully for statements that you write in one tone of voice but that your readers might "hear" in another. Users of electronic mail sometimes employ "emoticons" to signal the feeling that goes with a statement. Turn this page sideways to see the facial expressions represented by these examples:

Emoticons signal the writer's feelings and intent.	:-)	The writer is happy.
	:-(	The writer is sad.
	;-)	The writer is only kidding (a wink).
	>:->	The writer just made a really devilish remark.

GUIDELINE **4** **Say Things in Your Own Words**

No matter what style you choose, be sure to retain your own voice in your writing. You can do that even in your formal writing—for instance, in a scientific or engineering report. James Watson, winner of the Nobel Prize for his role in discovering the structure of DNA, praised Linus Pauling, three-time winner of the same prize, for his distinctive writing style in highly technical papers (Watson). When using a formal style, the objective is not to silence your own voice; it's to let your style sound like *you*, writing in a formal situation.

Try reading your draft aloud.

To check whether you are using your own voice, try reading your drafts aloud. Where the phrasing seems awkward or where the words are difficult for you to speak, you may have adopted someone else's voice—or slipped into bureaucratese, which reflects no one's voice. Reading your drafts aloud can also help you spot other problems with voice such as sarcasm or condescension.

Sometimes it's appropriate to suppress your own voice.

Despite the advice given in this guideline, it will sometimes be appropriate for you to suppress your own voice. For example, when a report, proposal, or other document is written by several people, the contributors usually strive to achieve a uniform voice so that all the sections will fit together stylistically. Similarly, certain kinds of official documents, such as an organization's policy statements, are usually written in the "employer's" style, not the individual writer's style. Except in such situations, however, let your own voice speak in your writing.

CONSTRUCTING SENTENCES

Aim for clear, interesting, emphatic sentences.

The four guidelines you have just read focus on social aspects of style: the way you present yourself in your writing and the relationship you establish there with your readers. When you are constructing your sentences, you need to focus also on another set of concerns: making your writing clear (so readers can read it easily), interesting (so readers are attentive and energized by your writing), and emphatic (so your readers will spot and remember your main points). The following six guidelines for constructing sentences are based primarily on what researchers have learned about the way the human mind processes information when it reads.

GUIDELINE **1** **Simplify Your Sentences**

Reading is work. Psychologists say that much of the work of reading is done by the short-term memory, which determines the meaning of each sentence as you read it. Short-term memory then forwards the meaning of each sentence to long-term memory, where the meanings you derive from individual sentences are integrated with one another and with other things you know.

By simplifying your sentences, you can ease the work your readers' short-term memories must perform to understand your message:

1. **Eliminate unnecessary words.** For short-term memory, every word represents work. Delete any word that doesn't help to convey your message.

| Original | The <u>physical size of the</u> workroom is too small <u>to accommodate</u> this equipment. | [1] |
| Shortened | The workroom is too small for this equipment. | [2] |

The writer of Sentence 1 used the first four words to specify the precise way in which the workroom is too small—in physical size. But if a room is too small for a piece of equipment, what feature of the room could the writer have in mind except its size? The first four words can be eliminated without changing the meaning.

2. **Substitute one word for several.** You can often replace an entire phrase with a single word.

Original	<u>Due to the fact that</u> the price of oil rose, Gulf Consolidated received many new orders for its fitting for oil rigs.	[3]
Shortened	<u>Because</u> the price of oil rose, Gulf Consolidated received many new orders for its fitting for oil rigs.	[4]
Original	They <u>do not pay attention to</u> our complaints.	[5]
Shortened	They <u>ignore</u> our complaints.	[6]

3. **Keep modifiers next to the words they modify.** Short-term memory relies on word order to indicate meaning. If you don't keep related words together, a sentence may end up saying something different from what you mean.

| Ambiguous sentence | A large number of undeposited checks were found in the file cabinets, <u>which were worth over $41,000.</u> | [7] |

According to the way our language works, Sentence 7 says that the file cabinets were worth over $41,000. Yet, the author meant that the *checks* were worth that amount. Of course, readers would probably figure out what the writer meant because it is more likely that the checks were worth that much money than that the file cabinets were. But readers arrive at the correct meaning only after performing work they would have been saved if the writer had kept related words together—in this example, by putting *which were worth over $41,000* after *checks*, rather than after *file cabinets.*

4. **Avoid long interjections between related words.** As its name suggests, short-term memory retains meaning for only a brief time, and it can hold only a small amount. Its limit is between five and nine bits of information at a time (Miller). If you write a sentence in which related words are too far apart, your readers' short-term memories may forget the first word by the time the second is reached.

| This interjection is too long. | A new factory that produces chemicals for the OPAS system, which enables large manufacturers of business forms to make carbonless copy paper as part of their own manufacturing process, began to operate last year. | [8] |

Most readers have to read that sentence twice before they understand it. The long clause following the subject, *factory,* pushes that word from their short-term memories before they reach the verb, *began.*

It's okay, however, to interject a small number of words between related words. In fact, this is one way of creating emphasis. For example, the following sentence emphasizes a point by placing it between the first and last parts of the verb phrase (*managed* and *to make*):

Short interjection is okay.   We managed, despite the recession, to make record profits that year.   **[9]**

5. **Combine short sentences to clarify meaning.** Often, combining two or more short sentences makes reading easier because it reduces the total number of words and helps the reader see the relationships among the points presented.

Separate   Water quality in Hawk River declined in March. This decline occurred because of the **[10–12]** heavy rainfall that month. All the extra water overloaded Tomlin County's water treatment plant.

Combined   Water quality in Hawk River declined in March because heavy rainfalls overloaded **[13]** Tomlin County's water treatment plant.

GUIDELINE **2** **Put the Action in Your Verbs**

Most sentences are about action. Sales rise, equipment fails, engineers design, managers approve. Clients praise or complain, and technicians advise. Yet, many people bury the action in nouns, adjectives, and other parts of speech. Consider the following sentence:

Original | Our department accomplished the <u>conversion</u> to the new machinery in two months.   **[14]**

It could be improved by putting the action (*converting*) into the verb:

Revised | Our department <u>converted</u> to the new machinery in two months.   **[15]**

Not only is the revised version briefer, it is also more emphatic and lively. Furthermore, according to researchers E.B. Coleman and Keith Raynor, when you put the action in your verbs, you can make your prose up to 25 percent easier to read.

To spot sentences that need to have their action moved to the verb, look for the following:

■ Sentences that begin with *it is* or *there are*

Original | <u>It is</u> because the cost of raw materials has soared that the price of finished goods is **[16]** rising.

Revised | Because the cost of raw materials has soared, the price of finished goods is rising.   **[17]**

Original | <u>There are</u> several factors causing engineers to question the strength of the dam.   **[18]**

Revised | Several factors cause engineers to question the strength of the dam.   **[19]**

■ Sentences that use some form of the verb *to be* (*is, was, will be*, etc.)

Original | The procedure <u>is a protection</u> against reinfection.   **[20]**

Revised | The procedure <u>protects</u> against reinfection.   **[21]**

■ Sentences in which an important word ends with one of the following suffixes: *-tion, -ment, -ing, -ion, -ance*

Original | Consequently, I would like to make a <u>recommendation</u> that the department hire two **[22]** additional programmers.

Revised | Consequently, I <u>recommend</u> that the department hire two additional programmers.   **[23]**

Although most sentences are about action, some aren't. For example, sentences that begin a paragraph, section, or larger unit usually serve as topic sentences that announce the focus of the sentences that follow. Moreover, they often provide a transition from the preceding section to the section that follows. To perform their functions, topic and transitional sentences often use some form of the verb *to be*.

Topic sentence using the There <u>are</u> three main reasons for the improved communications between corporate head- [24]
verb *to be*   quarters and out-of-state plants.

GUIDELINE **3** **Use the Active Voice Unless There Is Good Reason to Use the Passive Voice**

A second way to focus your sentences on action and actors is to use the active voice rather than the passive voice. To write in the active voice, place the actor—the person or thing performing the action—in the subject position. Your verb will then describe the actor's action.

Active voice

[25]

In the passive voice, the subject of the sentence and the actor are different. The subject is *acted upon* by the actor.

Passive voice

[26]

Here are some additional examples:

Passive voice | The Korean ore was purchased by us.   [27]
Active voice | We purchased the Korean ore.   [28]

Research shows that readers understand active sentences more rapidly than passive ones (Layton and Simpson). The active voice helps them see immediately what action a sentence describes and who performed it, thereby avoiding the vagueness and ambiguity that often characterize the passive voice. That's because with the active voice, you must always tell who the actor is. With the passive voice, you don't. "The ball was hit" is a grammatically correct sentence even if it doesn't tell who or what hit the ball. The writer may know who did the hitting, but the reader doesn't. With the active voice, the writer identifies the actor: "Linda hit the ball."

Avoiding the vagueness of the passive voice will be very important to you in many situations.

Passive voice | The operating temperatures must be checked daily to ensure the motor is not damaged.   **[29]**

Will the supervisor of the third shift know that he is the person responsible for checking temperatures? Sentence 29 certainly allows him to imagine that someone else, perhaps a supervisor on another shift, is responsible.

Although the passive voice generally impairs readability, there are some good uses for it. One occurs when you don't want to identify the actor:

Passive voice | The lights on the third floor have been left on all night for the past week, despite the ef- **[30]** forts of most employees to help us reduce our energy bills.

Sentence 30 is from a memorandum in which the writer urges all employees to work harder at saving energy but avoids causing embarrassment and resentment by naming the guilty parties. The passive voice serves that purpose very well. Also, consider this sentence:

Passive voice | I have been told that you may be using the company telephone for an excessive number of **[31]** personal calls.

Perhaps the person who told the writer about the breach of corporate telephone policy did so in confidence. If the writer decided that it would be ethically acceptable to communicate this news to the reader without naming the person who made the report, then she has used the passive voice effectively. (Be careful, however, to avoid using the passive voice to hide an actor's identity when it is unethical to do so—for instance, when trying to avoid accepting responsibility for your employer's actions.)

GUIDELINE 4   Emphasize What's Most Important

Another way to write clear, forceful sentences is to direct your readers' attention to the most important information you are conveying:

1. **Place the key information at the end of the sentence.** As linguist Joseph Williams points out, you can demonstrate to yourself that the end of the sentence is a place of emphasis by listening to yourself speak. Read the following sentences aloud:

   | Her powers of concentration are extraordinary.   **[32]**

   | Last month, he topped his sales quota even though he was sick for an entire week.   **[33]**

   As you read these sentences aloud, notice how you naturally stress the final words, *extraordinary* and *entire week.*

   To position key information at the end of a sentence, you may need to move other words or phrases to the beginning.

Original | The department's performance has been <u>superb</u> in all areas.   **[34]**

Revised | In all areas, the department's performance has been <u>superb</u>.   **[35]**

   Sometimes you can achieve the same effect by moving the key information from the beginning of the sentence to the end.

Original | The bright exterior design is one of the product's most appealing features to younger [36] customers.

Revised | One of the product's most appealing features to younger customers is its bright [37] exterior design.

2. **Place the key information in the main clause.** If your sentence has more than one clause, use the main clause for the information you want to emphasize.

Although our productivity was down, our profits were up. [38]

Although our profits were up, our productivity was down. [39]

In Sentence 38, the emphasis is on profits because *profits* is the subject of the main clause. Sentence 39 emphasizes productivity because *productivity* is the subject of the main clause. (Notice that in each of these sentences, the emphasized information is not only in the main clause but also at the end of the sentence.)

3. **Emphasize key information typographically.** Use boldface and italics. Be careful, however, to use typographical highlighting sparingly. When many things are emphasized, none stands out.

4. **Tell readers explicitly what the key information is.** A fourth way to emphasize key information is to announce its importance to your readers.

Economists pointed to three important causes of the stock market's decline: uncer- [40] tainty about the outcome of last month's election, a rise in inventories of durable goods, and—*most important*—signs of rising inflation.

GUIDELINE 5   Smooth the Flow of Thought from Sentence to Sentence

As your readers begin reading each new sentence, they need to figure out how the *new* information it contains relates to the *old* information in the preceding sentence. You can help them do that in several ways:

1. **Avoid needless shifts in topic.** The simplest relationship between two adjacent sentences is this: the first one says something about a particular topic, and the second says something more about the same topic.

The links of the drive chain must fit together firmly. They are too loose if you can [41] easily wiggle two links from side to side more than ten degrees.

Readers usually assume that the subject of a sentence is the topic. Consequently, you can help your readers rapidly detect the shared topic of adjacent sentences by putting that topic in the subject position of both sentences. For example, imagine that you have just written this sentence:

Topic (Subject) Our company's new inventory system

Comment reduces our costs considerably. [42]

And suppose that in your next sentence you wanted to communicate information that could be expressed either in this way:

> **Topic (Subject)** Thousands of dollars
>
> **Comment** have been saved by the system this year alone. [43]

or in this way:

> **Topic (Subject)** The system
>
> **Comment** has saved thousands of dollars this year alone. [44]

Sentences 43 and 44 contain the same information. However, Sentence 44 has the same topic—*system*—as Sentence 42, and Sentence 43 does not. Therefore, your readers would relate the old information in Sentence 42 more easily to the new information in Sentence 44 than to the same information in Sentence 43.

> Our company's new inventory system reduces costs considerably. [45–46]
> The system has saved thousands of dollars this year alone.

You can often achieve the same easy bridge from one sentence to the next by keeping the same *general* topic in the subject position of the adjacent sentences, even if you don't keep the exact same word:

Focus is maintained on one topic.

> The materials used to construct and furnish this experimental office are designed [47–50] to store energy from the sunlight that pours through the office's large windows. The special floor covering stores energy more efficiently than wood. The heavy fabrics used to upholster the chairs and sofas also capture the sun's energy. Similarly, the darkly colored paneling holds the sun's energy rather than reflecting it as lightly colored walls would.

In this paragraph, the subject of the first sentence is *materials*. Although the same word is not the subject of the sentences that follow, the subjects of all those sentences are kinds of materials, namely the *special floor covering, heavy fabrics,* and *darkly colored paneling.* Thus, although the specific word placed in the subject position of the various sentences changes, the general topic is the same.

The passive voice can help maintain focus.

One important implication of the preceding discussion is that you sometimes will be able to follow Guideline 5 only by using the passive voice. In the discussion of Guideline 3, you learned that it is generally desirable to use the active voice, not the passive. However, you also learned that sometimes the passive is more appropriate, even preferable, to the active. One such time occurs when the passive voice enables you to avoid a needless shift in the topic of two adjacent sentences. Consider the following paragraph:

Focus shifts in the third sentence.

> Tom works in the Paint Department. On Tuesday, he finished lunch late, so he took [51–54] a shortcut back to his work station. Fifteen yards above the factory floor, a can of paint slipped off a scaffold and hit him on the left foot. Consequently, at the busiest part of the year, he missed seventeen days of work.

The topic of most of the sentences in this accident report is "Tom" or "he." However, the third sentence shifts the topic from Tom to the can of paint. Furthermore, because the third sentence shifts, the fourth must also shift to bring the focus back to Tom. The writer could avoid these two shifts by rewriting the third sentence so that it is about Tom, not about the can of paint. That means making *Tom* the grammatical subject of the sentence, and, as a result, making the verb passive:

Better third sentence

> He was hit on the left foot by a can of paint that slipped off a scaffold fifteen yards above the factory floor. **[55]**

2. **Use transitional words.** The preceding discussion explains how you can help your readers follow your flow of thought when two adjacent sentences are about the same topic. In most communications, most of the sentences shift topics. One way to help your readers follow such shifts is to use transitional words. Here are some of the most commonly used transitional words:

Links in time	after, before, during, until, while
Links in space	above, below, inside
Links of cause and effect	as a result, because, since
Links of similarity	as, furthermore, likewise, similarly
Links of contrast	although, however, nevertheless, on the other hand

3. **Use echo words.** Another way to guide your readers from one sentence to the next is to use *echo words.* An echo word is a word or phrase that recalls to the readers' minds some information they've already encountered. For example:

> Inflation can be cured. The cure appears to require that consumers change their basic attitudes toward consumption. **[56–57]**

In this example, the noun *cure* at the beginning of the second sentence echoes the verb in the first. It tells readers that what follows in the second sentence will discuss the curing they have just read about in the first.

There are many other kinds of echo words:

Pronouns

> We had to return the copier. Its frequent breakdowns were disrupting work. **[58–59]**

Another word from the same "word family" as the word being echoed

> I went to my locker to get my lab equipment. My oscilloscope was missing. **[60–61]**

In this example, *oscilloscope* in the second sentence echoes lab equipment in the first.

A word or phrase that recalls some idea or theme expressed but not explicitly stated in the preceding sentence

> The company also purchased and retired 17,399 shares of its $2.90 convertible, preferred stock at $5.70 a share. These transactions reduce the number of outstanding convertible shares to 635,200. **[62–63]**

In this example, the words *these transactions* tell readers that what follows in the sentence concerns the purchasing and retiring that were discussed in the preceding sentence.

4. **Place transitional and echo words at the beginning of the sentence.** Transitional and echo words help readers most when they appear at the beginning of a sentence. In that position, they immediately signal the relationship between that sentence and the preceding one.

GUIDELINE **6** **Vary Your Sentence Length and Structure**

If all the sentences in a sentence group have the same structure, two problems arise: monotony sets in, and (because all the sentences are basically alike) you lose the ability to emphasize major points and de-emphasize minor ones.

You can avoid such monotony and loss of emphasis in two ways:

1. **Vary your sentence length.** Longer sentences can be used to show the relationships among ideas. Shorter sentences provide emphasis in a context of longer sentences.

Short sentences used for emphasis

> In April, many amateur investors jumped back into the stock market because they be- **[64–69]** lieved that another rally was about to begin. They noted that exports were increasing rapidly, which they felt would strengthen the dollar in overseas monetary markets and bring foreign investors back to Wall Street. Also, they observed that unemployment had dropped sharply, which they also predicted would be taken as an encouraging sign for the economy. <u>They were wrong on both counts.</u> Wall Street interpreted rising exports to mean that goods would cost more at home, and it predicted that falling unemployment would mean a shortage of workers, hence higher prices for labor. <u>Where amateur investors saw growth, Wall Street saw inflation.</u>

2. **Vary your sentence structure.** For example, the grammatical subject of the sentence does not have to be the sentence's first word. In fact, if it did, the English language would lose much of its power to emphasize more important information and to de-emphasize less important information.

One alternative to beginning a sentence with its grammatical subject is to begin with a clause that indicates a logical relationship.

Introductory clause

> <u>After we complete our survey,</u> we will know for sure whether the proposed site for **[70]** our new factory was once a Native American camping ground.

Introductory clause

> <u>Because we have thoroughly investigated all the alternatives,</u> we feel confident that a **[71]** pneumatic drive will work best and provide the most reliable service.

SELECTING WORDS

When selecting words, your first goal should be to enable your readers to grasp your meaning quickly and accurately. At the same time, you need to keep in mind that your word choices are one of the signals readers use to judge the voice of your writing, so you need to choose words that will create an effective and appropriate impression.

GUIDELINE **1** **Use Concrete, Specific Words**

One of the most important strategies for choosing words is to pick concrete, specific ones. Almost anything can be described either in relatively abstract, general words or in relatively concrete, specific ones. You may say that you are writing on

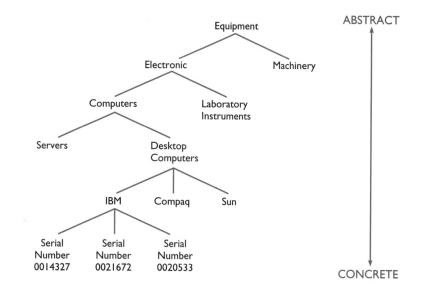

FIGURE 10.1

Hierarchy of Related Words That Move from Abstract to Concrete

a piece of *electronic equipment,* or that you are writing on *a laptop computer connected to a color laser printer.* You may say that your employer produces *consumer goods* or that it makes *men's clothes.*

When ranked according to degree of abstraction, groups of related words form hierarchies. Figure 10.1 shows such a hierarchy in which the most specific terms identify concrete items that we can perceive with our senses; Figure 10.2 shows a hierarchy in which all the terms are abstract but in which some are more specific than others.

When writing at work, you can usually strengthen your writing by using concrete, specific words rather than abstract, general ones. Concrete, specific words make it easier for your readers to understand precisely what you mean. If you say that your company produces television shows for a *younger demographic segment,* they won't know whether you mean *teenagers* or *toddlers.* If you say that you study *natural phenomena,* your readers won't know whether you mean *volcanic eruptions* or *the migration of monarch butterflies.*

Such vagueness can hinder readers from getting the information they need in order to make decisions and take action. Consider the following sentence from a memo addressed to an upper-level manager who wanted to know why production costs were up:

Original | The <u>cost</u> of one <u>material</u> has <u>risen recently.</u>   [72]

This sentence doesn't give the manager the information she needs to take any remedial action. In contrast, the following sentence, using specific words, suggests precisely what the situation is:

Revised | The cost of the <u>bonding agent</u> has <u>tripled</u> in the <u>past six months.</u>   [73]

■ **FIGURE 10.2**

Hierarchy of Related Words That Move From a General to a Specific Abstraction

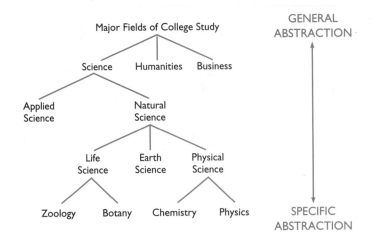

For another example, look at the original and revised versions of a sentence from a letter to state officials who are trying to decide whether to approve a series of construction projects proposed by an Alaskan mining company:

Original | Some of the planned construction may affect animals. [74]

Revised | Building the planned fence along the west side of the Hilton River access road may inter- [75]
rupt the natural migration of caribou, causing many to starve.

Of course, abstract and general terms do have important uses. For example, in scientific, technical, and other specialized fields, writers often are concerned with making general points, describing the general features of a situation, and providing general guidance for action. Your objective when choosing words is not to avoid abstract, general words altogether, but rather to avoid using words that are more abstract or more general than your purpose requires.

GUIDELINE **2** **Use Specialized Terms When—and Only When— Your Readers Will Understand Them**

A second way to make your writing clear and effective is to use the specialized terms of your own specialty wisely.

In some situations, specialized terms help you communicate effectively:

- **They convey precise, technical meanings economically.** Many terms have no exact equivalent in everyday speech and would take many sentences or even paragraphs to explain to someone who isn't familiar with them.
- **They can help you to establish credibility.** When you use the special terms of your field accurately, you show your fellow specialists that you are adept in it.

On the other hand, if you use technical terms when communicating to people who are unfamiliar with them, you will make your message very difficult to understand and use. Consider the following sentence:

> The major benefits of this method are smaller in-gate connections, reduced breakage, and minimum knock-out—all leading to great savings.

Although this sentence would be perfectly clear to any manager who works in a foundry that manufactures parts for automobile engines, it would be unintelligible to most other people because of the use of the specialized terms *in-gate connections* and *knock-out.*

How to Identify Words Your Readers Won't Know

When seeking to identify words you need to avoid, be sure to consider all specialized terms from your *readers'* point of view. Many recent college graduates are so used to talking with their instructors and with other students in their majors that they think that the specialized terms used in their fields are more widely understood than they actually are. On the job, remind yourself that you will often address people who are not in your field.

The task of identifying words readers may not know can be complicated by the fact that in many fields—perhaps including yours—some specialized terms are widely known but others are not. For instance, most people are familiar enough with chemistry to know what an *acid* is, and many have some sense of what a *base* is. But far fewer know what a *polymer* is. When addressing people who are not familiar with your specialty, you must distinguish between those technical terms your readers know and those they don't. To do this, you must have a fairly specific knowledge of your readers, especially of their level of familiarity with your field.

When addressing readers from another culture, ask someone familiar with that culture to review the words you've chosen. English words that sound like words in another language can have a completely different meaning. Only after Chevrolet introduced its Nova car to Latin America did it realize that in Spanish *"No va"* means "It doesn't go." Sales were slight until the name was changed (Grosse and Kujawa). In the 1920s, when Coca-Cola introduced its beverage in China, the company selected for its logo a series of Chinese characters that, when pronounced, sounded like the name of the beverage: *Ke Kou Ke La.* Later, they learned that the characters mean "Bite the wax tadpole." The characters used on Chinese Coke bottles today mean "Happiness in the mouth" (Ricks).

How to Explain Unfamiliar Terms If You Must Use Them

So far, this discussion has advised you to avoid using specialized terms when addressing readers who do not understand them. However, sometimes you may need to use such terms—for instance, when addressing a large audience that includes some people in your field and some outside of it or when explaining an entirely new subject not familiar to any of your readers.

In such cases, there are several ways to define the terms. Which one is appropriate will depend partly on the term and partly on the situation.

Ways to define terms your readers don't know.

1. **Give a synonym.** Example: On a boat, a rope or cord is called a *line.*
2. **Give a description.** Example: The *exit gate* consists of two arms that hold a jug while it is being painted and then allow it to proceed down the production line.
3. **Make an analogy.** Example: An atom is like a miniature solar system in which the nucleus is the sun and the electrons are the planets that revolve around it.
4. **Give a classical definition.** In a classical definition, you define the term by naming some familiar group of things to which it belongs and then identifying the key distinction between the object being defined and the other members of the group. Examples:

Word	Group	Distinguishing Characteristic
A crystal	solid	in which the atoms or molecules are arranged in a regularly repeated pattern
A burrow	hole in the ground	dug by an animal for shelter or habitation

---

GUIDELINE 3   **Use Words Accurately**

Whether you use specialized terms or everyday ones and whether you use abstract, general terms or concrete, specific ones, you must be careful to use all your words accurately. This point may seem obvious, but inaccurate word choice is all too common in on-the-job writing. For example, people often confuse *imply* (meaning to *suggest* or *hint,* as in "He implied that the operator had been careless") with *infer* (meaning *to draw a conclusion based upon evidence,* as in "We infer from your report that you do not expect to meet the deadline"). It's critical that you avoid such errors. They distract your readers from your message by drawing their attention to your problems with word choice, and they may lead your readers to believe that you are not skillful or precise in other areas—such as laboratory techniques or analytical skills.

How can you ensure that you use words accurately? There's no easy way. Consult a dictionary whenever you are uncertain. Be especially careful when using words that are not yet part of your usual vocabulary. Also, pay careful attention to the way words are used by other people.

GUIDELINE 4   **Choose Words with Appropriate Associations**

The three guidelines for choosing words that you have just read relate to the literal or dictionary meaning of words. At work, you must also consider the associations your words have for your readers. Two kinds of associations you should be especially sensitive to are *connotation* and *register.*

Connotation
Connotation is the extended or suggested meaning that a word has beyond its literal meaning. For example, according to the dictionary, *flatfoot* and *police detective*

Avoiding Sexist Language

Sexist language is language that reinforces stereotypes about women's qualities and capabilities. Because stereotypical assumptions about women (or any other group) can blind other people to a person's individuality, accomplishments, and potential, many employers consider sexist language to be unacceptable and unethical.

Here are four strategies for avoiding sexist language when you write at work.

Avoid Using the Word Man When Referring to Members of Both Sexes

Although the word man has traditionally been used to refer to people in general, it's now generally recognized that phrases such as man-made materials and mankind's scientific achievements perpetuate limiting stereotypes of male and female roles. After all, many synthetics were developed by women, and many scientists are female.

When seeking to avoid using man in this way, you should be especially alert to job titles and similar terms that include the word man. Try using business person, manager, or executive instead of businessman. Use firefighter, mail carrier, and salesperson instead of fireman, mailman, and salesman.

Also, beware of adjectives that incorporate the word man: Replace man-hours with working hours, man-made with synthetic, and man-sized job with large job.

Avoid Salutations That Imply the Reader of a Letter Is a Man

Once common in business letters, the salutations Dear Sir and Gentlemen are now rarely used be-cause they imply that the reader is male. Instead, you might use the title of the department or company you are addressing: Dear Personnel Department or Dear Switzer Plastics Company. Or you might use a job title: Dear College Recruiter or Dear Supervisor.

Avoid Using Sex-Linked Pronouns When Referring to Members of Both Sexes

When writing a sentence that refers to members of both sexes, avoid using pronouns like he or she that suggest that you are referring to only one sex.

One way to avoid using a sex-linked pronoun is to use a plural pronoun. Original: This survey shows that the consumer is worried that he won't get quick and courteous service during the warranty period. Revised: This survey shows that consumers are worried that they won't get quick and courteous service during the warranty period. Original: Our supermarkets cater to the affluent shopper. She looks for premium products and appreciates an attractive shopping environment. Revised: Our supermarkets cater to affluent shoppers. They look for premium products and appreciate an attractive shopping environment.

Another strategy is to use he or she and his or her. Original: Before the owner of a new business files the first year's tax returns, he might be wise to seek advice from a certified public accountant. Revised: Before the owner of a new business files the first year's tax returns, he or she might be wise to seek advice from a certified public accountant.

Refer to Individual Men and Women in a Parallel Manner

Another way to avoid sexist language is to refer to everyone in the same way, regardless of gender. For example, if you use full names for members of one sex, use full names for members of the other. Original: Christopher Sundquist and Ms. Tokagawa represented us at the trade fair. Revised: Christopher Sundquist and Anna Tokagawa represented us at the trade fair.

Similarly, if you use only first or last names for people of one sex, do the same for people of the other sex: The two leaders of the project are Neilson and Bledsoe or The two leaders of the project are Sheila and Randy.

Also, if you use courtesy titles (Mr., Ms.) for one sex, do the same for the other.

What about Miss, Mrs., and Ms.?

People are sometimes confused about whether to use the traditional terms Miss or Mrs. or the newer term Ms. In business, Ms. is becoming increasingly popular. People charge that using the older terms is a kind of sexism because it suggests that a woman's marital status is somehow relevant to the performance of her job. After all, they point out, all men, whether married or single, are addressed as Mr.

Although the term Ms. is now widely used, some women still prefer to be addressed as either Mrs. or Miss. Courtesy dictates that you follow the individual's preference if you know what it is.

are synonyms, but they connote very different things: *flatfoot* suggests a plodding, perhaps not very bright cop, while *police detective* suggests a highly trained professional.

Verbs, too, have connotations. For instance, to *suggest* that someone has overlooked a key fact is not the same as to *insinuate* that she has. To *devote* your time to working on a client's project is not the same as to *spend* your time on it.

Research on the impact of connotation

The connotations of your words can shape your audience's perceptions of your subject matter. To demonstrate this effect, researchers Raymond W. Kulhavy and Neil H. Schwartz wrote two versions of a description of a company that differed from one another in only seven words scattered throughout the 246 words in the entire description. In one version, the seven words suggested flexibility, such as *asked* and *should*. In the second version, those seven words were replaced by ones that suggested stiffness, such as *required* and *must*. Consider the following sentence from the first version:

First version   Our sales team is constantly trying to locate new markets for our various product lines.

In the second version of this sentence, the researchers replaced the flexible word *trying* with the stiff word *driving*.

Second version   Our sales team is constantly driving to locate new markets for our various product lines.

None of the substitutions changed the facts of the overall passage.

The researchers found that people who read the flexible version believed that the company would actively commit itself to the welfare and concerns of its employees, voluntarily participate in affirmative action programs for women and minorities, receive relatively few labor grievances, and pay its employees well. People who read that version also said they would recommend the company to a friend as a place to work. People who read the stiff version reported opposite impressions of the company. That people's impressions of the company could be affected so dramatically by just seven nonsubstantive words demonstrates the great importance of paying attention to the connotations of the words you use.

Register

Linguists use the term *register* to identify a second type of association exhibited by words. A word's register is the type of communication in which one expects the word to appear. At work, you need to use words whose register matches the type of communication you are preparing. In an advertisement, you might say that your restaurant gives *amazingly* good service, but you would not say the same thing about your engineering consulting firm in a letter to a prospective client. The word *amazingly* has the register of consumer advertising but not of letters to business clients.

If you inadvertently choose words with the wrong register, you may give the impression that you don't fully grasp how business is conducted in your field, and your credibility can be lost. As you choose words, be sensitive to the kinds of communications in which you usually see them used.

GUIDELINE **5** **Choose Plain Words over Fancy Ones**

Another way to make your writing effective and easy to understand is to avoid using fancy words where plain ones will do. At work, people often do just the opposite, perhaps because they think fancy words sound more official or make the writer seem more knowledgeable. The following list identifies some commonly used fancy words; it includes only verbs but might have included nouns and adjectives as well.

Fancy Verbs	Common Verbs
ascertain	find out
commence	begin
compensate	pay
constitute	make up
endeavor	try
expend	spend
fabricate	build
facilitate	make easier
initiate	begin
prioritize	rank
proceed	go
terminate	end
transmit	send
utilize	use

There are two important reasons for preferring plain words over fancy ones:

- **Plain words promote efficient reading.** Research has shown that even if your readers know both the plain word and its fancy synonym, they will still comprehend the plain word more rapidly (Klare).
- **Plain words reduce your risk of creating a bad impression.** If you use words that make for slow, inefficient reading, you may annoy your readers or cause them to conclude that you are behaving pompously, showing off, or trying to hide a lack of ideas and information behind a fog of fancy terms. Consider, for instance, the effect of the following sentence, which one writer included in a job application letter:

Pompous word choices

> I am transmitting the enclosed resume to facilitate your efforts to determine the pertinence of my work experience to your opening.

Don't misunderstand this guideline, however. It doesn't suggest that you should use only simple language at work. When addressing people with vocabularies comparable to your own, use all the words at your command, provided that you use them accurately and appropriately. This guideline merely cautions you against using needlessly inflated words that bloat your prose and may open you to criticism from your readers.

CONCLUSION

Your writing style can make a great deal of difference to the success of your writing. The voice you use, the sentence structures you employ, and the words you choose affect both your readers' attitudes toward you and your subject matter and also the readability and impact of your writing. This chapter has suggested many things you can do to develop an effective style. Underlying all these suggestions is the advice that you consider your stylistic decisions from your readers' point of view.

EXERCISES

1. Without altering the meaning of the following sentences, reduce the number of words in them.
   a. After having completed work on the data-entry problem, we turned our thinking toward our next task, which was the processing problem.
   b. Those who plan federal and state programs for the elderly should take into account the changing demographic characteristics in terms of size and average income of the composition of the elderly population.
   c. Would you please figure out what we should do and advise us?
   d. The result of this study will be to make total whitewater recycling an economical strategy for meeting federal regulations.

2. Rewrite the following sentences in a way that will keep the related words together.
   a. This stamping machine, if you fail to clean it twice per shift and add oil of the proper weight, will cease to operate efficiently.
   b. The plant manager said that he hopes all employees would seek ways to cut waste at the supervisory meeting yesterday.
   c. About 80 percent of our pulp, to be made into linerboard and corrugated cardboard (much of it used for beverage containers), supplies our plants for manufacturing packages.
   d. Once they wilt, most garden sprays are unable to save vegetable plants from complete collapse.

3. Rewrite the following sentences to put the action in the verb.
   a. The experience itself will be an inspirational factor leading the participants to a greater dedication to productivity.
   b. The system realizes important savings in time for the clerical staff.
   c. The implementation of the work plan will be the responsibility of a team of three engineers experienced in these procedures.
   d. Both pulp and lumber were in strong demand, even though rising interest rates caused the drying up of funds for housing.

4. Rewrite the following sentences in the active voice.
   a. Periodically, the shipping log should be reconciled with the daily billings by the Accounting Department.
   b. Fast, accurate data from each operating area in the foundry should be given to us by the new computerized system.
   c. Since his own accident, safety regulations have been enforced much more conscientiously by the shop foreman.
   d. No one has been designated by the manager to make emergency decisions when she is gone.

5. In three of the following pairs of sentences, the topic shifts from the first to the second sentence. Rewrite one or the other sentence so that the topics are the same.
   a. "Grab" samplers collect material from the floor of the ocean. Rock, sediment, and benthic animals can be gathered by these samplers at rates as high as 8,000 tons per hour.
   b. To fluoridate the drinking water, a dilute form of hydrofluorisilic acid is added directly to the municipal water supply at the main pump. An automatic control continuously meters exactly the right amount of the acid into the water.
   c. Fourteen variables were used in these calculations. The first seven concern the volume of business generated by each sales division each week.
   d. The city's low-income citizens suffer most from the high prices and limited selection of food products offered by commercial grocers. Furthermore, information concerning nutrition is difficult for many low-income citizens to find.

6. In the memo shown in Figure 10.3, identify places where the writer has ignored the guidelines given in this chapter. You may find it helpful to use a dictionary. Then write an improved version of the memo by following the guidelines in this chapter.

7. Create a one-sentence, classical definition for a word used in your field that is not familiar to people in other fields. The word might be one that people in other fields have heard of but cannot define precisely in the way specialists

■ **FIGURE 10.3**

Memo to Be Used in Exercise 6

MEMO

July 8, 19—

TO: Gavin MacIntyre, Vice President, Midwest Region

FROM: Nat Willard, Branch Manager, Milwaukee Area Offices

The ensuing memo is in reference to provisions for the cleaning of the six offices and two workrooms in the High Street building in Milwaukee. This morning, I absolved Thomas's Janitor Company of its responsibility for cleansing the subject premises when I discovered that two of Thomas's employees had surreptitiously been making unauthorized long-distance calls on our telephones.

Because of your concern with the costs of running the Milwaukee area offices, I want your imprimatur before proceeding further in making a determination about procuring cleaning services for this building. One possibility is to assign the janitor from the Greenwood Boulevard building to clean the High Street building also. However, this alternative is judged impractical because it cannot be implemented without circumventing the reality of time constraints. While the Greenwood janitor could perform routine cleaning operations at the High Street establishment in one hour, it would take him another ninety minutes to drive to and fro between the two sites. This is more time than he could spare and still be able to fulfill his responsibilities at the High Street building.

Another alternative would be to hire a full-time or part-time employee precisely for the High Street building. However, that building can be cleaned so expeditiously, it would be irrational to do so.

The third alternative is to search for another janitorial service. I have now released two of these enterprises from our employ in Milwaukee. However, our experiences with such services should be viewed as bad luck and not affect our decision, except to make us more aware that making the optimal selection among companies will require great care. Furthermore, there seems to be no reasonable alternative to hiring another janitorial service.

Accordingly, I recommend that we hire another janitorial service. If you agree, I can commence searching for this service as soon as I receive a missive from you. In the meantime I have asked the employees who work in the High Street building to do some tidying up themselves and to be patient.

in your field do. Underline the word you are defining. Then circle and label the part of your definition that describes the familiar group of items that the defined word belongs to. Finally, circle and label the part of your definition that identifies the key distinction between the defined word and the other items in the group. (Note that not every word is best defined by means of a classical definition, so it may

take you a few minutes to think of an appropriate word for this exercise.)

8. Create an analogy to explain a word used in your field that is unfamiliar to most readers. (Note that not every word is best defined by means of an analogy, so it may take you a few minutes to think of an appropriate word for this exercise.)

Drafting Visual Elements

CHAPTER 11
Drafting Visual Aids

REFERENCE GUIDE
Thirteen Types of Visual Aids

CHAPTER 12
Designing Pages and Documents

Drafting Visual Aids

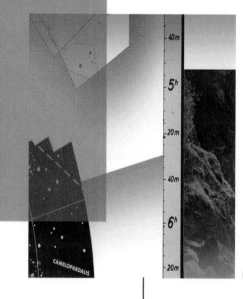

GUIDELINES

1 | Look for places where visual aids will help you achieve your communication objectives

2 | Choose visual aids appropriate to your objectives

3 | Make your visual aids easy to understand and use

4 | Use color to support your message

5 | Adapt existing visual aids to your purpose and readers

6 | Integrate your visual aids with your text

7 | When addressing an international audience, check your visual aids with persons from the other nations

Visual aids are an integral part of much on-the-job writing. In fact, the first thing to know about them is that usually they aren't *aids* at all. They often convey part of a message more clearly and usefully than words. Sometimes, they even carry the *entire* message.

For instance, if you've ever flown, you have probably reached into the pocket of the seat ahead of you to pull out instructions for exiting the plane in an emergency. The instruction sheets used by many airlines contain only pictures. Figure 11.1 shows an example. Wordless instructions are also used widely for products that are marketed internationally because the pictures can overcome language barriers.

Although you may never create a wordless communication, many times in your career you will surely need to design clear, useful visual aids and integrate them effectively into a communication. This chapter's seven guidelines will help you accomplish these goals whether you are preparing a written communication, an on-line document, or an oral presentation. The Reference Guide that follows this chapter provides additional advice about how to construct thirteen types of visual aids that are widely used in the workplace.

Chapters 15 and 16 provide additional advice for use with electronic communications and oral presentations.

GUIDELINE 1

Look for Places Where Visual Aids Will Help You Achieve Your Communication Objectives

Paradoxically, although contemporary society has become increasingly visual when taking in information, most of us still think primarily of words when we want to convey information to others. Consequently, an important step in creating reader-centered communications is to *search actively* for places where visual aids can help you achieve your communication objectives by replacing, supplementing, or reinforcing your prose (Shriver, 441).

Search actively for places to use visual aids.

Begin by thinking about some of the many ways you can assist your readers by using visual aids:

Ways you can use visual aids to help your readers

- **Show your readers how something looks or is constructed.** For example, Figures 11.2B, C, and D show readers the appearance of things with greater impact and clarity than words could achieve. Using Figure 11.2A, an engineer showed his readers the construction of the equipment he designed for using lasers to make computer chips.
- **Show your readers how to do something.** Ideal for instructions, visual aids explain operations that would be difficult to describe—and understand—in prose. For example, Figure 11.3 shows readers how to fasten a card fence inside a computer.
- **Explain a process.** Many processes are best understood visually. By reading Figure 11.4, people can quickly understand how seawater picks up chemicals as it loops through hot-spring systems under the ocean.
- **Show how something is organized.** For example, the diagram shown in Figure 11.5 explains the complex relationships among the computer programs and physical parts inside a cell phone.

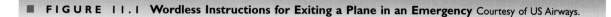

■ **FIGURE 11.1 Wordless Instructions for Exiting a Plane in an Emergency** Courtesy of US Airways.

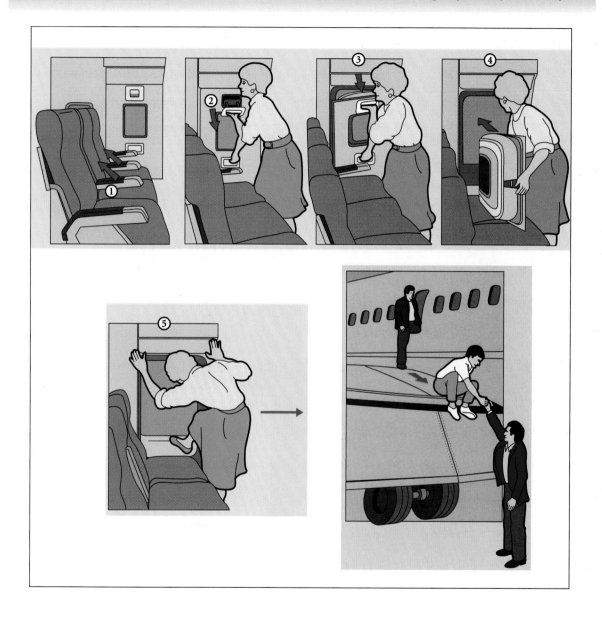

- **Display data so particular facts are easy to find.** Using the table shown in Figure 11.6, readers can determine quickly the time and temperature they should use when developing their own photographic film.
- **Show trends and other numerical relationships.** Various visual aids such as line graphs, bar graphs, and pie charts enable readers to grasp trends and other

(Text continues on page 279)

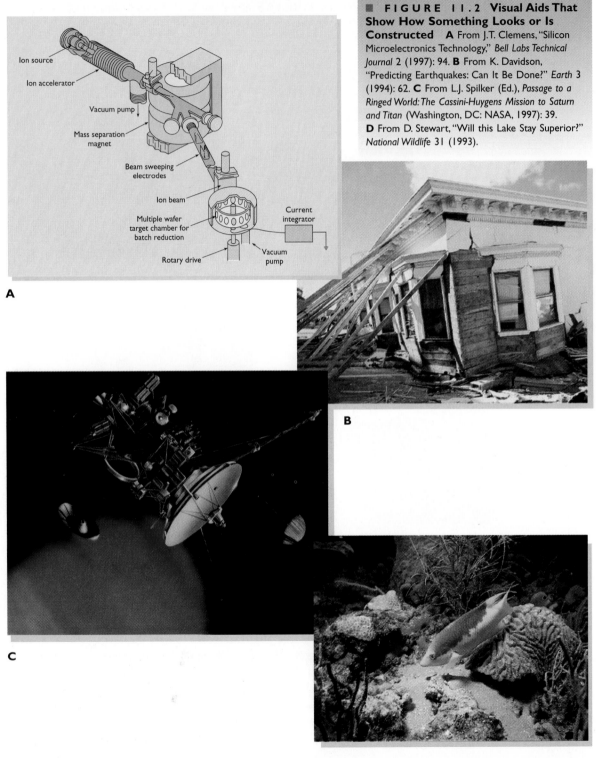

■ FIGURE 11.2 Visual Aids That Show How Something Looks or Is Constructed A From J.T. Clemens, "Silicon Microelectronics Technology," *Bell Labs Technical Journal* 2 (1997): 94. B From K. Davidson, "Predicting Earthquakes: Can It Be Done?" *Earth* 3 (1994): 62. C From L.J. Spilker (Ed.), *Passage to a Ringed World: The Cassini-Huygens Mission to Saturn and Titan* (Washington, DC: NASA, 1997): 39. D From D. Stewart, "Will this Lake Stay Superior?" *National Wildlife* 31 (1993).

■ **FIGURE 11.3 Drawing That Shows How to Do Something** From *Apple Computer Power Macintosh User's Manual for 7300 Series* (Cupertino, CA: Apple Computer, 1997) 206.

You may find it helpful to support the screw with the thumb of your other hand.

This figure shows the action from the same point of view that a person performing the task would have.

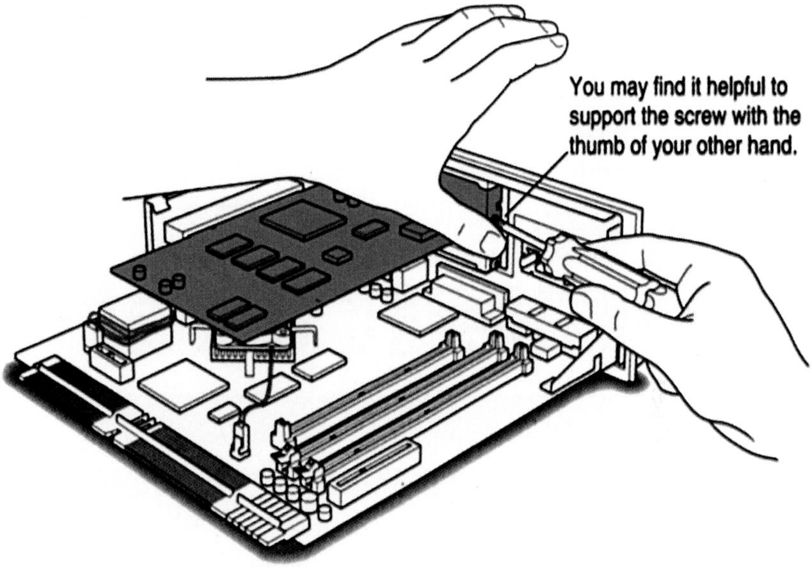

■ **FIGURE 11.4 Diagram That Explains a Process**

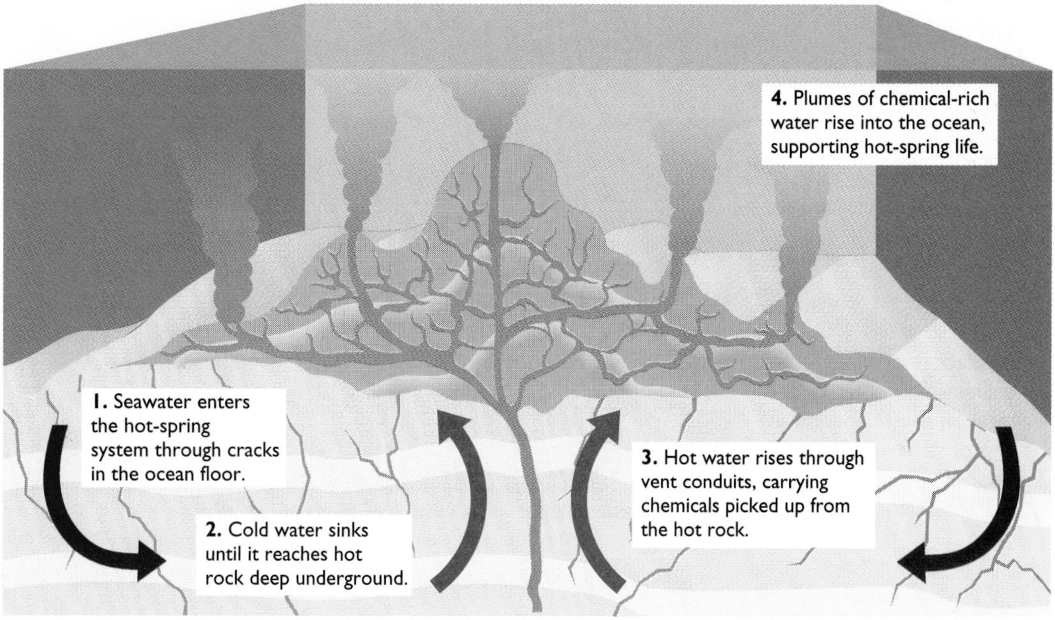

4. Plumes of chemical-rich water rise into the ocean, supporting hot-spring life.

By incorporating text into this drawing, the writer increases the ease with which readers can understand the process he describes.

1. Seawater enters the hot-spring system through cracks in the ocean floor.

2. Cold water sinks until it reaches hot rock deep underground.

3. Hot water rises through vent conduits, carrying chemicals picked up from the hot rock.

Hot rock deep underground causes seawater to loop through hot-springs, picking up heat and chemicals as it goes.

■ **FIGURE 11.5** **Diagram That Shows How Something Is Organized** Courtesy of Texas Instruments. From http://www.ti.com/sc/graphics/wireless/97/enable/rfgraph.gif.

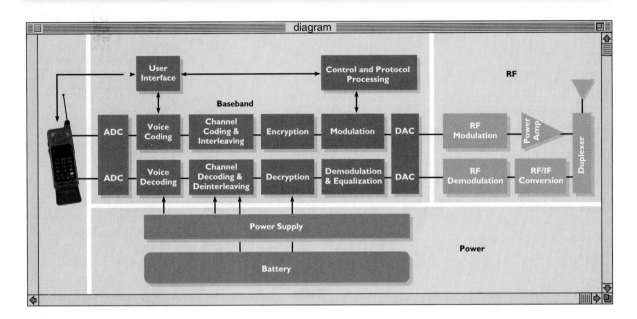

■ **FIGURE 11.6** **Visual Aid That Helps Readers Find Particular Facts** Courtesy of Eastman Kodak Company.

Boldface is used in the two columns for 68°F to highlight the temperature photographers prefer to use.

Kodak Developer	Developing Time (in Minutes)									
	SMALL TANK (Agitation at 30-Second Intervals)					LARGE TANK (Agitation at 1-Minute Intervals)				
	65°F (18° C)	68°F (20° C)	70°F (21° C)	72°F (22° C)	75°F (24° C)	65°F (18° C)	68°F (20° C)	70°F (21° C)	72°F (22° C)	75°F (24° C)
HC-110 (Dil B)	8½	**7½**	6½	6	5	9½	**8½**	8	7½	
D-76	9	**8**	7½	6½	5½	10	**9**	8	7	
D-76 (1:1)	11	**10**	9½	9	8	13	**12**	11	10	
MICRODOL-X	11	**10**	9½	9	8	13	**12**	11	10	
MICRODOL-X (1:3)*	—	—	15	14	13	—	—	17	16	
DK-50 (1:1)	7	**6**	5½	5	4½	7½	**6½**	6	5½	
HC-110 (Dil A)	4½†	**3¾†**	3¼†	3†	2½†	4¾†	**4¼†**	4†	3¾†	

* Gives greater sharpness than other developers shown in table.
† Avoid development times of less than 5 minutes if possible, because poor uniformity may result.

Note: Do not use developers containing silver halide solvents.

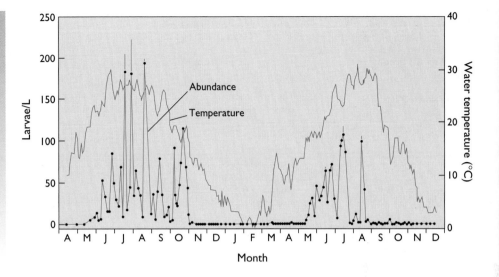

■ **FIGURE II.7**

Graph That Shows Relationships

From J.A. Stoeckel, D.W. Schneider, L.A. Soeken, K.D. Blodgett, and R.E. Sparks, "Larval Dynamics of a Riverine Metapopulation: Implications for Zebra Mussel Recruitment, Dispersal, and Control in a Large-River System," *Journal of the American Benthological Society* 16 (1997): 591.

numerical relationships much more quickly than they could from sentences. For example, a team of biological researchers used the graph shown in Figure 11.7 to help their readers see the relationship between river water temperature and the abundance of a particular kind of shellfish.

Use visual aids to make persuasive points.

When searching for opportunities to use visual aids, look also for places where they will support your persuasive points by conveying your data in a way that will impress your readers (Kostelnick and Roberts). For example, the manufacturer of a plastic insulating material used the bar graph shown in Figure 11.8 to persuade greenhouse owners that they could greatly reduce their winter heating bills by covering their greenhouses with the company's plastic sheets.

Plan your visual aids early.

Start looking for opportunities to use visual aids as soon as you begin to plan a communication. By deciding how to coordinate your prose and visual aids in this early stage, you can reduce the amount of revision required later. Also, if you need to ask an artist or photographer to prepare some of your visual aids, early planning will ensure that this person can meet your deadline.

GUIDELINE 2   Choose Visual Aids Appropriate to Your Objectives

After deciding where to use visual aids, you must select the type of visual aid that will most effectively communicate your message to your readers. Most information can be presented in more than one type of visual aid. For example, numerical data can be presented in a table, bar graph, line graph, or pie chart. The components of an electronic instrument can be represented in a photograph, sketch, block diagram, or schematic.

■ **FIGURE 11.8**

Visual Aid That Makes a Persuasive Point

Courtesy of Monsanto Company.

The brightest color is given to the 602 bars in order to emphasize the small amount of energy consumed when the 602 insulation is used.

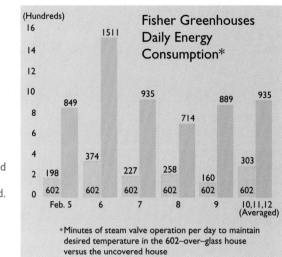

To determine which type to use, consider the objectives of your visual aid in exactly the same way you think about the objectives of the overall communication. Identify the task you want the visual aid to enable your readers to perform and determine how you want the visual aid to affect your readers' attitudes.

Consider Your Readers' Tasks

Different visual aids support different reading tasks. Consider, for example, Ben's choices.

Ben must decide how to display salary data.

Ben has surveyed people who graduated over the past three years from three departments in his college. Now he wants to report to the alumni what he has learned about their average starting salaries. He could do this with a table, bar graph, or line graph. Which would be best?

His choice should depend on the way his readers will want to use his data.

The answer depends on the way the alumni will want to use Ben's findings. If Ben's purpose is simply to enable the alumni to learn the average starting salary of people who graduated in their year from their department, he could use a table (see Figure 11.9). If he wants them to be able to compare the average starting salaries in their department with the average starting salaries of people who graduated in that same year from the other departments, he could use a bar graph. And if he wants them to be able to see how the average starting salary in their department changed over the years and to compare that change with the changes experienced by the other departments, he could use a line graph.

The Reference Guide that follows this chapter provides additional information about the reading tasks that are supported by these and several other types of visual aids.

■ FIGURE 11.9 **Three Ways of Showing Average Starting Salaries for Three Departments over Three Years**

A table helps a reader quickly find a specific piece of information, such as the average salary for a particular department in a specific year.

Department	Year of Graduation		
	1997	**1998**	**1999**
A	27,300	30,900	35,400
B	32,250	36,600	43,150
C	31,750	34,650	39,100

A bar graph helps a reader make comparisons, for instance a comparison among the average salaries of three departments for a particular year.

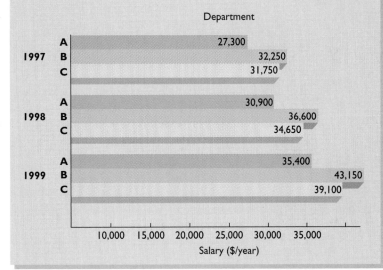

A line graph helps a reader see and compare trends.

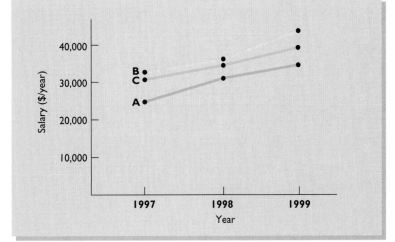

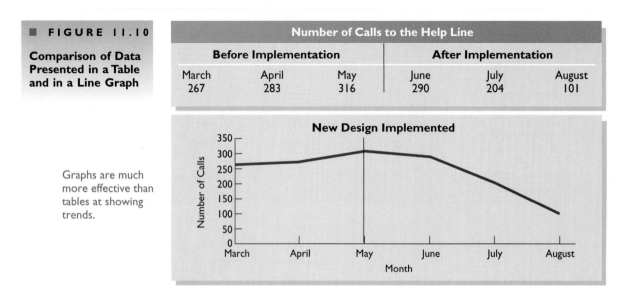

FIGURE 11.10

Comparison of Data Presented in a Table and in a Line Graph

Number of Calls to the Help Line					
Before Implementation			**After Implementation**		
March	April	May	June	July	August
267	283	316	290	204	101

Graphs are much more effective than tables at showing trends.

Consider Your Readers' Attitudes

When selecting the type of visual aid you will use, think also about the way you want to affect your readers' attitudes: pick the type of visual aid that most quickly and dramatically communicates the evidence that supports your persuasive point. Consider, for instance, Akiko's choices.

Akiko must select the type of visual aid with the highest visual impact.

> Akiko recommended a change in the design of one of her company's products. In order to show how the company has benefitted from this change, she has tallied the number of phone calls received by the company's toll-free help line during the months immediately before and after implementation of the new design. As Figure 11.10 shows, if Akiko presents her data in a table, her readers will have to do a lot of subtracting to appreciate the impact of her recommendation. If she presents her data in a line graph, they will be able to recognize her accomplishment at a glance.

Select visual aids your readers know how to interpret.

Of course, your readers will find your visual aids useful and persuasive only if they can understand them. Some types are familiar to us all, but others are more specialized, like those in Figure 11.11. Although they are very informative to people familiar with the symbols and conventions used, specialized visual aids will only baffle other persons. Either select visual aids your readers will understand or provide them with the explanations they need.

GUIDELINE 3 **Make Your Visual Aids Easy to Understand and Use**

Having chosen the *type* of visual aid you will use, you must design the aid itself. When doing so, remember that your visual aids, like your prose, should be easy for your readers to understand and use. Here are some suggestions.

■ **FIGURE 11.11 Specialized Visual Aids   A** From Burgess, "Organometallic Chemistry," *Chemistry and Industry* 24 (1997): 1004. **B** From National Aeronautics and Space Administration, "Asymetric Switching for PWM H-Bridge Power Circuit," *NASA Tech Briefs* 95-06 (1995): 13. **C** From H.V. Mahaney, "Thermal Modeling of the Infrared Reflow Process for Solder Ball Connect (SBC)," *IBM Journal of Research and Development* 37 (1993): 616. **D** From National Aeronautics and Space Administration, *Research and Technology Report: Goddard Space Flight Center* (Washington, DC: NASA, 1995) 3.

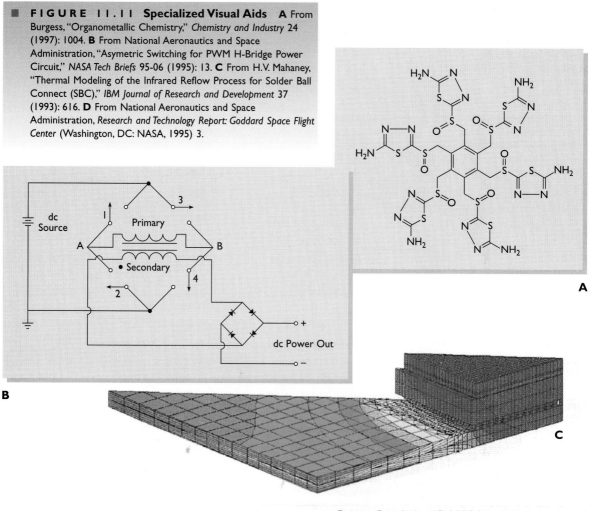

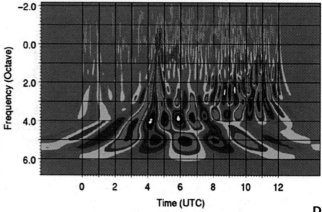

A

B

C

D

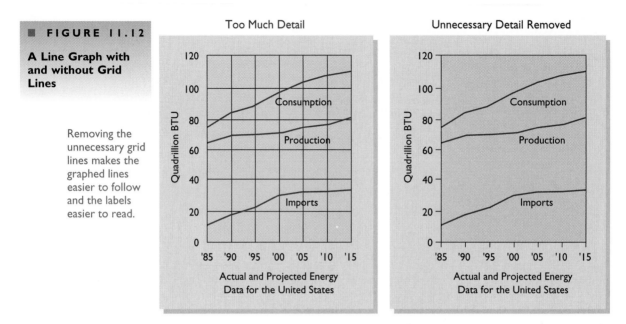

■ **FIGURE 11.12**

A Line Graph with and without Grid Lines

Removing the unnecessary grid lines makes the graphed lines easier to follow and the labels easier to read.

Design Your Visual Aids to Support Your Readers' Tasks

Imagine your readers trying to use your visual aid.

First, follow this familiar strategy: imagine your readers in the act of using your visual aid and then design it accordingly. For example, in drawings or photographs for step-by-step instructions, show objects from the same angle that your readers will see them when trying to perform the actions you describe.

Likewise, in a table, arrange the columns and rows in an order that will help your readers find the particular piece of information they are looking for. Maybe that means you should arrange the columns and rows in alphabetical order, according to a logical pattern, or by some other system. Use whatever arrangement your readers will find most efficient.

Similarly, when designing any other type of visual aid, remember that you are trying not only to display information but also to help your readers use it.

Make Your Visual Aids Simple

A second strategy for making your visual aids easy to understand and use is to keep them simple. Simplicity is especially important for visual aids that will be read on a computer screen or from a projected image because people have more difficulty reading from these media than from paper:

- **Don't cram in too much material.** Sometimes, two or three separate visual aids will communicate the same information more effectively than one.
- **Remove unnecessary details.** Like unnecessary words in prose, superfluous details in visual aids create extra, unproductive work for readers and obscure the really important information. Figure 11.12 shows how the elimination of extraneous detail can simplify a graph. As another example, Figure 11.13 shows two photographs and a line drawing of the same experimental apparatus used in new-product research.

■ **FIGURE 11.13**

Two Photographs and a Drawing of the Same Equipment

LESS EFFECTIVE PHOTOGRAPH

The cluttered background makes it difficult to identify the parts of the testing equipment.

MORE EFFECTIVE PHOTOGRAPH

Removal of the clutter allows the parts to be distinguished.

DRAWING

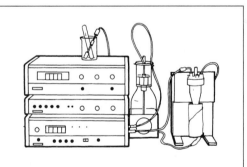

A line drawing shows very clearly some parts that are not obvious even in the uncluttered photograph.

Label the Important Content Clearly

By providing labels for the parts included in your visual aids, you can help your readers find the things they seek and understand what they see. To create labels, first determine which features need labeling by asking which features your readers will want to find or need help understanding. In a table, for instance, label every row and column. In a diagram, label every part that your readers will be interested in. But avoid labeling other features. Unnecessary labels clutter a visual aid and make it difficult to understand and use.

Some visual aids need no labels at all. For instance, the title for the visual aid may make clear what its important parts are (for example, "Figure 3.2. Dents Caused by Hail"). Or, the reference you make to the figure in your prose may serve the same purpose.

Wording and placing labels

After you've decided that a certain part needs a label, choose the appropriate word or words and place them where they are easy to see. If necessary, draw a line from the label to the part. Wherever possible, avoid labeling parts with letters or numbers that are explained in a separate key. Figure 11.14 shows how much more convenient it is for readers to have labels next to the parts they designate. Avoid placing a label on top of an important part of your figure.

Provide Informative Titles

Titles are the captions that tell readers what's in a figure. They help your readers find the visual aids they are looking for and know what the visual aids contain when they locate them. Typically, titles include both a number (for example, "Figure 3" or "Table 6") and a description ("Effects of Temperature on the Strength of M312").

Advice for writing titles

Make your titles as brief—yet informative—as possible. Avoid vague words. Don't say "Information on Computer Programs," but instead say "Comparison of the Speed and Capabilities of Three Database Programs."

Be consistent in the placement of your titles, for example, placing all of them above your figures or all below your figures.

For a long communication in which readers might seek a specific figure whose location won't be obvious from the regular table of contents, provide a separate list of the figures and the pages where they can be found.

Note, however, that some visual aids don't need a title. For instance, when you are including a very short table in your text, you can make its contents perfectly clear with a simple statement in the preceding sentence:

A table that needs no title

You will be pleased to see how well our top four salespersons did in June:

Chamberlain	$227,603
Tonaka	195,278
Gonzales	193,011
Albers	188,590

GUIDELINE 4 Use Color to Support Your Message

In recent years, there's been an explosion of color in workplace communications. Web pages and other on-screen communications are saturated with color. Color enlivens and enhances the many oral presentations made by individuals using computer programs such as PowerPoint. In addition, as color printing and copying become less expensive, even routine printed documents now incorporate multicolor designs in some organizations.

The widespread availability of color puts a new and powerful aid to communication at your disposal. With color you can clarify your messages, speed your

■ **FIGURE 11.14**

Labels Provided with and without a Key

From B. Margolin, "Analog, Mixed-Signal ICs Steering Drive-By-Wire Toward Reality," *Computer Design* 36 (1997): 31.

When labels are placed next to their parts, readers can easily match each part to its name.

Easy to Read: Labels Placed by Parts

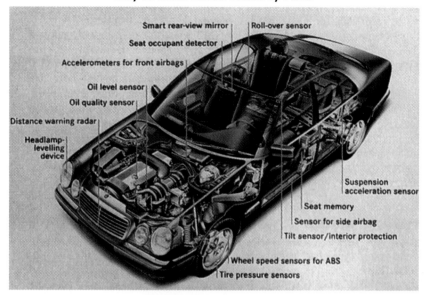

Sensors and Integrated Safety Devices

Less Easy to Read: Labels in a Key

When labels are placed in a key, readers must repeatedly shift their attention from the diagram to the key in order to learn the names of the parts.

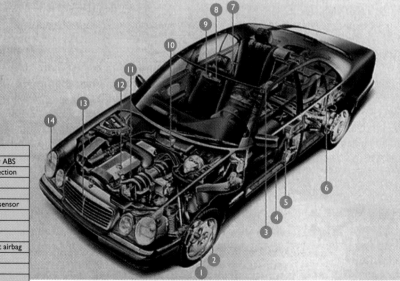

1	Tire pressure sensors
2	Wheel speed sensors for ABS
3	Tilt sensor/interior protection
4	Sensor for side airbag
5	Seat memory
6	Suspension acceleration sensor
7	Roll-over sensor
8	Smart rear-view mirror
9	Seat occupant detector
10	Accelerometers for front airbag
11	Oil level sensor
12	Oil quality sensor
13	Distance warning radar
14	Headlamp-levelling device

Sensors and Integrated Safety Devices

readers' comprehension, and make your information easy for your readers to use. Among other things, color can help you:

Some uses of color

- Highlight a point
- Tell the reader where to look first
- Group related items
- Establish hierarchies of importance
- Provoke an emotional response
- Make your communication look more polished and attractive

Guidelines for Using Color

The impact of color on readers is determined partly by physiology and partly by psychology. Based on what researchers know about these responses, the following suggestions will enable you to use color in a reader-centered way:

Misuse of color can diminish a communication's effectiveness.

1. **Use color primarily for clarity and emphasis, not decoration.** When used merely for decoration, color can create two problems. First, because color attracts the eye, it can draw a reader's eye to ornamentation rather than to more important content, thereby reducing the reader's ability to grasp your message.

   Second, attractive colors can actually make reading difficult, as was discovered by communication researcher Colin Wheildon. He showed people two versions of the same page, one printed in black and one in blue. The people said the blue one was more attractive, but those who actually read the blue version scored substantially lower on a comprehension test than those who read the black version. It is critical that you deploy colors in a way that promotes rather than hinders comprehension.

A color's appearance can change if the surrounding colors are changed.

2. **Choose color schemes, not just single colors.** Readers see a color in terms of its surroundings. To illustrate this point, design expert Jan V. White (15) uses blocks of color like those shown in Figure 11.15. The top pair of blocks in Figure 11.15 shows that the same shade of blue-gray appears lighter when seen against a dark color than when seen against a pale color. As the bottom pair of blocks demonstrates, the same pure color looks much different when surrounded by another shade of the same color than when surrounded by a complementary color.

   Here are some facts about color's effects on readers that you should keep in mind when choosing color schemes:

   - **Bright colors attract the eye more assertively than dull colors.** Use a bright color for accent and a dull color for background. Figure 11.16 shows how one writer used bright yellow to focus his readers' eyes to the central component in his illustration of a device for creating silicon-germanium crystals.
   - **Warmer and more intense colors appear closer to the reader than cooler and less intense colors.** When trying to communicate depth, use cooler, less intense colors for what appears more distant. Figure 11.17 shows how a group of scientists used a dull background and bright colors to make their image of a progenitor cell appear to advance toward their readers.

■ **FIGURE 11.15   Some Ways a Color's Appearance is Affected by the Surrounding Color** Based on J. V. White, *Color for the Electronic Age* (New York: Watson-Guptil, 1990): 16.

The same blue square appears brighter against a darker color (such as black) than it does against a lighter color (such as yellow).

The same orange square appears brighter against a different shade of its own color than it does against a complementary color (in this case green).

■ **FIGURE 11.16   Bright Colors Used to Focus Attention** From B. S. Meyerson, "High-Speed Silicon-Germanium Electronics," *Scientific American* 270 (1994): 67.

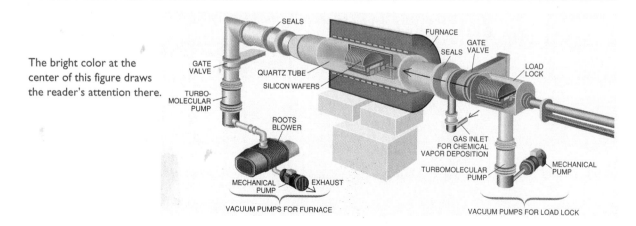

The bright color at the center of this figure draws the reader's attention there.

■ **FIGURE 11.17**

Bright Colors Used against a Dull Background to Make Important Material Advance toward the Reader

From M. Fischer, J. Goldschmitt, C. Peschel, J.P.G. Brakenhoff, K.J. Kallen, A. Wollmer, Grotzinger, and S. Rose-John, "A Bioactive Designer Cytokine for Human Hematopoietic Progenitor Cell Expansion," *Nature Biotechnology* 15 (1997): 142.

Bright colors appear to advance from a dark background.

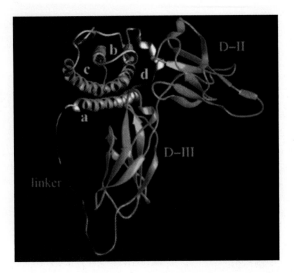

■ **Contrast creates emphasis.** To make something stand out, put it against a much different color rather than a very similar color.

Greater contrast creates more emphasis.

More Emphasis	Less Emphasis

3. **To promote easy reading, use a high contrast between text and background.** To comprehend a written message, readers must first pick out the letters from the background on which they are printed. We traditionally use black print on white paper because this color combination creates a very high contrast that makes letter identification easy. However, backgrounds of colors other than white are very common in Web pages and computer-projected visual aids for oral presentations. They often appear in printed documents also. In fact, even if you don't have a color printer, you can create gray backgrounds with many desktop publishing programs. The following chart shows how much more difficult black type becomes to read as the background becomes darker.

Reducing contrast reduces readability.

20%	This type is surprinted in black	This type is dropped out in white	20%
40%	This type is surprinted in black	This type is dropped out in white	40%

60%	This type is surprinted in black	This type is dropped out in white	60%
80%	This type is surprinted in black	This type is dropped out in white	80%
100%	This type is surprinted in black	This type is dropped out in white	100%

The same color can have different associations in different contexts and different cultures.

4. **Select colors with appropriate associations.** In many contexts, colors have specific associations and even symbolic meaning. When driving through a city, we associate red with "stop," and green with "go." As Jan V. White (20) points out, however, our associations with color vary from one context to another. In politics, blue is associated with conservatism and in business with stability, but to a doctor it connotes death. In other contexts, blue suggests sky, water, and cold. People's associations with colors are quite powerful, so be alert to them when selecting colors for your visual aids. Also, color associations vary from one culture to another. In many Western cultures, black is the color of death and mourning. In China, white is. If you are addressing an international audience, determine what your readers might associate with the colors you are thinking of using.

5. **Stick to a few colors.** An overabundance of colors can cause confusion. Colors can compete with one another for attention, leaving readers unsure of the visual hierarchy being established among the elements of a visual aid. Also, readers rely on color to establish patterns of meaning, as when one color is employed consistently to represent the raw materials used in a manufacturing process and another color is employed to represent the products of the process. If too many colors are used, such patterns are obscured—if they even existed in the first place. Usually it's better to use fewer colors, perhaps in a variety of shades, than to use a larger number of colors.

6. **Use color to unify your overall communication.** When choosing colors, think beyond the individual visual aids, and consider your communication as a whole. By using a limited group of colors, you can create visual unity, and by using these colors in a consistent pattern, you can help your readers understand your message.

When writing long documents, you can also employ color to help your readers use your communications efficiently. Figure 11.18 depicts several techniques for doing so for print documents. Consistent, strategic use of color can also unify the visual aids for oral presentations (Figure 11.19) and on-line documents (Figure 11.20).

■ **FIGURE 11.18**

Ways of Unifying a Printed Communication with Color

Based on Jan V. White, *Color for the Electronic Age* (New York: Watson-Guptill, 1990), 35, 40–43.

There are many ways to use color to unify a long communication visually.

Headers and Footers

Tabs and Locators

Marking Breaks between Sections

Highlighting a Key Section

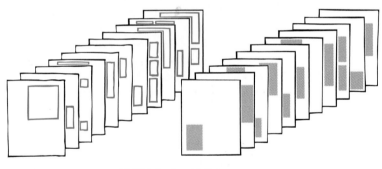

Highlighting Special Content

■ FIGURE 11.19

Ways of Unifying an Oral Presentation with Color

By using the same color scheme throughout this presentation, the writer created a visual unity among the slides.

To make reading easy, the writer used large letters and high contrast between background and the text.

The background pattern adds interest but is subtle enough to avoid distracting from the writer's message.

Consistent use of color and design elements unifies these slides for an oral presentation.

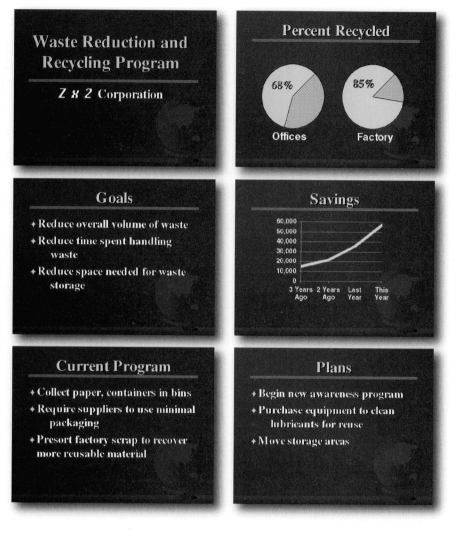

■ **FIGURE 11.20**

Ways of Unifying an On-line Communication with Color

These pages demonstrate the use of color to unify a Web site.

Note the various ways that black and the same shades of blue, yellow, and gray are worked into each of these pages.

The pages are also unified through the repetition of certain design elements and through the use of the same grid (see page 334).

GUIDELINE **5** **Adapt Existing Visual Aids to Your Purpose and Readers**

Computer technology has made it very easy to incorporate existing visual aids in your communications. Some organizations keep files of their electronic artwork for the very purpose of allowing it to be reused rather than redrawn. Scanners allow you to make electronic copies of print items, programs like Microsoft Word and PowerPoint include libraries of clipart, and Web sites include collections of art you can download. And it's easy to copy images from the Web pages you visit. With Netscape, for instance, you simply put your pointer on a Web page image, hold your button down until a pop-up menu appears, and select "Save."

When using existing visual aids, be sure to review the items from the perspective of your readers and purpose. Examine not only the contents but also the labels. If you can't adapt the visual aid sufficiently to serve your purposes, create a new one on your own.

Also, when using existing visual aids that aren't owned by your employer, look for copyright notices. Just because you can copy an image from a Web site doesn't mean that it's legal for you to do so. Also, document the sources of your visual aids.

GUIDELINE **6**

Integrate Your Visual Aids with Your Text

The first five guidelines in this chapter focus on visual aids in isolation from your prose. In contrast, this guideline asks you to think about your visual aids from the point of view of your readers in the act of reading your overall communication. It suggests that you integrate your visual aids with your prose so that they work together harmoniously to create a single, unified message. Here are four strategies you can follow:

- **Introduce your visual aids in your text.** When people read sequentially through a communication, they read one sentence and then the next, one paragraph and then the next, and so on. When you want the next element that they read to be a visual aid rather than a sentence or a paragraph, you need to direct their attention from your prose to the visual aid and also tell what they will find in the visual aid. There are various ways of doing that:

Two sentences

> In a market test, we found that Radex was much more appealing than Talon, especially among rural consumers. See Figure 3.

One sentence with an introductory phrase

> As Figure 3 shows, Radex was much more appealing than Talon, especially among rural consumers.

One sentence with the reference in parentheses

> Our market test showed that Radex was much more appealing than Talon, especially among rural consumers (Figure 3).

Sometimes your text reference to a visual aid will have to include information your readers need in order to understand or use the visual aid. For example, here is how the writers of an instruction manual explained how to use one of their tables:

Writer tells reader how to use the visual aid.

> In order to determine the setpoint for the grinder relay, use Table 1. First, find the grade of steel you will be grinding. Then read down column two, three, or four, depending upon the grinding surface you are using.

Whatever kind of introduction you make to a visual aid, place it at the exact point where you want your readers to focus their attention on the visual aid.

■ **State the conclusions you want your readers to draw.** Another way to integrate your visual aids into your text is to state explicitly the conclusions you want your readers to draw from them. Otherwise, they may draw conclusions that are quite different from the ones you have in mind.

For example, one writer included a graph that showed how many orders she thought her company would receive for its rubber hoses over the next six months. The graph showed that there would be a sharp decline in orders from automobile plants, and the writer feared that her readers might focus on that fact and miss the main point. So she referred to the graph in the following way:

Writer tells readers what conclusion to draw from the visual aid.

> As Figure 7 indicates, our outlook for the next six months is very good. Although we predict fewer orders from automobile plants, we expect the slack to be taken up by increased demand among auto parts outlets.

You might find it helpful to think of the sentences in which you explain a visual aid's significance as a special kind of topic statement. Just as in the topic statement at the head of a paragraph, you can tell your readers the points to be derived from the various facts that follow.

■ **When appropriate, include explanations in your figures.** Sometimes you can help your readers understand your message by incorporating explanatory statements into your figures. Figure 11.21 shows how paint powder is applied to cars in an automobile assembly line.

■ **Place your visual aids near your references to them.** When your readers come to a statement asking them to look at a visual aid, they lift their eyes from your prose and search for the visual aid. You want to make that search as short and simple as possible. Ideally, you should place the visual aid on the same page as your reference to it. If there isn't enough room, put the visual aid on the page facing or the page that follows. If you place the figure farther away than that (for instance, in an appendix), give the number of the page on which the figure can be found:

Direction to help reader find a visual aid

> A detailed sketch of this region of the new building's floor plan is shown in Figure 17 in Appendix C (page 53).

GUIDELINE 7   When Addressing an International Audience, Check Your Visual Aids with Persons from the Other Nations

Visual language, like spoken and written language, differs from nation to nation. For example, Dwight W. Stevenson reports that while people in Western nations typically read visual aids from left to right, the Japanese read them from right to left—the same way they read prose. Moreover, though many technical symbols are used worldwide, others are not.

The numbered explanations help readers understand the process by describing it step by step.

The boxed steps help readers identify and understand the function of two important parts of the paint facility.

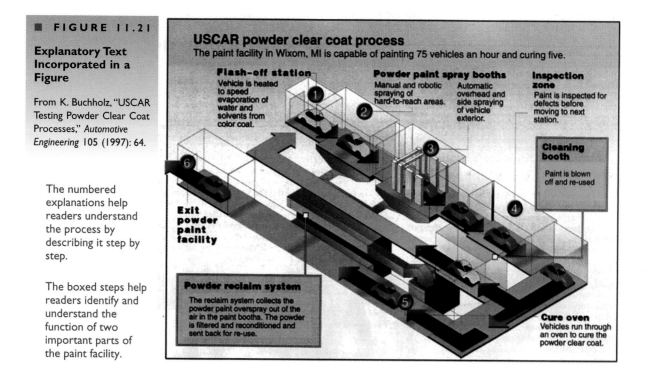

USCAR powder clear coat process
The paint facility in Wixom, MI is capable of painting 75 vehicles an hour and curing five.

Flash-off station
Vehicle is heated to speed evaporation of water and solvents from color coat.

Powder paint spray booths
Manual and robotic spraying of hard-to-reach areas.
Automatic overhead and side spraying of vehicle exterior.

Inspection zone
Paint is inspected for defects before moving to next station.

Cleaning booth
Paint is blown off and re-used

Exit powder paint facility

Powder reclaim system
The reclaim system collects the powder paint overspray out of the air in the paint booths. The powder is filtered and reconditioned and sent back for re-use.

Cure oven
Vehicles run through an oven to cure the powder clear coat.

Visual aids are interpreted differently in different cultures.

Drawings and photographs can be especially troublesome in international communication. A major U.S. corporation reports that it once encountered a problem with publications intended to market its computer systems abroad because they included photos of telephones used in the United States rather than the much different looking telephones used in the other countries. The design of many other ordinary objects differs from country to country. If you use a picture of an object that looks odd to people in your target audience, the effect you are striving for may be lost. Customs vary even in such matters as who stands and who sits in various working situations. Certain hand gestures that are quite innocent in the United States are regarded as obscene elsewhere in the world.

As explained in Guideline 4, colors, too, have different connotations in different cultures. While yellow suggests caution or cowardice in the United States, it is associated with prosperity in Egypt, grace in Japan, and femininity in several other parts of the world (Thorell and Smith).

The point is simple: whenever you are writing for readers in another country, discuss your plans with people familiar with that country's culture.

CONCLUSION

Visual aids can greatly increase the clarity and impact of your written communications. To use visual aids well, you need to follow the same reader-centered strategy that you use when writing your prose: think about the tasks your readers will perform while reading and think about the ways you want your communication to shape your readers' attitudes. Doing so will enable you to decide where to use visual aids, determine the most effective types of visual aids to use, make them easy to understand and use, and integrate them successfully with your prose.

The Reference Guide following this chapter supplements this chapter's general advice by providing detailed information about how to construct thirteen types of visual aids that are often used at work.

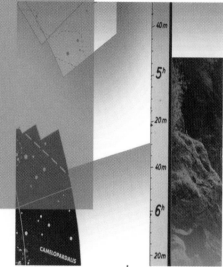

Reference Guide: Thirteen Types of Visual Aids

This Reference Guide presents detailed advice for constructing thirteen types of visual aids that are widely used on the job. The thirteen are organized according to the functions they most often perform in workplace writing.

Types of Visual Aids

Displaying data
Tables   Page 300
Bar graphs   Page 305
Pictographs   Page 308
Line graphs   Page 309
Pie charts   Page 311
Showing how something looks or is constructed
Photographs   Page 312
Drawings   Page 316
Screen shots   Page 315
Showing how to do something
Photographs   Page 317
Drawings   Page 317
Explaining a process
Flow charts   Page 321
Diagrams   Page 323
Providing management information
Organizational charts   Page 325
Schedule charts   Page 325
Budget statements   Page 326

Photographs and drawings appear in the list twice because, like many other forms of visual aids, they can be used for a variety of purposes.

DISPLAYING DATA

When you need to display data, consider using one of the following types of visual aids: tables, bar graphs, pictographs, line graphs, and pie charts. Figure VA.1 identifies applications for which each type is typically used.

TABLES

Tables are everywhere: on the side of your cereal box; in the owner's manual for your stereo, television, car, or computer; and in the reports, proposals, memos, letters, and instructions you will read (and write) at work.

Tables are used so often because they help writers achieve several common communication objectives:

■ **FIGURE VA.1**

Advice for Choosing among Various Ways of Displaying Numerical Data

Type	Typical Application	Comments
Table	Helps readers find particular facts in large sets of information	Not good for emphasizing trends or making comparisons unless only a few points are involved
Bar Graph	Helps readers compare quantities at a glance	Can also show trends if readers can easily draw lines mentally between the ends of the relevant bars
Pictograph	A type of bar graph that makes data more vivid by calling to mind the people and things discussed	In some situations, readers may think that a pictograph is unprofessional or otherwise inappropriate
Line Graph	Highlights trends and relationships among variables	Can display complex relationships more clearly than can other types of visual aids described here
Pie Chart	Shows how a whole has been divided into parts and indicates the relative sizes of the parts	Sometimes difficult for readers to compare the size of wedges accurately

■ **Tables present detailed facts in a concise, readable form.** Consider, for instance, the following passage:

Data presented in prose

> In 1992, the United States spent $833.6 billion on health care, which amounted to $3,144 per capita and 13.3 percent of the gross national product (GNP). In 1993, total expenditure increased to $892.3 billion, which was $3,331 per capita and 13.6 percent of the GNP. In 1994, the total expenditure was $949.4 billion, equaling $3,510 per capita and 13.7 percent of the GNP.

When placed in a table, this same information is organized and displayed in a manner that is much easier to read.

The same data presented in a table

	U.S. Health Care Expenditures		
Year	**Total Dollars (in billions)**	**Dollars Per Capita**	**Percent of GNP**
1992	833.6	3,144	13.3
1993	892.3	3,331	13.6
1994	949.4	3,510	13.7

■ **Tables also help readers find particular facts quickly.** To demonstrate this point, first use the prose version and then the table to locate the total amount of money spent in the United States on health care in 1993. Or, try to determine how the percentage of the Gross National Product spent on health care services changed from 1992 to 1994.

■ FIGURE VA.2

Table That Helps Readers Understand Options

From Thompson Electronics, *RCA Pro808A Camcorder User's Guide* (Indianapolis: Thompson Electronics, 1994) 30.

This table explains the preset recording modes for a camcorder.

It enables readers to quickly learn what each mode does and when it is best used.

The "Indicator" column shows the symbol that displays in the viewfinder when each mode is chosen; it illustrates the extensive use of drawings in technical writing.

Tables are often used in passages that group facts or present comparisons. See pages 193–196 and 205–208.

Preset Program Modes				
Mode	**Shutter Speed**	**Indicator**	**Auto Focus Area**	**Recording Conditions**
Auto mode	1/60 second.	None	Normal	Use under normal conditions.
Sports	1/60 ~ 1/250 second. (depending on brightness)		Center Frame Area Only (9 feet and farther)	For filming sporting events, football games, etc. • Colors may change if this mode is used indoors with fluorescent lighting.
Auto high speed shutter	1/250 ~ 1/10,000 second (depending on brightness)		Normal	For capturing fast movements such as a golf swing, tennis swing, etc. • Colors may change if this mode is used indoors with fluorescent lighting.
Close-up	1/60 second		2/5 inch~78 inches	For filming subjects, such as flowers or insects, at a short distance. • This mode automatically sets the zoom to the wide-angle position and focus to about 2 inches from the lens. The focus can then be adjusted on any subject in a range of 2/5 inch to 78 inches from the lens.

Tables can be just as effective at presenting information in words as in numbers. They are often used to help readers understand options and choose among them (Figure VA.2). They are also used in the troubleshooting sections of instruction manuals (Figure VA.3).

How to Construct a Table

To construct a table, you systematically arrange information in rows and columns, adding headings and other explanatory information as necessary.

Figure VA.4 (page 304) shows the basic structure of a table.

Word-processing programs make it very easy to create tables within a draft you are preparing or to import tables you've created in a spreadsheet program such as Microsoft Excel. Your challenge is to use the power of these computer programs to design tables that are easy to understand, easy to use, and attractive. The following guidelines will enable you to do that:

Guidelines for designing tables

- **Order items in a way your readers will find useful.** For example, in a table designed to show the research budgets of the nation's fifty largest biotechnology companies, you could arrange the companies alphabetically if your readers would want to quickly locate the sales output of a few specific companies. However, if your readers would want to compare companies in terms of the amounts they spend on research, you could order the companies from the highest to the lowest in terms of the research and development expenses.
- **Make the key information stand out visually.** Column and row headings are very important to readers. Consider using boldface, larger type, color, and rules (lines) to make them stand out. Use these same tools if you want to emphasize certain data with your table or to help readers find a particular row or column.
- **Label your columns and rows clearly.** From a reader's perspective, clear and precise labels are essential. If several columns are related, span them with a

■ **FIGURE VA.3**

Table That Provides Troubleshooting Information

Courtesy of MTD Products Incorporated.

The vertical and horizontal lines help readers quickly find the information they need.

Problem	Cause	Remedy
1 Engine fails to start.	A Blade control handle disengaged.	A Engage blade control handle.
	B Fuel tank empty.	B Fill tank if empty.
	C Spark plug lead wire disconnected.	C Connect lead wire.
	D Throttle control lever not in the starting position.	D Move throttle lever to "start" position.
	E Faulty spark plug.	E Spark should jump gap between control electrode and side electrode. If spark does not jump, replace the spark plug.
	F Carburetor improperly adjusted, engine flooded.	F Remove spark plug, dry the plug, crank engine with plug removed, and throttle in "off" position. Replace spark plug and lead wire and resume starting procedures.
	G Old stale gasoline.	G Drain and refill with fresh gasoline.
	H Engine brake engaged.	H Follow starting procedure.
2 Hard starting or loss of power	A Spark plug wire loose.	A Connect and tighten spark plug wire.
	B Carburetor improperly adjusted.	B Adjust carburetor. See separate engine manual.
	C Dirty air cleaner.	C Clean air cleaner as described in separate engine manual.
3 Operation erratic	A Dirt in gas tank.	A Remove the dirt and fill tank with fresh gas.
	B Dirty air cleaner.	B Clean air cleaner as described in separate manual.
	C Water in fuel supply.	C Drain contaminated fuel and fill tank with fresh gas.
	D Vent in gas cap plugged.	D Clear vent or replace gas cap.
	E Carburetor improperly adjusted.	E Adjust carburetor. See separate engine manual.
4 Occasionally skips (hesitates) at high speed	A Carburetor idle speed too slow.	A Adjust carburetor. See separate engine manual.
	B Spark plug gap too close.	B Adjust to .030".
	C Carburetor idle mixture adjustment improperly set.	C Adjust carburetor. See separate engine manual.

■ **FIGURE VA.4 Structure of a Typical Table**

Table number ——————————————————— Table 9

Title —————————————— **Operating Expenses for Centennial Power Company's Major Divisions
1997 and 1998**

Explanatory note————————————————— (in thousands of dollars)

Column headings

Stub heading

Row headings

Footnote letter

Row subheadings

Expense Category	Electricity		Natural Gas	
	1997	1998[a]	1997	1998[a]
Fuel and electric power purchased	913,732	837,446	—	—
Gas purchased for resale	—	—	221,052	276,472
Operation and maintenance[b]	998,698	917,184	152,663	157,831
Depreciation and amortization	257,013	248,267	24,866	26,275
Construction				
Willow Point Plant	15,989	26,257	—	—
Adamsville Plant	—	—	1,409	967
Taxes				
Federal taxes	309,500	362,861	30,152	29,854
Other taxes	774,238	750,726	100,989	100,814
Total Operating Expenses	**3,259,170**	**3,178,741**	**531,131**	**592,213**

Footnotes ——————— Notes

a. 1998 figures are unaudited.

b. Expenses for Centennial's General Utility Plant were allocated to the Electric and Natural Gas Divisions
based on the use made of the plant by each.

higher level heading that indicates that they go together. Similarly, use indentation or similar devices to group row headings that go together.

Avoid Unsorted Lists	Use Headings
Fruits	Nutritious Foods
Grains	Fruits
Legumes	Grains
Sweets	Legumes
Fat-Fried Products	Nonnutritious Foods
	Sweets
	Fat-Fried Products

■ **In longer tables, guide your readers' eyes across rows.** Leave a blank or insert a horizontal rule after every five rows or so. This will help your readers' eyes move across the rows. Of course, if the rows are grouped by some logical relationship, place the breaks between the groupings.

■ **When presenting data, indicate the units.** Make sure your readers know what each entry in your table represents: dollars, kilograms, percentage, and so on. When all the entries in a long column or row use the same units, it's usually best to identify the units in the heading to avoid cluttering the table. Use abbreviations only when you are certain your readers will understand them.

■ **Align entries in a way that supports easy reading.** Align numerical entries either on the units or on the decimal point:

23,418	2.79
5,231	618.0
17	13.517

■ Align words and phrases on the left-hand margin or center them in the column.

Acceptable	Acceptable
Marginally Acceptable	Marginally Acceptable
Unacceptable	Unacceptable

■ **Place explanatory notes where they are accessible, but not distracting.** In some tables, you will need to include notes that explain the labels or cite the sources of your information. If your notes are short, you can place them next to the appropriate title or headings. Otherwise, place them in footnotes at the bottom of your table. Use lowercase letters to label the footnotes if your readers might confuse a superscript number with a mathematical exponent. For example, "14^2" could be read as "fourteen squared" rather than the number 14 followed by a superscript. Using a lowercase letter avoids that confusion: "14^b."

■ **Where possible, keep your table on one page.** Consider breaking large tables into smaller, separate ones. If your table contains too many columns to fit on the page, turn it sideways.

Informal Tables

Sometimes you can create tables that are much simpler than those just described. Such "informal tables" need no row or column headings, no titles or notes. They are useful where the preceding sentence explains what the table is about and where the interpretation of the table is obvious. Here is an example showing how an informal table can be built into a paragraph.

Informal tables fit into the flow of your prose without figure numbers or titles.

Even more important, the sales figures demonstrate how our investment in technical research has helped several of our divisions become more competitive. The following figures show the increase in the market share enjoyed since the same quarter last year by three major divisions that have extensive research programs:

Strausland Microchips	7%
Minsk Machine Tools	5%
PTI Technical Services	4%

Note that such tables work only when they contain a single column of facts and when readers will readily understand them. If you think that such an informal table might confuse your readers, even momentarily, use a formal table instead.

BAR GRAPHS

Bar graphs are often used in passages that present comparisons. See pages 208–210.

Uses of bar graphs

Like a table, a bar graph can represent numerical quantities. However, a bar graph does it with rectangles called *bars*. The greater the quantity, the longer the bar. Here are some uses of bar graphs:

■ **To compare quantities at a glance.** Because the bars are drawn to scale, bar graphs can help readers tell immediately not only which quantities are the larger or smaller, but also how great the differences are (see Figure VA.5).

■ **To show trends.** If a series of bars is used to represent a quantity over time (such as average length of hospital stays in the United States from 1990–1996), readers will be able to detect overall trends (see Figure VA.6).

REFERENCE GUIDE: Thirteen Types of Visual Aids

■ **FIGURE VA.5**

Bar Graph Showing Comparison

Based on data from "Occupational Employment to 2005," *Monthly Labor Review* 118.11 (1995): 60–78.

A bar graph enables readers to compare quantities instantly.

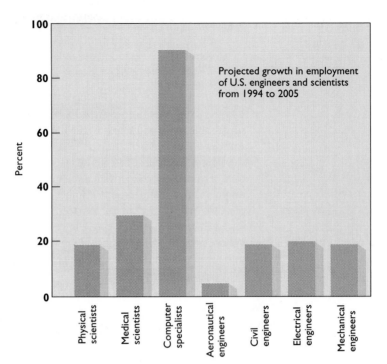

Projected growth in employment of U.S. engineers and scientists from 1994 to 2005

■ **FIGURE VA.6**

Bar Graph Showing a Trend

From A. Sesenig, S.K. Heffler, and C. Donham, "Hospital, Employment, and Price Indicators for the Health Care Industry," *Health Care Financing Review* 18 (1997): 234.

Because the heights of the bars change steadily, the trend becomes obvious to readers.

Average Hospital Length of Stay Among All Adults, Persons 65 Years of Age or Over, and Persons Under 65 years of Age: 1990–96

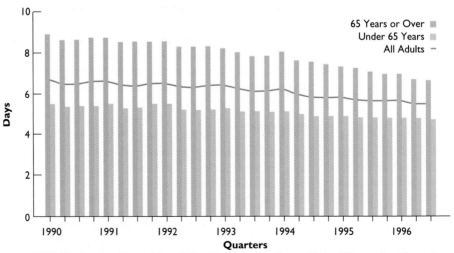

SOURCE: American Hospital Association, Trend Analysis Group: *National Hospital Panel Survey Reports.* January 1990–September 1996.

■ **FIGURE VA.7**

Bar Graph with Subdivided Bars

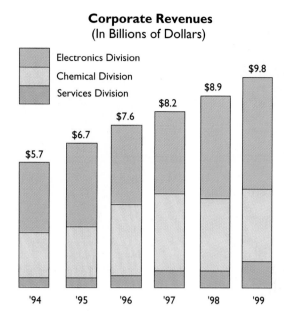

Corporate Revenues
(In Billions of Dollars)

Electronics Division
Chemical Division
Services Division

$5.7 $6.7 $7.6 $8.2 $8.9 $9.8

'94   '95   '96   '97   '98   '99

■ **To indicate the composition of a whole.** For instance, a bar that represents the entire revenue of a company might be subdivided to indicate the various sources of that revenue. A series of such bars can show the changing (or unchanging) composition of the company's revenue over time (see Figure VA.7).

How to Construct a Bar Graph

Desktop publishing and database programs enable you to create bar graphs quickly. The following guidelines and the "Focus on Ethics" (page 313) will help you use these computer tools to design bar graphs that represent your data clearly and accurately:

Guidelines for creating bar graphs

■ **Draw the horizontal and vertical axes so that your graph will be roughly square.**
■ **Decide whether to extend the bars vertically or horizontally.** Vertical bars are often used for height and depth, whereas horizontal bars are often used for distance, length, and time.
■ **Use tick marks to indicate quantities on the axis parallel to the bars.** Label them ($5 million, $10 million, etc.; 50 psi, 100 psi, etc.). Plan the tick marks so that the longest bar will extend nearly to the end of its parallel axis.
■ **Order the bars to suit your communication purpose.** For example, if you want your readers to discern rank orders, arrange the bars in order of length. If you want your readers to compare subgroups of quantities, group the appropriate bars together.
■ **Place labels next to the bars, when possible.** Generally, readers find such labels easier to use than a separate key. An exception occurs when you use the same groups of bars repeatedly, as in Figure VA.8. In that case, use distinctive shading, color, or cross-hatching to indicate each category within the group of bars and provide a key to the categories.

■ **FIGURE VA.8**

Multibar Graph

From U.S. Bureau of the Census, *Statistical Abstract of the United States, 116th Ed.* (Washington D.C.: U.S. Government Printing Office, 1996) 248.

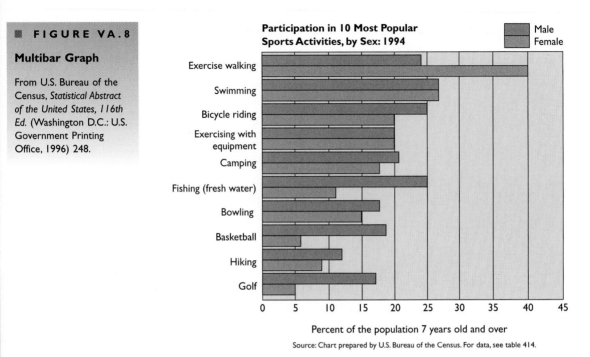

Participation in 10 Most Popular Sports Activities, by Sex: 1994

■ Male
■ Female

Exercise walking
Swimming
Bicycle riding
Exercising with equipment
Camping
Fishing (fresh water)
Bowling
Basketball
Hiking
Golf

0   5   10   15   20   25   30   35   40   45

Percent of the population 7 years old and over

Source: Chart prepared by U.S. Bureau of the Census. For data, see table 414.

Usually, it is unnecessary to include numbers that indicate the exact quantity represented by each bar. Provide exact quantities only if your readers are likely to want them.

PICTOGRAPHS

Pictographs are often used in passages that present comparisons. See pages 208–210.

Pictographs are a special kind of bar graph in which the bars are replaced by drawings that represent the thing being described. In Figure VA.9, for example, the number of barrels of oil used per capita in the United States is represented by drawings of oil barrels. The chief advantage of the pictograph is that the drawings symbolize concretely the quantities that your graph displays.

You will find pictographs especially useful where you want to do one or both of the following:

Pictographs can suggest the significance of data.

■ **To emphasize the practical consequences of the data represented.** For example, a pictograph that uses silhouettes of people to represent the workers who will be employed in a new plant emphasizes a benefit that the plant will bring to the community. You can select from a multitude of clipart symbols in desktop publishing and spreadsheet programs, as well as other sources.

■ **To make your data visually interesting and memorable.** Visual interest is especially important when you are addressing the general public. In some situations at work, however, readers expect a more abstract representation of information and would consider pictographs inappropriate.

■ **FIGURE VA.9**

Pictograph (Combined with Line Graph)

Design courtesy of B.P. America. Updated with data from U.S. Bureau of the Census, *Statistical Abstract of the United States, 117th Ed.* (Washington D.C.: U.S. Government Printing Office, 1997) 9, 582.

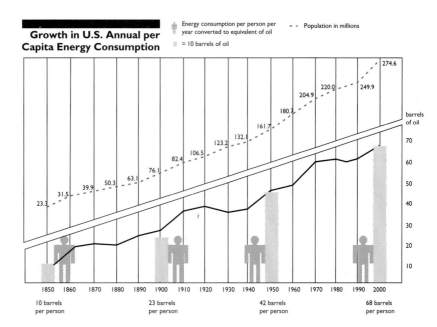

How to Construct a Pictograph
To create a pictograph, follow the procedure for creating a bar graph but substitute drawings for the bars.

LINE GRAPHS

A line graph shows how one quantity changes as a function of changes in another quantity. You can use line graphs for many purposes, including the following:

Line graphs are often used in passages that explain cause and effect. See pages 210–212.

- **To show trends and cycles.** When you want to show a pattern of change, line graphs can be very helpful.
- **To compare trends.** Line graphs are also very useful for showing readers how two or more trends relate to one another. For instance, using the graph shown in Figure VA.10, economists were able to demonstrate quite dramatically how the number of people employed as bank tellers has plummeted as the number of transactions at automated teller machines has risen.
- **To show how two or more variables interact.** Figure VA.11 (page 311) shows two line graphs, one used by a group of physicists studying cosmic rays (top), the other used by engineers experimenting with lasers (bottom).

How to Construct a Line Graph
In line graphs, you usually want to show how variations in one factor (the *dependent variable*) are affected by variations in another factor (the *independent variable*).

Guidelines for creating line graphs

- **Draw the horizontal and vertical axes so that your graph will be roughly square.**

■ **FIGURE VA.10 Line Graph Comparing Trends** From T.L. Morisi, "Commercial Banking Transformed by Computer Technology," *Monthly Labor Review* 119 (1996.8): 34.

Employment in commercial banks, seasonally adjusted, and number of ATM transactions, 1986–96

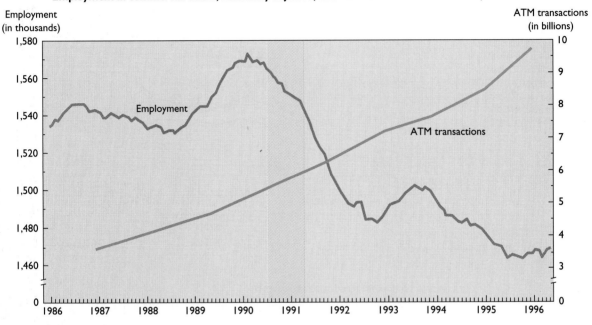

NOTE: The shaded area denotes a recession, as identified by the National Bureau of Economic Research.

SOURCES: Unpublished data from the Bureau of Labor Statistics Current Employment Statistics program; and *Bank Network News.*

- ■ **Indicate the quantities along each axis with tick marks placed at regular intervals.** Label the tick marks. Usually your graph will be less cluttered if you make the tick marks short (but still clearly visible). In some situations, however, your readers may find it easier to read a line graph if you extend the tick marks all the way across the graph to form a grid. If you do this, draw the grid with thinner lines than your plotted lines so that the plotted lines stand out.
- ■ **Start the axes at zero, where possible.** Otherwise readers may be misled about the proportions of changes shown. (See "Focus on Ethics" on page 313.) If the vertical axis does not begin at zero, alert your readers to that fact by using hash marks to indicate that the scale is not continuous from zero. Where you need to indicate some negative quantities, such as losses, or degrees below zero, use both positive and negative values on whichever of the axes needs them.
- ■ **Put labels next to the plotted lines and data points.** Generally, readers find such labels easier to use than a separate key.

■ **FIGURE VA.11**

Line Graphs Showing the Interaction among Variables

A From T. O'Halloran, P. Sokolsky, and S. Yoshida, "The Highest Energy Cosmic Rays," *IEEE Journal of Quantum Electronics* 34 (1998): 50. **B** From Z. Donko, L. Szalai, K. Rozsa, M. Ulbel, and M. Pockl, "High-Gain Ultraviolet Cu-II Laser in a Segmented Hollow Cathode Discharge," *Physics Today* 51 (1998): 32.

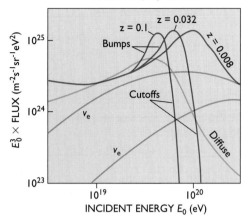

Expected Effects of GZK Cutoff on the Cosmic-Ray Spectrum

Careful placement of the labels and the use of colors make it easy to identify the lines in this complex graph.

The graphed lines emphasize the continuity among the data points.

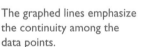

The *I*th threshold current and the *P*th threshold input for the λ = 270.3–nm transition.

PIE CHARTS

Pie charts are often used in passages that present comparisons. See pages 208–210.

Pie charts are a good choice when you want to show the composition of a whole—for example, the amount of money spent worldwide on different types of packaging for products (see Figure VA.12).

How to Construct a Pie Chart

A pie chart is simply a circle divided into wedges proportional to the amount of the total that each quantity represents:

■ **Arrange the wedges in a way that will help your readers perceive the rank order of the wedges and compare their relative sizes.** Often that means starting with the largest wedge near the top and proceeding clockwise in descending order of size.

■ **FIGURE VA.12**

Pie Chart

From N. Schneegens, "Charting a Course for the Future of Corrugated," *Pulp & Paper International* 39.11 (1997): 22.

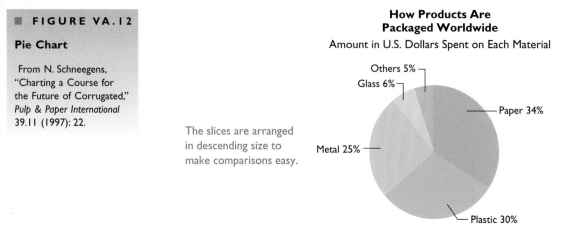

How Products Are Packaged Worldwide

Amount in U.S. Dollars Spent on Each Material

Others 5%
Glass 6%
Paper 34%
Metal 25%
Plastic 30%

The slices are arranged in descending size to make comparisons easy.

- **Label each wedge and give its percentage of the whole.** Depending on the size of a wedge, place its label inside or outside the circle.
- **Limit the number of wedges to about eight.**
- **Create an "Other" wedge if you have a collection of small quantities that would be difficult to distinguish.**

SHOWING HOW SOMETHING LOOKS OR IS CONSTRUCTED

Photographs and drawings are often used in passages that describe an object. See pages 198–202.

When you want to tell your readers what something looks like or how it is constructed, you may be able to communicate most effectively with a photograph or drawing. For communications involving computers, screen shots can be very useful to readers.

PHOTOGRAPHS

Photographs have become a very common element in workplace writing because scanners have made it so easy to transform photos into computer files so they can be incorporated directly into a word-processed communication. By showing *exactly* what something looks like, photographs can help you achieve many goals, including the following:

Uses of photographs

- **To indicate the appearance of something the readers have never seen.** Perhaps it's the inside of a human heart, the surface of one of the moons of Saturn, a new building purchased in another city, or a new product your company has just begun manufacturing.
- **To show how something is done.** For example, the photograph shown in Figure VA.13 shows readers how one of the steps in genetic engineering is performed.
- **To show the condition of something.** Photographs can help portray the condition of an object when that condition is indicated by the object's appearance. Maybe you want to show the result of the treatment of a skin ailment with a

Avoiding Graphs That Mislead

Visual aids can mislead as easily as words can. When representing information visually, you have an ethical obligation to avoid leading your readers to wrong conclusions.

Bar Graphs and Line Graphs
To design bar graphs and line graphs that convey an accurate visual impression, you may need to include zero points on your axes. In Graph A, where the X-axis begins at 85 percent instead of at zero, the difference between the two bars appears misleadingly large.

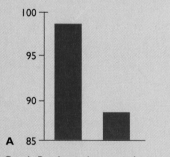

A

Graph B, where the x-axis begins at zero, gives a more accurate impression of the data represented.

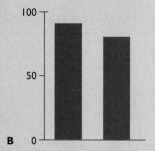

B

If you cannot use the entire scale, indicate that fact to your readers by using hash marks to signal a break in the axis and, if you are creating a bar graph, in the bars themselves.

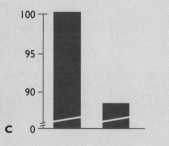

C

Note, however, that zero points and hash marks are sometimes unnecessary. For example, in some technical and scientific fields, certain kinds of data are customarily represented without zero points, so readers are not misled by their omission.

Pictographs
Pictographs can also mislead readers. Graph D, for example, shows the average percentage of an apple harvest that a grower should expect to be graded Extra Fancy. Graph D makes the percentage of Red Delicious apples seem much larger than the percentage for Golden Delicious, even though the actual difference is only 20 percent. That's because the picture of the Red Delicious apple is larger in height *and* width, so its area is much greater. Graph E shows how to accurately represent the data:

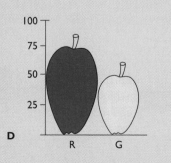

D

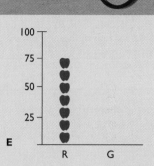

E

by making columns that differ in height alone.

Color
Like any other element of a graph, color can be used unethically. For example, because bright colors attract the eye, they can be used to distract the reader's focus from crucial bad news by emphasizing relatively unimportant news. Graph F shows an example, and Graph G shows how the problem can be corrected.

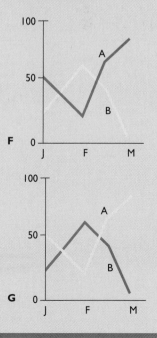

F

G

■ **FIGURE VA.13**

Photograph Used to Show How Something Is Done

From *Cincinnati Enquirer*, March 7, 1994, Sec. D, 1.

The photographer chose to record this action from an angle that shows all the important details about how the researcher performs this step.

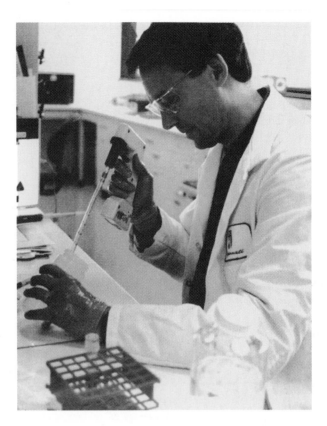

new drug your company is marketing, the damage to a shipment of products caused by improper handling, the progress being made on the construction of a new factory, or the difference between corn that has received sufficient water and corn that has not (see Figure VA.14).

■ **To help readers recognize something**. For instance, in a field guide for biologists, photographs like those displayed in Figure VA.15 help readers identify various species of frogs.

■ **To help readers locate something**. In an instruction manual, for instance, you might employ a photograph of an MRI (magnetic resonance imaging) machine to help a hospital's medical staff find the parts used to operate the unit (see Figure VA.16).

How to Create a Photograph

Here are some suggestions that will help you create effective photographs:

Guidelines for creating photographs

■ **Choose an appropriate angle of view**. If you want to help your readers recognize or find something, photograph it from the angle that your readers would take when looking for it.

■ **Eliminate unnecessary or distracting details**. Before taking your photograph, remove irrelevant objects from the area to be photographed or screen them

■ **FIGURE VA.14**

Photographs Used to Show the Condition of Something

Captions point out key features of the photographs and interpret their meaning for readers.

Watering regimen: 1 inch of irrigation water per week. Leaves green and pliable to the edges. Sheen on leaves indicates a healthy cuticle that is able to resist insects and disease.

Watering regimen: 3 weeks without water. Necrosis on leaf tips and margins, where water stress typically shows itself first. No sheen. Inner necrotic spots caused by disease that was able to penetrate the weakened cuticle.

■ **FIGURE VA.15**

Photographs Used to Help Readers Recognize Something

Poison arrow frog, *Dendrobates melanoleusos*, found in the rainforest of Guyana.

Red-eye leaf frog, *Agalychnis callidryas*, found on the Caribbean side of Costa Rica.

from view. If such objects show up in the photograph, crop them (trim them away) to focus your readers' attention on what you want them to see.

■ **Ensure that all relevant parts are clearly visible.** Don't let important parts get hidden (or half-hidden) behind other parts. Ensure that the important parts are in focus.

■ **Provide whatever labels your readers will need.** Be sure that all labels stand out from the background of the photograph. With some desktop publishing

REFERENCE GUIDE: Thirteen Types of Visual Aids

■ **FIGURE VA.16**

FIGURE VA.16

Photograph Used to Help Readers Locate Something

The labels are printed on a white background to make them stand out.

They are carefully placed where they will not cover an important part.

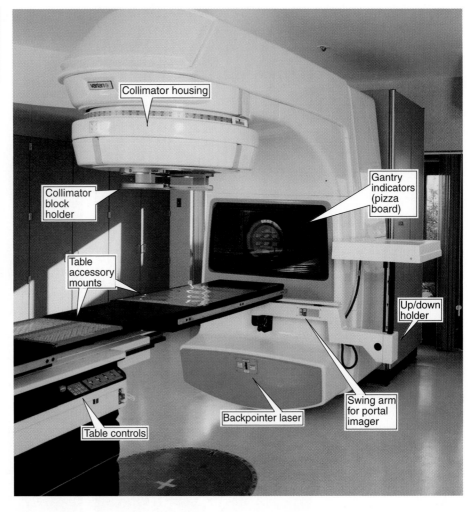

Collimator housing

Gantry indicators (pizza board)

Collimator block holder

Table accessory mounts

Up/down holder

Table controls

Backpointer laser

Swing arm for portal imager

programs, you can add these labels electronically. If you don't have that capability, print the labels on white strips of paper and paste them onto the photograph before you scan or photocopy it (see Figure VA.16).

DRAWINGS

Drawings are often more effective than photographs.

In some situations, drawings can be even more effective than photographs at showing how something looks or is put together. Often, you can prepare drawings more quickly, and they allow you to readily emphasize important details and omit distracting ones. Moreover, drawings enable you to show things that photographs cannot, such as the inner parts of an object. Figure VA.17 shows four drawings—one that takes an external view and three that take internal views: cutaway, cross-section, and exploded.

■ **FIGURE VA.17**

Four Types of Drawings

A From "Carousel Creates Continuous Ion Exchange," *Chilton's Food Engineering* 65 (1993): 80. **B** From M. Campanale, "Bearing the Load," *Byte* 23.2 (1998): 114. **C** From "Getting More Direct," *Automotive Engineering* 105.12 (1997): 84. Artwork courtesy of Audi. **D** From U.S. National Aeronautics and Space Administration, *Research and Technology Report: Goddard Space Flight Center* (U.S. Government Printing Office, 1996) 120.

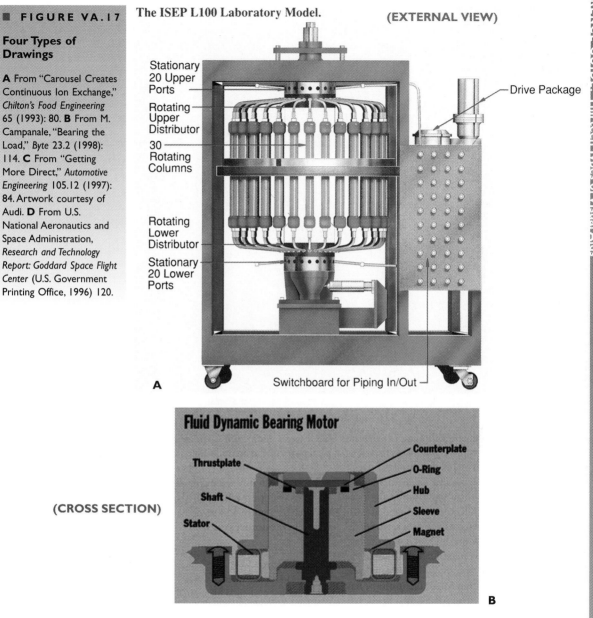

The ISEP L100 Laboratory Model.   (EXTERNAL VIEW)

Stationary 20 Upper Ports

Rotating Upper Distributor

30 Rotating Columns

Rotating Lower Distributor

Stationary 20 Lower Ports

Drive Package

Switchboard for Piping In/Out

A

Fluid Dynamic Bearing Motor

(CROSS SECTION)

Thrustplate

Shaft

Stator

Counterplate

O-Ring

Hub

Sleeve

Magnet

B

REFERENCE GUIDE: Thirteen Types of Visual Aids

FIGURE VA.17
(continued)

(CUTAWAY)

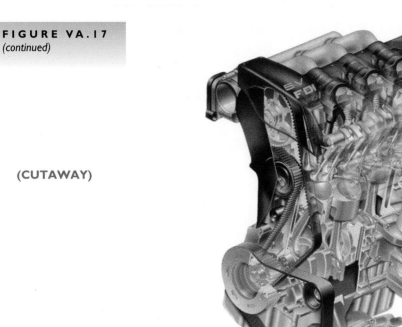

C

(EXPLODED VIEW)

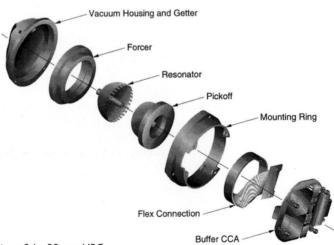

Vacuum Housing and Getter

Forcer

Resonator

Pickoff

Mounting Ring

Flex Connection

Buffer CCA

D

*Exploded view of the 30-mm HRG
mechanical components.*

This drawing helps car owners locate the reserve tank for radiator fluid.

Other parts are shaded to focus the readers' attention on the reserve tank.

The surrounding parts are sketched in vaguely to orient readers without confusing them with too much detail.

The drawing's angle of view approximates the one that owners would have when performing this task.

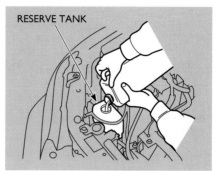
RESERVE TANK

How to Create a Drawing
Tailor your drawing to the use your readers will make of it:

Guidelines for creating a drawing

- **Choose the angle of view that your readers will find most helpful.** In many cases, this will be a "three-cornered" view, which shows, for example, two sides and the top of an object drawn in perspective. Such a view helps people see at a glance what the object looks like and how its major parts fit together. If you are preparing a drawing for a set of instructions, show the object from the same point of view that your readers will have when working with it.

Drawings allow you to include only the parts that are important to the reader.

- **Select your details.** Remember that your purpose is usually not to produce a perfectly realistic image of the object but to highlight its significant parts or features. If you want to make a relatively realistic drawing, you might trace the important features from a photograph. To emphasize significant details, you might draw them slightly larger than they actually are, draw them with a heavier line than you use for other parts, or point them out with labels.
- **Draw attention to key parts with color, shading, or the thickness of lines.**

Figure VA.18 shows a drawing that uses several of these techniques.

SCREEN SHOTS

Screen shots are images captured from a computer screen. They are especially useful in instructions for using computer software. After you've imported the image into a desktop publishing program, you can enlarge it, shrink it, or enhance it by cropping away unneeded elements or by making helpful additions. See Figure VA.19.

How to Use Screen Shots
When using screen shots, follow this advice, which is illustrated in Figure VA.19:

■ **FIGURE VA.19**

Screen Shots

A From Prentice-Hall, *Macromedia Director Version 4.0: Learning Director* (Upper Saddle, NJ: Prentice-Hall, 1995) 191. **B** From Apple Computer, *Power Macintosh User's Manual for Power Macintosh 7600 Series Computers* (Cupertino, CA: Apple Computer, 1996) 33.

The labels and arrows help readers understand the options available in the displayed window.

This screen shot shows what users will see when they click on the "Paint" option while working with a tutorial for Macromedia Director.

Zoom box

Destination color chip
Foreground color chip
Foreground color chip

Line width selector

This screen shot shows what users will see when they click on the "Look For" button on a Macintosh computer.

The labels provide instructions that guide the readers' actions.

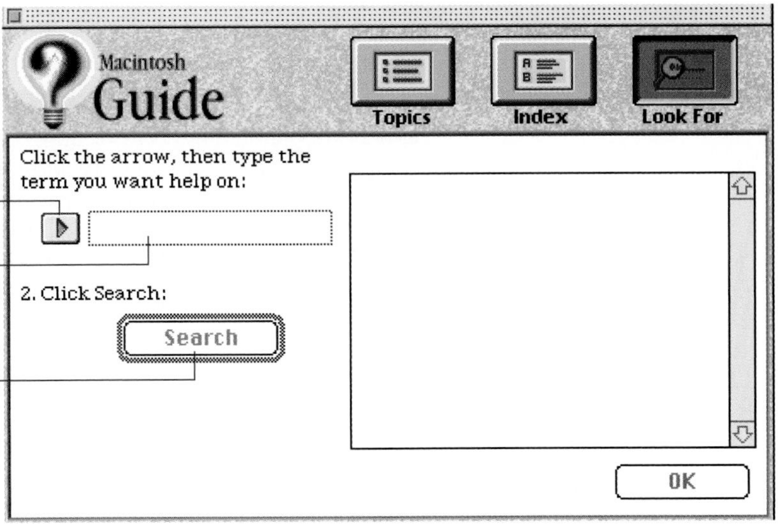

To activate the text box click here.

Type a word or phrase

. . . and then click here.

Guidelines for using screen shots

- **Show only what's important to readers.** Don't show the whole screen if only one window is important, and don't show a whole window if readers need to see only a part of it.
- **Add arrows, color, or other devices to guide your readers' attention to the key elements.**
- **Fill in fields with information that will help your readers.** For example, if readers are supposed to fill in a particular field in a certain way, let your screen shot illustrate that field filled in properly.

■ **FIGURE VA.20**

Drawing That Shows How to Do Something

From *The Home Depot, Improvement 123: Expert Advice from The Home Depot* (Des Moines: Meredith, 1995) 169.

This drawing aids readers by showing exactly how to hold the switch and by using the same angle of view that readers would have when performing the task.

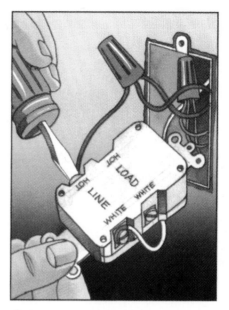

2 Pigtail all the black hot wires together and connect them to the terminal marked HOT LINE on the GFCI.

SHOWING HOW TO DO SOMETHING

When writing instructions, you will often need to show your readers how to perform some task. Photographs and drawings provide excellent means of doing this.

Photographs and drawings are often used with passages that explain a process. See pages 202–207.

PHOTOGRAPHS AND DRAWINGS

For general advice about preparing these forms of visual aids, see the preceding discussion of them (pages 312–317). Figure VA.20 presents a drawing that shows how to do something. It might have been replaced by a photograph with essentially the same design.

When preparing photographs and drawings for instructions, be especially careful to use the same angle of view that your readers will have and to include all details necessary to enable your readers to understand the action they are going to perform.

EXPLAINING A PROCESS

When you need to explain the succession of events in a process or procedure, consider using a flow chart or diagram. Flow charts can be especially useful for describing processes that have a fixed beginning and a fixed conclusion. Diagrams work well for *ongoing* processes, such as the operation of the food chain.

■ **FIGURE VA.21**

General Flow Chart

Courtesy of Zinc
Corporation of America.

Because the key parts are
clearly labeled, readers can
understand this figure even
if they don't understand
some of the special symbols.

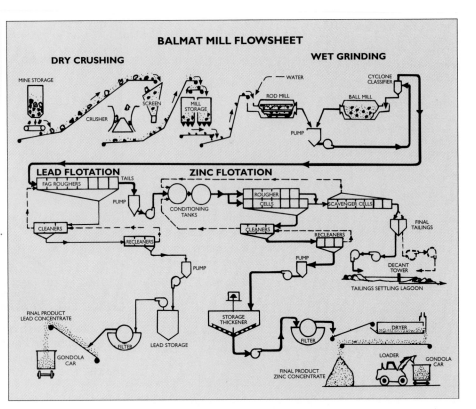

FLOW CHARTS

Flow charts and diagrams
are often used with
passages that describe a
process. See pages 202–
207.

The simplest flow charts use rectangles, circles, diamonds, or other geometric shapes
to represent events and arrows to indicate the progress from one event to another.
Sketches suggesting the appearance of objects also can be used (see Figure VA.21).

Some technical fields, such as systems analysis, have developed special techniques
for their flow charts (see Figure VA.22). They use agreed-upon sets of symbols to
represent specific kinds of events and outcomes, and they follow agreed-upon rules
for arranging these symbols on the page. If you are in a field that uses such specialized flow charts, include them when addressing your fellow specialists but not
when addressing people outside your specialty.

How to Create a Flow Chart
A few conventions govern the design of flow charts:

Guidelines for creating
flow charts

- **Place labels that identify the activities *inside* the boxes that represent those
  activities.**
- **Arrange the boxes so activity flows from left to right, or from top to bottom.** If
  your flow chart continues for more than one line, begin the second and subsequent lines at the left-hand margin or at the top of the chart (as in Figure VA.21).

■ **FIGURE VA.22** **Flow Chart Showing Special Techniques Used in Systems Analysis** From J.L. Whitten, L.D. Bentley, and K.C. Dittman, *Systems Analysis and Design Methods*, 4th Ed. (Boston: McGraw-Hill, 1998) 384.

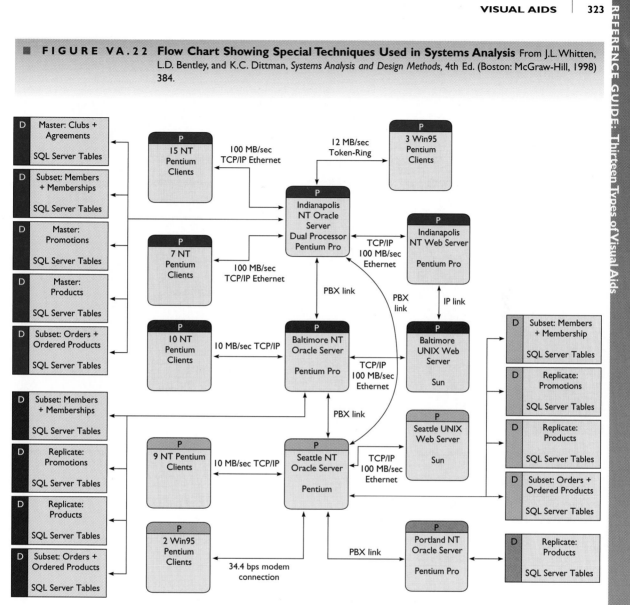

When you create a flow chart, be patient. It may take you several drafts to get the boxes the right size, to place the labels neatly inside them, and to arrange the boxes and arrows in an attractive and readily understandable way.

DIAGRAMS

Like flow charts, diagrams can be used to explain a process. Some diagrams are very pictorial, almost like drawings, and others are quite abstract. For example, Figure VA.23, which illustrates the carbon cycle, includes sketches of trees and an oil well, though it does not represent an actual scene.

■ **FIGURE VA.23** **Diagram That Does Not Use Specialized Symbols**

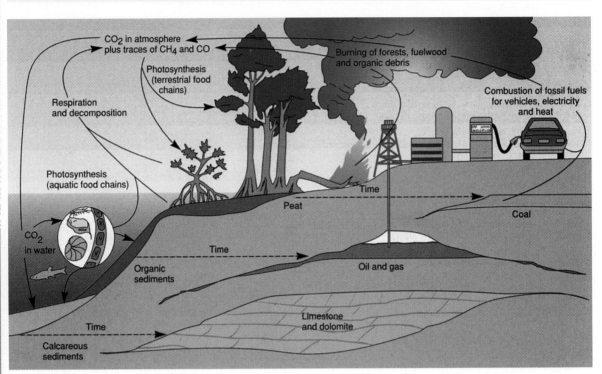

Atmospheric carbon dioxide is the "source" of carbon in the carbon cycle. It passes into ecosystems through photosynthesis and is captured in the bodies and products of living organisms. It is released to the atmosphere by weathering, respiration, and combustion. Carbon may be locked up for long periods in both organic (coal, oil, gas) and inorganic (limestone, dolomite) geological formations, which are, therefore, referred to as carbon "sinks."

How to Create a Diagram

The following suggestions will help you create diagrams that clearly explain processes to your readers:

Much creativity is required to design effective diagrams.

■ **Decide exactly what you want to show.** What are the events and objects that you want to show, and what relationships among them do you want to convey?

■ **Create an appropriate means to represent your subject.** You can represent objects and events with geometric shapes or with sketches that suggest their appearance. You can show relationships among objects and events by the way you arrange the shapes and by drawing arrows between them. Figure VA.23 illustrates these techniques. When designing a diagram, you may find it helpful to examine communications similar to yours that were written by other people.

■ **Provide the explanations readers will need in order to understand your diagram.** You may provide necessary explanations in the diagram itself, in a separate key, in the title, or in the accompanying text.

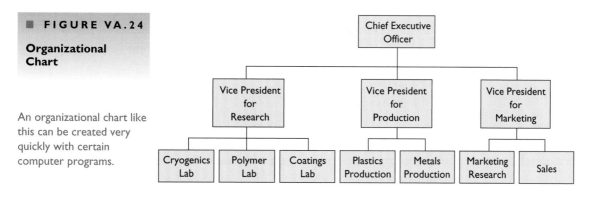

FIGURE VA.24

Organizational Chart

An organizational chart like this can be created very quickly with certain computer programs.

PROVIDING MANAGEMENT INFORMATION

Writers often need to explain the managerial aspects of the projects they are proposing or reporting about. The visual aids most often used for this purpose are organizational charts, schedule charts, and budget statements.

ORGANIZATIONAL CHARTS

An organizational chart uses rectangles and lines to tell how the people and departments in an organization are arranged into a managerial hierarchy. It shows, for example, how smaller units (such as departments) are combined into larger ones (such as divisions), and it indicates who reports to whom and who gives direction to whom (see Figure VA.24). Among the uses of organizational charts are these:

Uses of organizational charts

- To show the scope and arrangement of an organization
- To show the formal lines of authority and responsibility in an organization
- To provide a map of an organization so that readers can readily locate the particular people they want to contact

How to Create an Organizational Chart

Because of the hierarchical nature of most business organizations, organizational charts usually are pyramidal. You do not need to show every part of the organization, only those parts that are of interest to your readers. Sometimes, you may need to represent more than one kind of relationship. You can, for example, use solid lines to indicate relationships of direct authority and dashed lines to indicate close consultation or cooperation.

SCHEDULE CHARTS

A schedule chart identifies the major steps in a project and tells when they will be performed. As Figure VA.25 illustrates, a schedule chart enables readers to see what will be done, when each activity will start and end, and when more than one activity will be in progress simultaneously. (This particular type of schedule chart is called a *Gantt chart,* named for its inventor.)

■ FIGURE VA.25

Schedule Chart

Indenting is used to distinguish major tasks and subtasks.

Bars overlap because some tasks are performed simultaneously.

TASKS	WEEKS 1 2 3 4 5 6 7 8 9 10 11 12 13
Define Objectives	
Interview Users	
Analyze Present System	
Design	
Create Overall Design	
Code Programs	
Write Manual	
Test	
Review with Experts	
Give to Selected Users	
Revise	
Install	
Train Users	

Schedule charts are often used in proposals to show the projected plan of work. You can also use them in progress reports to show what you have accomplished and what you still have to do, and in final reports to describe the process you followed while working on a completed project.

How to Create a Schedule Chart

One of the principal considerations in creating a schedule chart is deciding how much detail to include—something that you can determine only on a case-by-case basis in light of your purpose and your readers' needs and expectations. Tasks are always listed along the vertical axis, with subtasks indented beneath them. The intervals (weeks, months) are usually marked off with vertical lines to help readers see exactly when tasks begin and end.

BUDGET STATEMENTS

A budget statement is a table that shows how money will be acquired or spent. It may be either very simple or very elaborate.

On the job, you may use budget statements in the following situations:

Uses of budget statements

- **To explain the expenses involved in a project or purchase**. You might prepare a budget statement when requesting funds or when reporting on the financial feasibility of a particular course of action.
- **To summarize the savings to be realized by following a recommendation you are making.** Because profits are a major goal of most organizations, budget statements are often prepared for this purpose.

■ **FIGURE VA.26**

Detailed Budget Statement

A detailed budget statement is a type of formal table (see pages 300–305).

Note that similar types of costs are grouped under common headings.

PROJECT COSTS	
Equipment	
4 KRN 3781 Robots ($37,000 apiece)	$148,000
1 Microcomputer with hard disk	6,500
4 Power supplies ($5,100 apiece)	20,400
Constructing (includes labor and supplies)	
Rewiring	7,100
Construction pads for mounting robots	3,000
Initial Programming (ten days at $125 per day)	1,250
Travel for Installation Personnel	
Airfare (two round trips)	400
Car rental	200
Living expenses (two people for five days at $150 per day)	1,500
TOTAL	$188,350

- **To report the costs that have been incurred in a project for which you are responsible.** Figure VA.26 shows an example of a budget statement prepared for this purpose.
- **To explain the sources of revenue associated with some project or activity.** For instance, you may use a budget statement when reporting your department's sales of products and services.

How to Create a Budget Statement

The following steps will enable you to prepare simple, informative budget statements (when accountants and auditors prepare budget statements, they sometimes use specialized conventions that are not discussed here):

Guidelines for creating budget statements

- Divide your page into two vertical columns.
- In the left-hand column, list the major categories of *expense*. If your readers will want additional detail, list the principal expenses that make up each major category. Make the major categories most prominent visually.
- In the right-hand column, write the *amount* of each expense. Align the figures on the decimal point.
- Indicate the total.
- To show *income* also, repeat Steps 2 through 4.

EXERCISES

1. Figure VA.27 shows a table containing information about enrollments in institutions of higher education in the United States. A writer might use that information in a variety of ways. For each of the uses listed below, decide whether the writer should present the information in a table, bar graph, pictograph, line graph, or pie chart.
   a. To show how steadily and dramatically the number of women age 35 and over who are enrolled in college has risen since 1987 and is expected to continue to rise through 2007.
   b. To provide a reference source in which researchers can find the numbers of men (or women) in a particular age group who were enrolled in college in a particular year.
   c. To enable readers to make a rough comparison of the 1995 enrollments of men in each age group with the 1995 enrollments of women in each age group.
   d. To enable educational planners to see what proportion of the men (or women) who are projected to enroll in 2002 is expected to be from each of the age groups. (To present this information, the writer would have to perform some mathematical calculations based on the data in Figure VA.27.)

2. Using the data provided in Figure VA.27, create bar graphs that show the following:
   a. The trend described in part a of Exercise 1.
   b. The comparisons described in part c of Exercise 1.
   c. The relationship between age and percentage of women students enrolled part-time in 2002.

3. The table in Figure VA.28 shows how much crude oil was produced by the world's leading producers in the years 1993 through 1997. Using that information, make the following visual aids. Be sure to provide all appropriate labels and a title for each.
   a. A bar graph showing how much crude oil was produced in 1997 by each of the top producers in that year.
   b. A pictograph showing how much crude oil was produced by Nigeria in each of the five years. (Because Figure VA.9 uses barrels to represent quantities of oil, use some other symbol for your pictograph.)
   c. A line graph showing trends in crude oil production in the following countries: the United States, the United Kingdom, China, Mexico, and Iran.

   d. A pie chart showing the proportions of the world's crude oil produced in 1997 by the following countries. For your convenience, the correct percentages are provided below:

Canada	.8
China	4.9%
Mexico	4.5%
Saudi Arabia	12.8%
United Kingdom	3.7%
United States	9.8%
Russia	8.8%
All other countries	52.7%

4. In textbooks, journals, or other publications related to your major, find and photocopy three photographs. For each photograph, answer the following questions:
   a. What does the photograph show, who is the intended audience, and how is the reader supposed to use or be affected by the photograph?
   b. What angle of view has the photographer chosen and why?
   c. What, if anything, has the writer done to eliminate unnecessary detail?
   d. Are all the relevant parts of the subject visible? If not, what is missing?
   e. Has the writer supplied helpful labels? Would any additional labels be helpful? Are any of the labels unnecessary?
   f. Could the writer have achieved his or her purpose more effectively by using a drawing or a diagram instead of a photograph? Why or why not?

5. Create a drawing to include in a set of instructions for operating one of the following pieces of equipment. Explain who your readers are and, if it isn't obvious, how they will use the equipment. Be sure to label the significant parts and include a figure title.

   ■ An instrument or piece of equipment used in your field
   ■ A power lawnmower
   ■ A clock radio
   ■ The subject of a set of instructions you are preparing for your writing class
   ■ Some other piece of equipment that has at least a half-dozen parts that should be shown in a set of instructions

■ FIGURE VA.27

Table for Use with
Exercise 1

Table 6. Enrollment in All Institutions of Higher Education by Age, Sex, and Attendance Status
50 States and D.C., fall 1987, 1992, 1995, 2002, and 2007
(in thousands)

SEX AND AGE	NUMBER (1,000)					PERCENT PART-TIME				
	1987	1992 est.	1995 est.	2002 proj.	2007 proj.	1987	1992 est.	1995 est.	2002 proj.	2007 proj.
Total	12,767	14,487	13,913	15,206	16,111	43.3	43.7	43.7	42.0	40.7
Men	5,932	6,524	6,186	6,605	6,939	39.1	39.8	40.3	40.3	39.7
14 to 17 years old	127	89	86	103	115	44.8	4.5	19.8	17.5	17.4
18 and 19 years old	1,427	1,305	1,294	1,505	1,620	13.9	13.5	14.8	14.3	14.5
20 and 21 years old	1,318	1,342	1,194	1,380	1,454	21.2	19.2	19.5	20.3	20.6
22 to 24 years old	995	1,272	1,116	1,148	1,245	34.8	32.8	33.4	35.0	35.3
25 to 29 years old	920	995	929	884	1,003	61.6	58.3	53.9	58.0	58.2
30 to 34 years old	520	628	601	586	550	73.2	72.1	69.7	71.5	71.6
35 years old and over	624	933	965	999	953	78.8	76.4	78.2	82.1	82.4
Women	6,835	7,963	7,727	8,601	9,172	47.0	46.8	46.5	43.3	41.4
14 to 17 years old	136	97	85	141	175	44.9	3.1	9.4	9.9	9.1
18 and 19 years old	1,585	1,479	1,534	1,816	1,977	15.4	15.3	15.1	14.4	14.4
20 and 21 years old	1,333	1,541	1,378	1,603	1,721	23.4	25.0	19.2	18.7	18.5
22 to 24 years old	984	1,255	1,131	1,202	1,359	45.5	41.0	39.3	36.9	35.7
25 to 29 years old	825	1,030	999	972	1,141	64.0	65.7	61.8	59.1	57.2
30 to 34 years old	703	828	810	826	799	80.2	71.6	71.6	68.5	66.7
35 years old and over	1,267	1,732	1,791	2,040	2,001	83.3	78.2	80.8	77.0	75.5

Source: U.S. Department of Education, National Center for Educational Statistics, Fall Enrollment in
Colleges and Universities survey and Integrated Secondary Education Data System (ISEDS) survey; and
U.S. Department of Commerce, Bureau of the Census, unpublished tabulations.

■ FIGURE VA.28

Table for Use with
Exercise 3

From U.S. Department of
Energy, "World Oil
Production," *Monthly
Energy Review, U.S. Energy
Department Report
DOE/EIA-0035* (September
1997): 131.

World Oil Production
Thousands of Barrels per Day

Country	1993	1994	1995	1996	1997
Saudi Arabia	8,198	8,120	8,231	8,218	8,474
United States	6,847	6,662	6,560	6,465	6,431
Russia	6,730	6,135	5,995	5,774	5,833
Iran	3,429	3,540	3,643	3,686	3,685
China	2,890	2,939	2,990	3,131	3,245
Venezuela	2,450	2,588	2,750	3,053	3,214
Norway	2,350	2,521	2,768	3,104	3,199
Mexico	2,673	2,685	2,618	2,855	2,970
United Kingdom	1,915	2,375	2,489	2,568	2,492
United Arab Emirates	2,159	2,193	2,279	2,278	2,317
Kuwait	1,852	2,025	2,057	2,062	2,075
Nigeria	1,960	1,931	1,993	2,188	2,286
Canada	1,679	1,746	1,805	1,823	1,847
Indonesia	1,511	1,510	1,503	1,547	1,572
Lybia	1,361	1,378	1,390	1,401	1,442
Total	48,004	48,348	49,071	50,153	51,082
Other	12,243	12,655	13,375	13,829	14,870
Grand Total	60,247	61,003	62,446	63,982	65,952

6. Draw a diagram that you might use in a report, proposal, instruction manual, or other communication written on the job. The diagram might be an abstract representation of some object, design, process, or other subject. Use special symbols if you wish. Explain what use you might make of the diagram. Also, explain how your readers might use it. Be sure to provide all appropriate labels and a figure title.

7. Create a flow chart for one of the following processes and procedures. State when you might use the flow chart and why. Be sure to provide appropriate labels and a figure title. Show no more than sixteen steps. If the process calls for more, show the major steps and omit the substeps.

   - Applying for admission to your college
   - Changing the spark plugs in a car
   - Making paper in a paper mill (begin with the trees in the forest)
   - Preparing to make an oral presentation in class or on the job. Your presentation should include visual aids. Start at the point where you decide that you are going to speak or are given the assignment to do so.
   - Explaining a process or a procedure that you will describe in a communication you are preparing for your writing class
   - Explaining some process or procedure that is commonly used in your field

8. Create an organizational chart for some organization that has at least three levels—perhaps a club you belong to or a company that employs you. Or visit an office or a store and ask someone there to provide you with information about its organizational hierarchy.

9. Make a schedule chart for an assignment you are preparing for your writing class. Cover the period from the date you received the assignment to the date you will turn it in. Be sure to include all major activities, such as planning, gathering information, bringing a draft to class for review, and so on.

10. Create a budget statement using the following data on the monthly costs that an electronics company would incur if it opened a new service center in a new city. Remember to group related expenses and to provide a total.

    Salary for central manager $5,450. Rent $1,900. Business tax (prorated) $1,250. Electricity (year-round average) $875. Water $245. Receptionist's salary $2,100. Office supplies $200. Car lease $500. Salary for technician $3,000. Salary for technician's assistant $1,800. Supplies for technician $300. Travel for monthly trip to main office by center manager $300. Car driving expenses $250. Telephone $330. Depreciation on equipment $1,700.

CHAPTER

Designing Pages and Documents

GUIDELINES

1	Begin by considering your readers and purpose
2	Align related visual elements with one another
3	Use contrast to establish hierarchy and focus
4	Use proximity to group related elements
5	Use repetition to unify your communication visually
6	Select type that is easy to read
7	Design your overall package for ease of use and attractiveness

You build your written messages out of *visual* elements. These visual elements are dark marks printed on a light background: words and sentences and paragraphs; drawings and graphs and tables. Whether you are writing for printed pages or for computer screens, your readers *see* your message before they read and understand it. And what they see has a powerful effect on the success of your communications.

IMPORTANCE OF GOOD DESIGN

Good design helps you achieve your communication objectives in several ways:

- **Good design helps readers understand your information.** For example, you can use visual design to signal the hierarchy of ideas and information in a report. This helps your readers understand what you are saying and what its significance is to them. Similarly, when writing instructions, you can place a direction and a figure next to each other to indicate that the two work together to explain a step.
- **Good page design helps readers locate information.** At work, readers often want to find part of a communication without reading all of it. With headings and other design elements, you can help them do that quickly.
- **Good design emphasizes the most important content.** By varying such things as the size and placement of the visual elements on the page, you can draw your readers' attention to certain elements, such as a warning in a set of instructions or a list of actions to take in a recommendation report.
- **Good design encourages readers to feel good about a communication and its subject matter.** You've surely seen pages—perhaps in a textbook or a set of instructions—that struck you as uninviting, even ugly. As a result, you may have been reluctant to read them. And undoubtedly you've seen other pages that you found attractive, which you probably approached more eagerly, more receptively. Good design can even affect the readers' attitude toward the subject matter, as demonstrated in an experiment in which researcher Karen Schriver asked people to comment on two visual designs for a set of instructions for a microwave oven. When people commented on the design they preferred, they also volunteered that the oven was easy to use—even though they had not seen the oven itself (302).

DESIGN ELEMENTS OF A COMMUNICATION

When designing communications, it's helpful to think of yourself as working primarily with six types of elements. To see the variety of ways in which these elements can be crafted to create effective, attractive, and interesting page designs, see Figure 12.1.

■ **FIGURE 12.1 Sample Page Designs** **A** From M. Baab, "PCs Take on New Roles in Automobile Manufacturing," *Design News* 53 (1998): 29. **B** From *NEXTSTEP: User's Guide* (Redwood City, CA: NEXT, 1994) 197. **C** From Y. Fukuoka, M. Shigematsu, M. Itoh, S. Homma, and H. Ikegami, "Effects of Football Training on Ventilatory and Gas Exchange Kinetics to Sinusoidal Work Load," *Journal of Sports Medicine and Physical Fitness* 37 (1997): 161. **D** From C. Zimmer, "A Sickle in the Clouds," *Discover Magazine* 19 (1998): 32. Illustration by Steve Kirk.

The six design elements of a page

- **Text.** Paragraphs and sentences.
- **Headings and titles.** Labels for sections of your communication.
- **Visual aids.** Drawings, graphs, tables, and so on—including their captions.
- **White space.** Blank areas.
- **Headers and footers.** The items, such as page numbers, that occur at the top or bottom of each page in a multipage document.
- **Physical features**. These include paper, which may take many shapes and sizes, and bindings, which come in many forms.

FOUR BASIC DESIGN PRINCIPLES

This chapter describes easy-to-follow strategies for coordinating these six basic elements to design effective communications. Much of this advice involves the application of four simple design principles identified by graphic artist Robin Williams.

Basic Design Principles
■ **Alignment** Everything placed on a page should have a visual connection with something else. You can establish these connections by aligning related elements with one another. **(Guideline 2)** ■ **Contrast** To establish a hierarchy of importance or to focus a reader's attention, you must make some things look different than others. You can establish difference by using contrast. **(Guideline 3)** ■ **Proximity** When two or more items on a page are closely related to one another, you should signal this relationship by placing them in close proximity with one another. **(Guideline 4)** ■ **Repetition** The pages in a document should look like they belong to a cohesive whole. You can provide this visual unity by repeating design elements from page to page. **(Guideline 5)**

GUIDELINE 1   Begin by Considering Your Readers and Purpose

To employ the four design principles effectively, you must have a clear understanding of what you are trying to achieve through your design. Therefore, you should begin your design work in the same way you begin making plans about what information to include and how to organize these contents: by reviewing your communication objectives so you have the following considerations clearly in mind.

- **Who your readers are.** Review their needs, attitudes, and expectations. All should influence your design decisions.
- **What tasks your communication should enable readers to perform.** If readers are going to use your communication as a reference work from which they will seek only specific pieces of information, you will need to design differently than if they will simply read it straight through.
- **How you want to influence readers' attitudes.** As mentioned above, design affects the way your readers feel. You need to create designs that will shape your readers' attitudes in the ways you desire.

GUIDELINE 2   Align Related Visual Elements with One Another

The first principle of visual design—alignment—provides you with a way to avoid the appearance that you have placed items on your pages arbitrarily. When the arrangement of the items on a page seems (or is) arbitrary, readers have difficulty discerning meaningful relationships, they find it hard to understand and use the information and ideas presented, and they may form an unfavorable impression of the communication as well as of the subject matter and the writer.

By comparing the two designs at the top of the facing page, you can see how readily alignment establishes connections among related items.

Arbitrary Placement

Martina Alverez

AAA Consultants, Inc.

4357 Evington Street
Minneapolis, MN 50517

(416) 232-9999

Alignment Establishes Relationships

Martina Alverez

AAA Consultants, Inc.

4357 Evington Street
Minneapolis, MN 50517
(416) 232-9999

In the right-hand design, alignment establishes relationships that are not evident in the left-hand design.

In the demonstration above, the right-hand design connects related items with one another by aligning them along the "invisible" line of either the left-hand or the right-hand margin. To coordinate the visual elements in the more complex page designs often required on the job, use additional vertical and horizontal lines. The resulting network of lines is called a *grid.* Here are three examples:

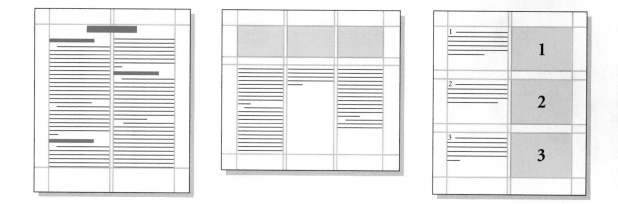

In the left-hand example, a pair of vertical grid lines used to create a simple, two-column page. The white space between the columns is called a *gutter.*

The center example represents a page in which the writer presents three figures, each accompanied by an associated block of text. To connect each figure to its text, the writer aligns each text-and-figure pair vertically in a column of its own, leaving varying amounts of white space at the bottoms of the columns.

The right-hand example represents a set of instructions in which the writer places all the directions in the left-hand column and all the illustrations in the right-hand column. To link each direction visually with its corresponding illustration, the writer aligns their tops along the same horizontal grid line. Horizontal gutters separate the direction-and-figure pairs from one another.

■ **FIGURE 12.2**

Grid Lines Used to Align the Elements of a Page

Grid lines create the visual structure of a page.

Visual elements are aligned with one another by being placed against the grid lines.

When visual elements extend across vertical grid lines, they usually go all the way to the far side of the adjacent area.

Sometimes writers break out of the basic grid pattern to emphasize one particular visual element.

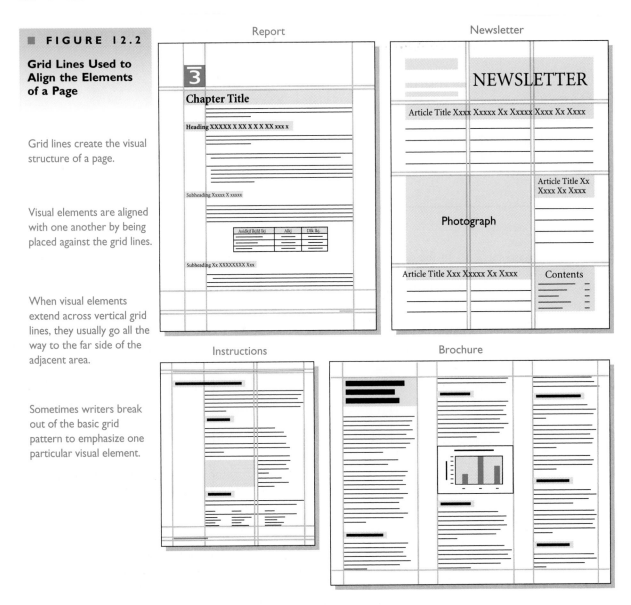

FIGURE 12.2

Grid Lines Used to Align the Elements of a Page

Using grid patterns creatively, you can build an unlimited variety of functional and attractive page designs. Figure 12.2 shows a few examples.

As you look at Figure 12.2, note that you can span two or more columns with a heading, figure, or other visual item as long as you still align the item within the grid system. Placing items across columns is one way of emphasizing them.

Items aligned against a left grid line are said to be *flush left*, and those against a right grid line are *flush right*. A centered item isn't aligned against a left or right grid line, of course, but its midpoint aligns with a line running down the column's center. Headers and footers align flush right or left in the top and bottom margins.

■ **FIGURE 12.3 Comparison of Irregularly Shaped Figures without and with Rectangular Enclosures** From Monarch Marking, *Operating Instructions for Model 100® Dial-A-Price Printer*, (Dayton, OH: by permission from Monarch Marking Systems, Inc).

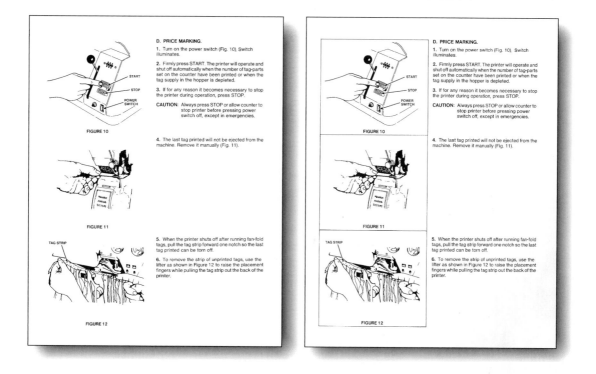

If your communication includes drawings or other visual aids that have irregular outlines, consider enclosing the figures in rectangles that run along the grid lines. In word-processing programs, you can easily do this by using the borders or frames feature. Figure 12.3 shows how such rectangles can anchor the figures in the framework of the page.

To create multicolumn pages, use the menu or button in your word-processing program that lets you choose the number of columns on a page and the width of the gutters that separate the columns. For designs that rely heavily on horizontal grid lines, use the program's feature that lets you create tables. The boundaries of the cells in the table will define your page's vertical and horizontal grid lines.

Word-processing programs make it easy to create grid lines for aligning the visual elements of your pages.

GUIDELINE 3   Use Contrast to Establish Hierarchy and Focus

Of the various items on a page, you will usually want some to stand out more than others. For instance, you may want to indicate that some items are at a higher level than others within your organizational hierarchy. Or you may want to focus attention on certain items, such as a warning in a set of instructions. However, nothing will stand out if everything on the page looks the same. To make some things stand out, you must use contrast, the second design principle.

No Contrast

Martina Alverez
AAA Consultants, Inc.

4357 Evington Street
Minneapolis, MN 50517
(416) 232-9999

Contrast Establishes Emphasis

Martina Alverez
AAA Consultants, Inc.

4357 Evington Street
Minneapolis, MN 50517
(416) 232-9999

Color, type size, and bold are used in the right-hand design to establish a focus and a visual hierarchy.

When deciding how to establish the visual hierarchy of your page, pay special attention to text items: paragraphs, headings, figure titles, and headers and footers. To create distinctions among these items, you can control four variables:

- **Size.** The size of type is measured in *points* and always refers to the height of the capital letters. The following line illustrates a range of type sizes. There are 72 points to an inch, so the right-hand letter is one inch high.

M	M	M	M	M	M	M	M	M	M
8	10	12	14	18	24	36	48	60	72

A variety of type sizes, measured in points

When trying to distinguish different elements (such as different levels of heading) by using different type sizes, be sure to select sizes that contrast enough for the difference to be immediately noticeable. On the other hand, consider the relationship of all the visual elements on the page to assure that differences in size aren't so great that the larger dominates attention. You want to create a hierarchy of meaning and attention, not create one or two elements that keep pulling the eye to them or that appear to be out of proportion with the rest of the page. As a rule of thumb, try keeping each type size no larger than one and one-half times the size of the next smaller size in your hierarchy.

- **Type treatment.** Use plain type (called *roman*) for most type. Create contrast for items that you want to stand out by printing them in bold or italics.
- **Color.** Emphasize some things by making them a different color. Black type and gray type aren't as distinguishable as black type and red type.
- **Typeface.** To help readers distinguish one kind of element on your page from another, you can use different typefaces for each. At work, this is often done to help headings stand out from paragraphs.

Of course, using different typefaces to distinguish different kinds of content will work only if there is enough contrast between the two typefaces. Consider the following six examples.

Times Roman	Helvetica
Baskerville	Geneva
Palatino	**Folio**

As you can see, the typefaces in each column look very similar to the others in the same column, so choosing two from the same column would not accomplish your objective. However, all of the typefaces on the left look quite distinct from all of those on the right. Here's why. The left-hand typefaces all have lines drawn across the ends of their strokes. These lines are called *serifs*, and typefaces with them are called *serif* typefaces. In contrast, all of the typefaces in the right-hand column have no serifs. They are called *sans serif* typefaces (in French, *sans* means "without").

To make headings look quite distinct from paragraphs, choose any of the multitude of sans serif typefaces for your headings and any of the many serif typefaces for your text.

To create even greater contrast among the visual elements on the page, you can use the variables of size, type treatment, type category, and color to reinforce one another. By coordinating these variables with one another, you can create distinctive appearances for a substantial number of visual elements, as the following table illustrates. Figure 12.4 shows a page created using this table.

Element	Size	Typeface	Type Category	Color
Paragraph	12 point	roman	serif (e.g., Times)	black
Headings First level	16 point	bold roman	sans serif (e.g., Helvetica)	blue
Second	14 point	bold roman	sans serif	blue
Figure titles	10 point	bold roman	sans serif	black
Footers	10 point	italic	sans serif	black

■ **FIGURE 12.4**

Coordination of Size, Typeface, Type Category, and Color to Reinforce One Another

Based on United States Consumer Product Safety Commision, *Protect Your Family from Lead in Your Home* (Washington DC: United States Environmental Protection Agency, 1995) 33–4.

These pages illustrate how typeface, size, style, and color can be coordinated to indicate a communication's organization.

They follow the styles described in the table on page 339.

Header in 14-point Helvetica italic

Text in 12-point Times

Section number in 14-point Helvetica

Section title in 20-point Helvetica bold

First level headings in 16-point Helvetica bold

Second level heading in 14-point Helvetica bold

Figure caption in 10-point Helvetica bold

Footer in 10-point Helvetica italic

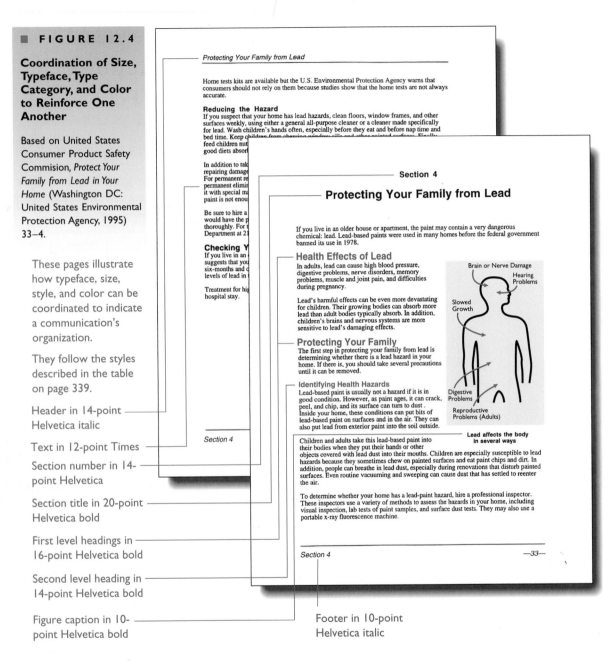

Protecting Your Family from Lead

Home tests kits are available but the U.S. Environmental Protection Agency warns that consumers should not rely on them because studies show that the home tests are not always accurate.

Reducing the Hazard
If you suspect that your home has lead hazards, clean floors, window frames, and other surfaces weekly, using either a general all-purpose cleaner or a cleaner made specifically for lead. Wash children's hands often, especially before they eat and before nap time and bed time. Keep children from chewing window sills and other painted surfaces. Finally, feed children nut... good diets absor...

In addition to tak... repairing damage... For permanent re... permanent elimin... it with special ma... paint is not enou...

Be sure to hire a... would have the p... thoroughly. For t... Department at 21...

Checking Y...
If you live in an... suggests that you... six-months and c... levels of lead in t...

Treatment for hi... hospital stay.

Section 4

Section 4

Protecting Your Family from Lead

If you live in an older house or apartment, the paint may contain a very dangerous chemical: lead. Lead-based paints were used in many homes before the federal government banned its use in 1978.

Health Effects of Lead
In adults, lead can cause high blood pressure, digestive problems, nerve disorders, memory problems, muscle and joint pain, and difficulties during pregnancy.

Lead's harmful effects can be even more devastating for children. Their growing bodies can absorb more lead than adult bodies typically absorb. In addition, children's brains and nervous systems are more sensitive to lead's damaging effects.

Protecting Your Family
The first step in protecting your family from lead is determining whether there is a lead hazard in your home. If there is, you should take several precautions until it can be removed.

Identifying Health Hazards
Lead-based paint is usually not a hazard if it is in good condition. However, as paint ages, it can crack, peel, and chip, and its surface can turn to dust . Inside your home, these conditions can put bits of lead-based paint on surfaces and in the air. They can also put lead from exterior paint into the soil outside.

Brain or Nerve Damage
Hearing Problems
Slowed Growth
Digestive Problems
Reproductive Problems (Adults)

Lead affects the body in several ways

Children and adults take this lead-based paint into their bodies when they put their hands or other objects covered with lead dust into their mouths. Children are especially susceptible to lead hazards because they sometimes chew on painted surfaces and eat paint chips and dirt. In addition, people can breathe in lead dust, especially during renovations that disturb painted surfaces. Even routine vacuuming and sweeping can cause dust that has settled to reenter the air.

To determine whether your home has a lead-paint hazard, hire a professional inspector. These inspectors use a variety of methods to assess the hazards in your home, including visual inspection, lab tests of paint samples, and surface dust tests. They may also use a portable x-ray fluorescence machine.

Section 4 —33—

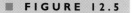

■ FIGURE 12.5

Icons Used to Aid Readers in Seeing the Structure of a Page

From Toshiba, *Satellite Pro 400CS/500 User's Guide* (Santa Ana, CA: Toshiba, 1996) xxvii, 134, 210.

The first sentence on page xxvii explains that the icons' purpose is to make "finding your way around" the guide easier.

The icons help readers distinguish special kinds of information from the rest of a page's contents:

- "Warnings" and "Cautions" that require attention.

- "Notes" that might be helpful but could be skipped.

Note how the rules (horizontal lines) also help to organize the information visually.

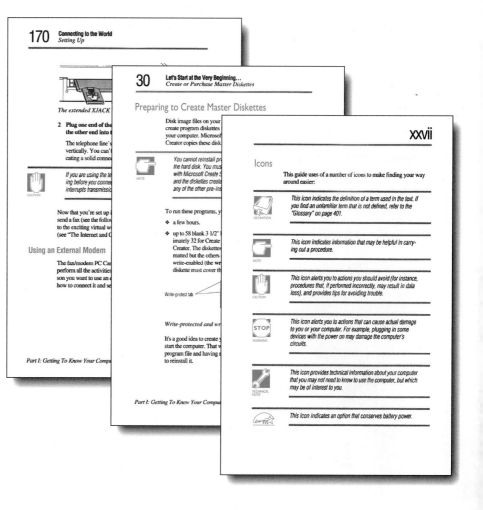

You can use the principle of contrast to distinguish other elements as well. For example, in a set of instructions, you can set off warnings in a box that might have a background in color. In a report, you might set off your tables from your paragraphs by using the same typeface for your tables that you use for your headings.

When working with the page design variables, remember that your reason for creating visually contrasting elements is to simplify the page for your readers so they can readily see the role played by each element on the page. Don't create so many distinctions that the page seems chaotic to readers. For example, in most cases, stick to only two colors for your type and only two typefaces.

Other tools you can use to organize a page visually include rules (lines) that mark the boundaries between sections of text and icons that serve as non-verbal headings to assist readers in locating a certain kind of information. See Figure 12.5.

GUIDELINE 4 **Use Proximity to Group Related Elements**

One goal of visual design is to help your readers see how your information is organized. The third design principle, proximity, provides an important strategy for accomplishing this goal. To apply this principle, group related items visually by placing them in close proximity to one another.

Not Grouped	Proximity Establishes Groupings
Martina Alverez AAA Consultants, Inc. 4357 Evington Street Minneapolis, MN 50517 (416) 232-9999	Martina Alverez AAA Consultants, Inc. 4357 Evington Street Minneapolis, MN 50517 (416) 232-9999

Here are some ways in which you can use the principle of proximity in your on-the-job communications:

- Use less white space below headings than above to place the heading in closer proximity to the text it labels than to the preceding section.
- Use less white space between titles and the figures they label than is used to separate the title and figure from adjacent items.
- In lists that have subgroups, use less white space between items within a subgroup than between one subgroup and another subgroup.

In Figure 12.6, notice how proximity helps to convey the organization of the page.

GUIDELINE 5 **Use Repetition to Unify Your Communication Visually**

In communications that are more than a page long, you should think not only about creating well-designed single pages but also about creating a well-designed set of pages.

When you are creating a set of pages, the chief goal is to make the pages harmonize visually in a way that supports the readers' use of them and is aesthetically pleasing. To achieve this goal, use the fourth design principle: repetition.

For instance, use the same grid pattern throughout. Similarly, use the same type treatment (typeface, size, color, etc.) for all major headings, for all second-level headings, all headers and footers, and so on. Such repetition enables your readers to "learn" the structure of your pages so that they immediately understand the organization of each new page as they turn to it. Repetition also creates visual harmony that is more pleasing aesthetically than would be a set of inconsistent designs.

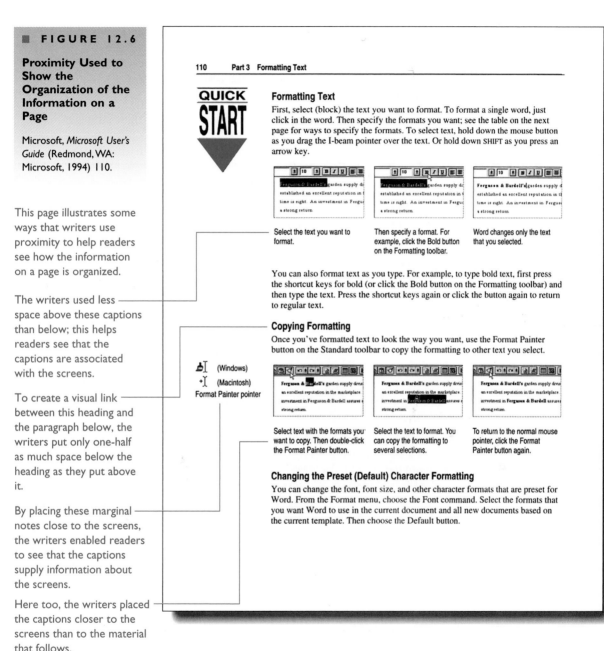

■ **FIGURE 12.6**

Proximity Used to Show the Organization of the Information on a Page

Microsoft, *Microsoft User's Guide* (Redmond, WA: Microsoft, 1994) 110.

This page illustrates some ways that writers use proximity to help readers see how the information on a page is organized.

The writers used less space above these captions than below; this helps readers see that the captions are associated with the screens.

To create a visual link between this heading and the paragraph below, the writers put only one-half as much space below the heading as they put above it.

By placing these marginal notes close to the screens, the writers enabled readers to see that the captions supply information about the screens.

Here too, the writers placed the captions closer to the screens than to the material that follows.

---

110   Part 3   Formatting Text

QUICK START

Formatting Text

First, select (block) the text you want to format. To format a single word, just click in the word. Then specify the formats you want; see the table on the next page for ways to specify the formats. To select text, hold down the mouse button as you drag the I-beam pointer over the text. Or hold down SHIFT as you press an arrow key.

Select the text you want to format.

Then specify a format. For example, click the Bold button on the Formatting toolbar.

Word changes only the text that you selected.

You can also format text as you type. For example, to type bold text, first press the shortcut keys for bold (or click the Bold button on the Formatting toolbar) and then type the text. Press the shortcut keys again or click the button again to return to regular text.

Copying Formatting

Once you've formatted text to look the way you want, use the Format Painter button on the Standard toolbar to copy the formatting to other text you select.

(Windows)
(Macintosh)
Format Painter pointer

Select text with the formats you want to copy. Then double-click the Format Painter button.

Select the text to format. You can copy the formatting to several selections.

To return to the normal mouse pointer, click the Format Painter button again.

Changing the Preset (Default) Character Formatting

You can change the font, font size, and other character formats that are preset for Word. From the Format menu, choose the Font command. Select the formats that you want Word to use in the current document and all new documents based on the current template. Then choose the Default button.

Of course, it's not possible to have exactly the same design for every page in a long communication. Often, such communications will have different types of pages. In long reports, for instance, each chapter may begin with a page that looks different from every other page in the chapter. Instruction manuals often have troubleshooting sections that present different kinds of information than the manuals' other pages do. For such communications, follow these two strategies:

■ Treat in the same way all elements that are shared by different types of pages. For instance, use the same style for all headings, even on different types of pages.

■ Use the same design for all pages of the same type (for example, all pages that begin a new chapter).

Figure 12.7 shows pages from a communication that used these strategies.

GUIDELINE **6**   **Select Type That Is Easy to Read**

We recognize letters by seeing their main lines. These lines are more obvious with some typefaces than with others, as you can see by comparing the two typefaces on the left with the two on the right:

Times Roman
All major lines of all the letters are clearly defined

Ultra
The second leg of the *u* is very thin, as is the cross-stroke of the *t*.

Script
The shape of the s is "hidden" by the ornate lines, and the circle of the *p* is not closed.

When we are reading only a few words, as when looking at a magazine ad, these differences are inconsequential. However, when we are reading an entire page, a full paragraph, or even a few sentences, type with the more distinct main lines is easier to read. Consequently, when choosing typefaces for your text, you should apply the following advice:

Basic principles of type selection

■ **Use a typeface with strong, distinct main lines.**

■ **Avoid italics for more than a sentence at a time.** Although they are great for emphasis, italics are difficult to read in long passages because they represent a "distorted" or "ornate" version of the alphabet that obscures the main lines.

■ **Avoid using all capital letters for more than a few words at a time.** Research has also shown that you should avoid using all capital letters for passages that are longer than a sentence because they are difficult to read in long stretches (Tinker). You can see why if you consider that in capitals the letters of the alphabet have shapes more similar to one another than the shapes in lowercase. For instance, a capital "D" and "P" are the same height and face the same direction, but lowercase "d" and "p" have much different heights and face in different directions. The greater similarity of capital letters makes it more difficult to distinguish one letter from another when they are printed in full sentences. And if you can't tell one letter from another easily, you also can't very rapidly figure out the word they spell.

After studying the extensive literature on the readability of different typefaces, Karen Schriver concludes that in extended text, serif type may be somewhat easier to read than sans serif, although the two categories can be read equally quickly in small amounts. Schriver notes, however, that several factors may come into play, including cultural preferences and familiarity with the typeface. In the United States, serif

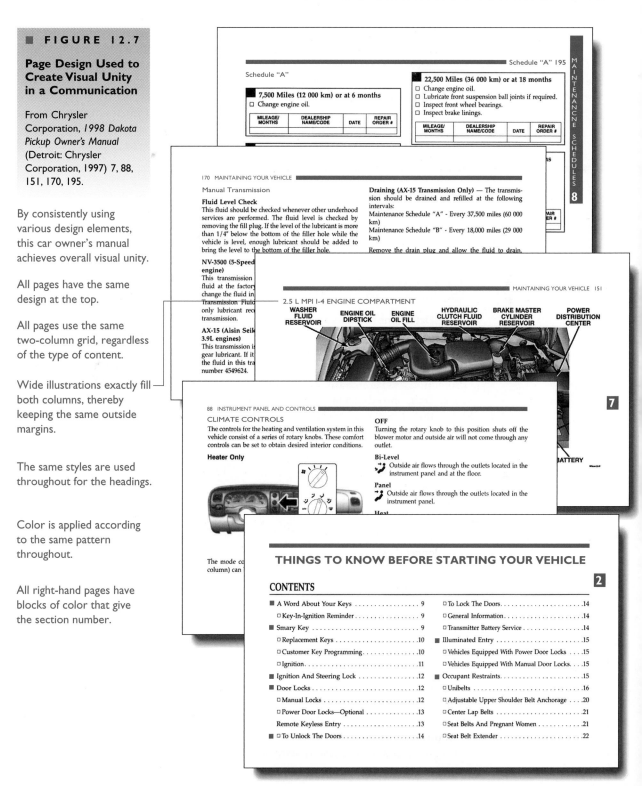

■ **FIGURE 12.7**

Page Design Used to Create Visual Unity in a Communication

From Chrysler Corporation, *1998 Dakota Pickup Owner's Manual* (Detroit: Chrysler Corporation, 1997) 7, 88, 151, 170, 195.

By consistently using various design elements, this car owner's manual achieves overall visual unity.

All pages have the same design at the top.

All pages use the same two-column grid, regardless of the type of content.

Wide illustrations exactly fill both columns, thereby keeping the same outside margins.

The same styles are used throughout for the headings.

Color is applied according to the same pattern throughout.

All right-hand pages have blocks of color that give the section number.

Use 10-point or 12-point type for text.

type is most common in published books, but in Europe publishers usually use sans serif type. She concludes that if you choose a typeface with strong, distinct lines, your text will be readable whether you select a serif or sans serif typeface.

Of course, no type will be legible unless it is large enough. Research has shown that in print communications, it's easiest to read passages printed in type that is between 8 points and 12 points high (Tinker). In most printed communications written at work, type smaller than 10 points is avoided, and type larger than 12 points is usually reserved for headings, titles, and the like. Type as small as 9 points may work in headers, footers, and the captions for figures.

For on-screen reading, choose type that is at least 12 points high, except for brief items such as figure captions and copyright notices.

PRACTICAL PROCEDURES FOR DESIGNING PAGES

You do not need any special artistic or technical skills to follow the first six guidelines for designing pages. Here are some practical procedures you can follow:

1. **Determine the amount of text and visual aids you will include.** This will help you determine how to coordinate your text and visual aids. If you are pairing specific blocks of text or visual aids across adjacent columns by using horizontal grid lines, identify the longest text passage that goes with a single illustration. Use the length of that passage as the standard for allocating space for all the other text passages.

2. **Draw thumbnail sketches of a variety of grid patterns.** Figure 12.8 shows nine thumbnail sketches exploring alternative ways of designing a single page. Sketches like these can help you quickly assess the various grid patterns you might use. Even when making thumbnail sketches, keep your communication's purpose and readers in mind, so you will know what material to emphasize and what relationships to make clear. Think, too, about how large you will need to make your illustrations so that all the details are legible. Finally, choose the design most likely to achieve your purpose.

3. **Make a full-size mockup of the design you have chosen.** A mockup is a full-size page that shows what a typical page will look like, though it need not contain the actual words and visual aids you will use in the finished communication. If you haven't written your text and created your visual aids yet, type nonsense words and draw rectangles where the visual aids will go.

4. **Evaluate your mockup.** Once you have created your mockup, you can judge how well its text, headings and titles, visual aids, and white space work together. If you're dissatisfied with the result, make adjustments. If possible, show your mockup to other people—preferably (in the spirit of continuous reader involvement) to members of your target audience.

5. **Create a style sheet.** After you've refined your mockup so that you believe it will successfully achieve your communication goals, use your word processor to create a style sheet that defines each of the text elements you have chosen. For example, designate the largest level of heading as "Heading 1," and then tell the typeface, size, treatment, margins, and indentations that you have selected for it.

■ **FIGURE 12.8**

Nine Thumbnail Page Designs for the Same Material

From Professor Joseph L. Cox III.

Each of these thumbnails represents a different way of arranging the same visual elements.

Note how changing the size and placement of an element alters the emphasis it receives.

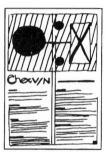

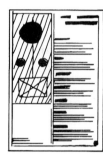
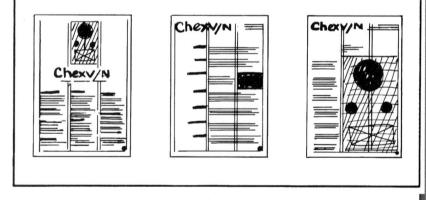

■ **FIGURE 12.9**

Style Sheet Created in Microsoft Word

List of styles created for this document

Name of the new style now being developed

Preview of the style's appearance

Details of the style

By selecting "FORMAT," you can obtain a list of options for defining the style.

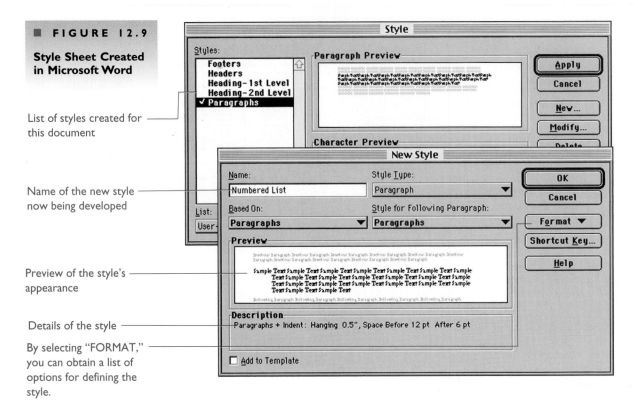

This step will allow you to format each element of your text simply by highlighting it and applying the appropriate style. It has the added advantage of letting you adjust your style without going through the entire text to change numerous items. For example, your style sheet will enable you to change all of the first-level headings at one time simply by redefining the style itself. Figure 12.9 shows a style sheet created in Microsoft Word.

6. **Test your final pages.** If your design is at all complex, as it might be if you were creating a set of instructions, test it out by asking one or more members of your target audience to try out your communication.

GUIDELINE **7** **Design Your Overall Package for Ease of Use and Attractiveness**

For some communications, you will need to think how to design not only the elements on the page but also the overall product that you will provide to your readers. Here, too, think about your communication from the perspective of your readers:

■ **Size.** Choose a size that your readers will find convenient in the situations in which they will use your communication. For example, if you are creating instructions that readers will use at a desk already crowded by a computer and a keyboard, imitate software manufacturers who print manuals that are smaller than 8 1/2 by 11 inches.

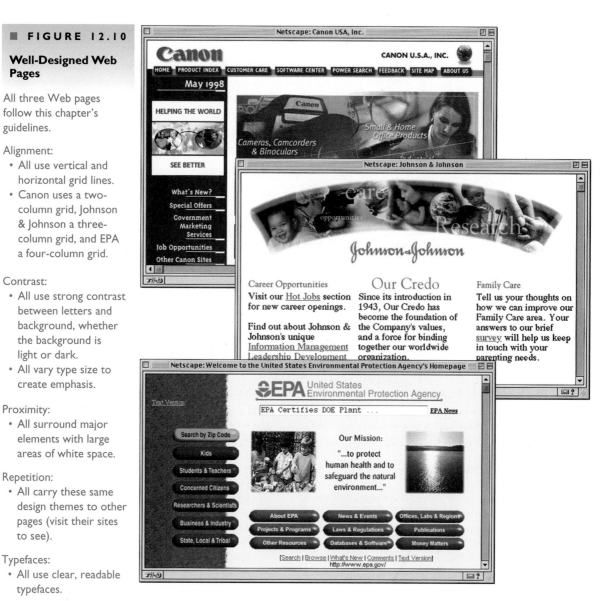

Well-Designed Web Pages

All three Web pages follow this chapter's guidelines.

Alignment:
- All use vertical and horizontal grid lines.
- Canon uses a two-column grid, Johnson & Johnson a three-column grid, and EPA a four-column grid.

Contrast:
- All use strong contrast between letters and background, whether the background is light or dark.
- All vary type size to create emphasis.

Proximity:
- All surround major elements with large areas of white space.

Repetition:
- All carry these same design themes to other pages (visit their sites to see).

Typefaces:
- All use clear, readable typefaces.

- ■ **Shape.** Choose a shape that will make it convenient for your readers to carry and store. If appropriate, for example, make it a shape that will fit into a shirt pocket or into a special case (such as the case for a notepad computer or a blood glucose monitor).
- ■ **Binding.** Some bindings stay open more easily than others. If your readers will want your communication to lie flat because they need to use both hands for something else, consider a spiral binding or three-ring binder.
- ■ **Paper.** If you are creating a shop manual that might be spilled on or a document that might be used outdoors, consider a coated paper that resists liquids and soil.

VISUAL DESIGN OF ON-LINE PAGES

As mentioned at the beginning of this chapter, the guidelines discussed here are just as valid for pages to be read on-line as for pages to be read on paper. Figure 12.10 (on the preceding page) shows sample on-line pages that follow this chapter's advice. However, there are additional considerations in the visual design of on-line pages. They are discussed in Chapter 15.

CONCLUSION

Every page that you write has some sort of page design. This chapter has explained how you can look at your pages in the way that graphic designers do, thinking about each visual element in terms of the way it affects your readers. By following this chapter's advice, you will be able to create page designs that help your readers read efficiently, emphasize the important contents of your communication, and create a favorable impression.

EXERCISES

1. Study the design of the sample pages shown in Figure 12.1. Identify the number of columns; the placement of text, headings, and visual aids; and any other important features of the design.

2. Figure 12.11 shows four package inserts for a prescription medication. All contain the same information, but each was prepared by a different graphic designer. Describe the page designs used in each. What purpose do you think each designer had in mind? Which design do you think works best? Worst? Why?

3. Find three different page designs. (Choose no more than one from a popular magazine; look at instructions, insurance policies, leases, company brochures, technical reports, and the like.) If your instructor asks, find all the samples in documents related to your major. Photocopy one page illustrating each design. Then, for each page, describe what you think is the purpose of the document and discuss the specific features of the page design that help or hinder the document from achieving that purpose.

4. This exercise will provide you with practice at evaluating and improving a page design.
   a. List the ways in which the design of the page shown in Figure 12.12 (page 355) could be improved.
   b. Redesign the page by following Steps 1 through 4 of the "Practical Procedures for Designing Pages." Specifically, do the following:
      ■ Create three thumbnail sketches for the page.
      ■ Create a full-size mockup of the best design.
   c. Display your mockup on the wall of your classroom along with the mockups prepared by the other students in your class. Decide which mockups work best. Discuss the reasons.

HYGROTON®
chlorthalidone usp | 50 mg. Tablets, 100 mg. Tablets | Oral Antihypertensive-Diuretic

DESCRIPTION
HYGROTON (chlorthalidone) is a monosulfamyl diuretic which differs chemically from thiazide diuretics in that a double-ring system is incorporated in its structure. It is 2-Chlor-5-(1-hydroxy-3-oxo-1-isoindolinyl) benzenesulfonamide, with the following structural formula:

ACTIONS
HYGROTON is an oral diuretic with prolonged action (48-72 hours) and low toxicity. The diuretic effect of the drug occurs within two hours of an oral dose and continues for up to 72 hours.

INDICATIONS
Diuretics such as HYGROTON are indicated in the management of hypertension either as the sole therapeutic agent or to enhance the effect of other antihypertensive drugs in the more severe forms of hypertension and in the control of hypertension of pregnancy.

CONTRAINDICATIONS
Anuria. Hypertensitivity to chlorthalidone. The routine use of diuretics in an otherwise healthy pregnant woman with or without mild edema is contraindicated and possibly hazardous.

WARNINGS
Should be used with caution in severe renal disease. In patients with renal disease, chlorthalidone or related drugs may precipitate azotemia. Cumulative effects of the drug may develop in patients with impaired renal function.

USAGE IN PREGNANCY: Reproduction studies in various animal species at multiples of the human dose showed no significant level of teratogenicity; no fetal or congenital abnormalities were observed.
NURSING MOTHERS: Thiazides cross the placental barrier and appear in cord blood and breast milk.

PRECAUTIONS
Periodic determination of serum electrolytes to detect possible electrolyte imbalance should be performed at appropriate intervals.
Chlorthalidone and related drugs may decrease serum PBI levels without signs of thyroid disturbance.

ADVERSE REACTIONS
Gastrointestinal System Reactions:
anorexia constipation
gastric irritation jaundice
nausea (intrahepatic
vomiting cholestatic
cramping jaundice)
diarrhea pancreatitis

Central Nervous System Reactions:
dizziness headache
vertigo xanthopsia
paresthesias

Hematologic Reactions:
leukopenia thrombocytopenia
agranulocytosis aplastic anemia

Other Adverse Reactions:
hyperglycemia muscle spasm
glycosuria weakness
hyperuricemia restlessness
impotence

Whenever adverse reactions are moderate or severe, chlorthalidone dosage should be reduced or therapy withdrawn.

DOSAGE AND ADMINISTRATION
Therapy should be individualized according to patient response. This therapy should be titrated to gain maximal therapeutic response as well as the minimal dose possible to maintain that therapeutic response.
Initiation: Preferably, therapy should be initiated with 50 mg. or 100 mg. daily. Due to the long action of the drug, therapy may also be initiated in most cases with a dose of 100 mg. on alternate days or three times weekly (Monday, Wednesday, Friday). Some patients may require 150 or 200 mg. at these intervals.
Maintenance: Maintenance doses may often be lower than initial doses and should be adjusted according to the individual patient. Effectiveness is well sustained during continued use.

OVERDOSAGE
Symptoms of overdosage include nausea, weakness, dizziness and disturbances of electrolyte balance.

HOW SUPPLIED
HYGROTON (chlorthalidone). White, single-scored tablets of 100 mg. and aqua tablets of 50 mg. in bottles of 100 and 1000; single-dose blister packs, boxes of 500; Paks of 28 tablets, boxes of 6.
CAUTION: Federal law prohibits dispensing without prescription.

ANIMAL PHARMACOLOGY
Biochemical studies in animals have suggested reasons for the prolonged effect of chlorthalidone. Absorption from the gastrointestinal tract is slow, due to its low solubility. After passage to the liver, some of the drug enters the general circulation, while some is excreted in the bile, to be reabsorbed later.

USV PHARMACEUTICAL MFG. CORP.
Manati, P.R. 00701

A

FIGURE 12.11   Package Inserts for a Prescription Medication From USV Pharmaceuticals.

hygroton* chlorthalidone usp

50 mg. tablets
100 mg. tablets

oral antihypertensive-diuretic

Description: *HYGROTON* (chlorthalidone) is a monosulfamyl diuretic which differs chemically from thiazide diuretics in that a double-ring system is incorporated in its structure. It is 2-Chlor-5-(1-hydroxy-3-oxo-1-isoindolinyl) benzenesulfonamide, with the following structural formula:

Actions: *HYGROTON* is an oral diuretic with prolonged action (48-72 hours) and low toxicity. The diuretic effect of the drug occurs within two hours of an oral dose and continues for up to 72 hours.

Indications: Diuretics such as HYGROTON are indicated in the management of hypertension either as the sole therapeutic agent or to enhance the effect of other antihypertensive drugs in the more severe forms of hypertension and in the control of hypertension of pregnancy.

Contraindications: Anuria. Hypersensitivity to chlorthalidone.

Warnings: Should be used with caution in severe renal disease. In patients with renal disease, chlorthalidone or related drugs may precipitate azotemia. Cumulative effects of the drug may develop in patients with impaired renal function.

The routine use of diuretics in an otherwise healthy pregnant woman with or without mild edema is contraindicated and possibly hazardous.

Usage in pregnancy: Reproduction studies in various animal species at multiples of the human dose showed no significant level of teratogenicity; no fetal or congenital abnormalities were observed.

Nursing mothers: Thiazides cross the placental barrier and appear in cord blood and breast milk.

Precautions: Periodic determination of serum electrolytes to detect possible electrolyte imbalance should be performed at appropriate intervals.

Chlorthalidone and related drugs may decrease serum PBI levels without signs of thyroid disturbance.

Adverse reactions:

Gastrointestinal System Reactions:
gastric irritation jaundice
anorexia constipation
nausea (intrahepatic
vomiting cholestatic
cramping jaundice)
diarrhea pancreatitis

Central Nervous System Reactions:
dizziness headache
vertigo xanthopsia
paresthesias

Hematologic Reactions:
leukopenia thrombocytopenia
agranulocytosis aplastic anemia

Other Adverse Reactions:
hyperglycemia muscle spasm
glycosuria weakness
hyperuricemia restlessness
impotence

Whenever adverse reaction are moderate or severe, chlorthalidone dosage should be reduced or therapy withdrawn.

Dosage and administration: Therapy should be individualized according to patient response. This therapy should be titrated to gain maximal therapeutic response as well as the minimal dose possible to maintain that therapeutic response.

Initiation: Preferably, therapy should be initiated with 50 mg. or 100 mg. daily. Due to the long action of the drug, therapy may also be initiated in most cases with a dose of 100 mg. on alternate days or three times weekly (Monday, Wednesday, Friday). Some patients may require 150 or 200 mg. at these intervals.

Maintenance: Maintenance doses may often be lower than initial doses and should be adjusted according to the individual patient. Effectiveness is well sustained during continued use.

Overdosage: Symptoms of overdosage include nausea, weakness, dizziness and disturbances of electrolyte balance.

How supplied: HYGROTON (chlorthalidone). White, single-scored tablets of 100 mg. and aqua tablets of 50 mg. in bottles of 100 and 1000; single-dose blister packs, boxes of 500; Paks of 28 tablets, boxes of 6.

Caution: Federal law prohibits dispensing without prescription.

Animal pharmacology: *Biochemical studies* in animals have suggested reasons for the prolonged effect of chlorthalidone. Absorption from the gastrointestinal tract is slow, due to its low solubility. After passage to the liver, some of the drug enters the general circulation, while some is excreted in the bile, to be reabsorbed later.

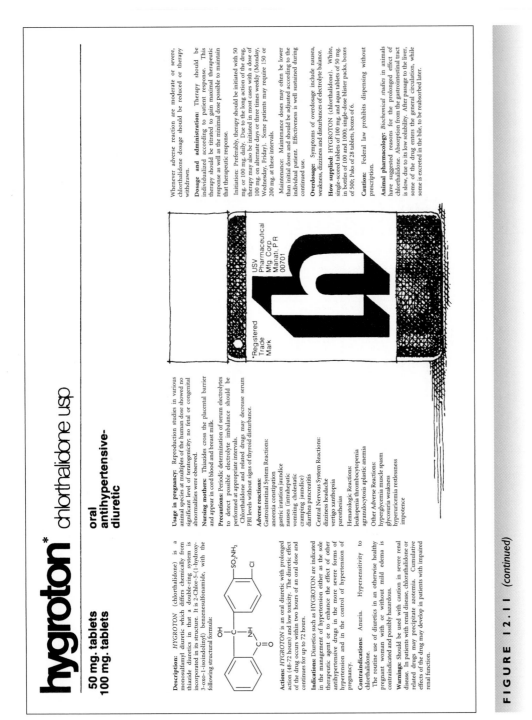

USV
Pharmaceutical
Mfg. Corp.
Manati, P.R.
00701

*Registered
Trade
Mark

FIGURE 12.11 *(continued)*

B

Hygroton®
chlorthalidone USP

50 mg. Tablets 100 mg. Tablets	Oral Antihypertensive-Diuretic	
Description	**Hygroton** (chlorthalidone) is a monosulfamyl diuretic which differs chemically from thiazide diuretics in that a double-ring system is incorporated in its structure. It is 2-Chlor-5-(1-hydroxy-3-oxo-1-isoindolinyl) benzenesulfonamide, with the following structural formula	
Actions	**Hygroton** is an oral diuretic with prolonged action (48-72 hours) and low toxicity. The diuretic effect of the drug occurs within two hours of an oral dose and continues for up to 72 hours	
Indications	Diuretics such as **Hygroton** are indicated in the management of hypertension either as the sole therapeutic agent or to enhance the effect of other	antihypertensive drugs in the more severe forms of hypertension and in the control of hypertension of pregnancy
Contraindications	Anuria. Hypertensivity to chlorthalidone	The routine use of diuretics in an otherwise healthy pregnant woman with or without mild edema is contraindicated and possibly hazardous
Warnings	Should be used with caution in severe renal disease. In patients with renal disease, chlorathalidone or related drugs may precipitate azotemia	Cumulative effects of the drug may develop in patients with impaired renal function
Usage in Pregnancy:	Reproduction studies in various animal species at multiples of the human dose showed no significant level of teratogenicity; no fetal or congential abnormalities were observed	
Nursing Mothers:	Thiazides cross the placental barrier and appear in cord blood and breast milk	
Precautions	Periodic determination of serum selectrolytes to detect possible electrolyte imbalance should be performed at appropriate intervals	Chlorthalidone and related drugs may decrease serum PBI levels without signs of thyroid disturbance
Adverse reactions: Gastrointestinal System Reactions:	anorexia vomiting gastric irritation cramping nausea diarrhea	constipation pancreatitis jaundice (intrahepatic cholestatic jaundice)
Central Nervous System Reactions:	dizziness headache vertigo xanthopsia paresthesias	
Hematologic Reactions:	leukopenia thrombocytopenia agranulocytosis aplastic anemia	
Other Adverse Reactions:	hyperglycemia weakness glycosuria restlessness hyperuricemia impotence muscle spasm	Whenever adverse reaction are moderate or severe, chlorthalidone dosage should be reduced or therapy withdrawn
Dosage and Administration	Therapy should be individualized according to patient response. This therapy should be titrated to gain maximal therapeutic response as well as	the minimal dose possible to maintain that therapeutic response
Initiation:	Preferably, therapy should be initiated with 50 mg. or 100 mg. daily. Due to the long action of the drug, therapy may also be initiated in most cases with a dose of 100 mg. on alternate days or	three times weekly (Monday, Wednesday, Friday). Some patients may require 150 or 200 mg. at these intervals
Maintenance:	Maintenance doses may often be lower than initial doses and should be adjusted according to	the individual patient. Effectiveness is well sustained during continued use
Overdosage	Symptoms of overdosage include nausea, weakness, dizziness and disturbances of electrolyte balance	
How Supplied	**Hygroton** (chlorthalidone). White, single-scored tablets of 100 mg. and aqua tablets of 50 mg in	bottles of 100 and 1000; single-dose blister packs, boxes of 500; Paks of 28 tablets, boxes of 6
Caution:	Federal law prohibits dispensing without prescription	

C

FIGURE 12.11 *(continued)*

Hygroton®
Chlorthalidone USP

50 mg. Tablets
100 mg. Tablets
Oral Antihypertensive-Diuretic

DESCRIPTION
HYGROTON (chlorthalidone) is a monosulfamyl diuretic which differs chemically from thiazide diuretics in that a double-ring system is incorporated in its structure. It is 2-Chlor-5-(1-hydroxy-3-oxo-1-isoindolinyl) benzenesulfonamide, with the following structural formula:

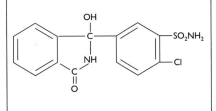

ACTIONS
HYGROTON is an oral diuretic with prolonged action (48-72 hours) and low toxicity. The diuretic effect of the drug occurs within two hours of an oral dose and continues for up to 72 hours.

INDICATIONS
Diuretics such as HYGROTON are indicated in the management of hypertension either as the sole therapeutic agent or to enhance the effect of other antihypertensive drugs in the more severe forms of hypertension and in the control of hypertension of pregnancy.

CONTRAINDICATIONS
Anuria.
Hypertensitivity to chlorthalidone. The routine use of diuretics in an otherwise healthy pregnant woman with or without mild edema is contraindicated and possibly hazardous.

WARNINGS
Should be used with caution in severe renal disease. In patients with renal disease, chlorathalidone or related drugs may precipitate azotemia. Cumulative effects of the drug may develop in patients with impaired renal function.
Usage in Pregnancy: Reproduction studies in various animal species at multiples of the human dose showed no dignificant level of teratogenicity; no fetal or congenital abnormalities were observed.
Nursing Mothers: Thiazides cross the placental barrier and appear in cord blood and breast milk.

PRECAUTIONS
Periodic determination of serum selectrolytes to detect possible electrolyte imbalance should be performed at appropriate intervals.
Chlorthalidone and related drugs may decrease serum PBI levels without signs of thyroid disturbance.

ADVERSE REACTIONS
Gastrointestinal Systems Reactions:
anorexia
gastric irritation
nausea
vomiting
cramping
diarrhea
constipation
jaundice (intrahepatic cholestatic jaundice)
pancreatitis
Central Nervous System Reactions:
dizziness
vertigo
paresthesias
headache
xanthopsia
Hematologic Reactions: leukopenia
agranulocytosis
thrombocytopenia
aplastic anemia

Other Adverse Reactions:
hyperglycemia
glycosuria
hyperuricemia
impotence
muscle spasm
weakness
restlessness
Whenever adverse reaction are moderate or severe, chlorthalidone dosage should be reduced or therapy withdrawn.

DOSAGE AND ADMINISTRATION
Therapy should be individualized according to patient response. This therapy should be titrated to gain maximal therapeutic response as well as the minimal dose possible to maintain that therapeutic response.
Initiation: Preferabley, therapy should be initiated with 50 mg. or 100 mg. daily. Due to the long action of the drug, therapy may also be initiated in most cases with a dose of 100 mg. on alternate days or three times weekly (Monday, Wednesday, Friday). Some patients may require 150 or 200 mg. at these intervals.
Maintenance: Maintenance doses may often be lower than initial doses and should be adjusted according to the individual patient. Effectiveness is well sustained during continued use.

OVERDOSAGE
Symptoms of overdosage include nausea, weakness, dizziness and disturbances of electrolyte balance.

HOW SUPPLIED
HYGROTON (chlorthalidone). White, single-scored tablets of 100 mg. and aqua tablets of 50 mg. in bottles of 100 and 1000; single-dose blister packs, boxes of 500; Paks of 28 tablets, boxes of

CAUTION: Federal law prohibits dispensing without prescription.

ANIMAL PHARMACOLOGY
Biochemical studies in animals have suggested reasons for the prolonged effect of chlorthalidone. Absorption from the gastrointestinal tract is slow, due to its low solubility. After passage to the liver, some of the drug enters the general circulation, while some is excreted in the bile, to be reabsorbed later.

USV PHARMACEUTICAL
MFG. CORP.
Manati, P.R. 00701

D

FIGURE 12.11 (continued)

■ **FIGURE 12.12**

Sample Page for Use with Exercise 4

4) Flatten the clay by pounding it into the table. Remember, work the clay thoroughly!!

4)

Slab Roller

The slab roller is a simple but very efficient mechanical device. A uniform thickness of clay is guaranteed. The ease of its operation saves countless hours of labor over hand rolling techniques.

1) The thickness of the clay is determined by the number of masonite® boards used. There are three $1/4$" boards and one $1/8$" board. They can be used in any combination to reduce or increase the thickness of the clay. If no boards are used, the clay will be 1" thick. If all the boards are used, the clay will be $1/8$" thick. So, for a $1/2$" thickness of clay, use two $1/4$" boards.

1)

2) The canvas cloths must be arranged correctly. They should form a sort of envelope around the wet clay. This prevents any clay from getting on the rollers and masonite® boards.

2)

3) Place the clay flat on the canvas near the rollers. It may be necessary to trim some of the clay since it will spread out as it passes through the rollers.

3)

4.

Evaluating and Revising

CHAPTER 13
Evaluating Drafts

CHAPTER 14
Revising

Evaluating Drafts

GUIDELINES

Guidelines for Checking

1 | Check from your readers' point of view—and your employer's

2 | Distance yourself from your draft

3 | Read your draft more than once, changing your focus each time

4 | Use computer aids to find (but not to cure) possible problems

Guidelines for Reviewing

1 | Discuss the objectives of the communication and the review

2 | Build a positive interpersonal relationship with your reviewers or writer

3 | Rank suggested revisions—and distinguish matters of substance from matters of taste

4 | Explore fully the reasons for all suggestions

Guidelines for User Testing

1	Pick test readers who truly represent your target readers
2	Ask your test readers to use your draft in the same ways your target readers will use it
3	Learn how your draft affects your test readers' attitudes
4	Interview your test readers after they've used your draft
5	Test early and often, when appropriate

CHAPTER

13

DEFINING
OBJECTIVES

PLANNING

DRAFTING

EVALUATING

REVISING

This chapter looks at the fourth major activity of writing: evaluating. When you evaluate something you are writing, you step back from your creative work at designing and drafting your message to determine how well it is likely to succeed at achieving its objectives. You can then use the results of your evaluation to revise your draft, which is the fifth writing activity.

OVERVIEW OF EVALUATION

Goals of evaluation: detect potential problems and discover ways to improve

At work, almost everyone evaluates almost everything they write. Often writers undertake these evaluations on their own initiative, realizing that they usually cannot produce a perfectly effective communication on the very first try. At other times, evaluation is required by the employer. In either case, the goals are the same: to detect potential problems and discover ways to improve.

The time and effort spent on evaluation vary from situation to situation.

In pursuit of these objectives, some communications receive a much more rigorous evaluation than others. Proposals, letters to clients, and manuals often go through many cycles of evaluation and revision that may last weeks. In contrast, internal memos and brief progress reports often receive only a quick going-over. The amount of time and effort invested depends on such considerations as the communication's objectives, the employer's standards for writing quality, and the severity of the consequences if problems slip through.

This chapter presents guidelines for the three most common evaluation methods.

> ### Evaluation Methods
>
> - **Checking**
>   Carefully examine your draft yourself.
> - **Reviewing**
>   Ask for advice about your draft from people who are *not* members of your target audience.
> - **User Testing**
>   Ask members of the target audience to use your draft so that you can determine how well it works.

CHECKING

The first thing to know about checking is that it is very difficult to recognize problems in your own writing. Consider Diane's situation.

Even though Diane proofread carefully, she missed an error.

> Diane is experiencing one of the most excruciating of all feelings. Ten minutes ago, she mailed an important report to a client. Now, as she puts a photocopy of it into her file, her eye catches an obvious error. How could she have missed it? She read and reread that report before mailing it, looking diligently for errors. And yet she let this one get past her.

Diane's experience is one we all have shared. Although we get plenty of practice checking our own writing at both school and work, errors still get by us. Why? Some clearly identifiable obstacles hinder our checking. The following guidelines identify those obstacles and help you overcome them.

GUIDELINE 1   Check from Your Readers' Point of View—And Your Employer's

One obstacle to effective checking is that writers tend to define the purpose of their checking too narrowly. They concentrate on spelling, punctuation, and grammar, forgetting to examine the effect a draft will have on their readers and their employer.

Take Your Readers' Point of View
The reason for examining your drafts from your readers' point of view is obvious: the ultimate test of your communication is whether it affects your readers in the way you defined when you established its objectives.

Review the enabling and persuasive elements of your communication's purpose.

Consequently, the first step in checking a draft is to refer to these objectives. If you wrote them down, pull out your notes. If you recorded them mentally, review them now. What tasks do you want your communication to help your readers perform? How do you want it to alter their attitudes?

Then, with your objectives fresh in mind, read your draft, trying to imagine your readers' moment-by-moment responses. If you've drafted a proposal, imagine the questions or objections your readers might raise. If you've drafted a set of instructions, try to follow them yourself. In every way you can, read as your readers will read.

Take Your Employer's Point of View

Also read your draft from your employer's point of view. Be sure to consider each of the following employer concerns:

Things to consider when evaluating from your employer's perspective

- **Impact on the organization**. Ask yourself which people and departments will be affected by the facts you provide and the recommendations you make. How will these individuals and groups respond to what you say? By anticipating conflicts and objections that your communication might stir up, you may be able to reduce their severity or avoid them altogether.
- **Commitments**. In many communications, you will make commitments on behalf of your department or employer. When writing a proposal to a client, you promise that your employer will provide certain goods or services. When you move to a managerial position, you may write policies that promise that the organization will take certain actions. As you check your draft, determine whether it makes any commitments. If so, ask whether you have the authority to do so, whether the commitment is in the best interest of your employer, and whether it is a commitment that your employer wishes to make.
- **Compliance**. Determine whether your draft complies with organizational policies governing communications. Be especially careful when working on a project that your employer considers to be sensitive. For example, for legal reasons your employer may want to restrict when and how you reveal information about a certain aspect of your work. This might happen, for instance, if you are working on a patentable project or a project regulated by a government body, such as a state or federal Environmental Protection Agency. Whatever the reason for your employer's policies, assure that your draft complies with them.

Also, be sure to check your draft against whatever regulations your employer has about writing style and format.

Distance Yourself from Your Draft

When we check, we often see what we intended, not what actually appears.

A second obstacle to effective checking is that we are too "close" to what we write. Because we know what we meant to say, when we check for errors we often see what we *meant* to write rather than what is actually there. A word is misspelled, but we see it spelled correctly. A paragraph is cloudy, but we see just the meaning we intended.

To distance yourself from your draft, try the following measures:

Ways to distance yourself from your draft

- **Let time pass.** As time passes, your memory of what you intended fades, and you become better able to see what you actually wrote. Set your draft aside, if for only a few minutes, before checking it. For longer, more complex communications, hours and days are better.

Evaluating from an Ethical Perspective

Whether you evaluate your draft by means of checking, testing, or reviewing, be sure to assess not only its effectiveness but also its potential impact on stakeholders.

Checking

If you have practiced continuous stakeholder involvement (see page 70), you will already have looked at your communication from the stakeholders' point of view. Early in your work on your communication, you will have identified its stakeholders and learned about the impact your message might have on them. Then, while drafting, you will have kept your stakeholders constantly in mind.

However, there are so many things to think about when writing that there's a chance you may have overlooked your stakeholders' concerns in some way. Therefore, when checking your draft, review your knowledge of your stake-holders and look one last time at your communication from their perspective.

Testing

The best way to determine whether you have adequately addressed your stakeholders' concerns is to ask them. Consequently, you should consider including stakeholders in the group of people with whom you share your draft when testing it.

Reviewing

When you review a draft written by someone else, ask the same questions you would ask when planning your own writing: Who will be affected? How? Should the stakeholders be consulted directly about the decisions and actions discussed in this communication? Can potential negative impacts on the stakeholders be reduced or eliminated? Is it ethical to do this at all?

Similarly, when something you've written is being reviewed, tell your reviewer who your communication's stakeholders are and how you think they might be affected by your communication.

Ethical problems can be difficult for writers and reviewers to discuss. None of us likes to be accused of acting unethically, so a writer may quickly become defensive. Furthermore, the writer and reviewer may hold quite different ethical principles. Consequently, whether you are the writer or the reviewer, you may find it helpful to refer to the ethical code of your employer or profession, rather than insist on your own ethical views. But remember that despite the difficulties of doing so, you have an obligation to raise ethical questions even if you have not been asked to do so.

■ **Read your draft aloud.** You can also distance yourself from your draft by reading it aloud, even if there is no one to listen. When you speak your words, you process them mentally in a somewhat different way than when you read them silently to yourself. You *hear* your words as well as see them. This small shift may seem trivial, but it can help you detect problems you might otherwise have overlooked. Where you stumble over your own words, your readers are likely to stumble, too. Reading aloud will also help you determine whether you have established an effective voice (see Chapter 10). There is no better way to find out how your voice will "sound" to your audience than to hear it read aloud.

GUIDELINE ③   Read Your Draft More Than Once, Changing Your Focus Each Time

Yet another obstacle to effective checking is summed up in the adage, "You can't do two things at once." To "do" something, according to researchers who study the way humans think, requires "attention." Some activities (like walking) require much less attention than others (like solving algebra problems). We *can* attend to several more-or-less automatic activities at once. However, when we are engaged in any activity that requires us to concentrate, we have difficulty doing anything else well at the same time (Anderson).

This limitation has important consequences. When you check a draft, you must concentrate on different things: spelling, the consistency of your headings, the clarity of your prose, and so on. When you concentrate on one aspect, you diminish your ability to concentrate on the others.

Read separately for substantive and mechanical matters.

You can overcome this limitation by reading through your draft at least twice, once for substantive matters (like clarity and persuasive impact) and once for mechanical ones (like correct punctuation and grammar). If you have time, you might read through it more than twice, sharpening the focus of each reading.

Double-check everything you are uncertain about.

Finally, be sure to double-check everything you are uncertain about. When you pause to ask yourself: "Is that word spelled correctly?" "Is that number accurate?" "Is that precisely what the lab technician told me?" you may cringe at the thought of getting out your dictionary, looking back through your calculations, or calling up the technician. You may be tempted to say, "Yeah, sure that's right. No need to double-check." Ignore that temptation. Trust the instinct that made you hesitate in the first place.

GUIDELINE ④   Use Computer Aids to Find (But Not to Cure) Possible Problems

Most word-processing programs offer a variety of aids that can be helpful when checking a draft—if you use them carefully:

- **Spell checkers.** Spell checkers identify possible misspellings by looking for words in your draft that aren't in their dictionaries. Consequently, they may also flag many correctly spelled words, such as proper names and technical terms not in ordinary usage.
- **Grammar checkers.** Grammar checkers identify sentences that might have any of a wide variety of problems with grammar or punctuation. For example, they highlight sentences that might be missing a period or that include an error in subject-verb agreement. Typically, grammar checkers also highlight sentences that the computer thinks (perhaps incorrectly) may be in the passive voice, and they indicate possible problems with word choice. See Figure 13.1.
- **Style checkers.** Some computer programs analyze various aspects of your writing that are related to style, such as the average paragraph, sentence, and word length. Using special formulas, they also compute scores that attempt to reflect the "readability" of a draft. See Figure 13.2.

■ FIGURE 13.1

Grammar Checker

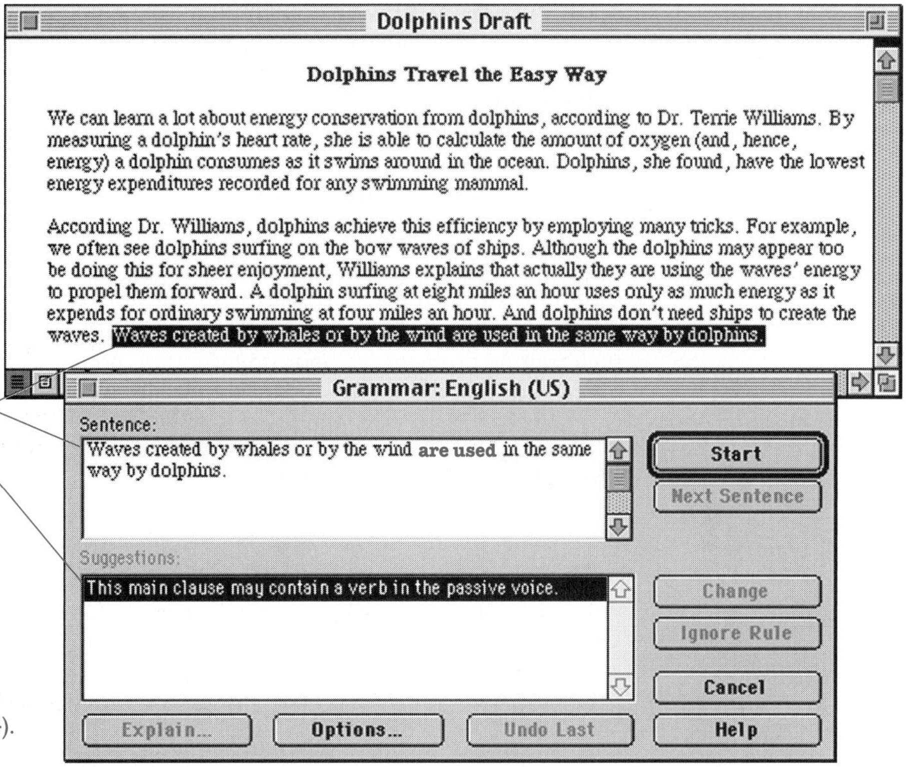

A grammar checker looks for sentences that seem to violate a set of rules it has been given.

If it finds one, it does the following:

- Highlights the sentence

- Explains the problem it may have found

Usually, grammar checkers look for misspellings also; note that it missed the use of the wrong "too" in the second line of the second paragraph (see the discussion of spell checkers on page 364).

■ FIGURE 13.2

Style Checker

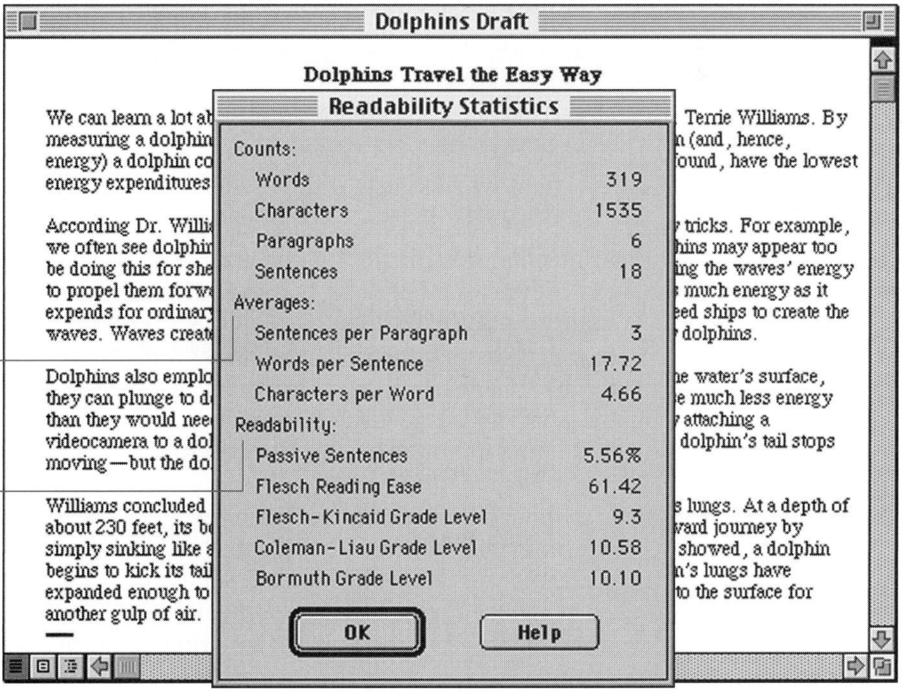

Style checkers provide statistics that are intended to help writers determine how difficult their prose is to read.

Typically, they calculate the average lengths of the paragraphs, sentences, and words.

They also employ these statistics to estimate the "readability" of the passage (usually expressed as "grade level").

The "Help" button provides explanations of the results.

After using a spell, grammar, or style checker, read over your draft carefully yourself.

All three types of aids can be helpful, if used with caution. They bring to your attention problems and even suggest possible solutions. But all three also have serious shortcomings. They just don't "know" enough. For example, spell checkers ignore words that are misspelled but look like other words, such as *forward* for *foreword* or *take* for *rake*—a shortcoming that can have serious consequences if you don't also perform your own careful proofreading. Similarly, grammar checkers can't tell whether you are using the word *fly* as a noun (the insect) or a verb (the way birds travel), nor can they distinguish a good use of the passive voice from a poor one. And style checkers can't tell a clearly written long sentence from a murky short one. Nor can they distinguish an easy long word, such as *excitement*, from a difficult short one, such as *erg*. Moreover, readability indexes don't even consider such writing problems as poor organization, poor use of topic sentences, or poor use of headings. These and similar limitations of on-line aids to checking mean that you must use them with great care. Don't accept any of their suggestions without careful review, and always read over your drafts carefully yourself.

REVIEWING

Reviewers may consider any aspects of a communication.

In reviewing, a writer gives his or her draft to one or more other people, who respond by suggesting revisions. Reviewers may include the manager and other members of the writer's own department, as well as many other individuals such as lawyers, public relations specialists, and upper-level executives. Different reviewers may be asked to focus on different things, according to their specialty, so that scientists or engineers perform a technical review, lawyers a legal review, and so on.

In the workplace, reviewers play either of two roles:

- **Coach.** As coaches, reviewers *suggest* improvements that the writer is free to accept or ignore.
- **Gatekeeper.** Gatekeepers possess the authority to require that the writer make the revisions they specify. When writers disagree with a gatekeeper, they can sometimes negotiate, but often they must simply accept the gatekeeper's judgment.

Reviewing can be quite extensive or quite quick.

As mentioned earlier in this chapter, some communications go through many cycles of review and revision that may take weeks or months. Lengthy review cycles sometimes result not from weak writing but from disagreements about what the communication should say and how it should say it. Alecia Swasy, a former reporter for the *Wall Street Journal*, describes a document written at Procter & Gamble that was reviewed and revised 460 times over six months before the reviewers approved it. Routine communications, however, are usually reviewed only one time by only one person.

On-line tools for reviewing

Although people continue to do much reviewing on paper copies of drafts, online tools are finding increasing use. Often, drafts are sent as e-mail enclosures, and comments are returned by e-mail. Some word processing programs allow reviewers to highlight certain words or sentences, open a special window, and enter a comment addressed to the writer. The writer can then click on the passage, which is

■ **FIGURE 13.3**

Reviewer's Comments Attached to a Draft

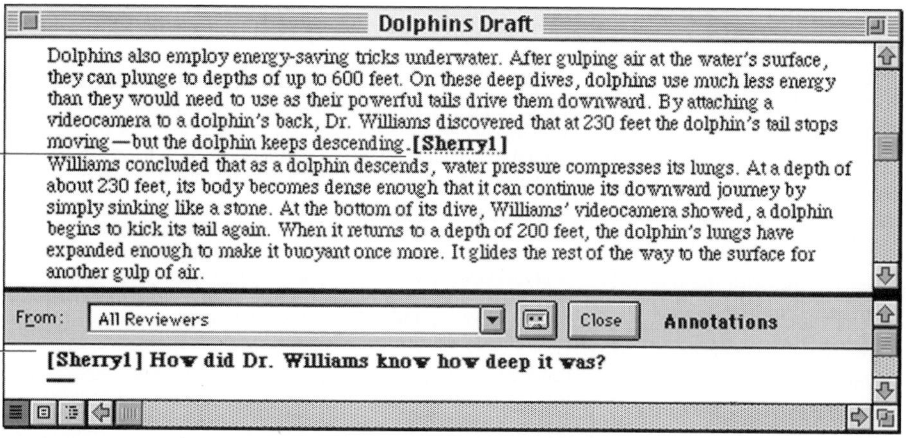

An annotation feature allows reviewers to place markers at spots where they wish to make comments for the writer.

They type the comments into a separate window.

```
[□]                        Dolphins Draft                              [■]
  Dolphins also employ energy-saving tricks underwater. After gulping air at the water's surface,
  they can plunge to depths of up to 600 feet. On these deep dives, dolphins use much less energy
  than they would need to use as their powerful tails drive them downward. By attaching a
  videocamera to a dolphin's back, Dr. Williams discovered that at 230 feet the dolphin's tail stops
  moving—but the dolphin keeps descending.[Sherry1]
  Williams concluded that as a dolphin descends, water pressure compresses its lungs. At a depth of
  about 230 feet, its body becomes dense enough that it can continue its downward journey by
  simply sinking like a stone. At the bottom of its dive, Williams' videocamera showed, a dolphin
  begins to kick its tail again. When it returns to a depth of 200 feet, the dolphin's lungs have
  expanded enough to make it buoyant once more. It glides the rest of the way to the surface for
  another gulp of air.

From:  [ All Reviewers                        ▼] [□] [ Close ]   Annotations
       [Sherry1] How did Dr. Williams know how deep it was?
       —
```

Each reviewer's name is placed by his or her comment.

By clicking on a marker in the text, the writer calls up the reviewer's comment.

The text can be viewed and printed with or without the markers and comments.

marked in color, to read the comment, as shown in Figure 13.3. Reviewers can also make changes directly in the electronic file of the writer's draft. To identify the changes that the reviewers have made, a writer uses a feature of his or her desktop publishing program that highlights all additions and deletions. See Figure 13.4.

The four guidelines that follow will help you obtain good advice from your reviewers, and they will aid you in giving good advice when you review the writing of others.

GUIDELINE ❶ **Discuss the Objectives of the Communication and the Review**

When you are the reviewer, begin by asking about the communication's objectives. You will need to possess very specific knowledge of the communication's audience and aims in order to judge whether it will achieve its purpose and to suggest revisions that will improve its likelihood of success.

Also discuss the scope and focus of the review. As a reviewer, you might comment on many aspects of a communication: organization, selection of material, accuracy, tone, spelling, page design, and so on. The writer may have a good sense of areas that most need attention. Although you should not necessarily restrict your attention to these areas, you may be able to save yourself considerable time if you know what they are. Similarly, if you are a gatekeeper, let the writer know the breadth of issues you will examine.

When you are the writer, and your reviewer doesn't ask about the communication's objectives or about your desires for the review, convey this information anyway. By doing so, you assure that the reviewer possesses the knowledge required to give you the best possible assistance.

■ **FIGURE 13.4**

Automatic Comparison of Drafts

To see what changes reviewers have made, a writer can compare the original draft with the one revised by the reviewers.

The computer identifies deletions and additions in a format chosen by the writer.

To help the writer find changes, the computer places markers next to all lines where changes occur.

Writers can also use this feature to compare their own drafts.

Dolphins Compare

Dolphins Travel the Easy Way

We can learn a lot about energy conservation from dolphins, according to Dr. Terrie Williams. By measuring a dolphin's heart rate, she is able to calculate the amount of oxygen (and, hence, energy) a dolphin consumes as it swims around in the ocean. Dolphins, she found, have the lowest energy expenditures recorded for any swimming mammal.

According Dr. Williams, dolphins achieve this efficiency by employing many tricks. For example, we often see dolphins surfing on the bow waves of ships. Although the dolphins may appear too be doing this for sheer enjoyment, Williams explains that actually they are using the waves' energy to propel them forward. A dolphin surfing at eight miles an hour uses only as much energy as it expends for ordinary swimming at four miles an hour. And dolphins don't need ships to create the waves. Waves created by whales or by the wind are used in the same way by dolphins **provide the same opportunity to hitch a ride.**

Dolphins also employ energy-saving tricks underwater. After gulping air at the water's surface, they can plunge to depths of up to 600 feet. On these deep dives, dolphins use much less energy than they would need to use as their powerful tails drive them downward. By attaching a videocamera and depth gage to a dolphin's back, Dr. Williams discovered that at 230 feet the dolphin's tail stops moving — but the dolphin keeps descending.

Williams concluded that as a dolphin descends, water pressure compresses its lungs. At a depth of about 230 feet, its body becomes dense enough that it can continue its downward journey by simply sinking like a stone. At the bottom of its dive, Williams' videocamera showed, a dolphin begins to kick its tail again. When it returns to a depth of 200 feet, the dolphin's lungs have expanded enough to make it buoyant once more. It glides the rest of the way to the surface—— **again using very little energy** —for another gulp of air.

GUIDELINE ❷ **Build a Positive Interpersonal Relationship with Your Reviewers or Writer**

Emotions are an important element in reviewing.

The relationship between writers and their reviewers is not only intellectual but also interpersonal and emotional. The quality of this human relationship can greatly affect the outcome of the review process. When writers feel criticized and judged rather than helped and supported, they become defensive and closed to suggestions. When reviewers feel that their suggestions are rebuffed rather than welcomed, they cease giving the advice the writer needs to hear. The following sections describe specific things you can do to build positive, productive relationships with your reviewers and writers.

When You Are the Writer

Ways to encourage your reviewers to help as much as they can

As a writer, interact with your reviewers in ways that encourage them to be thoughtful, supportive, and generous. Even when they are acting as gatekeepers, reviewers will be more helpful if they believe you will welcome their comments. Throughout your discussions with them, project a positive attitude, treating your reviewers as people who are on your side, not as obstacles to the completion of your work. Begin meetings by thanking them for their efforts. Paraphrase their comments to show that you are listening attentively and express gratitude for their suggestions.

When your reviewers offer comments, stifle any temptation to react defensively, for instance, by explaining why your original is better than a suggested revision. Even if you *know* a particular suggestion is wrong-headed, listen to it without argument. On the other hand, don't avoid entering into a dialogue with your reviewers. When they misunderstand what you are trying to accomplish, explain your aims. But do so in a way that indicates you are still open to suggestions. If your reviewers misunderstood what you were attempting, it's likely that you would benefit from some advice.

When You Are a Reviewer

When you are acting as a reviewer, there are some specific actions you can take to build a good relationship with the writer:

Ways to encourage openness to your suggestions

- **Begin with praise.** By doing so, you show the writer that you recognize the good things he or she has done and indicate your sensitivity to that person's feelings. In addition, some writers don't know their own strengths any better than they know their weaknesses. By praising what they have done well, you encourage them to continue doing it and you reduce the chance that they will weaken a strong segment of their communication by revising it.
- **Focus your suggestions on goals, not shortcomings.** For example, instead of saying, "I think you have a problem in the third paragraph," say "I have a suggestion about how you can make your third paragraph more understandable or persuasive to your readers."
- **Use positive examples from the writer's own draft to explain suggestions.** For example, if the writer includes a topic sentence in one paragraph but omits the topic sentence in another, you might cite the first paragraph as an example of a way to improve the second. By doing this, you indicate that you know the writer understands the principle but has slipped this one time in applying it.
- **Project a positive attitude toward the writer.** Even when acting as a gate-keeper, think of the writer as a person you want to help, not judge. If the writer feels you are taking a judgmental approach, he or she will almost surely become resentful and resist making the revisions you suggest.

GUIDELINE 3   Rank Suggested Revisions—And Distinguish Matters of Substance from Matters of Taste

By ranking your suggestions, you help both the writer and yourself work effectively.

One of the most helpful things you can do for writers is to rank your suggested revisions. By doing so, you help them decide which revisions will bring the greatest improvement in the least amount of time.

Also, many writers can face only a limited number of suggestions before feeling overwhelmed and defeated. As a reviewer, therefore, you should look over your list of suggestions to see which ones will make the greatest difference. Convey those to the writer. As for the rest, keep them to yourself or make it clear that they are less important than the others.

Ranking also helps you work productively. Often, you will not have time to review an entire draft in detail. Begin by scanning through the draft to identify the issues that most need attention, then focus your effort on them.

Distinguish matters of substance from matters of taste.

When ranking suggestions, distinguish those based on substantial principles of writing from those based on your personal taste. If, as a reviewer, you suggest changes that would merely replace the writer's preferred way of saying something with your own preferred way, you will be doing nothing to improve the writing—and you will almost certainly spark the writer's resentment. Unfortunately, it can often be difficult to determine whether we like a certain way of saying something because it is good in itself or because it matches our own style. When faced with that uncertainty, try to formulate a *reason* for the change. If all you can say is, "My way sounds better," you are probably dealing with a matter of taste. On the other hand, if you can offer a more objective reason—for instance, a reason based on one of the guidelines in this book—you are dealing with a matter of substance.

One caution, however. Sometimes your sense that something doesn't sound right is your first clue that there is a problem. For example, you may stumble over a sentence that doesn't sound right and discover, after closer examination, that it contains a grammatical error. It is important to follow up your instincts about how something sounds to see whether you can find an objective reason for your dissatisfaction. If so, tell the writer. If not, let the matter drop.

So far, the discussion of this guideline has focused on the reviewers' perspective. When you are the writer, you can be helped greatly by your reviewers' rankings of their suggestions. If your reviewers don't volunteer a ranking, request one.

GUIDELINE 4 **Explore Fully the Reasons for All Suggestions**

Explanations can be more valuable than the suggestions themselves.

The more fully writers and reviewers explore the *reasons* for the reviewers' suggested revisions, the more helpful the review will be. In fact, sometimes reviewers' explanations can be more valuable than the suggestions themselves. Perhaps their explanations will stimulate you to think of an even better way of solving the problem they have identified. Or they may help you recognize and avoid that problem in the future. Even when a particular suggestion seems useless to you, try to find out why the reviewers thought it was needed. Then devise your own solution to the problem that prompted them to make the suggestion in the first place.

When you are acting as a reviewer, it's also in your interest to provide a full explanation of your suggestions. If you don't explain the reasons for your suggestions, the writer may think that you are simply expressing a personal preference. As a result, the writer may dismiss your suggestions, leaving the draft weaker than it might otherwise have been.

Full explanations also help the writer learn to write better. For example, imagine that you suggest rephrasing a sentence so that the old information is at the beginning and the new information is at the end (see Chapter 10). The writer may agree that your version is better but not know the reason why, unless you explain the *principle* that you applied.

Some reviewers withhold such explanations because they think the reasons are obvious. However, reasons that are obvious to the reviewer are not necessarily obvious to the writer. Otherwise, the writer would have avoided the problem in the first place.

Phrase your suggestions from the intended readers' viewpoint.

Whenever possible, phrase your suggestions from the perspective of the intended readers. Instead of saying, "I think you should say it like this," say "I think your intended readers will be able to understand your point more clearly if you phrase it like this." Such a strategy will help the writer take a reader-centered approach to revising the draft. It will also help you present yourself not as a judge of the writer's writing, but as a person who wants to help the writer achieve his or her communication objectives.

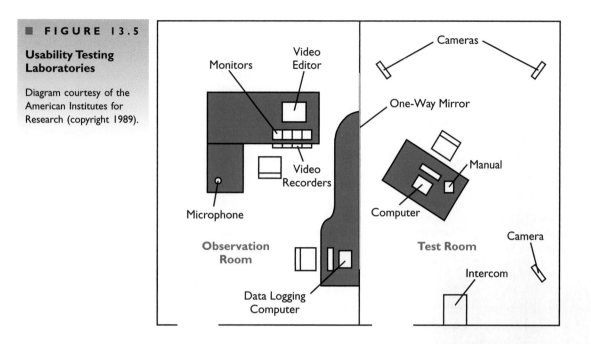

■ **FIGURE 13.5**

Usability Testing Laboratories

Diagram courtesy of the American Institutes for Research (copyright 1989).

USER TESTING

With testing—the third type of evaluation—you "try out" your plans and drafts by showing them to members of your target audience, whom you invite to share their reactions, requests, and suggestions.

Tests take many forms. In one type, you simply show an outline or draft to members of your target audience, asking each person to tell you what he or she thinks of it. You can also use questionnaires or a series of preplanned questions, or you can organize a focus group, in which you ask several people to meet to discuss an outline or draft. The remainder of this chapter explains how to design and conduct an especially valuable kind of test, called a *user test*.

USER TESTS

In a user test, you ask one or more people, called *test readers*, to read and use a draft of your communication in the way that your intended readers will read and use the finished document. Then, by means of various techniques, you gather information from your test readers that will serve as a basis for predicting reader response. If your test is well-constructed, where your test readers have problems, your intended audience probably will, too. Where things worked well for your test readers, they will probably work well for your audience.

User tests are becoming increasingly well known in industry. Some companies, such as IBM and Microsoft, even employ testing specialists who work in laboratories specifically designed for user testing. As shown in Figure 13.5, such laboratories are often equipped with video cameras and two-way mirrors that enable writers and testing specialists to monitor the readers' attempts to use the draft of a communication. However, you can learn a great deal of valuable information from user tests conducted without such elaborate equipment and facilities.

User tests can provide insights that other evaluation methods, such as checking and reviewing, cannot. That's because these other evaluation methods rely on *guesswork*—knowledgeable guesswork in many cases, but guesswork just the same. Consider, for example, Imogen's project.

When checking and reviewing, writers and reviewers can only guess at how the target readers will respond.

Imogen drafted a set of instructions that tell ordinary consumers how to install a car radio and CD player manufactured by her employer. Imogen then carefully checked her instructions herself, trying to view them from the standpoint of her intended readers. The best Imogen could do was guess whether the instructions would work for these consumers. The same is true for the people who reviewed her instructions: her boss and two engineers. They guessed, too.

A major limitation on the accuracy of their guesses is that Imogen and her reviewers already know how to install the equipment. Consequently, they know the meaning of directions that people without their expertise could find unclear, and they know how to perform certain steps even if the directions don't explain the steps precisely enough for less knowledgeable people to understand.

By asking members of her target audience to actually *use* the instructions to install the radio and CD player, Imogen can *see* how well her instructions will work—for at least a few of her intended readers. The insights she gains can be invaluable as she revises.

THE TWO MAJOR QUESTIONS YOU CAN ANSWER THROUGH USER TESTING

What, exactly, will Imogen try to learn from her user test? The key questions for almost all user tests are the same:

- "Is my communication good enough to send to my intended readers?"
- "How can I improve my communication?"

Is My Communication Good Enough?

One way to determine if your communication is good enough is to see if it meets some predetermined standard. For instance, Imogen decided that her instructions would be satisfactory if a typical reader could use them to install the radio and CD player within two hours. When communications are intended to teach, minimum test scores are often expressed in terms of the percentage of correct answers. Thus, a person who wrote a description of the electromagnetic fields surrounding the earth might say that the description was satisfactory if readers could answer correctly at least 75 percent of the questions on a test based on it. (Remember that the tests described in this chapter evaluate the communication, not its readers—a point you should emphasize to your test readers.)

To interpret the results, you will need to use good judgment and common sense. Suppose, for instance, that Imogen found that her readers took three hours, rather than two, to install the radio and CD player. If she observed that her readers worked steadily without having any trouble following her instructions, she might conclude that three hours were needed because the task was difficult, not because the instructions were written poorly. On the other hand, if she observed that the readers stumbled through the procedure because they had trouble understanding and using the instructions, she might conclude that her instructions were at fault.

How Can I Improve My Communication?

Naturally, if a user test shows that a draft is deficient in some way, the writer wants to know how to fix it. Moreover, writers often want to improve their communications even when a test shows that a draft is ready to be distributed. Accordingly, user tests are usually constructed not only to determine whether a draft is "good enough," but also to generate ideas for improvements even if it is.

GUIDELINE **1**   **Pick Test Readers Who Truly Represent Your Target Readers**

To construct a test that will accurately predict how your target readers will respond to your finished communication, you must pick test readers who truly represent this audience. If you are writing for plumbers, pick plumbers. If you are writing for adults who suffer from asthma, pick adult asthma sufferers. If you revise based on the responses of people who are not from your target audience, you may actually make your communication *less* effective for your intended readers.

When it's impossible to pick readers from your target audience, search for people who are as similar as possible to that audience. In your class, for instance, you may be writing a report to engineers who design robots. If you can't enlist such engineers as your test readers, you might use engineering seniors who have had coursework in robotics.

Even a single test reader can provide valuable insights.

How many test readers are enough? That depends on several factors. Generally, there is little variation from reader to reader in tests in which you ask people to follow step-by-step instructions. Two or three members of your target audience may be enough. But when you are testing people's understanding of the ideas or arguments presented in a longer communication, more variation among readers is likely to exist. Common practice, based on practical experience, suggests that about a dozen readers is a good number for such tests. However, don't let the fact that you can use only a few test readers stop you from testing. Testing with one reader is infinitely better than not testing at all, as you could readily see by conducting a user test for a set of instructions or other communication you are creating in your writing class.

GUIDELINE **2**   **Ask Your Test Readers to Use Your Draft in the Same Ways Your Target Readers Will Use It**

At work, user tests usually focus on the readers' efforts to carry out one or more of the following tasks:

- **Perform a procedure,** as when reading instructions.
- **Understand content,** trying to learn about something through reading.
- **Locate information,** as when looking for a certain fact in a reference manual.

For some communications, all three tasks are important. For example, the owner's manuals for some personal computers open with a section describing how computers work (the readers' chief task is to *understand*), proceed to step-by-step instructions (the readers' chief task is to *perform* a procedure), and conclude with a reference section (where the readers must *locate* the particular pieces of information they need).

You should test your communication's effectiveness at enabling your readers to perform each task it is intended to support. The following sections explain how to construct performance, understandability, and location tests.

Performance Tests

To test a communication's effectiveness at enabling readers to perform a procedure, give the communication to a few test readers and watch them use it. Performance tests produce the most useful results when they are designed in the following ways.

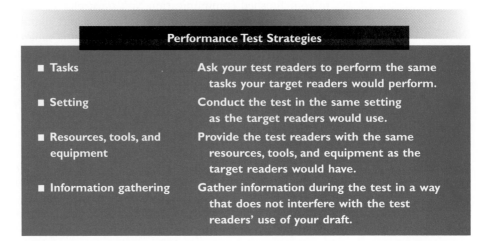

Performance Test Strategies

■ **Tasks**	Ask your test readers to perform the same tasks your target readers would perform.
■ **Setting**	Conduct the test in the same setting as the target readers would use.
■ **Resources, tools, and equipment**	Provide the test readers with the same resources, tools, and equipment as the target readers would have.
■ **Information gathering**	Gather information during the test in a way that does not interfere with the test readers' use of your draft.

To see how you might apply these strategies, consider the way Imogen tested her instructions for installing the car radio and CD player.

Imogen picked test users from her target audience.

She asked them to work in the same settings her target readers would use.

Imogen recruited two friends, Rob and Janice, as her test readers. Both owned cars, and neither had made a similar installation before, so they accurately represented her audience.

Imogen asked Rob and Janice to work alone because she imagined that most purchasers would do so. Rob installed the equipment in his garage at home, and Janice worked in the parking lot of her apartment building, typical of the work areas for

Imogen's target readers. Rob already had all the necessary tools, and Imogen supplied Janice with a phillips head screwdriver.

While Rob and Janice worked, Imogen observed; however, she was careful to stay completely out of their way. She took detailed notes throughout. Several times, Rob asked Imogen questions. Instead of answering, Imogen urged him to do his best without her help. If she had begun to provide oral instructions, she would no longer have been testing her written ones.

Imogen did assist both Rob and Janice at one point when it became clear that they could not understand the instructions at all. Without this help, they would have had to stop work, and Imogen couldn't have found out how well the rest of her instructions worked.

She observed their performance and gathered information without interfering or providing help.

She assisted only when the test would otherwise have had to stop.

So that she could later use her observational notes as efficiently as possible, Imogen recorded them on the form shown in Figure 13.6. In the left-hand column, she wrote down anything that Rob or Janice did that seemed to indicate that they were having difficulty. Later, she filled in the middle column with her estimate of the problem's cause. In the right-hand column she formulated possible solutions to the difficulties Rob and Janice experienced.

People conducting user tests also employ other techniques for gathering information, including the following:

- Asking readers to mark every place in the draft that seemed particularly good or caused them a problem (you would talk with them about the marks afterwards).
- Asking readers to speak their thoughts aloud as they work, so you can know what they are thinking at each moment.
- Videotaping.
- Interviewing test readers after the test (see Guideline 4).

Adjusting Performance Tests to Circumstances   Sometimes it may be impossible for you to ask test readers to use your communication in exactly the way that your target readers will.

Imogen couldn't reproduce actual problems.

She created a simulation that enabled her test readers to use her instructions in a realistic way.

Imogen's instructions included a troubleshooting section designed to enable consumers to repair some problems with their radios and CD players on their own. Ideally, Imogen would test this section by presenting test readers with several faulty radios and CD players, asking the readers to use her troubleshooting section to diagnose and repair the problems.

However, her employer was unwilling to spend time and money to provide such equipment. Therefore, Imogen prepared *written descriptions* of malfunctions and asked her test readers to use her troubleshooting section to diagnose the cause and describe the repair they would make.

■ **FIGURE 13.6** User Test Observation Sheet

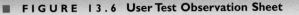

Observation Sheet for User Tests		
Problem (What difficulty did the reader have?)	**Interpretation** (What might have caused the difficulty?)	**Solution** (What might prevent this difficulty?)
After completing a step, Rob sometimes hunted around the page for his place.	1. The steps don't stand out plainly enough.	1. Enlarge the step numbers. 2. Print the steps in bold so they are easier to distinguish from the notes and cautions.
At Step 7, Rob couldn't find the hole for the mounting bracket.	1. Rob couldn't understand the figure.	1. Simplify the figure by eliminating unnecessary details.

After the test, you can ask the test reader to tell you what caused the problems you observed.

At work, circumstances may require you to adjust your test procedures in similar, creative ways.

Understandability Tests
In understandability tests, you ask members of your target audience to read your draft and then ask them questions designed to determine whether they have understood it accurately.

Norman is drafting a communication for which understandability is a major issue.

Norman has been assigned by his employer, an insurance company, to write a new, more comprehensible version of its automobile insurance policies. Before the company begins using Norman's version, however, the company wants to test it. Norman has placed an ad in the local newspaper and has arranged to have two dozen people read a draft and answer questions about it.

The following sections describe three kinds of tasks you can ask test readers to perform when you want to assess a communication's understandability. The sample questions all refer to the following paragraph from the insurance policy Norman drafted.

A passage Norman tested

> In return for your insurance payments, we will pay damages for bodily injuries or property loss for which you or any other person covered by this policy becomes legally responsible because of an automobile accident. If we think it appropriate, we may defend you in court at our expense against a claim for damages rather than pay the person making the claim. Our duty to pay or defend ends when we have given the person making a claim against you the full amount of money for which this policy insures you.

Ways to test
understandability

- **Ask your test readers to recognize a correct paraphrase.** By testing your readers' ability to recognize a paraphrase of your communication, you determine whether they have understood your communication well enough to recognize the same meaning expressed in different words. Avoid quoting directly because readers may recognize quotations through an act of memory without understanding its meaning. You may use either true-false or multiple-choice questions.

Sample questions

> **True or False:**
> We will defend you in court against a claim when we feel that is the best thing to do.
>
> When will we defend you in court? (A) When you ask us to. (B) When the claim against you exceeds $20,000. (C) When we think that is the best thing to do.

- **Ask your test readers to create a correct paraphrase.** By asking your test readers to paraphrase your communication, you can find out whether they understand it well enough to explain it in their own words. Here is a sample question:

Request for a paraphrase

> In your own words, tell when we will defend you in court.

  Presumably, if your readers provide a correct paraphrase, your communication is understandable; if they don't, it isn't. However, you must judge whether an unclear paraphrase is the result of faulty writing on your part or the result of the test readers' lack of skill at explaining things.

- **Ask your test readers to apply your information.** To test your readers' ability to apply information, you need to create a fictional situation in which the information can be used. Here is the situation Norman devised to test his readers' ability to understand one section of his draft insurance policy (not the section quoted above):

Situation used by Norman
to determine how easily
readers could apply
information in his draft

> You own a sports car. Your best friend asks to borrow it so he can attend his sister's wedding in another city. You agree. Before leaving for the wedding, he takes his girlfriend on a ride through a park, where he loses control of the car and hits a hot dog stand. No one is injured, but the stand is damaged. Is that damage covered by your insurance? Explain why or why not.

Location Tests

At work, you will sometimes write a communication in which your readers will want to find specific pieces of information without reading everything. Through a location test, you can determine how effective your headings, topic sentences, table of contents, and other navigational aids are in helping your readers quickly find what they need.

Location tests closely resemble performance tests. You give your communication to the test readers and ask them to find specific pieces of information as rapidly as possible. You might ask them to locate the pages on which specific pieces of information appear.

Question for a location test |

On which page do you find information about the liability insurance included in this policy?

Alternatively, you might describe a problem and ask your test readers to locate the page that tells them how to solve it.

Problem-solving task for a location test |

You are making preparations for a party. Because you are running late, you ask a friend to use your car to pick up some things at a bakery so you can finish putting up the decorations. On the way back, your friend hits a parked car while trying to avoid a child who has run into the street. Find the page that tells you whether or not we will pay for the damage to the other car.

Location tests can easily be combined with understandability and performance tests to simulate the real uses to which readers will put your communication. For example, Norman could make an understandability question out of the sample just given by rewriting the final sentence to say, "Will we pay for damage to the other car?"

GUIDELINE 3 **Learn How Your Draft Affects Your Test Readers' Attitudes**

As you learned in Chapter 3, the purpose of almost every communication has a persuasive element. Be sure to test your draft's effectiveness at influencing your readers' attitudes. At work, user tests usually focus on the readers' attitudes toward one or both of the following:

- The *subject matter* of the communication. For example, does this pamphlet by the National Cancer Institute change the readers' attitudes toward a possible ban on smoking in all public places?
- The *quality* of the communication. For example, do readers think this instruction manual is easy to use, complete, and accurate?

Compare Your Readers' Attitudes before and after Reading

To determine how a draft affects your test readers' attitudes, you must compare their attitudes before and after reading it. Consider a test conducted by Rachel, the author of the pamphlet on smoking mentioned above.

To find out whether her test readers changed their attitudes, Rachel must know what their attitudes were before reading her pamphlet.

Rachel learned that after reading her pamphlet, test readers were moderately in favor of banning smoking in all public places. Unless she knew what their attitudes were *before* reading her pamphlet, she could not conclude that their attitude toward a smoking ban had been caused by what she wrote. Maybe her test readers felt exactly the same way before reading, and her pamphlet made no difference. Or maybe they were strongly in favor of such a ban, and her pamphlet made them a little less so.

It would be possible for Rachel to ask her test readers after they've read the pamphlet how their current attitude compares with their attitude before reading it. There is a danger, however, in this procedure because readers sometimes misremember their earlier attitudes. It's more reliable to obtain comparable information both before and after their reading. Here are two ways to do that:

- **Interview before and after reading.** Use the same questions for both interviews. Begin with questions that relate to specific aspects of your draft. "Do you think that the rights of smokers would be unfairly ignored if smoking were banned in public places?" "Do you feel that these instructions are thorough? Clear? Helpful?"

  Follow up with a more open question, such as, "What else would you like to say about this subject (or this communication)?" Open questions can uncover additional insights into your readers' attitudes and their reactions to your communication.

  You can present such interview-type questions orally or in writing. In either case, prepare them in advance to make sure your questions will elicit the information you want.

- **Ask questions constructed around a scale.** When you ask your readers to answer questions on a scale, you are asking them to assign a number to their attitudes. To determine the effect of your communication, you can simply compare the numbers they assigned before reading your draft with the numbers they assigned afterwards.

Sample questions

Smoke in a room can harm the nonsmokers there.

Disagree   1   2   3   4   5   6   7   Agree

The rights of smokers would be unfairly ignored if smoking were banned in theaters, stores, offices, and other public places.

Disagree   1   2   3   4   5   6   7   Agree

A formal analysis of the results obtained in this way requires the use of statistics, which is outside the scope of this book. However, if you use ten or more readers, you can gain at least a general idea of your communication's effectiveness by comparing the average score before reading and the average score after reading.

GUIDELINE **4**   **Interview Your Test Readers after They've Used Your Draft**

By interviewing your test readers after they've used your draft, you can often obtain a wealth of insights you couldn't otherwise have discovered. Here are some things to inquire about:

Things to ask when interviewing test readers

- **What were your test readers thinking when you thought they were having problems?** If you use a form like that shown in Figure 13.6, you might go through each of the behaviors you noted in the left-hand column. Remember also to inquire about their evolving attitudes during reading.

- **How did they try to overcome problems that they encountered?** Their strategies may suggest ways you can improve the presentation of your information.

- **What do they think of revisions you have thought of making?** Even during the test, you may begin to devise revisions. Ask your test readers what they think of these ideas.
- **What do they suggest?** Readers often have excellent ideas about ways a communication can better meet their needs.

GUIDELINE **5** **Test Early and Often, When Appropriate**

When needed, use more than one test and more than one type of test.

When is the best time to conduct a user test? No single answer applies to all situations. If you feel confident about your overall approach in a communication, you may want to wait until you have a nearly final draft. However, if you are trying a new writing strategy or working with a long or complex document, you may want to conduct several kinds of tests throughout the writing process. For example, when writing a set of instructions, you could ask members of the target audience to look over your outline. Their comments can guide you not only as you revise your outline but also as you draft. After completing a draft of one section, you could ask several test readers to meet with you to discuss it. And when you've finished a full draft, you could conduct a user test.

CONCLUSION

This chapter has presented separate sets of guidelines for the three major methods of evaluating drafts—checking, reviewing, and testing. Through these methods, you can detect possible ways of improving your communications. To learn how to make the best use of these insights, read the next chapter on revising.

EXERCISES

1. Following the advice given in this chapter, carefully check a draft you are preparing for this class. Then give your draft to one or more of your classmates to review. Make a list of the problems they find that you overlooked. For three of those problems, explain why you missed them. If possible, pick problems that have different explanations.

2. The memo shown in Figure 13.7 contains 18 misspelled words. Find as many as you can. Unless you found all the words on your first reading, explain why you missed each of the words you overlooked. Based on your performance in this exercise, state in a sentence or two advice to your-

self about how to improve your reading for misspellings and typographical errors.

3. The memo shown in Figure 13.7 has several other problems, such as inconsistencies and missing punctuation. Find as many of those problems as you can.

4. This exercise will help you strengthen your ability to make constructive suggestions to a writer. (See this chapter's advice on reviewing other people's writing.)
   a. Exchange drafts with a classmate, together with information about the purpose and audience for the drafts.

■ FIGURE 13.7

Memo for Use in
Exercises 2 and 3

MARTIMUS CORPORATION
Interoffice Memorandum

February 19, 19—

From   T. J. Mueller, Vice President for Developmnet

To   All Staff

RE   PROOFREADING

Its absolutely critical that all members of the staff carefully proofread all communications they write. Last month we learned that a proposal we had submited to the U.S. Department of Transportation was turned down largely because it was full of careless errors. One of the referees at the Department commented that, "We could scarcely trust an important contract to a company that cann't proofread it's proposals any better than this. Errors abound.

We received similar comments on final report of the telephone technology project we preformed last year for Boise General.

In response to this widespread problem in Martinus, we are taking the three important steps decsribed below.

I. TRAINING COURSE

We have hired a private consulting form to conduct a 3-hour training course in editing and proofreading for all staff members. The course will be given 15 times so that class size will be held to twelve participants. Nest week you will be asked to indicates times you can attend. Every effort will be made to accommodate your schehule.

II. ADDITIONAL REVIEWING.

To assure that we never again send a letter, report, memorandum, or or other communication outside the company that will embarrass us with it's carelessness, we are establishing an additional step in our review proceedures. For each communication that must pass throug the regular review process, an additional step will be required. In this step, an appropriate person in each deparmtent will scour the communication for errors of expression, consistancy, and correctness.

III. WRITING PERFORMANCE TO BE EVALUATED

In addition, we are creating new personnel evaluation forms to be used at annual salary reviews. They include a place for evaluating each employees' writing.

III. Conclusion

We at Martimus can overcome this problem only with the full cooperation of every employe. Please help.

■ FIGURE 13.8

Memo for Use in
Exercise 5

INTERNATIONAL MANUFACTURING, INCORPORATED
New York, New York

Interoffice Correspondence

DATE   7 July 19—
FROM   S. Benjamin Bradstreet, Marketing Department
TO   Tom Wiley, New Factory Development Department

Your department's representative Dick Saunders called us on Tuesday, 5 July, from Manila, requesting some product information, an old formula, and information about the status of shipments to him. He also told us his projected return schedule.

First of all, he plans on returning to the States on 12 July, arriving in Chicago and then going directly to North Hampton, Massachusetts. He will stay at the Colonial-Hilton, (413) 586-1211, with Mr. Rossini of the Appliance Factories Group (13, 14, and 15 July).

A Victory luncheon is planned in Manila for Friday, 8 July, based on the anticipated success of our roofing factory there. General Tobias, the equivalent of our Secretary of Health and Human Services, is pleased with the factory and sees the work done this past week as the start of a production that will continue for some time.

Dick requested some additional information that is to be answered by means of a cable. This was to include when and how the Osprey drawings and the Quickmold release agent were shipped. He also wanted to know the exact cost of the release agent because it would be paid for with a check that he will carry back with him.

Dick said that Snyder and Leigh, of the American consulate, have been replaced by Wilson F. Brady. In future correspondence, we can use his name as a contact.

Dick said that they were having considerable success in making the shingles at the new roofing plant and that the 361 Filipinos will be able to take over full operation of the plant in a few days. These are the results that please General Tobias so.

Dick will return to New York on 18 July.

He said that the hard-rubber roofs installed last fall look good and that people are living in the houses. The only problem is some holes where nails were inadvertently pounded through in the wrong place.

Dick is also interested in a fire-retardant formula for the dry-blend phenolic system, and specifications for the Slobent 37, so he can find some locally available substitute before he leaves. He was aware of the retardant having a specific gravity of 2.4. Please send him the answers to these questions by cable.

b. Carefully read your partner's draft, playing the role of a reviewer. Ask your partner to read your draft in the same way.

c. Offer your comments to your partner.

d. Evaluate your success in delivering your comments in a way that makes the writer feel comfortable while still providing substantive, understandable advice. Do this by writing down three specific points you think you handled well and three ways in which you think you could improve. At the same time, your partner should be making a similar list of observations about your delivery. Both of you should focus on such matters as how you opened the discussion, how you phrased your comments, and how you explained them.

e. Talk over with your partner the observations that each of you made.

f. Repeat steps c through e, but have your partner give you his or her comments on your draft.

5. In this exercise, you are to prepare review comments for a writer. Depending on what your instructor asks you to do, you may present your comments orally or state them in a memo to the writer. In either case, be sure to follow all the suggestions for reviewing other people's writing. Remember that how you present your comments can be as important as what you suggest. For the sake of this exercise, imagine that you are a coach (not a gatekeeper), so that the writer is free to follow or ignore your suggestions.

The memo you are to review is shown in Figure 13.8. Direct your review comments to the writer, S. Benjamin Bradstreet, who works for a firm that builds manufac-

turing plants in foreign countries. Yesterday, Ben received a call from Dick Saunders, who has been in the Philippines for the past two years. Dick has been overseeing the construction of a factory that manufactures roof shingles from bagasse, the fibers left after the sugar has been squeezed out of sugar cane.

Dick happened to reach Ben while trying to call his own boss, Tom Wiley, who wasn't in. Dick asked Ben to take notes on their conversation and to forward them to Tom.

The audience for Ben's memo will include not only Tom, who will be interested in all the information it contains, but also several other people, who will be interested in only certain pieces of that information. These people include Tom's assistant, who will be responsible for sending the items Dick requests, and other men and women in the sales department who will be talking with Tom on the phone or in person while he is in the States.

6. Explain how you would test each of the following communications:

a. A display in a national park that is intended to explain to the public how the park's extensive limestone caves were formed.

b. Instructions that tell homeowners how to design and construct a patio. Assume that you must test the instructions without having your test readers actually build a patio.

7. Following the guidelines in this chapter, test one of the communications you are preparing for this class.

Revising

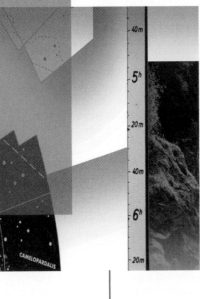

GUIDELINES

1	Adjust your effort to the situation
2	Make the most significant revisions first
3	Be diplomatic
4	To revise well, follow the guidelines for writing well
5	Revise to learn

DEFINING OBJECTIVES

PLANNING

DRAFTING

EVALUATING

REVISING

This chapter provides advice about the fifth major activity of writing: revising. When you revise, you improve a draft by changing it in ways that have been suggested by your evaluation of it.

Often, revising is a very straightforward activity. Writers simply proceed through their drafts, from beginning to end, making each change suggested by their checking, reviewing, or testing of it.

Sometimes, however, writers face complex decisions about what to revise and what not to revise. The need for these decisions can arise for any of the following reasons:

- When there isn't enough time to make all the revisions that checking, reviewing, or testing suggest.
- When the draft has been reviewed by two or more persons who give contradictory advice.
- When a reviewer, such as a boss, suggests changes that the writer believes will actually diminish the communication's effectiveness.

The guidelines in this chapter will help you deal effectively with these more complex revising situations.

GUIDELINE 1 **Adjust Your Effort to the Situation**

This guideline suggests that you approach revising as if you were an investor. As you begin revising any communication, let your first concern be the amount of time and energy you will invest in it rather than in your other duties.

Some students think it is peculiar to ask how good a communication needs to be. "After all," they observe, "shouldn't we try to make everything we write as good as it can be?" On the job, the answer is, "No."

Different communications need different levels of polish.

Of course, all your communications should clearly present their central points and achieve an appropriate tone. In the workplace, however, different communications need different levels of additional polish. For example, in most organizations, printed messages are expected to be error-free, but e-mail messages sent internally may contain spelling errors and grammatical mistakes as long as their meaning is clear and their tone inoffensive. Even among printed communications, different levels of polish are expected. In a survey of workers in a diverse mix of professions, researchers Barbara Couture and Jone Rymer found that three times as many employees "often" or "very often" make major revisions in communications they consider to be "special" as make major revisions in communications they consider to be "routine."

To determine how good a communication you are writing needs to be, do the following:

Ways to determine how good a communication needs to be

- **Think about your purpose.** How carefully does your communication need to be crafted to help your readers perform their tasks? To affect your readers' attitudes in the way you want?

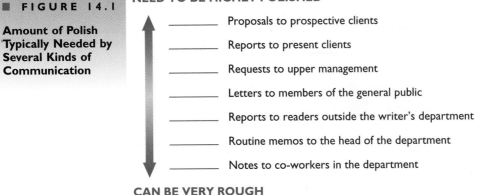

■ **FIGURE 14.1**

Amount of Polish Typically Needed by Several Kinds of Communication

NEED TO BE HIGHLY POLISHED

_____ Proposals to prospective clients

_____ Reports to present clients

_____ Requests to upper management

_____ Letters to members of the general public

_____ Reports to readers outside the writer's department

_____ Routine memos to the head of the department

_____ Notes to co-workers in the department

CAN BE VERY ROUGH

- **Consider general expectations about quality.** Generally, you need to polish your communications more thoroughly when addressing people at a higher level than at your own level in your organization, when addressing people outside your organization rather than inside, and when trying to gain something rather than give something (for example, when writing proposals rather than reports). These general expectations can be translated into a list that ranks some typical communications according to the level of polish they usually need (Figure 14.1).
- **Look at similar communications.** Often, the level of quality needed is determined largely by what's customary. By looking at communications similar to the one you're preparing, you can see what level of quality has succeeded in the past.
- **Ask someone.** Your boss or co-workers can be excellent sources of information about the level of quality needed. Better yet, follow the principle of *continuous reader involvement* by asking your intended readers how polished they want your communication to be.

Note, by the way, that there are sometimes good reasons for wanting your communication to go beyond the minimum level needed to make your communication "good enough."

Reasons for making your communications better than "good enough"

First, your writing is one of the major factors on which your job performance will be evaluated. In fact, people who are not involved with your work from day to day may base their opinion of your ability solely on your writing. Consequently, there's a real advantage to having your readers say not only, "We picked up a lot of useful information from your report," but also "And you wrote it so well!"

Second, communications prepared at work often have a wider audience than the writer assumes. Notes to co-workers and to your immediate manager can often be fairly rough. Sometimes, however, those people may pass your communications along to upper management or to members of other departments for whom you would want to prepare more polished communications. Therefore, when determining what level of quality to strive for, be sure to consider who your possible readers may be.

■ FIGURE 14.2

Amount of Improvement That Various Revisions Would Make in Wayne's Proposal

MAKE GREAT IMPROVEMENT

_____ Correcting errors in key statements

_____ Adding essential information that was overlooked

_____ Correcting misspellings

_____ Repairing obvious errors in grammar

_____ Fixing major organizational difficulties

_____ Supplying missing topic sentences

_____ Revising sentences that are tangled but still understandable

_____ Correcting less obvious problems in grammar

MAKE SMALL IMPROVEMENT

GUIDELINE **2**   ## Make the Most Significant Revisions First

After you've decided how much time and effort to invest in revising, determine which revisions to tackle first.

Why concern yourself with the order in which you make revisions? When revising, your goal is to achieve the greatest possible improvement in the least possible time. If you spend fifteen minutes on revisions that result in a small improvement rather than on ones that bring a large improvement, you have squandered your time.

Because the advice to make the most important revisions first sounds so sensible, you might wonder whether anyone ever ignores it. In fact, many people do. They begin by looking at the first paragraph, making revisions there, then proceeding through the rest of the communication in the same sequential way. That procedure works well enough if the most serious shortcomings occur in the opening paragraphs, but not if they come in later passages that the writers might not even reach before the time available for revising runs out. Furthermore, some problems—for instance, inconsistencies and organizational problems—require simultaneous attention to passages scattered throughout a communication, so that a sequential approach to revising may ignore them altogether.

To avoid the weak communications that can result from poorly planned revising, start by ranking all the modifications you might make.

How to Rank Revisions

The relative importance of a particular revision depends on several factors.

There is no single ranked list of revisions that you can apply to all communications. The importance of most revisions depends very much on the situation. For one thing, the relative importance of a certain revision is determined by the other revisions that are needed or desirable. Consider, for instance, the place of "supplying topic sentences" in the ranked list (Figure 14.2) that Wayne created after surveying the comments made by four reviewers of a proposal he had drafted. In comparison

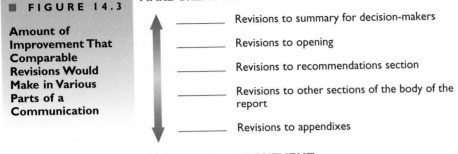

■ FIGURE 14.3

Amount of Improvement That Comparable Revisions Would Make in Various Parts of a Communication

MAKE GREAT IMPROVEMENT

_____ Revisions to summary for decision-makers

_____ Revisions to opening

_____ Revisions to recommendations section

_____ Revisions to other sections of the body of the report

_____ Revisions to appendixes

MAKE SMALL IMPROVEMENT

with the other items in the list, supplying topic sentences is *relatively* unimportant. However, in a draft with fewer problems in more critical areas, providing topic sentences might bring more improvement than any other revision Wayne could make.

Another factor affecting the relative importance of a revision is its location in a communication. An improvement in the opening summary, for example, would increase the effectiveness of a long report more than a similar revision made in an appendix. Likewise, revisions in passages that convey key points usually have greater impact than similar revisions in passages that provide background information and explanations. Figure 14.3 compares the amount of improvement that similar revisions would make in various parts of a typical communication.

A third factor can come into play when you are ranking revisions requested by reviewers: the importance of the person making the request. Sometimes, for obvious and practical reasons, you will want to give first attention to revisions requested by people in positions of authority, even if you would not otherwise have given those same revisions high priority.

If you have only a limited amount of time to revise, some of the revisions on your ranked list may never be made. By making such a list, however, you ensure that the revisions you do complete are the ones that will contribute most to making your communication work.

Be Sure to Correct Mechanical Problems

No matter how you rank other possible improvements, place the correction of mechanical problems at the top of your list, unless you are writing in a situation where you are sure that such problems won't matter. Here are the major mechanical problems you should focus on:

Mechanical issues to focus on

- **Correctness.** Be sure you are correct in matters where there are a clear right and wrong (as with spelling, grammar, and punctuation).
- **Consistency.** Where two or more items should have the same form, be sure they do. For instance, be sure that parallel tables look the same. Be sure that the figure after Figure 3 is correctly numbered as Figure 4. Similarly, if you tell your

readers to look on page 10 for a particular drawing, be sure that the drawing is on page 10, not on page 11.

- **Conformity.** Be sure that you have followed your employer's policies on such matters as the width of margins, the use of abbreviations, and the contents of title pages. This will be easy for you if your employer has put these policies in writing. If not, remember that your communication must still conform to your employer's informal policies and expectations.
- **Attractiveness.** Be sure that your communication looks neat and professional.

Check mechanical matters last.

Often, it's best to postpone your work on mechanical matters until the end of your work on a communication. There is no point in investing time in correcting passages that may later be deleted or changed. At the same time, if you ask others to evaluate your draft, either by reviewing it for you or by testing it, be sure to clear up mechanical problems in the draft you give them. If the errors remain, your readers may become distracted by them and miss more substantive issues.

GUIDELINE **3** **Be Diplomatic**

Writers are often perplexed about how to handle situations that require diplomatic finesse. One such situation arises when managers or other influential reviewers suggest revisions that the writers know will weaken their communications. Somehow the writers must persuade the reviewers to change their minds without giving offense. One diplomatic approach is to refer to the reader-centered guidelines in this book and explain the reasons for them.

Conflicting advice about writing may reflect conflicts over broader issues.

Another awkward situation arises when two reviewers make conflicting demands or give conflicting advice. Some conflicts of this sort can be resolved by reference to the communication's purpose or some principle of reader-centered writing. In other cases, the conflict may reflect an underlying dispute between the reviewers or the groups they represent. Communication specialist Stephen Doheny-Farina witnessed a months-long dispute in a small computer software company over the writing and revising of a business plan designed to raise money from investors. He reports that the dispute was actually over the mission, organization, and future plans of the company itself.

New employees have an especially difficult time recognizing where political controversies underlie conflicting advice from reviewers. Often, the tip-off is that the conflicting advice seems to relate to different views of what should be said rather than to the best way of saying it.

If you sense that you and your draft are caught in a crossfire between contending parties, you might ask the reviewers to explain the reasons for their advice. You may be able to fashion a statement that is acceptable to all parties. However, the large number of review cycles that some communications go through suggests that writers are not always able to succeed in fashioning a compromise. Sometimes you may have to ask the reviewers to talk directly with one another and then tell you what they have decided.

GUIDELINE **4** To Revise Well, Follow the Guidelines for Writing Well

This guideline suggests, quite simply, that when revising you should follow the same guidelines that you follow when drafting. For example, if you want to change your communication's contents, observe the guidelines in Chapters 4 and 5, "Planning to Meet Your Readers' Informational Needs" and "Planning Your Persuasive Strategies." Similarly, if you want to polish your paragraphs, sentences, or visual aids, follow the guidelines that pertain to them.

"Is that right?" you may be asking yourself. "Shouldn't a chapter on revising tell me how to rewrite a sentence, restructure a paragraph, and so on?" Not necessarily, at least not if you can find the most important advice about those very matters elsewhere in the same book, as you can in this one. Whether you are drafting or revising, the principles and guidelines for good communication remain the same. Where your evaluation shows that you might improve your communication, you need to apply the guidelines in a different way—not search for alternative guidelines.

GUIDELINE **5** Revise to Learn

The first four guidelines in this chapter have focused on ways in which revising can improve the effectiveness of your communications. Revising can also help you learn to write better.

Through revising you can learn new writing skills.

When revising, you will often be applying writing skills that you have yet to master fully. By consciously practicing those skills, you can strengthen them. Then you will be able to use them when you *draft*. For example, if you spend much of your revising time supplying topic sentences for your paragraphs, you probably do so because you have not yet learned to write topic sentences in your first drafts. Through the practice you receive when revising, you can master the use of topic sentences and learn to supply them automatically in your earliest drafts.

Because you can learn so much from revising, it can often be worthwhile to invest *extra* time in revising. Even if your communication is good enough to satisfy the needs and expectations of your readers and employer, consider revising it further for the sake of what you can learn by doing so.

CONCLUSION

This chapter has suggested that the complexities of working situations may require you to play several roles while revising. As an investor, you will need to decide how much time to devote to revising a draft. As a diplomat, you will need to negotiate with reviewers about changes they have requested or demanded. Furthermore, as part of your ongoing efforts to improve your professional skills, you will sometimes play the role of student, revising for the sake of what you can learn. Finally, as a writer, you always need to pursue the goal of creating communications that (despite deadlines and the demands of other people) will be understandable, useful, and persuasive to your readers.

Applications of the Reader-Centered Approach

CHAPTER 15
Communicating Electronically: E-Mail, Web Pages, and Web Sites

CHAPTER 16
Creating and Delivering Oral Presentations

CHAPTER 17
Creating Communications with a Team

Communicating Electronically: E-Mail, Web Pages, and Web Sites

GUIDELINES

Guidelines for Using E-Mail

1   See what other people are doing

2   Keep your messages brief

3   Make your messages easy to read on screen

4   Provide an informative, specific subject line

5   Take time to revise

6   Remember that e-mail isn't private

Guidelines for Designing Web Pages

1   Make your pages easy to read

2   Keep your pages short

3   Make your pages attractive

4   Limit loading time

5   Keep your pages up to date

Guidelines for Creating Web Sites

1 | Begin by considering your site's audience and purpose

2 | Meet your readers' informational needs

3 | Organize your site hierarchically

4 | Provide useful associative links

5 | Label your links clearly

6 | Provide many navigational aids

7 | Use a consistent visual design

8 | Enable readers to contact you

9 | Test your site

Want to contact a friend? Many students are more likely to do so by e-mail than by the Postal Service. Need to gather information for a report assigned by one of your professors? Even before they walk to the library, many students search the World Wide Web. At work, too, people rely extensively on computers when they need to share or obtain information. In many organizations, there's a computer on every desk, and employees are using them to do a substantial portion of the communicating they previously did on paper. Some employers have even adopted the goal of becoming "paperless."

In this chapter, you will learn how to work effectively in a workplace that is becoming more reliant on computer-based communication. First, you'll learn how to use e-mail effectively on the job, where conventions are distinctly different from those of the personal e-mail you may now exchange with friends and family members. You'll also find advice for creating informational Web sites of the kind that organizations use to provide information that their employees, customers, clients, vendors, and investors can use for practical purposes.

This chapter's guidelines supplement rather than supersede the other guidelines in this book.

You should view this chapter's guidelines as supplementary to those you've read elsewhere in this book for preparing paper-based communications. When writing for on-screen reading, you should follow the same basic process as described in other chapters: begin by learning about your audience and defining your purpose, create a plan, draft, evaluate your draft, and revise it. The guidelines in this chapter are designed to provide additional advice for addressing the special opportunities and challenges of preparing electronic communications.

■ **FIGURE 15.1**

E-Mail Message

Elena's short subject line states her main point.

Short paragraphs increase reading ease on computer screens; one-sentence paragraphs are often used in e-mail.

Because underlining and bold aren't available in e-mail, Elena emphasizes a word with asterisks.

Elena sticks to a single topic, using a separate message to discuss a related matter.

Armin's e-mail reply said simply, "Yes, please send information. Thanks."

Mail

Send Now | Quote | Attach | Address | Stop

Subject: Security System Needed for Research Labs

Addressing   Attachments

TO   Armin Weiss
FROM   Elena Gambaro

I think we should install a security system for the research labs in the Krantz Building.

Last week a technician from the plastics lab entered the enzyme lab without having the proper security authorization. This resulted from an innocent mistake. However, it shows how vulnerable we are to the loss of company secrets. Also, in the enzyme lab, untrained persons could accidentally expose themselves to *very* harmful substances.

My quick research suggests that computerized fingerprint-recognition systems are far superior to traditional keypad-and-password security systems. No one can steal a fingerprint, and the fingerprint systems retain the fingerprints of people who try to use them without authorization. Let me know if you'd like more information.

I also have concerns about safety in labs. I'll explain them in a separate e-mail.

USING E-MAIL

Advantages of e-mail over paper mail

When used effectively, e-mail has some notable advantages over paper mail. Most importantly, you can get your message to your readers almost instantly, and your readers can respond without having to print something out, put it into an envelope, and take it to the maildrop. Also, many people use e-mail in situations where previously they made a phone call because e-mail allows them to exchange information quickly without needing to be free at the same time as the other person. In addition, e-mail lets you send as attachments fully formatted documents, spreadsheets, and graphics over computer networks.

On the other hand, e-mail has some disadvantages. For example, readers can't scribble notes in the margin, and it's easy to send off messages that, on reflection, you would prefer to have proofread again—or not sent at all.

The following guidelines will help you work effectively with the special possibilities and limitations associated with on-screen correspondence. The e-mail message shown in Figure 15.1 illustrates their application.

GUIDELINE ① See What Other People Are Doing

Conventions for e-mail vary from one organization to another.

Despite the enormous amount of e-mail being exchanged, a uniform set of conventions for its use in the workplace has yet to emerge. Perhaps one never will. In some organizations, people use slang, abbreviations, and very clipped expressions when using e-mail. They don't polish their writing or even check their spelling. In these organizations, the informality of e-mail is often seen as one of its appealing features: writers can dash off their core message without investing time in careful revising. It can even become a substitute for discussion, with each member of a team sending messages to all the other team members simultaneously—and everyone contributing freely to the on-line conversation. In other organizations, however, e-mail is viewed more as a document than as a discussion. There, the writing of e-mail messages is very formal, and an informal e-mail note would seem glaringly out of place (Selber).

Because conventions vary so greatly from organization to organization, pay careful attention to the local customs concerning e-mail.

GUIDELINE ② Keep Your Messages Brief

Brevity is almost always valued at work, but especially with e-mail messages. Many people find it more difficult to read computer screens than printed documents. The letters of the words on screen are less distinct, the scrolling required for long communications makes it difficult to flip back and forth between sections, and people dislike sitting in one position for an extended period, as they must do when using a desktop computer. Here are some tips for keeping your messages brief (Weisband, Denning, and Berghel):

Keeping E-Mail Messages Brief

- Use a simple, three-part structure: succinctly state your topic, quickly summarize background information, and then state your main point and supporting material.
- Exclude any information that is not directly related to your topic.
- Stick to one topic. If you want to write about two things, send two messages.
- When quoting from a previous e-mail message (easy to do with most e-mail programs), include only the relevant lines, not the entire earlier message.

GUIDELINE ③ Make Your Messages Easy to Read on Screen

Compared to desktop publishing programs, most e-mail programs offer fewer options for enhancing readability and creating emphasis. Typically, you can't use bold or italics and can't change the type size or typeface. But there are a few things you can do to enhance readability:

Writing for On-Screen Reading

- Write short paragraphs.
- Put blank lines between paragraphs.
- Make headings for longer communications, putting each heading on a line of its own.
- Use lists.
- Use asterisks or other symbols around words or phrases you want to emphasize.

GUIDELINE **4**   **Provide an Informative, Specific Subject Line**

Readers use subject lines to decide whether to read e-mail messages.

Some people receive literally hundreds of e-mail messages a day. When reviewing their mailbox, their first task is to decide which messages to open and which to delete unopened. To make this decision, they see who sent each message and what the subject line says. You can assure that your important messages will be opened if you use your subject line to tell as exactly as possible what's in your message. When doing so, focus on saying things that will make clear to your readers that the contents are valuable to them.

Also, people often save some e-mail messages so that they can refer back to them at a later time. By writing informative, specific subject lines you help your readers quickly locate your message when they want to read it a second time.

GUIDELINE **5**   **Take Time to Revise**

Because e-mail can be written so quickly and because in many workplaces it's acceptable to send fairly rough prose, many people simply write their message and zip it off. If you do this, however, you risk sending unclear messages that will require additional correspondence to straighten out. Also, if you don't take time to reflect on your message, you may send a note while feeling anger or some other intense emotion. Messages sent under these circumstances can create hard feelings. Many e-mail programs allow you to write a message but to postpone sending it. Use this feature when you need to review your message carefully or cool down before mailing it.

GUIDELINE **6**   **Remember That E-Mail Isn't Private**

Many people believe that their e-mail is private. Perhaps they harbor this belief because the word *mail* suggests privacy since we know that the Postal Service is not permitted to read the letters we send. Or maybe, as Weisband suggests, people assume that because they use a password to enter their e-mail account, no one else has access to the mail in that account (40). Nonetheless, courts have held that employers have the right to look at all employee e-mail that is on or sent through a company computer (Berghel, 14). As one summer intern said ruefully, "It's very disconcerting to be told that the day before, some official of the company read all your e-mail, including all your gripes and all your jokes about the people in the next department—and management!"

Employers can read your e-mail messages.

Even if the e-mail in your mailbox isn't read by your employer, your messages may be read by many people you didn't intend to see it. With a mere click of the mouse, the persons to whom you send a message can forward it to anyone else who has e-mail capability.

To protect your own privacy and avoid embarrassment or misunderstanding, do the following:

Protecting Your Privacy with E-Mail

- Never include anything in an e-mail message that you aren't prepared for a large audience to read.
- Be careful about mixing personal and work-related topics in the same e-mail message.
- Never write something about a person that you wouldn't say directly to that person.
- Do not send e-mail when feeling a strong emotion.
- If an e-mail exchange becomes emotionally charged, talk to the person directly.
- Never include confidential information.

CREATING INFORMATIONAL WEB SITES

Despite some important differences, e-mail messages closely resemble those printed on paper. In contrast, the World Wide Web provides a fundamentally new way of communicating. It allows you to create messages that incorporate not only words and graphics but also animation, sounds, movies—all presented in a dazzling array of colors, if you wish. Moreover, you can create links that whisk your readers to other Web sites, whether created by you or by someone located on another continent.

In the workplace, Web pages serve practical purposes.

The rest of this chapter provides advice for creating informational Web sites, ones that your employer may want you to create for any of a wide variety of uses. The following sections describe how the World Wide Web works, explain how to create a single Web page, tell how to give that page an effective design, and then present guidelines for building sets of pages into an effective, job-related site.

HOW THE WORLD WIDE WEB WORKS

One of the most amazing things about the World Wide Web is that only two simple components orchestrate the eye-catching and mind-catching array of features and capabilities presented at many Web sites. These components are a Web page file and a Web browser.

A Web page file consists of commands that tell the browser how to create the images that you see on your screen. These commands are written in a computer language called *hypertext markup language* or *HTML.*

A Web browser performs three functions: it locates the Web page file for the page you want to visit, it copies the file to your computer's memory, and it uses the instructions in the file to construct the display you see on your screen.

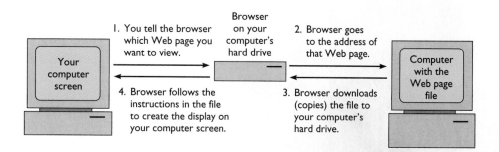

The interaction of these two elements—Web page files and Web browsers—allows you to view millions of pages created by thousands of individuals and organizations in hundreds of countries around the world.

CREATING A WEB PAGE

To create a Web page, you create the Web page file containing the HTML commands that tell a browser what you want it to display. You can write the HTML commands yourself or use a program that lets you design the appearance of the page and then translates your designs into a file with HTML commands. Some desktop publishing programs such as Microsoft Word do this, as do some specialized programs. One that you can download for free is:

Free program for creating Web pages | AOL Press   http://www.aolpress.com/press/index.html

Even if you use one of these special programs to create your Web page file, it's useful to know how the commands work so that you can solve problems in your file or imitate strategies you see on other people's pages.

How HTML commands work   Most HTML commands, called *tags,* appear in brackets, and most come in pairs that surround some part of the text. For example, if you want your file to instruct a browser to display a word in bold, you would surround that word with <b> and </b>. Pairs of bracketed tags also define the three parts of a Web page: the head, title, and body. Figure 15.2 shows a Web page that uses many common Web page features. Figure 15.3 shows the file that created this Web page.

■ **FIGURE 15.2**

Web Page Created by File in Figure 15.3

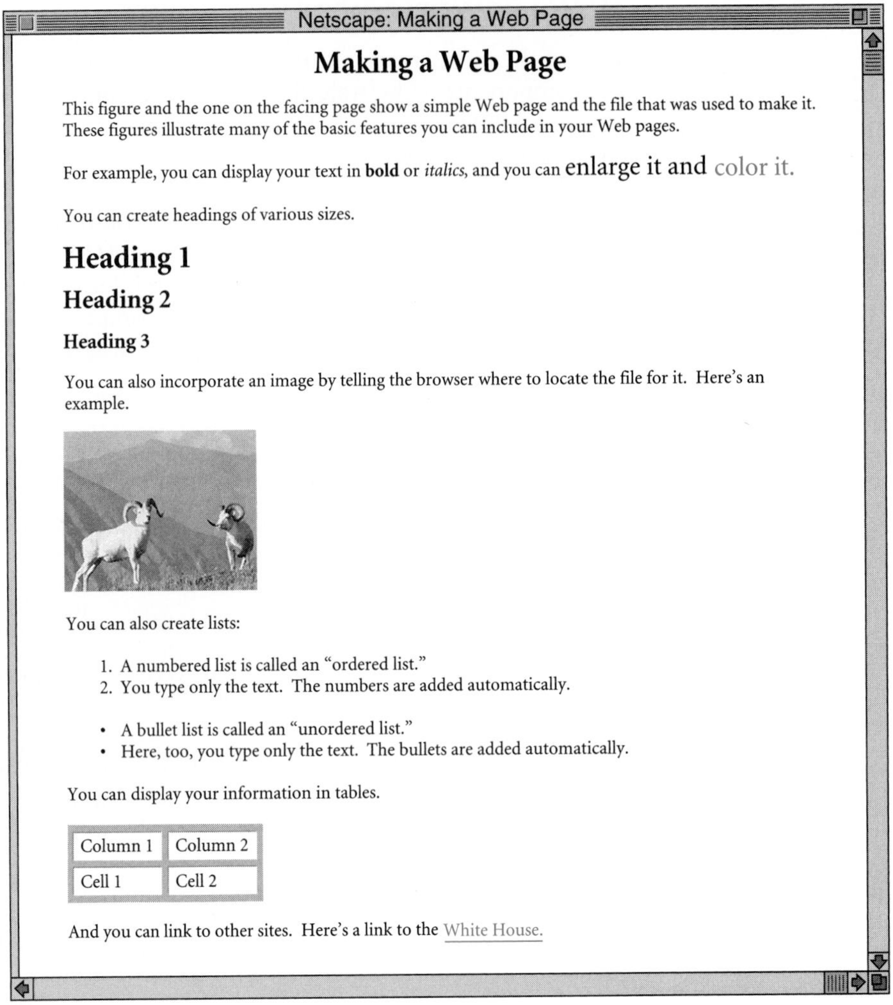

Netscape: Making a Web Page

Making a Web Page

This figure and the one on the facing page show a simple Web page and the file that was used to make it. These figures illustrate many of the basic features you can include in your Web pages.

For example, you can display your text in **bold** or *italics*, and you can enlarge it and color it.

You can create headings of various sizes.

Heading 1

Heading 2

Heading 3

You can also incorporate an image by telling the browser where to locate the file for it. Here's an example.

You can also create lists:

1. A numbered list is called an "ordered list."
2. You type only the text. The numbers are added automatically.

- A bullet list is called an "unordered list."
- Here, too, you type only the text. The bullets are added automatically.

You can display your information in tables.

Column 1	Column 2
Cell 1	Cell 2

And you can link to other sites. Here's a link to the White House.

Posting a Web page to a server

To make a Web page available to other people, you must post it to a computer that is operating as a World Wide Web server. Ask your professor or others at your college for instructions. However, before you post a page that you've made, you can view it on your own computer. Simply open your browser, go to the File menu, and choose a command that says "Open file in compositor," "Open file in browser," or something similar.

GUIDELINES FOR DESIGNING WEB PAGES

See pages 295 and 349 for additional well-designed Web pages.

When readers open your Web page, what will determine whether the page succeeds in achieving your objectives? The following guidelines provide many of the answers. Figure 15.4 (page 402) shows a Web page created in accordance with these guidelines.

■ **FIGURE 15.3**

File That Created the Web Page Shown in Figure 15.2

Tells the browser that this is a Web page

Tells the browser what words go in the bar at the top of the browser window

Sets the background color ("#FFFFFF" is the code for white)

Inserts a blank line

Tells the browser the location of the file for the image

Starts an ordered list (the browser will add the numbers automatically)

Starts an unordered list (the browser will add the bullets automatically)

Starts a table

Begins a table row

Tells what goes in a table cell

Instructs the browser to go to the address indicated when the user clicks on the link

```
<HTML>
<HEAD>
    <TITLE>Making a Web Page</TITLE>
</HEAD>
<BODY BGCOLOR="#FFFFFF">
    <H1><Center>Making a Web Page</Center></H1>
    This figure and the one on the facing page show a simple Web page and the file that was
    used to make it.  These figures illustrate many of the basic features you can include in
    your Web pages.
    <P>
    For example, you can display your text in <B>bold</B>or<i>italics</i>, and you can
    <BIG><BIG>enlarge it and <font color="#3399CC">color it.</font></BIG></BIG>
<P>
You can create headings of various sizes.
    <H1>Heading 1</H1>
    <H2>Heading 2</H2>
    <H3>Heading 3</H3>
You can also incorporate an image by telling the browser where to locate the file for it.
Here's an example.
    <P>
    <IMG SRC="TC4earth.gif">
    <P>
You can also create lists:
    <OL>
        <LI>A numbered list is called an "ordered list."
        <LI>You type only the text.  The numbers are added automatically.
    </OL>
    <UL>
        <LI>A bullet list is called an "unordered list."
        <LI>Here, too, you type only the text.  The bullets are added automatically.
    </UL>
You can display your information in tables.
    <P>
    <TABLE BORDER CELLPADDING="2">
        <TR>
            <TD>Column 1</TD>
            <TD>Column 2</TD>
        </TR>
        <TR>
            <TD>Cell 1</TD>
            <TD>Cell 2</TD>
        </TR>
    </TABLE>
    <P>
And you can link to other sites.  Here's a link to the<A HREF="http://www.whitehouse.gov">
White House</A>.
</BODY>
</HTML>
```

■ **FIGURE 15.4**

Well-Designed Home Page for a Web Site

This home page illustrates good web page design.

High contrast between letters and background promotes easy reading.

The design is simple, uncluttered.

All content can be read on one screen.

The list on the left-hand side provides links to the next level of pages; the same links appear on all other pages for easy navigation.

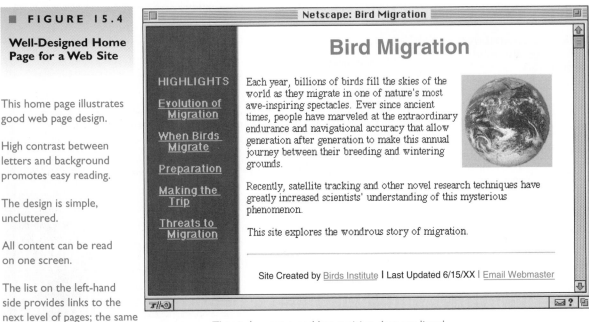

The site's creator and last revision date are listed.

The site includes a way for visitors to contact the creator.

GUIDELINE ❶ **Make Your Pages Easy to Read**

There are so many ways you can design any Web page that it's easy to lose sight of the factors that meet readers' most basic requirement: that the page be readable.

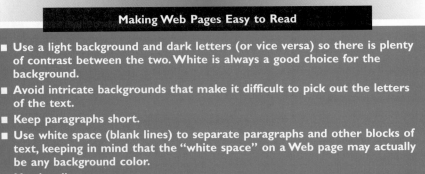

Making Web Pages Easy to Read

- Use a light background and dark letters (or vice versa) so there is plenty of contrast between the two. White is always a good choice for the background.
- Avoid intricate backgrounds that make it difficult to pick out the letters of the text.
- Keep paragraphs short.
- Use white space (blank lines) to separate paragraphs and other blocks of text, keeping in mind that the "white space" on a Web page may actually be any background color.
- Use headings.
- Use lists and tables, where appropriate.
- Don't fill the screen with text. Some sources recommend that only about 30 percent of the page be text.

GUIDELINE **2**   **Keep Your Pages Short**

Minimize the scrolling readers must do.

Words never run off the bottom of a Web page. With long pages, all readers need to do is to keep scrolling. However, scrolling creates problems for readers. First, they have to stop reading while scrolling because the type becomes unreadable when rolling down the screen. Second, after they've scrolled down a long page, it is difficult for them locate an earlier part that they'd like to look at again. Try to keep your Web pages to one or two screens. Do this by writing concisely, eliminating unnecessary information, and breaking long pages into separate, linked pages.

GUIDELINE **3**   **Make Your Pages Attractive**

For advice on visual design, see Chapter 12.

A cluttered or ugly design will discourage readers from using your Web page. Keep the number of elements on the page small, and use a limited number of grid lines. Choose pleasing color combinations and avoid clashing ones. Avoid garish backgrounds and continuously blinking or moving elements that distract a reader's eye from the text. Avoid large pictures that dominate the page and leave little room for text.

GUIDELINE **4**   **Limit Loading Time**

Visual elements can take a long time to load.

Readers' efficiency is diminished and their patience is taxed if they must wait a long time to load a Web page. In judging loading time, remember that some people may load your page over a slow network or with a slow modem.

To reduce loading time, avoid unnecessary visual aids. When using picture, movie, or sound files, pick the smallest ones that will meet your readers' needs. Also, browsers won't display a table until it is entirely loaded. Therefore, break long tables into separate ones so that the first part of the information can be viewed while the rest is being processed.

GUIDELINE **5**   **Keep Your Pages Up to Date**

The Web is in constant flux. You may alter parts of your site. Sites to which you have established links may change or disappear. New and better sites may be now available for linking. To keep your site up to date, periodically check your links to be sure they are still active and still contain the information they once did. Also, at the bottom of your page indicate when you last revised it so that readers can determine how current it is and whether it contains new information since they last visited.

GUIDELINES FOR CREATING WEB SITES

Web sites vary by size, purpose, and target audience.

In the workplace, a single Web page is rarely sufficient to meet a practical communication need. Consequently, organizations build Web sites out of interrelated sets of pages. Some Web sites have only a few pages, but others have thousands. Employers use these sites for a broad array of purposes, such as distributing internal information, communicating with clients and customers, and advertising products and services. Many organizations open their sites to the world. Others permit access only to authorized personnel because the site contains such things as proprietary research results, engineering plans, or sales data.

GUIDELINE 1

Begin by Considering Your Site's Audience and Purpose

Begin creating a Web site in the same way you would begin creating any other work-related communication: by thinking about your audience and purpose. Although many Web sites are created for entertainment, the ones you create in your career will almost certainly be addressed to people seeking information they can use in some practical way. Don't let the novelty of the Web or the features of other types of Web sites distract you from creating your site to meet the specific needs of the particular audience you are addressing.

GUIDELINE 2

Meet Your Readers' Informational Needs

The first challenge of creating a Web site is to get people to use it. In the work setting, they will visit your site for information. Make sure you provide what they want and that you enable them to get it quickly and in a way they will find useful. Avoid devoting too much of your pages to visuals, unless the visuals communicate information useful to your readers. Also, avoid making highly decorative pages when readers are consulting them for practical purposes. Finally, note that although lists help readers gather information quickly, too many lists become monotonous and difficult to use.

GUIDELINE 3

Organize Your Site Hierarchically

When visiting a Web site, readers are often seeking a particular piece of information. If your site has only a few pages, they will be able to locate that information quickly, provided that your home page includes a menu with links to every other page. If your site is larger, however, such a menu will be impractical. In this case, do the following:

For advice on organizational patterns, see the Reference Guide on organizing (page 194).

- **Organize hierarchically.** For instance, if you were designing a Web site for your college, you might group your pages into four main areas: academics, admissions, athletics, and resources, which would be listed on the home page. Someone who clicked on "academics" would come to another menu, listing its subtopics, such as degree programs, advising, and home pages for courses. Each of these, in turn, might have its own menu leading to its subtopics.
- **Use intuitive categories.** Create categories that your readers would intuitively think of when searching for a topic. This will enable them to predict which category contains the information they want (Shriver).
- **Keep the number of levels small.** Try to organize so that readers can reach their destination in no more than three clicks from the home page.

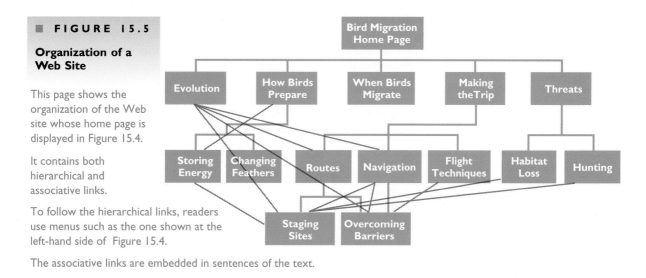

■ FIGURE 15.5

Organization of a Web Site

This page shows the organization of the Web site whose home page is displayed in Figure 15.4.

It contains both hierarchical and associative links.

To follow the hierarchical links, readers use menus such as the one shown at the left-hand side of Figure 15.4.

The associative links are embedded in sentences of the text.

GUIDELINE 4   Provide Useful Associative Links

One of the most powerful features of the World Wide Web is that it enables you to help readers link directly from one of your pages to a page on a related or supporting topic. For instance, in a paragraph that uses a term your readers might not understand, you can provide a link to the definition for the term. Similarly, if you were making a generalization in a report, you could provide a link to the data that supports your point. Because these links lead directly to information associated with the topic about which the reader is reading, these links are called *associative links.*

As you design your Web site, think about the associative links that readers are likely to find helpful. But don't use too many. A large number can be distracting. Also, if you want users to explore your site fully, be cautious about creating links that lead outside your Web site. Readers may not return.

Note that when you follow Guidelines 3 and 4, you provide your Web site with two distinct kinds of organization, each serving a different purpose for your readers. By providing a hierarchical organization (Guideline 3), you build a structure that helps readers to search systematically for information on a particular topic within your site. When you add associative links (Guideline 4), you enable readers to readily obtain additional information related to a topic they have already located and are now reading about. These are not competing organizational structures but complementary ones.

Figure 15.5 shows the hierarchical organization and associative links of a small Web site.

GUIDELINE 5   Label Your Links Clearly

Links are helpful only if readers can understand them. For each link, provide clear and ample information:

- **Highlight only the key words.** If you were to highlight all the words in the following sentence, your readers wouldn't know whether the link will lead to information on whales, the Bering Sea, or krill. Highlighting only key words makes clear what the topic of the link is.

Blue type indicates the link.

| When whales reach the northern Bering Sea, they feed on the plentiful <u>krill.</u>

- **Supply explanations of the links.** These are especially helpful for links included in a list.

| <u>International projects</u>—Read about our current projects in Europe and Asia.

- **Use precise, specific wording.** Choose words that tell exactly what the linked page will show.

GUIDELINE 6 **Provide Many Navigational Aids**

When they finish reading one page, readers often want to move to another area within a Web site for which there is no associative link. Provide the navigational aids that let them do that quickly and easily:

Navigational Aids

- Provide a link back to the home page, where the master menu is found.
- Provide links to submenus that users might find helpful.
- Provide an index, and a link to it on every page.
- Place navigational aids in the same place on every page so readers can find them easily. Typically these aids are located at the top or bottom of the page.

GUIDELINE 7 **Use a Consistent Visual Design**

Page 342 provides additional advice for creating visual unity among pages.

Page 295 shows a set of visually unified Web pages.

Using a consistent visual design from page to page helps to make a Web site visually pleasing and easy to use (Williams and Tollett). Employ the same typefaces and size for text throughout, and use the same colors for headings, background, and other features. From page to page, locate repeated elements in the same place and present them in the same appearance. In large sites, you may develop separate visual designs for different areas, but even then retain some visual elements in the various sections to unify them.

GUIDELINE 8 **Enable Readers to Contact You**

A key question readers ask when viewing a Web page is, "Who made it?" The answer plays a large role in determining whether they will spend time reading it and how much credibility they will attribute to it. Tell readers who you are. In addition,

Ethics of Web Site Creation

When you are creating a Web site, you encounter two sorts of ethical issues: those involved with what you borrow from other people when making your site and those involved with what you offer visitors to your site.

Ethics of Downloading

It's very easy to download images and text from someone else's Web site for incorporation into your own site. Many of the items available on the Web fall into the public domain, meaning that no one has a copyright on them and they can be used freely without permission.

However, much of what's on the Web is copyrighted. This includes not only text but technical drawings and photographs or frames from your favorite characters from the comic pages of the newspaper. It also includes many sound files, animations, and videos (Mohler). When you are thinking of using images from another site, check to see whether the site includes a copyright notice or request concerning use of its materials. Note, however, that what you may find at some sites has itself been copied from some other site, which may have restrictions that weren't observed by the creator of the site you are visiting.

Whenever you are unsure about whether permission is needed to use something, check with your instructor or other knowledgeable person—or simply request the permission.

Even when permission isn't needed, acknowledge your source when using something that clearly represents someone else's intellectual or creative effort. Appendix B tells how to cite Web sources.

Ethics of Posting

When you post something on the Web, keep in mind that other people may rely on your expertise and integrity. Be sure that you have checked your facts and that your information is up to date. Also, remember that all the other ethical considerations discussed in this book apply to Web communications just as much as to print communications. Don't post things that will harm other people.

---

let them know how to reach you or other appropriate persons at your employer's organization. An easy way to do that is to use the HTML tag that lets users click on a link to an e-mail form that is addressed to you:

HTML tag for letting visitors to your site send you e-mail | `<A HREF="mailto:your e-mail address">Send me an e-mail message</A>`

You may be able to provide visitors with additional information that they need, and they may have ideas for increasing the effectiveness of your site.

GUIDELINE 9   **Test Your Site**

On-line communications need to be tested just as much as paper communications do. Your test should certainly include verifying that all the links work. If possible, also view your site using both more sophisticated and less sophisticated hardware and software. Some features of Web sites cannot be viewed with all computers. Finally, conduct a user test of the kind described in Chapter 13. Design the test so that your test readers not only view the various pages but also use the variety of hierarchical and associative links you provide. Only by observing and talking with actual members of your target audience who have used your site can you determine how well it really meets your communication objectives.

■ FIGURE 15.6

Creating Your Own Web Page

1. Type this text:
   <html>
   <head>
   <title>Type the title of your Web page here.</title>
   </head>
   <body>
   Type the body of your text here.
   </body>
   </html>

2. Replace the sentence about the title with your name.

3. Replace the sentence about the body with whatever text you would like to include in your own homepage. Type as much as you want.

4. Use HTML tags shown in Figure 15.3 to give your text the appearance you would like.

5. Save the file as a "text" file. (For example, in Microsoft Word, choose "Save As" from the File menu, give your file a name, and from the pop-up menu for "Save as File Type," select "text.")

6. Open the file in your Web browser. For example, in Netscape choose "Open File in Browser" or something similar from the File menu.

7. Learn additional HTML tags. Use your browser's "View Source" or "View Page Source" option to view the tags used to create design features of the Web pages you visit.

8. Download images from the Web. Place your cursor on the image, hold down the mouse button until a pop-up menu appears, and choose "Save." See the "Focus on Ethics" on page 407 concerning the ethics of downloading.

EXERCISES

1. Visit a Web site, perhaps one related to your major or to a project you are conducting in this course.
   a. Evaluate one of the site's pages in terms of this chapter's guidelines for designing effective Web pages.
   b. Evaluate the site's overall design in terms of this chapter's guidelines for building effective Web sites.

2. Create your own Web page by following the instructions given in Figure 15.6.

3. Create your own Web site, following the guidelines given in the Web site assignment in Appendix C.

Creating and Delivering Oral Presentations

1 | Define your objectives

2 | Select the form of oral delivery best suited to your purpose and audience

3 | Focus on a few main points

4 | Use a simple structure—and help your listeners follow it

5 | Use a conversational style

6 | Look at your audience

7 | Prepare for interruptions and questions—and respond courteously

8 | Fully integrate visual aids into your presentation

9 | Rehearse

10 | Accept your nervousness—and work with it

n your career, you will almost certainly make many oral presentations. In some you may briefly and informally address individuals with whom you work closely every day. At other times, you may speak more formally to upper-level managers, clients, professional organizations, or the general public. Usually you will convey your entire message orally, but on other occasions your talk may supplement a report or proposal you have prepared on the same subject.

Compared to written communications, oral presentations are more personal and more interactive. You'll be able to see your audience's reactions even as you are speaking. Your listeners will usually have an opportunity to make comments and ask questions when you have finished, perhaps even before.

A listener-centered approach to oral presentations

This chapter presents advice that will help you plan and deliver oral presentations in any on-the-job situation. Its ten guidelines teach a listener-centered approach to speaking that parallels the reader-centered approach to writing.

GUIDELINE 1   **Define Your Objectives**

Begin work on an oral presentation in the same way you begin work on a written communication—by figuring out exactly what you want to accomplish and studying the situation in which you will communicate:

Key factors to consider

1. **Define your objectives.** First, think about who your listeners are and how you want to affect them. If you wish to review the procedures for doing these things, turn to Chapter 3.
2. **Think about what your listeners expect.** In addition to considering their expectations about such things as the topics you will cover and the way you will treat them, focus on your listeners' expectations about the amount of time you will speak. Even when you aren't given a time limit, your listeners are likely to have firm expectations about your presentation's length. Don't ruin an otherwise successful presentation by talking too long.

Know and stay within your time limit.

3. **Assess the scene of your talk.** Three aspects of the scene are especially important:
   Size of audience. The smaller your audience, the smaller your visual aids can be, the more likely your audience will expect you to be informal, and the more likely your listeners will interrupt you with questions.
   Location of your talk. If the room has fixed seats, you will have to plan to use visual aids in spots where they are visible to everyone. If you can move the seats, you will be able to choose the seating arrangement best suited to your presentation.
   Equipment available. The kinds of equipment that are available determine the types of visual aids you can use. You can't use a chalkboard or overhead projector if none is available.

GUIDELINE 2   **Select the Form of Oral Delivery Best Suited to Your Purpose and Audience**

At work, people generally use one of three forms of oral delivery: the scripted talk, the outlined talk, or the impromptu talk. Sometimes the situation and your listeners' expectations will dictate the form of talk you will give, but at other times you will be free to choose. The following paragraphs describe each type of delivery and provide information that will help you select among them.

Scripted Talk

With a scripted talk, you write out your entire message, word for word, in advance and then deliver it by reading the script or by reciting it from memory.

Because the scripted talk lets you work out your exact phrasing ahead of time, it is ideal for presenting complex information and speaking when a small slip in phrasing could be embarrassing or damaging. Also, with a scripted talk you can be sure of making all your major points and, if you timed your rehearsals, keeping within your time limit.

The scripted talk is also a good choice when you expect to be extremely nervous, as might happen when you are addressing a large or unfamiliar audience. Even if you become too unsettled to think straight, you will have all your words spelled out in front of you.

On the other hand, scripted talks take a long time to prepare, and you cannot alter them in response to audience reactions. Even more importantly, they are difficult to compose and deliver in a natural speaking style that maintains the interest of your audience. Rehearsals are a must.

Scripted talks offer security but can be rigid.

Outlined Talk

To prepare an outlined talk, you do what the name implies: prepare an outline, perhaps very detailed, of what you plan to say.

At work, outlined talks are more common than scripted talks. You can create them more quickly, and you can deliver them in a "speaking voice," which helps increase listener interest and appeal. Furthermore, outlined talks are very flexible. In response to your listeners' reactions, you can speed up, slow down, eliminate material, or add something that you discover is needed. Outlined talks are ideal for situations in which you speak on familiar topics to small groups, as in a meeting with other people in your department.

The chief weakness of the outlined talk is that it is so flexible that unskilled speakers can easily run over their time limit, leave out crucial information, or have difficulty finding the phrasing that will make their meaning clear. For these reasons, you may want to avoid giving outlined talks on unfamiliar material or in situations where you might be so nervous that you become tongue-tied or forget your message.

Outlined talks offer flexibility within a general framework.

Impromptu Talk

An impromptu talk is one you give on the spur of the moment with little or no preparation. At most, you might jot down a few notes beforehand about the points you want to cover.

The impromptu talk is well suited to situations in which you are speaking for a short time on a subject so familiar that you can express yourself clearly and forcefully with little or no forethought.

The chief disadvantage of the impromptu talk is that you prepare so little that you risk treating your subject in a disorganized, unclear, or incomplete manner. You may even miss the mark entirely by failing to address your audience's concerns at

Impromptu talks are ideal for topics you know well.

all. For these reasons, the impromptu talks given at work are usually short, and they are usually used in informal meetings where listeners can interrupt to ask for additional information and clarification.

GUIDELINE **3** ## Focus on a Few Main Points

For a variety of reasons, it is often more difficult for people to understand what they hear than what they read:

Difficulties That Listeners Face

- Listeners have more difficulty than readers in concentrating for extended periods. Whereas people can read for hours at a time, many listeners have trouble concentrating for more than 20 minutes.

- A talk proceeds at a steady pace, so listeners have no chance to pause to figure out a difficult point.

- If listeners fail to understand a point or let their attention wander, they cannot flip the pages back and reread the passage. The talk goes forward regardless.

Pick points relevant to your listeners' interests and needs.

For these reasons, you need to take special care to make your oral presentations easy to understand, especially if they are longer than a few minutes. One important strategy is to concentrate on only a few major points. Many experienced speakers limit themselves to three or, at most, four. Of course, major points may have subpoints, but their number should be limited also. And it is always important for you to choose points that are directly relevant to your listeners' interests and needs. For instance, when making a recommendation for overcoming a problem in your employer's organization, your first point might be that the problem has two major features, your second might be that there are three principal causes of the problem, and your third might be that you have three recommendations for overcoming it.

GUIDELINE **4** ## Use a Simple Structure—And Help Your Listeners Follow It

If your listeners are to understand and remember your presentation fully, they must be able to organize your points in their own minds. They stand the best chance of doing this if they can follow the structure of your talk. However, as listeners try to discern your presentation's structure, they must proceed without the help of paragraph breaks, headings, indentations, and similar aids that readers have.

Consequently, you can increase the understandability and memorability of your presentations by employing a simple structure that's easy to follow. A widely used structure consists of three major parts:

Simple Structure for Oral Presentations

Introduction	Introduces your topic and discusses its background briefly.
Body	Organized around your three or four main points, which you elaborate and explain.
Conclusion	Sums up your main points.

Even when you employ a very simple organizational pattern, you must still help your readers discern it. This means forecasting the structure in the introduction, clearly signaling transitions throughout, and summarizing the structure (and the main points) in the conclusion. Figure 16.1 (page 414) describes and illustrates techniques for providing these forms of guidance for your listeners.

Note that although the advice you have just read will serve you very well when you are speaking to audiences in the United States and several other Western countries, it may not work in some other cultures where traditions about oral presentations may be much different. For example, Wolvin and Oakley report that in China a talk may have the following structure:

Typical Structure of a Chinese Talk

KI	An introduction offering an observation of a concrete reality.
SHO	A story.
TEN	A shift or change in which a new topic is brought into the message.
KETSU	A gathering of loose ends, a "nonclusion."
YO-IN	A last point to think about, which does not necessarily relate to the rest of the talk

In this style of Chinese presentation, the main points are never stated explicitly, nor is the structure of the talk previewed or reviewed by the speaker. To create an effective talk for an international audience, you will need to research the traditions and expectations of your listeners' culture.

GUIDELINE **5**   ## Use a Conversational Style

For most talks, a conversational style works best. It helps you express yourself clearly and directly, and it helps you build rapport with your listeners. In contrast, a more abstract, impersonal style can lead you to make convoluted statements that are difficult to understand and can cause you to speak in ways that leave your listeners feeling that you are talking *at* them rather than *with* them.

■ **FIGURE 16.1**

Signaling the Structure of Oral Presentations

General Strategies	Techniques
Forecast the structure	■ In the introduction, tell what the structure will be: "In the rest of my talk, I will take up the following three topics: ..." ■ Show a visual aid that outlines the major parts of your talk.
Signal transitions	■ Announce transitions explicitly. "Now I would like to turn to my second topic, which is..." ■ Show a visual aid that announces the next topic and, perhaps, lists its subtopics. ■ Highlight your main points. Your discussion of each main point is a major section of your talk: "I'm going to shift now to the second cause of our problem, a cause that is particularly important for us to understand." ■ Pause before beginning the next topic. This pause will signal your listeners that you have completed one part of your presentation. ■ Slow your pace and speak more emphatically when announcing your major points, just as you would when shifting to a new topic in conversation. ■ Move about. If you are speaking in a setting where you can move around, signal a shift from one topic to another by moving from one spot to another.
Review	■ In your conclusion, remind listeners explicitly about what you've covered: "In conclusion, I've done three main things during this talk: ..."

Although people often associate a conversational style with informality, the two are not synonymous. The two keys to a conversational style are that you do the following: speak directly to your readers and express yourself in the same simple, natural, direct way you do in conversation. The following suggestions will help you do these things:

Ways to develop a conversational style

- **While preparing your talk, imagine that members of your audience are right there listening to the words you are planning to speak.**
- **Use the word *you* or *your* in the first sentence.** Thank your listeners for coming to hear you, praise something you know about them (preferably something related to the subject of your talk), state why they asked you to address them, or talk about the particular goals of theirs that you want to help them achieve.
- **Continue using personal pronouns throughout.** Let the use of *you* or *your* in the first sentence establish a pattern of using personal pronouns *(I, we, our, you, your)* throughout.
- **Use shorter, simpler sentences than you might use when writing.**

■ **Choose words your listeners will understand immediately.** This will be especially important when your listeners include persons who are not native speakers of English. Check with a member of the audience or with someone who is very familiar with your listeners when you are not sure whether your listeners will understand your terminology.

Use your voice as you would in conversation.

As you strive to create a conversational style, remember that the way you use your voice can be as important as the words and phrasing you select. Listen to yourself and your friends converse. Your voices are lively and animated. To emphasize points, you change the pace, the rhythm, and the volume of your speech. You draw out words. You pause at key points. Your voice rises and falls in the cadence of natural speech.

Using your voice in the same way during your oral presentations can help you keep your listeners' interest, clarify the connections between ideas, identify the transitions and shifts that reveal the structure of your talk, and distinguish major points from minor ones. It can even enhance your listeners' estimate of your abilities. Researcher George B. Ray found that listeners are more likely to believe that speakers are competent in their subject matter if the speakers vary the volume of their voices than if the speakers talk in a monotone.

Show your feelings.

Also, exhibit enthusiasm for your subject. One characteristic of conversation is that we let people know how we feel as well as what we think. Do the same in your oral presentations, especially when advocating ideas, making recommendations, or promoting your employer's products and services. If you express enthusiasm about your topic, you increase the chances that your listeners will share your feelings.

Use gestures.

One last way to achieve a conversational speaking style is to use gestures. In conversation, you naturally make many movements—pointing to an object, holding out your arms to show the size of something, and so on. Similarly, when making oral presentations, avoid standing stiffly and unnaturally. Use natural gestures to help hold your listeners' attention and to make your meaning and feelings clear.

GUIDELINE 6 Look at Your Audience

One of the most effective ways of building rapport with your listeners is to look at them while you speak. There are several reasons why this eye contact is so important:

■ It enables you to create a personal connection with your listeners. You show that you are interested in them as individuals, both personally and professionally.
■ It helps you make a favorable impression on them. In one study, researcher S. A. Beebe asked two groups of speakers to deliver the same seven-minute talk to various audiences. One group was instructed to look often at their listeners, the other group was told to look rarely. Beebe found that the speakers who looked more often at their listeners were judged to be better informed, more experienced, more honest, and friendlier than those who used less eye contact.
■ It enables you to judge how things are going. You can see the eyes fastened on you with interest, the nods of approval, the smiles of appreciation, or the puzzled looks and the wandering attention. These signals enable you to adjust your talk, if necessary.

Of course, you don't need to look at your audience constantly. If you are using an outline or a script, you will want to refer occasionally to your notes, but not rivet your gaze on them.

If you have difficulty looking at your listeners when you speak, here are some strategies you can use:

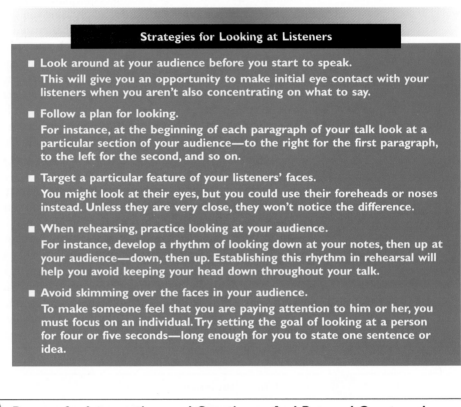

Strategies for Looking at Listeners

- **Look around at your audience before you start to speak.**
  This will give you an opportunity to make initial eye contact with your listeners when you aren't also concentrating on what to say.

- **Follow a plan for looking.**
  For instance, at the beginning of each paragraph of your talk look at a particular section of your audience—to the right for the first paragraph, to the left for the second, and so on.

- **Target a particular feature of your listeners' faces.**
  You might look at their eyes, but you could use their foreheads or noses instead. Unless they are very close, they won't notice the difference.

- **When rehearsing, practice looking at your audience.**
  For instance, develop a rhythm of looking down at your notes, then up at your audience—down, then up. Establishing this rhythm in rehearsal will help you avoid keeping your head down throughout your talk.

- **Avoid skimming over the faces in your audience.**
  To make someone feel that you are paying attention to him or her, you must focus on an individual. Try setting the goal of looking at a person for four or five seconds—long enough for you to state one sentence or idea.

GUIDELINE 7 **Prepare for Interruptions and Questions—And Respond Courteously**

Questions are very common at work.

Audiences at work often ask questions and make comments. In fact, most of the talks you give there will be followed by discussion periods during which members of your audience will ask you for more information, discuss the implications of your talk, and even argue with you about points you have made. This give-and-take helps explain the popularity of oral presentations at work: they permit speaker and audience to engage in a discussion of matters of common interest. Part of preparing to deliver a talk is preparing yourself for questions and discussions. In a sense, you do this when you plan the presentation itself, at least if you follow Chapter 4's advice that you begin planning your communication by thinking about the various questions that your readers will want it to answer. Usually, however, you will not have time in your talk to answer all the questions you expect that your listeners might ask. The questions you can't answer in your talk are ones your listeners may raise in a question period. Prepare for them by planning your responses.

Respond to questions in ways that maintain good relations.

When a member of the audience asks a question—even an antagonistic one—remember that you want to maintain good relations with all your listeners. If you are speaking in a large room, be sure that everyone hears the question. Either ask the questioner to speak loudly or repeat the question yourself. If people hear only your answer, they may have no idea what you are talking about. Respond to all questions courteously. Remember that the questions and comments are important to the people who ask them, even if you don't see why. Give the requested information if you can. If you don't know how much detail the questioner wants, offer some and then ask the questioner if he or she wants more. If you don't know the answer to a question, say so.

Some speakers ask that questions and comments be held until after they have finished. Others begin by inviting their listeners to interrupt when they have a question. By doing so, they are offering to help listeners understand what is being said and relate it to their own concerns and interests. Sometimes listeners will interrupt without being invited to do so. Such interruptions require special care. Speak to the person immediately. If you are planning to address the matter later in your talk, you may want to ask the questioner to wait for your response. If not, you may want to respond right away. After you do so and resume your talk, be sure to remind your listeners of where you broke off: "Well, now I'll return to my discussion of the second of my three recommendations."

GUIDELINE 8 **Fully Integrate Visual Aids into Your Presentation**

You can greatly increase the effectiveness of your oral presentations by using visual aids to present your message to your listeners' eyes as well as their ears. A study conducted at the Wharton Applied Research Center found that speakers who use visual aids are judged by their listeners to be

- Better prepared
- More professional
- More persuasive
- More credible
- More interesting

than speakers who don't use visual aids (Jewett and Margolis; Andrews and Andrews).

The following sections provide advice for planning, designing, and displaying visual aids.

Look for Places Where Visual Aids Can Contribute

Begin planning your visual aids very early.

Visual aids are most effective when they are fully integrated into your oral presentation. To achieve this total integration, begin them early. If you begin by sketching out the verbal portion of your talk, for instance, begin looking for places where visual aids will help as soon as you know how your talk will be structured. Alternatively, you can begin work on your presentation by deciding which visual aids will work best and then building the verbal portion around them.

In either case, look early for places where visual aids can contribute to your presentation in each of the following ways:

- **Explain your subject matter.** In an oral presentation, visual aids can be as useful as in a written communication for helping you convey data, portray the appearance of an object, illustrate the steps in a process, and explain a difficult concept. Look for places where a picture really will be worth a thousand words.
- **Highlight your main points.** By displaying key data, summarizing your conclusions, listing your recommendations, and making other critical points in your visual aids, you give them more emphasis than you could with spoken words alone.
- **Describe the structure of your talk.** Some of the visual aids in your presentation can serve the same purpose as the headings in your printed communications: they can help your listeners see the structure of your talk and understand how each part fits in. For example, you might begin your talk with a slide that announces the major topics you will be discussing. If your talk is long, you might preface each major part with a visual aid that identifies the subtopics you will explore.
- **Hold your listeners' attention.** Listeners are more likely than readers to let their eyes wander—and when they look away from you, their thoughts may drift off as well. Visual aids provide them with a second place to gaze that is directly related to your message. If the visual aids are interesting (visually, intellectually, or both), so much the better.
- **Help you remember what you want to say.** Visual aids can function as your speaking notes. If you forget what you planned to say next, a glance at the visual aid you are displaying can bring you back on track.

Although you should look for opportunities to use visual aids, employ them only when they have a genuine contribution to make. Mixing passages with and without visual aids is a way you can add variety and interest to your talk.

Use a Storyboard

Devised by people who write movie and television scripts, storyboards are an excellent tool for planning the verbal and visual dimensions of a presentation simultaneously. Storyboards are divided into two columns, one showing the words and other sounds an audience will hear, and the other describing (in words or sketches) what the audience will see as those words are spoken. By reading a storyboard, someone can tell what an audience will hear and view at each moment.

A simple way to make a storyboard is to fold a piece of paper down the middle. On the left, outline your talk. On the right, list the visual aids you plan to use as you discuss each topic. Figure 16.2 shows part of a storyboard that includes the script for a talk and notes on the visual aids.

Select the Medium Best Suited to Your Purpose, Audience, and Situation

In the workplace, people use many different media for the visual aids that are part of their oral presentations. The four most common are computer projections made with programs such as PowerPoint and Persuasion, overhead transparencies, chalkboards or dryboards, and handouts. Figure 16.3 summarizes the chief advantages and disadvantages of each.

■ **FIGURE 16.2**

Storyboard for an Oral Presentation

Using a storyboard, writers can carefully coordinate their words with their visual aids.

The right-hand column of the storyboard identifies the visual aid to be shown while corresponding text is spoken.

For this presentation, the speaker used PowerPoint, which allowed the speaker to show a slide with a title and then "build" the slide by adding additional lines of text at appropriate moments.

Programs such as PowerPoint also allow speakers to plan their slides and then add notes that the speakers can print below a paper copy of the slides; these notes can serve to remind the speakers of what they want to say while each slide is displayed.

Talk to Company Steering Committee on
Future Computer Projects

Good morning. I want to thank Mr. Chin for inviting me to speak to you this morning about two projects that my staff in the Computing Services Department thinks will increase our company's productivity considerably.

As you know, people in our company use computers for many different purposes: our managers use computers to create budgets and schedules; our researchers use them to analyze their data; our marketing staff uses them to understand our customers and potential customers; our development teams use them to design products; our manufacturing people use them to control production lines; and everybody uses them for word processing and e-mail.

Show slide entitled "Uses of Computers." List: Management Functions, Research Analysis, Marketing Analysis, Design, Production, Word Processing.

We estimate, however, that at present the company is realizing only about two-thirds of the labor-saving capability of present-day computer technology. There are two reasons for this shortfall.

Show pie chart illustrating that only 2/3 of capability is used.

First, despite promises by software manufacturers, there remains a great deal of incompatibility among applications. Partly, this occurs because people use different platforms—Mac, PC, Sun, and so on—and even (in some cases) different operating systems on the same platform. Also, new releases of some software are not fully compatible with earlier versions. Consequently, work done with an old version of a program may be lost or converted at great expense of time and patience. Also, people in the company who have different versions of the same program may have difficulty sharing their work.

Show slide entitled "Computer Barrier #1: Incompatibility."

Add subheadings: Between Programs and Platforms.

Add subheading: Between Releases.

A second major reason for our failure to realize the full potential of computing technology is that different people use the same data in different ways. For example, the marketing and production divisions use the same sales data, but for much different purposes. As a result, the same data may be processed several times by different units within the company—and this happens each time the data are updated.

Show slide entitled "Computer Barrier #2: Multiple Processing of Same Data."

Today, I want to describe two major projects the Computing Services Department believes will overcome these barriers to full workplace productivity.

Show slide entitled "Proposed Projects."

[Note: This storyboard continues for six more pages.]

When choosing the medium that is most suitable to your presentation, consider the following criteria:

Criteria for selecting media for visual presentations

■ **Your purpose and audience.** A computerized presentation is appropriate when you need to impress, as with a formal presentation or in a sales meeting, but at a small meeting in your own department, overhead transparencies or a handout may be much more suitable.

FIGURE 16.3

Advantages and Disadvantages of Several Media

Medium	Advantages and Disadvantages
Computer projections (for example, PowerPoint, Persuasion)	**Advantages** Enable you to create very polished-looking slides without the aid of a graphic artist Enable you to provide visual harmony to your presentation by using a single, colorful design for all your slides Allow you to prepare slides quickly by typing words and inserting other content directly into them Enable you to expand your media by incorporating tables, graphs, photos, sound, animation, and movies Allow you to use special aids such as a remote control for changing slides and a laser pointer for highlighting elements on the screen **Disadvantages** Special equipment is required for projecting the slides for your audience Must be delivered in a dark room, making it difficult for your listeners to take notes or see you Slides cannot be altered or reordered during a presentation to accommodate audience response Preparation can be time consuming Ability to create special effects leads some speakers into making overly elaborate presentations that detract from their content
Overhead transparencies	**Advantages** Can be made simply by copying a word-processed page onto an acetate sheet with an ordinary copy machine Projectors are available in almost every organization Can reorder the slides and draw on them with markers even as you are giving your talk **Disadvantages** Require some preparation Look plain, especially compared to computerized presentations Can't include motion or sound

FIGURE 16.3
(continued)

Medium	Advantages and Disadvantages
Chalkboard and dryboard	**Advantages** Require no preparation Very flexible Can be used to record contributions from audience Work well for small meetings and discussion sessions **Disadvantages** Can be used only for words and line drawings Can delay presentation while you pause to do your writing Can leave you speaking to the board rather than your audience
Handouts	**Advantages** Give readers something to take away that provides key information from your talk Aid listeners with notetaking **Disadvantages** Require preparation May tempt audience to read ahead rather than listening to what you are saying

- **Your listeners' expectations.** If you provide glitz when your listeners expect simplicity, your credibility will diminish, just as it will if you keep pausing to draw diagrams on the board for listeners who expect you to have prepared your visual aids in advance.
- **Your resources.** The amount of time you have, the size of your budget, and the unavailability of equipment may limit your choices.

Remember that you can use more than one medium in a presentation. For instance, when speaking to a group of managers, a chemical engineer used slides to show photographs of the crystals grown in an experiment, overhead transparencies to explain the process used, and a handout containing detailed data that her audience could study later.

Make Your Visual Aids Easy to Read and Understand

It is much more difficult to comprehend the visual aids in an oral presentation than it is to comprehend the visual aids in a printed communication such as a proposal or report. Listeners must study the visual aids from a distance, which may make your writing and symbols difficult for them to see. Also, listeners must look at the visual aids while you are talking, so they have to concentrate on both at once. In addition, listeners have only a brief time to see the visual aids—and that time is determined by your pace in speaking, not their pace in comprehending. Consequently, you should design your visual aids for immediate understanding.

The table at the top of page 422 gives some ways to make it easy for your listeners to read and understand your visual aids. Figure 16.4 shows slides from a PowerPoint presentation that illustrate their application.

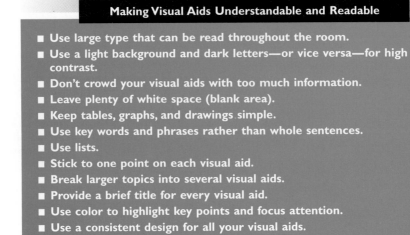

Making Visual Aids Understandable and Readable

- Use large type that can be read throughout the room.
- Use a light background and dark letters—or vice versa—for high contrast.
- Don't crowd your visual aids with too much information.
- Leave plenty of white space (blank area).
- Keep tables, graphs, and drawings simple.
- Use key words and phrases rather than whole sentences.
- Use lists.
- Stick to one point on each visual aid.
- Break larger topics into several visual aids.
- Provide a brief title for every visual aid.
- Use color to highlight key points and focus attention.
- Use a consistent design for all your visual aids.
- Avoid long series of text-only visual aids.
- Proofread.

■ **FIGURE 16.4 Presentation Slides Made with PowerPoint**

With PowerPoint and similar programs, you can change the format of your slides with a few clicks.

These formats were chosen from a library provided by PowerPoint; you can also make your own quite easily.

The figure is a piece of clipart that comes with the program and can be easily inserted.

It's also possible to insert tables, graphs, pictures, movies, and sounds.

These slides are for projection from a computer; the program also makes overhead transparencies and 35 mm slides.

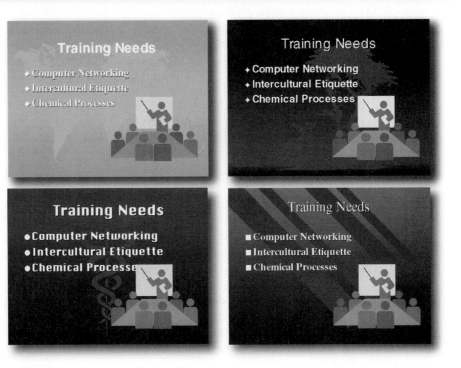

Test Your Visual Aids

Like any other element of a communication, visual aids should be tested beforehand to make sure that they will do what you want them to do. Show them to other people, preferably members of your target audience. Such testing is particularly important if you are speaking to an international audience. Especially in visual aids that show people or workspaces, it is easy to accidentally violate a taboo or otherwise offend or irritate listeners from another culture. Even if you blunder in a way that only draws chuckles, you will have reduced the effectiveness of your presentation.

Prepare Your Stage

When you deliver a talk at work, you are a little like a stage performer, with some words to deliver and some props (your visual aids) to manage. Any difficulties with your visual aids can interfere with your listeners' ability to concentrate on and understand your message. Therefore, arrive at the site of your presentation with plenty of time to set up and test any equipment you will use and to arrange your materials so you can work with them smoothly during your presentation.

Present Your Visual Aids Effectively

During your talk, use your visual aids in ways that support and reinforce your presentation, rather than detract from it:

- **Display a visual aid only when you are talking about it.** If you talk about one thing but display a visual aid about something else, each person in your audience must choose whether to listen to your words or read your visual aid. Either way, your audience may miss part of your message.
- **Leave each visual aid up long enough for your listeners to digest its contents.** Sometimes this will require you to stop speaking while your listeners study your visual aid.
- **Explain the key points in your visual aids.** If you want your readers to notice a particular trend, compare certain figures, or focus on a particular feature in a drawing, say so explicitly.
- **Use the same words and phrases in your visual aids and in your spoken comments.** What your listeners see and what they hear should reinforce one another, not leave them puzzled about whether what they are reading corresponds to what you are saying.

Look at Your Audience Most of the Time

When displaying visual aids, some speakers break their connection with their listeners. Usually this happens because the speakers lose eye contact with their listeners by turning to look at a chalkboard or projection screen. For this reason, some speakers feel that they must face forward absolutely all the time.

However, it is sometimes natural and appropriate to turn and look at your visual aids—just as your listeners are looking at them. For instance, you may want to locate the answer to a question or point to an important piece of information. When you turn away from your listeners, however, do so only briefly and speak loudly enough that you can still be heard by the people who are now behind you.

Give Your Listeners Something to Take Away

No matter how skillfully you design the oral and visual dimensions of your presentation, your listeners are likely to forget some of your message after they leave the room where you are speaking. You can overcome this problem by passing out a summary of your key points—or even your entire script—for your listeners to file for future reference.

However, handouts can also be a distraction. Your listeners may start to read the handout, rather than listen to you. For that reason, some communication specialists urge speakers to distribute their handouts only after they have finished speaking. However, if you give your listeners an outline of your talk before you begin, you help them understand your talk's structure and scope and assist them in taking notes. To help you prepare an outline for distribution during your talk, PowerPoint and similar programs automatically generate pages with miniature versions of your slides and blank spaces for notes.

Handouts are especially useful when you are addressing an international audience whose members may not be able to follow everything you say. In this case, if you are speaking from a complete script, the script itself is the best handout, along with copies of your key visual aids. If you are not speaking from a script, create a more detailed outline of what you plan to say than you otherwise would. Consider using full sentences—even in an outline—rather than words or brief phrases.

GUIDELINE 9   Rehearse

All of your other good preparations can go for naught if you are unable to deliver your message in a clear and convincing manner. Whether you are delivering a scripted or outlined talk, consider the following advice:

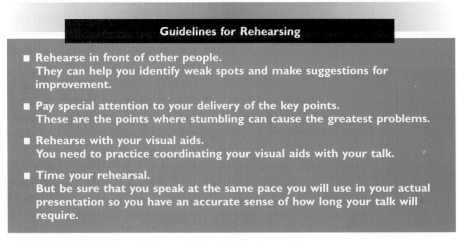

Guidelines for Rehearsing

- **Rehearse in front of other people.**
  They can help you identify weak spots and make suggestions for improvement.

- **Pay special attention to your delivery of the key points.**
  These are the points where stumbling can cause the greatest problems.

- **Rehearse with your visual aids.**
  You need to practice coordinating your visual aids with your talk.

- **Time your rehearsal.**
  But be sure that you speak at the same pace you will use in your actual presentation so you have an accurate sense of how long your talk will require.

GUIDELINE **10**   **Accept Your Nervousness—And Work with It**

This guideline is difficult for many novice speakers to follow. But it is very important. Not only is nervousness unpleasant to experience, it can lead to distracting and unproductive behaviors that greatly impair the effectiveness of your talk. These include:

- Looking away from your listeners instead of looking into their eyes.
- Speaking in an unnatural or forced manner.
- Exhibiting a tense or blank facial expression.
- Fidgeting, rocking, and pacing.

How should you deal with nervousness? First, accept it. It's natural. Even practiced speakers with decades of experience sometimes feel nervous when they face an audience. If you fret about being nervous, you merely heighten the emotional tension. Also, keep in mind that your nervousness is not nearly so obvious to your listeners as it is to you. Even if they do notice that you are nervous, they are more likely to be sympathetic than displeased. Furthermore, a certain amount of nervousness can help you. The adrenaline it pumps into your system will make you more alert and more energetic as you speak.

Here are some strategies for reducing your nervousness and controlling the pacing, fidgeting, and other undesirable mannerisms it fosters:

Controlling Nervousness

- **Avoid rushing from a previous activity to your talk.**
- **Devote a few minutes before your talk to relaxing, for instance, by taking a walk, chatting with a friend, or spending a quiet moment alone.**
- **Arrive early to give yourself plenty of time to set up.**
- **Remind yourself that your listeners are there to learn from you, not to judge you.**
- **Try to speak with audience members before your presentation begins so that you will already have started a conversation with a few of your listeners.**
- **When it's time to begin, pause before you start your talk. Look at your audience, say "Hello," and adjust your outline or notes as you accustom yourself to standing before your listeners.**

MAKING TEAM PRESENTATIONS

At work, team presentations are as common as team writing. They occur, for example, when a project team reports on its progress or results, when various departments work together on a joint proposal, or when a company is selling a technical product (such as customized software) that requires participation of employees from several units of the company.

Team presentations are so common because it is usually more effective to have several members make a presentation than to have one person speak for all team members. In a team presentation, each topic can be discussed by the person who is most expert in it. Moreover, the use of a variety of speakers can help retain the audience's attention.

The following sections provide advice for creating and delivering effective team presentations.

PLAN THOROUGHLY

When making team presentations, plan as carefully as you would if preparing a team-written document. Devoting a team meeting to making plans can be very helpful. Decide which topic each team member is to discuss, which points are to be made, and how each part fits with the others. Set a time limit for each part, so that the total presentation doesn't run too long. Also, decide whether the team is going to ask the audience to hold questions until the end or invite the audience to interrupt the speaker with questions. In either case, provide time for the interchange between the team and its listeners.

ALLOW FOR INDIVIDUAL DIFFERENCES

In a team-written project, the goal is usually to produce a document with a single voice for the entire document. In team presentations, however, each speaker can speak in his or her own style and voice, provided that the general tone of the presentation is relatively consistent.

MAKE EFFECTIVE TRANSITIONS BETWEEN SPEAKERS

By carefully planning the transitions from one speaker to the next, a team can substantially increase the effectiveness of its presentation. Switch speakers where you are making a major shift in topic. This will help the audience discern the overall structure of the presentation. Also, have both speakers explain how the two parts of the presentation fit together. For example, the speaker who is finishing might say, "Now, Ursula will explain how we propose to solve the downtime problem I have just identified." The next speaker might then say, "In the next few minutes, I'll outline our three recommendations for dealing with the downtime problem Jefferson has described."

SHOW RESPECT FOR ONE ANOTHER

Your team can increase the effectiveness of your presentation if each member shows, perhaps implicitly, respect for the others. If team members seem confident of one another's contributions and capabilities, your audience is more likely to adopt the same attitudes.

REHEARSE TOGETHER

Rehearsals are crucial to the success of team presentations. Team members can help one another polish their individual contributions and ensure that all the parts are coordinated in a way that the audience can easily understand. Moreover, they can see to it that the entire presentation can be completed in the time allotted. Running overtime is a common and serious problem for groups that have not worked together previously.

CONCLUSION

Making oral presentations can be among your most challenging—and rewarding—experiences at work. By taking a listener-centered approach that is analogous to the reader-centered approach described elsewhere in this book, and by striving to communicate simply and directly with your audience, you will prepare talks that your listeners will find helpful, informative, interesting, and enjoyable.

EXERCISES

1. Outline a talk to accompany a written communication that you have prepared or are preparing in one of your classes. The audience for your talk will be the same as for your written communication. The time limit for the talk will be ten minutes. Be sure that your outline indicates the following:

   ■ The way you will open your talk
   ■ The overall structure of your talk
   ■ The main points from your written communication that you will emphasize
   ■ The visual aids you will use

   Be ready to explain your outline in class.

2. Imagine that you must prepare a five- to ten-minute talk on some equipment, process, or procedure. Identify your purpose and readers. Then write a script or an outline for your talk (whichever your instructor assigns). Be sure to plan what visual aids you will use and when you will display each of them.

3. Standing in front of your class, deliver the talk you prepared in Exercise 1 or 2. Let your classmates and instructor play the role of your intended audience. When preparing your talk, be sure to rehearse it more than once, timing it to see that you can stay within your time limit. After your talk, take questions from your audience, who

will be asking the types of questions your intended listeners would ask.

4. At work, you will sometimes be asked to contribute to discussions about ways to make improvements. For this exercise, you are to deliver a five-minute impromptu talk describing some improvement that might be made in some organization you are familiar with. Topics you might choose include ways of improving efficiency at a company that employed you for a summer job, ways of improving the operation of some club you belong to, and ways that a campus office can provide better service to students.

   In your talk, clearly explain the problem and your solution to it. Your instructor will tell you which of the following audiences you should address in your talk:

   ■ Your classmates in their role as students. You must try to persuade them of the need for, and the reasonableness of, your suggested action.

   ■ Your classmates, playing the role of the people who actually have the authority to take the action you are suggesting. You should take one additional minute at the beginning of your talk to describe these people to your classmates.

CHAPTER 17

Creating Communications with a Team

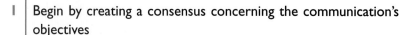

GUIDELINES

1	Begin by creating a consensus concerning the communication's objectives
2	Involve the whole team in planning
3	Make a project schedule
4	Share leadership responsibilities
5	Make meetings efficient
6	Encourage debate and diversity of ideas
7	Be sensitive to possible cultural and gender differences in team interactions
8	Use computer support for collaboration when it's available

With satisfaction and pride, Jack sets his copy of the report down on his desk. For the past three months, he and four co-workers have labored together to evaluate three possible plans for creating a high-speed computer network for their employer's headquarters building. Together they researched, together they evaluated, and together they wrote the 60-page report with which Jack is now so pleased. Such group efforts are very common at work. The evaluation report was Jack's fourth collaborative communication project in the past twelve months. Two of the others were written reports, and one was an oral presentation that he and several co-workers created and delivered together. For Jack, as for most professionals, the ability to work effectively on communication teams is an indispensable skill.

Advantages of creating communications with a team

Employees work together on communication teams for several reasons. Many projects benefit greatly from the expertise of people specializing in several fields. Other projects are simply too large to be completed on time without the combined efforts of several people. Just as important, experience has shown that groups can generate a larger and more creative pool of ideas than can one person working alone. For this last reason, management theory and practice increasingly emphasize teamwork over individual efforts in all areas, including writing and speaking.

Despite these good reasons for establishing communication teams, the thought of working on one can create anxiety. Jack experienced such apprehensions the first time his boss assigned him to a team. Because Jack hadn't gained any experience with writing groups in school, he didn't know what to expect. He feared that others in the group might overrule his good ideas or that his ideas might be accepted but blended in with the others so that he wouldn't receive the recognition he deserved. He also feared that he might be left with a huge portion of the work because others would not feel as committed to the project as he did. In fact, Jack has encountered some of these problems while working on teams, but overall he has found teamwork to be quite satisfying. And he has earned a reputation for being an effective writing-team member, a quality he hadn't previously realized that he possessed or that his employer valued.

SPECIAL CHALLENGES OF TEAM PROJECTS

All of the advice given in other chapters applies just as validly to communications you co-author as it does to those you prepare by yourself. That's because, at one level, communicating collaboratively involves exactly the same process as communicating independently. You need to define your objectives, plan a strategy for meeting those objectives, and then draft, evaluate, and revise the communication in which you carry out that strategy.

Some additional tasks required for team efforts

However, when you join with others to form a communication team, you and your teammates have some additional tasks to perform. Imagine that your team is preparing a brief, written communication that can be completed in a single meeting. You and your teammates might discuss your subject matter until a consensus is reached about what to say. Then, one person could draft what he or she thinks the team has decided. The team then edits the draft and adjourns. Even when a team works on such brief communications, the writing skills required include those necessary to run the meeting efficiently, obtain good contributions from all team members, negotiate conflicting ideas about the communication's content, and draft something that all present will find acceptable.

Other communication projects, like Jack's, are too large to be completed in a single meeting. In fact, some are huge. The proposals from companies that wanted to build the space shuttle for the National Aeronautics and Space Administration (NASA) were thousands of pages long, required contributions from hundreds of people, and cost millions of dollars to prepare. When working on large projects, a team will typically alternate between work done as a group and work done independently by individual team members. Consequently, in addition to needing all the special skills required for team writing on brief communications, the team members face the additional challenges of figuring out how to coordinate group efforts and individual work and how to create a single, unified communication from sections drafted by different people, each with a distinctive personal style.

This chapter's eight guidelines will help you and your teammates work productively together on either written or oral communications. For additional advice about creating oral communications as a team, see Chapter 16.

GUIDELINE **1** **Begin by Creating a Consensus Concerning the Communication's Objectives**

The first activity of the communication process—defining objectives—is even more important when you are participating on a team than when you are preparing a communication individually. Because each member brings a unique perspective to the task, the team can build on one another's ideas and insights to achieve a particularly comprehensive view of the communication's readers and purpose. This is especially helpful with long, complex communications, such as formal reports and proposals.

Failure to achieve consensus about objectives can cause many problems.

However, differences among the team members' perspectives may also create problems. If each member insists on emphasizing his or her own perspective on the communication, the team may have difficulty determining what's important to the people whose perspective matters most: the readers.

Moreover, even when the team agrees on a specific set of objectives, team members may interpret them differently. For example, the members of a writing team might agree that the readers of their report will want to know the research procedures the team used. But some team members might think the readers want a nontechnical explanation, while others may think a technical one is appropriate.

No matter who drafts the description of the research procedures, some of the team members are likely to say it doesn't achieve the communication's objectives. The work may need to be redone, and feelings are likely to be strained as a result.

To avoid such problems, urge members of your communication teams to follow these four suggestions:

> ### Defining Objectives as a Team
>
> 1. Take time to explore the diverse views of all team members regarding your communication's objectives.
>
> 2. Keep talking until consensus is reached.
>
> 3. Discuss communication strategies the team might use to achieve its objectives. Such discussion may reveal unexpected differences among team members that can then be addressed openly.
>
> 4. Remain open to new insights about your readers and purposes as your work progresses. But remember that individual team members must share these insights so all can agree on the modified definition of objectives.

GUIDELINE **2**   ## Involve the Whole Team in Planning

One major advantage of planning as a team is identical with a major advantage of defining objectives as a team: many minds working together will almost always generate better results than could one person working alone. Another major advantage stems from the way teams often organize their work. On almost all large projects and on many small ones, teams often divide research, drafting, and other tasks among their members. When this occurs, each team member must be clear about what the team wants him or her to produce. Otherwise, the person may spend hours on work the team will ask to have redone. Such misunderstandings bruise feelings and waste time. Here are four suggestions for avoiding such problems:

Suggestions for planning team projects

- **Discuss plans in detail.** The key to avoiding misunderstandings is to plan in sufficient detail. Vague plans leave the door wide open for problems. For each part of a communication, team members should discuss what topics are to be covered, what sources should be consulted, what main points are to be highlighted, and what visual aids are to be included.

  Such detailed team planning often triggers ideas and suggestions that may not have occurred to one person working alone. In addition, it informs each team member about exactly what his or her efforts are supposed to produce. Moreover, it can enable team members to see at the outset how their sections are supposed to fit together, so that less editing time is required later to achieve a harmonious document.

- **Write an outline.** One way to focus your team's planning efforts on the details of your report is to write an outline together. Outlining also gives everyone a written record of what the team decided, so no one forgets while doing independent work.

- **Create a storyboard.** Your team can also plan together by using the "storyboard" technique devised by James R. Tracey and now widely employed in industry. After the team has prepared a written outline, it assigns each section to one of the team members. Before the next team meeting, the member

■ **FIGURE 17.1**

Storyboard for Use by Writing Teams

Before anyone begins drafting, team members can use a storyboard to decide together what the content of each section will be.

This process helps each team member draft sections that will fit together tightly and require a minimum of revision.

Storyboard	
Project _____	Writer _____
Section _____	Subsection _____

TOPIC:
Thesis Statement:

Main Subpoints to Be Made   Figure

1.

2.

3.   Figure Title

responsible for a given section fills out a set of standard, one-page forms, preparing one form for each segment of the section. On the form, the writer indicates the segment's title or topic, its main point (or thesis), its subpoints, and the figures it will include. See Figure 17.1.

When all members have completed their storyboards, the team meets again to review the results. Some teams copy and circulate the storyboards before the meeting. Some tape them on the walls in the order in which they will appear in the finished communication. Team members then jot down their comments on the storyboards and discuss their ideas. This process often uncovers overlap, omissions, and inconsistencies. Typically, it produces many new ideas as well. After revision, the storyboards can serve as guides to drafting.

■ **Use a style guide.** To achieve a uniform style in their communications, teams often need to do a lot of editing. Your teams can reduce that work by giving each member a style guide before drafting begins.

Style guides tell how to handle details in a consistent fashion. For example, they explain what abbreviations to use, whether to spell out numbers or use numerals, what the headings should look like, and how tables and graphs should be designed. If drafting will be done on a computer, a style guide may specify such things as the margins, font, and type size to be used.

Some employers publish their own style guides or specify that employees should use an appropriate general one, such as the *Chicago Manual of Style,* the *CBE Style Guide* (for writers in the biological sciences), or the *APA Style Manual* (for writers in the social sciences). If your employer doesn't use a specific style guide, your team can create one, perhaps by delegating the responsibility to one member.

GUIDELINE **3** **Make a Project Schedule**

Schedules are helpful for almost any team project that requires more than one meeting, but especially for projects in which some of the tasks will be performed by individual team members working independently. The schedule lets each person know exactly when his or her work must be completed, and it enables every team member to see the adverse consequences of missing any deadline along the way. When creating a schedule, include the following three elements:

Suggestions for creating a project schedule for your team

- **Time to define the project's objectives, probably at the first meeting.** If the project leader has already defined the objectives, he or she should take time to discuss them with the team. Alternatively, the entire team can define the communication's objectives by discussing its purpose and readers. In either case, this definition of objectives can serve as a beacon to guide both group discussions and individual work throughout the entire project.
- **Frequent checkpoints.** The team needs to meet often enough to see that the work that individual members are doing independently is proceeding in the way the team wants. The early discovery of problems helps the individual as much as it helps the team because the individual is saved from investing additional time doing work that will have to be redone. Frequent meetings also give the team ample opportunity to refine or alter its plans *before* team members have devoted overly large amounts of energy and creativity to work that later would have to be changed substantially.
- **Time to edit the drafts for consistency and coherence.** When you write alone, you usually don't need to edit for consistency because you will probably have written consistently in the first place. But on a group project, different sections are written by different people, each with a distinctive, individual style. Even if the team uses a style guide, sharp differences may appear between sections. The editing required to smooth out these differences might be assigned to one team member, or it might be undertaken by the whole team acting as an editorial committee. Whichever approach your team takes, it will need to provide time in its schedule for this work.

Create a team schedule as soon as possible.

The best time to make a schedule is at the very beginning of the specialized, technical work that will produce much of the content of the communication. For instance, Jack's team made its schedule when it first received its assignment to investigate the networking alternatives. This enabled the team to create a schedule that integrated writing activities with the research and other work that the team was to conduct. When teams instead plan to do all of the writing work at the end of the project, they frequently leave too little time for writing. Consequently, their communication is either done poorly or late—outcomes that you and your teammates will surely want to avoid.

GUIDELINE **4** **Share Leadership Responsibilities**

Communication experts Kenneth D. Benne and Paul Sheats have identified a wide range of roles that team members must play if they are going to maximize their productivity. Many are described below.

Type	Roles and Their Contributions
Task roles	
Initiators	offer new ideas, propose new solutions, and restate old issues in a novel way. They provide creativity and direction as the team ponders its subject matter and the strategies for communicating about it.
Information seekers	request clarification and additional information. They ensure that the team members understand all relevant factors — including their subject matter, readers, and communication alternatives.
Information givers	furnish the facts needed by the team, sometimes on their own initiative, sometimes in response to information seekers.
Opinion seekers	ask others to express their judgments, values, and opinions.
Opinion givers	share their views about what the team's decisions should be.
Clarifiers	clear up misunderstanding or confusion by explaining points or providing additional information.
Summarizers	consolidate the team's deliberations by stating concisely what has been said or decided. They help team members see what has been accomplished so the team can proceed to the next task.
Energizers	motivate the team to take action, often by communicating a sense of enthusiasm or by emphasizing its commitment to its goals.
Group maintenance roles	
Encouragers	offer warmth, praise, and recognition during team discussions. They support quieter team members, whom they gently encourage to join in.
Harmonizers	help team members explore differences of opinion without hurting one another's feelings. They detect and reduce friction by helping the team to focus on ideas rather than on personalities.
Feeling expressers	share their own feelings or vocalize those of the team, thereby enabling members to deal with emotions that might interfere with the team's ability to work together productively.
Compromisers	volunteer concessions of their own positions on controversial issues and suggest a middle ground when other team members seem stuck in opposing positions. They help all team members realize that they are contributing even when their ideas are altered.
Gatekeepers	encourage all team members to participate, and they create opportunities for silent members to speak.

The roles fall into two groups: *task roles,* which keep the team moving toward its goal, and *group maintenance roles,* which assure good working relationships among the team members. See Figure 17.2.

Teams often work best when all members share leadership responsibilities.

The most important thing for you and your teammates to remember is that these roles are all leadership roles for which team members all should take responsibility when the need arises. In this way, your whole team shares leadership responsibility. Teams are usually stronger when their members share leadership rather than rely on one person to provide it all.

GUIDELINE **5** ## Make Meetings Efficient

Nothing is more precious to a communication team than time. Because it's usually so hard to find moments when all members are free, every one of these moments should be used well. Also, every member usually has so many other responsibilities that meetings must be productive to justify the minutes and hours taken away from other duties. Here are four strategies for making meetings productive:

Suggestions for conducting efficient meetings

- **Prepare an agenda.** Before the meeting, have someone prepare an agenda by listing the major issues to be discussed. Then, open the meeting by having the team review the agenda to be sure everyone agrees on what is to be accomplished. As the meeting proceeds, team members can then keep the discussion on track by referring to the agenda.
- **Bring discussions to a close.** Communication teams sometimes keep debating a topic even after everything useful has been said. When a discussion becomes repetitious, you can focus the team's attention on the decision to be made by saying something like, "We seem to have explored the options pretty thoroughly. Let's make a decision."

   Some teams go right on talking even after they have reached consensus. If your team does that, try formalizing the agreement by saying, "I think I hear everyone agreeing that. . . ." If someone objects, the team can clear up any point that still needs to be resolved. Otherwise, the team can move on to the next item of business.
- **Sum up.** After all the topics have been covered to everyone's satisfaction, sum up the results of the meeting. Such a summation consolidates what the team has accomplished and reinforces its decisions.
- **Set goals for the next meeting.** Before the meeting breaks up, make sure everyone knows exactly what he or she is to do before the next meeting. This helps assure that when you meet again, you will have new ideas and material to discuss.

There's one caution, however. In your quest for efficiency, remember that even at work a writing team is a social group in which friendliness and interest in one another are natural and desirable. In your attempts to be efficient, don't take the fun out of the occasion. On the other hand, don't let the fun take up so much of the meeting that people feel exasperated because so little was accomplished.

GUIDELINE **6** ## Encourage Debate and Diversity of Ideas

As mentioned above, one of the chief benefits of group work is that many people bring their expertise and creativity to a project. To take full advantage of that benefit, all team members must offer their ideas freely—even if the ideas conflict with one another. In fact, debate and disagreement can be very useful if carried out in a courteous and nonthreatening way. Debate ensures that the team won't settle for the first or most obvious suggestion. It also enables your team to avoid "groupthink," a condition in which everyone uncritically agrees at a time when critical thinking is really what's needed.

Encouraging debate and diversity of ideas can be difficult. Some people are naturally shy about speaking, and many avoid disagreeing, especially if they fear that their ideas will be treated with hostility rather than openness and politeness. To promote healthy debate and the consideration of a rich diversity of ideas, you and your teammates can use these four strategies:

Ways to encourage debate and diversity of ideas

- **Invite everyone to speak.** The quiet members of a team often have good ideas but are timid about offering them. They may need to be invited before they will speak up. You might simply say, "What do you think of that idea, Keith?" or "What have you been thinking about this topic, Jessica?" If some team members are very talkative, you may have to create a place for the quiet person in the team's conversation by interrupting the more talkative people. You might say, "I've liked the things Lynn has had to say, but I wonder what Pat's ideas are," or "Let's take a minute to hear what Terry feels about the ideas we've been discussing." Another way of inviting everyone to speak is to establish an operating procedure that gives each person an equal amount of time to talk about every major new topic before the floor is opened to a more general discussion.

- **Listen with interest and respect.** When a team member does speak, it is critical that others respond with interest and respect—even if they disagree with what the person is saying. If someone feels that his or her ideas have been treated rudely or harshly, that person is unlikely to contribute openly again.

Show that you welcome each person's contributions.

One simple way to indicate that you welcome someone's contribution is to make remarks that show you are paying attention. If you agree with the person, say such things as "That's interesting," "I hadn't thought of that," or even simply "Uh-huh."

If you disagree, indicate that you welcome the person's contribution by showing that you want to understand the person's position fully. Ask questions if you are unclear about anything. Or, paraphrase the person's position, perhaps after saying something like, "What I think I hear you saying is. . . ." If you have misunderstood, the speaker can then correct you. Maybe you don't disagree after all. But even if you do, *hear the person out*. Don't cut the speaker off. If you won't listen, others won't speak, and then your team will lose its good ideas as well as its not-so-good ones.

Maintaining eye contact makes people feel you are listening attentively to them.

In addition to sounding interested, look interested in what others are saying. That will encourage them to share their ideas. Start by maintaining eye contact. Researchers have discovered that when speakers think they are receiving more eye contact, they also think their listeners are more attentive (Kleck and Nuessle). Researchers have also found that people believe that listeners who maintain lots of eye contact are friendlier than those who maintain less eye contact (Kleinke, Bustos, Meeker, and Staneski).

Another way to show your interest is to refrain from nervous gestures. Researchers have found that speakers feel uncomfortable if their listeners engage in such nervous gestures as cleaning their fingernails, drumming their fingers, or holding their hands over their mouths (Mehrabian). Replace such gestures with notetaking, or assume a relaxed but alert posture.

Listen actively.

The listening strategies described above are sometimes referred to as *active listening skills* because they involve positive actions you can take to understand other people and to show them you want to hear their message accurately. The term *active listening* is particularly appropriate because it can remind you that in team meetings you should put as much effort into listening as you put into speaking.

- **Be considerate when discussing drafts.** Team meetings can become particularly awkward when drafts produced by members working independently are reviewed by the group as a whole. Many people almost automatically resist any suggestion for change in their drafts. This resistance is entirely understandable. The writers have invested considerable personal creativity and effort in the project and so are reluctant to see that work undone. Furthermore, writers sometimes feel that the team is criticizing their overall writing ability when it requests changes. The resulting defensive responses by the writers can prevent needed improvements and undermine the mutual goodwill that is essential to effective teamwork.

  On the other side, the people reviewing another team member's work often avoid suggesting changes because they sympathize with the drafter's anxiety and fear a conflict. "We just can't think of any way to make this better," they say— no matter how badly improvements are needed.

  Such resistance by the writer and other team members can be very counterproductive. Most drafts can be improved, and open discussion of them can discover how that can be done.

Open your comments on drafts with a positive statement.

  The most effective way to promote an open discussion is to be considerate of one another's feelings. Present your ideas for changing a draft as suggestions or options: "Here's another way you could say that." When discussing options, focus on the *positive* reasons for choosing one option over another. Avoid making statements that sound like criticism of the writer's work. Also, accompany suggestions with praise for what is strong in the writer's draft. Indicate that you are offering ideas for improving a draft that is basically good, not corrections for a draft that is fundamentally bad.

  You can also be considerate of others' feelings when your draft is being reviewed by the team. Help the other team members feel comfortable by being open, not defensive. Make them feel that their ideas are welcomed rather than resented.

- **Treat drafts as team property, not individual property.** Another way to promote open discussion is to encourage team members to give up their sense of personal "ownership" of the material they draft. While still taking pride in your contributions, you and your teammates can try to see your drafts as something you've created for the team so that the drafts are the group's property, not your personal property. This doesn't mean that you and your teammates should give up supporting the strong points of your own drafts if you think they have been underestimated. It means that when the team is reviewing your draft, you should join in a *reasoned* discussion of the best way to write "our" communication rather than struggle to protect "my" writing from assaults by others. Your

Swapping responsibilities can diminish the sense of personal ownership.

openness about your draft will encourage others to take the same attitude concerning theirs.

Your team can also reduce the troublesome sense of personal ownership by agreeing to swap responsibilities at a certain point. For example, after second drafts are written, the first section might become the responsibility of the person who drafted the second section, the second section might become the responsibility of the person who drafted the third section, and so on. Also, the team members can agree that at some point everyone's drafts will be combined for editing and polishing by the whole group or by an individual the group designates. At that point, the draft clearly becomes *group* property, not *individual* property.

GUIDELINE 7 **Be Sensitive to Possible Cultural and Gender Differences in Team Interactions**

Different people approach team projects in different ways. It's very helpful to any team for all members to be aware of their own predispositions and to be sensitive to those of others. The team's goal should be to interact in ways that allow each member to make his or her maximum contribution. For this to happen, various individuals may need to adapt their customary ways of interacting. For example, because they are eager to contribute, some members may speak immediately on each issue that arises. An advantage to the team of this strategy is that these individuals quickly put ideas on the table for others to consider and, perhaps, build on. However, this strategy also has the potential to discourage other members from saying anything. Perhaps these other members fear that the matter has already been settled or are hesitant to contradict the first speaker. The challenge faced by a team is to develop an approach to conducting its interactions that gets the fullest possible contribution from all members.

To succeed in encouraging maximum participation by all team members, each person must be sensitive and responsive to the individual styles of everyone else. It can be helpful to remember that a person's style may be significantly influenced by gender and cultural background.

Gender and Collaboration

For example, research shows that many men state their ideas and opinions as assertions of fact. When exploring ideas, they may argue over them in a competitive manner. In contrast, many women offer their ideas tentatively, introducing them with statements such as "I think," or "I'm not sure about this, but. . . ." If there is disagreement, they may support part or all of the other person's ideas and seek to reach consensus (Lay).

Although it would be counterproductive to assume that all men or all women behave in these ways, knowing about such general patterns can enable you to increase your sensitivity to your own habits and to recognize the different practices of others. A key point is to avoid valuing your own mode of interacting as necessarily the best one. As mentioned above, you can help to create successful team interactions by adapting your own modes and supporting people with different modes so that all can contribute to the maximum of their potential.

Culture and Collaboration

On the job, you will almost certainly find yourself engaged in some form of international or intercultural collaboration. In companies with international operations, collaboration between offices can also mean collaboration between residents of different countries. Moreover, many workers in the United States and Canada were born and raised elsewhere in the world or have grown up in families or neighborhoods deeply influenced by other cultures.

Recognizing cultural differences

Writing researcher Deborah S. Bosley has identified some of the ways in which people from non-Western cultures may behave differently than people from Western cultures when working on writing teams:

- **May not say "no" even when "no" is really what they mean.** In some cultures, people do not say "no" even in response to direct questions. Instead, they indicate "no" only indirectly in order to save face for themselves and for the other person.
- **May avoid making alternative suggestions.** To avoid embarrassing others, people in some cultures avoid saying anything that might be interpreted as disagreement.
- **May be reluctant to admit a lack of understanding or ask for clarification.** In some cultures, people avoid asking questions because it would be rude to imply that the speaker doesn't know what he or she is talking about or hasn't succeeded in explaining things clearly.
- **May avoid debating ideas.** Whereas members of work teams in some Western cultures debate ideas freely as a way of exploring ideas, people from certain other cultures regard such behavior as disloyal and unacceptable.

Responding to possible cultural differences

When you work on an international or intercultural writing team, try to avoid using Western standards to interpret and evaluate the ways non-Western people relate to the group. If one of the members is quiet, instead of concluding that the person is indifferent or bored, remind yourself that he or she may simply be interacting in a way that is expected in his or her culture.

Later, talk with the person about his or her feelings about team projects so you can be sure you understand them. Also, share your own assumptions about group work, but not in a way that is intended to coerce or judge the other person. Part of the experience of working on intercultural writing teams is learning about the customs of people in other cultures—and sharing with people from other cultures the customs in your own.

GUIDELINE 8 **Use Computer Support for Collaboration When It's Available**

A fascinating variety of computer programs offer support for teams that are creating communications together. Here are some examples:

Examples of computer support for team projects

- E-mail allows teams members to share ideas and drafts without meeting. Using a program called a *listserve,* an individual can send an e-mail message to a single address from which it will be forwarded automatically to all other team members.

Figure 13.3 (page 367) shows how writers can use a word-processing program to add comments to a team-written draft.

- Some software allows all team members to participate simultaneously in an on-line discussion even though each person is in a different location.
- Some corporations use teleconferencing rooms so team members in locations distant from one another can converse even as they use computer software to draft or edit a document together.
- Word-processing programs allow all team members to work on a single draft. Each person's suggested revisions are shown in a different color, so team members can identify the revisions' sources. These programs also allow an individual to attach a written or voice annotation to a specific place in a communication, thereby enabling other team members to read or hear the person's comments while simultaneously looking at the passage under discussion.

The advantages of these electronic tools can be enormous. Some let you "converse" with one another even if you are not working at the same time. Others allow you to "meet" together even if you aren't in the same location. Although some of these tools are associated with expensive software programs, others are included in standard products such as Microsoft Word, Excel, and WordPerfect. When working with a team, explore the electronic tools that can increase the efficiency of your team.

Because many of these tools rely on e-mail or similar capabilities for conveying messages electronically, follow Chapter 15's guidelines for using e-mail. These will help you communicate effectively and avoid inadvertently offending other team members.

CONCLUSION

Team writing is very common in the workplace. Although all the guidelines in this book apply to team writing as well as to individual writing, team projects require some additional skills. The eight guidelines presented in this chapter will help you create team efforts in which the team members work together productively and enjoy their mutual effort.

PART VIII

Superstructures

CHAPTER 18
Reports

REFERENCE GUIDE
Three Types of Special Reports

CHAPTER 19
Proposals

CHAPTER 20
Instructions

Reports

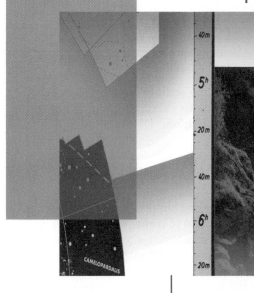

SUPERSTRUCTURE

Introduction

Method of Obtaining Facts

Facts

Discussion

Conclusions

Recommendations

R eports are among the most common types of communication prepared at work. They come in many varieties. Here are some examples:

- A 100-page report on a seven-month project testing a special method of venting high-thrust engines for use in space vehicles.
- A 12-page report based on library research concerning new techniques of genetic engineering used for food crops.
- A two-paragraph report based on a manufacturing engineer's visit to a new plant that is about to be put into service.
- A 200-page report addressed to the general public concerning the environmental impact of mining certain portions of public land in Utah.

As these examples suggest, reports differ from one another in many ways, including subject matter, length, purpose, information sources, number and kind of readers, and the circumstances that led to their preparation.

YOUR READERS WANT TO USE THE INFORMATION YOU PROVIDE

Despite their differences, almost all reports share one important feature: their readers want to put the information the reports contain to some professional or practical use. The precise use varies, of course, from situation to situation. For example, readers sometimes want to use a report's information to solve an organizational problem (where typical goals are to increase efficiency and profit), a social problem (where a typical goal is to improve the general health and welfare of a group of people), or an ethical problem (where a typical goal is to see that people are treated justly and respectfully).

Despite the many differences in readers' goals, most successful reports prepared at work share certain characteristics. You can understand why if you follow Chapter 3's advice to think of your readers as persons who ask questions. At a general level, report readers almost always ask the same basic set of six questions. The general superstructure for reports is a conventional pattern that both readers and writers have found to be successful for answering these questions. In fact, each of the six major elements of the superstructure is matched to one of them.

READERS' SIX BASIC QUESTIONS

The readers' six basic questions are as follows. All six reflect readers' overriding goal of using the information and ideas that you provide as a guide for future action:

Report readers' questions focus on the future.

- **What will we gain from reading your report?** Most people at work want to read only those communications that are directly useful to them. Therefore, you need to explain your communication's relevance to the readers' responsibilities, interests, and goals.
- **Are your facts reliable?** Readers want to be certain that the facts you supply will provide a sound basis for their decisions or actions.

- **What do you know that is useful to us?** Readers don't want to read everything you know about your subject; they want you to tell them only the facts they can put directly to use. (Example: "The most important sales figures for this quarter are as follows: . . .")
- **How do you interpret those facts from our point of view?** Facts alone are meaningless. To give facts meaning, people must interpret them by pointing out relationships or patterns among them. (Example: "The sales figures show a rising demand for two products but not for two others.") Usually, your readers will want you to make those interpretations rather than leave that work to them.
- **How are those facts significant to us?** Readers generally want you to go beyond an interpretation of the facts to explain what the facts mean in terms of the readers' responsibilities, interests, or goals. (Example: "The demand for one product falls during this season every year, though not quite this sharply. The falling sales for the other may signal that the product is no longer competitive.")
- **What do you think we should do?** Because you will have studied the facts in detail, readers will usually assume that you are especially well qualified to make recommendations. (Example: "You should continue to produce the first product, but monitor its future sales closely. You should find a way to improve the second product or else quit producing it.")

Of course, these six questions are very general. For large reports, writers need to take hundreds, even thousands, of pages to answer them. That's because readers often seek answers to these basic questions by asking a multitude of more specific, subsidiary questions. But these six questions are the general ones that should guide your overall work on any report.

GENERAL SUPERSTRUCTURE FOR REPORTS

The questions report readers ask are linked in the following way with the six elements of the report superstructure:

Report Superstructure	
Report Element	**Readers' Question**
Introduction	What will we gain from reading your report?
Method of obtaining facts	Are your facts reliable?
Facts	What do you know that is useful to us?
Discussion	How do you interpret those facts from our point of view?
Conclusions	How are those facts significant to us?
Recommendations	What do you think we should do?

For a general discussion of how to use superstructures, see Guideline 4 in Chapter 4, pages 92–93.

As you examine the elements of the report superstructure, remember that a superstructure is not the same as an outline. The six elements may be arranged in many ways, and one or more of them may be omitted if circumstances warrant. In some brief reports, for example, the writers begin with a recommendation, move to a paragraph in which the facts and conclusions are treated together, and state the sources of their facts in a concluding, single-sentence paragraph. Also, people sometimes present two or more of the six elements under a single heading. For instance, they may include in their introduction information about how they obtained their facts, and they frequently present and interpret their facts in a single section of their report.

The various ways of combining these elements into a particular report are discussed at the end of this chapter. First, however, each of the six elements is described individually, with particular attention to the ways each might be developed in a report in which all six appear separately.

INTRODUCTION

For additional advice on writing an introduction, see Chapter 8, "Beginning a Communication."

In the introduction of a report, you answer your readers' question, "What will we gain from reading your report?" In some reports, you can answer this question in a sentence or less. Consider, for instance, the first sentence of a report written by Lisa, an employee of a university's fund-raising office, who was asked to investigate the university's facilities and programs in horseback riding. Because her reader, Matt, had assigned her to prepare the report, she could tell him what he would gain from it simply by reminding him why he had requested it:

Lisa's opening sentence | In this report, I present the information you wanted to have before deciding whether to place new university stables on next year's list of major funding drives.

For a further explanation of this writing strategy, see pages 222–224.

In longer reports, your explanation of the relevance of your report to your readers may take many pages, in which you tell such things as (1) what problem your report will help solve, (2) what activities you performed toward solving that problem, and (3) how your readers can apply your information in their own efforts toward solving the problem.

Besides telling your readers what your communication offers them, your introduction may serve many other functions. The most important of these is to state your main points. In most reports, your main point will be your major conclusions and recommendations. Although you should postpone a full discussion of these topics to the end of your report, your readers will usually appreciate a brief summary of them in your introduction. Lisa provided such a summary in the second, third, and fourth sentences of her horseback riding report:

Summary of conclusions | Overall, it seems that the stables would make a good fund-raising project because of the strength of the current programs offered there, the condition of the current facilities, and the existence of a loyal core of alumni who used the facilities while undergraduates.

Summary of recommendations | The fund raising should focus on the construction of a new barn, costing $125,000. An additional $150,000 could be sought for a much-needed arena and classroom, but I recommend that this construction be saved for a future fund-raising drive.

In brief reports (for example, one-page memos), a statement of your main points may even replace the conclusions and recommendations that would otherwise appear at the end.

Four other important functions that an introduction may serve are to explain how the report is organized, outline its scope, encourage openness to your message, and provide background information the readers will need in order to understand the rest of the report. You will find a detailed discussion of these functions in Chapter 8.

METHOD OF OBTAINING FACTS

Your discussion of your method of obtaining the facts in your report can serve a wide variety of purposes. Report readers want to assess the reliability of the facts you present: your discussion of your method tells them how and where you got your facts. It also suggests where your readers can find additional information. If you obtained your information from printed sources, for example, you can direct your readers to those sources. If you obtained your information from an experiment, survey, or other special technique, your account of your method may help others design similar projects.

Lisa explained how she gathered her information this way:

Lisa's methods | I obtained the information given below from Peter Troivinen, Stable Manager. Also, at last month's Alumni Weekend, I spoke with a half-dozen alumni interested in the riding programs. Information about construction costs comes from Roland Taberski, whose construction firm is experienced in the kind of facility that would be involved.

FACTS

Your facts are the individual pieces of information that you gathered. If your report, like Lisa's, is based on interviews, your facts are what people told you. If your report is based on laboratory, field, or library research, your facts are the verifiable pieces of information you gathered: the laboratory data you obtained, the survey responses you recorded, or the knowledge you assembled from printed sources. If your report is based on your own efforts to design a new product, procedure, or system, your facts are the details of what you designed or created. In sum, your facts are the separate pieces of information you present as objectively verifiable.

You may present your facts in a section of their own, or you may combine your presentation of your facts with your discussion of them, as explained next.

DISCUSSION

Your discussion gives meaning to your facts.

Taken alone, facts mean nothing. They are a table of data, a series of isolated observations, or pieces of information without meaning. Therefore, an essential element of every report you prepare will be a discussion in which you interpret your facts in a way that is significant to your readers.

Relationship between facts and discussion

Sometimes, writers have trouble distinguishing between the presentation and the discussion of their facts. The following example may help to make the distinction clear. Imagine that you observed that when the temperature on the floor of your factory is 65°F, workers produce 3 percent rejected parts; when it is 70°F, they produce 3 percent rejected parts; when it is 75°F, they produce 4.5 percent rejected parts; and when it is 80°F, they produce 7 percent rejected parts. Those would be your facts. If you were to say, "As the temperature rises above 70°F, so does the percentage of rejected parts," you would be interpreting those facts. Of course, in many reports you will be dealing with much larger and more complicated sets of facts that require much more sophisticated and extended interpretation. But the basic point remains the same: when you begin to make general statements based upon your facts, you are interpreting them for your readers. You are discussing them.

In many of the communications you write, you will weave your discussion of the facts together with your presentation of them. In such situations, the interpretations often serve as the topic sentences of paragraphs. Here, for example, is a passage in which Lisa mixes facts and discussion:

| Interpretation | The university's horseback riding courses have grown substantially in recent years, due largely to the enthusiastic and effective leadership of Mr. Troivinen, who took over as Stable Manager five years ago. When Mr. Troivinen arrived, the university offered three |
| Facts | courses: beginning, intermediate, and advanced riding. Since then two courses have been added, one in mounted instruction and one in the training of horses. |

Whether you integrate your presentation and discussion of the facts or treat them separately, it is important to remember that your readers count on you not only to select facts that are relevant to them, but also to discuss those facts in a way that is meaningful to them.

CONCLUSIONS

Like interpretations, conclusions are general statements based on your facts. However, conclusions focus on answering the readers' question, "How are those facts significant to us?" In her report, for instance, Lisa provided many paragraphs of information about the university riding programs, the state of the current stable facilities, and the likely interest among alumni in contributing money for new facilities. After reading her presentation and discussion of those facts, Lisa's reader, Matt, might ask, "But how, exactly, does all this affect my decision about whether to start a fund-raising project for the stables?" Lisa answers that question in her conclusions:

| Lisa's conclusions | In conclusion, my investigation indicates that the university's riding programs could benefit substantially from a fund-raising effort. However, the appeal of such a program will be limited primarily to the very supportive alumni who used the university stables while students. |

Such brief, explicit statements of conclusions are almost always desired and welcomed by report readers.

RECOMMENDATIONS

Just as conclusions grow out of interpretations of the facts, recommendations grow out of conclusions. They answer the readers' question, "If your conclusions are valid, what do you think we should we do?" Depending on many factors, including the number and complexity of the things you are recommending, you may state your recommendations in a single sentence or in many pages.

As mentioned above, you can help your readers immensely by stating your major recommendations at the beginning of your report. In a short report, this may be the only place you need to present them. On the other hand, if your communication is long, or if a full discussion of your recommendations requires a great deal of space, you can summarize your recommendations at the beginning of your report and then treat them more extensively at the end. This is what Lisa did when she summarized her recommendations in two sentences in the first paragraph of her introduction and then presented and explained them in three paragraphs at the end of her report. To be sure that her reader could readily find this fuller discussion, she placed it under the heading "Conclusions and Recommendations," and she began the first paragraph with the words, "I recommend."

Although readers usually want recommendations in reports, you may encounter some situations in which you will not want to include them. That might happen, for instance, in either of these situations:

When you should not include recommendations

■ The decision being made is clearly beyond your competence, and you have been asked to provide only a small part of the information your readers need to make the decision.

■ The responsibility for making recommendations rests with your boss or other people.

In the usual situation, however, your recommendations will be welcomed. If you are uncertain about whether to provide them, ask your boss or the person who asked you to prepare the report. Don't omit your recommendations out of shyness or because you don't know whether they are wanted.

SAMPLE OUTLINES AND REPORT

The sample outlines show some ways the superstructure is adapted for specific situations.

A superstructure is not the same thing as an outline. The six elements of the general superstructure for reports can be incorporated into many organizational patterns. Figure 18.1 illustrates one possibility. It shows the outline for a report written by Brian, who works in the Human Resources Department of Centre Corporation. Much to the credit of Brian's department, the company's executive management recently decided that developing the full potential of all the company's employees would be a major corporate goal. As a first step, the executive management asked Brian's department to study employee morale. Brian has organized his report on the study into six sections that correspond directly to the six elements of the general superstructure.

Figure 18.2 shows the much different outline for Lisa's report to Matt on the university fund-raising campaign. Like Brian's report, Lisa's has six sections. However, those sections do not bear a one-to-one relationship with the six elements of the general superstructure—although all six elements are present. In her opening section, Lisa explains what the reader will gain from her communication and describes her methods for gathering facts. In each of the next four sections, she

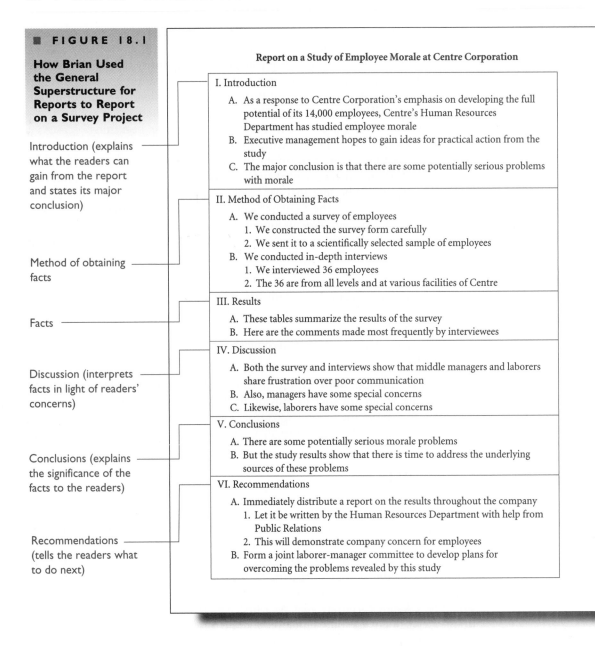

How Brian Used the General Superstructure for Reports to Report on a Survey Project

Introduction (explains what the readers can gain from the report and states its major conclusion)

Method of obtaining facts

Facts

Discussion (interprets facts in light of readers' concerns)

Conclusions (explains the significance of the facts to the readers)

Recommendations (tells the readers what to do next)

Report on a Study of Employee Morale at Centre Corporation

I. Introduction

  A. As a response to Centre Corporation's emphasis on developing the full potential of its 14,000 employees, Centre's Human Resources Department has studied employee morale

  B. Executive management hopes to gain ideas for practical action from the study

  C. The major conclusion is that there are some potentially serious problems with morale

II. Method of Obtaining Facts

  A. We conducted a survey of employees

    1. We constructed the survey form carefully

    2. We sent it to a scientifically selected sample of employees

  B. We conducted in-depth interviews

    1. We interviewed 36 employees

    2. The 36 are from all levels and at various facilities of Centre

III. Results

  A. These tables summarize the results of the survey

  B. Here are the comments made most frequently by interviewees

IV. Discussion

  A. Both the survey and interviews show that middle managers and laborers share frustration over poor communication

  B. Also, managers have some special concerns

  C. Likewise, laborers have some special concerns

V. Conclusions

  A. There are some potentially serious morale problems

  B. But the study results show that there is time to address the underlying sources of these problems

VI. Recommendations

  A. Immediately distribute a report on the results throughout the company

    1. Let it be written by the Human Resources Department with help from Public Relations

    2. This will demonstrate company concern for employees

  B. Form a joint laborer-manager committee to develop plans for overcoming the problems revealed by this study

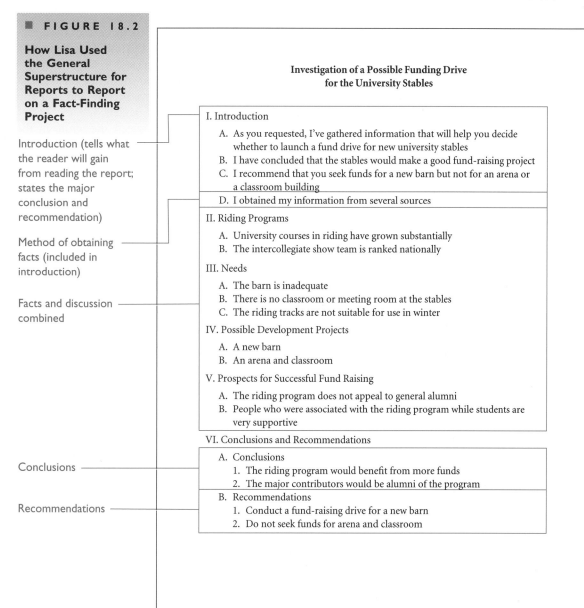

■ FIGURE 18.2

How Lisa Used the General Superstructure for Reports to Report on a Fact-Finding Project

Introduction (tells what the reader will gain from reading the report; states the major conclusion and recommendation)

Method of obtaining facts (included in introduction)

Facts and discussion combined

Conclusions

Recommendations

**Investigation of a Possible Funding Drive
for the University Stables**

I. Introduction

    A. As you requested, I've gathered information that will help you decide whether to launch a fund drive for new university stables

    B. I have concluded that the stables would make a good fund-raising project

    C. I recommend that you seek funds for a new barn but not for an arena or a classroom building

    D. I obtained my information from several sources

II. Riding Programs

    A. University courses in riding have grown substantially

    B. The intercollegiate show team is ranked nationally

III. Needs

    A. The barn is inadequate

    B. There is no classroom or meeting room at the stables

    C. The riding tracks are not suitable for use in winter

IV. Possible Development Projects

    A. A new barn

    B. An arena and classroom

V. Prospects for Successful Fund Raising

    A. The riding program does not appeal to general alumni

    B. People who were associated with the riding program while students are very supportive

VI. Conclusions and Recommendations

    A. Conclusions

        1. The riding program would benefit from more funds

        2. The major contributors would be alumni of the program

    B. Recommendations

        1. Conduct a fund-raising drive for a new barn

        2. Do not seek funds for arena and classroom

mingles her presentation of the facts with her discussion of them; each of these sections is built around one of the major focuses of her investigation. In her last section, Lisa combines her conclusions and her recommendations.

As these two outlines suggest, when writing a report you should be certain that your communication contains all six elements of the superstructure and that you organize them in a way that is suited to your purpose and readers.

Figure 18.3 (pages 453–458) shows Lisa's full report, which she wrote in the memo format.

CONCLUSION

The general superstructure for reports is a versatile and flexible pattern for organizing information. Many specialized variations of this superstructure have evolved. The Reference Guide that follows this chapter describes three of the most common ones: empirical research reports, feasibility reports, and progress reports.

Note to the Instructor: Appendix C contains a report-writing project and cases that involve report writing. In addition, the printed *Instructor's Manual* contains a "Planning Guide for Reports," and the book's Web site offers a copy you can download, edit to suit your course, and distribute electronically to your students. Also, the Web site provides additional cases you can download and edit to suit your course.

■ **FIGURE 18.3**

Report That Uses the General Superstructure

Lisa's introduction explains the significance of her report to her reader and summarizes her conclusions and recommendations.

Lisa explains her method of obtaining facts.

Lisa begins the first of four sections that present and discuss her findings.

MEMORANDUM

**Central University
Development Office**

FROM: Lisa Beech   February 26, 19—
TO: Matt Fordyce, Director of Funding Drives
SUBJECT: POSSIBLE FUNDING DRIVE FOR UNIVERSITY STABLES

In this report, I present the information you wanted to have before deciding whether to place new university stables on next year's list of major funding drives. Overall, it seems that the stables would make a good fund-raising project because of the strength of the current programs offered there, the condition of the current facilities, and the existence of a loyal core of alumni who used the facilities while undergraduates. The fund raising should focus on the construction of a new barn, costing $125,000. An additional $150,000 could be sought for a much-needed arena and classroom, but I recommend that this construction be saved for a future fund-raising drive.

I obtained the information given below from Peter Troivinen, Stable Manager. Also, at last month's Alumni Weekend, I spoke with a half-dozen alumni interested in the riding programs. Information about construction costs comes from Roland Taberski, whose construction firm is experienced in building the kind of facility that would be involved.

RIDING PROGRAMS

Begun in 1936, Central University's riding programs fall into two categories: regular university courses offered through the stable, and the university's horse show team, which competes nationally through the Intercollegiate Horse Show Association.

University Courses

The university's horseback riding courses have grown substantially in recent years, due largely to the enthusiastic and effective leadership of Mr. Troivinen, who took over as Stable Manager five years ago. When Mr. Troivinen arrived, the university offered three courses: beginning, intermediate, and advanced riding.

■ **FIGURE 18.3**
(continued)

February 26, 19—   Page 2

Since then two courses have been added, one in mounted instruction and one in the training of horses. In all riding courses, students may choose either English or Western style.

In the past five years, the number of students taking a horseback riding course for college credit has more than doubled from 310 to 725. That has placed a tremendous burden on both the stable and the horses.

Intercollegiate Show Team

When Mr. Troivinen began working at the stable, he helped students form an intercollegiate show team, which originally had six members. It now has over one hundred, making it one of the largest in the country. Furthermore, the team has become competitive both regionally and nationally. Three years ago it was first in the region; two years ago it was third in the nation in English; and last year it was first in the nation in Western.

NEEDS

Mr. Troivinen and the alumni identify three major problems facing the equestrian programs: poor barn facilities, lack of a classroom and meeting room, and lack of an all-weather riding arena.

Barn

Clearly, the most pressing problem facing the equestrian programs is the size of the barn. The barn does not provide adequate stabling for the increased number of horses Mr. Troivinen has purchased in response to the rising number of riders in classes and on the horse show team. To provide at least some space for these horses, he has made some modifications to the barn. When originally built, the barn had six box stalls and two tie stalls. Box stalls are the best housing for most horses because they allow the horses to move around. Tie stalls have many uses, including providing a place for horses between classes and while they are being curried. However, tie stalls are not desirable for permanent housing because the horses' heads are tied at all times. Mr. Troivinen has had to convert all but one of the box stalls to tie stalls in order to make room for the additional horses. Also, some horses are now kept in the aisles.

Lisa begins the second section that reports and discusses her findings.

■ FIGURE 18.3
(continued)

February 26, 19—   Page 3

The barn is now full, so that no additional horses can be purchased to meet the student demand for riding courses. As a result, many of the horses work seven hours a day instead of the more reasonable four or five that is standard for the type of horse used for riding. With a seven-hour workload, the chances of health problems increase—and the workload of a sick horse must be shifted to other horses. Also, with this workload, the horses grow tired by the afternoon classes and they are no longer willing to cooperate with their riders. Consequently, the riders (especially beginning riders) have trouble getting their horses to perform. However, the only way to increase the number of horses now would be to tie them up in enclosures along a fence behind the barn. Mr. Troivinen is reluctant to do that because horses kept there would have no shelter from the weather.

Other problems with the barn include the following:

- **Storage space for feed is too small.** Hay, grain, and the special feeds required for some of the horses are stored in the aisle at one end of the barn. Horses that get loose during the night sometimes eat the feed until they get sick.

- **Lack of storage place for equipment.** Saddles and bridles are kept along the aisles, where they are exposed to damage from bites or kicks of passing horses. Moreover, other necessary equipment can't be purchased because there is no place to store it.

- **Lack of a wash area.** Washing has to be done in the courtyard, where drainage is poor and there is no place to tie the horses. As a result, the horses rarely get a bath, rendering them more susceptible to fungus and skin disease.

Classroom and Meeting Room

At present, there is no classroom for riding classes. In good weather the classes meet outdoors, and in bad weather they meet in the aisles of the barn. For the basic and intermediate riding classes, that is not a great problem. It is a problem, however, for the advanced riding class and the elementary training class, where lectures, films, and other indoor instruction are appropriate.

■ **FIGURE 18.3**
(continued)

February 26, 19—   Page 4

Also, there is no meeting room for the riding club, which in addition to its regular business meetings sometimes has guest speakers and films. The nearest rooms they can use for these purposes are classrooms in Haddock Hall, a quarter mile from the barn.

Riding Tracks

Riding is done on four outdoor cinder tracks. Therefore, student interest is very low during winter sessions, when the weather is cold and the riding tracks are often muddy or even covered with snow and ice. Snow and ice create additional problems. They greatly increase the chances that a horse will slip, injuring itself and its rider. Also, snow builds up on the horses' feet, impairing their movements. When that happens, riding is restricted to the slower gaits of walk and trot, so students don't receive the full content of the course they are taking. Finally, the cold air of winter is hard on the horses' lungs.

POSSIBLE DEVELOPMENT PROJECTS

Mr. Troivinen has identified two subjects for a possible fund drive: a new barn to replace the old one and a riding arena with a classroom and viewing area attached.

Barn

Lisa begins her third section on her findings.

According to both Mr. Troivinen and the alumni I spoke with, an adequate barn would be a 70 × 170-foot steel building. The building would contain 32 box stalls, 27 tie stalls, 3 storage rooms for equipment, another storage area for feed, and a washing area for bathing the horses. Like the present barn, it would also include an office for the Stable Manager.

The stall area and aisles would have dirt floors to provide good drainage. The other areas would have regular concrete floors, except the washing area, which would need a special nonslip concrete floor. The building could be faced with wood siding and roofed with wood shingles to help it blend in with its setting.

The cost of such a barn would be about $125,000. Small savings could be realized by replacing some of the box stalls with tie stalls, which cost about one-third as much, but as explained above the tie stalls are not as desirable.

■ FIGURE 18.3
(continued)

February 26, 19—   Page 5

Arena and Classroom

An indoor riding facility could be provided by building an 80 × 200-foot arena. It would be used for riding instruction, team practice, and horse shows. Like the barn, this could be a steel building covered on the outside with appropriate siding and roofing. It would have a dirt floor.

The arena would have no seating area, under the assumption that a classroom would be attached to its side. The classroom would extend for 40 feet along one wall of the arena, and would be 30 feet deep. Along the common wall, it would have a 30-foot window through which students could watch demonstrations and spectators could watch horse shows. The room would be equipped with a movie screen and restroom facilities. It would also provide a meeting room for the horse show club. The arena and classroom together would cost about $150,000.

PROSPECTS FOR SUCCESSFUL FUND RAISING

This is the last section in which Lisa presents and discusses her findings.

When I spoke with alumni at last month's Alumni Weekend, I found that a fund-raising drive for the stables would not be widely appealing to Central's general alumni. Many alumni perceive that contributions to such a drive would benefit only a relatively small number of students, primarily those on the riding team.

However, I also found that alumni who have been involved in the riding programs over the years are very supportive, especially alumni from more than ten years ago, when students who owned their own horses could board them at the barn. These alumni are particularly impressed with the success of the intercollegiate show team. In the past few months, one alumnus has pledged $4000 toward the new barn, and the parents of a current member of the riding club have donated a new treadmill, valued at over $5000, which will be used to train young horses. Mr. Troivinen has a long list of alumni who have expressed support for the program.

CONCLUSIONS AND RECOMMENDATIONS

Lisa explicitly states her conclusions.

In conclusion, my investigation indicates that the university's riding programs could benefit substantially from a fund-raising effort. However, the appeal of such a program will be limited primarily to the very supportive alumni who used the university stables while students.

■ **FIGURE 18.3**
(continued)

Lisa presents her
detailed
recommendations.

February 26, 19—   Page 6

Therefore, I recommend that we conduct a fund-raising drive focused on the barn alone, leaving the arena and classroom for a future program. The drive should be announced to all alumni in one of the brief sketches in the brochure we send to all alumni each year to describe our development plans. The description should emphasize the classes taught and the need to provide better housing for the horses.

A more extensive description of the project should be prepared for alumni known to be interested in the riding programs. In addition to the information provided to all alumni, the description should emphasize the success of the horse show team and appeal to the desire of the alumni to have a top-quality equestrian program at their alma mater.

Though Mr. Troivinen will be disappointed by a decision not to seek funds for the arena and classroom next year, I am sure that he will work with us enthusiastically and effectively in the fund-raising drive I have outlined.

Reference Guide:
Three Types
of Special Reports

CONTENTS

Empirical Research Reports

Feasibility Reports

Progress Reports

Ｔhis Reference Guide describes the superstructure for three types of specialized reports:

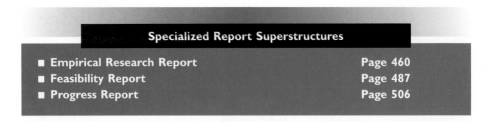

Specialized Report Superstructures

■ **Empirical Research Report**   **Page 460**
■ **Feasibility Report**   **Page 487**
■ **Progress Report**   **Page 506**

Each is a variation on the general superstructure for reports discussed in Chapter 18. If you have not already done so, you should read that discussion because it provides information not repeated here that will help you write these three types of reports effectively.

EMPIRICAL RESEARCH REPORTS

In empirical research, the investigators gather information through carefully planned, systematic observations or measurements. When scientists send a satellite to investigate the atmosphere of a distant planet, when engineers test jet-engine parts made of various alloys, when pollsters ask older citizens what kinds of outdoor recreation they participate in, and when sociologists observe people's behavior at baseball games, they all are conducting empirical research. In your career, you will almost certainly perform some type of empirical research—and report on it in writing. This section describes the superstructure you can use for those reports.

TYPICAL WRITING SITUATIONS

Research to support decision-making

Empirical research has two distinct purposes. Most aims to help people make practical decisions. For example, the engineers who test jet-engine parts are trying to help designers determine which alloy to use in a new engine. Similarly, the researchers who study older persons' recreational activities are trying to help decision-makers in the state park system determine what sorts of services and facilities to provide for senior citizens.

Research to extend human knowledge

A smaller portion of empirical research aims not to support practical decisions but rather to extend human knowledge. Here researchers set out to learn how fish remember, what the molten core of the earth is like, or why people fall in love. Such research is usually reported in scholarly journals, such as the *Journal of Chemical Thermodynamics,* the *Journal of Cell Biology,* and the *Journal of Social Psychology,* whose readers are concerned not so much with making practical business decisions as with extending the frontiers of human understanding.

These two aims of research sometimes overlap. Some organizations sponsor basic research in the hope that what is learned can later be turned to practical use.

Likewise, some practical research produces results that help explain something about the world in general.

THE QUESTIONS READERS ASK MOST OFTEN

Whether it aims to support practical decisions, extend human knowledge, or achieve some combination of these two purposes, almost all empirical research is reported in the same superstructure. That's largely because the readers of reports on all types of empirical research tend to ask the same seven general questions:

- **Why is your research important to us?** Readers concerned with solving specific practical problems want to know what problems your research will help them address. Readers concerned with extending human knowledge want to know what your research contributes to that pursuit.
- **What were you trying to find out?** A well-designed empirical research project is based on carefully formulated research questions that the project will try to answer. Readers want to know what those questions are so they can determine whether they are significant.
- **Was your research method sound?** Unless your method is appropriate to your research questions and unless it is intellectually sound, your readers will not place any faith in your results or in your conclusions and recommendations.
- **What results did your research produce?** Naturally, your readers will want to learn what results you obtained.
- **How do you interpret those results?** Your readers will want you to interpret your results in ways that are meaningful to them.
- **What is the significance of those results?** What answers do your results imply for your research questions, and how do your results relate to the problems your research was to help solve or to the area of knowledge it was meant to expand?
- **What do you think we should do?** Readers concerned with practical problems want to know what you advise them to do. Readers concerned with extending human knowledge want to know what you think your results imply for future research.

SUPERSTRUCTURE FOR EMPIRICAL RESEARCH REPORTS

To answer their readers' questions, writers of empirical research reports use a superstructure that contains seven elements. The table at the top of the next page shows how each of these elements corresponds with one of the readers' seven questions.

Remember that a superstructure is not an outline; you may combine the elements of a superstructure in many ways (see pages 449–452).

Much of the following advice about using this superstructure is illustrated through the use of two sample reports. The first is presented in full on pages 469–486. Its aim is practical. It was written by engineers who were developing a satellite communication system that will permit companies with large fleets of trucks to communicate directly with their drivers at any time (Anderson, Frey, and Lewis). In the report, the writers tell decision-makers and other engineers in their organization about the first operational test of the system, in which they sought to answer several practical engineering questions.

Superstructure for Empirical Research Reports

Report Element	Readers' Question
Introduction	Why is your research important to us?
Objectives of the research	What were you trying to find out?
Method of obtaining facts	Was your research method sound?
Facts	What results did your research produce?
Discussion	How do you interpret those results?
Conclusions	What is the significance of those results?
Recommendations	What do you think we should do?

The aim of the second sample report is to extend human knowledge. In it, researcher Robert B. Hayes describes his study of the ways people develop friendships. Selected passages from this report, which appeared in the *Journal of Personality and Social Psychology,* are quoted throughout this section.

Introduction

For additional advice on writing an introduction, see Chapter 8, "Beginning a Communication."

In the introduction to an empirical research report, you should seek to answer the readers' question, "Why is this research important to us?" Typically, writers answer that question in two steps: they announce the topic of their research and then explain the importance of the topic to their readers.

Announcing the Topic   You can often announce the topic of your research simply by including it as the key phrase in your opening sentence. For example, here is the first sentence of the report on the satellite communication system:

Topic of report | For the past eighteen months, the Satellite Products Laboratory has been developing a system that will permit companies with large, nationwide fleets of trucks to communicate directly to their drivers at any time through a satellite link.

Here is the first sentence of the report on the way people develop friendships:

Topic of report | Social psychologists know very little about the way real friendships develop in their natural settings.

Explaining the Importance of the Research   To explain the importance of your research to your readers, you can use either or both of the following methods: tell how your research is relevant to your organization's goals, and review the previously published literature on the subject:

- **Relevance to organizational goals.** In reports written to readers in organizations (whether your own or a client's), you can explain the relevance of your research by relating it to some organizational goal or problem. Sometimes, in fact, the importance of your research to the organization's needs will be so obvious to your readers that merely naming your topic will be sufficient. At other times, you will need to discuss at length the relevance of your research to the organization. In the first paragraph of the satellite report, for instance, the writers mention the potential market for the satellite communication system they are developing. That is, they explain the importance of their research by saying that it can lead to a profit. For detailed advice about how to explain the importance of your research to readers in organizations, see Guideline 1 of Chapter 8, "Beginning a Communication."

■ **Relevance to existing knowledge.** A second way to establish the importance of your research is to show the gap in current knowledge that it will fill. The following passage from the opening of the report on the friendship study illustrates this strategy.

The writer tells what is known about his topic.

The writer identifies the gaps in knowledge that his research will fill.

> A great deal of research in social psychology has focused on variables influencing an individual's attraction to another at an initial encounter, usually in laboratory settings (Bergscheid & Walster, 1978; Bryne, 1971; Huston & Levinger, 1978), yet very little data exists on the processes by which individuals in the real world move beyond initial attraction to develop a friendship; even less is known about the way developing friendships are maintained and how they evolve over time (Huston & Burgess, 1979; Levinger, 1980).

The writer continues this discussion of published research for three paragraphs. Each follows the same pattern: it identifies an area of research, tells what is known about that area, and identifies gaps in the knowledge — gaps that will be filled by the research the writer has conducted. These paragraphs serve an important additional function performed by many literature reviews: they introduce the established facts and theories that are relevant to the writer's work and necessary to an understanding of the report.

Objectives of the Research

Every empirical research project has carefully constructed objectives. These objectives define the focus of your project, influence the choice of research method, and shape the way you interpret your results. Readers of empirical research reports want and need to know what the objectives are.

The following example from the satellite report shows one way you can inform your readers about your objectives:

Statement of research objectives

> In particular, we wanted to test whether we could achieve accurate data transmissions and good-quality voice transmissions in the variety of terrains typically encountered in long-haul trucking. We wanted also to see what factors might affect the quality of transmissions.

When reporting on research that involves the use of statistics, you can usually state your objectives by stating the hypotheses you were testing. Where appropriate, you can explain these hypotheses in terms of existing theory, again citing previous publications on the subject. The following passage shows how the writer who studied friendship explains some of his hypotheses. Notice how the author begins with a statement of the overall goal of the research:

Overall goal

First objective (hypothesis) —

Second objective —
(hypothesis)

Third objective —
(hypothesis)

> The goal of the study was to identify characteristic behavioral and attitudinal changes that occurred within interpersonal relationships as they progressed from initial acquaintance to close friendship. With regard to relationship benefits and costs, it was predicted that both benefits and costs would increase as the friendship developed, and that the ratings of both costs and benefits would be positively correlated with ratings of friendship intensity. In addition, the types of benefits listed by the subjects were expected to change as the friendships developed. In accord with Levinger and Snoek's (1972) model of dyadic relatedness, benefits listed at initial stages of friendship were hypothesized to be more activity centered and to reflect individual self-interest (e.g., companionship, information) than benefits at later stages, which were expected to be more personal and reciprocal (e.g., emotional support, self-esteem).

Method

Readers of your empirical research reports will look for precise details concerning your method. Those details serve three purposes. First, they let your readers assess the soundness of your research design and its appropriateness for the problems you are investigating. Second, the details enable your readers to determine the limitations that your method might place on the conclusions you draw. Third, they provide information that will help your readers repeat your experiment if they wish to verify your results or conduct similar research projects of their own.

The nature of the information you should provide about your method depends on the nature of your research. The writers of the satellite report provided three paragraphs and two tables explaining their equipment (truck radios and satellite), two paragraphs and one map describing the eleven-state region covered by the trucks, and two paragraphs describing their data analysis.

Often a description of empirical research methods uses the pattern for organizing a description of a process (see pages 202–207).

The writer of the friendship study used much simpler methods and therefore could describe them quite briefly.

> At the beginning of their first term at the university, first-year students selected two individuals whom they had just met and completed a series of questionnaires regarding their relationships with those individuals at 3-week intervals through the school term.

In the rest of that paragraph, the writer explains that the questionnaires asked the students to describe such matters as their attitudes toward each of the other two individuals and the specific things they did with each of them. However, that paragraph is just a small part of the researcher's account of his method. He then provides a 1200-word discussion of the students he studied and of the questionnaires and procedures he used.

How can you decide which details to include? The most obvious way is to follow the general reporting practices in your field. Find some research reports that use a method similar to yours and see what they report. Depending on the needs of your readers, you may need to include some or all of the following:

Elements of your method to describe

- Every aspect of your procedure that you made a decision about when planning your research.
- Every aspect of your method that your readers might ask about.

- Any aspect of your method that might limit the conclusions you can draw from your results.
- Every procedure that other researchers would need to understand in order to design a similar study.

Results

The results of empirical research are the data you obtain. Although the results are the heart of any empirical research report, they may take up a very small portion of it. Generally, results are presented in one of two ways:

For information on using tables and other visual aids for reporting numerical data, see pages 300–312.

- **Tables and graphs.** The satellite report, for instance, uses two tables. The report on friendship uses four tables and eleven graphs.
- **Sentences.** When placed in sentences, results are often woven into a discussion that combines data and interpretation, as the next paragraphs explain.

Discussion

Sometimes writers briefly present all their results in one section and then discuss them in a separate section. Sometimes they combine the two in a single, integrated section. Whichever method you use, your discussion must link your interpretative comments with the specific results you are interpreting.

One way of making that link is to refer to the key results shown in a table or other visual aid and then comment on them as appropriate. The following passage shows how the writers of the satellite report did that with some of the results they presented in one of their tables:

Writers emphasize a key result shown in a table.

Writers draw attention to other important results.

Writers interpret those results.

As Table 3 shows, 91% of the data transmissions were successful. These data are reported according to the region in which the trucks were driving at the time of transmission. The most important difference to note is the one between the rate of successful transmissions in the Southern Piedmont region and the rates in all the other regions. In the Southern Piedmont area, we had the truck drive slightly outside the ATS-6 footprint so that we could see if successful transmissions could be made there. When the truck left the footprint, the percentage of successful data transmissions dropped abruptly to 43%.

When you present your results in prose only (rather than in tables and graphs), you can weave them into your discussion by beginning your paragraphs with general statements that serve as interpretations of your data. Then, you can cite the relevant results as evidence in support of the interpretations. Here is an example from the friendship report:

General interpretation

Specific results presented as support for the interpretation

Intercorrelations among the subjects' friendship intensity ratings at the various assessment points showed that friendship attitudes became increasingly stable over time. For example, the correlation between friendship intensity ratings at 3 weeks and 6 weeks was .55; between 6 weeks and 9 weeks, .78; between 9 weeks and 12 weeks, .88 (all $p < .001$).

In a single report, you may use both of these methods of combining the presentation and discussion of your results.

Conclusions

Besides interpreting the results of your research, you need to explain what those results mean in terms of the original research questions and the general problem you set out to investigate. Your explanations of these matters are your conclusions.

For example, if your research project is sharply focused on a single hypothesis, your conclusion can be very brief, perhaps only a restatement of your chief results. However, if your research is more complex, your conclusion should draw all the strands together.

Link your conclusions to your objectives.

In either case, the presentation of your conclusions should correspond very closely to the objectives you identified toward the beginning of your report. Consider, for instance, the correspondence between objectives and conclusions in the satellite study. The first objective was to determine whether accurate data transmissions and good-quality voice transmissions could be obtained in the variety of terrains typically encountered in long-haul trucking. The first of the conclusions addresses that objective:

Conclusions from the satellite report

The Satellite Product Laboratory's system produces good-quality data and voice transmissions throughout the eleven-state region covered by the satellite's broadcast footprint.

The second objective was to determine what factors affect the quality of transmissions, and the second and third conclusions relate to it:

The most important factor limiting the success of transmissions is movement outside the satellite's broadcast footprint, which accurately defines the satellite's area of effective coverage.

The system is sensitive to interference from certain kinds of objects in the line of sight between the satellite and the truck. These include trees, mountains and hills, overpasses, and buildings.

The satellite research concerns a practical question. Hence its objectives and conclusions address practical concerns of particular individuals—in this case, the engineers and managers in the company that is developing the satellite system. In contrast, research that aims primarily to extend human knowledge often has objectives and conclusions that focus on theoretical issues.

For example, at the beginning of the friendship report, the researcher identifies several questions that his research investigated, and he tells what answers he predicted his research would produce. In his conclusion, then, he systematically addresses those same questions in terms of the results his research produced. Here is a summary of some of his objectives and conclusions. (Notice how he uses the technical terminology commonly employed by his readers.)

	Objective	Conclusion
Conclusions from the friendship report	As they develop friendships, do people follow the kind of pattern theorized by Guttman, in which initial contacts are relatively superficial and later contacts are more intimate?	Yes. "The initial interactions of friends . . . correspond to a Guttman-like progression from superficial interaction to increasingly intimate levels of behavior."

Do *both* the costs (or unpleasant aspects) and the benefits of personal relationships increase as friendships develop?

Yes. "The findings show that personal dissatisfactions are inescapable aspects of personal relationships and so, to some degree, may become immaterial. The critical factor in friendships appears to be the amount of benefits received. If a relationship offers enough desirable benefits, individuals seem willing to put up with the accompanying costs."

Are there substantial differences between the friendships women develop with one another and the kind men develop with one another?

Apparently not. "These findings suggest that—at least for this sample of friendships—the sex differences were more stylistic than substantial. The bonds of male friendship and female friendship may be equally strong, but the sexes may differ in their manner of expressing that bond. Females may be more inclined to express close friendships through physical or verbal affection; males may express their closeness through the types of companionate activities they share with their friends."

Typically, in presenting the conclusions of an empirical research project directed at extending human knowledge, writers discuss the relationship of their findings to the findings of other researchers and to various theories that have been advanced concerning their subject. The writer of the article on friendship did that. The table you have just read presents only a few snippets from his overall discussion, which is several thousand words long and is full of thoughts about the relationship of his results to the results and theories of others.

In the discussion section of their empirical research reports, writers sometimes discuss any flaws in their research method or limitations on the generalizability of their conclusions. For example, the writer on friendship points out that his subjects all were college students and that most lived in dormitories. It is possible, he cautions, that what he found while studying this group may not be true for other groups.

Recommendations

The readers of some empirical research reports want to know what, based on the research, the writer thinks should be done. This is especially true when the research is directed at solving a practical problem. Consequently, such reports usually include recommendations.

Recommendations of the satellite report

For example, the satellite report contains three. The first is the general recommendation that work on the project be continued. The other two involve specific actions that the writers think should be taken: design a special antenna for the trucks and develop a plan that tells what satellites would be needed to provide coverage throughout the 48 contiguous states, Alaska, and southern Canada. As is common in research addressed to readers in organizations, these recommendations concern practical business and engineering decisions.

Even in reports designed to extend human knowledge, writers sometimes include recommendations. These usually convey their ideas about future studies that should be made, adjustments in methodology that seem to be called for, and the like. In the last paragraph of the friendship report, for instance, the writer suggests that additional studies be made of different groups (not just students) in different settings (not just college) to establish a more comprehensive understanding of how friendships develop.

SAMPLE RESEARCH REPORT

Figure SR.1 (pages 469–486) shows the full report on the truck-and-satellite communication system, which is addressed to readers within the writers' own organization. To see examples of empirical research reports presented as journal articles, consult journals in your field.

Note to the Instructor: For an assignment involving an empirical research report, you can ask students to write on research they are conducting in their majors, or you can have them do the formal report project or the user test report project described in Appendix C. In addition, several cases in Appendix C can be written using the superstructure for empirical research reports. The printed *Instructor's Manual* contains other suitable cases as well as a "Planning Guide for Empirical Research Reports," and this book's Web site offers a copy you can download, edit to suit your course, and distribute to your students. Also, the Web site provides additional cases you can download and edit to suit your course.

■ **FIGURE SR.I**

Empirical Research Report

Cover

ELECTRONICS CORPORATION OF AMERICA

Truck-to-Satellite Communication System: First Operational Test

September 30, 19—

Internal Technical Report

Number TR-SPL-0931

■ **FIGURE SR.1**
(continued)

Title page

ELECTRONICS CORPORATION OF AMERICA

**Truck-to-Satellite Communication System:
First Operational Test**

September 30, 19—

Research Team
Margaret C. Barnett
Erin Sanderson
L. Victor Sorrentino
Raymond E. Wu

Internal Technical Report
Number TR-SPL-0931

Read and Approved:

_____   _____
Laboratory Director   Date

■ **FIGURE SR.I**
(continued)

Topic of report

Method

Results and
discussion

Conclusions

Recommendations

EXECUTIVE SUMMARY

For the past eighteen months, the Satellite Products Laboratory has been developing a system that will permit companies with large, nationwide fleets of trucks to communicate directly to their drivers at any time through a satellite link. During the week of May 18, we tested our concepts for the first time, using the ATS-6 satellite and five trucks that were driven over an eleven-state region with our prototype mobile radios.

More than 91% of the 2500 data transmissions were successful and more than 91% of the voice transmissions were judged to be of commercial quality. The most important factor limiting the success of transmissions was movement outside the satellite's broadcast footprint. Other factors include the obstruction of the line of sight between the truck and the satellite by highway overpasses, mountains and hills, trees, and buildings.

Overall, the test demonstrated the soundness of the prototype design. Work on it should continue as rapidly as possible. We recommend the following actions:

- Develop a new antenna designed specifically for use in communications between satellites and mobile radios.

- Explore the configuration of satellites needed to provide thorough footprint coverage for the 48 contiguous states, Alaska, and Southern Canada at an elevation of 25° or more.

i

■ **FIGURE SR.1**
(continued)

Cross-reference to
related reports

Acknowledgments

FOREWORD

Previous technical reports describing work on this project are TR-SPL-0785, TR-SPL-0795 through TR-SPL-0798, TR-SPL-0823, and TR-SPL-0862.

We could not have conducted this test without the gratifying cooperation of Smithson Moving Company and, in particular, the drivers and observers in the five trucks that participated. We are also grateful for the cooperation of the United States National Aeronautics and Space Administration in the use of the ATS-6 satellite.

The test described in this report was supported through internal product development funds.

ii

■ **FIGURE SR.I**
(continued)

Table of contents

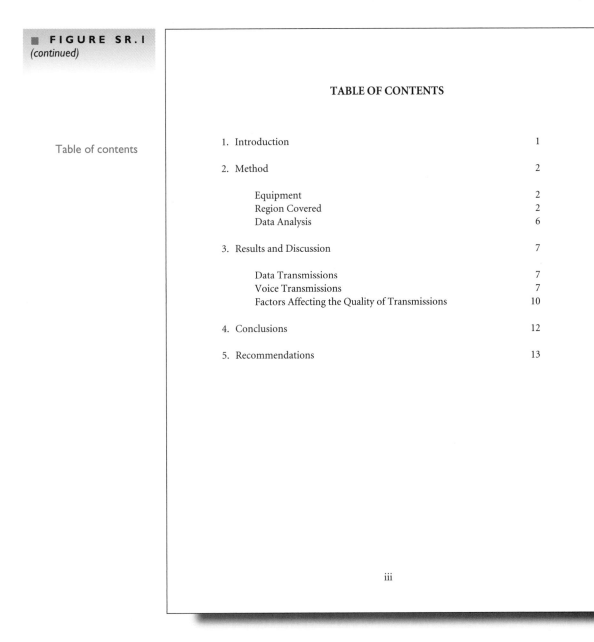

TABLE OF CONTENTS

1. Introduction   1

2. Method   2

    Equipment   2
    Region Covered   2
    Data Analysis   6

3. Results and Discussion   7

    Data Transmissions   7
    Voice Transmissions   7
    Factors Affecting the Quality of Transmissions   10

4. Conclusions   12

5. Recommendations   13

iii

REFERENCE GUIDE: Three Types of Special Reports

■ **FIGURE SR.1**
(continued)

Topic of report ——————

Significance of project ——————
to the organization

Objectives of test

Key findings

Section 1

INTRODUCTION

For the past eighteen months, the Satellite Products Laboratory has been developing a system that will permit companies with large, nationwide fleets of trucks to communicate directly to their drivers at any time through a satellite link. Several trucking lines and supermarket chains have expressed an interest in such a service. At present, they can communicate with their long-distance drivers only when the drivers pull off the road to phone in, meaning that all contacts are originated by the drivers, not the central dispatching service. The potential market for such a satellite service also includes many other companies and government agencies (such as the National Forest Service) that desire to communicate with trucks, cars, boats, or trains that regularly operate outside the very limited range of urban cellular telephone systems.

This report describes the first operational test of the system we have developed. Such tests were particularly important to conduct before continuing further with the development of this system because our system is much different from those currently being used with commercial satellites. Specifically, our system will transmit to mobile ground stations by using the short antennas and the low power provided by conventional terrestrial broadcasting systems.

In particular, we wanted to test whether we could achieve accurate data transmissions and good-quality voice transmissions in the variety of terrains typically encountered in long-haul trucking. We wanted also to see what factors might affect the quality of transmissions.

The test results indicate that our design is basically sound, although a new mobile antenna needs to be designed and the satellite configuration needs to be examined.

1

■ **FIGURE SR.1**
(continued)

Overview of method

Forecasting statement
for section

Paragraph is organized
from general to
particular (as are all
others).

Reference to technical
data in table

Use of large station
is justified.

Section 2

METHOD

In this experiment, we tested a full-scale system in which five trailer trucks communicated with an earth ground station via a satellite in geostationary orbit 23,200 miles above the earth. This section describes the equipment we used, the area covered by the test, and the data analyses we performed.

Equipment

The five trucks, operated by Smithson Moving Company, were each equipped with a prototype of our newly developed 806 megahertz (MHz) two-way mobile radio equipment. Each radio had a speaker and microphone for voice communications, along with a ten-key keyboard and digital display for data communications. Equipped with dipole antennas, the radios broadcast at 1650 MHz with 12 to 15 watts of power. They received signals at 1550 MHz and had an equivalent antenna temperature of 800°K, including feedline losses. Technical specifications for the receivers and transmitters of these radios are given in Table 1.

The satellite used for this test was the ATS-6, which has a larger antenna than most commercial communication satellites, making it more sensitive to the low-power signals sent from the mobile stations. Technical specifications for its receiver and transmitter are given in Table 2.

Through the ATS-6 satellite, the five trucks communicated with the Earth Ground Station in King of Prussia, Pennsylvania. This facility is a relatively large station, but not larger than is planned for a fully operational commercial system.

Region Covered

The five trucks drove throughout the region covered by the "footprint" of ATS-6. The footprint is shown as the area within the oval in Figure 1. It is defined as the area in which the broadcast signals received are within at least 3 dB of the signal received at the center of the beam. In all, the trucks covered eleven states: Georgia, South Carolina, North Carolina, Tennessee, Virginia, West Virginia, Ohio, Indiana, Illinois, Iowa, and Nebraska.

2

■ **FIGURE SR.I**
(continued)

Table 1

Specifications for Satellite-Aided Mobile Radio

Transmitter

Frequency	1655.050 MHz
Power Output	16 watts nominal
	12 watts minimum
Frequency Stability	±0.0002% (−30° to +60°C)
Modulation	$16F_3$ Adjustable from 0 to ±5 kHz swing FM with instantaneous modulation limiting
Audio Frequency Response	Within +1 dB and −3 dB of a 6 dB/octave pre-emphasis from 300 to 3000 HZ per EIA standards
Duty Cycle	EIA 20% Intermittent
Maximum Frequency Spread	±6 MHz with center tuning
RF Output Impedance	50 ohms

Receiver

Frequency	1552.000 MHz
Frequency Stability	±0.0002% (−30° to +60°C)
Noise Figure	2.6 dB referenced to transceiver antenna jack
Equivalent Receiver Noise Temperature	238° Kelvin
Selectivity	−75 dB by EIA Two-Signal Method
Audio Output	5 watts at less than 5% distortion
Frequency Response	Within +1 and −8 dB of a standard 6 dB per octave deemphasis curve from 300 to 3000 Hz
Modulation Acceptance	±7 kHz
RF Input Impedance	50 ohms

3

■ **FIGURE SR.I**
(continued)

Table 2

**Performance of ATS-6 Spacecraft L-Band Frequency
Translation Mode**

Receive

Receiver Noise Figure (dB)	6.5
Equivalent Receiver Noise Temperature (°K)	1005
Antenna Temperature Pointed at Earth (°K)	290
Receiver System Temperature (°K)	1295
Antenna Gain, peak (dB)	38.4
Spacecraft G/T, peak (dB/°K)	7.3
Half Power Beamwidth (degrees)	1.3
Gain over Field of View (dB)	35.4
Spacecraft G/T over Field of View (dB/°K)	4.3

Transmit

Transmit Power (dBw)	15.3
Antenna Gain, peak (dB)	37.7
Effective Radiated Power, peak (dBw)	53.0
Half Power Beamwidth (degrees)	1.4
Gain over Field of View (dB)	34.8
Effective Radiated Power over Field of View (dBw)	50.1

4

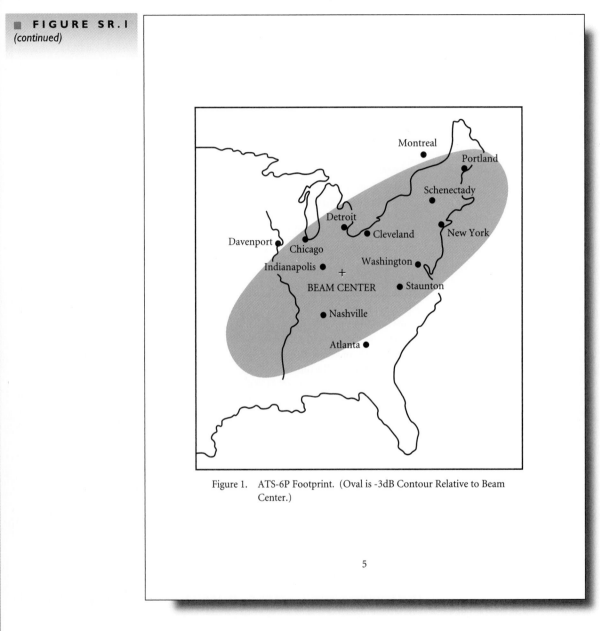

Figure 1. ATS-6P Footprint. (Oval is -3dB Contour Relative to Beam Center.)

5

■ **FIGURE SR.I**
(continued)

Within this region, the trucks drove through the kinds of terrain usually encountered in long-haul trucking, including both urban and rural areas in open plains, foothills, and mountains.

Data Analysis

All test transmissions were recorded at the earth station on a high-quality reel-to-reel tape recorder. The strength of the signals received from the trucks via the satellite was recorded on a chart recorder that had a frequency response of approximately 100 hertz. In addition, observers in the trucks recorded all data signals received and all data codes sent. They also recorded information about the terrain during all data and voice transmissions.

We analyzed the data collected in several ways:

- To determine the accuracy of the data transmissions, we compared the information recorded by the observers with the signals recorded on the tapes of all transmissions.

- To determine the quality of the voice transmissions, we had an evaluator listen to the tape using high-quality earphones. For each transmission, the evaluator rated the signal quality on the standard scale for the subjective evaluation of broadcast quality. On it, Q5 is excellent and Q1 is unintelligible.

- To determine what factors influenced the quality of the transmissions, we examined the descriptions of the terrain that the observers recorded for all data transmissions that were inaccurate and all the voice communications that were rated 3 or less by the evaluator. We also looked for relationships between the accuracy and quality of the transmissions and the distance of the trucks from the edge of the broadcast footprint of the ATS-6 satellite.

Presentation of data analyses parallels the list of objectives in the indtroduction.

6

■ **FIGURE SR.I**
(continued)

Section 3

RESULTS AND DISCUSSION

Background for results
and discussion section

In total, the test transmissions took 603 hours of satellite time. They included 690 data communications and 5351 seconds of voice communications. This section reports and discusses the results of these transmissions and examines the factors that influence transmission quality.

Data Transmissions

Key result is
presented first.

Other results are
mentioned.

Other results are
interpreted.

As Table 3 shows, 91% of the data transmissions were successful. These data are reported according to the region in which the trucks were driving at the time of transmission. The most important difference to note is the one between the rate of successful transmissions in the Southern Piedmont region and the rates in all the other regions. In the Southern Piedmont area, we had the truck drive slightly outside the ATS-6 footprint so that we could see if successful transmissions could be made there. When the truck left the footprint, the percentage of successful data transmissions dropped abruptly to 43%. If transmissions in that area are eliminated from the calculations, 95% of all data transmissions were successful.

Voice Transmissions

Result is given.

Result is interpreted.

The success rate for the voice transmissions was also very high. As the two left-hand columns of Table 4 show, 91% of the communications were rated as Q4 or Q5. That is a very good rating because Q3 is usually considered adequate to provide useful commercial communications. As with data communications, the rate of successful transmissions drops off sharply in the Southern Piedmont area, where the truck involved left the ATS-6 footprint. If the transmissions made in the South Piedmont area are eliminated from the calculations, the system produced voice communications rated a Q4 or Q5 96% of the time.

Summary emphasizes
major results.

Thus, within the footprint of the satellite, 95% or more of the transmissions of both data and voice were of commercial quality. That success rate is very good: the specifications for the mobile radio systems used by police and fire departments usually require only 90% effectiveness for the area covered.

7

Table 3

Success in Decoding DTMF Automatic Transmitter

REGION	STATES	ATS TRANSMISSIONS		ELEVATION
		Sent by Vehicle	Received and Decoded Correctly	Angle to Satellite (°)
Open Plains	Indiana, Ohio, Nebraska, Illinois, Iowa	284	283 (100%)	17–26
Western Appalachian Foothills	Ohio, Tennessee	55	53 (96%)	15–19
Appalachian Mountains	West Virginia	112	93 (83%)	15–17
Piedmont	Virginia, North Carolina	190	178 (97%)	11–16
Southern Piedmont	Georgia, South Carolina	49	21 (43%)	17–18
TOTAL		690	628 (91%)	

8

■ **FIGURE SR.I**
(continued)

Table 4
Quality of Voice Communication Signal[1]

Area	Transmission Time (Seconds)	No Blockage Time (Secs)		Trees			Mountains and Hills			Overpasses (Momentary Dropouts)			Buildings		
		Q5	Q4	Q3	Q2	Q1	Q3	Q2	Q1	Q3	Q2	Q1	Q3	Q2	Q1
Open Plains	2481	2334	73	1	1	0	4	1	3	13	2	20	15	10	4
Western Foothills	344	322	2	0	0	0	6	12	13	0	0	0	0	0	0
Appalachian Mountains	1037	614	267	42	17	0	20	31	37	0	2	7	0	0	0
Piedmont	1219	481	623	5	15	19	25	16	10	4	1	4	8	4	1
Southern Piedmont	270	0	149	109	3	12	0	0	0	0	0	2	0	0	0
TOTAL TIME (seconds)	5351	3751	1114	157	36	31	55	60	63	17	5	33	23	14	5

[1]Total times in seconds for each quality of received signals. Q5 is excellent; Q1 is unintelligible.

9

REFERENCE GUIDE: Three Types of Special Reports

Most important factor
is presented first.

Reference to detailed
data in table

Key result is presented
and explained.

Factors Affecting the Quality of Transmissions

The factor having the largest effect on transmission quality is the location of the truck within the footprint of ATS-6. The quality of transmissions is even and uniformly good throughout the footprint, but almost immediately outside of it the quality drops well below acceptable levels.

Several factors were found to disrupt transmissions even when the trucks were in the satellite's footprint. Table 4 shows what these factors are for the 4% of the transmissions in the footprint that were not of commercial quality. In all cases the cause is some object passing in the line of sight between the satellite and the truck.

Trees caused 45% of the disruptions, more than any other source. At the frequencies used for broadcasting in this system, trees and other foliage have a high and very sharp absorption. Of course, the tree must be immediately beside the road and also tall enough to intrude between the truck and the satellite, which is at an average elevation of 17° above the horizon. And the disruption caused by a single tree will create only a very brief and usually insignificant dropout of one second or less. Only driving past a group of trees will cause a significant loss of signal. Yet this happened often in the terrain of the Appalachian Mountains and the South Piedmont.

We believe we could eliminate many of the disruptions caused by trees if we developed an antenna specifically for use in communications between satellites and mobile radios. In the test, we used a standard dipole antenna. Instead, we might devise a Wheeler-type antenna that is omnidirectional in azimuth and with gain in the vertical direction to minimize ground reflections.

Mountains and hills caused 36% of the disruptions. That happened mostly in areas where the satellite's elevation above the horizon was very low. Otherwise a hill or mountain would have to be very steep to block out a signal. For example, if a satellite were only 17° above the horizon, the hill would have to rise over 1500 feet per mile to interfere with a transmission—and the elevation would have to be precisely in a line between the truck and the satellite.

10

Most of the disruptions caused by mountains and hills can be eliminated by using satellites that have an elevation of at least 25°. That would place them above all but the very steepest slopes.

Highway overpasses accounted for 11% of the disruptions, but these disruptions had little effect on the overall quality of the broadcasts. As one of the test trucks drove on an open stretch of interstate highway, the signal was strong and steady, with fading less than 2 decibels peak-to-peak. About two seconds before the truck entered the overpass, there was detectable but not severe multipath interference. The only serious disruption was a one-second dropout while the truck was directly under the overpass. This one-second dropout was so brief that it did not cause a significant loss of intelligibility in voice communications. Only a series of overpasses, such as those found where interstate highways pass through some cities, cause a significant problem.

Finally, buildings and similar structures accounted for about 8% of the disruptions. These were experienced mainly in large cities, and isolated buildings usually caused only brief disruptions. However, when the trucks were driving down city streets lined with tall buildings, they were unable to obtain satisfactory communications until they were driven to other streets.

11

■ **FIGURE SR.I**
(continued)

The presentation of conclusions parallels the list of objectives in the introduction.

Section 4

CONCLUSIONS

This test supports three important conclusions:

• The Satellite Products Laboratory's system produces good-quality data and voice transmissions through the eleven-state region covered by the satellite's broadcast footprint.

• The most important factor limiting the success of transmissions is movement outside the satellite's broadcast footprint, which accurately defines the satellite's area of effective coverage.

• The system is sensitive to interference from certain kinds of objects in the line of sight between the satellite and the truck. These include trees, mountains and hills, overpasses, and buildings.

12

■ **FIGURE SR.1**
(continued)

Overall
recommendation
is given first.

Section 5

RECOMMENDATIONS

Based on this test, we believe that work should proceed as rapidly as possible to complete an operational system. In that work, the Satellite Products Laboratory should do the following things:

1. Develop a new antenna designed specifically for use in communications between satellites and mobile radios. Such an antenna would probably eliminate many of the disruptions caused by trees, the most common cause of poor transmissions.

2. Define the configuration of satellites needed to provide service throughout our planned service area. We are now ready to determine the number and placement in orbit of the satellites we will need to launch in order to provide service to our planned service area (48 contiguous states, Alaska, Southern Canada). Because locations outside of the broadcast footprint of a satellite probably cannot be given satisfactory service, our satellites will have to provide thorough footprint coverage throughout all of this territory. Also, we should plan the satellites so that each will be at least 25° above the horizon throughout the area it serves; in that way we can almost entirely eliminate poor transmissions due to interference from mountains and hills.

13

FEASIBILITY REPORTS

A feasibility report is an evaluation of the practicality and desirability of pursuing some course of action. Imagine, for instance, that you work for a company that designs and builds sailboats. The company thinks it might reduce manufacturing costs without hurting sales if it uses high-strength plastics to manufacture some parts traditionally made from metal. Before making such a change, however, the company wants you to answer several questions: Would plastic parts be as strong, durable, and attractive as metal ones? Is there a supplier who would make the plastic parts? Would the plastic parts really be less expensive than the metal ones? Would boat buyers accept the change? The company will use the information and analyses you provide in your report as the primary basis for deciding whether to pursue this course of action.

In this section, you will learn how to prepare effective feasibility reports.

TYPICAL WRITING SITUATION

All feasibility reports are written to help decision-makers choose between two or more courses of action. Even when a feasibility report focuses on a single course of action, the readers are always considering a second course—namely, to leave things the way they are. Often, however, your readers will already have decided that some change is necessary and will be choosing between two or more alternatives to the status quo.

THE QUESTIONS READERS ASK MOST OFTEN

As decision-makers think about the choices they must make, they ask many questions. From situation to situation, their basic questions remain the same, and the superstructure for feasibility reports is a widely used way of providing the answers. Here are the readers' typical questions:

- **Why is it important for us to consider these alternatives?** Decision-makers ask this question because they want to know why they have to make any choice in the first place. They may need a detailed explanation of the problem before they appreciate the urgency of considering alternative courses of action. On the other hand, if they are already familiar with the problem, they may need only to be reminded of what it is.
- **Are your criteria reasonable and appropriate?** To help your readers choose between alternative courses of action, you must evaluate the alternatives in terms of specific criteria. At work, people want these criteria to reflect the needs and aims of their organization. And they want you to tell them explicitly what the criteria are so they can judge them.
- **Are your facts reliable?** Decision-makers want to be sure that your facts are reliable before they take any action based on those facts.
- **What are the important features of the alternatives?** So that they can understand your detailed discussion of the alternatives, readers want you to highlight the key features of each alternative.

- **How do the alternatives stack up against your criteria?** The heart of a feasibility study is your evaluation of the alternatives in terms of your criteria. Your readers want to know the results.
- **What overall conclusions do you draw about the alternatives?** Based on your detailed evaluation of the alternatives, you will reach some general conclusions about the merits of each. Decision-makers need to know your conclusions because these overall judgments form the basis for decision-making.
- **What do you think we should do?** In the end, your readers must choose one of the alternative courses of action. Because of your expertise on the subject, they want you to help them by telling what you recommend.

SUPERSTRUCTURE FOR FEASIBILITY REPORTS

The superstructure for feasibility reports provides a framework that writers and readers both have found effective for answering these questions. Each element corresponds with one of the questions decision-makers ask when trying to decide about future action:

Superstructure for Feasibility Reports	
Report Element	**Readers' Question**
Introduction	Why is it important for us to consider these alternatives?
Criteria	Are your criteria reasonable and appropriate?
Method	Are your facts reliable?
Overview of alternatives	What are the important features of the alternatives?
Evaluation	How do the alternatives stack up against your criteria?
Conclusions	What overall conclusions do you draw from the alternatives?
Recommendations	What do you think we should do?

Of course, you may combine the elements in different ways, depending on the situation. For instance, you may integrate your conclusions into your evaluation, or you may omit a separate discussion of your criteria if they need no special explanation. But when preparing any feasibility report, you should consciously determine whether to include each of the seven elements, based on your understanding of your purpose, audience, and situation.

Remember that a superstructure is not an outline; you may combine the elements of a superstructure in many ways (see pages 449–452).

Introduction

For additional advice on writing an introduction, see Chapter 8, "Beginning a Communication."

In the introduction to a feasibility report, you should answer your readers' question, "Why is it important for us to consider these alternatives?" The most persuasive way to answer this question is to identify the problem your feasibility report will help your readers solve or the goal it will help them achieve: to reduce the number of rejected parts, to increase productivity, and so on. Beyond that, your introduction should announce the alternative courses of action you studied and tell generally how you investigated them.

Consider, for example, the way Phil, a process engineer in a paper mill, wrote the introduction of a feasibility report he prepared. (Phil's entire report appears at the end of this section, pages 499–505.) Phil was asked to study the feasibility of substituting one ingredient for another in the furnish for one of the papers the mill produces (*furnish* is the combination of ingredients used to make the pulp for paper):

<table>
<tr><td style="text-align:right">Problem</td><td>At present we rely on the titanium dioxide (TiO_2) in our furnish to provide the high brightness and opacity we desire in our paper However ... the price of TiO_2 has been rising steadily and rapidly for several years. We now pay roughly $1400 per ton for TiO_2, or about 70¢ per pound.</td></tr>
<tr><td style="text-align:right">Possible solution</td><td>Some mills are now replacing some of the TiO_2 in their furnish with silicate extenders. Because the average price for silicate extenders is only $500 per ton, well under half the cost of TiO_2, the savings are very great.</td></tr>
<tr><td style="text-align:right">What Phil did to investigate the possible solution</td><td>To determine whether we could enjoy a similar savings for our 30-pound book paper, I have studied the physical properties, material handling requirements, and cost of two silicate extenders, Tri-Sil 606 and Zenolux 26 T.</td></tr>
</table>

Generally, the introduction to a long feasibility report (and most short ones) should also include a preview of the main conclusions and, perhaps, the major recommendations. Phil included his major conclusion:

Phil's main point

> I conclude that one of the silicate extenders, Zenolux 26 T, looks promising enough to be tested in a mill run.

As another example, consider the way Ellen wrote the introduction of a feasibility report she prepared for the board of directors of the bank where she works. Ellen was asked to evaluate the feasibility of opening a new branch in a particular suburban community. She began by announcing the topic of her report:

Ellen's introduction

> This report discusses the feasibility of opening a branch office of Orchard Bank in Rolling Knolls, Tennessee.

Then, after giving a sentence of background information about the source of the bank's interest in exploring this possibility, Ellen emphasized the importance of conducting a feasibility study:

> In the past, Orchard Bank has approached the opening of new branches with great care, which is undoubtedly a major reason that in the twelve years since its founding it has become one of Tennessee's most successful small, privately owned financial institutions.

Ellen also included her major conclusions:

> Overall, the Rolling Knolls location offers an enticing opportunity, but would present Orchard Bank with some challenges it has not faced before.

She ended her introduction with a brief summary of her major recommendation:

> We should proceed carefully.

The introduction of a feasibility report is often combined with one or more of the other six elements, such as a description of the criteria, a discussion of the method of obtaining facts, or an overview of the alternatives. It may also include the various kinds of background, explanatory, and forecasting information that may be found in the beginning of any technical communication (see Chapter 8).

Criteria

Criteria are the standards of evaluation.

Criteria are the standards that you apply in a feasibility study to evaluate the alternative courses of action you are considering. For instance, to assess the feasibility of opening the new branch office, Ellen used many criteria, including the existence of a large enough market, the possibility of attracting depositors away from competitors, the likelihood that profits on deposits at the branch would exceed the expenses of operating it, and the reasonableness of the financial outlay required to open the office. If she had found that the proposed branch failed to meet any of those criteria, she would have concluded that opening it was not feasible. Likewise, Phil evaluated the two silicate extenders by applying several specific criteria.

Two Ways of Presenting Criteria   There are two common ways of telling your readers what your criteria are:

- **Devote a separate section to identifying and explaining them.** Writers often do this in long reports or in reports in which the criteria themselves require extended explanation.
- **Integrate your presentation of them into other elements of the report.** Phil did this in the following sentence from the third paragraph of his introduction:

Phil names his three criteria.

> To determine whether we could enjoy a similar savings for our 30-pound book paper, I have studied the physical properties, material handling requirements, and cost of two silicate extenders, Tri-Sil 606 and Zenolux 26 T.

For each of the general criteria named in this sentence, Phil had some more specific criteria, which he described when he discussed his methods and results. For instance, at the beginning of his discussion of the physical properties of the two extenders, he named the three properties he evaluated.

Importance of Presenting Criteria Early   Whether you present your criteria in a separate section or integrate them into other sections, you should introduce them early in your report. There are three good reasons for doing this. First, because your readers know that the validity of your conclusion depends on the criteria you use to evaluate the alternatives, they will want to evaluate the criteria themselves. They will ask, "Did you take into account all the considerations relevant to this decision?" and "Are the standards you are applying reasonable in these circumstances?"

Second, your discussion of the criteria tells readers a great deal about the scope of your report. Did you restrict yourself to technical questions, for instance, or did you also consider relevant organizational issues such as profitability and management strategies?

The third reason for presenting your criteria early is that your discussion of the alternative courses of action will make much more sense to your readers if they know in advance the criteria by which you evaluated the alternatives.

Sources of Your Criteria   You may wonder how to come up with the criteria you will use in your study and report. Often, the person who asks you to undertake a study will tell you what criteria to apply. In other situations, particularly when you are conducting a feasibility study that requires technical knowledge that you have but your readers don't, your readers may expect you to identify the relevant criteria for them.

In either case, you are likely to refine your criteria as you conduct your study. The writing process itself can help you refine your criteria because as you compose you must think in detail about the information you have obtained and decide how best to evaluate it.

Four Common Types of Criteria   As you develop your criteria, you may find it helpful to know that, at work, criteria often address one or more of the following questions:

- **Will this course of action really do what's wanted?** This question is especially common when the problem is a technical one: Will this reorganization of the department really improve the speed with which we can process loan applications? Will the new type of programming really reduce computer time?
- **Can we implement this course of action?** Even though a particular course of action may work technically, it may not be practical. For example, it may require overly extensive changes in operations, equipment, or materials that are not readily available, or special skills that employees do not possess.
- **Can we afford it?** Cost can be treated in several ways. You may seek an alternative that costs less than some fixed amount or one that will save enough to pay for itself in a fixed period (for example, two years). Or you may simply be asked to determine whether the costs are "reasonable."
- **Is it desirable?** Sometimes a solution must be more than effective, implementable, and affordable. Many otherwise feasible courses of action are rejected because they create undesirable side effects. For example, a company might reject a plan for increasing productivity because it would impair employee morale.

Ultimately, your selection of criteria for a particular feasibility study will depend on the problem at hand and on the professional responsibilities, goals, and values of the people who will use your report. In some instances, you will need to deal only with criteria related to the question, "Does it work?" At other times, you might need to deal with all the criteria mentioned above, plus others. No matter what your criteria, however, announce them to your readers before you discuss your evaluation.

Method
By explaining how you obtained your facts, you answer your readers' question, "Are your facts reliable?" That is, by showing that you used reliable methods, you assure your readers that your facts form a sound basis for decision-making.

You may refine your criteria while you are writing your report.

The source of your facts will depend on the nature of your study—library research, calls to manufacturers, interviews, meetings with other experts in your organization, surveys, laboratory research, and the like.

The amount of detail to provide depends on the situation.

How much detail should you provide about your methods? That depends on your readers and the situation, but in every case your goal is to say enough to satisfy your readers that your information is trustworthy. For example, Ellen used some fairly technical procedures to estimate the amount of deposits that Orchard Bank could expect from a new branch in Rolling Knolls, Tennessee. However, because those procedures are standard in the banking industry and well known to her readers, she did not need to explain them in detail.

In contrast, Calvin needed to provide a great deal of information about his methods in a feasibility report that he prepared for his employer, a manufacturer of packaged mixes for cakes, breads, and cookies. Calvin's assignment was to determine the feasibility of making a new, low-gluten muffin mix for a new line of products for people with special health conditions. To evaluate the alternative muffin mixes, Calvin used several test procedures common in the food industry. However, to persuade his very demanding readers that his results were valid, he had to explain in detail how he obtained them. Readers in another organization might have required less detail to accept the validity of his findings.

Descriptions of methods are often combined with other sections.

Where is the best place to describe your methods? The best place for describing your methods depends partly on how many techniques you used. If you used only one or two techniques—say, library research and interviews—you might describe each in a separate paragraph or section near the beginning of your report, perhaps in the introduction. On the other hand, if you used several different techniques, each pertaining to a different part of your analysis, you might describe each of them at the point where you present and discuss the results you obtained.

Of course, if your methods are obvious, you may not need to describe them at all. You must always be sure, however, that your readers know enough about your methods to accept your facts as reliable.

Overview of Alternatives

Ensure that your readers understand the alternatives before you begin evaluating them.

Before you begin your detailed evaluation of the alternatives, you must be sure that your readers understand what the alternatives are. Sometimes you need to devote only a few words to that task. Imagine, for instance, that you work for a chain of convenience stores that has asked you to investigate the feasibility of increasing starting salaries for store managers as a way of attracting stronger applicants for job openings. Surely your readers will not require any special explanation to understand the course of action you are assessing.

However, you may sometimes need to provide extensive background information or otherwise explain the alternatives to your readers. George needed to do so when he wrote a report on the feasibility of replacing his employer's building-wide telephone system. That's because the alternative systems he considered are complex and differ from one another in many ways. By providing an initial overview of the alternative telephone systems he was considering, George helped his readers piece together the more detailed comments he later made in his point-by-point evaluation of the systems.

Of course, if George's readers had already understood the alternative systems, he would not have needed to explain them, no matter how complex the alternatives were. Your job is to ensure that your readers understand the alternatives before you begin evaluating them, whether it takes just a few words or many pages of explanation.

Evaluation

The heart of a feasibility report is the detailed evaluation of the course or courses of action you studied. Most writers organize their evaluation sections around their criteria. For example, in her study of the feasibility of opening a new branch office, Ellen devoted one section to the size of the market, another to the competition, a third to prospective income and expenses, and so on. Similarly, in his report on alternative telephone systems, George organized his evaluation around his criteria: ability to handle voice communication, ability to handle data communication, and so on.

The following sections offer three pieces of advice that will help you present your evaluations clearly and effectively.

For a full discussion of the divided and alternating patterns of organization, see pages 208–209.

Choose Carefully between the Divided and Alternating Patterns   In reports in which you are comparing two or more alternatives, you can organize your evaluation according to either the divided pattern or the alternating pattern. Choose the pattern that will enable your readers to read, understand, and use your information most efficiently. For example, George knew that readers of his report on the telephone systems would want to compare the systems directly in terms of each of their specific criteria. Because many of the comparisons involved complex details, George felt that he could help his readers by using the alternating pattern, which enabled him to present each set of relevant details in one place.

On the other hand, Calvin used the divided pattern in his evaluation of the alternative recipes for low-gluten muffins. Each individual test on each muffin mix produced a single, specific result that could be communicated in only a few words. He judged that his readers would have difficulty building a coherent understanding of each muffin's strengths and weaknesses if he used the alternating pattern. By using the divided pattern, he presented all the results for a particular mix in one brief passage. Then, in his conclusions, Calvin was able to compare the mixes quickly by citing the most significant differences among them.

Dismiss Obviously Unsuitable Alternatives   Sometimes you will want to mention several alternatives but treat only one or a few thoroughly. Perhaps your investigation showed that the other alternatives failed to meet one or more of the critical criteria so that they should not be considered seriously.

Usually, it makes no sense to discuss obviously unsuitable alternatives at length. Instead, you might explain briefly the alternatives that you have dismissed and tell why you dismissed them. This entire discussion might take only a sentence or a paragraph. You might include it in the introduction (when you are talking about the scope of your report) or in your overview of the alternatives.

It is usually not wise to postpone your mention of unsuitable alternatives until the end of your report. If you do, some of your readers may keep asking, "But why didn't you consider so and so?" That question may distract them as they read the important sections of your report.

Put Your Most Important Points First   The final piece of advice for presenting your evaluation of alternatives is to remember the guideline in Chapter 7 that urged you to begin each segment of your communications with the most important information. This advice applies to the entire segment in which you evaluate the alternatives, as well as to its parts. By presenting the most important information first, you save your readers the trouble of trying to figure out what generalizations they should draw from the details you are presenting. For instance, in her report to the bank Ellen begins one part of her evaluation of the Rolling Knolls location by saying:

See Guideline 3 in Chapter 7, page 173.

> Beginning of Ellen's evaluation

> The proposed Rolling Knolls branch office would be profitable after three years if Orchard Bank successfully develops the type of two-pronged marketing strategy outlined in the preceding section.

Ellen then spends two pages discussing the estimates of deposits, income, and expenses that support her overall assessment.

Similarly, Phil begins one part of his evaluation of the silicate extenders in this way:

> Beginning of Phil's evaluation

> With respect to material handling, I found no basis for choosing between Zenolux and Tri-Sil.

Phil then spends two paragraphs reporting the facts he has gathered about the physical handling of the two extenders.

Conclusions

Your conclusions constitute your overall assessment of the feasibility of the alternative courses of action you studied. You might present your conclusions in two or three places in your report. You should certainly mention them in summary form near the beginning. If your report is long (say, several pages), you might also remind your readers of your conclusions at the beginning of the evaluation segment. Finally, you should provide detailed discussion of your conclusions in a separate section following your evaluation of the alternatives.

Recommendations

Tell what you think your readers should do, based on your study.

It is customary to end a feasibility report by answering the decision-makers' question, "What do you think we should do?" Because you have investigated and thought about the alternatives so thoroughly, your readers will place special value on your recommendations. Depending on the situation, you might need to take only a single sentence or many pages to present your recommendations.

Sometimes your recommendations will pertain directly to the course of action you studied: "Do this" or "Don't do this." At other times you may perform a preliminary feasibility study to determine whether a certain course of action is promising enough to warrant a more thorough investigation. In that case, your recommendation would focus not on whether to pursue a certain course of action but on whether to continue studying it. Ellen's report about opening a new bank office is of that type. She determined that there was a substantial possibility of making a profit with the new branch, but felt the need for expert advice before making a final decision. Consequently, she recommended that the bank hire a marketing agency to evaluate the prospects.

Sometimes you may discover that you were unable to gather all the information you needed to make a firm recommendation. Perhaps your deadline was too short or your funds too limited. Perhaps you uncovered an unexpected question that needs further investigation. In such situations, you should point out the limitations of your report and let your readers know what else they should find out so they can make a well-informed decision.

SAMPLE OUTLINES AND REPORT

The seven elements of the superstructure for feasibility reports can be incorporated into many different organizational patterns. Figures SR.2 and SR.3 illustrate some of the possibilities by showing you the outlines for the reports by George and Calvin.

In his report on the telephone systems (Figure SR.2), George uses seven sections that correspond directly to the seven elements of a feasibility report (page 488). In contrast, Calvin uses only four sections in his report on the muffin mixes (Figure SR.3). He does this by combining some of the superstructure's elements: in the opening section, he presents both the introduction and the overview; in the next section, he describes both his method of obtaining facts and his criteria; and in the final section, he intertwines his conclusions and recommendations.

In her report on the new branch office for the bank (Figure SR.4), Ellen uses six sections but devotes three of them to her evaluation of alternatives. In contrast, both George and Calvin devote only a single section to evaluation.

You will find many other differences among these three outlines. The most important points to note are (1) that all three reports contain all seven elements of a feasibility report and (2) that the superstructure can be applied in many different ways to suit the purpose and readers of a particular report.

Figure SR.5 (pages 496–505) shows the feasibility report written by Phil on the silicate extenders.

Note to the Instructor: For an assignment involving a feasibility report, you can use the formal report project in Appendix C. Also, several cases in Appendix C can be written using the superstructure for feasibility reports. The printed *Instructor's Manual* contains a "Planning Guide for Feasibility Reports," and the book's Web site offers an on-line version you can download, edit to suit your course, and distribute electronically to your students. Also, the Web site provides additional cases you can download and edit to suit your course.

■ **FIGURE SR.2**

How George Used the Superstructure for Feasibility Reports in His Comparison of Three Phone Systems

Introduction (explains importance of considering the alternatives)

Method of obtaining facts

Criteria used to evaluate alternatives

Overview of alternatives

Evaluation of alternatives (uses alternating pattern)

Conclusions

Recommendations

Feasibility of Installing a New Building-Wide Phone System at Whitney Industries

I. Background

    A. Purpose of report is to analyze alternative phone systems for Whitney Industries
    B. Present phone system has many problems
    C. Additional capabilities will be required in future

II. Investigative Procedures

    A. Audited performance of present system
    B. Asked managers to predict future needs
    C. Contacted selected vendors

III. Characteristics Sought in Phone System

    A. Required
    B. Optional

IV. Comparison of Alternatives

    A. Choices considered
        1. Upgrade present system
        2. Replace with System X
        3. Replace with System Y
    B. Point-by-point comparison
        1. Basic capabilities
          -Voice communication
          -Data communication
          -Call forwarding
          -Multiple-party calls
        2. Expandability
        3. Service
        4. Cost

V. Conclusions

VI. Recommendations

    A. Choose System X
    B. Form a steering committee for implementation

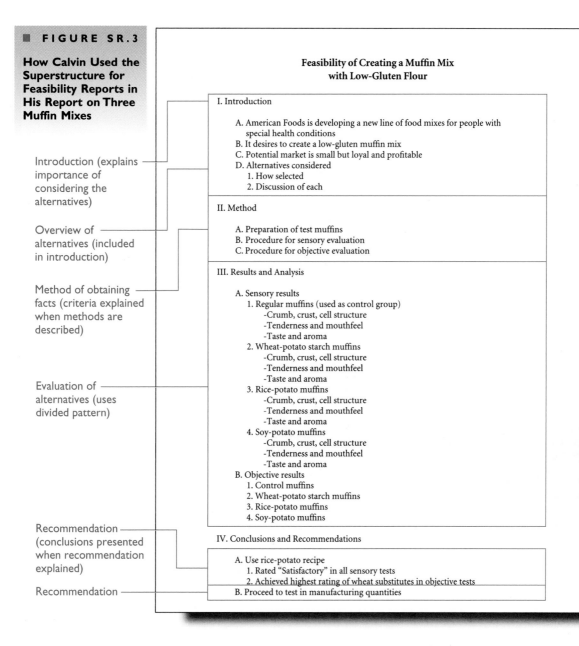

■ FIGURE SR.3

How Calvin Used the Superstructure for Feasibility Reports in His Report on Three Muffin Mixes

Introduction (explains importance of considering the alternatives)

Overview of alternatives (included in introduction)

Method of obtaining facts (criteria explained when methods are described)

Evaluation of alternatives (uses divided pattern)

Recommendation (conclusions presented when recommendation explained)

Recommendation

Feasibility of Creating a Muffin Mix
with Low-Gluten Flour

I. Introduction

  A. American Foods is developing a new line of food mixes for people with
     special health conditions
  B. It desires to create a low-gluten muffin mix
  C. Potential market is small but loyal and profitable
  D. Alternatives considered
    1. How selected
    2. Discussion of each

II. Method

  A. Preparation of test muffins
  B. Procedure for sensory evaluation
  C. Procedure for objective evaluation

III. Results and Analysis

  A. Sensory results
    1. Regular muffins (used as control group)
      -Crumb, crust, cell structure
      -Tenderness and mouthfeel
      -Taste and aroma
    2. Wheat-potato starch muffins
      -Crumb, crust, cell structure
      -Tenderness and mouthfeel
      -Taste and aroma
    3. Rice-potato muffins
      -Crumb, crust, cell structure
      -Tenderness and mouthfeel
      -Taste and aroma
    4. Soy-potato muffins
      -Crumb, crust, cell structure
      -Tenderness and mouthfeel
      -Taste and aroma
  B. Objective results
    1. Control muffins
    2. Wheat-potato starch muffins
    3. Rice-potato muffins
    4. Soy-potato muffins

IV. Conclusions and Recommendations

  A. Use rice-potato recipe
    1. Rated "Satisfactory" in all sensory tests
    2. Achieved highest rating of wheat substitutes in objective tests
  B. Proceed to test in manufacturing quantities

REFERENCE GUIDE: Three Types of Special Reports

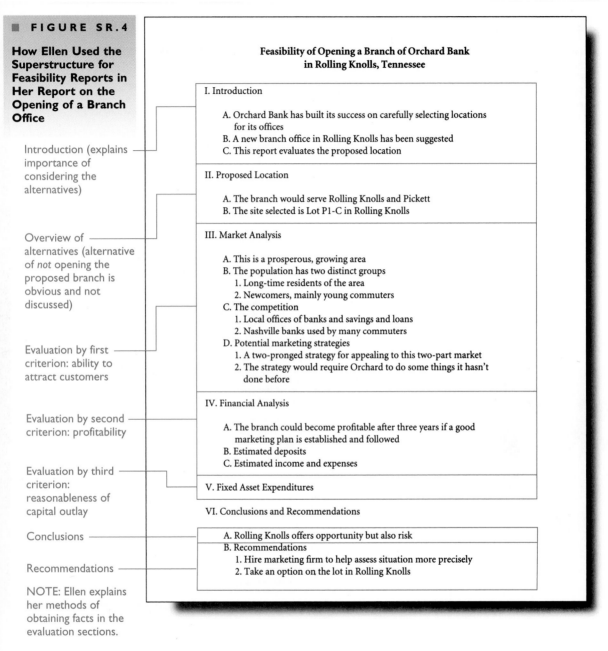

■ **FIGURE SR.4**

How Ellen Used the Superstructure for Feasibility Reports in Her Report on the Opening of a Branch Office

Introduction (explains importance of considering the alternatives)

Overview of alternatives (alternative of *not* opening the proposed branch is obvious and not discussed)

Evaluation by first criterion: ability to attract customers

Evaluation by second criterion: profitability

Evaluation by third criterion: reasonableness of capital outlay

Conclusions

Recommendations

NOTE: Ellen explains her methods of obtaining facts in the evaluation sections.

Feasibility of Opening a Branch of Orchard Bank in Rolling Knolls, Tennessee

I. Introduction

    A. Orchard Bank has built its success on carefully selecting locations for its offices
    B. A new branch office in Rolling Knolls has been suggested
    C. This report evaluates the proposed location

II. Proposed Location

    A. The branch would serve Rolling Knolls and Pickett
    B. The site selected is Lot P1-C in Rolling Knolls

III. Market Analysis

    A. This is a prosperous, growing area
    B. The population has two distinct groups
        1. Long-time residents of the area
        2. Newcomers, mainly young commuters
    C. The competition
        1. Local offices of banks and savings and loans
        2. Nashville banks used by many commuters
    D. Potential marketing strategies
        1. A two-pronged strategy for appealing to this two-part market
        2. The strategy would require Orchard to do some things it hasn't done before

IV. Financial Analysis

    A. The branch could become profitable after three years if a good marketing plan is established and followed
    B. Estimated deposits
    C. Estimated income and expenses

V. Fixed Asset Expenditures

VI. Conclusions and Recommendations

    A. Rolling Knolls offers opportunity but also risk
    B. Recommendations
        1. Hire marketing firm to help assess situation more precisely
        2. Take an option on the lot in Rolling Knolls

■ **FIGURE SR.5**

Feasibility Report

REGENCY INTERNATIONAL PAPER COMPANY

Memorandum

FROM: Phil Hines, Process Engineer
TO: Jim Shulmann, Senior Engineer
DATE: December 13, 19—

SUBJECT: **FEASIBILITY OF USING SILICATE EXTENDERS
FOR 30-POUND BOOK PAPER**

Summary

Entire report is summarized in 125 words.

I have investigated the feasibility of using a silicate extender to replace some of the TiO_2 in the furnish for our 30-pound book paper. Because the cost of the extenders is less than half the cost of TiO_2, we could enjoy a considerable savings through such a substitution.

The tests show that either one of the two extenders tested can save us money. In terms of retention, opacity, and brightness, Zenolux is more effective than Tri-Sil. Consequently, it can be used in smaller amounts to achieve a given opacity or brightness. Furthermore, because of its better retention, it will place less of a burden on our water system. With respect to handling and cost, the two are roughly the same.

I recommend a trial run with Zenolux.

Summary emphasizes conclusions and recommendations.

Introduction

At present we rely on the titanium dioxide (TiO_2) in our furnish to provide the high brightness and opacity we desire in our paper. However, as Figure 1 shows (at the end of this report), the price of TiO_2 has been rising steadily and rapidly for several years. We now pay roughly $1400 per ton for TiO_2, or about 70¢ per pound.

Problem

■ **FIGURE SR.5**
(continued)

Silicate Extenders   Page 2

Possible solution — Some mills are now replacing some of the TiO$_2$ in their furnish with silicate extenders. Because the average price for silicate extenders is only $500 per ton, well under half the cost of TiO$_2$, the savings are very great.

What writer did to investigate possible solution (general criteria) — To determine whether we could enjoy a similar savings for our 30-pound book paper, I have studied the physical properties, material handling requirements, and cost of two silicate extenders, Tri-Sil 606 and Zenolux 26 T.

Major conclusion and recommendation — I conclude that one of the silicate extenders, Zenolux 26 T, looks promising enough to be tested in a mill run.

Tests of Physical Properties

Criteria for evaluating physical properties — The three physical properties I tested are retention, opacity, and brightness.

General result — In all three areas, Zenolux is superior.

Retention

Reason for testing retention — As with any ingredient in our furnish, we must be concerned with the proportion of a silicate extender that will be retained in the paper and the proportion that will be left in the water, where it is wasted and may cause problems in our water system.

Method — To test retention of the two silicate extenders, I made two dozen handsheets, each containing the equivalent of 3 grams of oven-dried pulp and 2 grams of oven-dried extender. By weighing the finished handsheets, I determined how much silicate extender had been lost from each.

Evaluation of results and discussion — The results showed that the average retention for Zenolux was 75%, whereas the average retention for Tri-Sil was 51%. Higher retention should result in higher opacity and brightness because more particles remain in the furnish to prevent clumping of the TiO$_2$.

Opacity

Method of opacity testing — To determine the effectiveness of each extender in preventing light from passing through the paper, I conducted a two-stage test of opacity. First, I investigated the opacity of TiO$_2$, Tri-Sil, and Zenolux when each is used alone. To do that, I made the following sets of handsheets:

■ **FIGURE SR.5**
(continued)

Method of opacity
testing (continued)

Evaluation of results
(detailed results given
in figure)

Overall evaluation
of material handling

Results concerning
material handling
(method not mentioned
because it is obvious)

Silicate Extenders   Page 3

- 8 handsheets containing each of the following loadings of TiO_2: 2%, 4%, 6%, 8%, 10%, 12%, 14%, and 16%.
- 8 handsheets containing each of the same loadings of Tri-Sil.
- 8 handsheets containing each of the same loadings of Zenolux.

I stored the handsheets at the standard conditions of 50% relative humidity and 23°C for 24 hours. Then, I found the TAPPI opacity of each handsheet. The results, given for the average opacity at each loading, are shown in Figure 2. Again, Zenolux is superior to Tri-Sil.

In the second stage of the opacity test, I made two additional sets of handsheets:

- 5 handsheets with each of the following pigment loadings: 100% TiO_2 and 0% Tri-Sil; 75% TiO_2 and 25% Tri-Sil; 50% TiO_2 and 50% Tri-Sil; 25% TiO_2 and 75% Tri-Sil; and 0% TiO_2 and 100% Tri-Sil.
- 5 handsheets with each of the same proportions of TiO_2 and Zenolux.

As Figure 3 shows, Zenolux is again superior.

Brightness

Using the three sets of handsheets employed in the first-stage opacity tests, I calculated the GE brightness achieved by each of the three pigments. Figure 4 shows the results. Although not as bright as TiO_2, Zenolux is brighter than Tri-Sil.

Using the two sets of handsheets employed in the second-stage opacity tests, I examined the brightness of each of the ratios of TiO_2 to the extenders. The results, shown in Figure 5, indicate that, as expected, TiO_2 with Zenolux is brighter than TiO_2 with Tri-Sil.

Material Handling

With respect to material handling, I found no basis for choosing between Zenolux and Tri-Sil. Both are available from suppliers in Chicago. Both are available in dry form in bags and as a slurry in bulk hopper cars. Zenolux slurry is

REFERENCE GUIDE: Three Types of Special Reports

■ **FIGURE SR.5**
(continued)

Results concerning
material handling
(continued)

Conclusion

Results and
explaination that
support the conclusion

Recommendation

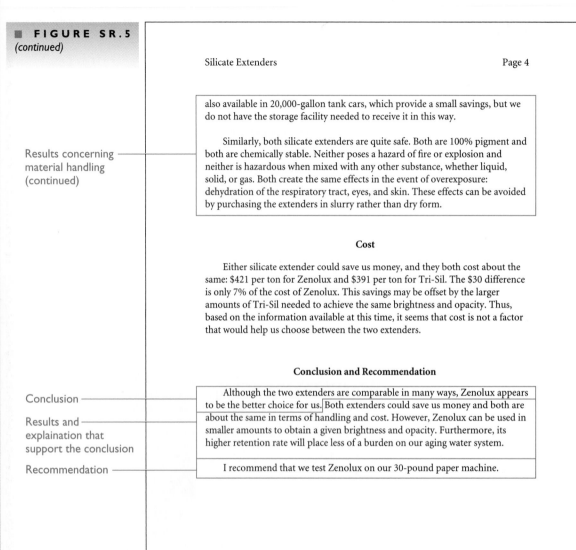

Silicate Extenders   Page 4

also available in 20,000-gallon tank cars, which provide a small savings, but we
do not have the storage facility needed to receive it in this way.

Similarly, both silicate extenders are quite safe. Both are 100% pigment and
both are chemically stable. Neither poses a hazard of fire or explosion and
neither is hazardous when mixed with any other substance, whether liquid,
solid, or gas. Both create the same effects in the event of overexposure:
dehydration of the respiratory tract, eyes, and skin. These effects can be avoided
by purchasing the extenders in slurry rather than dry form.

Cost

Either silicate extender could save us money, and they both cost about the
same: $421 per ton for Zenolux and $391 per ton for Tri-Sil. The $30 difference
is only 7% of the cost of Zenolux. This savings may be offset by the larger
amounts of Tri-Sil needed to achieve the same brightness and opacity. Thus,
based on the information available at this time, it seems that cost is not a factor
that would help us choose between the two extenders.

Conclusion and Recommendation

Although the two extenders are comparable in many ways, Zenolux appears
to be the better choice for us. Both extenders could save us money and both are
about the same in terms of handling and cost. However, Zenolux can be used in
smaller amounts to obtain a given brightness and opacity. Furthermore, its
higher retention rate will place less of a burden on our aging water system.

I recommend that we test Zenolux on our 30-pound paper machine.

■ **FIGURE SR.5**
(continued)

Silicate Extenders   Page 5

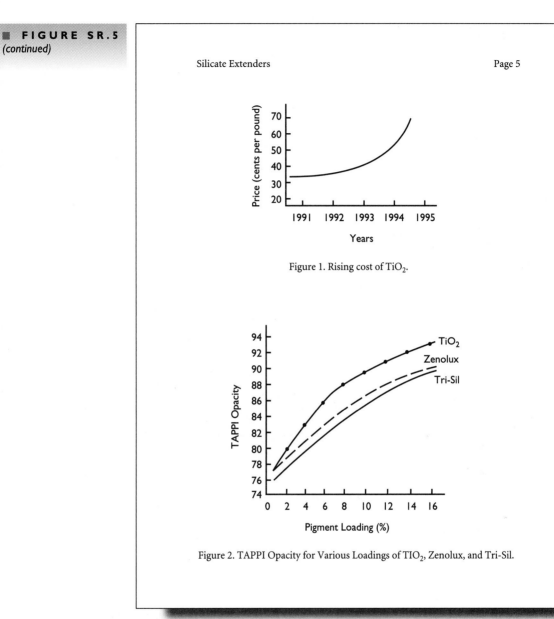

Figure 1. Rising cost of TiO_2.

Figure 2. TAPPI Opacity for Various Loadings of TIO_2, Zenolux, and Tri-Sil.

■ **FIGURE SR.5**
(continued)

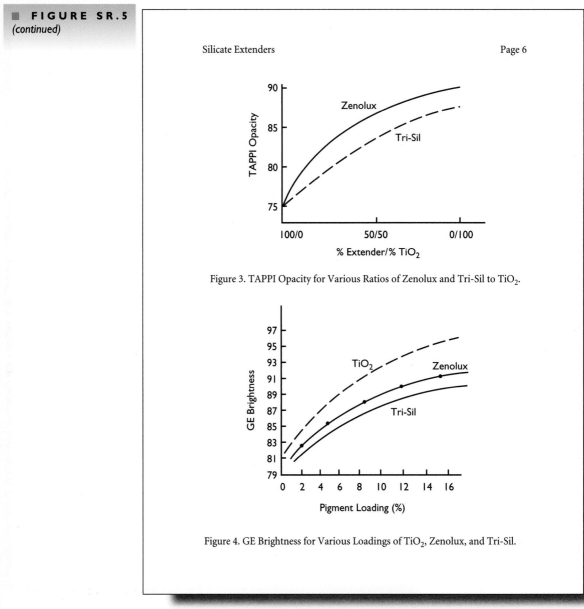

Silicate Extenders   Page 6

Figure 3. TAPPI Opacity for Various Ratios of Zenolux and Tri-Sil to TiO_2.

Figure 4. GE Brightness for Various Loadings of TiO_2, Zenolux, and Tri-Sil.

■ **FIGURE SR.5**
(continued)

Silicate Extenders   Page 7

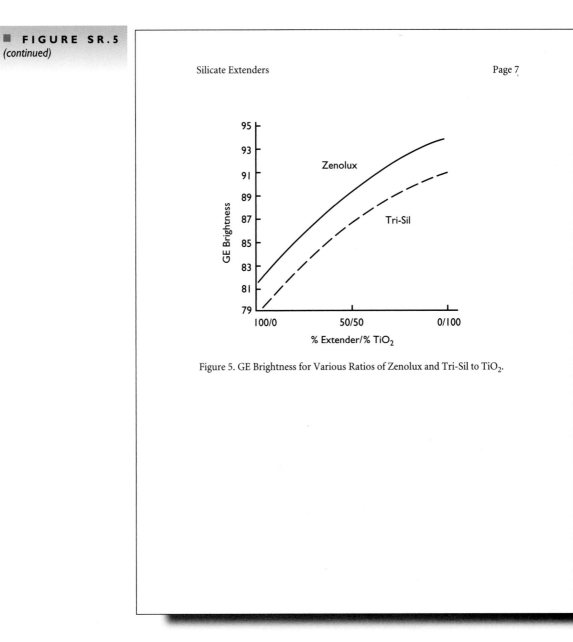

Figure 5. GE Brightness for Various Ratios of Zenolux and Tri-Sil to TiO_2.

REFERENCE GUIDE: Three Types of Special Reports

PROGRESS REPORTS

A progress report is a report on work you have begun but not yet completed. The typical progress report is one of a series submitted at regular intervals, such as every week or month.

TYPICAL WRITING SITUATIONS

Some progress reports concern a single project.

Progress reports are prepared in two types of situations. In the first, you tell your readers about your progress on *one particular project.* Lee is a geologist employed by an engineering consulting firm. His employer has assigned him to study the site that a large city would like to use for a civic center and large office building. The city is worried that the site might not be geologically suited for such construction. Every two weeks, Lee must submit a progress report to his supervisor and to the city engineer. His supervisor uses the report to make sure that Lee is conducting the study in a rapid and technically sound manner. The city engineer uses the report to see that Lee is proceeding according to schedule. She also looks for indications about the likely outcome of the study. Other work could be accelerated or halted as a result of Lee's preliminary findings.

Some progress reports concern all projects worked on during a single period.

In the second type of situation, you prepare progress reports that tell about your work on *all* your projects. Many employers require their workers to report on their activities at regular intervals all year round, year in and year out. Jacqueline is a person who must write such progress reports (often called *periodic reports*). She works in the research division of a large manufacturer of consumer products, where she manages a department that is responsible for improving the formulas for the company's laundry detergents—making them clean better and smell better, making them less expensive to manufacture, and making them safer for the environment. At any one time, Jacqueline's staff is working on between ten and twenty different projects.

As part of her regular responsibilities, Jacqueline must write a report every two weeks to summarize the progress on each of the projects. Her reports go to many readers, including the following: her immediate superiors, who want to be sure that her department's work is proceeding satisfactorily; researchers in other departments, who want to see whether her staff has made discoveries that they can use in the products they are responsible for (for example, dishwashing detergents); and corporate planners, who want to anticipate changes in formulas that will require alterations in production lines, advertising, and so on.

As the examples of Lee and Jacqueline indicate, progress reports may differ in many ways: they may cover one project or many; they may be addressed to people inside the writer's organization or outside it; and they may be used by people who have a variety of reasons for reading them, such as learning what they need to know to manage and to make decisions.

Although progress reports talk about the past, they are used to make decisions about the future.

READERS' CONCERN WITH THE FUTURE

Despite their diversity, however, almost all progress reports have this in common: their readers are primarily concerned with the *future.* That is, even though most progress reports talk primarily about what has happened in the past, their readers usually want that information so that they can plan for the future.

For example, from your report they may be trying to learn the things they need to know in order to manage *your* project. They will want to know, for instance, what they should do (if anything) to keep your project going smoothly or to get it back on track. The progress reports written by Lee and Jacqueline are used for this purpose by some of their readers.

Other readers may be reading your progress reports to learn what they need to know in order to manage *other* projects. Almost all projects in an organization are interdependent with other projects. For instance, maybe you are conducting a marketing survey whose results will be used by another group as it designs an advertising campaign. If you have fallen behind your schedule, the other group's schedule may need to be adjusted.

Your readers may also be interested in the preliminary results of your work. Suppose, for instance, that you complete one part of a research project before you complete the others. Your readers may very well be able to use the results of that part immediately. The city engineer who reads Lee's reports about the possible building site wishes to use each of Lee's results as soon as it is available.

THE QUESTIONS READERS ASK MOST OFTEN

Your readers' concern with the implications of your progress for their future work and decisions leads them to want you to answer the following questions in your progress report. If your report describes more than one project, your readers will ask these questions about each of them:

- **What work does your report cover?** To be able to understand anything else in a progress report, readers must know what project or projects and what time period the report covers.
- **What is the purpose of the work?** Readers need to know the purpose of your work to see how it relates to their own responsibilities and to the other work, present and future, of the organization.
- **Is your work progressing as planned or expected?** Your readers will want to determine if adjustments are needed in the schedule, budget, or number of people assigned to the project or projects on which you are working.
- **What results have you produced?** The results you produce in one reporting period may influence the shape of work in future periods. Also, even when you are still in the midst of a project, readers will want to know about any results they can use in other projects now, before you finish your overall work.
- **What progress do you expect during the next reporting period?** Again, your readers' interests will focus on such management concerns as schedule and budget and on the kinds of results they can expect.
- **How do things stand overall?** This question arises especially in long reports. Readers want to know what the overall status of your work is, something they may not be able to tell readily from all the details you provide.
- **What do you think we should do?** If you are experiencing or expecting problems, your readers will want your recommendations about what should be

done. If you have other ideas about how the project could be improved, they, too, will probably be welcomed.

SUPERSTRUCTURE FOR PROGRESS REPORTS

The conventional superstructure for progress reports provides a very effective framework for answering your readers' questions about your projects:

Superstructure for Progress Reports	
Report Element	**Readers' Question**
Introduction	**What work does your report cover?**
	What is the purpose of the work?
Facts and discussion	
Past work	**Is your work progressing as planned or expected?**
	What results have you produced?
Future work	**What progress do you expect during the next reporting period?**
Conclusions	**In long reports—How do things stand overall?**
Recommendations	**What do you think we should do?**

Introduction

In the introduction to a progress report, you can address the readers' first two questions. You can usually answer the question, "What work does your report cover?" by opening with a sentence that identifies the project or projects your report concerns and what time period it covers.

Sometimes you will not need to answer the second question—"What is the purpose of the work?"—because all your readers will already be quite familiar with its purpose. At other times, however, it will be crucial for you to tell your work's purpose because your readers will include people who don't know or may have forgotten it. You are especially likely to have such readers when your progress reports are widely circulated in your own organization or when you are reporting to another organization that has hired your employer to do the work you describe. You can usually explain purpose most helpfully by describing the problem that your project will help your readers solve.

The following sentences show how one manager answered the readers' first two questions:

Remember that a superstructure is not an outline; you may combine the elements of a superstructure in many ways (see pages 449–452).

For additional advice about writing an introduction, see Chapter 8, "Beginning a Communication."

Project and period covered —

Purpose of project —

> This report covers the work done on the Focus Project from July 1 through September 1. Sponsored by the U.S. Department of Energy, the Focus Project aims to overcome the technical difficulties encountered in constructing photovoltaic cells that can be used to generate commercial amounts of electricity.

Of course, your introduction should also provide any background information your readers will need in order to understand the rest of your report.

Facts and Discussion

In the facts and discussion section of your progress report, you should answer these readers' questions: "Is your work progressing as planned or as expected?" "What results have you produced?" and "What progress do you expect during the next reporting period?"

Answering Your Readers' Questions   Because the work to be accomplished during each reporting period is usually planned in advance, you can indicate your progress by comparing what happened with what was planned. Where there are significant discrepancies between the two, your readers will want to know why. The information you provide about the causes of problems will help your readers decide how to remedy them. It will also help you to explain any recommendations you make later in your report.

When you are discussing preliminary results, be sure to explain them in terms that will enable your readers to recognize their significance. Let your readers know whether the preliminary results are tentative or certain. That information will help them decide whether they can use the results.

Providing the Appropriate Amount of Information   How much information should you include in your progress reports? Generally, readers prefer brief reports. Although you need to provide your readers with specific information about your work, don't include details unless they will help readers to decide how to manage your project or unless you believe readers will be able to make immediate use of them. As you work on a project, many minor events will occur, and you will have lots of small setbacks and triumphs along the way. Avoid discussing such matters. No matter how important these details may be to you, they are not likely to be interesting to your readers. Stick to the information your readers can use.

Organizing the Discussion   You can organize your discussion segment in many ways. One way is to arrange it around time periods:

I. What happened during the most recent time period
II. What's expected to happen during the next time period

You will find that this organization is especially well suited for progress reports dealing with a single project that has distinct stages. However, you can also expand this structure for reports that cover either several projects or one project in which several tasks are performed simultaneously:

I. What happened during the most recent time period
  A. Project A (or Task A)
  B. Project B
II. What's expected to happen during the next time period
  A. Project A
  B. Project B

When you prepare a report that covers more than one project or more than one task, you might consider organizing it around those projects or tasks:

I. Work on Project A (or Task A)
   A. What happened during the last time period
   B. What's expected to happen during the next time period
II. Work on Project B
   A. What happened during the last time period
   B. What's expected to happen during the next time period

This organization works very well in reports that are more than a few paragraphs long because it keeps all the information on each project together, making the report easy for readers to follow.

Emphasizing Important Findings and Problems   As mentioned, your findings and problems are important to your readers. Be sure to highlight them and discuss them in sufficient detail to satisfy your readers' needs and desires for information.

Conclusions

Your conclusions are your overall views on the progress of your work. In short progress reports, there may be no need to include any conclusions, but if your report covers several projects or tasks, conclusions may help your readers understand the general state of your progress.

Recommendations

If you have any ideas about how to improve the project or increase the value of its results, your readers will want you to include them. Your recommendations might be directed at overcoming some difficulty that you have experienced or anticipate encountering in the future. Or they might be directed at refocusing or otherwise altering your project.

A Note on the Location of Conclusions and Recommendations

For most of your readers, your conclusions and recommendations are the most important information in your progress report. Therefore, you should usually include them at the beginning, either in the introduction or at the head of your discussion section. If they are brief, this may be the only place you need to state them. If they are long or if your readers will be able to understand them only after reading your discussion section, it's best to present your conclusions and recommendations at the end of your report, while still including a summary of them at the beginning.

TONE IN PROGRESS REPORTS

You may wonder what tone to use in the progress reports you prepare. Generally, you will want to persuade your readers that you are doing a good job. That is especially likely when you are new on the job and when your readers might discontinue a project if they feel that it isn't progressing satisfactorily.

Because of this strong persuasive element, some people adopt an inflated or highly optimistic tone. This sort of tone, however, can lead to difficulties. It might lead you to make statements that sound unbusinesslike—more like advertising copy than a professional communication. Such a tone is more likely to make your readers suspicious than agreeable. Also, if you present overly optimistic accounts of what can be expected, you risk creating an unnecessary disappointment if things don't turn out the way you seem to be promising. And if you consistently turn in overly optimistic progress reports, your credibility with your readers will quickly vanish.

In progress reports, it's best to be straightforward about problems so that your readers can take appropriate measures to overcome them and so that they can adjust their expectations realistically. You can sound pleased and proud of your accomplishments without exaggerating them.

SAMPLE OUTLINES AND REPORT

The outlines of two progress reports prepared by Erin and Lloyd will suggest how the four elements of the superstructure for progress reports can be adapted to different situations. Erin is reporting on her investigation of problems with a hot saw, the machine that cuts white-hot ingots of metal in a steel mill (Figure SR.6), and Lloyd is submitting a weekly update on a project to introduce a new line of high-fashion women's clothes (Figure SR.7).

Notice that Erin organizes her report around time periods, devoting one section to her past work and a separate section to her future work. In contrast, Lloyd organizes his report around major activities: manufacturing, marketing, and so on. Within the section on manufacturing, he talks about past work (emphasizing a problem) and about future work; he even makes a recommendation there, rather than at the end.

When using the superstructure as a guide in preparing progress reports, try to be as responsive to your purpose and your readers as Erin and Lloyd have been to theirs.

Figure SR.8 (page 512) shows the full progress report Erin submitted to her manager.

Note to the Instructor: Appendix C contains a project that involves writing a progress report. Also, the printed *Instructor's Manual* contains a "Planning Guide for Progress Reports." This book's Web site provides a copy you can download, edit to suit your course, and distribute electronically to your students.

REFERENCE GUIDE: Three Types of Special Reports

■ FIGURE SR.6

Outline for Erin's Progress Report on Increasing Efficiency

Erin's full report is shown in Figure SR.8. page 514.

Introduction (Erin explains work covered and its purpose; she tells the period covered)

Past work (Erin emphasizes her accomplishments)

Future work (she tells specifically what she will do)

Conclusions (Erin indicates that she's behind schedule, she asks for assistance, and she describes actions that can be taken immediately)

Progress on Efficiency Project

I. Introduction

    A. I am reporting on the efficiency project
    B. This report covers my work for the past two weeks
    C. I focused on the hot saw

II. Past Work

    A. I discovered a problem with the location of the tools
    B. I discovered a problem with the blades our supplier provides

III. Future Work

    A. During the next two weeks, I will visit Winnipeg to check on their hot-saw process
    B. I will also check on their loading dock procedures

IV. Conclusions

    A. I'm behind schedule; please let Larry help me for a few days
    B. I have two recommendations
        1. Build a tool stand next to the hot saw
        2. Look for a new supplier or get ours to meet our specifications

■ **FIGURE SR.7**

Outline of Lloyd's Progress Report on Introducing a New Line of Clothes

Introduction (explains work covered and its purpose)

Past work (emphasizes problem)

Future work (explains problem that could arise)

Recommendations

Past work (briefly recounts accomplishments)

Conclusion (tells how things stand overall)

Progress on Development of New Line of Clothes

I. Introduction
   A. I am reporting on progress during the past month on the High Look project
   B. The report covers the activities of all the groups working under me to introduce our line of high-fashion clothes for women

II. Manufacturing
   A. Huge problem
      1. Last week, garment workers at the Saucon factory went on a wildcat strike
      2. Saucon is making 65% of our dresses and 45% of our blouses
      3. Garments are going to arrive late at retail stores if the strike continues another two days; that would decrease sales by very large amounts
      4. This morning, Saucon management predicted no quick settlement

   B. Recommendations
      1. Contract with Webster Corporation to begin manufacturing the garments if we can get the fabrics
      2. Immediately begin picking alternative fabrics

III. Marketing
   A. Orders continue to arrive
   B. We will probably make waves, if we can get our goods to market

IV. Designs for Next Year
   A. Progressing on schedule
   B. Designers are playing with ideas for High Look

V. All Other Areas: Proceeding Well

VI. Conclusion
   A. Although things are going well in most areas, we face a major crisis if our initial offering fails to sell because our goods don't make it to retailers on time
   B. Let's do something

■ **FIGURE SR.8**

Erin's Progress Report on Increasing Efficiency

An outline of Erin's progress report is shown in Figure SR.6, page 512.

Erin reminds her reader of the purpose of her work.

She tells what she has done during the most recent period.

Erin reports the results she has obtained so far.

Erin explains what she will do during the coming period and explains why she's behind schedule.

She tells how things stand with her overall project and identifies help she needs.

She identifies actions that can be taken immediately.

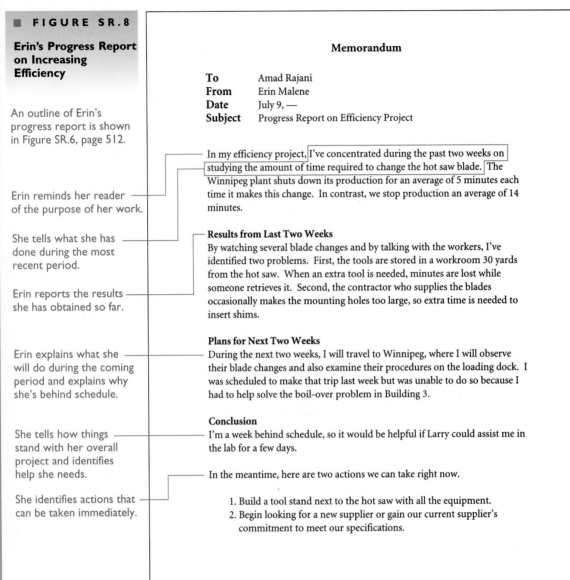

Memorandum

To	Amad Rajani
From	Erin Malene
Date	July 9, —
Subject	Progress Report on Efficiency Project

In my efficiency project, I've concentrated during the past two weeks on studying the amount of time required to change the hot saw blade. The Winnipeg plant shuts down its production for an average of 5 minutes each time it makes this change. In contrast, we stop production an average of 14 minutes.

Results from Last Two Weeks
By watching several blade changes and by talking with the workers, I've identified two problems. First, the tools are stored in a workroom 30 yards from the hot saw. When an extra tool is needed, minutes are lost while someone retrieves it. Second, the contractor who supplies the blades occasionally makes the mounting holes too large, so extra time is needed to insert shims.

Plans for Next Two Weeks
During the next two weeks, I will travel to Winnipeg, where I will observe their blade changes and also examine their procedures on the loading dock. I was scheduled to make that trip last week but was unable to do so because I had to help solve the boil-over problem in Building 3.

Conclusion
I'm a week behind schedule, so it would be helpful if Larry could assist me in the lab for a few days.

In the meantime, here are two actions we can take right now.

1. Build a tool stand next to the hot saw with all the equipment.
2. Begin looking for a new supplier or gain our current supplier's commitment to meet our specifications.

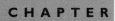 CHAPTER 19

Proposals

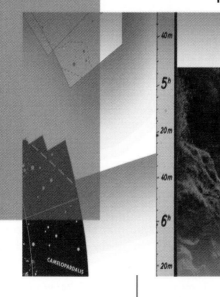

SUPERSTRUCTURE

Introduction

Problem

Objectives

Solution

Method

Resources

Schedule

Qualifications

Management

Costs

When you write a proposal, you make an offer and try to persuade your readers to accept it. You say that, in exchange for money or time or something else from your readers, you will give them something they want, make something they desire, or do something they wish to have done.

Throughout your career, you will have many occasions to make such offers. You may think up a new product you could develop—if your employer will give you the time and funds to do so. Or you may devise a plan for increasing your employer's profits—if your employer will authorize you to put it into effect. If you join one of the many companies that sell their products and services by means of proposals (rather than through advertising), you may offer to provide those products and services to your employer's prospective clients and customers.

In this chapter, you will learn about the conventional superstructure for writing proposals. This superstructure will help you persuade people to accept your offer and invest their money, time, and trust in your ideas and in your employer's products and services.

THE VARIETY OF PROPOSAL-WRITING SITUATIONS

As the second paragraph of this chapter suggests, you may be called on to write proposals in a wide variety of situations. Here are some of the ways in which these situations differ:

- Your readers may be employed in your own organization or in other organizations.
- Your readers may have asked you to submit a proposal, or you may submit it to them on your own initiative.
- Your proposal may be in competition against others, or it may stand or fall on its own merits.
- Your proposal may have to be approved by people in your organization before you submit it to your readers, or you may be authorized to submit it directly yourself.
- You may have to follow regulations governing the content, structure, and format of your proposal, or you may be free to write your proposal as you think best.
- After you have delivered your proposal to your readers, they may follow any of a wide variety of methods for evaluating it.

To illustrate these variables in actual proposal-writing situations, the following paragraphs describe the circumstances in which two successful proposals were written. The information provided here will be useful to you later in this chapter, where several pieces of advice are explained through the example of these proposals.

EXAMPLE SITUATION I

Helen wanted permission to undertake a special project. She thought her employer should develop a computer program that employees could use to reserve conference rooms. On several occasions, she had arrived at a conference room she had reserved only to find that someone else had reserved it also. Because she is employed to write computer programs, she is well qualified to write this one. However, her work is assigned to her by her boss, and she cannot write the scheduling program without permission from him and from his boss. Consequently, she wrote a proposal to them.

Helen is proposing a project to her own employer. The only "cost" will be the time she spends on it.

As she writes, Helen has to think about only two readers because her boss and her boss's boss would decide about her proposed project without consulting other people. Because her employer has no specific guidelines for the way such internal proposals should be written, she could have used whatever content, structure, and format she thought would be most effective. Furthermore, she did not need anyone's approval to submit her proposal to people within her own department, although she would need approval before sending a proposal to another department.

Finally, Helen did not have to worry about competition from other proposals because hers would be considered on its own merits. However, her readers would approve her project only if they were persuaded that the time she would spend writing the program would not be better spent on her regular duties. (Helen's entire proposal is presented at the end of this chapter.)

EXAMPLE SITUATION 2

Three persons are proposing a project to a federal agency, which will consider the proposal competitively.

The second proposal was written under very different circumstances. To begin with, it was written by three people, not just one. The writers were a producer, a scriptwriter, and a business manager at a public television station that seeks funds from nonprofit corporations and the federal government to produce television programs. The writers had learned that the U.S. Department of Education was interested in sponsoring programs about environmental concerns. To learn more about what the department wanted, the writers obtained copies of its "request for proposals" (RFP). After studying the RFP, they decided to propose to develop a program that high school teachers and community leaders could use to teach about hazardous wastes.

In their proposal, the writers addressed an audience very different from Helen's. The Department of Education receives about four proposals for every one it can fund. To evaluate these proposals, it follows a procedure widely used by government agencies. It sends the proposals to experts around the country. These experts, called *reviewers*, rate and comment on each proposal. Every proposal is seen by several reviewers. Then the reviews for each proposal are gathered and interpreted by staff members at the department. The proposals that have received the best reviews are funded. To secure funding, the writers of the environmental proposal needed to persuade their reviewers that their proposed project came closer to meeting the objectives of the Department of Education than did at least three-quarters of the other proposed projects.

Before the writers could even mail their proposal to the department, they had to obtain approval for it from several administrators at the television station. That's because the proposal, if accepted, would become a contract between the station and the Department of Education.

PROPOSAL READERS ARE INVESTORS

The descriptions of the proposals written by Helen and by the employees of the public television station illustrate some of the many differences that exist in proposal-writing situations. Despite these differences, however, almost all proposal-writing situations have two important features in common—features that profoundly affect the way you should write your proposals:

- In proposals, you ask decision-makers to invest some resource, such as time or money, so that the thing you propose can be done.
- Your readers will make their investment decisions *cautiously.* Their resources are limited, so if they decide to invest in your project, resources will not be available for others. For example, to let Helen spend two weeks creating the new scheduling program, her bosses had to decide that she would not spend that time on the other projects the department had. To spend money on the environmental project, the DOE had to turn down other proposals seeking those same dollars.

THE QUESTIONS READERS ASK MOST OFTEN

The questions decision-makers ask when they consider a proposal generally concern the following three topics:

- **Problem.** Your readers will want to know why you are making your proposal and why they should be interested in it. What problem, need, or goal does your proposal address—and why is it important to them?
- **Solution.** Your readers will want to know exactly what you propose to make or do and how it relates to the problem you describe. They will ask, "What kinds of things will a successful solution to this problem have to do?" and "How do you propose to do those things?" They will examine your responses carefully, trying to determine whether your overall strategy and your specific plans are likely to work.
- **Costs.** Your readers will want to know what it will cost to implement your proposal and whether the cost will be worth it to them.

In addition, if you are proposing to perform some work (rather than supply a product), your readers will want an answer to this question:

- **Capability.** If your readers pay or authorize you to perform the work, how will they know whether they can depend on you to deliver what you promise?

STRATEGY OF THE CONVENTIONAL SUPERSTRUCTURE FOR PROPOSALS

The conventional superstructure for proposals provides a framework for answering those questions—one that has been found successful in repeated use in the kinds of situations you will encounter on the job. This superstructure, which is summarized at the top of the next page, includes ten topics. In some proposals you may need to include information on all ten, but in others you will need to cover only some of them. Even in the briefest proposals, however, you will probably need to treat the following four: introduction, problem, solution, costs.

Whichever question you are answering, remember that a proposal is a highly persuasive communication. To write successfully, you must not only provide facts

Superstructure for Proposals		
Topic	**Readers' Question**	**Your Persuasive Point**
*Introduction	What is this communication about?	Briefly, I propose to do the following.
*Problem	Why is the proposed project needed?	The proposed project addresses a problem, need, or goal that is important to you.
Objectives	What features will a solution to the problem need in order to be successful?	A successful solution can be achieved if it has these features.
*Solution	What will your proposed solution look like?	Here's what I plan to produce, and it has the features necessary for success.
Method Resources Schedule Qualifications Management	Are you going to be able to deliver what you describe here?	Yes, because I have a good plan of action (method); the necessary facilities, equipment, and other resources; a workable schedule; appropriate qualifications; and a sound management plan.
*Costs	What will it cost?	The cost is reasonable.

*Topics marked with an asterisk are important in almost every proposal, whereas the others are needed only in certain ones.

but also weave those facts into an argument that strongly supports the persuasive points listed in the right-hand column of the above chart. Your goal is to lead your readers through the following sequence of thought:

Ideal sequence of readers' thoughts while reading a proposal

1. The readers learn generally what you want to do. (Introduction)
2. The readers are persuaded that there is a problem, need, or goal that is important to them. (Problem)
3. The readers are persuaded that the proposed action will be effective in solving the problem, meeting the need, or achieving the goal that they now agree is important. (Objectives, Solution)
4. The readers are persuaded that you are capable of planning and managing the proposed solution. (Method, Resources, Schedule, Qualifications, Management)
5. The readers are persuaded that the cost of the proposed action is reasonable in light of the benefits the action will bring. (Costs)

There is no guarantee, of course, that your readers will read your proposal from front to back or concentrate on every word. Long proposals usually include a summary or abstract at the beginning. Instead of reading the proposal straight through, many readers will read the summary, perhaps the first few pages of the body, and then skim through the other sections.

In fact, in some competitive situations, readers are *prohibited* from reading the entire proposal. For instance, companies competing for huge contracts to build parts of space shuttles for the National Aeronautics and Space Administration (NASA) submit their proposals in three volumes: one explaining the problem and their proposed solution, one detailing their management plan, and one analyzing their costs. Each volume (sometimes thousands of pages long) is evaluated by a separate set of experts: technical experts for the first volume, management experts for the second, and budget experts for the third.

Even when readers do not read your proposal straight through—and even when your proposal is only a page or two long—the account given above of the relationships among the parts will help you write a tightly focused proposal in which all the parts support one another.

SUPERSTRUCTURE FOR PROPOSALS

Remember that a superstructure is not an outline. For general advice about using superstructures, see pages 91–92.

The rest of this chapter describes in detail each of the ten topics that comprise the conventional superstructure for proposals. As you read, keep in mind that the conventional superstructure is only a general plan. You must use your imagination and creativity to adapt it to particular situations.

In addition, as you plan and write your proposal, remember that the ten topics identify kinds of information you need to provide, not necessarily the titles of the sections you include. In brief proposals, some parts may take only a sentence or a paragraph, or several sections may be grouped together. For instance, writers often combine their introduction, their discussion of the problem, and their explanation of their objectives under a single heading, which might be "Introduction," "Problem," or "Need."

INTRODUCTION

At the beginning of a proposal, you want to do the same thing that you do at the beginning of anything else you write on the job: tell your readers what you are writing about. In a proposal, this means announcing what you are proposing.

How long and detailed should the introduction be? In proposals, introductions are almost always rather brief. By custom, writers postpone the full description of what they are proposing until later, after they have discussed the problem their proposal will help solve.

You may be able to introduce your proposal in a single sentence as Helen did:

Helen's introduction

I request permission to spend two weeks writing, testing, and implementing a program for scheduling conference rooms in the plant.

When you are proposing something more complex, your introduction will probably be longer. You may want to provide background information to help your readers understand what you have in mind. Here, for example, is the introduction from the proposal written by the employees of the public television station to the Department of Education:

Introduction to the television writers' proposal

Chemicals are used to protect, prolong, and enhance our lives in numerous ways. Recently, however, society has discovered that some chemicals also present serious hazards to human health and the environment. In the coming years, citizens will have to make many difficult decisions to solve the problems created by these hazardous substances and to prevent future problems from occurring.

 To provide citizens with the information and skills they will need to decide wisely, WPET Television proposes to develop an educational package entitled "Hazardous Substances: Handle with Care!" This package, designed for high school students, will include five 15-minute videotape programs and a thorough teacher's guide.

For more ideas on writing introductions, see Chapter 8, "Beginning a Communication."

PROBLEM

Once you've announced what you're proposing, you must persuade your readers that it will address some problem that is significant to *them*. Your description of the problem is crucial to the success of your proposal. Although you might persuade your readers that your proposed project will achieve its objectives and that its costs are reasonable, you cannot hope to win approval unless you show that it is worth doing from your readers' point of view.

Often this requires considerable creativity and research. The following paragraphs offer advice that applies to each of three situations you are likely to encounter on the job: when your readers define the problem for you, when your readers provide you with a general statement of the problem, and when you must define the problem yourself.

When Your Readers Define the Problem for You

You need to do the least research about the problem when your readers define it for you. For instance, your readers might issue an RFP that explains in complete detail some technical problem they would like your firm to solve. In such situations, your primary objective in describing the problem will be to show your readers that you thoroughly understand what they want.

When Your Readers Provide a General Statement of the Problem

The writers read the RFP to determine the department's goals.

At other times, your readers may describe the problem only vaguely. This happened to the three television writers who submitted the environmental education proposal. In its RFP, the Department of Education provided only the general statement that it perceived a need for "educational resources that could be used to teach about the relation of the natural and man-made environments to the total human environment." Each group that wished to submit a proposal had to identify a more specific problem that the Department would find important.

The writers used the RFP when deciding how to describe the problem they would solve.

Finding a problem that *someone else* thinks is important can be difficult. Often, it will require you to hunt for clues to your readers' values, attitudes, concerns, and opinions. You may have to interview people (including your target readers, where possible), visit the library, or search the Web. The television writers found their major clue in the following statement, which appeared elsewhere in the RFP: "Thus, environmental education should be multifaceted, multidisciplinary, and issue-oriented." This statement suggested to the writers that they should define the problem as the need experienced by some group of people to gain the multifaceted, multidisciplinary knowledge that would enable them to make good decisions about a practical environmental issue.

But who would that group be? And what is the environmental issue this group needs to address? First, the television writers selected an issue faced by many communities: how to handle and regulate hazardous substances that are produced or stored within their boundaries. This issue seemed ideal because citizens can make good decisions about hazardous substances only if they possess "multifaceted, multidisciplinary" knowledge from such fields as health, economics, and technology. Next, the writers also decided to target their project to high school students. These students seemed like a perfect group to address because they soon would be eligible to vote on questions involving hazardous substances in their communities. Finally, through research, the writers determined that, in fact, no such materials existed. They really were needed.

Thus, by working creatively from the Department of Education's vague statement, the television writers identified a specific problem that their proposed project would help to solve: the lack of educational materials that high school teachers can use to provide their students with the multifaceted, multidisciplinary knowledge that the students need in order to make wise decision, as voters, concerning the hazardous substance issues that face their communities.

When You Must Define the Problem Yourself

The reasons you offer your readers for supporting your proposal may be different from your reasons for writing it.

In other situations, you may not have the aid of explicit statements from your readers to help you formulate the problem. This is most likely to happen when you are preparing a proposal on your own initiative, without being asked by someone else to submit it. Describing the problem in such situations can be particularly challenging because the argument that will be persuasive to your readers might be entirely distinct from your own reasons for writing the proposal.

Think about Helen's situation, for instance. She originally came up with the idea of writing the program for scheduling conference rooms because she felt frustrated and angry on the many occasions when she went to a meeting room she had reserved only to find that someone else had reserved it too. Her bosses, however, are not likely to approve the scheduling project simply to help Helen avoid frustration. For the project to appeal to them, it must be couched in terms that are allied to *their* responsibilities and professional interests.

First strategy: identify goals you will help your readers achieve.

In such situations, you can pursue two strategies to define the problem. The first is to think about how you can make your proposed project important to your readers. What goals or responsibilities do your readers have that your proposal will help them achieve? What concerns do they typically express that your proposal could help them address? A good place to begin is to think about some of the standard concerns of organizations: efficiency and profit.

When Helen did this, she realized that from her employer's point of view, the problems involved with scheduling conference rooms were creating great inefficiencies. Time was wasted while all the people who appeared for a meeting looked around for another place to meet.

Second strategy: talk with your readers before you begin writing.

A second strategy for defining the problem is to speak with the people to whom you will send your proposal. This conversation can have two advantages. First, it will let you know whether or not your proposal has at least some chance of succeeding. If it doesn't, it's best to find out before you invest time writing it. Second, by talking with people who will be readers of your proposal, you can find out how the problem appears to them.

When Helen spoke to her boss, he mentioned something she hadn't thought of before. Sometimes the rooms are used for meetings with customers. When customers see confusion arising over something as simple as meeting rooms, they may wonder if the company has similar problems that would affect its products and services.

OBJECTIVES

When using the conventional superstructure for proposals, writers usually state the objectives of their proposed solution after describing the problem they are proposing.

Your statement of objectives plays a crucial role in the logical development of your proposal: it links your proposed action to the problem by telling how the action will solve the problem. To make that link tight, you must formulate each of your objectives so that it grows directly out of some aspect of the problem you describe. Here, for example, are three of the objectives that the writers devised for their proposed environmental education program. To help you see how these objectives grew out of the writers' statement of the problem, each objective is followed by the point from their problem statement that serves as the basis for it. (The writers did not include the bracketed sentences in the objectives section of their proposal.)

Objectives of the environmental education proposal

1. To teach high school students the definitions, facts, and concepts necessary to understand both the benefits and risks of society's heavy reliance upon hazardous substances. [This objective is based on the evidence presented in the problem section that high school students do not have that knowledge.]
2. To employ an interdisciplinary approach that will allow students to use the information, concepts, and skills from their science, economics, government, and other courses to understand the complex issues involved with our use of hazardous substances. [This objective is based on the writers' argument in the problem section that people need to understand the use of hazardous substances from many points of view to be able to make wise decisions about them.]
3. To teach a technique for identifying and weighing the risks and benefits of various uses of hazardous substances. [This objective is based on the writers' argument in the problem section that people must be able to weigh the risks and benefits of the use of hazardous substances if they are to make sound decisions about that use.]

The writers created similar lists of objectives for the other parts of their proposed project, each based on a specific point made in their discussion of the problem.

Like the writers at the television station, Helen built her objectives squarely on her description of the problem. She also took into account something she learned through her research: even with a computerized system, managers wanted a single person in each department to coordinate room reservations. They didn't want each individual employee to be able to enter changes into the system. Similarly, you will need to consider the concerns of your readers when framing the objectives for your proposals. Here are two of Helen's objectives:

Helen's objectives

1. To maintain a completely up-to-date schedule of reservations that can be viewed by salaried personnel in every department. [This objective corresponds to her argument that the problem arises partly because there is no convenient way for people to find out what reservations have been made.]
2. To allow designated persons in every department to add, change, or cancel reservations through their terminals. [This objective relates to Helen's discovery that the managers want a single person to handle room reservations in each department.]

In proposals, writers usually describe the objectives of their proposed solution without describing the solution itself at all. The television writers, for example, wrote their objectives so that their readers could imagine achieving them through the creation of a textbook, an educational movie, a series of lectures, or a Web site—as well as through the creation of the videotape programs that the instructors proposed. Similarly, Helen described objectives that might be achieved by many kinds of computer programs. She withheld her ideas about the design of her program until the next section of her proposal.

The purpose of separating the objectives from the solution is not to keep readers in suspense. Rather, this separation enables readers to evaluate the aims of the project separately from the writers' particular strategies for achieving those aims.

Proposal writers usually present their objectives in a list or state them very briefly. For instance, Helen used only a paragraph to present her objectives. The members of the television group presented all their objectives in three pages of their 98-page proposal.

SOLUTION

When you describe your solution, you describe your plan for achieving the objectives you have listed. For example, Helen described the various parts of the computer program she would write, explaining how they would be created and used. The television writers described each of the four components of their environmental educational package. Scientists seeking money for cancer research would describe the experiments they wish to conduct.

When describing your solution, you must persuade your readers of two things:

■ **That the solution will successfully address each of the objectives.** For instance, to be sure that the description of their proposed educational program matched their objectives, the writers included detailed descriptions of the following: the definitions, facts, and concepts that their videotape program would teach (Objective 1), the strategy they would use to help students take an interdisciplinary approach to the question of hazardous waste (Objective 2), and the technique for identifying and weighing risks and benefits that they would help students learn (Objective 3).

- **That your proposed solution offers a particularly desirable way of achieving the objectives.** For example, the television writers planned to use a case-study approach in their materials, and in their proposal offered this explanation of the advantages of the case-study approach they planned to use:

Television writers' argument for the special desirability of their solution

> Because case studies represent real-world problems and solutions, they are effective tools for illustrating the way that politics, economics, and social and environmental interests all play parts in hazardous substance problems. In addition, they can show the outcome of the ways that various problems have been solved—successfully or unsuccessfully—in the past. In this way, case studies provide students and communities with an opportunity to learn from past mistakes and successes.

When describing your solution, you may find it helpful to use the strategies for describing an object or process (pages 198–207).

Of course, you should include such statements only where they won't be perfectly obvious to your readers. In her proposal, Helen did not include any because she planned to use standard practices whose advantages would be perfectly evident to her readers, both of whom had spent several years doing exactly the kind of work Helen is doing now.

METHOD

Readers of proposals sometimes need to be assured that you can, in fact, produce the results that you promise. That happens especially in situations where you are proposing to do something that takes special expertise.

To assure themselves that you can deliver what you promise, your readers will look for information about several aspects of your project: your method or plan of action for producing the result; the facilities, equipment, and other resources you plan to use; your schedule; your qualifications; and your plan for managing the project. This section is about method; the other topics are discussed in the sections that follow.

To determine how to explain your proposed method, imagine that your readers have asked you, "How will you bring about the result you have described?"

In some cases, you will not need to answer that question. For example, Helen did not talk at all about the programming techniques she planned to use because her readers were already familiar with them. On the other hand, they did not know how she planned to train people to use her program. Therefore, in her proposal she explained her plans for training.

In contrast, the television writers had an elaborate plan for creating their educational materials. An important part of their plan, for instance, was to use three review teams: one to assess the accuracy of the materials they drafted, another to advise about the effectiveness of the videotapes, and a third to advise about the effectiveness of the community film and the discussion leader's guide. In their proposal, they described these review teams in great detail.

When describing your method, you may find it helpful to use the strategies for describing a process (page 205).

In addition, the writers described each phase of their project to show that they would conduct all phases in a way that would lead to success. These phases include research, scripting, review, revision, production, field-testing, revision, final production, and distribution. When you write proposals, you may have to supply similar detailed descriptions of your method for creating your solution.

RESOURCES

By describing the facilities, equipment, and other resources to be used for your proposed project, you assure your readers that you will use whatever special equipment is required to do the job properly. If part of your proposal is to request that equipment, tell your readers what you need to acquire and why.

If no special resources are needed, you do not need to include a section on resources. Helen did not include one. In contrast, the television writers needed many kinds of resources. In their proposal, they described the library facilities that were available for their research. Similarly, to persuade their readers that they could produce high-quality programs, they described the videotaping facilities they would use.

SCHEDULE

Proposal readers have several reasons for wanting to know what your schedule will be. First, they want to know when they can enjoy the final result. Second, they want to know how you will structure the work so they can be sure that the schedule is reasonable and sound. In addition, they may want to plan other work around the project: When will your project have to coordinate with others? When will it take people's attention from other work? When will other work be disrupted and for how long? Finally, proposal readers want a schedule so they can determine if the project is proceeding according to plan.

For information on creating a schedule chart, see page 325.

The most common way to provide a schedule is to use a schedule chart, which is sometimes accompanied by a prose explanation of its important points.

QUALIFICATIONS

When they are thinking about investing in a project, proposal readers want to be sure that the proposers have the experience and capabilities to carry it out successfully. For that reason, a discussion of the qualifications of the personnel involved with a project is a standard part of most proposals. For example, the television writers discussed their qualifications in two places. First, in a section entitled "Qualifications," they presented the qualifications of each of the eight key people who would be working on the project. In addition, they included a detailed resume for each participant in an appendix.

The television writers discussed their qualifications in two places.

In other situations, much less information might be needed. For instance, Helen's qualifications as a programmer were evident to her readers because they were employing her as one. If that experience alone were enough to persuade her readers that she could carry out the project successfully, Helen would not have needed to include any section on qualifications. However, her readers might have wondered whether she was qualified to undertake the particular program she proposed because different kinds of programs require different knowledge and skills. Therefore, Helen wrote the following:

Helen's statement of her qualifications

> As you know, although I usually work with the Windows operating system, I am also familiar with UNIX, which is used on the computer on which the schedule will be placed. In addition, as an undergraduate I took a course in scheduling and transportation problems, which will help me here.

In some situations, your readers will want to know not only the qualifications of the people who will work on the proposed project, but also the qualifications of the organization for which they work.

MANAGEMENT

When you propose a project that will involve more than about four people, you can make your proposal more persuasive by describing the management structure of your group. Proposal readers realize that on complex projects even the most highly qualified people can coordinate their work effectively only if a well-designed project management plan is in place. In projects with relatively few people, you can describe the management structure by first identifying the person or persons who will have management responsibilities and then telling what their duties will be. In larger projects, you might need to provide an organizational chart for the project and a detailed description of the management techniques and tools that will be used.

For information on creating an organizational chart, see page 325.

Because her project involved only one person, Helen did not establish or describe any special management structure. However, the television writers did. Because they had a complex project involving many parts and several workers, they set up a project planning and development committee to oversee the activities of the principal workers. In their proposal, they described the makeup and functions of this committee, and in the section on qualifications, they described the credentials of the committee members.

COSTS

As emphasized throughout this chapter, when you propose something, you are asking your readers to invest resources, usually money and time. Naturally, then, you need to tell them how much your proposed project will cost.

For information on creating a budget statement, see page 326.

One way to discuss costs is to include a budget statement. Sometimes, a budget statement needs to be accompanied by a prose explanation of any unusual expenses and the method used to calculate costs.

In proposals where dollars are not involved, information about the costs of required resources may be provided elsewhere. For instance, in her discussion of the schedule for her project, Helen explained the number of hours she would spend, the time that others would spend, and so on.

In some proposals, you may demonstrate that the costs are reasonable by also calculating the savings that will result from your project.

SAMPLE PROPOSAL

Figure 19.1 shows the proposal written by Helen.

Note to the Instructor: An assignment that involves writing a proposal is included in Appendix C, and a case on proposal writing is included in the *Instructor's Manual.* Also, the printed *Instructor's Manual* contains a "Planning Guide for Proposals." In addition, this book's Web site provides additional cases you can download and edit to suit your course.

PARKER MANUFACTURING COMPANY

Memorandum

TO: Floyd Mohr and Marcia Valdez
FROM: Helen Constantino
DATE: July 14, 19—
RE: Proposal to Write a Program for Scheduling Conference Rooms

In the introduction, Helen tells what she is proposing and what it will cost.

I request permission to spend two weeks writing, testing, and implementing a program for scheduling conference rooms in the plant. This program will eliminate several problems with conference room schedules that have become acute in the last six months.

Present System

Because her introduction includes much background information, Helen makes a separate section for it; she labels the section "Present System" rather than "Background" to provide her readers with a more precise heading.

At present, the chief means of coordinating room reservations is the monthly "Reservations Calendar" distributed by Peter Svenson of the Personnel Department. Throughout each month, Peter collects notes and phone messages from people who plan to use one of the conference rooms sometime in the next month. He stores these notes in a folder until the fourth week of the month, when he takes them out to create the next month's calendar. If he notices two meetings scheduled for the same room, he contacts the people who made the reservations so they can decide which of them will use one of the other seven conference rooms in the new and old buildings. He then prints the calendar and distributes it to the heads of all seventeen departments. The department heads usually give the calendars to their secretaries.

Someone who wants to schedule a meeting during the current month usually checks with the department secretary to see if a particular room has been reserved on the monthly calendar. If not, the person asks the secretary to note his or her reservation on the department's copy of the calendar. The secretary is supposed to call the reservation in to Peter, who will see if anyone else has called about using that room at that time.

■ **FIGURE 19.1**
(continued)

For her problem
section, Helen also
uses a more precise
heading.

Problem ————

Helen describes the ————
consequences of the
problem that are
important to her
readers.

Helen ties the
objectives of her
proposed project
directly to the points
she raised when
describing the problem.

Problems with the Present System

The present system worked adequately until about six months ago, when two
important changes occurred:

- The new building was opened, bringing nine departments here from
  the old Knoll Boulevard plant.
- The Marketing Department began using a new sales strategy of bringing
  major customers here to the plant.

These two changes have greatly complicated the work of scheduling rooms. In
the past, though secretaries rarely called Peter Svenson with reservations for the
current month, few problems resulted. Now, with such greatly increased use of
the conference rooms, employees often schedule more than one meeting for the
same time in the same room. That problem has always created some loss of
otherwise productive work time. Now, if one of the meetings involves customers
brought here by the Marketing Department, we end up giving a bad impression
of our ability to manage our business.

A related problem is that even when concurrent meetings are scheduled for
different rooms, both may be planning to use the same audiovisual equipment.

Objectives

To solve our room scheduling problems, we need a reservation system that will
do the following:

- provide a single, up-to-date room reservation schedule for the entire
  company, thereby ending the confusion caused by having a
  combination of departmental and central calendars
- allow a designated person in each department to add, change, or cancel
  reservations with a minimum of effort
- show the reservation priority of each meeting so that people scheduling
  meetings with higher priority (such as those with potential customers)
  will be able to see which scheduled meetings they can ask to move to
  free up a room

2

After stating the general nature of her proposed project, Helen links the features of her product to the objectives she identified earlier.

Proposed Solution

I propose to solve our room scheduling problems by creating a centralized reservation system on the VAX computer. Because every department has at least one terminal networked to this computer, a designated person in each department will be able to enter, alter, or cancel reservations quickly and easily. The program will automatically revise the reservation list every time someone makes an addition or other change so people anywhere in the company can view a completely updated schedule at any time. When they enter a reservation, people will include information about the priority of their meeting, so that other individuals will be able to view this information if they are having trouble finding a place for their own meeting. The program will also be able to handle reservations for audiovisual equipment, thereby ending problems in that area. This computer program will have the added advantage of freeing Peter Svenson from the time-consuming task of manually maintaining the monthly reservations calendar.

Method for Developing the Program

I propose to create and implement the program in three steps: writing it, testing it, and training people in its use.

Helen provides an overview of her method, then explains each step.

Writing the Program

The program will have three routines. The first will display the reservations that have been made. When users access the program, the system will prompt them to tell which day's schedule they want to see and whether they want to see the schedule organized by room or by the hour. The calendar will display a name for the meeting, the name of the person responsible for organizing it, and the audiovisual equipment needed.

The second routine will handle entries and modifications to the schedule. When users call up this program, they will be asked for their company identification number. To prevent tampering with the calendar, only people whose identification number is on a list given to the computer will be able to proceed. To make, change, or cancel reservations, users will simply follow prompts given by the system.

3

■ **FIGURE 19.1**
(continued)

Once a user completes his or her request, the system will instantly update the calendar that everyone can view. In this way, the calendar will always be absolutely up-to-date.

The third routine is for administration of the system. It will be used only by someone in the Personnel Department. Through it, this person can add and drop people from the list of authorized users. The person will also be able to see who made each addition, change, or deletion from the schedule. That information can be helpful if someone tampers with the calendar.

Testing the Program

Helen has already planned the testing.

I will test the program by having secretaries in four departments use it to create an imaginary schedule for one month. The secretaries will be told to schedule more meetings than they usually do to be sure that conflicts arise. They will then be asked to reschedule some meetings and cancel some others.

Training

Training in the use of the program will involve preparing a user's manual and conducting training sessions. I will write the user's manual, and I will work with Joseph Raab in the Personnel Department to design and conduct the first training session. After that, he will conduct the remaining training sessions on his own.

Resources Needed

Resources

To write this program, I will need no special resources. Testing and training will require the cooperation of other departments. I have already contacted four people to test the program, and Vicki Truman, head of the Personnel Department, has said that Joseph Raab can work on it because that department is so eager to see Peter relieved of the work he is now having to do under the current system.

4

■ **FIGURE 19.1**
(continued)

In her schedule, Helen also tells the cost (in hours of work).

Qualifications

Schedule

I can write, test, and train in eight eight-hour days, beginning on August 15.

Task	Hours
Designing Program	12
Coding	24
Testing	8
Writing User's Manual	12
Training First Group of Users	8
Total	64

The eight hours estimated for training includes the time needed both to prepare the session and to conduct it one time.

Qualifications

As you know, although I usually work with our IBM system, I am also familiar with the VAX computer on which the schedule will be placed. In addition, as an undergraduate I took a course in scheduling and transportation problems, which will help me here.

Conclusion

I am enthusiastic about the possibility of creating this much-needed program for scheduling conference rooms and hope that you are able to let me work on it.

5

Instructions

CAMELOPARDALIS

SUPERSTRUCTURE

Introduction

Description of the Equipment

List of Materials and Equipment Needed

Directions

Troubleshooting

I nstructions come in many lengths, shapes, and levels of complexity. They range from the terse directions on a shampoo bottle ("Lather. Rinse. Repeat.") to the huge manuals that are hundreds or thousands of pages long for servicing airplane engines, managing large computer systems, and performing biomedical procedures.

Most employees write instructions sometimes.

Although some instructions are prepared by professional writers and editors, most other employees also need to prepare instructions sometimes. Whether you are developing a new procedure, training a new co-worker, or preparing to leave for vacation, you may need to provide written directions to someone else. You may even be called on to create instructions for people who will read and use them on a computer screen rather than on paper.

This chapter's advice applies to both printed and on-line instructions.

This chapter provides advice that you will find valuable regardless of the subject or size of the instructions you write. The advice given in the first part of this chapter applies equally to instructions written for paper and for computer screens. A special section at the end of the chapter provides additional suggestions for on-line instructions.

FOUR IMPORTANT POINTS

Readers of instructions are particularly challenging people to write for. Often, they don't want to read at all, preferring to rely on their common sense rather than on instructions. When they do read, they repeatedly shift their attention between reading and actually performing the task: they read a step, then do the step, read the next step, then do it. All this means that you must write instructions that attract and hold the attention of impatient readers, communicate with great clarity to people who don't want to spend any time at all figuring out what you mean, explain exactly what the readers will need in order to perform the next step in the procedure, and help the readers quickly find their place each time they look back to your directions after completing another step in their task.

This chapter describes the general superstructure for instructions, which will help you successfully address the challenges of instruction writing. While working with this superstructure, keep the following general advice in mind:

1. **Remember the persuasive element of purpose.** As you learned in Chapter 3, on-the-job writing has two elements of purpose: enabling and persuasive. When writing instructions, many people focus so sharply on the enabling element (enabling their readers to perform a procedure) that they forget about the persuasive element—the way they want their instructions to shape their readers' attitudes. Don't commit this oversight.

   Instructions must persuade as well as instruct.

   When writing instructions, you'll often need to shape your readers' attitudes. Sometimes your persuasive aim will be simply to get your readers to read your instructions at all. Also, if you know that your readers will have any anxieties about being able to perform the task successfully, you'll need to allay these feelings so that your readers can concentrate more fully on the task. And if you are preparing instructions for one of your employer's products, you'll want your readers to feel so good about the product that they will buy from your employer again and recommend that others do likewise.

For advice about creating visual aids, see Chapter 11.

2. **Use plenty of visual aids.** For many purposes, well-designed visual aids are much more effective than words. For example, words cannot show readers where the parts of a machine are located, how to grasp a tool, or what the result of a procedure should look like. It's especially helpful to use visual aids when preparing instructions for readers who speak other languages. Sometimes visual aids can even carry all the information your readers need (see Figure 11.1 on page 271).

For advice about designing pages, see Chapter 12. Chapter 15 gives additional suggestions for designing Web pages.

3. **Design your pages to support your readers' reading activities.** Whether your instructions consist of paper pages or Web pages, a carefully planned page design can help your readers find their places as they bounce back and forth between reading about steps and performing those steps. Good page design also helps readers see the connections between related blocks of information such as a written direction and the drawing that accompanies it.

For advice about how to test your draft, see Chapter 13.

4. **Test your instructions.** Instructions can be surprisingly difficult to write. Words and illustrations that we think are easy to understand can baffle our readers. And we can too easily omit a step that seems obvious to us, only to find out later that our readers needed to have it explained. The best way to prevent such outcomes is to ask members of your target audience to try out a draft of your instructions so you can determine whether they will really work for your intended readers.

SUPERSTRUCTURE FOR INSTRUCTIONS

The conventional superstructure for instructions contains the following elements:

Superstructure for Instructions	
Topic	**Readers' Questions**
Introduction	Will these instructions help me? How can I use them effectively?
Description of the equipment	Where are the parts that I'll be working with while I repair or use this equipment?
List of materials and equipment needed	What material and equipment should I collect before I begin?
Directions	Once I'm ready to start, what—exactly—do I do?
Troubleshooting	Something isn't working correctly: how can I fix it?

Many instructions contain only the directions.

The simplest instructions contain only the directions. More complex instructions contain some or all of the other four elements listed above. And some instructions also include such additional elements as covers, title pages, tables of contents, appendixes, lists of references, glossaries, lists of symbols, and indexes.

To determine which elements to include in any instructions you write, follow this familiar advice: consider your purpose and the aims and needs of your readers.

INTRODUCTION

The effectiveness of your instructions can depend substantially on your decision about what—if anything—to provide as introductory material. An unneeded or overly long introduction may prompt readers to toss your instructions aside before reading even a single direction. Conversely, if you fail to provide needed information, you may make it impossible for your readers to perform their tasks.

The following sections describe the elements most commonly included in introductions, together with suggestions for deciding whether your readers need each of them.

Possible Introduction Topics

- **Subject**
- **Aim (purpose or outcome of the procedure described)**
- **Intended readers**
- **Scope**
- **Organization**
- **Usage (advice about how to use the instructions most effectively)**
- **Conventions (explanations of short-cut expressions and other conventions used in the instructions)**
- **Motivation (reasons why readers should use the instructions rather than ignore them)**
- **Safety**

Subject

Often the title of your instructions will fully convey their subject. Especially in longer instructions, however, you may need to announce the subject in an introduction. Here is the first sentence from the 50-page operator's manual for a 10-ton machine used in the manufacture of automobile and truck tires:

Opening sentence that announces the subject

> This manual tells you how to operate the Tire Uniformity Optimizer (TUO).

The first page of the manual for a popular word-processing program reads:

> The Microsoft Word User's Guide contains detailed information about using Microsoft® Word for Windows™ and Microsoft Word for Apple® Macintosh®.

Aim

From the beginning, your readers will want to know the purpose or outcome of the procedure described in your instructions. When the purpose or outcome isn't obvious from the title, announce it in the introduction. You may be able to convey your instructions' aim by listing the major steps in the procedure or the capabilities of the equipment whose operation you are describing. Here is the second sentence of the manual for the Tire Uniformity Optimizer:

Depending upon the options on your machine, it may do any or all of the following jobs:

A list of the purposes for which readers can use the equipment

- Test tires
- Find irregularities in tires
- Grind to correct the irregularities, if possible
- Grade tires
- Mark tires according to grade
- Sort tires by grade

Intended Readers

Readers sometimes ask, "Is this manual for me?"

When they pick up instructions, people often want to know whether the instructions are directed to them or to people who differ from them in interests, responsibilities, level of knowledge, or some other variable.

Sometimes, they can tell merely by reading the instructions' title. For instance, the operator's manual for the Tire Uniformity Optimizer is obviously addressed to people hired to operate that machine.

Identify special knowledge that is required.

In contrast, people who consult instructions for a computer program may wonder whether the instructions assume that they know more (or less) about computers than they actually do. In such situations, answer their question in your introduction. Readers who don't already possess the required knowledge can then seek help or acquire the necessary background. To illustrate, here is part of the introduction to on-line instructions for AOL Press, a program for making Web pages.

Description of the target audience from on-line instructions

Our assumptions about you:

- We assume that you know how to use your computer and its operating software.

- We assume that you know how to use one of the popular word-processing software packages, such as Microsoft Word.

- We *do not* assume that you are familiar with the World Wide Web and with the concept of navigating through information with hypertext.

Scope

By telling the scope of your instructions, you help readers know whether the instructions contain directions for the specific tasks they want to perform. The manual for the Tire Uniformity Optimizer describes the scope of its instructions in the third and fourth sentences:

Statement of scope

This manual explains all the tasks you are likely to perform in a normal shift. It covers all of the options your machine might have.

A manual for Microsoft NT, a computer operating system, describes its scope in this way:

Scope of Part I —

In Part I, you'll learn the basic features of Windows NT 4.0, including the new Windows 95 interface. Designed to get you up-to-speed quickly and easily, Part I provides the step-by-step procedures you'll need to get started. Part II lists the system requirements for running this new version, and then guides you through installing this new operating system.

Scope of Part II —

Organization

By explaining how the instructions are organized, an introduction can help readers understand the overall structure of the tasks they will perform and locate specific pieces of information without having to read the entire set of instructions.

Often introductions explain scope and organization together. If you look back at the statement of scope from the Microsoft NT manual, you will see that it simultaneously describes the manual's organization: it announces that the manual is organized into two parts, each with two types of content.

Similarly, the introduction to the Tire Uniformity Optimizer devotes several sentences to explaining that manual's organization, and this information also fills out the readers' understanding of the manual's scope.

Paragraph describing a manual's organization

The rest of this chapter introduces you to the major parts of the TUO and its basic operation. Chapter 2 tells you step-by-step how to prepare the TUO when you change the type or size of tire you are testing. Chapter 3 tells you how to perform routine servicing, and Chapter 4 tells you how to troubleshoot problems you can probably handle without needing to ask for help from someone else. Chapter 5 contains a convenient checklist of the tasks described in Chapters 3 and 4.

Usage

Your readers will want to know how to use your instructions as efficiently and effectively as possible. If the best method is simply to follow the directions from beginning to end, you don't need to tell them anything at all. However, if you know of a better way to use your instructions, share it with your readers. Here's the advice given in the on-line instructions for AOL Press:

Advice about how to use the instructions

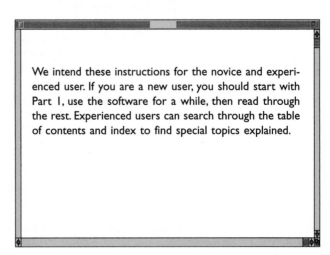

We intend these instructions for the novice and experienced user. If you are a new user, you should start with Part I, use the software for a while, then read through the rest. Experienced users can search through the table of contents and index to find special topics explained.

Conventions

Some instructions use special conventions or terms that enable them to communicate succinctly. If you employ such shortcuts that your readers don't already know, be sure to include an explanation in your introduction.

The introduction to the on-line manual for AOL Press explains some of its conventions as follows:

Explanation of conventions
used in an on-line manual

Following the heading that introduces a task are either sequential steps or option steps, each with its distinctive style:

1. Numbered paragraphs, like this one, designate step-by-step instructions. Follow them to learn how the tools work.

2. Menu commands are shown with arrows, for example **File→Save** means you should pull down the **File** menu and choose the **Save** option.

■ Paragraphs with a bullet, like this one, are optional steps. Usually there is a sequence. Do one or more of the steps to cause the designated action or actions.

Motivation

As pointed out above (and as you may know from your own experience), some people are tempted to toss instructions aside and rely on their common sense. A major purpose of many introductions is to persuade readers to *read* the instructions. You can do this by employing an inviting and supportive tone and by creating attractive design. You can also include statements that tell readers directly why it is important to pay attention to the instructions. The following example is from instructions for a ceiling fan that purchasers install themselves.

Statement of scope

We're certain that your Hampton Bay fan will provide you with many years of comfort, energy savings, and satisfaction. To ensure your personal safety and to maximize the performance of your fan, please read this manual.

Motivation to read the
instructions

Safety

Your readers depend on you to prevent them from taking actions that could spoil their results, damage their equipment, or cause them injury. Moreover, product liability laws require companies to pay for damages or injuries that result from inadequate warnings in their instructions.

To satisfy your ethical and legal obligations, you must provide prominent, easy-to-understand, and persuasive warnings. If a warning concerns a general issue that covers the entire set of instructions (e.g., "don't use this electrical tool while standing on wet ground"), place it in your introduction. If it pertains to a certain step, place it before that step. The following guidelines apply to warnings in either location:

- **Make your warnings stand out visually.** Try printing them in large, bold type and surrounding them with a box (Velotta). Sometimes, writers use the following international hazard alert symbol to draw attention to the warning.

You may also include an icon to convey the nature of the danger. Here are some icons developed by Westinghouse.

Electrical Shock   Fire   Eye Protection

- **Place your warnings so that your readers will read them before performing the action the warnings refer to.** It won't help your readers to discover the warning after the step has been performed and the damage has been done.
- **State the nature of the hazard and the consequences of ignoring the warning.** If readers don't know what could happen, they may think that it's not important to take the necessary precautions.
- **Tell your readers what steps to take to protect themselves or avoid damage.**

The box and international hazard icon draw attention to the warning.

Initial statement tells what readers can do to avoid the hazard.

Readers are told the possible consequences of ignoring the warning.

⚠ **DANGER**

Wear safety goggles when performing the next step. Flying chips could damage eyesight or cause blindness.

In many professions, writers distinguish among various types of warnings to indicate the severity of the hazard. Although these classification systems usually use the same words (*caution, warning,* and *danger*), there are no standard definitions for these words. However, here is one set of definitions that is widely used (Sides):

- **Caution.** Alerts readers that they may spoil the results if they do not follow the directions exactly.

Be sure to clean the flask with alcohol before adding the reagent. Otherwise, you may get false readings.

- **Warning.** Alerts readers that they may damage equipment if they do not follow the directions exactly.

When performing the next step, **do not use detergents** to clean the reservoir. They contain chemicals that may damage the seals.

- **Danger.** Alerts readers to the danger of injury or death.

These canisters contain ammonia, which is highly explosive. Handle them with extreme caution. If they are damaged, they could explode, causing injury or death.

Note that the word in the rectangle changes to reflect the severity of the hazard.

Sample Introductions

Figure 20.1 shows the introduction to the instruction manual for the Tire Uniformity Optimizer. The introduction to another manual appears in Figure 8.4 (page 234).

Notice that the manual for the Tire Uniformity Optimizer uses the word *Introduction* and the introduction to the Detroit Diesel Engine Series 53 manual (Figure 8.4) is headed "General Information." The material that this chapter refers to as the *introduction* is called many other names in other instructions. Sometimes, it is given no title at all.

DESCRIPTION OF THE EQUIPMENT

To describe equipment, use the pattern for describing an object (page 198) or use a photograph or drawing (pages 312–319).

To be able to operate or repair a piece of equipment, readers need to know the location of its parts. Sometimes, they need to know the function as well. For this reason, instructions often include a description of the equipment to be used. For example, the first page of the manual for the Tire Uniformity Optimizer displays a photograph of the machine with its major parts labeled. In some instructions, such illustrations are accompanied by written explanations of the equipment and its parts.

LIST OF MATERIALS AND EQUIPMENT NEEDED

Tell your readers what they need *before* they need it.

Some procedures require materials or equipment that readers wouldn't normally have at hand. If yours do, include a list of these items. Be sure to present the list *before* giving your step-by-step instructions. This will save your readers from the unpleasant surprise of discovering that they cannot go on to the next step until they have gone to the shop, supply room, or store to obtain an item that they didn't realize they would need.

DIRECTIONS

At the heart of a set of instructions are the step-by-step directions that tell readers what to do. The following guidelines suggest detailed strategies for writing direc-

■ **FIGURE 20.1**

Introduction to the Instruction Manual for the Tire Uniformity Optimizer

From Akron Standard, *Operator's Manual for the Tire Uniformity Optimizer* (Akron, OH: Akron Standard, 1986) 1.

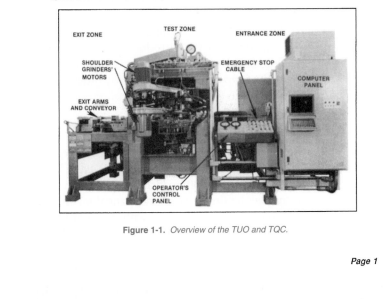

Chapter 1— Introduction

This manual tells you how to operate the Tire Uniformity Optimizer (TUO) and its controller, the Tire Quality Computer (TQC). The TUO has many options. Depending upon the options on your machine, it may do any or all of the following jobs:

- Tests tires
- Finds irregularities in tires
- Grinds to correct the irregularities, if possible
- Grades tires
- Marks tires according to grade
- Sorts tires by grade

This manual explains all the tasks you are likely to perform in a normal shift. It covers all of the options your machine might have.

The rest of this chapter introduces you to the major parts of the TUO and its basic operation. Chapter 2 tells you step-by-step how to prepare the TUO when you change the type or size of tire you are testing. Chapter 3 tells you how to perform routine servicing, and Chapter 4 tells you how to trouble-shoot problems with the TUO. Chapter 5 contains a convenient checklist of the tasks described in Chapter 3.

Major Parts of the TUO

You can find the major parts of the TUO by looking at Figure 1-1. To operate the TUO, you will use the Operator's Control Panel and the Computer Panel.

EXIT ZONE TEST ZONE ENTRANCE ZONE

SHOULDER GRINDERS' MOTORS

EMERGENCY STOP CABLE

COMPUTER PANEL

EXIT ARMS AND CONVEYOR

OPERATOR'S CONTROL PANEL

Figure 1-1. *Overview of the TUO and TQC.*

Page 1

tions that your readers will find easy to understand and use. Figure 20.2 illustrates much of this advice.

1. **Write each direction for rapid comprehension and immediate use.** When using your instructions, readers will be impatient to complete their tasks. During the time they are reading (not doing) they will want to learn very quickly what they need to do next.

   ■ **In each direction, give your readers just enough information to perform the next step.** If you give more, they may forget some or become confused. If you give less, they may be unable to perform the step.

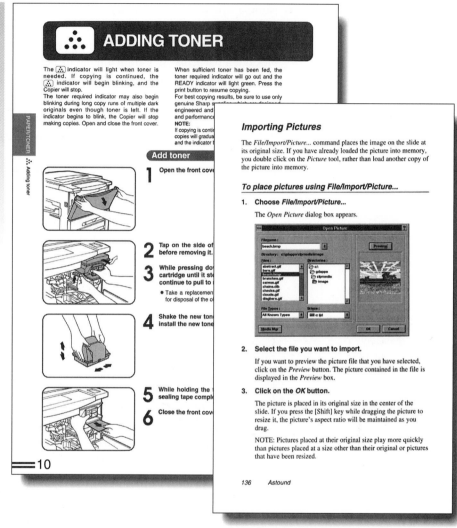

FIGURE 20.2

Well-Designed Presentation of Procedures

From Sharp Electronics, *Plain Paper Copier Model SF-2–22 Operation Manual* (Mahwah, NJ: Sharp Electronics, 1998) 10. And from Astound, *Gold Disk Astound Version 2.0 for Windows: Tutorials, User's Guide, Media Manager* (Mississauga, Ontario, Canada: Astound, 1995) 136.

Though very different in design, both are easy to read and use because they apply the principles discussed on pages 535–538.

Step numbers are prominent, easy to see.

Each step describes only one action.

Each direction is short and easy to comprehend.

Directions are on a line of their own, separate from explanations, to make them easy to read.

Figures provide additional guidance.

■ **Present the steps in a list.** A list format helps readers see exactly what they must read in order to perform the next step.

■ **Use the active voice and the imperative mood.** Active, imperative verbs give commands: "*Stop* the engine." (This is much simpler than, "The operator should then stop the engine.")

■ **Highlight key words.** In some instructions, a direction may contain a single word that conveys the critical information. You can speed the readers' task by using boldface, all-capital letters or a different typeface to make this word pop off the page. Example: Press the **RETURN** key.

2. **Help your readers locate the next step quickly.** There are many things you can do to help your readers as they turn their eyes away from the task and back to your text:

- **Number the steps.** With the aid of numbers, readers will not have to reread earlier directions to figure out which one they last read.

- **Put blank lines between steps.** This white space makes it easy for readers to pick out a particular step from among its neighbors.

- **Give one action per step.** It's difficult to find a direction that is hidden after another direction.

- **Put step numbers in their own column.** Instead of aligning the second line of a direction under the step number, align it with the text of the first line. Not this:

Step number is obscured.

> 2. To quit the program, click the CLOSE button in the upper right-hand corner of the window.

But this:

Step number is in its own column.

> 2. To quit the program, click the CLOSE button in the upper right-hand corner of the window.

3. **Within steps, distinguish actions from supporting information.**

- **Present actions before responses.** As the following example shows, you make reading unnecessarily difficult if you put the response to one step at the beginning of the next step.

The computer response obscures the action to be performed.

> 4. Press the RETURN key.
> 5. The Customer Order Screen will appear. Click on the TABS button.

Instead, put the response after the step that causes it.

Improved placement of the computer reaction lets the actions stand out.

> 4. Press the RETURN key.
>   The Customer Order Screen will appear.
> 5. Click on the TABS button.

- **Make actions stand out visually from other material.**
  In the following example, boldface is used to signal to the readers that the first part of Step 4 is an action and the second part is the response.

Use boldface and layout to make actions stand out.

> **4. Press the RETURN key.** The Customer Order Screen will appear.

You can also use layout to make such distinctions.

> **4. Press the RETURN key.**
> - The Customer Order Screen will appear.

And you can use similar techniques when explaining steps.

> **7. Enter ANALYZE.** This command prompts the computer to perform seven analytical computations.

4. **Group related steps under action-oriented headings.** By arranging the steps into groups, you divide your procedure into chunks that readers are likely to find manageable. Also, you help them *learn* the procedure so that they will be able to perform it without instructions in the future. Moreover, if you use action-oriented headings and subheadings for the groups of steps, you aid readers who need directions for only one part of the procedure. The headings enable them to locate quickly the information they require.

To create action-oriented headings, use participles, not nouns, to describe the task. For example, use *Installing* rather than *Installation* and use *Converting* rather than *Conversion*.

■ FIGURE 20.3

Drawing That Shows Readers Where to Locate Parts of a Camcorder

From Thompson Electronics, *RCA Pro808A Camcorder User's Guide* (Indianapolis: Thompson Electronics, 1994) 28.

This figure helps readers locate controls used to focus their camcorders.

The labels are placed far enough from the drawing to stand out distinctly.

To avoid ambiguity, arrows lead directly to each labeled part.

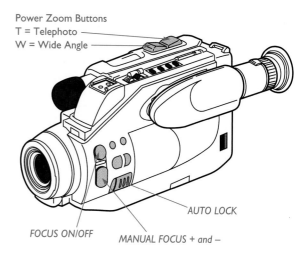

Power Zoom Buttons
T = Telephoto
W = Wide Angle

AUTO LOCK

FOCUS ON/OFF   MANUAL FOCUS + and −

Here are some of the action-oriented headings and subheadings from Chapter 4 of the Microsoft NT manual.

The first word in each heading and subheading is a participle.

Setting Up Your Computers on Your Network
   Connecting to Computers on Your Network
  Sharing Your Printer
    Viewing Network Drives
    Using Dial-Up Networking
  Using Peer Web Services
   Installing Peer Web Services
   Configuring and Administering Peer Web Services

5. **Use many visual aids.** Drawings, photographs, and similar illustrations often provide the clearest and simplest means of telling your readers such important things as:

   Chapter 11 tells how to design effective visual aids for instructions.

   ■ **Where things are.** For instance, Figure 20.3 shows the readers of an instruction manual where to find two control switches.

   ■ **How to perform steps.** For instance, by showing someone's hand performing a step, you provide your readers with a model to follow as they attempt to follow your directions (see Figure 20.4).

   ■ **What should result.** By showing readers what should result from performing a step, you help them understand what they are trying to accomplish and help them determine whether they have performed the step correctly (see Figure 20.5).

   Chapter 12 provides detailed advice for using page design to help readers see which figure goes with which text.

6. **Present branching steps clearly.** Sometimes instructions include alternative courses of action. For example, while performing a chemical analysis, there might be one procedure if the acidity of a solution is at a normal level, and there might be another if the acidity is high. In such a situation, avoid listing only one of the alternatives.

■ **FIGURE 20.4**

Drawings That Show How to Do Something

From Lifescan, *Obtaining a Blood Sample* (Milpitas, CA: Lifescan, 1998).

These instructions tell people with diabetes how to obtain the drop of blood they need in order to test their insulin levels.

The Lancet is a sharp needle used to prick the skin.

Each drawing shows exactly how to hold the PENLET.

The drawing for Step 4 highlights the placement of the PENLET against the side of a finger.

The drawing for Step 5 emphasizes that the drop of blood must hang from the finger so that it may be applied to a test strip (in the next part of the procedure).

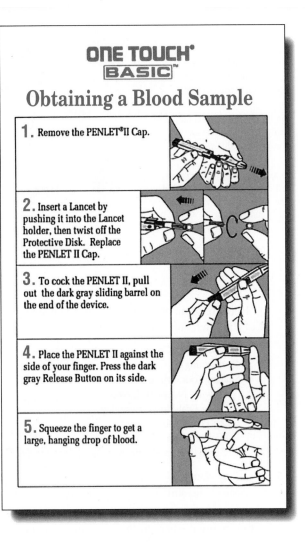

ONE TOUCH® BASIC™

Obtaining a Blood Sample

1. Remove the PENLET®II Cap.

2. Insert a Lancet by pushing it into the Lancet holder, then twist off the Protective Disk. Replace the PENLET II Cap.

3. To cock the PENLET II, pull out the dark gray sliding barrel on the end of the device.

4. Place the PENLET II against the side of your finger. Press the dark gray Release Button on its side.

5. Squeeze the finger to get a large, hanging drop of blood.

Possibly confusing direction

| 6. If the acidity is high, follow the procedure described on page 20.

Instead, describe the step that enables readers to determine which alternative to choose (in the example, *checking the acidity* is that step) and then format the alternatives clearly:

Revised direction

| 6. Check the acidity.
■ If it is high, follow the procedure described on page 20.
■ If it is normal, proceed to Step 7.

Follow the same logic with other places where your instructions branch into two or more directions. The following example is from instructions for a computer program.

| 9. Determine which method you will use to connect to the Internet:
■ If you will use PPP (Point to Point Protocol), see Chapter 3.
■ If you will use SLIP (Serial Line Internet Protocol), see Chapter 4.

■ **FIGURE 20.5**

Drawing That Shows a Successful Outcome

From Apple Computer, *Power Macintosh User's Manual for the 7300 Series* (Cupertino, CA: Apple Computer, 1997) 9.

This figure is part of the set-up instructions for a computer; it assists new owners in determining whether they have correctly connected their cables.

The monitor cable and port are highlighted because new owners can be confused about which of two ports receives that cable.

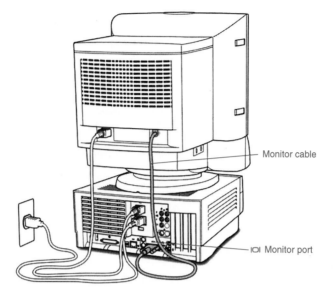

Monitor cable

|O| Monitor port

7. **Tell what to do in the case of a mistake or unexpected result.** Try to anticipate the places where readers might make mistakes in following your instructions. If it is not obvious how to correct or compensate for a mistake, tell them how to do so. Similarly, tell them what to do when a correct action does not produce the expected result:

> 5. Depress and release the RUN switches on the operator's panel.
>
> **NOTE:** If the machine stops immediately and the FAULT light illuminates, reposition the second reel and repeat Step 5.

TROUBLESHOOTING

The troubleshooting section of a set of instructions tells readers what to do if things don't work out as expected—if the equipment fails to work properly or if the results are unsatisfactory. Often, a table format works best. Figure 20.6 shows the troubleshooting section of the manual for the Tire Uniformity Optimizer.

PHYSICAL CONSTRUCTION OF INSTRUCTIONS

The physical construction of instructions is an important element of their design. Computer manuals are often printed in a small format because readers use them on crowded desktops. Cookbooks are sometimes printed on glossy paper to withstand kitchen spills. Be sure to adapt your instructions to the environment in which they will be used.

Chapter 4—Trouble-shooting

This chapter tells you what to check when trouble-shooting the TQC. It lists the problems that may occur, the probable causes, and the remedies.

The first list in this chapter consists of the error messages that appear on the CRT when a problem occurs. Next to the error messages are the causes of the problem and the possible remedies. A list of all the error messages can be found in Appendix B. The second list consists of observable phenomena that are listed in order of normal TQC operation.

One easily-solved problem is caused by entering entries too quickly to the TQC through the keyboard. If the operator does not wait for the TQC to respond to one request before entering another, errors and inaccurate data will result. Make sure you allow sufficient time for the TQC to respond to your input before you press another key.

Warning

EXTERNAL TEST EQUIPMENT CAN DAMAGE THE TQC. If you use external equipment to trouble-shoot the TQC, make sure that it does not introduce undesired ground currents or AC leakage currents.

Trouble-shooting with Error Messages

Power-up Error Messages

Error Message	Probable Cause	Remedy
BACKUP BATTERY IS LOW	1. Battery on Processor Support PCB.	1. Replace the battery on the Processor Support PCB.
CONTROLLER ERROR	1. PC interface PCB. 2. Processor Support PCB.	1. Swap the PC Interface PCB. 2. Swap the Processor Support PCB.
EPROM CHECKSUM ERROR	1. Configuration tables. 2. Analog Processor PCB.	1. Check the configuration tables. 2. Swap the Analog Processor PCB 88/40.
KEYBOARD MALFUNCTION: PORT	1. Keyboard or keyboard cable. 2. Processor Support PCB.	1. Check the keyboard and cable. 2. Swap the Processor Support PCB.
RAM FAILURE AT 0000:	1. Main Processor 86/30.	1. Swap the 86/30.
RAM FAILURE AT 1000:	1. Main Processor 86/30.	1. Swap the 86/30.
TIGRE PROGRAM CHECKSUM ERROR	1. TIGRE program.	1. Reenter the TIGRE program or debug the program.

Table 4-1. *Power-up error messages.*

Page 59

WRITING ON-LINE INSTRUCTIONS

As explained at the beginning of this chapter, all the advice you have read so far applies not only to printed instructions but also to on-line ones.

On-line instructions are becoming increasingly common. Often they are included within the computer programs. Also, many sites on the World Wide Web provide instructions meant for on-screen use. Some organizations provide on-line instructions to guide their employees through various technical processes.

To create on-line instructions, you can use any of several computer programs designed for that purpose. For a lot less money, you can design a Web site that presents the instructions your readers need.

The following guidelines for creating on-line instructions supplement the guidelines given earlier in this chapter:

For detailed advice on creating on-line communications, see Chapter 15's discussion of Web site design.

Guidelines for On-Line Instructions

1. **Keep each unit of instruction to screen size or smaller.** Eliminate scrolling by using a compact page design and by dividing larger tasks into smaller ones.

2. **Use a consistent design on all instructional pages.** This helps readers quickly locate the information they need.

3. **When writing instructions for a computer program, let readers see their work areas simultaneously with the directions.** Don't make the instructions window so large that it hides the window that readers are using to perform their task.

4. **Provide a map or table of contents on the home page.** This will enable readers to locate the specific part of the instructions that interests them.

5. **Provide navigational aids within the instructions.** On every page include links to the home page and to other pages of interest.

6. **Conduct a user test.** As with any instructions, the on-line variety should be tested by members of the target audience working under conditions identical to those of the anticipated actual use.

SAMPLE INSTRUCTIONS

Figure 20.7 shows a set of instructions written by a student. Figure 20.8 shows part of the on-line instructions for Harvard Graphics. Figure 20.9 shows two screens from on-line instructions contained in a Web site created by a student.

Note to the Instructor: Appendix C contains an instruction-writing project. In addition, the printed *Instructor's Manual* includes a "Planning Guide for Instructions," and the Web site for this book has a version you can download and edit to match your approach to this chapter. The Web site also includes exercises that involve editing word-processed drafts of instructions.

Text continued on page 557

Determining the Percentages of Hardwood and Softwood Fiber in a Paper Sample

These instruction tell you how to analyze a paper sample to determine what percentage of its fibers is from hardwood and what from softwood. This information is important because the ratio of hardwood to softwood affects the paper's physical properties. The long softwood fibers provide strength but bunch up into flocks that give the paper an uneven formation. The short hardwood fibers provide an even formation but little strength. Consequently, two kinds of fibers are needed in most papers, the exact ratio depending on the type of paper being made.

Importance of the procedure is explained.

To determine the percentages of hardwood and softwood fiber, you perform the following major steps: preparing the slide, preparing the sample slurry, placing the slurry on the slide, staining the fibers, placing the slide cover, counting the fibers, and calculating the percentages. The procedure described in these instructions is an alternative to the test approved by the Technical Association of the Pulp and Paper Industry (TAPPI). The TAPPI test involves counting fibers in only one area of the sample slide. Because the fibers can be distributed unevenly on the slide, that procedure can give inaccurate results. The procedure given here produces more accurate results because it involves counting all the fibers on the slide.

Overview of the procedure and important background information

EQUIPMENT

All equipment is listed before the directions.

Microscope	Hot plate
Microscope slide	Paper sample
Microscope slide cover	Blender
Microscope slide marking pen	Beaker
Acetone solvent	Eyedropper
Clean cloth	Graff "C" stain
	Pointing needle

FIGURE 20.7
(continued)

2

PREPARING THE SLIDE

1. **Clean slide.** Using acetone solvent and a clean cloth, remove all dirt and fingerprints. NOTE: Do not use paper towel because it will deposit fibers on the slide.

Explanation of reason for the caution

2. **Mark slide.** With a marking pen, draw two lines approximately 1.5 inches apart across the width of the slide.

3. **Label slide.** At one end, label the slide with an identifying number. Your slide should now look like the one shown in Figure A.

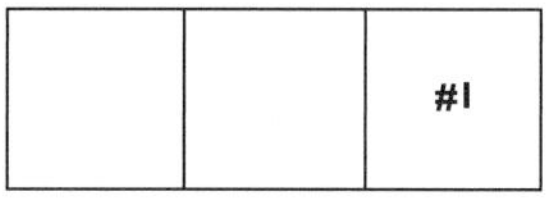

Figure is placed immediately after its mention in text.

#1

Figure A

4. **Turn on hot plate.** Set the temperature at warm. NOTE: Higher temperatures will "boil" off the softwood fibers that you will later place on the slide.

5. **Place the slide on hot plate.** Leave the slide there until it dries completely, which will take approximately 5 minutes.

6. **Remove slide from hot plate.** Leave the hot plate on. You will use it again shortly.

PREPARING THE SAMPLE SLURRY

1. **Pour 2 cups of water in blender.** This measurement can be approximate.

2. **Obtain paper sample.** The sample should be about the size of a dime.

3. **Tear sample into fine pieces.**

4. **Place sample into blender.**

5. **Turn blender on.** Set blender on high and run it for about 1 minute.

6. **Check slurry.** After turning the blender off, see if any paper clumps remain. If so, turn the blender on for another 30 seconds. Repeat until no clumps remain.

7. **Pour slurry into beaker.**

FIGURE 20.7
(continued)

3

Helpful suggestion
to readers

Desired result
explained

Action to be taken
if desired result
is not achieved

PLACING THE SLURRY ONTO THE SLIDE

1. Suck slurry into eyedropper.

2. **Place 3 ml of slurry onto slide between the lines you marked on it.** This measurement can be approximate.

3. Place slide onto black paper.

4. **Check slide.** It should have between 300 and 1,000 fibers.
   - **If it has too few, use the eyedropper to add more slurry.**
   - **If it has too many, use the eyedropper to remove some slurry.**

When done, your slide should look like the one shown in Figure B.

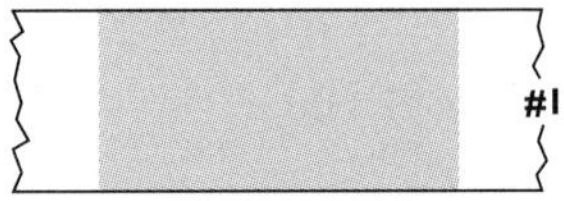

#1
Figure B

5. **Place slide on hot plate.** Leave it there until all the water has evaporated, which will take about 1 hour.

6. **Remove slide from hot plate.**

7. **Turn off hot plate.**

NOTE: If you cannot complete the entire procedure, in one session, this is a good place to stop. The rest of the steps take about 1 hour.

STAINING THE FIBERS

1. **Place 3 drops of Graff "C" stain onto fibers.**

2. **Spread stain.** With the pointing needle, spread the stain evenly over the fibers, using the motion in Figure C.

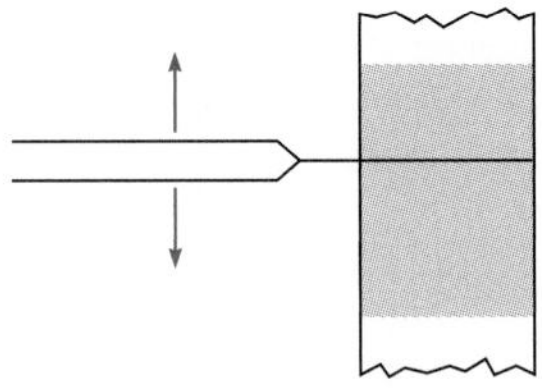

Figure C

PLACING THE SLIDE COVER

1. **Place one end of slide cover onto one of the lines you marked on the slide.** See Figure D.

FIGURE 20.7
(continued)

Figure is used to show a step not easily described in words.

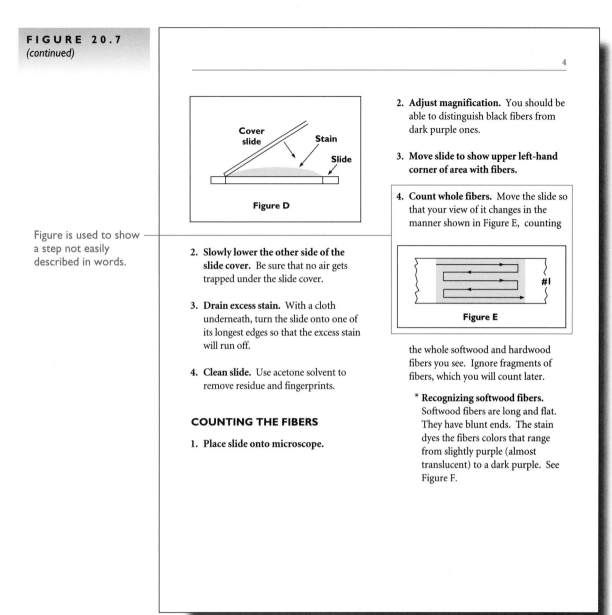

4

2. Adjust magnification. You should be able to distinguish black fibers from dark purple ones.

3. Move slide to show upper left-hand corner of area with fibers.

4. Count whole fibers. Move the slide so that your view of it changes in the manner shown in Figure E, counting

Figure D

2. Slowly lower the other side of the slide cover. Be sure that no air gets trapped under the slide cover.

3. Drain excess stain. With a cloth underneath, turn the slide onto one of its longest edges so that the excess stain will run off.

4. Clean slide. Use acetone solvent to remove residue and fingerprints.

Figure E

the whole softwood and hardwood fibers you see. Ignore fragments of fibers, which you will count later.

COUNTING THE FIBERS

1. Place slide onto microscope.

* **Recognizing softwood fibers.** Softwood fibers are long and flat. They have blunt ends. The stain dyes the fibers colors that range from slightly purple (almost translucent) to a dark purple. See Figure F.

FIGURE 20.7
(continued)

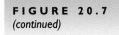

5

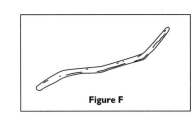

Figure F

* **Recognizing hardwood fibers.**
Hardwood fibers are much smaller
than softwood fibers. Their ends
come to a point, and the stain dyes
them deep black. See Figure G.

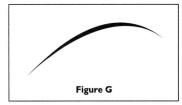

Figure G

5. **Count fragments.** Fragments result
from refining. Count them while
moving the slide in the way shown in

Figure E. Count softwood fragments
until they equal a typical whole
softwood fiber on the slide. Do the
same for the hardwood fragments.

CALCULATING THE PERCENTAGES

1. **Multiply the total number of
hardwood and softwood fibers by the
appropriate factors.**

   - Number of softwood fibers
     $\times 1.5 = X$

   - Number of hardwood fibers
     $\times 0.2 = Y$

2. **Determine the percentages.**

   - Percentage of softwood
     $= X/(X + Y) \times 100\%$

   - Percentage of hardwood
     $= Y/(X + Y) \times 100\%$

■ **FIGURE 20.8**

On-Line Instructions

Courtesy of Harvard Graphics

The opening page of the tutorial provides an overview of the topics covered.

Each topic is associated with a distinctive icon.

The appropriate icon is used on each page.

To create visual unity, all pages have the same overall design.

Link to related topics help users find all the information they need.

Pictures help users locate the buttons they need to find.

Each step describes a single action.

Blank lines between steps increase readability.

Each page is short enough to be read without scrolling.

Harvard Graphics Help

File Edit Bookmark Options Help

Contents | Search | Back | Print

Working with Harvard Graphics

You can get step-by-step Help for working with Harvard Graphics. What do you want to do?

Create a presentation

Change the look of a presentation

Work with charts

Work with text, graphics, or symbols

Print a presentation

Work with other applications

Create S

Customi

Note
■ To look for a t

Harvard Graphics Help

File Edit Bookmark Options Help

Contents | Search | Back | Print

Changing Effects for a Single Slide

Individual slide transition effects override the default effects for the ScreenShow.

To change slide effects for a single slide:

1. Click

2. In the slide list, select the slide.

3. Select the draw and eras

4. Type the time you want the **Display time** box.

5. Click **OK**.

Related Topic
Changing default slide effect

Harvard Graphics Help

File Edit Bookmark Options Help

Contents | Search | Back | Print

Organizing the Slides in a Presentation

Use the Slide Sorter to view all of a presentation at once and to easily rearrange, delete, and copy slides.

To display the Slide Sorter:

Click

To move a slide:

Drag the slide where you want it to go, and release the mouse button.

To delete, copy, or paste slides:

1. Select one or more slides.

To select:	Do this:
A single slide	Click it
Non-adjacent slides	Hold down Shift as you click each slide
Adjacent slides	Drag a selection box around the slides

2. Use the Edit menu to cut, copy, or paste.

■ **FIGURE 20.9 On-Line Instructions Created by a Student** Courtesy of Amy Beaton

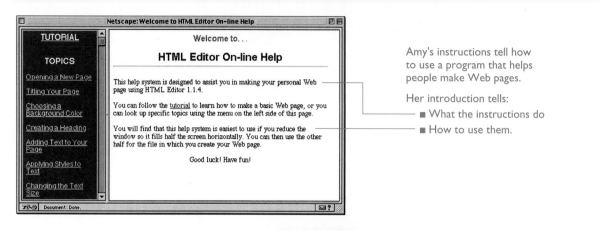

Amy's instructions tell how to use a program that helps people make Web pages.

Her introduction tells:
- What the instructions do
- How to use them.

Amy uses the same basic design for all pages.

Most of her screens require no scrolling (though the menu on the left must be scrolled).

Note her use of visual aids.

On each screen, Amy provides two ways of navigating her instructions:
- The menu at right provides rapid access to specific topics.
- The links at the bottom guide the reader through a step-by-step process.

Figure 12.10 shows screens from another set of on-line instructions.

EXERCISES

1. Find and photocopy a short set of instructions (five pages or less). Analyze the instructions, noting how the writers have handled each element of the superstructure for instructions. If they have omitted certain elements, explain why you think they did so. Comment on the page design and visual aids (if any). Then evaluate the instructions. Tell what you think works best about them and identify ways you think they can be improved.

2. Choose one:
   a. Find a set of instructions designed to be read on the World Wide Web and discuss ways they might be changed to be effective in print.
   b. Find a set of print instructions and discuss ways they might be changed to make them as effective as possible if viewed on the World Wide Web.

3. Explore the on-line instructions for a program on your computer. Evaluate them in light of the guidelines on page 549. What design features seem to you to be especially effective? How might they be improved? Consider the guidelines given on page 549 and your own experience as you try to follow the instructions in your own user test of them.

Appendixes

APPENDIX A
Formats for Letters, Memos, and Books

APPENDIX B
Documenting Your Sources

APPENDIX C
Projects and Cases

559

Formats for Letters, Memos, and Books

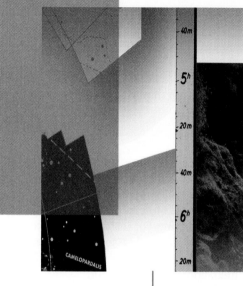

CONTENTS

Letter Format

Memo Format

Book Format

F ormats are conventional packages for presenting messages. This appendix is about the three formats most often employed at work:

Formats		
Letter	Used primarily for short communications sent outside the organization	Page 562
Memo	Used primarily for short, internal communications	Page 567
Book	Used for communications addressed inside or or outside the organization that are long enough to have a cover and binding	Page 569

Many employers distribute instructions that tell employees how to prepare each of these formats. These instructions, sometimes called *style guides,* describe everything from the width of margins to the placement of headings. Of course, the instructions vary somewhat from company to company. For instance, on the cover of a report, one employer may want the title placed in a certain location, and another employer may want it placed somewhere else. In a letter, one employer may want the first line of a paragraph to be indented, and another may not.

Despite these variations, most business letters, memos, and formal reports look very much alike. The formats described in this chapter reflect common practices in the business world. You will have little trouble adapting them to other, slightly different versions if the need arises.

LETTER FORMAT

Letters are ordinarily used to send relatively short messages to customers, clients, government agencies, and other readers outside the writer's organization. Two variations of the letter format are shown in Figures A.1 and A.2. Both variations have the same parts:

- **Heading.** The heading gives your address (but not your name) and the date. It may also include your e-mail address. Spell out all words (*Street,* not *St.*), except that you may use the Postal Service's two-letter abbreviations for the states (*TX* for *Texas*). If you are writing on letterhead stationery that already includes your company's name, address, and phone number, you will need to add only the date.
- **Inside address.** The inside address gives the name and address of the person to whom you are writing. Where appropriate, include the person's title and position. By custom, the titles *Mr., Mrs., Ms.,* and *Dr.* are abbreviated, but other

Text continued on page 565

■ **FIGURE A.1**

Block Format for Letters

Letterhead

Date

Inside address

Subject line

Salutation

Signature block

Enclosure notation

Distribution list

Typist identification

SUPERIOR FABRICATION COMPANY

176 Lafayette Court
Baton Rouge, Louisiana 70816
517-235-9008

October 17, 19—

Mr. Anthony Fazio
Capra Consultants, Incorporated
9223 Taft Street
Grand Rapids, Michigan 49507

Subject: Request for Proposal

Dear Mr. Fazio:

We invite you to submit a proposal for the design and implementation of an inventory control system.

We manufacture conduit used to run electrical and computer cabling through walls, floors, and ceilings; some is also used in outdoor applications, such as the lighting systems in athletic stadiums. Although we build many products to standard specifications, we also custom design a substantial amount. Our product inventory includes over 8,000 items, and we use over 700 different materials. We are seeking a new inventory system because we too often discover that we don't have materials needed to fill a rush order from a customer. Since most of the materials we use are made specifically for us by our suppliers, it can take up to 30 days for the needed supplies to arrive.

We want the inventory control system to tell us when to reorder commonly used materials from our suppliers. We would also like it to help us determine how many of our most frequently requested products we should keep on hand.

The enclosed documents describe our current inventory system. If you are interested in submitting a proposal, please call so I can send you additional information.

Sincerely,

Francis V. Sullivan

Francis V. Sullivan
Project Engineer

Enclosures (2)

cc. T. L. Klein

FVS/tm

■ **FIGURE A.2**

Modified Block Format for Letters (paragraphs may be indented)

MIAMI UNIVERSITY

Department of English
Bachelor Hall
Oxford, Ohio 45056
313 529-5221

October 12, —

Mr. Paul Ring
P.O. Box 143
Watson, Illinois 62473

Dear Mr. Ring:

I am delighted that you wish to learn about Miami University's master's degree program in technical and scientific communication. This professional, practice-oriented program prepares people for careers in which they will help specialists in scientific, technical, and other fields communicate their knowledge in an understandable and useful way. The job market for our graduates is excellent.

People studying with us complete three semesters of course work and an internship. Within this framework, we strive to tailor each student's course of study to his or her particular interests and career objectives. Consequently, our graduates work in a wide variety of jobs and deal with many types of communication. These types include instruction manuals for computers and other high-tech equipment, informational booklets given to cancer patients, technical advertising, corporate procedure books, and technical reports and proposals in many fields, such as chemistry, aerospace engineering, pharmaceuticals, environmental protection, and health care. A special feature of our program is that it prepares people to advance rapidly in the profession—to management, policy-making roles, or ownership of their own communication companies.

We welcome applications from people with undergraduate degrees in many different subjects, including English and the other humanities, communication, natural and social sciences, engineering and other technical fields, art, business, and education. We strive to obtain graduate assistantships or other financial aid for every student accepted into the program who requests it.

I am enclosing a booklet describing our MTSC program in detail. If you wish to learn about similar programs at other schools, you may want to purchase a copy of *Academic Programs in Technical Communication,* which is sold by the Society for Technical Communication, 901 N. Stuart Street, Suite 904, Arlington, VA 22203-1854.

If you have any question about the MTSC program, please feel welcome to write, call, or visit.

Sincerely,

Robert R. Johnson, Director
Master's Degree Program in Technical
    and Scientific Communication

Enclosure: Booklet

Excellence is Our Tradition

titles are usually written out in full: *Professor, Senator.* The reader's title is usually typed before his or her name, and the reader's position is typed after it.

Reader's title ——— [Professor] Helen O. Jowarski, [Chair] ——— Reader's position
Computer Engineering Department

- If you are writing to an organization but do not know the name of the person to contact, you may address your letter to the organization or to a specific department in it.

- **Subject line.** A subject line focuses the reader's attention on the topic of your message and makes it easier to locate your letter in the file. Make it brief and begin with the word *Subject* or *Re,* followed by a colon: *Re: Continuing Problems with the SXD.*

  Phrase your subject line in the same reader-centered way you phrase the rest of your communication. Avoid phrases like "Responses to Your Questions." Instead, use precise phrases, such as "Near-Term Risks of Investing in Southeast Asia." Be brief but specific.

  Although subject lines are helpful to readers, many letters are sent without them. If you are unsure about whether to include one, consider the custom in your organization and the extent to which a subject line will help your reader.

- **Salutation.** By custom, a salutation includes the word *Dear,* usually followed by the reader's title, last name, and a colon: *Dear Mr. Dobcheck:.*

  If you know your reader well enough to use his or her first name in conversation, you may use it in your salutation. In that case, use a comma rather than a colon: *Dear Leon,.*

  If you do not know the name of the appropriate person to address, avoid using *Dear Sir* or *Gentlemen.* These salutations are considered objectionable because of the assumption they make about the sex of the addressee. Instead use the name of the department or organization in the salutation: *Dear Customer Relations Department:.*

- **Body.** The body of a letter contains your message. Except in rare instances, it is single-spaced with a double space between paragraphs. The paragraphs are usually ten lines or fewer. However, use longer paragraphs if you feel they are better suited to your message.

  Customarily the body of a letter consists of a beginning, a middle, and an end. In most letters, the beginning is one paragraph long. It announces the writer's reason for writing. In letters between people who communicate frequently, it may include personal news. The main discussion of the writer's topic is usually contained in the middle section. The final paragraph usually includes a social gesture—thanking the other person for writing, expressing a willingness to be of further assistance, or the like.

- **Complimentary close.** The complimentary close consists of one of several familiar phrases, such as *Yours truly, Sincerely,* or *Cordially.* The first letter of the first word is capitalized. The complimentary close is followed by a comma.

  When you are writing to someone you do not know, select one of the more formal phrases for your complimentary close, such as *Sincerely* or *Sincerely yours.* When writing to an acquaintance, use a more informal phrase, such as *Cordially* or *With best wishes.*

■ **Signature block.** Your name appears twice in the signature block: once in handwriting (with a pen) and once typed. Together, the complimentary close and signature block look like this:

Complimentary close	Sincerely yours,	Cordially,
Signature	*Raphael Goodman*	*Constance Idanopolis*
Typed name	Raphael Goodman	Constance Idanopolis
Title	Senior Auditor	Head, Sales Division

■ **Special notations.** On occasion, you may include certain informative notations after the signature block. If you are enclosing items with your letter, you may want to note that fact. You may also specify how many items you are enclosing or what the items are: *Enclosure: 2 brochures.*

Also, if you are going to send copies of the letter to other people, you may list their names in alphabetical order. The abbreviation *c,* followed by a colon, appears before the names: *c: T. K. Brandon.*

Occasionally, other notations are included, such as the initials of a typist or the electronic file for the letter.

ARRANGEMENT OF LETTERS ON THE PAGE

The customary margins for page-length letters are 1 to 1½ inches on the top and sides. Typically, the bottom margin is ½ inch deeper than the top margin. With letters that are shorter than a full page, you might position the middle line a few lines above the middle of the page.

When you write a letter that is longer than one page, use plain paper for the second and subsequent pages rather than letterhead stationery. Use the "header" feature in your word-processing program to print the name of the addressee, the page number, and the date. Here is one commonly used arrangement:

Header for top of second and subsequent pages.	Hasim K. Lederer	2	November 16, 19–—

Always start second and subsequent pages a line or two below the header, even if that leaves a lot of blank space at the bottom of the page. If only your complimentary close and signature block appear on the final page, insert returns at the top of the first page so that more material is pushed to the final page.

FORMAT FOR ENVELOPES

The letters you write at work should be sent in business-sized envelopes (9½ by 4⅛ inches). Figure A.3 shows the placement of the address and the return address.

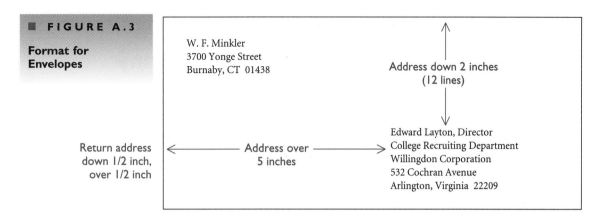

■ **FIGURE A.3**

Format for Envelopes

W. F. Minkler
3700 Yonge Street
Burnaby, CT 01438

Address down 2 inches
(12 lines)

Return address down 1/2 inch, over 1/2 inch

Address over 5 inches

Edward Layton, Director
College Recruiting Department
Willingdon Corporation
532 Cochran Avenue
Arlington, Virginia 22209

MEMO FORMAT

Along with e-mail (see Chapter 15), memos are an important medium for communications addressed to co-workers, managers, and other people inside the writer's organization. Figure A.4 shows an example.

The following sections describe the major parts of a memo:

- **Heading.** The distinguishing characteristic of the memo is its heading, which looks like a form that has slots for the writer's name, the reader's name, and the date. Addresses are not included because the message is being sent internally.

  In the past, memos were usually written on forms that had the heading already printed on them. Now, it's just as common for people to store the format in their word-processing program so they can simply summon it each time they want to draft a new memo.

- **Subject line.** As in a letter, you can use a subject line to indicate the topic of your memo. In fact, subject lines are more commonly used in memos than in letters, and many companies include a spot for a subject line on their preprinted memo forms.

- **Body.** The body of a memo closely resembles the body of a letter. The beginning is usually a brief statement of the purpose of the communication, and the middle gives the gist of the message. The ending is usually more or less perfunctory, with perhaps a brief reminder of what is to happen next.

- **Signature.** There are several common ways of signing a memo. In some organizations, writers sign only their initials, while in others they sign their full names. They may sign at the bottom of the memo or next to their name in the heading.

- **Special notations.** Memos may include the same kinds of notations that sometimes appear in letters. See page 563.

ARRANGEMENT OF MEMOS ON THE PAGE

The body of a memo begins two or three lines below the heading, regardless of the amount of blank space that this might leave on the rest of the page.

Rentscheller Company

Interoffice Memorandum

To   Dwight Levy
From   Natalie Sebastian
Date   June 16, 19—

Subject   Radon Testing

I've completed the radon testing you requested in our Worthington warehouse. Results showed slightly elevated radon concentrations.

As you know, radon is a naturally occurring radioactive gas that is present throughout the environment. It can accumulate, sometimes to dangerous concentrations, in enclosed places, such as the basements of houses and other underground structures.

The normal, or "background" level of radon in our region is 0.40 ± 0.13 pCi/L (picocuries per liter of air). On all four above-ground floors of the warehouse, radon concentrations were within this range. However, our tests showed somewhat elevated concentrations on the two underground floors. On Floor A, the readings were 0.63 pCi/L, and on Floor B, they were 0.70 pCi/L. Although these readings are well below the levels considered dangerous, it does seem advisable to reduce them, especially since radon concentrations can vary and may be higher at other times of the year.

The easiest way to reduce radon concentrations on Floors A and B is to increase the volume of fresh, outside air that circulates through these floors. We can do that by detaching the ventilation ducts for these floors from the ventilation system used for the rest of the building. We can then re-route the ducts to two new, high-capacity blowers.

I can prepare cost estimates, if you wish.

When a memo runs to more than one page, the additional pages carry the same sort of header as is used in letters. See page 566.

BOOK FORMAT

Communications in this format have many of the features of books you buy for your classes: bindings, a protective and informative cover, a table of contents, and separate chapters or sections for each major block of information.

Some communications prepared in this format are very brief—ten pages or fewer. Others are hundreds of pages long. The pages are usually written on 8½-by-11-inch paper, often on only one side of the sheet. The binding may be a set of staples or a plastic spine. Communications presented in book format often contain summaries and appendixes.

Reports and proposals prepared in this format are often called *formal* reports or *formal* proposals, and instructions presented in this format are usually called *instruction manuals.*

Overall, communications in the book format are thought of as having three parts: front matter, the body of the communication, and back matter. A communication presented in this format is often accompanied by a letter of transmittal.

FRONT MATTER

Front matter consists of the cover, title page, executive summary, table of contents, and list of figures and tables.

Cover

Figures A.5 and A.6 show typical covers, one for a report and one for an instruction manual. Covers are usually printed on heavy, flexible paper called *cover stock.*

The cover should carry the title of the communication along with other information that will help people who might want to file it for later use. For instance, you might give both your own organization's name and the name of the organization for which the communication was prepared.

You can create your cover by preparing your material with a word-processing program. If your computer's printer won't print on cover stock, you can print it on regular paper, then photocopy it onto heavier paper. Some companies have covers set in type by a printer, in which case you can tell the printer what you want.

Title Page

The title page of a formal report repeats the information on the cover. It may also include the following items:

- **Names of the authors and other contributors.**
- **Addresses of the authors and of the organization for which they work.**
- **Cross-referencing material.** In a report, you might give the name of the contract under which the work was prepared (for example, Contract Number WEI-377-B) or the titles of related reports. In a proposal, you might give the

FIGURE A.5 Cover of a Formal Report

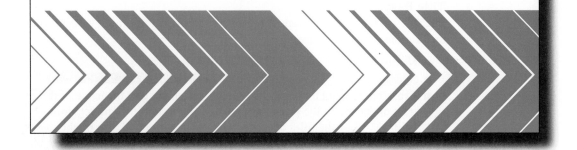

United States Environmental Protection Agency	Office of Research and Development Washington, DC 20460	EPA/600/R-93?165 September 1993

EPA

Evaluation of an Automated Sorting Process for Post-Consumer Mixed Plastic Containers

■ **FIGURE A.6 Cover of an Instruction Manual** Courtesy of Detroit Diesel Allison Division, General Motors Corporation.

DETROIT DIESEL
Series 53 Service Manual
Sections 1-3

title or number of the document issued by your readers when they asked you to submit your ideas to them. In an instruction manual, you would surely give the model number of the equipment described.

- **File number.** Some organizations assign file numbers to the reports, manuals, and other communications produced by their staffs.
- **Copyright notice.** If your employer claims a copyright on your material, include a copyright notice on the title page. Such notices contain the word *Copyright* or the symbol ©, the date of the copyright, and the name of the organization.
- **Notice of restrictions on distributing or photocopying.** If the communication contains information that your employer does not want its competitors to obtain, such a notice should appear on the title page.

Figure A.7 shows the title page of the report whose cover is shown in Figure A.5. This report was prepared by two researchers working under a contract with the U.S. Environmental Protection Agency (EPA). In addition to the information given on the cover, the title page gives the names and addresses of the authors, the name and address of the person in the EPA who was responsible for overseeing the report, and the contract number under which the authors prepared the report.

Figure A.8 shows the title page of the instruction manual whose cover is shown in Figure A.6. It adds the following information: the file number of the manual; the address, telephone, and fax numbers of the manufacturer; and copyright and trademark notices.

Executive Summary

The executive summary conveys the essence of a communication in a short space, usually one page or less. Almost all reports and proposals presented in the book format begin with a summary. For advice about writing summaries, see Guideline 7 in Chapter 8 (page 232). Figure A.9 shows the summary (here called an *abstract*) from the EPA report. This summary identifies the contents of the report for readers who want to learn quickly how the tests were run and what the test results were.

Table of Contents

A table of contents serves two purposes. Obviously, it helps readers who do not want to read the whole communication but want to find particular parts of it. In addition, it assists readers who want an overview of the communication's scope and contents before they begin reading it in its entirety.

Make your table of contents by creating an outline of your section or chapter titles and your headings. However, if your table of contents runs more than a page or two, you may want to leave out the lowest levels of headings. Just make sure your table of contents reflects the organization of the report and enables your readers to find the specific pieces of information they seek. Usually, this will require you to include at least two heading levels.

Figure A.10 shows the table of contents from the report whose cover is shown in Figure A.5. Notice how the writers use extra white space to set off the front matter from the body of the report and to set off other major parts. You will find other tables of contents in Figures 7.11 and 7.13 (pages 183 and 186).

■ FIGURE A.7 Title Page of the Report Whose Cover Is Shown in Figure A.5

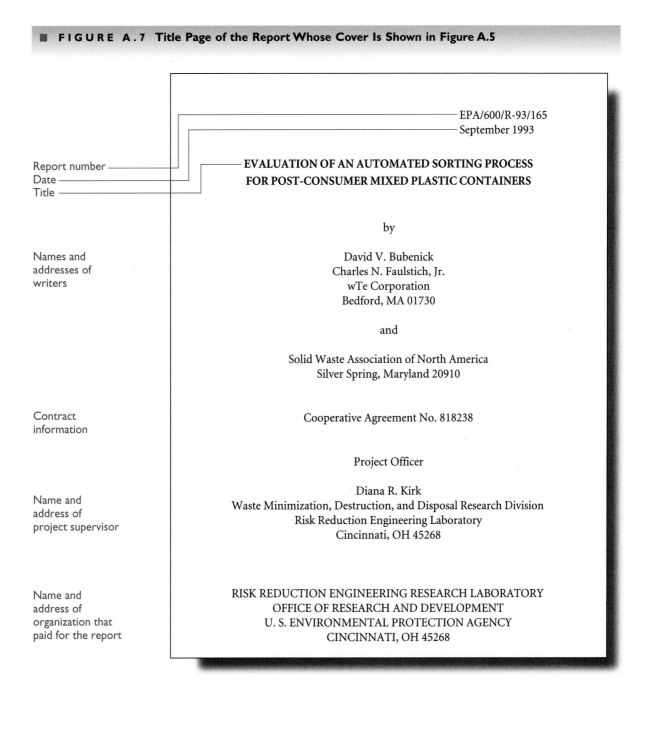

Report number

Date

Title

EPA/600/R-93/165
September 1993

**EVALUATION OF AN AUTOMATED SORTING PROCESS
FOR POST-CONSUMER MIXED PLASTIC CONTAINERS**

by

Names and
addresses of
writers

David V. Bubenick
Charles N. Faulstich, Jr.
wTe Corporation
Bedford, MA 01730

and

Solid Waste Association of North America
Silver Spring, Maryland 20910

Contract
information

Cooperative Agreement No. 818238

Project Officer

Name and
address of
project supervisor

Diana R. Kirk
Waste Minimization, Destruction, and Disposal Research Division
Risk Reduction Engineering Laboratory
Cincinnati, OH 45268

Name and
address of
organization that
paid for the report

RISK REDUCTION ENGINEERING RESEARCH LABORATORY
OFFICE OF RESEARCH AND DEVELOPMENT
U. S. ENVIRONMENTAL PROTECTION AGENCY
CINCINNATI, OH 45268

■ FIGURE A.8 Title Page of the Instruction Manual Whose Cover Is Shown in Figure A.6

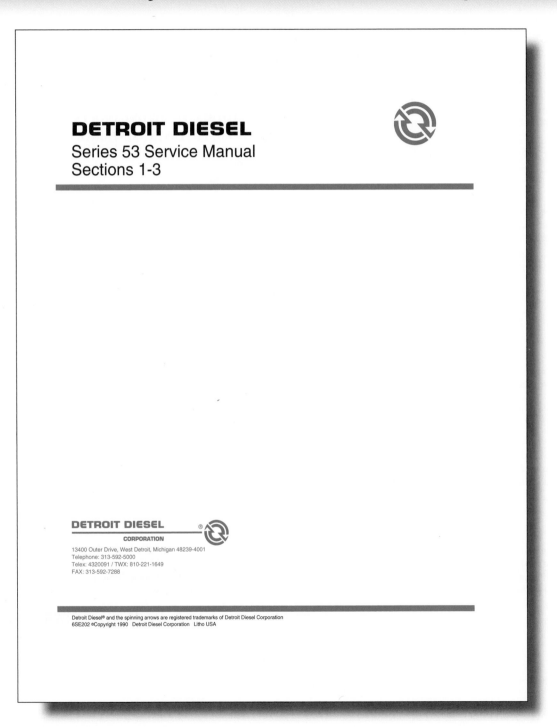

DETROIT DIESEL
Series 53 Service Manual
Sections 1-3

DETROIT DIESEL
CORPORATION

13400 Outer Drive, West Detroit, Michigan 48239-4001
Telephone: 313-592-5000
Telex: 4320091 / TWX: 810-221-1649
FAX: 313-592-7288

Detroit Diesel® and the spinning arrows are registered trademarks of Detroit Diesel Corporation
6SE202 ©Copyright 1990 Detroit Diesel Corporation Litho USA

■ **FIGURE A.9**

Summary from the Report Whose Cover Is Shown in Figure A.5

Objectives

Method

Results

Conclusions

Contract information (common in abstracts for reports sponsored by government agencies)

ABSTRACT

This project evaluates a proof-of-concept, pilot-scale, automated sorting system for mixed post-consumer plastic containers developed by the Rutgers University Center for Plastics Recycling Research (CPRR). The study evaluates the system's ability to identify and separately recover five types of plastic containers representative of those found in plastics recycling programs. It also addresses the system's potential for full-scale commercial application.

Three series of tests were performed: single composition, short-term tests; mixed composition, short-term tests; and mixed composition, extended tests. A total of 82 test runs were performed during which 66,632 bottles were processed.

The five bottle types considered were natural HDPE, PVC, clear PET, green PET, and opaque HDPE. The containers recovered at each product collection station were counted and the results compared to pre-established recovery goals. Bottle counts were then converted to weight recoveries using average bottle weights. The resulting product purity/contamination weight percents were compared to allowable product contamination limits representative of industry practice. From a detailed videotape analysis of a representative test, an exact profile of bottle feed timing and sequence was reconstructed. This analysis provided valuable insight into system feed and transport dynamic as well as an understanding of how product contamination occurs.

The system produced statistically reproducible results and proved to be mechanically reliable. However, it failed to achieve all of the commercial-level container recovery and product contamination limit goals. It was concluded that bottle singulation and spacing greatly influenced the effectiveness of the identification/separation equipment.

This work was submitted by wTe Corporation in fulfillment of Contract No. 850-1291-4. The contract was administered by the solid Waste Association of North America and sponsored by the U.S. Environmental Protection Agency. This report covers from May, 1992 to July, 1993.

■ **FIGURE A.10**

Table of Contents of the Report Whose Cover Is Shown in Figure A.5

Front matter ───

Body of report, organized according to the superstructure for empirical research reports (see page 460).

Note that the writers varied the superstructure to put their conclusions and recommendations second, to meet the needs of readers who want to focus on practical outcomes of the research.

Supplementary elements

CONTENTS

Preface		iii
Abstract		iv
List of Figures		vi
List of Tables		vii
Acknowledgments		viii
1.	Introduction	
	Background	1
	Project overview	1
	Technology status	2
2.	Conclusion and Recommendations	
	Conclusions	4
	Recommendations	4
3.	System Description	5
4.	Testing Methodology	
	Project objectives	14
	Quality assurance objectives	15
	Feed material	15
	Product contamination	17
	Tests performed	18
	Data reduction, calculation, and validations methods	22
5.	Test Results	
	Single-composition tests	29
	Mixed-composition, short-term tests	32
	Mixed-composition, extended (2,000 bottles) tests	38
6.	Commercial Potential	
	Pilot system design comments and suggestions	49
	Equipment cost estimate	52
	References	55
	Appendixes	
	A. Test Data as Collected for Extended (2,000 Bottles) Tests	
	B. Extended Test Results, Outliers Not Included	63
	Glossary of Terms	74

List of Figures and Tables

To help your readers find a particular table, drawing, or other graphic aid in your communication, include in the front matter a list of figures and tables. Such lists appear after the table of contents. Figure A.11 shows the list of figures from the EPA report whose cover is shown in Figure A.5. That report also contains a list of tables, with the same format.

BODY

The body is made up of the chapters or sections that constitute the bulk of your communication.

For advice on how to organize the body, see Chapter 4, "Planning to Meet Your Readers' Informational Needs," and Chapter 5, "Planning Your Persuasive Strategies." You might also refer to the conventional superstructures described in Chapters 18 through 20. Or you might devise your own structure.

Writing the Introduction

All communications written in the book format have an introduction. Various titles are used: "Introduction," "Problem," "Need," "Background," and so on. The contents of introductions vary widely, depending on the writer's purpose and readers. For guidelines on writing introductions, see Chapter 8 on "Beginning a Communication." For suggestions about the contents of introductions for specific kinds of communications, see Chapters 18 through 20 on conventional superstructures.

Don't hesitate to repeat in your introduction material from your summary. Although most readers will read your summary immediately before reading your introduction, the custom is to write the introduction as if the readers were beginning there—even if the first sentence of the summary and the first sentence of the introduction are exactly the same.

Writing the Conclusion

Many communications, but not all, end with a conclusion. For advice about how to conclude a communication in the book format, see Chapter 9 on "Ending a Communication."

Writing the Chapters

In the book format, begin each chapter on a new page and give it its own number. Usually, arabic numerals (1, 2, . . .) are used for chapter numbers, although roman numerals are sometimes used. Figure A.12 shows the first page of a chapter in the EPA report, and Figure A.13 shows the first page from a chapter in the instruction manual whose cover is shown in Figure A.6. The chapters in this manual (called *sections*) are so long that each has its own table of contents.

Your chapters may vary considerably in length. For instance, in the table of contents shown in Figure A.10, the "Introduction" is three pages long, the chapter on "Testing Methodology" is fifteen pages long, and the chapter on "Test Results" is twenty pages long.

Don't worry if your chapters vary in length—even if one or more of them is less than a page long. Remember that you break your communications into chapters in

■ FIGURE A.11

List of Figures from
the Report Whose
Cover Is Shown in
Figure A.5

List of Figures

Number		Page
1	Process flow diagram	7
2	Equipment layout	8
3	Feed bin, infeed conveyor, and oversize discharge chute	9
4	Infeed arrangement viewed from C4/C5 transition	9
5	Dual discharge chutes and underside of infeed conveyor	10
6	Conveyors C4b, C4c, C5, and C6	10
7	Green PET, clear PET, and PVC identification/separation stations	11
8	PVC and clear PET product chutes, conveyor C7 in foreground	11

■ FIGURE A.12

First Page of a
Chapter in the
Report Whose Cover
Is Shown in Figure
A.5

Section 1

INTRODUCTION

BACKGROUND

The significant difference in plastic resin properties require that post-consumer plastic containers be separated by resin type before they can be processed into a form that can be used as a substitute for virgin resin. Until recently, manual sorting has been the only method commercially available for accomplishing this separation. Manual sorting has been found to be less than ideal, however, owing to high labor and training expenses and its susceptibility to error. While some identification/separation errors involving polyethylene terphthalate (PET) and high density polythylene (HDPE) can be tolerated, very few such errors involving polyvinyl chloride (PVC) can be tolerated due to the physical/chemical incompatibility of PVC with PET. Compounding the manual separation problem is the visual similarity of some PVC and PET bottles.

Automated sorting systems are the latest technological development for the recycling of post-consumer plastic containers. These systems hold the promise of fast, cost-effective and accurate resin separation from a mixed plastic container feed stream. The pilot automated sortation system for mixed post-consumer plastic containers developed by the Rutgers University Center for Plastics Recycling Research (CPRR) is one of the first such systems developed during the past few years, and is believed to be the first system to be rigorously tested by an independent party.

The Rutgers system integrates equipment that separates whole, uncrushed, mixed rigid plastic containers into the five most common household plastic bottle types: PVC, clear PET, green PET, natural HDPE, and opaque HDPE. A bottle presentation subsystem and an identification/separation subsystem comprise the overall system. The bottle presentation subsystem incorporates material-handling equipment for the purpose of presenting the bottles to the identification/separation subsystem in an orderly and uniform manner, with each container separate and distinct from its predecessor and from its follower. The identification/separation subsystem consists of equipment for selectively identifying and removing bottles from the feed stream.

The system uses various techniques to perform the identification and separation of plastic containers. First, oversize containers consisting predominantly of natural HDPE milk and water jugs are removed by mechanical means. X-ray fluorescent is then used to identify the chlorine atom-containing bottles, namely PVC and air jets force the detached containers away from the flow stream. Optical sensors then detect the transparent clear and green PET bottles which are also removed from the flow stream by air jets. The remaining containers consist primarily of opaque HDPE bottles which are collected at the end of the presentation subsystem.

■ FIGURE A.13

First Page of a
Chapter in the
Instruction Manual
Whose Cover Is
Shown in Figure A.6

SECTION 2

FUEL SYSTEM AND GOVERNORS

CONTENTS

Fuel System. 2
Fuel Injector (Crown Valve) 2.1
Fuel Injector (Needle Valve) 2.1.1
Fuel Injector Tube. 2.1.4
Fuel Pump 2.2
Fuel Pump Drive 2.2.1
Fuel Strainer and Fuel Filter. 2.3
Fuel Cooler. 2.5.1
Mechanical Governors 2.7
Limiting Speed Mechanical Governor (In-Line Engine) 2.7.1
Limiting Speed Mechanical Governor (6V Engine) 2.7.1.1
Limiting Speed Mechanical Governor (8V Engine) 2.7.1.2
Limiting Speed Mechanical Governor (Variable Low-Speed) 2.7.1.3
Limiting Speed Mechanical Governor (Fast Idle Cylinder) 2.7.1.4
Limiting Speed Mechanical Governor (Variable High-Speed) 2.7.1.5
Variable Speed Mechanical Governor (6V Engine) 2.7.2.1
Variable Speed Mechanical Governor (Enclosed Linkage) (In-Line Engine). 2.7.2.2
Variable Speed Mechanical Governor (Open Linkage Engine) (In-Line). 2.7.2.4
Variable Speed Mechanical Governor (8V Engine) 2.7.2.5
Constant Speed Mechanical Governor (In-line Engine) 2.7.3

Hydraulic Governors 2.8
SG Hydraulic Governor 2.8.1
Hydraulic Governor Drive. 2.8.3
Hydraulic Governor Synchronizing Motor. 2.8.4

Fuel Injector Control Tube 2.9
Shop Notes—Troubleshooting Specifications—Service Tools 2.0

order to help your readers find information and understand the structure of your communication. The chapters should reflect the logic of the communication, even if this means that they do not divide it into approximately equal parts.

BACK MATTER

Almost every communication written in the book format contains all the elements you have read about so far—cover, title page, summary, table of contents, list of figures and tables, and body. The major exceptions are that shorter communications often omit the list of figures and tables and that instruction manuals do not include summaries.

Many communications in book format also contain one or more of the following supplementary elements: appendixes; list of references, endnotes, or bibliography; glossary or list of symbols; and index.

Appendixes

Appendixes can help you overcome one of the more common problems that vex people who are writing long communications. Sometimes you may find that you want to make certain information available to your readers but feel that it would be cumbersome to include it in the body of your communication. The following paragraphs describe three typical situations:

1. **When you must include detailed information that would interfere with your general message.** Imagine that you are preparing a report on a research project and need to include a two-page account of the calculations you used to analyze your data. Some of your readers might want to check your calculations, and others might want to use them in another experiment. However, you realize that your readers will have trouble following the thread of your research strategy if they are diverted by the details of your calculations. To solve this problem, present the calculations in an appendix.

   Other kinds of detailed information that are often placed in appendixes include the following:

   - Detailed data obtained in a research study
   - Detailed drawings and illustrations
   - Lengthy tables of values that a reader would refer to while operating certain equipment or performing some procedure
   - Detailed descriptions of the professional qualifications of the people who will work on a proposed project

2. **When your readers are unlikely to read the body of an overly long communication.** Sometimes you may find yourself addressing readers who will not read the body of a communication if it is too long. In fact, some readers may even set a limit to the length of what they will read. In such situations, you can relegate all secondary information to appendixes. You might end up with a report that has a one-page summary, a fifteen-page body, and sixty (or more) pages of appendixes. You might even print the appendixes on paper of a different color, so your readers will know at a glance how long the body of the communication is.

3. **When you write a communication that must serve the diverse needs of different readers.** For instance, when you are writing a proposal that will be read by both a decision-maker and a technical adviser, some information may be irrelevant to the decision-maker but essential to the technical adviser. First decide who your primary reader is. Then place material directed mainly to that reader in the body, and place material directed to other readers in appendixes.

Some writers include appendixes to present all kinds of material that *no* reader is likely to need. Avoid using appendixes for material that doesn't belong *anywhere* in your communication.

If you decide to include appendixes, be sure to tell your readers where they are. List them in your table of contents (see Figure A.10). Give each appendix an informative title that indicates clearly what it contains. Also, mention each appendix in the body of your report at the point where your readers might want to refer to it:

> Printouts from the electrocardiogram appear in Appendix II.
>
> Appendix A contains the names and addresses of companies in our area that provide the type of service contract that we recommend.

In the book format, each appendix begins on its own page. Arrange and label the appendixes in the same order in which they are mentioned in the body of the communication. If you have only one appendix, label it simply "Appendix." If you have more than one, you may use roman numerals, arabic numerals, or capital letters to label them:

> Appendix I, Appendix II . . .
> Appendix 1, Appendix 2 . . .
> Appendix A, Appendix B . . .

List of References, Endnotes, or Bibliography

Sometimes you may want to direct your readers' attention to other sources of information on your subject. You may want to acknowledge the sources of the information you have included or help your readers learn more about your topic. In letters and memos, such references are often worked into the body of the communication. In the book format, however, they are often gathered in a list of references, an endnotes section, or a bibliography.

In the book format, reference lists and bibliographies usually follow the body of the communication or appear immediately after the appendixes. Sometimes, however, a separate list or bibliography appears at the end of each chapter.

To learn what sources to mention and how to construct reference lists, endnotes, and bibliographies, see Appendix B.

Glossary or List of Symbols

When you are writing at work you will sometimes use special terms or symbols that may not be familiar to some of your readers. You may explain such terms and symbols either in the body of your communication or in a separate glossary or list of symbols.

If you are using a special term or symbol only once or in only one small segment of your communication, your readers will probably have no use for a glossary or a list of symbols. You can simply include your explanation in the text.

However, if you are going to use a term or a symbol throughout a long communication, you will help your readers by including a glossary or a list of symbols. Imagine that you are writing an instruction manual in which special terms appear on pages 3, 39, and 72, and in twelve other places. You might define each term the first time that it appears, in the hope that your readers will remember the definition when they encounter it again. They may not remember it thirty or forty pages later, however. Or they may go directly to one of the other pages without ever reading page 3 because the particular information they want is located elsewhere in your manual.

In either case, your readers will have to scan the pages of your text to find the definition. By defining each term in a glossary, you provide the definition in a place that is easy to find.

Glossaries and lists of symbols are also useful in communications in which some of your readers need explanations and some don't.

Figure A.14 shows the first page of the glossary from the EPA report previously mentioned. The author has used boldface for the terms so that readers can find them easily. Alternatively, you might use underlining or put the terms in one column and the definitions in another.

By custom, glossaries and lists of symbols may be placed either at the beginning of a communication (for instance, directly before the introduction) or at the end. In either case, be sure to include them in your table of contents.

Index

An index provides readers with a quick route to specific pieces of information. Here is a procedure for determining what items to include in your index:

1. **Identify all the specific kinds of information your readers might seek when using your communication as a reference document.**
2. **List the words your readers might use while searching for those kinds of information.** Because readers might use any of a variety of words to search for particular information, include *all* the most likely terms with cross-references to the main entry. Be sure to include words readers might use even if you have not used them in your text. Imagine that you are writing a marketing brochure for a chain of garden shops. If you have a section on trees and expect that some readers may look under the word *Evergreen* in the index for information that you've indexed under *Conifers,* include an entry for *Evergreen* that directs them to the *Conifer* entry.

   Some word-processing programs can help you create an index by generating a list of the words used in your communication. From this list, you can index those that will help your readers find the information they desire.
3. **Where possible, use headwords to gather related terms.** For example, use *Conifers* as a headword for *Fir, Cedar, Redwood,* and so on. If an entry is under a headword where some readers may not think to look for it, be sure to use cross-references.

■ FIGURE A.14

First Page of the
Glossary of the
Report Whose Cover
Is Shown in Figure
A.5

GLOSSARY OF TERMS

Availability — The probability that equipment will be capable of performing its specified function when called upon at any random point in time. Calculated as the ratio of run time to the sum of run time and downtime.

Bottle — A single plastic container, also referred to as a container.

Cascade — To sequentially increase the belt speed in a series of conveyors.

Contamination — Bottles improperly removed at a station.

Effective Bottle Feed Rate — The average rate at which a specific type of bottle is fed during a mixed composition test. Calculated as the total number of bottles of a specific type fed divided by the total run time for a specific test.

Extended Test — A test series consisting of many replicates at pre-selected conditions.

Fed — Refers to bottles removed from the feed bin by conveyor C2 and either removed by the oversize station, spilled, or delivered to conveyor C3.

Confidence Interval — The range in which an estimated population statistic is expected to fall with a specified degree of confidence based on sample statistics. Confidence intervals can be calculated for statistics such as the population mean and standard deviation. The confidence interval for the mean is calculated using the Student's t Distribution, and the confidence interval for the standard deviation is calculated using the Chi-Square Distribution. The 95 percent confidence interval is a range around the statistics such that 2.5 percent of the area under the distribution curve falls in each "tail" of the distribution. For example, if the sample mean is 90 and the 95 percent confidence interval is calculated to be the mean plus or minus 2, one would be 95 percent confident that the population mean would be within the range 88 to 92.

Confidence Limit — The value below and above the sample statistics defining the limits of the confidence interval.

Maintainability — A measure of the ease with which an equipment item or system can be maintained in proper running condition. Measured by parameters such as the Preventive Maintenance Ratio, the Corrective Maintenance Ratio, the Maintainability Index, the Mean Time to Repair, and the Mean Time Between Maintenance Actions.

Mistake — This is a bottle erroneously removed at a station.

74

Figure A.15 shows the first page of the index of the instruction manual whose cover is shown in Figure A.6.

PRINTING

Communications written in the book format may be single-spaced or double-spaced. If you single-space, leave a blank line between paragraphs.

PAGE NUMBERING

You can number the pages in the body of your communication in either of two ways. First, you can give the first page of your introduction the number *1* and then number all the following pages in sequence.

Or you can begin a new sequence on the first page of each chapter. To do this, give each page a number that has two parts. The first part tells the chapter number, and the second part tells the number of the page within the chapter. Thus, *page 1–2* is the second page of Chapter 1, and *page 3–4* is the fourth page of Chapter 3.

In the book format, pages that appear before the first page of the body either are given no numbers or are numbered in lowercase roman numerals (*i, ii, iii,* and so on). Page numbering in the appendixes and other back matter follows the system used in the body.

LETTER OF TRANSMITTAL

When you prepare communications in the book format, you will often send them (rather than hand them) to your readers. In such cases, you will want to accompany them with a letter (or memo) of transmittal.

Although the exact contents of a letter of transmittal depend on your purpose and situation, a typical one would contain some of the following elements:

- **Introduction.** In the introduction, you would mention the accompanying communication and perhaps explain or remind your readers of its topic. Here is an example written to a client:

  > In response to your recent request for proposals, BioLabs is pleased to submit the enclosed plan for continuously monitoring effluent from your Eaton plant for various pollutants, including heavy metals.

- **Body.** In the body of your letter, you might describe the purpose, contents, or special features of the communication. For instance, the writers of a research report who want their readers to note the most important consequences of their findings might briefly explain their findings and list their recommendations. (In this case, the letter would repeat some of the information contained in the summary; such repetition is common in letters of transmittal.)

- **Closing.** Transmittal letters commonly end with a short paragraph (often one sentence) that states the writer's willingness to work further with the reader or promises to answer any questions the reader may have.

Figure A.16 shows a letter of transmittal prepared in the workplace; Figure A.17 shows one prepared by a student.

DETROIT DIESEL 53

ALPHABETICAL INDEX

<table>
<tr><td>Subject</td><td>Section</td></tr>
</table>

A

Accessory drive	.1.7.7
Accumulator—Hydrostarter	.12.6.1
Air box drains	.1.1.2
Air cleaner	.3.1
Air compressor	.12.4
Air inlet restriction	.15.2
Air intake system	.3
Air shutdown housing	.3.3
Air Silencer	.3.2
Alarm system	.7.4.2
Alternator—battery-charging	.7.1

B

Balance shaft	.1.7.2
Balance weights—front	.1.7
Battery—storage	.7.2
Bearings:	
Camshaft and balance shaft	.1.7.2
Clutch pilot	.1.4.1
Connecting rod	.1.6.2
Connecting rod (clearance)	.1.0
Crankshaft main	.1.3.4
Crankshaft main (clearance)	.1.0
Crankshaft outboard	.1.3.5.1
Fan hub	.5.4
Idle gear—engine	.1.7.4
Belt adjustment—fan	.15.1
Bilge pump	.12.2
Block—cylinder	.1.1
Blower (In-line and 6V)	.3.4
Blower (8V)	.3.4.1
Blower drive gear	.1.7.6
Blower drive shaft	.1.7.6
Blower end plates	.3.0
Bluing injector components	.2.0
Breather—crankcase	.4.8
By-pass valve—oil filter	.4.2

C

Cam followers	.1.2.1
Camshaft	.1.7.2
Camshaft and balance shaft gears	.1.7.3
Cap—coolant pressure control	.5.3.1
Cautions	.*
Charging pump—Hydrostarter	.12.6.1

Charts:

Engine coolants	.13.3
Engine operating conditions	.13.2
Injector timing gage	.14.2
Lubrication	.15.1
Model description	.*
Preventive maintenance	.15.1
Cleaner—air	.3.1
Clearance—exhaust valve	.14.1
Clutch pilot bearing	.1.4.1
Cold weather operation—Hydrostarter	.12.6.1
Cold weather starting	.12.6
Compression pressure	.15.2
Compressor—air	.12.4
Connecting rod	.1.6.1
Connecting rod bearings	.1.6.2
Converter—Torqmatic	.8
Coolant—engine	.13.3
Coolant—filter	.5.7
Cooler—fuel	.2.5.1
Cooler—oil (engine)	.4.4
Cooling system	.5
Coupling—drive shaft	.1.4.2
Cover—engine front (lower)	.1.3.5
Cover—engine front (upper)	.1.7.8
Cover—valve rocker	.1.2.4
Crankshaft	.1.3
Crankshaft oil seals	.1.3.2
Crankshaft pulley	.1.3.7
Crankshaft timing gear	.1.7.5
Crankshaft vibration damper	.1.3.6
Cross section view of engines	.*
Cylinder block	.1.1
Cylinder head	.1.2
Cylinder liner	.1.9.3
Cylinder—misfiring	.15.2

D

Damper—vibration	.1.3.6
Description—general	.*
Diesel principle	.*
Dipstick—oil level	.4.6
Drains—air box	.1.1.2
Drive—accessory	.1.7.7
Drive—fuel pump	.2.2.1
Drive—hydraulic governor	.2.8.3
Drive—blower	.3.4
Dynamometer test	.13.2.1

*General Information and Cautions Section

May, 1990   **Page 1**

■ FIGURE A.16

Letter of Transmittal Written at Work

ELECTRONICS CORPORATION OF AMERICA
MEMORANDUM

To   Myron Bronski, Vice-President, Research
           MCB
From   Margaret C. Barnett, Satellite Products Laboratory

Date   September 30, 19 —

Re   REPORT ON TRUCK-TO-SATELLITE TEST

On behalf of the entire research team. I am pleased to submit the attached copy of the operational test of our truck-to-satellite communication system.

The test shows that our system works fine. More than 91% of our data transmissions were successful, and more than 91% of our voice transmissions were of commercial quality. The test helped us identify some sources of bad transmissions, including primarily movement of a truck outside the "footprint" of the satellite's strongest broadcast and the presence of objects (such as trees) in the direct line between a truck and the satellite.

The research team believes that our next steps should be to develop a new antenna for use on the trucks and to develop a configuration of satellites that will place them at least 25° above the horizon for trucks anywhere in our coverage area.

We're ready to begin work on these tasks as soon as we get the okay to do so. Let me know if you have any questions.

Encl: Report (2 copies)

■ **FIGURE A.17**

Letter of Transmittal Written by a Student

Tricia identifies the enclosed proposal.

She summarizes its major points.

Complimentary close.

Box 114, Bishop Hall
Miami University
Oxford, Ohio 45056
December 10, 19—

Professor Thomas B. Weissman
Department of English
Miami University
Oxford, Ohio 45056

Dear Professor Weissman:

I am enclosing my final project for your technical writing course, a proposal for a crime prevention program directed to elderly citizens of Oxford. As you recall, I have developed this proposal at the request of the City Manager, Tom Dority.

While working on this project, I learned that persons sixty-five and older comprise 18 percent of the nonstudent population of Oxford. Experience nationwide suggests that these individuals are particularly vulnerable to crime but that much of that crime can be prevented through simple precautions. I propose that the City of Oxford help protect its elderly by participating in two nationwide programs, Whistle Alert and Operation Safe Return, and that the city offer a series of nine presentations on crime prevention for the elderly. The entire effort could be supported by donated supplies and services, with no cost to the City of Oxford.

Throughout my work on this project, I received much help from the Oxford Police Department's crime prevention officer, Dwight Johnson. I have also been assisted by the staff at the Oxford Senior Citizens Center.

I believe there is a reasonable chance that the city will accept my plan. Officer Johnson has already said he likes it.

Thank you very much for you help and encouragement.

Sincerely,

Tricia Daniels

Tricia Daniels

Enclosure: Final Project

Documenting Your Sources

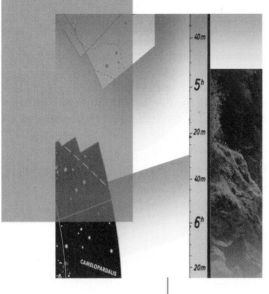

CONTENTS

Choosing a Format for Documentation

Deciding Where to Place In-Text Citations

Using the APA Documentation Style

Using the MLA Documentation Style

In many of the communications you will write at work, you will want to tell your readers about other sources of information concerning your subject. You may have any of the following reasons for wanting to do so:

- **To acknowledge the people and sources that have provided you with ideas and information.** For a discussion of this reason for citing your sources, see "Focus on Ethics" on page 133.
- **To help your readers find additional information about something you have discussed.**
- **To persuade your readers to pay serious attention to a particular idea.** By showing that an idea was expressed by a respected person or in a respected publication, you are arguing that the idea merits acceptance.
- **To explain how your research contributes to the development of new knowledge in your field.** In research proposals and in research reports published in professional journals, writers often include a literature survey to demonstrate how their own research advances knowledge. For more information on using references in this way, see the discussion of literature surveys in the discussion of empirical research reports, page 459.

CHOOSING A FORMAT FOR DOCUMENTATION

There are numerous formats for documentation, some very distinct from one another and some differing only in small details. No one format is the best for all situations. To document correctly, you must use the particular format that is required or most appropriate for the particular circumstances in which you are writing. Most organizations specify the documentation style they want their employees to use. Also, when writing to people in another organization, you may find that they have their own preferences or requirements, which you should follow.

To describe the documentation format they prefer, many organizations issue style guides that detail their rules and provide sample citations. Other organizations ask writers to follow a style guide published by a professional organization such as the American Psychological Association (APA) or the Modern Language Association (MLA). The rest of this appendix explains the APA and MLA styles. Most other documentation styles resemble one of these two.

DECIDING WHERE TO PLACE IN-TEXT CITATIONS

In both styles, you cite a source by putting the name of the author at the appropriate place in the body of your communication (the APA style includes the year of publication also). This citation refers your readers to the full bibliographic information that you provide in an alphabetical list of sources at the end of your communication. Between the two styles there are many differences in the way you write the in-text citations and the entries in the reference list. However, the rules for placing the in-text citations are the same for both.

Your primary objective when placing citations in your communications is to make clear to your readers what part of your text each citation is referring to. This is easy with citations that pertain to a single fact, sentence, or quotation. You simply place your citation immediately after the appropriate material (note that the APA style for formatting these citations is used in the following examples):

> According to F. C. Orley (1998, p. 37), "We cannot tell how to interpret these data without conducting further tests."

> Researchers have shown that a person's self-esteem is based upon performance (Dore, 1994), age (Latice, 1998), and weight (Swallen & Ditka, 1995).

If your citation refers to material that appears in several sentences, place the citations in a topic sentence that introduces the material. Your readers will then understand that the citation covers all the material that relates to that topic sentence. As a further aid to your readers, you may use the author's name (or a pronoun) in successive sentences:

> A much different account of the origin of oil in the earth's crust has been advanced by Thomas Gold (1983). He argues that . . . To critics of his views, Gold responds . . .

USING THE APA DOCUMENTATION STYLE

The following sections explain how to write in-text citations and the entries in a reference list using the APA style.

WRITING APA IN-TEXT CITATIONS

To write an APA in-text citation, enclose the author's last name and the year of publication in parentheses *inside* your normal sentence punctuation. Place a comma between the author's name and the date. Use *p.* if you are citing a specific page, and use *pp.* if citing more than one page.

> The first crab caught in the trap attracts others to it (Tanner, 1998, pp. 33–34).

If you incorporate the author's name in the sentence itself, give only the year and pages (if any) in parentheses:

> According to Tanner (1998, pp. 33–34), the first crab caught in the trap attracts others to it.

Here are some other types of citations:

(Hoeflin & Bolsen, 1997)	Two authors
(Wilton, Nelson, & Dutta, 1932)	First citation for three, four, or five authors
(Wilton et al., 1932)	Second and subsequent citations for three to five authors

(Norton et al., 1994)	First and subsequent citation for six or more authors (*et al.* is an abbreviation for the Latin phrase *et alii*, which means "and others")
(Angstrom, 1998, p. 34)	Reference to a particular page
(U.S. Department of Energy, 1997)	Government or corporate author
("Geologists discover," 1998)	No author listed (use the first few words of the title). In the example, the words from the title are in quotation marks because the citation is to an article; if it were to a book, the words would be in italics with no quotation marks.
(Justin, 1998; Skol, 1972; Weiss, 1996)	Two or more sources cited together (arrange them in alphabetical order)

In some communications, you may cite two or more sources by the same author. If they were published in *different* years, your readers will have no trouble telling which work you are referring to. If they were published in the *same* year, you can distinguish between them by placing lowercase letters after the publication dates in your citations and in your reference list:

(Burkehardt, 1998a)
(Burkehardt, 1998b)

WRITING AN APA REFERENCE LIST

Illustrated and explained below are APA reference list entries for the most common types of print, electronic, and other sources. To create entries that are not listed here, follow the logic of these examples or else consult the *Publication Manual of the American Psychological Association*, available in the reference section of most libraries. Figure B.1 (page 593) shows how to arrange these entries in your reference list.

Print Sources

1. Book, One Author—APA

Jacobs, J. R. (1998). *The scientific revolution: Aspirations and achievements, 1500–1700*. Atlantic Highlands, NJ: Humanities Press.

- Give the author's last name followed by a comma and initials (not full first or middle names).
- Place the copyright date in parentheses, followed by a period.
- Italicize or underline the title, and capitalize only the first word of the title, the first word of the subtitle (if any), and proper nouns.
- Follow the city of publication with a comma and the two-letter postal abbreviation for the state (however, do not give the state for cities such as New York that are well known for publishing).
- Indent the second and subsequent lines.

■ **FIGURE B.1**

APA Reference List

Second and subsequent lines are indented.

For the second and subsequent items by the same person, the author's name is repeated.

Items by corporate and government groups are alphabetized by the groups' names (spelled out).

Items without authors are alphabetized by the title.

References

Abernethy, B., Kippers, V., Mackinnon, L. T., Neal, R. J., & Hanrahan, S. (1997). *The biophysical foundations of human movement.* Champaign, IL: Human Kinetics.

Gould, S. J. (1995). *Dinosaur in a haystack: Reflections in natural history.* New York: Norton.

Gould, S. J. (1989). *Wonderful life: The Burgess Shale and nature of history.* New York: Harmony.

International Business Machines. (1998, March). *IBM web design guidelines.* [On-line]. Available: http://www.ibm.com/IBM/HCI/guidelines/web/web_design.html

McLaurin, J., & Chakrabartty, A. (1997). Characterization of the interactions of Alzheimer β-amyloid peptides with phospholipid membranes. *European Journal of Biochemistry, 245,* 355–363.

Rethinking traditional design. (1997). *Manufacturing Engineering, 118*(2), 50.

2. Book, Two or More Authors—APA

Talbert, S. H., & Betzalel, A. (1996). *Elementary mechanics of plastic flow in metal forming.* New York: Wiley.

Abernethy, B., Kippers, V., Mackinnon, L. T., Neal, R. J., & Hanrahan, S. (1997). *The biophysical foundations of human movement.* Champaign, IL: Human Kinetics.

3. Anthology or Essay Collection—APA

Lutz, P. L., & Musick, J. A. (Eds.). (1997). *The biology of sea turtles.* Boca Raton, FL: CRC Press.

■ If there is only one editor, use this abbreviation: (Ed.).

4. Second or Subsequent Edition—APA

Olin, H. B., Schmidt, J. J., & Lewis, W. H. (1995). *Construction: Principles, materials and methods* (6th ed.). New York: Van Nostrand Reinhold.

5. Government Report—APA

Frankforter, J. D., & Emmons, P. J. (1997). *Potential effects of large floods on the transport of atrazine into the alluvial aquifer adjacent to the Lower Platte River, Nebraska* (U.S. Geological Survey Water-Resources Investigation Report 96–4272). Denver, CO: U.S. Geological Survey.

- If the report doesn't list an author, use the name of the agency that published it as the author. If it is a United States government agency, use the abbreviation "U.S." Example: "U.S. Geological Survey."
- If the report has an identifying number, place it immediately after the title.

6. Corporate Report—APA

Daimler-Benz AG. (1997). *Environmental report 1997.* Stuttgart, Germany: Author.

- List the names of the individual authors rather than the corporation if the names are given on the title page.
- If the names of the individual authors aren't given on the title page, list the corporation as the author. (In the example, "Daimler-Benz AG" is the name of a company.)
- When the author and publisher are the same, use the word *Author* as the name of the publisher.

7. Essay in a Book—APA

Sullivan, P. (1996). Ethics in the computer age. In J. M. Kizza (Ed.), *Social and ethical effects of the computer revolution* (pp. 288–297). Jefferson, NC: McFarland.

8. Paper in a Proceedings—APA

Youra, S. (1996). Placing writing in engineering education. In R. Pose & A. Jawary (Eds.), *Proceedings of the Australian Communication Conference* (pp. 59–76). Melbourne, Australia: Monash University.

9. Encyclopedia Article—APA

Rich, E. (1996). Artificial intelligence. In *Encyclopedia Americana* (Vol. 2, pp. 407–412). Danbury, CT: Grolier.

10. Pamphlet or Brochure—APA

Ohio Department of Natural Resources. (1996). *Ring-necked pheasant management in Ohio.* [Pamphlet]. Columbus, OH: Author.

- When the author and publisher are the same, use the word *Author* as the name of the publisher.

11. Article in Journal That Numbers Its Pages Continuously through Each Volume—APA

McLaurin, J., & Chakrabartty, A. (1997). Characterization of the interactions of Alzheimer β-amyloid peptides with phospholipid membranes. *European Journal of Biochemistry, 245,* 355–363.

- After the journal's name, add a comma and the volume number (in italics).
- The word *Alzheimer* is capitalized because it is a proper name.

12. Article in Journal That Numbers Its Pages Separately for Each Issue—APA

Bradley, J., & Soulodre, G. (1997). The acoustics of concert halls. *Physics World, 10*(5), 33–37.

- After the journal title, include the volume number, followed by the issue number (in parentheses).
- Put the volume number—but not the issue number—in italics.

13. Article in a Popular Magazine—APA

Cowley, G. (1997, April 28). Cardiac contagion. *Newsweek, 129,* 69–70.

- Give the full date of the issue, placing the year first.
- Provide the volume number (in the example: 129) but not the issue number.

14. Newspaper Article—APA

Wade, N. (1997, May 24). Doctors record signals of brain cells linked to memory. *New York Times* [National edition], p. A8.

- In front of the page number for newspapers, write "p." (for one page) or "pp." (for more than one page).

15. Article with No Author Listed—APA

Rethinking traditional design. (1997). *Manufacturing Engineering, 118*(2), 50.

- Begin with the article's title. This example gives the issue number in parentheses because the journal numbers its pages separately for each issue (see Example 12 above).

Electronic Sources

Because placing a period at the end of an Internet address can cause confusion, final periods are omitted in APA entries for on-line sources.

16. Text Available Only at a World Wide Web Site—APA

International Business Machines. IBM web design guidelines. (1998, March). [On-line]. Available: http://www.ibm.com/IBM/HCI/guidelines/web/web_design.html

17. Text Downloaded from an FTP Site—APA

Modjeska, D., & Marsh, A. (1997, July). Structure and memorability of Web sites. University of Toronto Computer Systems Research Institute. Available FTP: ftp://ftp.cs.toronto.edu/csri-technical-reports/364

18. On-Line Journal Article That Is Not Available in Print—APA

Toll, D. (1996). Artificial intelligence applications in geotechnical engineering. *Electronic Journal of Geotechnical Engineering.* [On-line serial]. Available: http://geotech.civen.okstate.edu/ejge/JournTOC.htm

19. On-Line Journal Article That Is Also Available in Print—APA

Reid, M. E., Green, C. A., Hoffer, J., & Øyen, R. (1996). Effect of pronase on high-incidence blood group antigens and the prevalence of antibodies to pronase-treated erythrocytes. *Immunohematology, 12,* 139–142. Available: http://biomed.redcross.org/immunohematology/issues.htm

20. On-Line Posting at a Newsgroup—APA

Cite in the text only, not in the reference list:

(D. J. Young, on-line newsgroup posting, November 10, 1997, Logging on our national forests, Usenet alt.great-lakes)

21. CD-ROM—APA

"Rainforest." (1997). *Encarta '97* [CD-ROM]. Redmond, WA: Microsoft.

22. E-mail—APA

Cite in the text only, not in the reference list:

(M. Grube, e-mail to Justin Timor, December 4, 1998)

Other Sources

23. Letter—APA

The APA style includes references to letters only in parentheses in the text, not in the reference list. The parenthetical citation in the text includes the author's initials as well as his or her last name and an exact date.

(L. A. Cawthorne, personal communication, August 24, 1998)

24. Interview—APA

The APA style treats interviews the same way it treats letters (see above).

USING THE MLA DOCUMENTATION STYLE

The following sections explain how to write in-text citations and the entries in a reference list using the MLA style.

WRITING MLA IN-TEXT CITATIONS

A basic MLA citation contains two kinds of information: the author's name and the specific page or pages on which the cited information is to be found. Enclose these in parentheses—with no punctuation between them—and place them *inside* your normal sentence punctuation. If you are citing the entire work, omit the page numbers. The following citation refers the reader to pages 33 and 34 of a work by Tanner:

> The first crab caught in the trap attracts others to it (Tanner 33–34).

If you incorporate the author's name in the sentence itself, give only the page numbers in parentheses:

> According to Tanner, the first crab caught in the trap attracts others to it (33–34).

Here are some other types of citations:

(Hoeflin and Bolsen 167)	Two authors
(Wilton, Nelson, and Dutta 222)	Three, four, or five authors
(Norton et al. 776)	For six or more authors (*et al.* is an abbreviation for the Latin phrase *et alii*, which means "and others")
(U.S. Department of Energy 4–7)	Government or corporate author
("Geologists Discover" 31)	No author listed (use the first few words of the title). In the example, the words from the title are in quotation marks because the citation is to an article; if it were to a book, the words would be in italics with no quotation marks.
(Justin 23; Skol 1089; Weiss 475)	Two or more sources cited together (arrange them in alphabetical order)

In some of your communications, you may cite two or more sources by the same author. If they were published in *different* years, your readers will have no trouble telling which work you are referring to. If they were published in the *same* year, distinguish between them by placing a comma after the author's name, followed by a few words from the title.

(Burkehardt, "Gambling Addiction")
(Burkehardt, "Obsessive Behaviors")

WRITING AN MLA REFERENCE LIST

The following sections describe how to write entries for the most common types of print, electronic, and other sources. To create entries that are not listed here, follow the logic of these examples or else consult the *MLA Style Manual,* available in the reference section of most libraries. Figure B.2 (page 598) shows how to arrange these entries in your reference list.

■ FIGURE B.2

MLA Reference List

References

Abernethy, Bruce, Vaughn Kippers, Laurel Traeger Mackinnon, Robert J. Neal, and Stephanie Hanrahan. *The Biophysical Foundations of Human Movement.* Champaign, IL: Human Kinetics, 1997.

Gould, Stephen Jay. *Dinosaur in a Haystack: Reflections in Natural History.* New York: Harmony, 1995.

---. *Wonderful Life: The Burgess Shale and Nature of History.* New York: Norton, 1989.

International Business Machines. *IBM Web Design Guidelines.* 12 Mar 1998 <http://www.ibm.com/IBM/HCI/guidelines/web/web_design.html>.

McLaurin, JoAnne, and Avijit Chakrabartty. "Characterization of the Interactions of Alzheimer β-amyloid Peptides with Phospholipid Membranes." *European Journal of Biochemistry* 245 (1997): 355–63.

"Rethinking Traditional Design." (1997). *Manufacturing Engineering* 118.2, (1977): 50.

Second and subsequent lines are indented.

For the second and subsequent items by the same person, the author's name is replaced by three hyphens, followed by a period.

Items by corporate and government groups are alphabetized by the groups' names (spelled out).

Items without authors are alphabetized by the title.

Print Sources

1. Book, One Author—MLA

Jacobs, James R. *The Scientific Revolution: Aspirations and Achievements, 1500–1700.* Atlantic Highlands, NJ: Humanities Press, 1998.

- Give the author's last name followed by a comma and then the first and middle names or initials—exactly as they appear on the title page.
- In the title, capitalize all major words.
- Follow the city of publication with a comma and the two-letter postal abbreviation for the state (however, do not give the state for cities such as New York that are well known for publishing).
- Indent all lines after the first one.

2. Book, Two or Three Authors—MLA

Talbert, Samuel H., and Avitzur Betzalel. *Elementary Mechanics of Plastic Flow in Metal Forming.* New York: Wiley, 1996.

Abernethy, Bruce, Vaughn Kippers, Laurel Traeger Mackinnon, Robert J. Neal, and Stephanie Hanrahan. *The Biophysical Foundations of Human Movement.* Champaign, IL: Human Kinetics, 1997.

- Give the first author's last name in *reverse* order (last name first).
- Give the names of additional authors in *normal* order (first name first).

3. Anthology or Essay Collection—MLA

Lutz, Peter L., and John A. Musick, eds. *The Biology of Sea Turtles.* Boca Raton, FL: CRC Press, 1997.

- Use the abbreviation "ed." for a single editor and "eds." for multiple editors.

4. Second or Subsequent Edition—MLA

Olin, Harold B., John J. Schmidt, and Walter H. Lewis. *Construction: Principles, Materials and Methods.* 6th ed. New York: Van Nostrand Reinhold, 1995.

5. Government Report—MLA

Frankforter, J. D., and P. J. Emmons. *Potential Effects of Large Floods on the Transport of Atrazine into the Alluvial Aquifer Adjacent to the Lower Platte River, Nebraska* (U.S. Geological Survey Water-Resources Investigation Report 96–4272). Denver, CO: US Geological Survey, 1997.

- If the report doesn't list an author, begin the entry with the name of the government, followed by a period and the name of the agency that issued the document. If it is a United States government agency, spell out "United States" followed by a period and then the agency's name. Example: "United States. Geological Survey."
- If the report has an identifying number, place it immediately after the title.
- In the example, the authors' initials (not first and middle names) are given because that is how their names appear on the title page.

6. Corporate Report—MLA

Daimler-Benz AG. *Environmental Report 1997.* Stuttgart, Germany: Daimler-Benz AG, 1997.

- List the names of the individual authors rather than the corporation if the names are given on the title page.
- If the names of the individual authors aren't given on the title page, list the corporation as the author. (In the example, "Daimler-Benz AG" is the name of a company.)

7. Essay in a Book—MLA

Sullivan, Patricia. "Ethics in the Computer Age." *Social and Ethical Effects of the Computer Revolution.* Ed. Joseph Migga Kizza. Jefferson, NC: McFarland, 1996. 288–97.

- Use the abbreviation "Ed." for a single editor and for multiple editors.

8. Paper in a Proceedings—MLA

Youra, Steven. "Placing Writing in Engineering Education." *Proceedings of the Australian Communication Conference.* Ed. Ronald Pose and Anita Jawary. Melbourne, Australia: Monash University, 1996. 59–76.

9. Article in an Encyclopedia, Dictionary, or Similar Reference Work—MLA

Rich, Elaine. "Artificial Intelligence." *Encyclopedia Americana.* 1996 ed.

- If no author is listed, begin with the article's title.
- If entries in the work are arranged alphabetically, do not give volume or page number.
- When citing familiar reference works, give the edition number (if provided) and year of publication, but not the publisher or city of publication.

10. Pamphlet or Brochure— MLA

Ohio State. Department of Natural Resources. *Ring-Necked Pheasant Management in Ohio.* Columbus: State of Ohio, 1996.

- If the pamphlet or brochure doesn't list an author, begin the entry with the name of the government or other organization that published it, followed by a period and the name of the agency that issued the document.
- If the pamphlet or brochure lists no author and no publisher, begin with the document's title.

11. Article in Journal That Numbers Its Pages Continuously through Each Volume—MLA

McLaurin, JoAnne, and Avijit Chakrabartty. "Characterization of the Interactions of Alzheimer β-amyloid Peptides with Phospholipid Membranes." *European Journal of Biochemistry* 245 (1997): 355–63.

- Place the article's title in quotation marks and capitalize all major words.
- After the journal's name, give the volume number, followed by the year (in parentheses).
- For page numbers larger than 99, give only the last two digits unless more are needed. Examples: "355–63" and "394–405."

12. Article in Journal That Numbers Its Pages Separately for Each Issue—MLA

Bradley, John, and Gilbert Soulodre. "The Acoustics of Concert Halls." *Physics World* 10.5 (1997): 33–37.

- After the volume number, add a period and the issue number. (In the example, "10.5" signifies volume 10, issue 5.)

13. Article in a Popular Magazine—MLA

Cowley, Geoffrey. "Cardiac Contagion." *Newsweek* 28 Apr. 1997: 69–70.

- Give the full date of the issue, beginning with the day and abbreviating the month.
- Do not give the issue or volume number.

14. Newspaper Article—MLA

Wade, Nicholas. "Doctors Record Signals of Brain Cells Linked to Memory."
New York Times 24 May 1997, natl. ed.: A8.

- If the newspaper lists an edition (for example, "late edition") in the masthead, place a comma after the date and add the edition's name, using abbreviations where reasonable. In the example, "natl. ed." indicates "national edition."

15. Article with No Author Listed—MLA

"Rethinking Traditional Design." *Manufacturing Engineering* 118.2 (1997): 50.

- Begin with the article's title.
- This example gives the issue number ("2") because the journal numbers its pages separately for each issue (see Example 12, above).

Electronic Sources

16. Text Available Only at a World Wide Web Site—MLA

International Business Machines. *IBM Web Design Guidelines*. 12 Mar. 1998
<http://www.ibm.com/IBM/HCI/guidelines/web/web_design.html>.

17. Text Downloaded from an FTP Site—MLA

Modjeska, David, and Anna Marsh. "Structure and Memorability of Web
Sites." University of Toronto Computer Systems Research Institute. 14 July
1997. 15 Dec. 1998. Available: <ftp://ftp.cs.toronto.edu/csri-technical-
reports/364>.

18. On-Line Journal Article That Is Not Available in Print—MLA

Toll, David. "Artificial Intelligence Applications in Geotechnical Engineering."
Electronic Journal of Geotechnical Engineering 1 (1996). 12 Nov. 1997
<http://geotech.civen.okstate.edu/ejge/JournTOC.htm>.

19. On-Line Journal Article That Is Also Available in Print—MLA

Reid, M. E., C. A. Green, J. Hoffer, and R. Øyen. "Effect of Pronase on High-
incidence Blood Group Antigens and the Prevalence of Antibodies to
Pronase-treated Erythrocytes." *Immunohematology* 12 (1996): 139–42.
4 Aug. 1998 <http://biomed.redcross.org/immunohematology/issues.htm>.

20. On-Line Posting at a Newsgroup—MLA

Young, Darren, J. "Logging on Our National Forests." On-line posting. 10 Nov.
1997. 27 Aug. 1998 <news:alt.great-lakes>.

Because material that is available on the World Wide Web changes continuously, always include the date you last accessed the item you are citing; place this date before the URL or other information about the location of the source.

The first date tells when the text was posted; the second (before the URL) tells when it was accessed.

To prevent confusion about punctuation in Internet addresses, the MLA style encloses these addresses in angled brackets: < >.

21. CD-ROM—MLA

"Rainforest." *Encarta '97.* CD-ROM. Redmond, WA: Microsoft, 1998.

■ For a CD-ROM that you accessed through a network (for example, at your library), add the date you last accessed it.

22. E-mail—MLA

Grube, Melvin. E-mail to Justin Timor. 4 Dec. 1998.

Other Sources

23. Letter—MLA

Cawthorne, Linda A. Letter to the author. 24 Aug. 1998.

24. Interview—MLA

Cawthorne, Linda A. Telephone interview. 24 Aug. 1998.

Projects and Cases

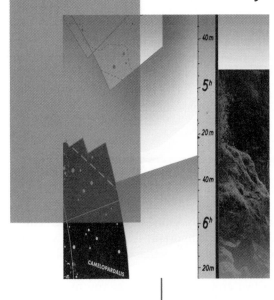

PROJECTS

Project 1   Resume and Job Application Letter

Project 2   Informational Web Site

Project 3   Informational Page

Project 4   Unsolicited Recommendation

Project 5   Brochure

Project 6   Instructions

Project 7   User Test and Report

Project 8   Project Proposal

Project 9   Progress Report

Project 10 Formal Report or Proposal

Project 11 Oral Briefing I: Project Plans

Project 12 Oral Briefing II: Project Results

CASES

Case 1 Electromagnetic Fields

Case 2 Company Day Care

Case 3 Ethics Report

Case 4 Corporate Credo

Case 5 International Issue Report

Case 6 Propose Your Own Business

This appendix contains writing and speaking assignments that your instructor might ask you to complete. All share this important feature: all ask you to communicate to particular people for specific purposes that closely resemble the purposes you will have for writing in your career.

The eighteen assignments fall into two groups. The first asks you to write or speak to real people about situations that are drawn from your own experience or that you learn about while working on your assignment. These assignments enable you to prepare communications that will actually help you or someone else. The second group includes case studies that ask you to communicate in fictitious (but realistic) situations.

Some of the assignments contain specifications about such things as length and format. Your instructor may change these specifications to tailor the assignments to your writing course.

Note to the Instructor: You will find helpful notes about these assignments in the *Instructor's Manual*. The book's Web site includes versions of these assignments you can download and adapt to your course. It also includes additional assignments.

PROJECTS

PROJECT **1** **Resume and Job Application Letter**

Write a resume and job application letter addressed to some *real* person in an organization with which you might actually seek employment. If you graduate this year, you will probably want to write for a full-time, permanent position. If you aren't about to graduate, you may want to apply for a summer position or an internship. If you are presently working, imagine that you have decided to change jobs, perhaps to obtain a promotion, secure higher pay, or find more challenging and interesting work.

To complete this project, you may need to do some research. Among other things, you will have to find an organization that really employs people in the kind of job you want, and you will need to learn something about the organization so you can persuade your readers in the organization that you are knowledgeable about it. Many employers publish brochures about themselves; your campus placement center or library may have copies. Many employers also post company Web sites. If the sources you find don't give the name of some specific person to whom you can address your letter, call the organization's switchboard to ask for the name of the employment director or the manager of the particular department in which you would like to work. While you work on this assignment, keep this real person in mind—even if you will not actually send your letter to him or her.

Your letter should be an original typed page, but your resume may be a high-quality photocopy of a typed original. Remember that the appearance of your resume, letter, and envelope will affect your readers, as will your attention to such details as grammar and spelling. Enclose your letter and resume in an envelope complete with your return address and your reader's name and address. You will find information about the formats for letters and envelopes in Appendix A.

As part of your package, include the names, addresses, and phone numbers of three or four references. These may be included within your resume. If you choose instead to have your resume say, "References available upon request," enclose a copy of the list of references you would send if the list were requested by an employer. Throughout your work on this project, you should carefully and creatively follow the advice given in Chapter 2 on resumes and letters of application.

P R O J E C T ② Informational Web Site

For this project, you are to create an informational Web site on a topic that interests you. Begin by identifying a target audience, purpose, and subject for your site. The subject may be related to your major or to something you enjoy and know a lot about. Your site should have the following elements:

- Four or more pages, one of which is a home page (entitled "index.html").
- Links among your pages.
- One or more links to other Web sites related to your topic.
- At least one image.

To count as a "page" in this project, a page must fill one window on a computer screen when the window is at its maximum size. The material in the window must include some text, but may also contain one or more images.

All pages, including the home page, should be informative, not just entertaining. The text is to be text you have written, not text you have downloaded or otherwise copied from someone else (see the "Focus on Ethics" on page 403). You may obtain your images by downloading them from the Web, provided that you are sure they are not copyrighted and that use of them is not otherwise restricted.

Avoid movies, large images, and other items that consume much memory and take a long time to load.

Your site may include a link to your personal Web page. However, your personal Web page does not count among the four that must be about your subject.

Your site should possess the following characteristics:

- All information is presented in a way that is suited to your audience and purpose.
- The text is accurate, informative, and well written.
- The pages are easy to read and use when accessed on a computer screen.
- Pages are easy to navigate individually and as a group.
- The site is well organized, with both hierarchical and associative links (as described in Chapter 15).
- The pages are unified with one another in terms of visual design, writing style, and purpose.

Turn in the following items:

- A memo to your instructor that identifies the audience and purpose of your site.
- A diskette with all files for your site. Be sure your name is on the diskette. If your instructor permits, you may instead post your site on a server and include the URL in your memo.

PROJECT **3** **Informational Page**

Project created by Jennie Dautermann

A bus schedule, a chart comparing the features of competing computer programs, and the centerfold in a natural history magazine that uses a time-line, diagrams, and words to explain the evolution of horses—all these are "informational pages." They convey a complex set of information or ideas principally by means of visual design, rather than relying solely on sentences and paragraphs.

For this assignment, you are to create an informational page addressed to some specific set of readers. Use tables or charts. Mix diagrams with words. Or use other ways of presenting information visually to achieve your communication objectives. But use only one side of one sheet of paper.

When planning your informational page, think carefully about how your readers will use your information and about how you can use visual design to make the facts you present as easily accessible, understandable, and useful as possible. The advice given in Chapters 11 ("Using Visual Aids") and 12 ("Designing Pages") can be especially helpful.

Here are informational pages you might create; note that each targets a specific group of readers:

- An explanation of a basic concept in your major, addressed to students who have just begun course work in it
- An explanation of a concept from your major that is important for members of the general public to understand as they make practical decisions

- A description of a process that would be important for clients or customers to know if they are going to purchase products or services from the kind of employer you would like to work for after graduation
- A reference card describing the computer labs on your campus, addressed to students who would want to use the labs
- A study guide that might help someone in one of your courses learn a topic that will be on an exam

---

PROJECT **4** **Unsolicited Recommendation**

This assignment is your chance to improve the world—or at least one small corner of it. You are to write a letter of 400 to 800 words in which you make an unrequested recommendation for improving the operation of some organization with which you have personal contact—perhaps the company that employed you last summer, a club you belong to, or your sorority or fraternity.

There are four important restrictions on the recommendation you make:

1. Your recommendation must concern a real situation in which your letter can *really* bring about change. As you consider possible topics, focus on situations that can be improved by the modest measures that you can argue for effectively in a relatively brief letter. It is not necessary, however, that your letter aim to bring about a complete solution. In your letter, you might aim to persuade *one* of the key people in the organization that your recommendation will serve the organization's best interests.
2. Your recommendation must be unsolicited; that is, it must be addressed to someone who has not asked for your advice.
3. Your recommendation must concern the way an organization operates, not just the way one or more individuals think or behave.
4. Your recommendation may *not* involve a problem that would be decided in an essentially political manner. Thus, you are not to write on a problem that would be decided by elected officials (such as members of Congress or the city council), and you may not address a problem that would be raised in a political campaign.

Of course, you will have to write to an *actual* person, someone who, in fact, has the power to help make the change you recommend. You may have to investigate to learn who that person is. Try to learn also how that person feels about the situation you hope to improve. Keep in mind that most people are inclined to reject advice they haven't asked for; that's part of the challenge of this assignment. From time to time throughout your career, you will find that you want to make recommendations that your reader hasn't requested.

In the past, students have completed this assignment by writing on such matters as the following:

- A no-cost way that the student's summer employer could more efficiently handle merchandise on the loading dock

- A detailed strategy for increasing attendance at the meetings of a club the student belonged to
- A proposal that the Office of the Dean of Students establish a self-supporting legal-aid service for students

Bear in mind that one essential feature of a recommendation is that it compares two alternatives: keeping things the way they are now and changing them to the way you think they should be. You will have to make the change seem to be the better alternative *from your reader's point of view*. To do this, you will find it helpful to understand why the organization does things in the present way. By understanding the goals of the present method, you will probably gain insight into the criteria that your reader will apply when comparing the present method with the method you recommend.

When preparing this project, follow the advice about the letter format given in Appendix A. Exercise 4 in Chapter 5 shows an unsolicited recommendation written by a student in response to this assignment.

PROJECT **5** **Brochure**

Create a brochure about some academic major or student service on your campus. Alternatively, create a brochure for a service organization in your community.

Begin by interviewing people at the organization to learn about their aims for such a brochure. Then follow the advice given in Chapter 3 ("Defining Your Objectives") to learn about the target audience for the brochure. Remember that to be effective the brochure must meet the needs of both the organization and the readers.

Use a folded 8½-by-14-inch sheet of paper so that there are three columns (or panels) on each side of the sheet. When the brochure is folded, the front panel should serve as a cover. In addition to any artwork you may decide to include on the cover, use at least one visual aid (such as a table, flow chart, drawing, or photograph) in the text of the brochure. Note that your cover need not have any artwork; it may consist solely of attractively lettered and arranged words that identify the topic of your brochure. Along with your brochure, turn in copies of any existing brochures or other printed material you used while working on this project.

Your success in this project will depend largely on your ability to predict the questions your readers will have about your subject—and on your ability to answer those questions clearly, concisely, and usefully. Also, think very carefully about how you want your brochure to alter your readers' attitudes about your subject. Remember that, along with the prose, the neatness and visual design of your brochure will have a large effect on your readers' attitudes.

PROJECT **6** **Instructions**

Write a set of instructions that will enable your readers to operate some device or perform some process used in your major. The procedure must involve at least twenty-four steps.

With the permission of your instructor, you may also choose from topics that are not related to your major. Such topics might include the following:

- Using some special feature of a word-processing or spreadsheet program
- Operating a piece of equipment used in your major
- Changing a bicycle tire
- Rigging a sailboat
- Starting an aquarium
- Some other procedure of interest to you that includes at least twenty-four steps

Your instructions should guide your readers through some specific process that your classmates or instructor could actually perform. Do not write generic instructions for performing a general procedure. For instance, do not write instructions for "Operating a Microscope" but rather for "Operating the Thompson Model 200 Microscope."

Be sure to divide the overall procedure into groups of steps, rather than presenting all the steps in a single list. Use headings to label the groups of steps.

When preparing your instructions, pay careful attention to the visual design of your finished communication. You must include at least one illustration, and you may rely heavily on figures if they are the most effective way for you to achieve your objectives. In fact, your instructions need not contain a single sentence.

Finally, your instructor may require you to use a page design that has two or more columns (rather than having a single column of type that runs all the way from the left-hand margin to the right-hand margin). In a two-column design, you might put all of your steps in the left-hand column and all of your accompanying illustrations in the right-hand column. Alternatively, you might mix both text and figures in both columns. Large figures and the title for the instructions can span both columns.

You may use the format for your instructions that you believe will work best—whether it is a single sheet of 8½-by-11-inch paper, a booklet printed on smaller paper, or some other design.

Don't forget that your instructions must be accurate.

Note to the Instructor: If you wish to make this a larger project, increase the minimum length of the procedure about which your students write. In this case, you may also want to specify that they create an instruction manual rather than, for example, an instruction sheet.

PROJECT **7**   **User Test and Report**

As you learned in Chapter 13, one excellent way to evaluate a draft is to conduct a user test in which you give your draft to members of your target audience, asking them to use it in the same way that your target readers will use the final draft. For this assignment, you are to conduct a user test of a nearly finished draft of a project you are preparing in this course (or another course, if your instructor permits), then report the results in a memo to your instructor. Instructions make an excellent subject for a user test, but other communications can be evaluated in this way also.

For your test, use a draft that is as close as possible to what you envision for your final draft. Ask two people to serve as your test readers, and arrange for them to work independently. If you cannot recruit test readers who are from your target audience, choose people who resemble the target readers as closely as possible. Similarly, if you cannot arrange for your test readers to read in exactly the same circumstances that your target readers will, simulate those conditions in some reasonable way. Also use simulation if your communication involves a potentially dangerous step (such as jacking up a car or pouring a strong acid from one container to another) that might result in injury to your test readers if they make a mistake. For advice on conducting user tests, see page 366.

Write your report in the memo format and use the superstructure for empirical research reports. To make your report readable and informative for your instructor, consider the following advice concerning the sections of your report:

- **Introduction.** Remind your instructor of the topic and target audience of the communication you are testing.
- **Objectives.** Identify the objectives of your communication (see Chapter 3) and those of your test. Remember that even instructions have a persuasive purpose as well as an enabling purpose.
- **Method.** Describe your draft (how closely does it resemble your planned final draft?), your test readers (who were they, and why are they good representatives of your target audience?), the location of your test (how closely does it resemble the setting in which your target readers will use your communication?), and your procedure (what did you ask your test readers to do, and how did you gather information from them?).
- **Results and discussion.** Report the results your test produced (where did your test readers have difficulties, and what did they say about your communication?) and tell what these indicate about your communication. Be quite specific in this section.
- **Conclusion.** Tell what you learned overall from your test and indicate the specific revisions you will make as a result of what you learned.

PROJECT ⑧ **Project Proposal**

Write a proposal seeking your instructor's approval for a project you will prepare later this term.

Your work on this proposal serves three important purposes. First, it provides an occasion for you and your instructor to agree about what you will do for the later project. Second, it gives you experience at writing a proposal, a task that will be very important to you in your career. Third, it gives you a chance to demonstrate your mastery of the material in Chapters 3 ("Defining Your Objectives"), 4 ("Planning to Meet Your Readers' Informational Needs"), and 5 ("Planning Your Persuasive Strategies").

Notice that while working on this assignment, you will have to define the objectives of two different communications: (1) the *proposal* you are writing now, which is addressed to your instructor, and (2) the *project* you are seeking approval to write, whose purpose and audience you will have to describe to your instructor in the proposal.

When writing your proposal, you may think of your instructor as a person who looks forward with pleasure to working with you on your final project and wants to be sure that you choose a project from which you can learn a great deal and on which you can do a good job. However, until your instructor learns from your proposal some details about your proposed project, his or her attitude toward it will be neutral. While reading your proposal, your instructor will seek to answer many questions, including the following:

- What kind of communication do you wish to prepare?
- Who will its readers be?
- What is its purpose?
    - What is the final result you want it to bring about?
    - What task will it enable its readers to perform?
    - How will it alter its readers' attitudes?
- Is this a kind of communication you will have to prepare at work?
- Can you write the communication effectively in the time left in the term using resources that are readily available to you?

For additional insights into the questions your instructor (like the reader of any proposal) will ask, see Chapter 19 ("Proposals").

Your proposal should be between 400 and 800 words long. Write it in the memo format (see Appendix A), use headings, and include a schedule chart.

PROJECT **9** **Progress Report**

Write a report of between 400 and 800 words in which you tell your instructor how you are progressing on the writing project you are currently preparing. Be sure to give your instructor a good sense not only of what you have accomplished but also of what problems you have encountered or anticipate. Use the memo format (see Appendix A).

PROJECT **10** **Formal Report or Proposal**

Write an empirical research report, feasibility report, or proposal. Whichever form of communication you write, it must be designed to help some organization—real or imaginary—solve some problem or achieve some goal, and you must write it in response to a request (again, real or imaginary) from the organization you are addressing.

A real situation is one you have actually encountered. It might involve your employer, your major department, or a service group to which you belong—to name just a few of the possibilities. Students writing on real situations have prepared projects with such titles as:

- **"Feasibility of Using a Computer Database to Catalog the Art Department's Slide Library."** The students wrote this feasibility report at the request of the chair of the Art Department.
- **"Attitudes of Participants in Merit Hotel's R.S.V.P. Club."** The student wrote this empirical research report at the request of the hotel, which wanted to find ways of improving a marketing program that rewarded secretaries who booked their companies' visitors at that hotel rather than at one of the hotel's competitors.
- **"Expanding the Dietetic Services at the Campus Health Center: A Proposal."** The student wrote this proposal to the college administration at the request of the part-time dietitian employed by the Health Center.

An imaginary situation is one that you create to simulate the kinds of situations that you will find yourself in once you begin your career. You pretend that you have begun working for an employer who has asked you to use your specialized training to solve some problems or answer some questions that face his or her organization. You may imagine that you are a regular employee or that you are a special consultant. Students writing about imaginary situations have prepared formal reports with titles such as:

- **"Improving the Operations of the Gift Shop of Sea World of Ohio."** The student who wrote this proposal had worked at this shop for a summer job; she imagined that she had been hired by the manager to study its operation and recommend improvements.
- **"Performance of Three Lubricants at Very Low Temperatures."** The student wrote this empirical research report about an experiment he had conducted in a laboratory class. He imagined that he worked for a company that wanted to test the lubricants for use in manufacturing equipment used at temperatures below $-100°F$.
- **"Upgrading the Monitoring and Communication System in the Psychology Clinic."** The student who wrote this report imagined that she had been asked by the Psychology Clinic to investigate the possibility of purchasing equipment that would improve its monitoring and communication system. All of her information about the clinic and the equipment were real.

For this project, use the book format (see Appendix A). Remember that your purpose is to help your readers make a practical decision or take a practical action in a real or imaginary organization. The body of your report should be between twelve and twenty pages long (not counting cover, executive summary, title page, table of contents, appendixes, and similar parts).

PROJECT ⑪ **Oral Briefing I: Project Plans**

At work, you will sometimes be asked to report in brief talks about projects upon which you are working. For this assignment, you are to give an oral briefing to the class about your final project. Here are the things you should cover:

- **What kind of communication are you writing?** Who will your readers be? What role will you be playing? Identify your readers by telling what organization they are in and what positions your key readers hold. Describe your role by saying whether you are imagining that you work for the company as a regular employee or have been hired as a consultant. Tell who you report to.
- **What organizational problem will your communication help your readers solve?** What need or goal will it help them satisfy or reach? Provide full background so your classmates can understand the situation from your readers' point of view.
- **What are you doing to solve the problem?**
  Your research activities: What kind of information are you gathering and how, or what kind of analysis are you providing and why?
  Your writing activities: How do you plan to organize and present your information? What will your communication look like?
- **What is the gist of your message to your readers?** What are the main points you are planning to make?

As you prepare and deliver your oral briefing, pretend that you are interviewing for a job (or for a new job) and that the prospective employer has asked you to give an oral briefing about a project of yours for which you are now writing a report or proposal. The members of your class can play the role of the people your employer has asked to attend your presentation. Pretend that your classmates have not heard about your project as yet, even though you may have already discussed it in class several times. This means that you will have to provide all the background information that will enable your listeners to understand the organizational situation in which you are writing.

As the name implies, a "briefing" is a brief presentation. Make yours between four and five minutes long—no longer. Gauge the time by making timed rehearsals. In your briefing, use at least one visual aid. It might show an outline for your project, or it might be one of the visual aids you will use within your project. You may present this visual aid as a poster, overhead transparency, or handout, and you may use more than one visual aid if doing so will increase the effectiveness of your briefing.

PROJECT ⑫ **Oral Briefing II: Project Results**

At work, people often present the results of their major projects twice: once in a written communication and a second time in an oral briefing that covers the major points of the written document. In some ways, this briefing is like an executive summary—an overview of all the important things presented in more detail in writing.

For this assignment, you are to give an oral briefing on one of your writing projects. Address the class as if it were the same audience that you address in writing, and imagine that the audience has not yet read your communication.

Limit your briefing to four or five minutes—no longer (see the last paragraph of Project 11). Use at least one visual aid.

CASES

C A S E   **1**   **Electromagnetic Fields**

Based on an idea by Michael Aplin, Laura Boring, Tricia Fries, Federico Reyes, and Eric Schweitzer

You work for the power company that provides electricity to the area in which you now live. Over the past few years, the company has received a growing number of letters and phone calls from customers seeking information about the possible harmful effects of electromagnetic fields.

Electromagnetic fields (EMFs) are created whenever electricity moves through a wire. Concern about the possible danger of EMFs first arose in the 1970s, when two researchers found a possible link between living near high-voltage power lines and a rise in the rate of childhood leukemia. Since then, many other scientists have investigated possible harmful effects of EMFs, including those created by household appliances, such as hair dryers, television sets, and microwave ovens. So far, scientists agree on only one thing: conclusive results have not been achieved. Different studies produce conflicting results. Yet public worry is great enough that, in some parts of the country, houses near high-voltage power lines sell for less than comparable houses in other neighborhoods. Also, in some locales, parents have insisted that power lines be moved away from schools.

Because the power company that employs you has continued to receive inquiries about EMFs, it has decided to initiate a public information campaign on the subject. Under normal conditions, this entire project would have been conducted by the Public Relations Department, but it has an overabundance of other projects, so you have been asked to help with some of the preliminary work. Oliver Thomas, department director, has called you into his office to explain.

"In order to design an effective information campaign, we need to learn a number of things about our customers. Therefore, we'd like you to design and carry out a telephone survey for us."

"What kinds of things do you want me to ask about?" you inquire.

"Well, for example, we need to find out how much our customers already know about EMFs so we can determine what we need to tell them. We also need to learn how concerned they are about EMFs. Researchers say that members of the public have a variety of responses to perceived health and environmental risks—ranging from acceptance to fear to outrage. To shape our messages effectively, we need to know what our customers' present attitudes are. This information will also help us determine whether we should construct a public information program that responds only to inquiries or create a much more expensive one that might, for instance, reach every customer several times through a variety of media.

"In addition, we need to learn where to present our message. Should we rely heavily on television or newspapers? Magazines? Direct mail letters?"

After a pause, Oliver Thomas continues. "We also have the problem that our customers may not perceive us as a credible source for information about the health effects of EMFs. First, they may think we're really not qualified to speak on the issue because we aren't scientists. Furthermore, they may think that we aren't a trustworthy source for information about the possibly harmful effects of our own service."

"Anything else?" you ask.

"There's much more we could ask about, but these are the most important points. Furthermore, we want to keep our survey short. When telephone surveys are long, people are much less willing to cooperate. Besides, we don't want to irritate our customers; many of them are already upset about the recent rate increase that the Public Utilities Commission authorized us to institute."

"Fine," you say. "I'll make a short survey."

"Oh, and one more thing. When you've completed your survey, please report on it in a memo addressed to the entire Public Relations Department. The eight of us always look these things over together. Some of our people don't know much about EMFs, so you'll need to provide some background information. Also, everyone in the department likes to see the detailed survey results. I guess they think they may be able to come up with some novel interpretation of the data. And we'll all want to know what you recommend."

After drafting your survey questions and having them approved by Oliver Thomas, you made your telephone calls, obtaining the results given below.

Assignment

Using the memo format and the superstructure for empirical research reports, write your report addressed to the Public Relations Department. Be sure to create informative, easy-to-interpret visual aids for presenting the survey results.

Survey Results

Have you read or heard about electromagnetic fields?

Yes	88%
No	7%
Don't know	5%

(This question was asked of 300 people. All subsequent questions were asked only of the 264 who responded "Yes.")

Do you believe electromagnetic fields created by power lines and household appliances can harm human health?

Yes	48%
No	22%
Don't know	30%

On a scale of 1 (least concerned) to 5 (most concerned), how concerned are you about electromagnetic fields?

1	16%
2	24%
3	37%
4	17%
5	6%

From what sources have you obtained your information about electromagnetic fields?

Magazines	68%
Television	53%
Newspapers	46%
Schools	30%
Work	24%
Conversation	22%
Radio	18%

On a scale of 1 (least qualified) to 5 (most qualified), how **well qualified** is each of the following sources to provide information about electromagnetic fields?

The Power Company		Newspapers and Television		A Local University	
1	2%	1	25%	1	1%
2	4%	2	34%	2	3%
3	14%	3	25%	3	12%
4	51%	4	8%	4	38%
5	26%	5	0%	5	26%
No opinion	3%	No opinion	8%	No opinion	20%

On a scale of 1 (least qualified) to 5 (most qualified), how **trustworthy** is each of the following sources when it comes to providing information about electromagnetic fields?

The Power Company		Newspapers and Television		A Local University	
1	6%	1	3%	1	1%
2	23%	2	5%	2	0%
3	38%	3	19%	3	3%
4	17%	4	31%	4	52%
5	2%	5	28%	5	35%
No opinion	14%	No opinion	14%	No opinion	9%

CASE   **2**   **Company Day Care**

Case developed by Martin Tadlock

After graduating from college, you were hired as the Special Assistant to the President of PrimeCare, Inc., which owns and operates twelve nursing homes throughout your state. The central office, where you work, oversees all twelve PrimeCare facilities.

Your job is to conduct special research projects for the company president, Walter Henocker, and other executive officers of PrimeCare. This morning, Jan Debliss, Personnel Director, has called you into her office.

"Well, how do you think things are going—after being here for one whole month?" she asks.

"Not bad," you reply. "I've really learned a lot. Everyone has been very helpful getting me on my feet and used to the way things work around here. I'm happy."

"Good," Jan says. "I hope you're feeling ready to help me solve a rather pressing problem. Usually, I'd handle it myself, but I've been snowed under with all the problems we're having on the new record-keeping system and the opening of the new nursing home. In addition, tomorrow I begin a two-week vacation. So I thought I would ask for your help."

"I'd be glad to help," you reply.

"Good," Jan answers. "Let me tell you what I'm looking for and then turn you loose on it.

"We've been having problems finding employees for the day shift. We've also been having problems with absenteeism among the day-shift employees we now have. In fact, the absenteeism has gotten so bad that a lot of the time we aren't fully staffed, and supervisors must call off-duty or second- and third-shift employees to fill in. We're concerned that patients aren't getting the full care they should because we're always shorthanded. Also, these staffing problems are causing added workloads for the employees who do show up consistently as scheduled, and that's killing staff morale."

Your mind is racing along at top speed now, trying to figure out how to solve such a problem. Jan continues.

"During last month's meeting of the directors of PrimeCare's twelve homes, the directors agreed that the biggest reason employees give for absenteeism is problems with child care. As you know, most of PrimeCare's employees are young women who work as nursing assistants. Many have young children—preschoolers—and they leave their children with family or friends who act as unpaid sitters. But if the sitter is busy or the kid's sick, the mother stays with the child and won't show up for work. And we can't pay high enough wages for our employees to go out and pay $2 an hour for paid sitters, which is what they have to do if no family or friends are available. This makes it hard to find employees for the day shift.

"One of the center directors suggested that we look into providing child care services for our employees. Not only would it cut down on absenteeism, it would also boost morale and give us a benefit to offer, helping to make up for the low salary we pay. It won't cost the company much, if anything, because we get a matching state grant for any money we spend on such a service."

Jan pauses, which gives you a chance to jump into the conversation.

You ask, "You mean setting up a nursery in an empty room right in each of the nursing homes?"

"Yes, that's one possibility," Jan replies, "but there could be several ways to provide the service. That's where you come in. I'd like you to find out what you can about corporate child care. I read somewhere that over 2,500 employers offer some kind of child-care assistance to their employees now, and the number is growing."

"It sounds like a good idea," you interject. "What should I do with the information once I find it?"

"Well, I'd like you to write it up in a report that tells me what you find out and also recommends a child-care service that you think would work for us."

You are wondering if there is more to this than you think. So you ask, "You mean like a report summarizing what other places have done with child care for their employees, with a recommendation included?"

"Yes," Jan answers. "Just send me a memo summarizing how other places provide child care for their employees and recommend the service that would work best for us. But don't report everything you find out about the services other places provide. We can't handle some huge, expensive thing like some corporations can. However, we can provide up to $800 per facility each month and have it matched by the state. We don't have any start-up money, and the state won't provide any, but at least the monthly funds are available. So focus on services that we could afford, perhaps by adapting them to our situation."

As Jan speaks, you realize that she probably has some information that could help you, and maybe even an opinion about what PrimeCare should do. You ask, "Is there any type of child-care service that you think would be especially good for us?"

"Well, frankly, I think that setting up a day-care service in each of our twelve homes would be an excellent way to meet our needs. Although I haven't had much time to investigate the matter, I have found that we could probably do it cheaply. Our present insurance would cover an in-house service, so we wouldn't have to face any additional expense there. Also, each of our homes has one room that could be used for this purpose. Though they aren't outfitted with the furniture or equipment needed for day care, they all meet the state's requirements, so we could get a day-care license without any additional expense."

Though this sounds good, you wonder about one thing: "But if we don't have any furniture or equipment, how could we get it? You said we won't have any start-up money."

"Well, that could be a problem," Jan responds. "We might be able to get donations from community people. The senior citizens' center near one of our facilities has already offered some things. And once we have the rooms outfitted, our only operating expenses would be pay for staff; supplies like paper, crayons, and Kleenex; and food—snacks and lunches—for the children. We may even be able to staff the centers partly with volunteers."

"It all sounds great," you observe. "Why not save some time by having me study ways to set up in-house services without investigating other alternatives?"

"Well, there are two reasons. First, some directors think such a service would cost more money than we will have. And, to tell the truth, I haven't had a chance to calculate the actual costs myself, though I'm pretty sure I'm right. Second, some directors feel uneasy about settling on a specific method of providing day-care assistance until all reasonable possibilities have been investigated. They fear that if we focus immediately on one alternative, we may overlook others that would better serve both the employees and the company. So, I need to have you get information on several possible ways of providing our employees with child-care assistance. That's what the directors want, and, after all, they are the people who will decide what we will do."

"I see," you reply. After a short pause, you ask, "Is there anything you can tell me about the number of employees who would use a child-care service at each facility?"

"Yes," Jan says. "We talked informally about all of this at the last directors' meeting. The director who brought it up gave me a sheet with a few figures based on his facility. Maybe it will help you."

Jan stands up and hands you a sheet scribbled with some figures about the Charleston Avenue PrimeCare facility. She starts toward the door, your signal that the conversation is over.

Jan says, "Have the memo on my desk when I return from vacation in two weeks. I'd like to be able to use your memo to decide what to recommend to the next directors' meeting. In fact, if I agree with your recommendation, I'll just pass your memo along with a note from me."

"Okay," you reply. "The memo will be waiting for you when you return."

On Jan's note sheet you find the following information about the Charleston Avenue facility.

Number of Day-Shift Employees

Nurses	17	Day-shift jobs vacant:	4	Nurse's Aides
Nurse's Aides	41		1	Housekeeping
Housekeeping	15		2	Nurses
Kitchen	13			
Maintenance	2	Absent days last month:	18	
Secretaries	2			
Therapists	3			
Social Relief	1			
Management	2			
	96			

Day Shift
72 employees paid less than $7/hour
24 with children under 6 years of age (28 total children)

24 employees paid more than $7/hour
6 with children under 6 years of age (7 total children)

Child Care Budget (monthly)
$800 local from PrimeCare for each facility
$800 state match for each facility
$1,600

What can we provide?
—within budget?
—22 employees say they will use/need in-house day-care services
—together they have 27 kids under 6
—volunteers?

Assignment

1. Write the report Jan Debliss has requested. Make it between 700 and 1200 words long.
2. Use the general superstructure for reports (see Chapter 18). Include the following sections:

■ **Introduction.** In it, review your assignment and describe the most important features of the problem that your research is intended to help the company solve. If you think you can make your memo more effective by briefly stating your recommendation here, do so. Do not give this section a heading.

■ **Method.** Tell how you got your information. Do not include full bibliographic citations, but name the journals and other sources you consulted. This will be a short section, perhaps only one sentence long.

■ **Findings.** Discuss each of the major alternatives you think will most interest Jan Debliss and the directors. This section should include the alternative(s) you will recommend. Be sure to describe each alternative in a way that lets your readers know what it involves. Also, be sure to evaluate each of the alternatives from PrimeCare's point of view. This will be your longest section.

■ **Recommendation.** State what you think PrimeCare should do (even though your recommendation may already be evident from your discussion of the alternatives). Your recommendation may involve a combination of two or more of the alternatives you described in the preceding section, or it may focus on just one alternative. Be sure that your readers understand how your recommended service would be implemented at PrimeCare; to do that, you may need to provide information not already given in your "Findings" section.

3. Use the memo format, including centered headings (all caps, bold). You may include subheadings (initial caps, flush left, bold).

C A S E   **3**   **Ethics Report**

Identify an ethical issue that is faced by employers in your field. Then imagine that your employer has asked you to write a 300–800 word memo analyzing that issue. Who are the various groups of stakeholders? What are the goals, needs, concerns, and values of each group of stakeholders? Even though you may favor one position or another, write your report in a way that each of the various groups of stakeholders will see as balanced. You may conclude by stating the position you advocate and explaining why.

Some possible topics are suggested below. Whatever topic you select, remember to imagine that you are working for a specific company, so that you are to consider the issues as they arise for that specific organization:

■ Use of animals to test for possible harmful effects on humans of cosmetics and household cleaners (imagine that you work for a company that makes these products or for a lab that conducts the tests)

■ Pollution or environmental disruption caused by your employer (a paper mill, toy factory, engineering consulting firm, etc.)

■ Product safety

■ Conflicts of interest

■ Advertising claims and deception (stick to advertisements for the specific kinds of products marketed by your current or future employer)

■ Requests for days off by employees who observe religious holidays that the traditional business calendar does not recognize

- Requests by gay and lesbian employees who are in long-term, committed relationships that their partners receive the same health care and other benefits that are given to partners of married employees
- Requests for extended leaves or shortened work weeks from employees who want to spend more time at home caring for their small children
- Uncertainty about how to deal with clients in another country (pick one) where it is customary to give "business gifts" that would be considered bribes in the United States

---

C A S E   **4**   **Corporate Credo**

Imagine that a vice president has asked for your help in developing a corporate credo or ethics code for the organization that employs you (see the example on page 102). Locate two professional codes of ethics that apply to your field or to fields closely allied with yours; professors in your major department and reference librarians can help you with this. Then, in your memo to the vice president, do one of the following things, depending on your instructor's directions:

1. Evaluate the two codes, with the aim of helping shape the vice president's thinking about the code for your organization.
2. Using the codes you have researched and your own sense of what an ethics code should do, identify the topics that your organization's code should cover, tell why, and discuss some of the major issues that should be considered under each topic.
3. Using the codes you have researched and your own sense of what an ethics code should do, propose a code that you have developed for your organization.

Whichever alternative you choose, be sure to consider all the various stakeholders in actions taken by your employer. If you work for a large and diverse company, you might choose to recommend an ethics code only for the part of the business in which you are employed.

C A S E   **5**   **International Issue Report**

Identify an international or intercultural issue that is faced by employers in your field. Then imagine that your employer has asked you to write an analysis of that issue and its impact on your employer's business.

Here are some possible topics; you are welcome to propose others to your instructor. For whatever topic you pick, focus on a specific country:

- Changes required in marketing strategy
- Modifications required in product design
- Differences in management technique
- Laws or regulations that affect the conduct of business in the other country
- Problems that can arise in communications between locations in the United States and locations in the other country
- Other issues that could affect the success of your company's operations in another country

CASE ⑥ **Propose Your Own Business**

For this assignment, you are to write a proposal that seeks a loan to start a student-created business in your city.

Imagine that in the hope of fostering the entrepreneurial spirit of students, a dozen prosperous alumni have persuaded your school to set aside space in a building near the center of your campus to provide rent-free space for several student-created businesses. Calling themselves the Delphi Group, these alumni will also make interest-free loans to the students who set up these businesses. The only stipulation is that repayment begin no later than one year after the students receive the money.

Because the Delphi Group expects a large number of requests for the space and the loans, its members have decided to establish a competition in which interested students submit proposals describing the businesses they would like to start. After reading these proposals, the Delphi Group will select the four that seem most likely to succeed.

You are to write a formal proposal to submit in this competition. To assure that you have an appropriate business to propose, you will need to submit a brief description of it for your instructor's review and approval.

Proposal Content

The Delphi Group has specified that the proposals should be between fourteen and twenty double-spaced pages (not counting front matter or appendixes). Proposals are to include the following chapters. Note that this organization is simply a variation on the superstructure for proposals that is described in Chapter 19.

Introduction   Briefly explain that you are responding to the Delphi Group's request for proposals and name the kind of business you would like to start. Tell how much money you want to borrow. Forecast the contents of the rest of your proposal. This chapter should not exceed one page.

Market Analysis   Provide persuasive evidence that a market exists for the business you are proposing. Who will purchase your products or services? What are the important characteristics of these people from the point of view of your proposed business?

Note to the Instructor: The *Instructor's Manual* discusses guidance you can give your students concerning this research.

Also, discuss any competition that exists and explain your reasons for thinking that you can compete effectively against it. If there isn't any competition, tell whether a similar business has been tried in your community but has failed. Explain what makes you think your business is more likely to succeed.

This chapter should be as long as is required to persuade your readers that a substantial market exists for the business you are proposing.

Proposed Business   Because the Delphi Group will be extremely interested in the soundness of your business plan, this chapter should be the longest in your proposal. Cover the following topics:

- **Products or services.** Tell specifically and in detail what your business will sell. Relate these products or services directly to your market analysis.
- **Business site.** Describe the physical layout of your business and its decor in a way that persuades that they will make your business efficient and appealing to its target market. Identify the equipment and furniture you will need to purchase. Include a floor plan that shows the overall dimensions of the area you will use and the arrangement of items within that area.
- **Marketing plan.** Tell how you will attract customers. Include both your plans for attracting attention to your business as it first opens and the on-going marketing plan you will follow thereafter.
- **Staffing and management.** Indicate how many people you will hire and what their duties will be. If your employees will need to have any special qualifications, name them. Be sure that you have someone to perform each of the functions required to run a business even if you don't assign one person to each function. For example, even if you don't plan to hire a full-time accountant, tell how your accounting will be done. Your staff may be as small as two people (yourself and one other person), provided that the two of you can perform all the required activities and provide coverage for all the hours that the business will be open.

Also, describe your business's management structure, keeping the structure as simple as possible.

Schedule   Provide a prose overview and a Gantt chart of the major events in the development of your business. Begin with the approval of your proposal and continue to the point where your business is fully established and you can start making payments on your loan. Include such events as outfitting and decorating your business location, lining up suppliers, hiring employees, preparing your marketing materials, and opening for the first day of business. Indicate the duration of each event.

This chapter should not exceed three pages, including the Gantt chart.

Qualifications   Explain your qualifications to run the business you propose. If you would need to gain additional knowledge, tell what it is and describe how you will get it (for instance, by taking a certain course). This chapter should not exceed one page.

Budget   Explain the projected expenses and income for your business. When discussing *initial expenses,* list major categories (such as furniture, equipment, initial supplies); you do not need to identify each separate item. You may provide rough estimates of costs as long as you have a basis for believing your estimates to be reasonable.

When discussing *operating expenses,* consider only the cost of replenishing supplies and paying salaries. Assume that utilities, janitorial services, and other miscellaneous operating needs will be provided for free by your school; do not include them in your budget.

When discussing *projected income,* state your assumptions about how much business you will do, what your profit margin will be, and so on. Here, too, rough estimates are acceptable, provided that you have a basis for believing them to be reasonable.

Remember that your business may build slowly and that consequently it may be months before your income can cover operating expenses completely. If this is the case, your loan request should include the money you need to operate during this period.

Present your financial plans in a way that will persuade the Delphi Group that you can begin repaying the loan one year after receiving it.

Your budget chapter should not exceed three pages, including prose and tables. If you feel that additional details about your budget would be persuasive, include them in an appendix (which does not count as part of the fourteen to twenty pages required for the body of the report).

Conclusion   Briefly summarize your proposal and bring it to an appropriate end. This chapter should not exceed one page.

Format

The Delphi Group has specified that all proposals should use the format described in the style guide distributed by your instructor.

Note to the Instructor: The *Instructor's Manual* includes suggestions about this style guide, and the Web site for this book contains a sample you can download and modify as you wish.

ACKNOWLEDGMENTS

Figure 1.1
Courtesy of Hewlett Packard.

Figure 4.1
"What to Report" by James W. Souther. From *Westinghouse Engineer*, 22, 4-5, 108-11. Copyright © 1962. Reprinted by permission of Westinghouse Electric Corporation.

Figure 4.5
Reprinted with permission from Microsoft Corporation.

Figure 5.1
Reprinted with permission from Welch's Foods, Inc.

Figure 5.2
Courtesy of Johnson & Johnson Company.

Figure 5.3
Courtesy of Procter & Gamble.

Figure RM.4
DIGITAL, Alta Vista and the Alta Vista logo are trademarks or service marks of Digital Equipment Corporation. Used with permission.

Figure RM.5
DIGITAL, Alta Vista and the Alta Vista logo are trademarks or service marks of Digital Equipment Corporation. Used with permission.

Figure RM.6
WhaleNet/Williamson Photo. Wheelock College, Boston, MA

Figure RM.7
Copyright © 1998 by the Yahoo Corporation. Reprinted by permission. All rights reserved.

Figure RM.8
Courtesy of the Miami University Library.

Figure RM.9
Courtesy of the Miami University Library.

Figure RM.10
Courtesy of the Miami University Library.

Figure RM.11
Courtesy of the Miami University Library.

Figure PO.1
From "Wavelet Applications in Medicine," by Metin Akay, *IEEE Spectrum*, 50-51 (1977, May). Copyright © 1977 IEEE.

Figure PO.2
Utilization of Emergent Aquatic Plants for Biomass Energy Systems Development (Golden, Colo: Solar Energy Research Institute, 1983). Reprinted with permission.

Figure PO.3
Courtesy of Daimler-Benz AG.

Figure PO.4
From Apple Computer Power Macintosh User's Manual for 7300 Series. (Cupertino, CA: Apple Computer, 1997) 1, 3, 4, 7, 11, 14. Copyright © 1997 by Apple Computer. Reprinted with permission.

Figure PO.5
From Cochran, William (1997, July), "Extrasolar Planets," *Physics World*, July, 1997, p. 31-35. Copyright © 1997 by the Institute of Physics Publishing, Bristol, England.

Figure PO.7
"Death of Dinosaurs: A True Story?" by Boyce Rensberger from *Science Digest*, 94,5, May 1986. Reprinted by permission of the Author.

Figure 7.7
Courtesy of DELL Computer Corporation.

Figure 7.10
Courtesy of the State of Ohio Department of Highway Safety.

Figure 7.11
"Sample Table of Contents that Contains All Three Kinds of Headings." From a National Audubon Society brochure. Copyright © 1993. Reprinted by permission of the National Audubon Society.

Figure 7.14
From Windows NT Server 4.0 Administrator's Bible by Robert Cowart and Kenneth Gregg. Copyright © 1996 IDG Books Worldwide, Inc. All rights reserved. Reproduced here by permission of the publisher. Access www.idgbooks.com.

Figure 8.1
Based on J. C. Mathes and Dwight W. Stevenson, *Designing Technical Reports* 2/e. Copyright © 1991 by Mathes & Stevenson. Reprinted by permission of Allyn & Bacon.

Figure 8.4
General information from *Detroit Diesel Engines Series 53 Service Manual*. Copyright © 1990. Reprinted courtesy of Detroit Diesel Corporation.

Figure 11.1
Courtesy of USAirways.

Figure 11.2A
Reprinted by permission of Lucent Technologies, from *Bell Labs Technical Journal, Autumn,* 1997, p. 94.

Figure 11.2B
"The Loma Preita Earthquake." Copyright © 1994. Reprinted by permission of Bonnie Kamin.

Figure 11.2C
Courtesy of NASA.

Figure 11.2D
© Mike Bacon/Tom Stack & Associates.

Figure 11.3
Copyright © 1997 by Apple Computer. Reprinted with permission.

Figure 11.5
Courtesy of Texas Instruments.

Figure 11.6
Reprinted courtesy of Eastman Kodak Company.

Figure 11.8
Courtesy of the Monsanto Company.

Figure 11.11A
From *Chemistry and Industry,* no. 24, 10004, 1997, December. Reprinted with permission.

Figure 11.11B
Courtesy of NASA.

Figure 11.11C
Specialized Visual Aids: "Thermal Modeling of the Infrared Reflow Process for Solder Ball Connect (SBC)," reprinted by permission from *IBM Journal of Research and Development,* 37, 616, 1993. Copyright 1993 International Business Machines Corporation.

Figure 11.11D
Courtesy of NASA.

Figure 11.14
Copyright © 1997 Penn Well Publishing Company, reprinted from *Computer Design,* 36,31, 1997, December, with permission.

Figure 11.15
Courtesy of Jan V. White.

Figure 11.16
Copyright © 1994 by Ian Warpole/Scientific American, Inc. All rights reserved.

Figure 11.17
Fig. 1-A, "Molecular model of H-IL-6" from "A bioactive designer cytokine for human hematopoietic progenitor cells expansion," by Martina Fischer, Jutta Goldschmitt *et al, Nature Biotechnology,* Vol. 15, February, 1997.

Figure 11.18
Courtesy of Jan V. White.

Figure 11.20
Ways of Unifying an On-line Communication with Color: reprinted by permission from three IBM web pages of IBM Online. Copyright 1998 International Business Machines Corporation.

Figure 11.21
Copyright © 1997 Society of Automotive Engineers International (SAE), Warrendale, PA.

Figure VA.2
Courtesy of Thomson Consumer Electronics.

Figure VA.3
Courtesy of MTD Products, Inc.

Figure VA.8
Courtesy of the American Hospital Association, the American Hospital Publishing, Inc., Chicago, IL.

Figure VA.9
Courtesy of Standard Oil Company.

Figure VA.10
From T. L. Morisi, "Commercial Banking Transformed by Computer Technology," Monthly Labor Review 119 (1996: 8): 34.

Figure VA.11
Reprinted by permission. Copyright © 1985 by Macmillan Journals Limited. Courtesy of Dr. William L. Farrar, National Cancer Institute.

Figure VA.12
Charting a course for the future of corrugated, *Pulp & Paper International,* 39, 22 (1997). Copyright © 1997 by Miller Freeman, Inc. Reprinted with permission.

Figure VA.13
Copyright © 1994. Reprinted by permission of the *Cincinnati Enquirer* and Marion Merrell Dow, Inc.

Figure VA.14
© Grant Heilman Photography.

Figure VA.15
© Michael Fogden/Animals Animals/Earth Scenes.

Figure VA.16
© Garrison/Hewitt Photography.

Figure VA.17A
External View. "Carousel Creates Continuous Ion Exchange," from *Chilton's Food Engineering,* Vol. 65, No. 10:80, June, 1993. Reprinted by permission of Advanced Separation Technologies, Inc.

Figure VA.17B
Cross-Section. *BYTE* Magazine, February 1998. Reproduced with permission. Copyright © 1998 by The McGraw-Hill Companies, Inc., New York, NY, USA. All rights reserved.

Figure VA.17C
Cutaway. Courtesy of Audi of America, Inc.

Figure VA.17D
Exploded View. From U.S. National Aeronautics and Space Administration (1996). *Research and Technology Report: Goddard Space Flight Center,* U.S. Government Printing Office, 120.

Figure VA.18
Courtesy of Honda Motor Company of America.

Figure VA.19A
Copyright © 1995 by Macromedia, Inc.

Figure VA.19B
Copyright © 1996 by Apple Computer. Reprinted with permission.

Figure VA.20
This is copyrighted material of Meredith Corporation, used with their permission. All rights reserved.

Figure VA.21
Courtesy of Zinc Corporation of America.

Figure VA.22
Flow Chart showing special techniques used in system analysis from *Systems Analysis and Design Methods (4th edition)*, by J. L. Whitten, L. D. Bentley, & K. C. Dittman, 1998, p. 384. Copyright © 1998 McGraw-Hill, Inc. Reprinted by permission of The McGraw-Hill Companies.

Figure VA.23
Diagram that does not use specialized symbols: Fig. 3.15: The Carbon Cycle from *Environmental Science: A Global Concern* (4th ed.), by William P. Cunningham & Barbara W. Saigo, 1997. Copyright © 1997 McGraw-Hill, Inc. Reprinted by permission of The McGraw-Hill Companies.

Figure 12.1A
Copyright © 1998 by *Design News*. Reprinted with permission.

Figure 12.1B
Copyright © 1994 by Next Software, Inc.

Figure 12.1C
"Effects of football training on ventilatory and gas exchange kinetics to sinusoidal work load," *Journal of Sports Medicine and Physical Fitness,* (1997) Vol. 2, No. 3, p. 161. Copyright © 1997 by Edizioni Minerva Medica. Reprinted with permission.

Figure 12.1D
Article: Carl Zimmer, copyright © 1998. Reprinted by permission of *Discover Magazine*. Illustrations: Steven Kirk, copyright © 1998. Reprinted by permission of *Discover Magazine*.

Figure 12.3
Reprinted by permission of Monarch Marketing Systems, a Pitney Bowes Company.

Figure 12.5
Reprinted by permission of Toshiba America, Inc., New York.

Figure 12.6
Reprinted with permission from Microsoft Corporation.

Figure 12.7
Copyright © 1997 Chrysler Corporation.

Figure 12.8
Courtesy of Professor Joseph L. Cox III.

Figure 12.9
Reprinted with permission from Microsoft Corporation.

Figure 12.10A
Courtesy of Johnson & Johnson.

Figure 12.10B
Courtesy of Canon, Inc.

Figure 12.11
Courtesy of USV Pharmaceuticals.

Figure 13.1
Reprinted with permission from Microsoft Corporation.

Figure 13.2
Reprinted with permission from Microsoft Corporation.

Figure 13.3
Reprinted with permission from Microsoft Corporation.

Figure 13.4
Reprinted with permission from Microsoft Corporation.

Figure 13.5
Copyright © 1989 American Institutes for Research.

Figure 16.4
Reprinted with permission from Microsoft Corporation.

Figure 20.1
Used with permission of Eagle-Picher Industries, Inc., Akron Standard.

Figure 20.2A
Reproduced with the permission of Sharp Electronics Corporation.

Figure 20.2B
Courtesy of Astound Technologies Corporation.

Figure 20.3
Courtesy of Thomson Consumer Electronics.

Figure 20.4
Courtesy of Johnson & Johnson.

Figure 20.5
Copyright © 1996 by Apple Computer. Reprinted with permission.

Figure 20.6
Used with permission of Eagle-Picher Industries, Inc., Akron Standard.

Figure 20.8
Harvard Graphics Help, copyright © 1997 by Software Publishing Corporation.

Figure A.6
Cover of *Detroit Diesel Engines Series 53 Service Manual.* Copyright © 1990. Reprinted courtesy of Detroit Diesel Corporation.

Figure A.8
Title of *Detroit Diesel Engines Series 53 Service Manual.* Copyright © 1990. Reprinted courtesy of Detroit Diesel Corporation.

Figure A.13
From *Detroit Diesel Engines Series 53 Service Manual.* Copyright ©
1990. Reprinted courtesy of Detroit Diesel Corporation.

Figure A.15
From *Detroit Diesel Engines Series 53 Service Manual.* Copyright ©
1990. Reprinted courtesy of Detroit Diesel Corporation.

pg. 121
Coles, William Jr. & Jame Vopat, *What Makes Writing Good? A
Multiperspective.* Copyright © 1985 D. C. Heath & Company.
Reprinted with permission of Houghton Mifflin Company.

pg. 123
Survey results are from The Gallup Organization, Inc. *The
American Public's Attitude Toward Organ Donation and
Transplantation* conducted for the Partnership for Organ
Donations, Boston, MA, February 1993. Used with permission.

REFERENCES

Anderson, John R. "Attention and Sensory Information Processing." *Cognitive Psychology and Its Implications.* 4th ed. New York: W.H. Freeman, 1995. 40–48.

Anderson, Paul V. "What Survey Research Tells Us about Writing at Work." *Writing in Nonacademic Settings.* Eds. Lee Odell and Dixie Goswami. New York: Guilford P, 1985. 3–85.

Anderson, Roy E., Richard L. Frey, and James R. Lewis. *Satellite-Aided Mobile Communications Limited Operational Test in the Trucking Industry.* Schenectady, NY: General Electric Co., 1980.

Andrews, Deborah C., and William D. Andrews. *Business Communication.* 2nd ed. New York: Macmillan, 1992.

Anonymous. Personal interview with corporate executive who requested that the company remain anonymous.

"AOL Press: Welcome." *America On-Line.* 1 April 1998 <http://www.aolpress.com/press/2.0/usrguide/preface.htm/>.

Barnum, Carol M. "Working with People." *Techniques for Technical Communicators.* Eds. Carol M. Barnum and Saul Carliner. New York: Macmillan, 1993. 122–125.

Barnum, Carol M., and Robert Fischer. "Engineering Technologists as Writers: Results of a Survey." *Technical Communication* 31 (Second Quarter 1984): 9–11.

Bazerman, Charles. *Shaping Written Knowledge: The Genre and Activity of the Experimental Article in Science.* Madison: U of Wisconsin P, 1988.

Beebe, S. A. "Eye Contact: A Nonverbal Determinant of Speaker Credibility." *Speech Teacher* 23 (1974): 21–25. Cited in *Louder Than Words.* Marjorie Fink Vargas. Ames, IA: Iowa State UP, 1986.

Beer, David F., and David McMurrey. *A Guide to Writing as an Engineer.* New York: Wiley, 1997.

Benson, Philippa J. "Writing Visually: Design Considerations in Technical Publications." *Technical Communication* 32, (Fourth Quarter 1985): 37.

Berghel, Hal. "E-mail—The Good, the Bad, and the Ugly." *Communication of the ACM* 40 (April 1997): 4.

Bevlin, Marjorie E. *Design Through Discovery.* Ft. Worth, TX: Holt, Rinehart & Winston, 1989.

Boiarsky, Carolyn. *Technical Writing.* Boston: Allyn & Bacon, 1993.

Bosley, Deborah S. "Cross-Cultural Collaboration: Whose Culture Is It, Anyway?" *Technical Communication Quarterly* 2 (1993): 51–62.

Bostrom, Robert N. *Persuasion.* Englewood Cliffs, NJ: Prentice-Hall, 1981.

Bransford, J. D., and M. K. Johnson. "Contextual Prerequisites for Understanding: Some Investigations of Comprehension and Recall." *Journal of Verbal Learning and Verbal Behavior* 11 (1972): 717–26.

Brislin, Richard W. *Cross-Cultural Encounters.* New York: Pergamon, 1981.

Coleman, E. B. "The Comprehensibility of Several Grammatical Transformations." *Journal of Applied Psychology* 48 (1964): 186–90.

Couture, Barbara, and Jone Rymer. "Situational Exigence: Composing Processes on the Job by Writer's Role and Task Value." *Writing in the Workplace: New Research Perspectives.* Ed. Rachel Spilka. Carbondale, IL: Southern Illinois UP, 1993.

Covey, Stephen R. *The Seven Habits of Highly Effective People.* New York: Simon & Schuster, 1989.

Cross, Geoffrey A. "The Interrelation of Genre, Context, and Process in the Collaborative Writing of Two Corporate Documents." *Writing in the Workplace: New Research Perspectives.* Ed. Rachel Spilka. Carbondale, IL: Southern Illinois UP, 1993. 141–52.

Denning, Peter J. "A World Lit by Flame." *Communications of the ACM* 36 (December 1993): 12.

DiMario, Michael F. "Prepared Statement Before the Subcommittee on Legislative Branch Appropriations." *Committee on Appropriations U.S. Senate on Appropriations Estimates for Fiscal Year 1988.* 5 June 1997 <http://www.access.gpo.gov/public-affairs/appfy98.html/>.

Doheny-Farina, Stephen. *Rhetoric, Innovation, Technology: Case Studies of Technical Communication in Technology Transfers.* Cambridge, MA: MIT, 1992.

Ede, Lisa, and Andrea Lunsford. *Singular Texts/Plural Authors: Perspectives on Collaborative Writing.* Carbondale, IL: Southern Illinois UP, 1990.

Faigley, Lester, and Thomas P. Miller. "What We Learn from Writing on the Job." *College English* 44 (1982): 557–69.

Filho, Spartaco Astolfi, et al. "Stable Yeast Transformants That Secrete Functional a-Amylase Encoded by Cloned Mouse Pancreatic cDNA." *Biotechnology* 4 (1986): 311–15.

Flower, Linda, John R. Hayes, and Heidi Swarts. "Revising Functional Documents." *New Essays in Technical and Scientific Communication.* Eds. Paul V. Anderson, R. John Brockmann, and Carolyn R. Miller. Farmingdale, NY: Baywood, 1983. 41–58.

Foreman, K. M. *Preliminary Design and Economic Investigations of Diffuser Augmented Wind Turbines (DAWT).* Golden, CO: Solar Energy Research Institute, 1981.

General Electric Company. *Refrigerator Use and Care Guide.* Louisville, KY: General Electric, 1995.

Gilbert, Jersey. "The Best Jobs in America." *Money* 23.3 (March 1994): 70–73.

Golen, Steve, Celeste Powers, and M. Agnes Titkemeyer. "How to Teach Ethics in a Basic Business Communication Class." *Journal of Business Communication,* 22 (1985): 75–84.

Gralla, Preston. *How the Internet Works.* Emeryville, CA: Zip-Davis, 1996.

Grosse, Robert, and Duane Kujawa. *International Business: Theory and Managerial Applications.* Burr Ridge, IL: Richard D. Irwin, 1988.

Haneda, Saburo, and Hirosuke Shima. "Japanese Communication Behavior as Reflected in Letter Writing." *Journal of Business Communication* 19 (1983): 19–32.

Harcourt, J., A. C. Krizan, and P. Merrier. "Teaching Resumé Content: Hiring Officials' Preferences Versus College Recruiters' Preferences." *Business Education Forum* 45.7 (1991): 13–17.

Hays, Robert B. "A Longitudinal Study of Friendship Development." *Journal of Personality and Social Psychology* 48 (1985): 909–24.

Herzberg, Frederick. *Work and the Nature of Man.* Cleveland: World, 1968.

Ishii, Satoshi. "Thought Patterns as Modes of Rhetoric: The United States and Japan." *Intercultural Communication: A Reader.* Eds. Larry A. Samovar & Richard E. Porter. 4th ed. Belmont, CA: Wadsworth, 1985. 97–102.

Jones, Dan. *Technical Writing Style.* Boston: Allyn & Bacon, 1998.

Kachru, Yamuna. "Writers in Hindi and English." *Writing Across Languages and Cultures: Issues in Contrastive Rhetoric.* Ed. Alan Purves. Thousand Oaks, CA: Sage, 1988. 109–37.

Kelman, H. C., and C. I. Hovland. "Reinstatement of the Communicator in Delayed Measurement of Opinion Change." *Journal of Abnormal and Social Psychology* 48 (1953): 327–35.

Kelton, Robert W. "The Internal Report in Complex Organizations." *Proceedings of the 30th International Technical Communication Conference.* Washington, DC: Society for Technical Communication, 1984. RET54–57.

Killingsworth, Jimmie, and Michael K. Gilbertson. *Signs, Genre and Communities in Technical Communication.* Amityville, NY: Baywood, 1992.

Kintsch, Walter, and Teun van Dijk. "Toward a Model of Text Comprehension and Production." *Psychology Review* 85 (1978): 363–94.

Klare, George R. "Readable Technical Writing: Some Observations." *Technical Communication* 24.2 (1977, 2nd Quarter): 2.

———. "The Role of World Frequency in Readability." *Elementary English* 45 (1968): 12–22.

Kleck, R. E., and W. Nuessle. "Congruence between Indicative and Communicative Functions of Eye-Contact in Interpersonal Relations." *British Journal of Social and Clinical Psychology* 6 (1967): 256–66.

Kleinke, C. L., A. A. Bustos, F. B. Meeker, and R. S. Staneski. "Effects of Self-Attributed Gaze on Interpersonal Evaluations between Males and Females." *Journal of Experimental Psychology* 9 (1973): 154–63.

Kostelnick, Charles, and David D. Roberts. *Designing Visual Language: Strategies for Professional Communicators.* Needham Heights, MA: Allyn & Bacon, 1998.

Kulhavy, Raymond W., and Neil H. Schwartz. "Tone of Communications and Climate of Perceptions." *Journal of Business Communication* 18 (Winter 1981): 17–24.

Lauer, J. "Persuasive Writing on Public Issues." *Composition in Context.* Eds. R. Winterowd and V. Gillespie. Carbondale, Il: Southern Illinois UP, 1994.

Lay, Mary M. "Interpersonal Conflict in Collaborative Writing: What Can We Learn from Gender Studies." *Journal of Business and Technical Communication* 3.2 (1989): 5–28.

Layton, Pamela, and Adrian J. Simpson. "Deep Structure in Sentence Comprehension." *Journal of Verbal Learning and Verbal Behavior* 14 (1975): 658–64.

Locker, Kitty O. *Business and Administrative Communication.* 4th ed. New York: McGraw-Hill, 1997.

Lustig, Myron W., and Jolene Koester. *Intercultural Competence: Interpersonal Communication Across Cultures.* New York: HarperCollins, 1993.

Mancusi-Ungaro, Harold R., Jr., and Norman H. Rappaport. "Preventing Wound Infections." *American Family Physician* 33 (April 1986): 152.

Mathes, J. C., and Dwight W. Stevenson. *Designing Technical Reports.* 2nd ed. New York: Macmillan, 1991.

Maslow, Abraham H. *Motivation and Personality.* New York: Harper & Row, 1970.

Mehrabian, Alan. *Nonverbal Communication.* Chicago: Aldine, 1972.

Miller, Carolyn R. "Genre as Social Action." *Quarterly Journal of Speech* 70 (1984): 151–67.

Miller, George A. "The Magic Number Seven, Plus or Minus Two: Some Limits of Our Capacity for Processing Information." *The Psychology of Communication.* New York: Basic Books, 1967. 14–44.

Miller, Gerald R. "On Being Persuaded: Some Basic Distinctions." *Persuasion: New Directions in Theory and Research.* Eds. Michael E. Roloff and Gerald R. Miller. Thousand Oaks, CA: Sage, 1980. 11–28.

Mohler, James L. *Teach Yourself How to Become a Webmaster in 14 Days.* Indianapolis: Sams.net, 1997.

Munter, Mary. *Business Communication: Strategy and Skill.* Englewood Cliffs, NJ: Prentice-Hall, 1987.

Murray, Raymond L. *Understanding Radioactive Waste.* Columbus, OH: Battelle, 1982.

Nash, Bruce, and Allan Zullo. *The Misfortune 500.* New York: Pocket Books, 1988.

Nishiyama, Kazuo. "Intercultural Problems in Japanese Multinationals." *Communication: The Journal of the Communication Association of the Pacific* 12 (1983): 58.

Northy, Margot. "The Need for Writing Skill in Accounting Firms." *Management Communication Quarterly* 3 (1990): 480.

Office of Cancer Communications. *Taking Time: Support for People with Cancer and the People Who Care About Them.* Bethesda, MD: National Cancer Institute, 1983.

Patterson, Valerie. "Resumé Talk from Recruiters" (Journal). Miami University: CPPO, 1996.

Petty, Richard E., and John T. Cacioppo. "Consequences of the Route to Persuasion," "Motivational Approaches," and "The Elaboration Likelihood Model of Persuasion." *Communication and Persuasion: Central and Peripheral Routes to Attitude Change.* New York: Springer-Verlag, 1986. 1–24; 126–61; 213–54.

Pinelli, T. E., Myron Glassman, Walter E. Oliu, and Rebecca O. Barlcaly. *Technical Communications in Aeronautics: Results of an Exploratory Study* (TM-101626). Washington, DC: National Aeronautics and Space Administration, 1989.

Ray, George B. "Vocally Cued Personality Prototypes: An Implicit Personality Theory Approach." *Communication Monographs* 53 (1986): 266–76.

Raynor, Keith. "Visual Attention in Reading: Eye Movements Reflect Cognitive Processes." *Memory and Cognition* 5 (1977): 443–48.

Ricks, David A. *Big Business Blunders: Mistakes in Multinational Marketing.* Burr Ridge, IL: Dow Jones-Irwin, 1983.

Rogers, Carl R. "Communication: Its Blocking and Its Facilitation." *Harvard Business Review* 30 (1952): 46–50.

Roth, Lorie. "Education Makes a Difference: Results of a Survey of Writing on the Job." *Technical Communication Quarterly* 2 (1993): 177–184.

Roth, Robert F. *International Marketing Communications.* Chicago: Crain, 1982.

Ruch, William V. *Corporate Communications: A Comparison of Japanese and American Practices.* Westport, CT: Quorum, 1984.

———. *International Handbook of Corporate Communication.* Jefferson, NC: McFarland, 1989.

Savin, Harris B., and Ellen Perchonock. "Grammatical Structure and the Immediate Recall of English Sentences." *Journal of Verbal Learning and Verbal Behavior* 4 (1965): 348–53.

Scannella, William J. *An Internship in Technical Communications with the Engineering Mechanics and Life Management Section of the General Electric Company's Aircraft Engine Business Group.* Miami University, OH: Master's degree internship report, 1989.

Schriver, Karen. *Dynamics of Document Design: Creating Text for Readers.* New York: Wiley, 1997.

Scott, Mary, and Howard Rothman. *Companies with a Conscience: Intimate Portraits of Twelve Companies that Make a Difference.* New York: Carol, 1992.

Selber, Stuart. E-mail to the author. 31 March 1998.

Selzer, Jack. "What Constitutes a "Readable" Technical Style?" *New Essays in Technical and Scientific Communication.* Eds. P. V. Anderson, R. J. Brockmann, and C. R. Miller. Farmingdale, NY: Baywood, 1983. 71–89.

Sides, Charles H. *How to Write Papers and Reports about Computer Technology.* Philadelphia: ISI, 1984.

Smart, Graham. "Genre as Community Invention: A Central Bank's Response to Its Executives' Expectations as Readers." *Writing in the Workplace: New Research Perspectives.* Ed. Rachel Spilka. Carbondale, IL: Southern Illinois UP, 1993. 124–40.

Smith, Frank. "Word Identification." *Understanding Reading.* 5th ed. Hillsdale, NJ: Erlbaum, 1994. 119–31.

Smith, Laura B. "A User's Guide to PCC (Politically Correct Communiqué)." *PCWeek* 10.25 (28 June 1993): 204.

Spilka, Rachel. "Moving Between Oral and Written Discourse to Fulfill Rhetorical and Social Goals." *Writing in the Workplace: New Research Perspectives.* Ed. Rachel Spilka. Carbondale, IL: Southern Illinois UP, 1993. 71–83.

Sternthal, B., R. Dholakia, and C. Leavitt. "The Persuasive Effect of Source Credibility: Tests of Cognitive Response." *Journal of Consumer Research* 4 (1978): 252–60.

Stevenson, Dwight W. "Audience Analysis Across Cultures." *Journal of Technical Writing and Communication* 13 (1983): 319–30.

Suchan, James, and Robert Colucci. "An Analysis of Communication Efficiency Between High-Impact and Bureaucratic Written Communication." *Management Communication Quarterly* 2 (1989): 464–73.

Swasy, Alecia. *Soap Opera: The Inside Story at Procter & Gamble.* New York: Times Books, 1993.

Thorell, L. G., and W. J. Smith. *Using Computer Color Effectively: An Illustrated Reference.* Englewood Cliffs, NJ: Prentice Hall, 1990.

Tinker, Miles A. *Legibility of Print.* Ames: U of Iowa P, 1969.

Toulmin, Stephen, Richard Rieke, and Allan Janik. *An Introduction to Reasoning.* 2nd ed. New York: Macmillan, 1984.

van Dijk, Teun. *Macrostructures: An Interdisciplinary Study of Global Structure in Discourse, Interaction, and Cognition.* Hillsdale, NJ: Erlbaum, 1980.

———. "Semantic Macrostructures and Knowledge Frames in Discourse Comprehension." *Cognitive Processes in Comprehension.* Eds. Marcel Adam Just and Patricia C. Carpenter. Hillsdale, NJ: Erlbaum, 1977. 3–32.

Varner, Iris I. "A Comparison of American and French Business Correspondence." *Journal of Business Communication* 25.4 (1988): 59.

Velotta, Christopher. "Safety Labels: What to Put in Them, How to Write Them, and Where to Place Them." *IEEE Transactions on Professional Communications* 30 (1987): 121–26.

Warren, E. K., L. Roth, and M. Devanna. "Motivating the Computer Professional." *Faculty R&D* New York: Columbia Business School, 1984 (Spring): 8.

Watson, Charles E. *Managing with Integrity: Insights from America's CEO's.* New York: Praeger, 1991.

Watson, James D. *The Double Helix: A Personal Account of the Discovery of the Structure of DNA.* New York: Atheneum, 1968.

"Weak Writers." *The Wall Street Journal* (14 June 1985): A1.

Webster, Tony, and Barbara Larter. *Dynamics of Desktop Publishing Design.* Redwood City, CA: M&T Books, 1989.

Weisband, Suzanne P., and Bruce A. Reinig. "Managing User Perception of E-mail Privacy." *Communications of the ACM* 38.12 (1995).

Wells, Baron, Nelda Spinks, and Janice Hargrave. "A Survey of the Chief Personnel Officers in the 500 Largest Corporations in the United States to Determine Their Preferences in Job Application Letters and Personal Resumés." *ABCA Bulletin* 14.2 (June 1981): 3–7.

Westinghouse Corporation. *Danger, Warning, Caution: Product Safety Label Handbook.* Author, 1981.

White, Jan V. *Color for the Electronic Age.* New York: Watson-Guptill, 1990.

Williams, Joseph M. *Style: Ten Lessons in Clarity and Grace.* 4th ed. New York: HarperCollins, 1994.

Williams, Robin. *The Non-Designer's Design Book.* Berkeley, CA: Peachpit P, 1994.

Williams, Robin, and John Tollett. *The Non-Designer's Web Book.* Berkeley, CA: Peachpit P, 1998.

Wolvin, Andrew D., and Carol Oakley. *Listening.* Dubuque, IA: Brown, 1985.

Zimmerman, Mark. *How to Do Business with the Japanese.* New York: Random House, 1985.

INDEX

Abbreviations, of state names, 562
Abstracts, 84, 153–54. *See also* Summaries
Abstract words, concrete words and, 260–62
Accuracy, in word choice, 264
Action
  future, in communication ending, 244
  writing as, 10–11, 57–58
Action verbs, 21, 254–55
Active listening, 436–37
Active voice. *See also* Passive Voice
  identifying, 255
  reasons for using, 272–73
  versus passive voice, 21, 255–56
Advisers. *See* Readers' roles
Alignment, 334–37
AltaVista, 144, 146, 147
Alternating pattern, of comparisons,
  208–09. *See also* Divided pattern
American Psychological Association (APA),
  style guide of, 590
Analogy
  comparison, 208
  to explain unfamiliar words, 264
Anderson, John R., 364
Anderson, Paul V., 4
Anderson, Roy E., 461
Andrews, Deborah C., 417
Andrews, William D., 417
Anonymous, 297
AOLpress, 399
Appearance. *See also* Page design; Visual aids
  importance of, 17, 389
  of resume, 38
  visual aids showing, 308–17
Appendixes, in formal reports, 581–87
Applications. *See* Job application letter
Argumentation. *See* Persuasion; Reasoning
Assignments *See* Cases; Projects
Assistance, asking others for, 71
Associations
  connotation, 264–66
  of words, 264–66
  register, as type of, 266
  with color, 291
Attitudes. *See also* Persuasion; Readers' attitudes
  changes in, 60–61, 99–100
    reinforce, 61, 99
    reverse, 61, 99
    shape, 61, 99
  in oral presentations, 415
  readers' attitudes, 60–61
    toward a communicator, 61
    toward subject, 61, 251
    toward writer, 61

    toward writer's organization, 61
  shaping in ending, 243
  shaping through persuasion, 99–100
  testing draft's impact on, 378–79
  visual aids and, 282
  writer's attitude, 251
Attractiveness, revising for, 389
Author-date citations. *See* Documentation
  of sources
Authorship, co-authorship and, 8

Background information
  describing situations, 231
  general principles, 231
  helps readers, 231
  in beginning, 231
  in proposals, 520
  in reports, 447
  technical terms, 231
Bar graphs. *See* Visual aids
Barclay, Rebecca O., 4
Barnum, Carol M., 4
Be, use of verb, 254–55
Beebe, S. A., 415
Beer, David F., 4, 5
Beginning a communication, 220–37. *See*
  also Introduction
  background information in, 231
  describing benefits of communication,
    232
  explaining what will follow, 226–27
    organization of communication, 227
    scope of communication, 227
  for international readers, 236–37
  functions of, 221
  guidelines
    adapt your beginning to your readers'
      cultural background, 236–37
    adjust the length of your beginning to
      your readers' needs, 231–32
    encourage openness to your message,
      227–30
    for longer communications, begin with
      a summary, 232–36
    give your readers a reason to pay atten-
      tion, 221–26
    provide necessary background infor-
      mation, 231
    state your main point, 226
    tell your readers what to expect, 226–27
  helping reader solve problem, 232–37
    abbreviated beginning and, 224–25
    problem definition in unsolicited com-
      munications, 225
  in book format, 577

  length of, 231–32
  of service manual, 234
  referring to readers' request in, 232
  stating a main point, 226
  summary as, 232–36
  topic announcement in, 221
Benefits for readers. *See* Persuasion
Benne, Kenneth D., 433
Berghel, Hal, 14
Bibliographies. *See* Documentation of
  sources
Binding, 349
Boiarsky, Carolyn, 9
Book format. *See* Formats
Bosley, Deborah S., 439
Bostrom, Robert N., 112
Bottom line. *See also* Direct and indirect or-
  ganizational patterns
  defined, 91
  where to place, 91–92, 226
Bottom-up processing, 168
Brainstorming
  examples, 137–38
  procedure for, 137
  to generate ideas, 136–38
Bransford, J. D., 164
Brislin, Richard W., 120
Brochure
  examples, 101, 103, 182
  headings in, 179
Budget statements. *See* Visual aids
Bureaucratese, 250
Business Periodicals Index, 153
Bustos, A. A., 436

Cacioppo, John T., 99, 104
Cases. *See also* Projects
  advising Patricia, 50
  announcing the smoking ban, 76
  company day care, 616–20
  corporate credo, 621
  debating a company drug-testing pro-
    gram, 123
  electromagnetic fields, 614–16
  ethics report, 620–21
  filling the disabled-learning classroom, 97
  increasing organ donations, 124–26
  international issue report, 621
  propose your own business, 622–24
  selecting the right forklift truck, 23–24
Catalog, Library, 150–53
  guidelines for using, 151–53
Catalog, of U.S. government publications,
  155

Center for Business Ethics, 12
Chalkboards, 421
Chapters. *See* Paragraphs, sections and
   chapters
Charts. *See also* Organizational charts
   flow charts, 139–40, 321–23
   organizational, 325
   pie, 301, 311–12
   schedule, 325–26
Checking drafts
   defined, 361
   difficulty of, 361
   from ethical point of view, 363
   guidelines
      check from your readers' point of
         view—and your employer's, 361–62
      distance yourself from your draft,
         362–63
      read your draft more than once,
         changing your focus each time,
         364
      use computer aids to find (but not to
         cure) possible problems, 364–66
China, 291, 413
Citizen, employees' status as, 13
Claims. *See* Reasoning
Classification. *See* Organizational patterns
Cluster sketch, 140, 141
Co-authorship. *See* Collaboration
Coach, 366
Coleman, E.B., 254
Collaboration
   common at work, 8, 429
   computer use, 439–40
   defining objectives with, 430–31
   drafting with a team, 431
      listening in meetings, 436–37
      meetings, 435
      oral presentations with team, 425–27
      planning with, 431–32
      roles for team members, 434
      scheduling work, 433
   guidelines
      be sensitive to possible cultural and
         gender differences in team interac-
         tions, 438
      begin by creating a consensus concern-
         ing the communication's objectives,
         430
      encourage debate and diversity of
         ideas, 435
      involve the whole team in planning,
         431
      make a project schedule, 433
      make meetings efficient, 435
      share leadership responsibilities, 433
      use computer support for collabora-
         tion when it's available, 439
Color
   associations with, 291, 297
   color schemes, 288–90

guidelines for using
   choose color schemes, not just single
      colors, 288
   select colors with appropriate associa-
      tions, 291
   stick to a few colors, 291
   to promote easy reading, use a high
      contrast between text and back-
      ground, 290
   use color primarily for clarity and em-
      phasis, not decoration, 288
   use color to unify your overall com-
      munication, 291
impact of surrounding colors on, 288
international readers and, 291, 297
in oral presentations, 422
readability of text and, 288, 290, 422
uses in visual aids, 288
Colucci, Robert, 21
Columns. *See* Grids
Common knowledge, crediting sources and,
   133
Companies with a Conscience, 12
Comparison. *See* Organizational patterns
Complex audience, 66
Computers. *See also* Computers, writing
   with
   and collaboration, 439–40
   computerized full-text sources and, 155
   library catalogs on, 150–51
Computers, writing with
   as medium of communication, 5
   checking drafts with, 364–66
   collaboration with, 336–37, 439–40
   designing pages with, 337, 346
   outlining with, 94
   reviewing with, 366–67
   style sheets, 346–47
Concrete words, 260–62
Conformity with policy, 389
Connotation, 264–65
Consistency, revising for, 388–89
Context, readers', 64–65
Continuous reader involvement, 17, 70, 71
Continuous stakeholder involvement, 70, 363
Contrast
   page design 338–41
   visual aids for oral presentation, 422
   Web pages, 402
Conversational style, for oral presentations,
   413–15
Copyright, 292, 407, 572
Corporate credo, 100, 102, 621
Correctness, revising for, 389
Counterarguments. *See also* Persuasion
   addressing readers', 102–06
   avoiding negative thoughts and, 105
   letter addressing, 105–06
Couture, Barbara, 385
Cover
   of formal report, 569–70

of instructional manual, 571
Covey, Stephen R., 119
Credibility
   establishing at beginning, 229–30
   sales letter building, 114–15
   of writer, 112–19
   word choice and, 262–63
Cross, Geoffrey A., 9
Cross-section view, in drawings, 318
Cultural background, 7, 189, 236–37, 438
Culture. *See also* International oral presen-
   tations; International readers
   tations; International readers
Cutaway view, in drawings, 319

Deadlines, 9
Decision-makers. *See* Readers' roles
Deficiency needs, 101
Definition, to explain unfamiliar words, 264
Description
   of equipment, in instructions, 541
   of mechanism, 198–202
   of object, 198–202
   of process, 202–07
   to explain unfamiliar words, 264
Descriptive summary. *See* Summaries
Desktop publishing. *See* Computers, writing
   with
Devanna, M., 101
Dholakia, Ruby, 109
Diagrams. *See* Visual aids
Dinsmore, Jonathan, 6
Diplomacy, 389
Direct and indirect organizational patterns,
   109–11, 170–73, 228–29. *See also*
   Bottom line
Distance, between writer and reader, 249
Divided pattern, of comparisons, 208–209.
   See also Alternating pattern
Documentation families, 9
Documentation of sources
   APA documentation style, 591–96
   choosing a format, 590
   deciding what to acknowledge, 133
   ethics, 133
   MLA documentation style, 596–602
   placing in-text citations, 590–91
   purposes, 133, 590
   sample reference lists, 593, 598
Drawings. *See* Visual aids

E-mail
   emoticons, 251
   emotions and, 251
   guidelines
      keep your messages brief, 396
      make your messages easy to read on
         screen, 396–97
      provide an informative, specific subject
         line, 397
      remember that e-mail isn't private,
         397–98

see what other people are doing, 396
take time to revise, 397
uses, 366, 395
Echo words, 259
Ede, Lisa, 8
Emoticons, 251
Emphasis
color and, 290
end of communication as, 239
sentence length and, 257
in sentences, 256–57
in tables, 302
typographic, 257, 337
Empirical research reports. *See also*
Reports
defined, 460
elements and their relationship to readers' questions, 462
planning guide, 468
questions readers ask, 461
sample, 469–82
superstructure for
conclusions, 466–67
discussion, 465
introduction, 462–63
method, 464–65
objectives of research, 463–64
recommendations, 467–70
results, 465
typical writing situations, 460–61
Enabling element of purpose. *See* Purpose
Ending a communication
aims of, 239, 245
guidelines
after you've made your last point, stop,
240
follow applicable social conventions,
244–45
focus on a key feeling, 243
identify any further study that is
needed, 244
refer to a goal stated earlier in your
communication, 241–43
repeat your main point, 240
summarize your key points, 241
tell your readers how to get assistance
or more information, 243–44
tell your readers what to do next, 244
Endnotes. *See* Documentation of sources
Enthusiasm, in oral presentations, 415
Envelope, format for, 566–67
Ethics
citizenship and, 13
company goals and, 100
confronting unethical practices, 229
documenting sources and, 133
ethical issues at work, 5
evaluating drafts and, 362
graphs and, 313
human consequences of work and, 12,
70, 87, 190

identifying communication impact on
stakeholders, 70
job search and, 34
of persuasion, 119
process strategy for writing, 70
sexist language and, 265
stakeholders and, 70, 363
stereotypes and, 242
your values and, 11–12
Evaluating drafts, 359–80. *See* Checking
drafts; Reviewing drafts; Testing
drafts
Evidence. *See* Reasoning
Executive summary, 235, 572, 575
Expectations about communications
as guide for choosing voice, 249–50
as guide for determining quality needs,
386
as guide for planning, 94–96
dealing with ineffective expectations and
regulations, 250
how to learn, 96, 386
oral presentations, 410, 421
reasons for, 96
sources of, 96
what they might be, 94, 248, 386, 410, 421
Exploded views, in drawings, 319
External views, in drawings, 318
Eye contact, 415

Feasibility reports. *See* Reports
defined, 487
elements and their relationship to readers' questions, 488
planning guide, 495
questions readers ask, 487–88
sample outlines, 495–98
sample report, 499–505
superstructure for
conclusions, 494
criteria, 490–91
evaluation, 493–94
introduction, 488–90
method, 491–92
overview of alternatives, 492–93
recommendations, 494–95
typical writing situation, 487
Figures. *See* Visual aids
Fischer, Robert, 4
Fit, 111
Flow charts. *See* Visual aids
Footers, 333, 336
Footnotes. *See* Documentation of sources
Forecasting statements, 414
Formality, degree of, 249
Formal reports. *See subtopic* book format
under Formats; Reports
Formats. *See also* Page design
book format
appendixes, 581–82
back matter, 581–88

body, 577–81
chapters, 577–81
conclusion, 577. *See also* Ending a
communication
cover, 569–71
defined, 562–69
executive summary, 572. *See*
Summaries
front matter, 569–77
glossary or list of symbols, 582–83
introduction, 577. *See* Beginning a
communication
list of figures or tables, 577
page numbering, 585
printing, 585
reference list, endnotes, or bibliography, 582. *See also* Documentation of
sources
table of contents. *See* Table of contents
title page, 569
transmittal letter, 585, 587, 588. *See*
Transmittal letters
choosing the appropriate, 562
letter format
block format, 563
body, 565
complimentary close, 562–66
envelope, 566–67
heading, 562
inside address, 562–65
modified block format, 564
placement of text on first page, 566
salutations, 565
signature block, 566
special notations, 566
subject line, 565
top of second and subsequent pages,
566
memo format
body, 567
heading, 567
placement of text on first page, 567
signature, 567
special notations, 567
subject line, 567
style guides, 562. *See also* Style guides
France, 49, 236
Freewriting, 138–39
Frey, Richard L., 461

Gantt charts, 325
Gatekeepers, reviewers as, 366
Gender
mention of, 242
writing teams and, 438
Generalization(s)
at beginning of segments, 170–73
importance of positioning, 172
in persuasive writing, 172
topic statement as, 173
when not to present first, 173

General superstructure. *See* Superstructures
Genres, 92
Gestures, 415
Gilbert, Jersey, 6
Glassman, Myron, 4
Glossaries, 582–83
Golen, Steve, 12
Gralla, Preston, 142
Grammar checkers, 364–66
Graphs. *See* Visual aids
Grids
    columns in, 335
    creativity and, 336
    on graph, 284
    thumbnail sketches of, 346–47
    to coordinate visual elements, 334–37
Grosse, Robert, 263
Growth needs
    as benefit for readers, 101–03
    recruiting brochure stressing, 103
Group writing. *See* Collaboration
Gutter, 335

Handouts, for oral presentations, 421, 424
Haneda, Saburo, 236
Harcourt, J., 28
Hays, Robert B., 462
Headers, 333, 336
Headings
    and topic sentences, 188
    as transitions, 179
    consistency of, 179, 342
    design of, 183
    in letters, 179
    in table of contents, 183, 186
    levels for, 183
    number of, 183
    outlining system in, 183
    parallel, 179
    phrasing, 179
    questions in, 179
    showing organizational hierarchy, 183
    typefaces and, 191, 338–40
    visual design of, 338–40
Her, use of, 265
Herzberg, Frederick, 100
Hierarchy
    contrast and, 337–41
    headings showing, 184
    in comparisons, 210
    indentation to show, 188–89
    of related words moving from abstract to
        concrete, 261
    of related words moving from general to
        specific abstraction, 261–62
    of topic statements, 170
    organizing communications hierarchi-
        cally, 88–89
    page design and, 337–41
High-impact writing techniques, 21
His, use of, 265

HOTBOT, 146
Hovland, C.I., 112
Humor, stereotypes in, 242

Idea tree, 141
Illustrations. *See* Page design; Visual aids
Imperative mood, in instructions, 543
Implementers. *See* Readers' roles
Impromptu oral presentation, 411
Indentation, to show organization, 188–89
Indirect organizational pattern. *See* Direct
    and indirect organizational patterns
Informal tables, 305
Informal style, conversational style and, 249
Informative summary, 232
Instruction manuals. *See also* Instructions
    book format and, 569
    cover of, 571
    title page of, 574
Instructions. *See also* Instruction manuals
    elements and their relationship to read-
        ers' questions, 535
    on-line, 549, 555, 556
    persuasive element of purpose in, 534
    page design, 535
    samples, 546, 550–54, 555, 556
    superstructure for
        description of equipment, 541
        directions, 541–47
        introduction, 536
        list of materials and equipment, 544
        troubleshooting, 303, 547
    tables in, 302
    testing, 535
    visual aids for, 277, 302, 303, 319, 320,
        321, 535, 545, 546, 547
    warnings to readers, 539–41
    wordless, 275
Interjections, 253–54
International collaboration, 439
*International Handbook of Corporate
    Communication,* 64
International oral presentations
    checking visual aids, 423
    choosing words for, 415
    customary organization differs, 413
    handouts with, 424
International readers
    addressed often at work, 7
    blunders when writing to, 263, 297
    foreign language ability a plus, 35
    have drafts reviewed by someone from
        the culture, 297–98
    organizing for, 190
    persuading, 119–20
    United States has an international work-
        force, 64
    visual aids for, 274, 291, 297–98
    writing customs vary from country to
        country, 63–64
        beginning of a communication, 236–37

resumes, 49
    style, 250
Interruptions, during oral presentations,
    416–17
Interviewing
    conducting an interview, 155–58
    determining readers' attitudes through,
        378–79, 521
    with test readers, 379–80
Introduction. *See* Beginning a communica-
    tion
Investors, proposal readers as, 517–18
Ishii, Satoshi, 190

Janik, 107
Japan
    communication beginning in, 236–37
    patterns of writing in, 189
Jewett, 417
Job application letter
    defining objectives of, 43–44
    drafting, 44–46
    planning for, 44
    reviewing, 46–47
    samples of, 47, 48

Kachru, Yamuna, 191
Kant, Immanuel, 119
Kelman, H.C., 112
Kelton, Robert W., 166
Keywords
    in headings, 179
    in scannable resumes,
    Internet search and, 142
    library research and, 151
    searches, 146–47, 151–53
Kleck, R. E., 436
Kleinke, C. L., 436
Koester, Jolene, 7, 120, 190
Kostelnick, Charles, 279
Krizan, A. C., 28
Kujawa, Duane, 263
Kulhavy, Raymond W., 266

Labels
    on visual aids, 285–86. 307, 310, 312,
        315–16, 322
Lauer, Janice, 119
Lay, Mary M., 438
Leavitt, Clark, 109
Legal concerns, 10
Length
    of beginning, 231–32
    of e-mail, 396
    of oral presentation, 410
    of summary, 236
    of Web page, 403
    of written communications, 236
    sentence, 260, 364–66
Letter format. *See* Formats
Lewis, James R., 461

Librarians, reference, 149–50, 155
Library
  computerized full-text resources, 155
  government documents in, 154–55
  information source in, 149
  library catalog in, 150–53
  periodical indexes and abstracts, 153–54
  reference works in, 154
  research aids in, 149
Line graphs. *See* Visual aids
Line of reasoning. *See* Reasoning
Listener-centered approach, to oral presen-
    tations, 410
Listening, 436–37
Lists
  kinds of, 188
  parallelism in, 188–89
  to help readers find information, 19
  to reveal organization, 188
Literature reviews, in empirical research re-
    port, 463
Location tests, 377–78
Low-impact writing techniques, 21
Lunsford, Andrea, 8
Lustig, Myron W., 7, 120, 190

Main point
  delay presenting, 109–11
  highlighting, 418
  in heading, 179
  repeating as an ending, 240
  stating at beginning, 226
Management information, presenting
  budget statements, 326–27
  organizational charts for, 325
  schedule charts, 325–26
Manuals. *See* Instruction manuals;
    Instructions
Margins, 566
Margolis, 417
Maslow, Abraham H., 100
Matalene, Carolyn B., 626
Mathes, J. C., 8, 223, 250
Matrix, 140
McMurrey, David, 4, 5
Mechanics. *See also* Style
  checking for, 364
  computer aids for checking, 364–66
  grammar, 364
  revising
    attractiveness, 389
    conformity to policy, 389
    consistency, 388–89
    correctness, 388
    spelling, 364
Mechanism, description of
  example, 203–04
  extended description of an object, 202
Meeker, F. B., 436
Meeting Readers' Informational Needs
  guidelines

answer your readers' questions, 83–86
include the additional information
    your readers need, 86–87
look for a technical writing superstruc-
    ture you can adapt, 92–93
organize to support your readers' tasks,
    88–92
outline, if this would be helpful, 94
plan your visual aids, 93–94
take regulations and expectations into
    account, 94–96
Meetings
  cultural differences, 438
  debate and discussion during, 435–38
  efficient, 435
  gender differences, 436–37
  listening, 436
Mehrabian, Alan, 436
Memo format. *See* Formats
Merrier, P., 28
Miller, Carolyn R., 92
Miss, use of term, 265
Modern Language Association (MLA), style
    manual of, 590, 597
Modifiers, placement of, 253
Mood, imperative, in instructions, 543
Motivation
  employee, growth needs and, 101
  for reading instructions, 539
Mr., use of term, 265
Mrs., use of term, 265
Ms., use of term, 265
Multibar graph. *See* Visual aids
Multicolumn format. *See also* Page design
  created with desktop computers, 237
  methods of creating, 335–37
Munter, Mary, 101
Murray, Raymond L., 241

NASA, 155
National Park Service, 155
National Technical Information Service, 155
Neild, Julie, 6
Nervousness, during oral presentations, 425
Nishiyama, Kazuo, 190
Northy, Margot, 4
Notes, in tables, 305. *See also*
    Documentation of sources;
    Footnotes
Nuessle, W., 436

Oakley, Caroline Gwynn, 413
Objectives, defining
  asking others about purpose and readers,
    71
  from ethical point of view, 70
  guidelines
    ask others to help you understand your
      readers and their context, 71
    focus on what you want to happen
      while your readers are reading, 57–58

identify the tasks your readers will per-
    form while reading, 58–60
learn about the context in which your
    readers will read, 64–65
learn who all your readers will be,
    65–69
learn your readers' important charac-
    teristics, 61–64
remain open to new insights and infor-
    mation, 71
tell how you want to change your read-
    ers' attitudes, 60–61
job application letter, 43–44
oral presentations, 410
page design, 334
reader-centered approach to defining ob-
    jectives, 56
resume, 26–27
stakeholders and, 70
uses of objectives
  example, 71–74
  in evaluating, 363, 367
  in planning, 83, 88
  in research, 129
  in revising, 385
  throughout the writing process, 56
  when creating visual aids, 274
worksheet, 73–74, 75
Objectivity, degree of, 249
Oliu, Walter E., 4
Oral presentations
  collaborative, 425–27
  for international audiences, 413, 415, 423,
    424
  guidelines for designing and using visual
    aids
    give your listeners something to take
      away, 424
    look at your audience most of the
      time, 423
    look for places where visual aids can
      contribute, 417–18
    make sure your visual aids are easy to
      understand, 421–22
    present your visual aids effectively, 423
    select the medium best suited to your
      purpose, audience, and situation,
      418–21
    test your visual aids, 423
    use a story board, 418
  guidelines for preparing and delivering
    accept your nervousness—and work
      with it, 425
    define your objectives, 410
    focus on a few main points, 412
    fully integrate visual aids into your
      presentation, 417–24
    look at your audience, 415–16
    prepare for interruptions and ques-
      tions—and respond courteously,
      416–17

Oral presentations, *continued*
  rehearse, 424
  select the form of oral delivery best suited to your purpose and audience, 410–12
  use a conversational style, 413–15
  use a simple structure and help your listeners follow it, 412–13
  impromptu talk, 411–12
  listener-centered approach to, 410
  outlined talk, 411
  scripted talk, 411
  unifying with color and design, 291, 293
Organization. *See also* Organizational patterns; Paragraphs, sections and chapters; Revealing organization, Superstructures
  conventional strategies as aids, 189
  for international readers, 189–91
  importance
    affects readers' attitudes, 109
    supports readers' tasks, 88
  logical versus effective, 88
  of oral presentation, 412
  outlining, 94
  superstructures as aids, 92–93
  tables of contents, 184, 186, 572, 576, 580
Organizational charts. *See also* Visual aids
  to identify members of complex audience, 67–69
Organizational goal stressing benefits of, 100
Organizational patterns
  cause and effect
    example, 211, 213–14
    guidelines for describing, 210
    guidelines for persuading, 212
    purposes, 210
  classification
    aims, 195
    examples, 196, 197, 199, 200
    formal defined, 195
    guidelines for formal, 196–97
    guidelines for informal, 197–98
    informal, defined, 197
    principle of, 195
  combining, 215–17
  comparison
    alternating and divided, 208
    defined, 208
    examples, 208, 211
    guidelines, 209–10
    how it works, 208–09
    purposes, 208
  partitioning (description of an object)
    defined, 198–99
    examples, 202, 203–04
    guidelines, 201
    how it works, 198–99
    purposes, 198
  problem and solution

example, 216
    guidelines for describing, 214
    guidelines for persuading, 214–15
    purposes, 212
  segmentation (description of a process)
    defined, 202
    examples, 205, 206, 207
    guidelines, 205
    purposes, 202
  uses, 189
Organizing to create favorable response, 109–11
  creating tight fit among communication parts, 111
  direct and indirect patterns of, 109–11
Organizing to support readers' tasks, 88–92
  give bottom line first, 91–92
  grouping, 89–91
  hierarchical organization, 88–89
Outlined oral presentations, 411
Outlining, 94, 431
Outlining programs (computer), 94, 95
Overhead transparencies, 420
Overseas employment, writing for, 49
Ownership sharing in team writing, 437–38

Page design
  arranging prose to reveal hierarchy, 188–89
  computer program used for, 337
  consistent, 342–44
  elements of, 333
  guidelines
    align related visual elements with one another, 334–37
    begin by considering your readers and purpose, 334
    design your overall package for ease of use and attractiveness, 348–50
    select type that is easy to read, 344–46
    use contrast to establish hierarchy and focus, 337–41
    use proximity to group related elements, 342
    use repetition to unify your communication visually, 342–44
  gutters, 335
  importance of, 332
  in instructions, 535
  mockups, 346
  practical procedures for, 346–48
    thumbnail sketches, 346–47
  principles, 334
Page numbering, 585
Paper, 349
Paragraphs, sections, and chapters. *See also* Organizational patterns; Segments
  defined as segments, 166
  guidelines
    begin by announcing your topic, 167–70

consider your readers' cultural background when organizing, 189
  consult conventional strategies when faced with organizational difficulties, 189
  move from most important to least important, 173–74
  present your generalizations before your details, 170–73
  reveal your organization, 174–89
Parallelism
  in headings, 179
  in lists, 188–89
  in resume, 34–35
  to avoid sexism, 265
Partitioning. *See* Organizational patterns
Passive voice. *See also* Voice
  versus active voice, 255–56
Patterson, Valerie, 43–44
Pauling, Linus, 252
Performance tests, 374–76
Personality, voice and, 249
Persuasion. *See also* Attitudes, Readers' attitudes, Reasoning
  aimed at altering attitudes, 107
  as a general objective, 60, 82, 105
  benefits for readers to emphasize growth needs, 101–03
    emphasize in beginning, 222
    organizational goals, 100
  concerns of readers
    how they arise, 103–04
    importance of addressing, 104
    predicting what they will be, 104
  counterarguments by readers
    how they arise, 103–04
    importance of addressing, 104
    predicting what they will be, 104
  ethics of, 119
  guidelines
    adapt your persuasive strategies to your readers' cultural background, 119–20
    address your readers' concerns and counterarguments, 103–06
    create an effective relationship with your readers, 112–19
    emphasize benefits for your readers, 100–03
    organize to create a favorable response, 109–111
    show that your reasoning is sound, 106–109
  how persuasion works, 99–100
  initial generalizations to increase persuasiveness, 172
  international readers and, 119–20
  persuading about a problem and its solution, 212–16
  persuading about cause and effect, 210–12

resistance to changing attitudes, 104
three kinds of attitude changes, 60, 61. 99
visual aids and, 289
Persuasion (computer program), 418
Persuasive element of purpose, 60, 82, 99.
    See also Objectives, defining;
    Planning
Petty, Richard E., 99, 104
Phantom readers, 65
Photographs. *See* Visual aids
Pictographs. *See* Visual aids
Pie charts. *See* Visual aids
Pinelli, T. E., 4
Plagiarism, crediting sources and, 133
Plain English, 250
Planning. *See also* Outlining
    before using sources, 129–30
    benefits of, 82
    computers, writing teams, and, 439–40
    for interviewing, 156
    outlines and, 94
    of persuasive strategies, 98–126
        answer your readers' questions, 83–86
        include the additional information
            your readers need, 86–87
        look for a technical writing superstruc-
            ture you can adapt, 92–93
        organize to support your readers' tasks,
            88–92
        outline, if this would be helpful, 94
        plan your visual aids, 93–94
        take regulations and expectations into
            account, 94–96
    storyboard for, 418–19, 431–32
    style guide for, 96
    superstructures for, 92–93
    for oral presentations, 426
    of visual aids, for oral presentations,
        417–18
    with writing team, 431–32
Policies, compliance with, 362, 389
Postscript. *See* Letter format
Power, and credibility of writer, 113
PowerPoint (computer program), 292, 418,
    421–22
Powers, Celeste, 12
Prioritizing, of revisions, 387–89
Problem and solution. *See* Organizational
    Patterns
Problem-solving, as beginning of communi-
    cation, 222–26
Procter & Gamble, document review at, 366
Progress reports. *See also* Reports
    defined, 506
    elements and their relationship to read-
        ers' questions, 508
    planning guide, 571
    questions readers ask, 507–08
    readers' concern with the future, 06–07
    sample outlines, 511–13
    sample report, 514

superstructure for
    conclusions, 510
    facts and discussion, 509–10
    introduction, 08–09
    recommendations, 510
    tone, 510–11
    typical writing situation, 506
Projects. *See also* Cases
    brochure, 608
    formal report or proposal, 611–12
    informational page, 696–07
    informational Web site, 605–06
    instructions, 608–09
    oral briefing
        project plans, 612–13
        project results, 613
    progress report, 611
    project proposal, 610–11
    resume and letter of application, 604–05
    unsolicited recommendation, 607–08
    user test and report, 609–10
Pronouns
    as echo words, 259
    personal, 249, 414
    sex-linked, 265
Proposals
    defined, 516
    elements and their relationship to read-
        ers' questions, 519
    planning guide, 527
    questions readers ask, 518
    readers as investors, 517–18
    sample, 528–32
    strategy of conventional superstructure,
        518–20
    superstructure for
        costs, 527
        introduction, 520–21
        management, 527
        method, 525
        objectives, 523–24
        problem, 521–23
        qualifications, 526–27
        resources, 526
        schedule, 526
        solution, 524–25
    variety of writing situations, 516–17
Proximity, 342
Purpose. *See* Objectives

Questionnaires. *See* Questions; Surveys
Questions
    as topic statement, 170
    during oral presentations, 416–17
    for user tests, 378–80
    in headings, 179
    in surveys, 159–61
    interviewing and, 156–57

Ray, George B., 415
Raynor, Keith, 254

Readability
    color, text, and, 290–91, 421–22
    formulas, 364–66
    of e-mail, 396–97
    of typefaces, 344–46
Reader-centered approach to writing
    continuous reader involvement, 71
    defined, 11
    overview, 16–17
Reader-centered writing, general techniques
    explain relevance, 21
    focus on key information, 18–21
    make reading easy, 21
Readers. *See also* Readers' attitudes; Readers'
    characteristics; Readers' questions;
    Readers' roles; Readers' tasks
    at work compared with at school, 6–7
    changing attitudes of, 60–61
    complex audiences, 66–69
    continuous involvement of, 17, 70, 71
    create meaning, 11
    diversity of, 7
    future, 65–66
    identifying all, 65–69
    identifying types, 67
    phantom, 65
    react on a moment-by-moment basis,
        14–16
    responses are shaped by situation, 13–14
Readers' attitudes; *See also* Attitudes,
    Persuasion
    affected by organization, 109–11
    affected by page design, 332
    as guide for checking, 361
    focusing on when defining objectives, 60
    predicting initial one, 228
    strategies for encouraging open ones,
        228–30
    testing to determine effects on, 378–79
    using endings to shape, 243
    ways they can change, 61, 99
    what they are about, 60–61, 99
Readers' characteristics
    cultural background, 63–64
    familiarity with specialty, 63
    familiarity with topic, 62–63
    personal preferences, 63
    professional roles, 61–62
    special factors, 64
Readers' questions
    importance of addressing in persuasive
        communications, 103–05
    portraying readers as asking, 59, 83–86
    typical ones asked
        arising from readers' limited knowl-
            edge of specialty, 86
        arising from readers' professional roles,
            83–85
        arising from readers unfamiliarity with
            subject, 85–86
    use in identifying readers' tasks, 59

Readers' questions, *continued*
  ways readers look for answers, 59
  ways readers use answers, 60
  when reading empirical research reports, 462
  when reading feasibility reports, 488
  when reading general reports, 445
  when reading instructions, 535
  when reading job application letters,
  when reading progress reports, 508
  when reading proposals, 519
  when reading resumes, 26–27
Readers' roles
  advisers
    defined, 84
    questions typically asked, 84
  decision-makers
    defined, 83
    questions typically asked, 83–84
  implementers
    defined, 84
    questions typically asked, 84–85
  importance of defining, 83
Readers' tasks
  as guide for designing visual aids, 280
  as guide in organizing, 88–92
  bottom-up and top-down mental pro-
    cessing of messages, 168–69
  building mental hierarchies, 88–89
  determining relevance, 21
  finding main point, 18–19, 91–92
  locating needed information, 18
  when reading resumes,
Reading aloud
  for checking, 363
  in user testing, 375
Reasoning
  claims
    defined, 107
    relationship to evidence, 107–08
  evidence
    defined, 107
    relationship to claims, 107–08
    reliability, 108
    sufficiency, 108
  flaws
    false assumptions, 108–09
    insufficient evidence, 108
    line of reasoning not appropriate to
      case at hand, 108
    line of reasoning not sound, 108
    overgeneralizing, 109
    unreliable evidence, 108
  how it works, 107–08
  importance at work, 107
  line of reasoning
    appropriateness to case at hand, 108
    defined, 107
    relationship to claims and evidence,
      107
Redundancy, 236

Reference librarians, 149–50
Reference lists. *See* Documentation of
    sources
Register of words, 266
Regulations. *See* Expectations about com-
    munications
Rehearsing oral presentations, 424, 427
  with readers, 112
Repetition, 342–44
Reports. *See also* Empirical research reports;
    Feasibility reports; Formats; Progress
    reports
  elements of and their relationship to
    readers' questions, 445
  guide for future action, 444
  planning guide, 452
  questions readers ask, 444–45
  sample outlines, 450–51
  sample report, 453–58
  superstructure
    conclusions, 448
    discussion, 447–48
    facts, 447
    introduction, 446–47
    method of obtaining facts, 447
    recommendations, 448–49
  superstructure's relationship to other re-
    port superstructures, 449–50
  variety of report-writing situations, 444
Research
  documenting sources, 133
  ethics, 133
  evaluating results, 131
  goals, 128
  guidelines
    begin interpreting your research results
      even as you obtain them, 131–32
    carefully evaluate what you find, 131
    check each source for leads to other
      sources, 131
    define your research objectives,
      128–29
    plan before you begin, 129–30
    take careful notes, 132
  methods
    conducting a survey, 158–62
    exploiting your own memory and cre-
      ativity, 136–41
    interviewing, 155–58
    searching the Internet, 142–49
    using the library, 149–55
Resumes. *See also* Drafting a resume
  design of appearance, 38
  employer interest in,
  employer reading habits and,
  evaluating, 38–39
  examples of,
  experiential, 28, 30–36
  functional, 28, 36–38
  organization
    activities, 35

  contact information, 30
  education, 31–32
  personal data, 35
  professional objective, 30
  references, 35
  sequencing of data,
  special abilities, 35
  work experience, 32–35
  length, 28
  objectives, 39
  scannable, 39–42
  Web page, 43
Revealing organization
  forecasting statements, 175–78
  headings, 179–88
  importance, 174
  of oral presentations, 413
  transitions, 178–79
  visual design, 188–89
Reviewing drafts
  alternative roles for reviewers, 366
  computers and, 366–67
  defined, 361, 366
  from ethical point of view, 363
  guidelines
    build a positive interpersonal relation-
      ship with your reviewers or writer,
      368–69
    discuss the objectives of the communi-
      cation and the review, 367–68
    explore fully the reasons for all sugges-
      tions, 370
    rank suggested revisions—and distin-
      guish matters of substance from
      matters of taste, 369–70
  job application letters, 46
  outlining as an aid, 94
  resumes, 38
  very common on the job, 9, 360, 366
  why employers require reviews, 366
Revising. *See also* Evaluating drafts
  complexities, 385
  defined, 385
  guidelines
    adjust your effort to the situation,
      385–7
    be diplomatic, 389
    make the most significant revisions
      first, 387–89
    revise to learn, 390–91
    to revise well, follow the guidelines for
      writing well, 390
  investment of time, 385
Ricks, David A., 120, 263
Roberts, David D., 142
Rogers, Carl R., 112
Roles
  created by voice, 250–51
  readers'
    advisers, 84
    decision-makers, 83–84

implementers, 84–85
professional, 61–62
of writer of persuasive communication, 112–119
Rothman, Howard, 12
Ruch, William V., 64, 236–250
Rymer, Jone, 385

Salutations
in letters, 565
Miss, Mrs., Mr, and Ms., 265
sexism in, 265
Sans serif typefaces, 339
Scene, of oral presentations, 410
Schedule
for team projects, 433
in proposals, 526
schedule charts, 325–26
Schedule charts. *See* Visual aids
School. *See* Writing at work
Schriver, Karen, 274
Schwartz, Neil H., 266
Scott, Mary, 12
Scripted oral presentations, 411
Search engines, 142
Sections. *See* Paragraphs, sections and chapters
Segments. *See also* Paragraphs, sections and chapters
characteristics, 166
defined, 166
demands on readers, 166
Segmentation. *See* Organizational patterns
Selber, Stuart, 396
Sentences. *See also* Topic statements
avoiding bureaucratese, 250
begin with *it is*, 254
guidelines
emphasize what's most important, 257
put the action in your verbs, 254–55
simplify your sentences, 252–54
smooth the flow of thought from sentence to sentence, 257–59
use the active voice unless there is good reason to use the passive voice, 255–56
vary your sentence length and structure, 260
length in oral presentations, 414
topic and comment, 257–59
transitional, 255
two goals when writing, 252
with verb *to be*, 254
Serif typefaces, 339
Sexist language, 265
Sheats, Paul, 433
Shima, Hirosuke, 236
Smart, Graham, 92
Smith, Laura B., 251
Smith, W. J., 298
Society for Technical Communication, 6

Software. *See* Computers, writing with; Desktop publishing programs
Source notes. *See* Bibliographies; Endnotes; Footnotes; Reference lists
Souther, James W., 84–85
Spain, communication beginning in, 236
Spell checkers, 364–66
Spiders, 142
Spinks, Nelda, 43
Stakeholders, 70, 87, 363
Staneski, R. S., 436
Stereotypes, 242
Sternthal, Brian, 109
Stevenson, Dwight W., 8, 223, 250, 297
Storyboard,
for planning, 418–19, 431–32
for visual aids, 418–19
Style. *See also* Sentences; Voice; Words
bureaucratese and, 250
computer programs for checking, 364
dimensions, 248
for oral presentations, 413–15
Style guides
APA *Style Guide*, 590
employers', 96, 562
for planning, 96
for term projects, 432
MLA Style Manual
restrictions, expectations, and, 96
Style checkers, 364–66
Subjectivity, 249
Suchan, James, 21
Summaries
as beginning of communication, 232–36
as ending, 241
descriptive, 235–36
executive, 235, 572
features of, 232
informative, 232
length of, 236
Superstructures
as aid to planning, 92–93
of empirical research reports, 462
of feasibility reports, 488
for instructions, 535
of progress reports, 508
for proposals, 93, 519
for reports, 445
Surveys, 158–62
Swasy, Alecia, 366
Synonyms, to explain unfamiliar words, 264

Tables of contents, 184, 186, 572, 576, 580
Tables. *See* Visual aids
Talks. *See* Oral presentations
Tasks. *See* Readers' tasks
Teams. *See* Collaboration
Technical communication careers, 6
Testing. *See* User testing
Thorell, L. G., 298

Thumbnail sketches, 346–47
Time limits, 410
Titkemeyer, M. Agnes, 12
Title page
of formal report, 569, 573
of instruction manual, 574
To be, topic sentence using, 254
Tone. *See also* Voice
checking, 363
in progress reports, 510–11
in job application letters, 46–48
Top-down processing, 168–69
Topic statements
as generalizations, 171–72
forecasting, 176
headings and, 188
how they help readers, 19, 167
in three levels of outline, 171
positioning of, 167
Toulmin, Stephen, 107
Tracey, James R., 431
Transitions
between speakers in team oral presentations, 426
headings as, 179
in oral presentations, 414
in sentences
echo words, 259
placement of transitional and echo words, 259
topic shifts, 257–59
transitional words, 259
Transmittal letters, for formal reports, 585, 587, 588
Tree diagram. *See* Idea tree
Typography
adjusting to show organization, 339
for emphasis in sentences, 257
serif and sans-serif typefaces, 339
size for headings, 183, 339
using easy-to-read typefaces, 344–45
on visual aids, 422

Understandability, 420–21
Understandability test, 376–77
Unifying communications visually, 342–44
Unsolicited communications
defining problem in, 225
example, 117–18
User testing
defined, 361, 371
from ethical point of view, 363
guidelines
ask your test readers to use your draft in the same ways your target readers will use it, 373–78
interview your test readers after they've used your draft, 379–80
learn how your draft affects your test readers' attitudes, 378–79

User testing, *continued*
    pick test readers who truly represent your target readers, 373
    test early and often, when appropriate, 376
    location test, 377–78
    of instructions, 535
    of visual aids, 423
    performance test, 374–76
    questions testing can answer, 372–73
    understandability test, 376–77

Values. *See* Ethics
van Dijk, Tuen, 92
Varner, Iris I., 236
Velotta, Christopher, 540
Verbs
    action, 21, 254–55
    active vs. passive voice, 21, 255–56
    fancy and common, 267
    in resume, 34
Visual aids
    aligning on page, 334–47
    attitudes and, 282
    bar graphs, compare with line graphs and tables, 280–81
        constructing, 307–08
        examples, 280, 281, 306–09
        misleading, 313
        multibar, 308
        pictographs as, 308
        uses, 307
        with subdivided bars, 307
    budget statements
        creating, 327
        examples, 327
        uses, 326–27
    chalkboards, 421
    color in, 286–91
    computerized projections for oral presentations. *See also* Persuasion and PowerPoint, 419–420
    diagrams
        creating, 324
        examples, 324
        uses, 323
    drawings
        compared with photographs, 285, 316
        creating, 284, 317
        cross-section, 318
        cutaway, 319
        examples, 318–21
        explanations in, 296–97, 319
        exploded, 319
        external, 318
        for international communications, 297–98
        uses, 316, 317
    dryboard, 421
    explanations in, 296, 324
    flow charts

    constructing, 322
    examples, 322–23
    use, 139, 321–22
    for displaying data, 300–05
    for international audiences, 297–98
    guidelines (general)
        adapt existing visual aids to your purpose and readers, 292
        choose visual aids appropriate to your objectives, 279–82
        integrate your visual aids with your text, 292–97
        look for places where visual aids will help you achieve your communication objectives, 274–79
        make your visual aids easy to understand and use, 282–86
        use color to support your message, 286–91
        when addressing an international audience, check your visual aids with persons from the other nations, 297–98
    guidelines (oral presentations)
        give your listeners something to take away, 424
        look at your audience most of the time, 423
        look for places where visual aids can contribute, 417–18
        make sure your visual aids are easy to understand, 421–22
        present your visual aids effectively, 423
        select the medium best suited to your purpose, audience, and situation, 418–21
        test your visual aids, 423
        use a story board, 418
    in instructions, 535
    in oral presentations, 417–24
    labelling, 285–86
    line graphs
        compared with tables and bar graphs, 280–81
        constructing, 309–10
        examples, 281, 310–11
        misleading, 313
        pictograph and, 309
        uses, 301, 309
    organizational charts
        creating, 325
        examples, 68, 325
        uses, 67–69, 325
    overhead transparencies, 419, 420
    photographs
        compared with drawings, 285, 316
        creating, 284, 314–16
        examples, 285, 314–16
        for international communications, 297–98
        uses, 312, 314, 317

    pictographs
        constructing, 309
        misleading, 313
        uses, 301, 308
    pie charts
        constructing, 311–12
        example, 312
        uses, 301, 311
    planning, 93–94
    rehearsing oral presentations with, 424
    schedule charts
        creating, 326
        examples, 326
        uses, 325–26
    simplicity, 284–85
    specialized, 282–83
    supporting readers' tasks, 28, 279–82, 300–05
    tables
        as aid to gathering information, 141
        compared with bar and line graphs, 280–81
        compared with prose presentation, 301
        constructing, 284, 302–05
        examples, 301–05
        informal, 305
        structure of, 304
        uses, 141, 301–02
        word data in, 302
    tasks of reader, 280–81
    titles, 286
    uses, 274–79, 417–418
    wordless instructions, 274–75
Voice. *See also* Active voice; Passive voice
    attitude toward subject and, 249
    customs and, 249
    distance between writer and reader, 249
    formality of, 249
    guidelines for choosing your voice
        consider how your attitude toward your subject will affect your readers, 251
        consider the roles your voice creates for your readers and you, 250–51
        find out what's expected, 249–250
        say things in your own words, 252
    objectivity of, 249
    professional relationship with readers, 249
    purpose and, 249
    reader's personality and, 139
    reading aloud in evaluation and, 252
    roles created by, 250–51
    subject and, 249
    subjectivity of, 249
    using your own words and, 252
    writer's personality and, 139

Warnings, in instructions, 539–41
Warren, E. K., 101
Watson, Charles E., 12

Watson, James D., 252
Web pages
  color in, 290
  create your own, 408
  guidelines for designing
    keep your pages short, 403
    keep your pages up to date, 403
    limit loading time, 403
    make your pages attractive, 403
    make your pages easy to read, 402
  how they work, 399–400
  posting, 400
  tags, 400–01
  viewing, 400
Web sites
  create your own, 605–06
  guidelines for designing
    begin by considering your site's audience and purpose, 404
    enable readers to contact you, 406–07
    label your links clearly, 405–06
    meet your readers' informational needs, 404
    organize your site hierarchically, 404–05
    provide many navigational aids, 406
    provide useful associative links, 405
    test your site 407
    use a consistent visual design, 406
  links, 405–06

navigational aids, 406
Weisband, Suzanne P., 398
Wells, Baron, 43
Wharton Applied Research Center, 417
Wheildon, Colin, 288
Whistle-blowing, ethics and, 229
White, Jan V., 291
White space, 333, 422. *See also* Margins
Williams, Joseph M., 256
Williams, Robin, 333
Wolvin, Andrew D., 413
Words
  as links, 259
  defining, 264
  echo, 259
  explaining unfamiliar, 263–64
  for oral presentations, 415
  guidelines for selecting
    choose plain words over fancy ones, 267
    choose words with appropriate associations, 264–66
    use concrete, specific words, 260–62
    use specialized terms when—and only when—your readers will understand them, 262–64
    use words accurately, 264
  identifying those unknown to readers, 263
  register, 266

sexist, 259
synonyms, 264
in tables, 302
transitional, 259
your own, 252
Word associations. *See* Associations; Word(s)
Work experience. *See* Professional experience
World Wide Web. *See also* Computers; Web pages; Web sites
  how it works, 139
  libraries linked to it, 149
  research on, 142–49
Writing at work
  action, 10–11
  compared with school, 5–10
  ethics and, 12–13
  hours spent, 116
  importance in career, 4–5
  percentage of time spent, 4
Writing process
  at work compared with at school, 7–9
  objectives as guide, 71–72
  reader-centered, 16–17

Yahoo, 144